That You May Grow Thereby

By

Greg Litmer

Truth
Publications

*Taking His hand,
helping each other home.*™

ISBN 10: 1-58427-230-9

ISBN 13: 978-158427-230-4

First Printing: 2008

Truth Publications, Inc.
CEI Bookstore
220 S. Marion St., Athens, AL 35611
855-492-6657
sales@truthpublications.com
www.truthbooks.com

What This Book Is about

This book has been a labor of love and is the result of over thirty-one years of preaching the word of God. It is a compilation of bulletin articles, magazine articles, and poems that I have written over the years, with just a very few of my favorites from my son, my wife, and a friend. I make no claim of originality, except perhaps in the matter of organization. Every sermon I have heard, every magazine article I have read, every commentary and other books in my library that I have used so extensively, have contributed to this work. I could not begin to recognize all that have contributed in that way. While all major contributions to an article have been noted, it is possible and even probable, that over the many years I used a sentence or two without remembering to note its source. Should this have happened, I apologize. At the same time I cannot be effusive enough in expressing my love and appreciation for all of the wonderful men of God from whom I have learned so much over the decades.

Anything of mine that you find in this book that you would like to use in your bulletins, sermons, or some other way, you have my permission to use. However, you may not reproduce the entire book or use any of it in material you plan to sell without written permission from the Guardian of Truth Foundation.

This book is dedicated to Vicky, my lifelong companion, my collaborator, and my best friend.

That You May Grow Thereby

Happy New Year!

"Happy New Year!" That is a statement that we hear every January 1st. I believe that it has many different meanings and nuances to the people who say it. For some it is a celebratory exclamation—they have made it to another year. For others it can be almost a statement of relief, not so much that they made it to a new year, but that they made it through the old one. If you live any length of time on this old earth, you will come to find that some years are just harder than others. Some years are just filled with more difficulties, setbacks, even tragedies.

Then again, for all of us, "Happy New Year" expresses hope perhaps more than any other emotion. While we don't know what the future holds, on January 1st we look to the year ahead that seems so full of potential and hope. We make New Year's Resolutions, which almost always involve something good we intend to do in the year that lies before us. O yes, in many ways, January 1st represents one of the most important motivating factors that exists for man—hope.

In many ways, hope is the peculiar possession of the Christian. It is so much more than a simple wish for something. When we speak of the hope of the Christian we are talking about an earnest and eager anticipation. It is not a wish; it is an expectation, built upon the firmest of foundations. William Bradbury, in his song "The Solid Rock," put it so beautifully when he wrote, "My hope is built on nothing less than Jesus' blood and righteousness."

The New Year, if God permits it to unfold in its entirety, may be for us a year of prosperity and personal success. On the other hand, it could be a year of financial reversals and family tragedy. The truth is that we simply do not know. However, faithful children of God can hold on to one thing with absolute certainty. No matter what the New Year holds—whether great material gain or poverty, unbounded happiness or heartrending sorrow—the child of God has hope that no one can take away. Peter put it this way in 1 Peter 1:3-5:

> "Blessed be the God and Father of our Lord Jesus Christ, which according to his abundant mercy hath begotten us again unto a lively hope by the resurrection of Jesus Christ from the dead, to an inheritance incorruptible, and undefiled, and that fadeth not away, reserved in heaven for you, who are kept by the power of God through faith unto salvation ready to be revealed in the last time."

Can you think of a more uplifting and encouraging way to approach a new year than to do so with the hope of a Christian, "which hope we have as an anchor of the soul, both sure and steadfast" (Heb. 6:19)?

January 2

Don't Give Up

Don't give up until the task is done.
Don't lay your weapon down until the battle's won.

The crucible of controversy requires your best.
In the heat of the conflict is no time to rest.

When your heart is broken over those who stray,
That is all the more reason that *you* must stay.

Don't give up until the task is done.
Don't lay your weapon down until the battle's won.

January 3

"When the Perfect Comes" (1)

There has been a tremendous increase in the number of people who claim to worship Jesus Christ and who also claim to possess miraculous spiritual gifts. By "miraculous spiritual gifts" I am referring to those gifts given through the Spirit that were outside of the normal functions of nature. Paul listed nine of them in 1 Corinthians 12:10, "For to one is given the word of wisdom through the Spirit, and to another the word of knowledge according to the same Spirit; to another faith by the same Spirit, and to another gifts of healing by the one Spirit, and to another the effecting of miracles, and to another prophecy, and to another the distinguishing of spirits, to another various kinds of tongues, and to another the interpretation of tongues."

Do not mistake the "wisdom" and the "knowledge" mentioned in these verses by Paul with wisdom and knowledge gained through the normal process of study and experience. This was "wisdom" and "knowledge" granted directly by the Spirit without the normal process. Do not confuse the "faith" Paul mentioned with the faith that all Christians must have to be saved. This was miraculous faith of some sort—perhaps a miracle-working faith. The point is that all of the things Paul mentioned were miraculous gifts.

This increase in the number of people claiming such gifts is frequently referred to as the "Charismatic Movement," based upon one of the Greek words for gift, "charisma." It is no longer confined to back road, country churches. It is no longer found strictly among Pentecostal groups. The movement has crossed into the mainstream denominational churches. Even the Roman Catholic Church has various charismatic segments among it.

The question that I would like to consider is whether or not these gifts are actually being exercised today. Are there those who possess the miraculous spiritual gifts as certain of the brethren did in the first century? Have the gifts ceased to be active? If they have ceased, when did it occur, and how do we know?

Turn to 1 Corinthians 13, which is the middle chapter of Paul's discussion concerning miraculous spiritual gifts. In it he presents what he calls "a still more excellent way." He writes of love, and the abiding nature of it. Paul wrote, "Love never fails," but that was not the case with the gifts. We find in verses 8-13:

> Love never fails; but if there are gifts of prophecy, they will be done away; if there are tongues, they will cease; if there is knowledge it will be done away. For we know in part, and we prophesy in part; but when the perfect comes, the partial will be done away. When I was a child, I used to speak as a child, think as a child, reason as a child; when I became a man, I did away with childish things. For now we see in a mirror dimly, but then face to face; now I know in

part, but then I shall know fully just as I also have been fully known. But now abide faith, hope, love, these three; but the greatest of these is love.

The obvious place to focus is found in verse 10. What is "the perfect" or in the Greek *to teleion*? Many commentators, and certainly all of the charismatic commentators, view "the perfect" as a reference to Christ and His second coming. I disagree with that. In *Vine's Expository Dictionary of New Testament Words, teleios* is defined as "signifies having reached its end, finished, complete, perfect." He comments on its use in 1 Corinthians 13:10 by saying, "referring to the complete revelation of God's will and ways, whether in the completed Scriptures or in the hereafter." The truth is, "the perfect" refers to the end of a process or of a development—and that can be of either people or things. It refers to the completed revelation of the Word of God.

The second coming is not a process—it will be an instantaneous event. Later on in this letter Paul describes the second coming as occurring, "in a moment, in the twinkling of an eye, at the last trumpet" (15:52).

We might also mention that *to teleion* is in neuter gender and nothing suggests that it applies to a person—Christ.

January 4

"When the Perfect Comes" (2)

Continuing our look at 1 Corinthians 13:8-13, we see in verse 11 Paul writing about the time of the spiritual gifts as the infancy or childhood of the church. Once the revelation was completed the church would be in its manhood. If we consider Paul's illustration of a mirror in verse 12, it will help us to understand. If you have ever stood before a fogged mirror in a steamy bathroom on a cold morning, you know that you cannot see yourself very well. Eventually the condensation on the mirror begins to fade, and bit by bit you can see yourself more clearly. Finally the mirror is completely fog-free, and you can see everything. That is the way the revelation was given. Not all at one time but bit by bit, until finally they could look into the "perfect law, the law of liberty" and see themselves in the mirror of God's Word.

It is important also to consider how faith and hope will abide after the second coming. Do not be misled by the use of the word "now" in verse 13. Its use is logical, not temporal. Let me present another example of the same us-age and then explain what it means. In John 18:36 we find, "Jesus answered, My kingdom is not of this world. If My kingdom were of this world, then My servants would be fighting, that I might not be delivered up to the Jews; *but as it is*, My kingdom is not of this realm." The phrase, "but as it is" is translated from the same word as "now" in 1 Corinthians 13:13. The idea is that even though the miraculous gifts would pass away, faith, hope, and love would abide. Of the three, love is the greatest.

Now if "when the perfect comes" refers to Christ at His second coming, how can faith abide? Paul wrote in 2 Corinthians 5:7, "for we walk by faith, not by sight." When Jesus returns, we shall see Him. Revelation 1:7 tells us, "Behold, He is coming with the clouds, and every eye shall see Him, even those who pierced Him, and all the tribes of the earth will mourn over Him. Even so, Amen." Remember the Hebrew writer's words in Hebrews 11:1, "Now faith is the assurance of things hoped for, the conviction of things not seen." When Jesus comes in the second coming, it will be a matter of sight, not faith.

Again, if "when the perfect comes" refers to Christ at His second coming, how can hope abide? In Romans 8:24 Paul wrote, "For in hope we have been saved, but hope that is seen is not hope; for why does one also hope for what he sees?" It really cannot be denied. 1 Corinthians 13:13 clearly teaches that "hope" is to exist after "the perfect comes." But hope cannot exist after a per-son has attained what he or she hoped for.

The truth is that miraculous spiritual gifts do not exist today. They were for the infancy of the church. They were given to assist in the revelation and to confirm that which was revealed (Mark 16:20; Heb. 2:3-4). When the revela-tion was completed, the gifts were no longer needed, and the God-ordained time of their cessation had arrived.

January 5

Help with 1 Corinthians 13:9-13

For we know in part, and we prophesy in part. But when that which is perfect is come, then that which is in part shall be done away. When I was a child, I spake as a child, I understood as a child, I thought as a child: but when I became a man, I put away childish things. For now we see through a glass darkly; but then face to face; now I know in part; but then shall I know even as I am known. And now abideth faith, hope, charity, these three: but the greatest of these is charity.

This is one of those controversial passages that is frequently misunderstood and misapplied in the religious world. The question revolves around "that which is perfect." Does it refer to the second coming of Christ, sometimes referred to as the Parousia; or does it refer to the completed revelation?

The Greek word translated as "perfect" is *teleios*. It refers to the end of a process or development (either of people or things). Vine's defines it as having reached its end, finished, complete, perfect." When the word is used of a person, it has reference to attaining the full limits of stature. When it is used of things, it has reference to completion.

Hebrews 5:12-14 is another passage where *teleios* is used, and will help to show how the word refers to the end of a process or development. This passage reads, "For when for the time ye ought to be teachers, ye have need that one teach you again which be the first principles of the oracles of God; and are become such as have need of milk, and not of strong meat. For everyone that useth milk is unskillful in the word of righteousness: for he is a babe. But strong meat belongeth to them that are *of full age*, even those who by reason of use have their senses exercised to discern both good and evil."

One does not arrive at "full age" suddenly when it comes to the knowledge of and the ability to use the Word of God. No, "full age" comes about as the result of a process, "reason of use." The process is what brings a person to the point of being able to use his or her knowledge "to discern both good and evil."

In 1 Corinthians 13:10 the Greek is as follows, *hotan de elthe to teleion, to ek merous katargethesetai. To ek merous* is translated "that which is in part." Mike Willis' exegesis of this particular verse (and, indeed, the entire passage) is right on the money. He wrote,

> Precisely what is described as *to teleios* must be learned from the context. The phrases *to teleion* and *to merous* are put in contrast with each other, and therefore, must be used together in defining what each is. If I can identify what *to ek merous* is, then I will know what *to teleion* is—it must refer to perfection or completeness in the same realm as that realm which was denoted by *to ek merous*. We know what *to ek merous* is; it is used to describe the manner in which

God revealed Himself to man through spiritual gifts. Hence, *to ek merous* is the partial revelation of God's will to men. *To teleion*, therefore, is the completed or perfected revelation of God's will to man. . . . Let us suppose that we have a pie of unknown kind. If I can identify one part of it, I will know what the rest of it is. . . . If I can identify the one slice of pie as cherry pie, I will know that the whole pie is cherry pie. Similarly, if I can identify the *to ek merous*, I will know what the *to teleion* is. *To teleion* must refer to completeness, wholeness, or perfection in the same realm as that referred to be *to ek merous*.

"But I can positively identify *to ek merous* as prophecy, the word of knowledge, and tongue speaking (v. 8, remember that these three gifts are used representatively in this text for the sum total of all the gifts); hence, *to ek merous* is the way of spiritual gifts as the *in part* method of God revealing His will to man.

If *to ek merous* refers to the *in part revelation*, then *to teleion* must be identified as the *completed revelations*, just as surely as if I identified the one piece of pie as cherry pie guarantees that the rest of the pie is cherry pie. *To teleion*, therefore, refers to God's completed revelation. . . .Hence, Paul is saying that when God's revelation was completed, the miraculous spiritual gifts would cease" *(A Commentary on Paul's First Epistle to the Corinthians*, 463, 464, 465).

Another difficulty which must be dealt with by those who see the "perfect" as referring to the second coming involves the word "now" in verse 13. The Greek is *nun*, and it has logical rather than temporal force in this verse. A similar passage is found in John 18:36, "Jesus answered, My kingdom is not of this world: if my kingdom were of this world, then would my servants fight, that I should not be delivered to the Jews: but *now* is my kingdom not from hence." The idea behind the word is "now however," or "now therefore," or "seeing that it is so." Thus, back in 1 Corinthians 13:13, we have the spiritual gifts passing away but faith, hope, and love abiding. How is hope going to abide after the return of Jesus? What is seen is not hoped for.

January 6

It Is Not Supposed to Be This Way!

It is sometimes necessary to expose false doctrine and, motivated by love, stand toe to toe with the purveyor of what is untrue. This is nothing new. The Apostle Paul found it necessary to clearly identify certain individuals, such as

Hymenaeus and Philetus, as well as the error that they taught. John warned of extending the boundaries of fellowship beyond the boundaries of truth in 2 John 9-11 when he wrote, "Anyone who goes too far and does not abide in the teaching of Christ, does not have God; the one who abides in the teaching, he has both the Father and the Son. If anyone comes to you and does not bring this teaching, do not receive him into your house, and do not give him a greeting; for the one who gives him a greeting participates in his evil deeds."

Sometimes when brethren are determined to cling to what is not true and to practice that which is not authorized, division becomes necessary. I cannot engage in that which I know to be unauthorized nor can I uphold the hands of those who are teaching what I know to be untrue. All division is heart-rending. Long time friendships will probably end. Perhaps even families will be torn apart. Division brings tears to the hearts of faithful children of God—but if it must be, it must be!

However, in the absence of doctrinal issues, why are there "church troubles"? Why do congregations end up torn by bitterness and strife? Why is it true that in most major metropolitan areas it is possible to find several "conservative" churches that have started as often-rancorous splits, *with no doctrinal reason*? Why are there brethren who will not talk to each other, refuse to step foot in various church buildings, and have nothing good to say about each other—*when there are no significant doctrinal differences among them*? It is not supposed to be this way!

I have seen churches split, brethren "jumping" each other in the church building after services, and gossip flying to the point that it brought tears to its victim. I have been in worship services where the tension was so evident that concentrating on the worship of the Lord was almost impossible. I have heard brethren seem to take a perverse delight in troubles that another "faithful" congregation was having. I have seen all of this take place and *none of it has anything to do with a doctrinal issue!* It is not supposed to be this way!

Please do not misunderstand me. When doctrine that is not according to truth is being espoused and practices are being advocated that are not authorized by the gospel of Christ, we must either correct that false teaching and eliminate the unauthorized practice, or separate ourselves. But even that must be done with love and true concern for the souls of those with whom we disagree.

I did not "grow up" in the church. I was born and raised a Roman Catholic. I must say that I never knew true love among people who were not related physically until I was baptized into Christ and added by the Lord to His church. Faithful brethren are the best people on earth. They are my family! At the same time I must sadly say that I never knew true hatred either, until I saw and experienced the way that some brethren will treat each other. It is not supposed to be this way!

So I have repeatedly asked myself "Why?" I have prayerfully asked God to help me to understand. The easiest answer is "lack of love," and that is true. For brethren to treat each other in such an ungodly manner is evidence of a lack of love for God, for Christ, for the Word of God, and for everything that is right and proper according to it. But it is also evidence of an over-abundance of love—*love for self!* In every single instance of "church trouble" of which I have been aware, it has come about because for some *self was more important—more important than the truth, more important than God, more important than the Lord, and more important than those whom Jesus died to purchase.*

January 7

"My Grace Is Sufficient for Thee"

When sickness enters into our lives,
And we cannot function as we would,
We turn to our Heavenly Father on our knee,
And He says, "My grace is sufficient for thee."

As we walk down the hospital corridors,
And see the tears in brethren's eyes,
In despair we may turn to Elijah's juniper tree,
But He says, "My grace is sufficient for thee."

When to the funeral home we are called,
And at the casket we all meet,
The Word teaches us that this is as it must be;
And God says, "My grace is sufficient for thee."

Church Trouble

"There's no trouble like church trouble!" That is an expression that I have both heard and used over the years, and in many ways it is true. "Church trouble" is heart wrenching; it tears at our insides and can make us physically sick. One of the problems is that it is just so hard to understand, and if we find ourselves in it we ask, "Why is this happening?" I guess I have been blessed. I preached for twenty-four years before I encountered any "church trouble" to speak of, but when it came, it came with a vengeance. I couldn't find any comfort when I tried to reason it out or deal with it on my own. Emotions, both good and bad, can and did get in the way. It was only when I went even deeper into the Word of God that comfort and encouragement were found.

First of all, almost from the very beginning, folks have sought to change God's prescribed method of worship and substitute their own ideas. We saw it with Cain and Abel. It is clear from the account that Abel did what *God* wanted, and his sacrifice was accepted. Cain did what *he* wanted, and his sacrifice was refused. Nadab and Abihu sought to change God's authorized form of worship by using fire from an unauthorized source. Over and over again the Israelites ventured into the realm of idolatry, changing God's prescribed methods of worship and going after other gods. If we examine it closely, we find that one of the primary reasons for doing that was a desire to be like everybody else.

This desire to change is by no means confined to the Old Testament. In his farewell address to the Ephesian elders Paul said, "Take heed therefore unto yourselves, and to all the flock, over the which the Holy Ghost hath made you overseers, to feed the church of God, which he hath purchased with his own blood. For I know this, that after my departing shall grievous wolves enter in among you, not sparing the flock. Also of your own selves shall men arise, speaking perverse things, to draw away disciples after them. Therefore watch, and remember, that by the space of three years I ceased not to warn every one night and day with tears" (Acts 20:28-31). This was a clear prediction of "church trouble."

The church at Corinth in the first century had "church trouble." A brief outline shows they were divided, suffering from "preacheritis" in chapter 1.

They were tolerating sin in the camp in chapter 5. Chapter 6 points out that they were going to law one against another. There were marriage problems mentioned in chapter 7. Some were having difficulty making the adjustment from idolatry to the truth, as dealt with in chapters 8 through 10. Some got mad and denied Paul's apostleship in chapter 9. Some were saying that the Lord's Supper was part of a common meal, so Paul had to deal with that in chapter 11. There were women who were acting out of place according to chapter 14. Some were even denying the general resurrection to come, as told in chapter 15. This was a church that had "trouble"!

January 9

More about Church Trouble

There were those who were guilty of teaching false doctrine, disseminating an idea that was just not true, in the church at Galatia, causing tremendous problems. In 2 Thessalonians 2:7 Paul wrote, "For the mystery of iniquity doth already work: only he who now letteth will let, until he be taken out of the way." There were already those who were departing from the faith, and that causes "church trouble." 1, 2, and 3 John show that the early church had to deal with the false teaching of the Gnostics who had made their way into the church. That would create "church trouble." Think of the letters to the churches of Asia in Revelation 2 and 3. Only the churches at Smyrna and Philadelphia did not receive rebukes.

The point I am making is that "church trouble" is nothing new. There have been, and there always will be, those who are not satisfied with God's revealed word. There have been, and there always will be, those who generate "church trouble" wherever they go. The important thing is not to despair when it happens. Does it hurt? Oh, yes it does! Can it destroy long-standing friendships and relationships? Yes, it certainly can. But here we are, 2,000 years removed from the "church trouble" of the first century, and the Lord's church is still here. There are still faithful brethren who will stand upon God's word no matter what. There are still brethren who will join hands against Satan (and it is naïve to think that he doesn't come to church) and *stand!*

Faithful brethren, when "church trouble" happens, do not despair! Do not give up! Do not throw your hands up in exasperation and say, "I don't know how much more of this I can take!" No—speak up! Take your stand! Remember Ephesians 6:13-17, "Wherefore take unto you the whole armor of God, that ye may be able to withstand in the evil day, and having done all, to stand. Stand therefore, having your loins girt about with truth, and having on the breastplate of righteousness; and your feet shod with the preparation of the gospel of peace; above all, taking the shield of faith, wherewith ye shall be able to quench all the fiery darts of the wicked. And take the helmet of salvation, and the sword of the Spirit, which is the word of God."

When "church trouble" happens, just *stand on the truth*, and you will be okay. No matter what happens, each of us can do what is right. When and if "church trouble" happens, speak up to those involved. Let your stand and your position be made known. And never gossip—speak directly to those involved.

January 10

But He Is Already Gone!

True Bible students recognize that the Scriptures teach the need for discipline in the church. Discipline itself is a somewhat generic word with a much wider meaning than folks are normally inclined to give it. *Webster's New Universal Unabridged Dictionary* gives the following definitions:

1. Training to act in accordance with rules; drill; 2. Activity, exercise, or a regimen that develops or improves a skill; training; 3. Punishment inflicted by way of correction and training; 4. The rigor or training effect of experience, adversity, etc; 5. Behavior in accord with rules of conduct; 6. A set or system of rules and regulations; 7. Eccles. The system of government regulating the practice of a church as distinguished from its doctrine; 8. An instrument of punishment, esp. a whip or scourge, used in the practice of self-mortification or as an instrument of chastisement in certain religious communities; 9. A branch of instruction or learning; 10. To train by instruction and exercise; drill; 11. To bring to a state of order and obedience by training and control; 12. To punish or penalize in order to train and control; correct; chastise.

Obviously, not all of those definitions are germane to the biblical concept of discipline, but many of them are. The Hebrew word equivalent to our word "discipline" is *musar*. It comes from "yasar," meaning "to bind, to tame; hence to correct, chastise, instruct, admonish." The words are used in the Old Testament concerning the disciplinary action of a parent toward his child and of the disciplinary action of God toward His people.

The Greek equivalent of "discipline" is *paideia*, meaning "to bring up, rear a child; to train and teach, educate; to chasten, discipline." This word is used to refer to bringing a child up in the *nurture* and admonition of the Lord in Ephesians 6:4. Forms of this word are used eight times in Hebrews 12:5-11, where the necessity of discipline by both earthly parents and God is discussed. Discipline involves all of the training done, up to and including withdrawal.

In 2 Thessalonians 3:6 we read, "Now we command you, brethren, in the name of our Lord Jesus Christ, that ye withdraw yourselves from every brother that walketh disorderly (leads an unruly life, NASB), and not after the tradition which he received of us." Here we see one type of individual Christian that is to be withdrawn from, the one who walks disorderly. The Bible also teaches us to exercise this final step of discipline with those who refuse to correct personal offenses against brethren in Matthew 18:15-17. Those who cause divisions contrary to the gospel are subject to being marked according to Romans 16:17-18. Also to be withdrawn from are those who are factious, teaching heresy. This involves those teaching error and seeking to influence others to follow their same false teaching. Consider Titus 3:10. There are others as well who should have such steps taken toward them, but this gets the idea across.

If there was no other scriptural reason to do this than the fact that it is commanded, that would be more than sufficient. A passage like 2 Thessalonians 3:6 is as clear and explicit as Acts 2:38. However, failure to do such shows a lack of love and concern for the erring brother or sister. In 1 Corinthians 5 Paul was writing about a brother who was caught up in a sin of immorality and was not repenting. He wrote in verse 5, "To deliver such an one unto Satan for the destruction of the flesh, that the spirit may be saved in the day of the Lord Jesus." The primary purpose of such a step is to save the individual from eternal damnation.

"But He Is Already Gone!"
A Closer Look at 2 Thessalonians 3:6

Now I want to go back to 2 Thessalonians 3:6 and examine a few of the words used in that passage a bit more closely. First we note the word "command." This is an injunction, not a suggestion or an option. We note the phrase, "in the name of our Lord Jesus Christ." This simply means by His authority, by the authority of Jesus Christ. Note, "withdraw yourselves." This is actually a nautical term, denoting "to shorten the sails," metaphorically to keep out of the way, withdraw from, to avoid intercourse and fellowship with. Focus now on "walketh disorderly." The proper idea of this word is that of soldiers who do not keep the ranks or who are irregular in any way. Finally, note "after the tradition which he received of us." That is the doctrine of Christ that Paul delivered unto them. When it comes to taking this sort of action in this sort of case, we have a choice. We can either obey the Lord or not obey Him. That truly is what it boils down to.

The statement, or something similar to it, is often made that, "You can't withdraw from someone who has already left the congregation." That sounds reasonable, but such should never be said or believed if it cannot be backed up with book, chapter, and verse. Where does the New Testament speak of one "quitting" or walking away from a faithful congregation of the Lord's people to engage in unauthorized activities, and their actions removing the responsibility toward them of the last faithful congregation of which they were a part? How much more "disorderly" and "out of rank" can a person get than to walk away from the Lord's church to participate in man-made traditions and practices in religion? Since it is a military term, what would happen to one engaged in legitimate military service if he or she simply walked away, went AWOL?

Can a person who wants to continue in fornication simply say he is leaving the congregation and consequently not be subject to withdrawal? Should we just let him go, or should we do what the Lord commands? Such reasoning says that all a person has to do is say, "I'm leaving," and all of our responsibility toward them is ended. That is not true! Love demands that we take the final step in an effort to save their soul, and quite frankly, ours as well. I have searched for thirty years now and have not found the passage that says a person can just walk away and our responsibility toward them is ended. Have you found it?

An Unbridled Tongue

Is it possible that some don't know the damage that can be done by a loose tongue? Is it possible that some don't know that they will be held accountable for weakening the faith of another because they did not restrain their lips? Let's let God through Solomon tell us some more.

In Proverbs 6:12-14 we read, "A worthless person, a wicked man, is the one who walks with a false mouth, who winks with his eyes, who signals with his feet, who points with his fingers; who with perversity in his heart devises evil continually, who spreads strife." In chapter 11:9 we find, "With his mouth the godless man destroys his neighbor, but through knowledge the righteous will be delivered." Chapter 16:28 says, "A perverse man spreads strife, and a slanderer separates intimate friends." How about one more? Chapter 20:19 informs us, "He who goes about as a slanderer reveals secrets, therefore do not associate with a gossip." *Amen, I say; and again I say, "Amen!"*

Whispering, backbiting, gossiping, and the lack of common sense and restraint with the tongue can do irreparable damage. It can be like a fire gone out of control, or perhaps a more appropriate image is that of a wind blowing trash, debris, and garbage all over a city.

I like what Solomon wrote in Proverbs 17:27-28: "He who restrains his words has knowledge, and he who has a cool spirit is a man of understanding. Even a fool, when he keeps silent, is considered wise; when he closes his lips, he is counted prudent."

I will freely tell you that I am about to take a passage out of its context, but hopefully you will be able to understand why. In Matthew 5:29-30 Jesus said, "And if your right eye makes you stumble, tear it out, and throw it from you; for it is better for you that one of the parts of your body perish, than for your whole body to be thrown into hell. And if your right hand makes you stumble, cut it off, and throw it from you; for it is better for you that one of the parts of your body perish, than for your whole body to go into hell."

We understand that Jesus is not really saying to pluck out your eye or to cut off your hand. He is emphasizing how serious a matter sin is and how much more important the spiritual is than the physical. I believe in some cases we could say, "If your computer, with its e-mail, causes you to sin, *throw it away!* If your telephone or cell phone causes you to stumble, destroy it, smash it, *throw it away!* It is better for you to go through life without e-mail and a telephone than for your whole body to go into hell because of them."

January 13

"Be Not Many of You Teachers"

One of the more interesting warnings that we find in Scripture is in James 3:1: "Let not many of you become teachers, my brethren, knowing that as such we shall incur a stricter judgment." To begin to understand the meaning of what James is saying, it is essential to keep it in its context. How does it fit with what we read in chapters 2 and 3? In the context, the point is made that words without works are worthless, just as faith apart from works is dead. The blessings of Christ come to those who hear and do, not to those who hear and do not. Even those whose very work is to use "words" to teach the truth must remember what a very weighty responsibility that involves and not rush into it without the necessary preparation and a thorough understanding and appreciation for the work they are doing.

Reading the New Testament epistles gives the indication that in the first century there were some of the brethren who desired attention and influence that came from the more visible types of functions. 1 Corinthians 14 addresses that tendency, as does the passage under consideration now. 1 Timothy 1:5-7 says, "But the goal of our instruction is love from a pure heart and a good conscience and a sincere faith. For some men, straying from these things, have turned aside to fruitless discussion, wanting to be teachers of the Law, even though they do not understand either what they are saying or the matters about which they make confident assertions." There was a real danger of some doing teaching when they just weren't qualified or prepared to do it.

The truth is that not all disciples are equipped to be public teachers of the word. Remember 1 Corinthians 12:17? It says, "If the whole body were an eye, where would the hearing be? If the whole were hearing, where would the sense of smell be?" There are other duties and activities in the church that are equally vital, and if one is not particularly adept in one area, he or she may be exceptional in another.

Every time I stand before a group of people, either to teach a Bible class or to present a lesson in our worship services, I pause to remind myself of the awesome responsibility I have assumed. The subjects with which a Bible teacher deals are eternal in nature, and this is why James tells us that those who do so "shall incur a stricter judgment." The phrase literally means "greater judgment." The word translated "judgment" here almost always means condemnation. The word is *krima*, from *krino*, meaning to separate or distinguish. The idea is that at the great Day of Judgment, the Lord "will separate" those who have been teachers of the Word from those who have not, and will then hold them accountable for that action. The consequences of teaching that which is false can be fatal—and those who teach without proper preparation and mislead their listeners must answer under a "stricter judgment." I am reminded of what Jesus said in Matthew 18:5-7, "And whoever receives one such child in My name receives Me; and whoever causes one of these little ones who believe in Me to stumble, it is better for him that a heavy millstone be hung around his neck, and that he be drowned in the depth of the sea. Woe to the world because of its stumbling blocks! For it is inevitable that stumbling blocks come; but woe to that man through whom the stumbling block comes!"

As teachers of the Word, either through public Bible classes or as presenters of sermons, we must also be prepared for a "stricter judgment" for those we teach. Indeed, in Luke 8:18 Jesus exhorted all to "take care how you listen." In 1 John 4:1 we are told, "Beloved, do not believe every spirit, but test the spirits to see whether they are from God; because many false prophets have gone out into the world." Those that we teach have the responsibility to "examine the Scriptures daily, to see whether these things are so" (Acts 17:11). If we assume the task of teaching, we must expect our words to be closely examined, debated, and dissected. Indeed, what we say publicly is fair game. I have been confronted in the back and in the front of auditoriums after services, sometimes rationally and sometimes irrationally. I have had people make broad demonstrations of how they felt about what I had to say. That is just the way it goes.

Does this mean that a teacher or preacher must be perfect? I pray not, for I have made many mistakes and have needed to correct them. I have changed views as my understanding of Scripture matured and will continue to do so. However, it does mean that all who choose to teach publicly must appreciate how serious a matter it truly is and make certain that the proper study has been done and the proper preparation made.

January 14

More Important Than Myself (Phil. 2:3)

If I can learn to truly regard others "as more important" than myself, then I will have taken a giant step toward living day by day as a faithful child of God. I struggle with this concept in some aspects and don't struggle with it in others. How can I view the person who has nothing and lives off of the government as more important than myself? How can I consider a person who does not match my intellectual abilities and talents as more important than myself? I can do it by looking at Jesus, that's how. How do I compare to Jesus? Like a drop of water in the bottom of an otherwise empty 50-gallon drum. I am nothing, and the Lord died for me. One person wrote that the person who is able to think this way is "the one who is so conscious of his dependence on God, and of his own imperfections and nothingness, that his own gifts only remind him that others must have gifts also, while his sense of his own utter nothingness suggests to him that these gifts may well be superior to his own, and higher in nature and degree."

Thinking this way, it becomes possible for me to "not merely look out for your own personal interests, but also for the interests of others." Paul's point is that the feelings, interests, and needs of our brethren are to be put before and above our own. That does not mean to ignore our own needs, but to subordinate them to the needs of others. In Romans 12:10 Paul put it this way, "Be devoted to one another in brotherly love; give preference to one another in honor."

Just think of how this understanding would affect our conduct in very practical ways. All of the sick would be visited and cared for just because we would be thinking about them. No one's burdens would have to be borne alone—because brothers and sisters would always be there with arms extended to help pick them up. We would all be present at every service that our health allowed because we would be most concerned about considering one another, to "provoke unto love and to good works" (Heb. 10:24). Arguments concerning non-doctrinal issues would be laid aside; they would cease, because the brethren involved in them would be most concerned about the others. Even when I have been sinned against, if I understand Paul's teaching in Philippians 2, than I am going to be most concerned about the spiritual welfare of the other person. That changes my entire attitude.

When I live my life recognizing that I am to follow the example of Jesus and to see others as more important than myself, I will engage in personal evangelism even when it is inconvenient or makes me feel uncomfortable. I will be moral and conduct myself as a child of God should every minute of every day because I want to give the best possible example that I can to every one with whom I come into contact. Christianity is not about me—that proved to be a hard lesson for me to learn. It is about the other person.

January 15

Duties of Elders (1)

The eldership (the plurality of elders overseeing a local congregation) is an executive body, not a legislative body. We are under the *"law of faith"* (Rom. 3:27), and the responsibility of the elders is to see to it that every law of the Lord Jesus Christ is carried out. The elders do not have the power or authority to make laws.

In Hebrews 13:17 we read, "Obey them that have the rule over you, and submit yourselves: for they watch for your souls, as they that must give account, that they may do it with joy, and not with grief: for that is unprofitable for you." Two of the duties of the elders are set forth in this verse. They are to "rule," meaning "to lead, to go before; to have authority over."

1 Peter 5:3 points out that this is not to be a tyrannical rule. It is not as though Christ made the elders "lords" over the flock.

Hebrews 13:17 also points out that the elders have the responsibility of "watching" on behalf of the soul of each member in the congregation. While the nature of this article precludes a thorough examination of the passage,

Ezekiel 33 sets forth in a powerful way some of the responsibilities of a watchman, including warning and exhortation. We know as well that they must watch for false teachers entering into the flock, and that they must also watch their own lives (Acts 20:28-31).

Peter tells us in 1 Peter 5:1-2, "The elders which are among you I exhort, who am also an elder, and a witness of the sufferings of Christ, and also a partaker of the glory that shall be revealed: feed the flock of God which is among you, taking the oversight thereof, not by constraint, but willingly: not for filthy lucre, but of a ready mind." The word "feed" is from the Greek *poimaino*, meaning, "to act as a shepherd." That is a responsibility of the elders that encompasses many things.

First of all, shepherds lead—they do not drive their flocks. Elders are to be examples to the flock, they are "out in front," leading the congregation. An elder should live in such a manner that he would be able to ask the congregation to "Be followers of me, even as I also am of Christ" (1 Cor. 11:1). The Bible indicates several areas in which they must be exemplary. For instance, in their personal conduct and character, their habits and their speech. They should be examples in attendance at all services, in personal evangelism, in visiting the sick, in their family relationships, in making peace. In every day activities in the community, in their jobs, recreation, and so forth, they must serve as good examples.

January 16

Duties of Elders (2)

As shepherds, elders must protect the "flock" in the face of all danger, including false teachers (Acts 20:28-31). They must care for the people that they oversee, knowing each member and watching to see that none stray from the flock (Heb. 13:17). They must see to it that the congregation is fed and that what they are fed is the unadulterated, full counsel of God (Acts 20:27-28).

One of the qualifications for a man who is appointed as an elder in the Lord's church is that he be "apt to teach" (1 Tim. 3:2). That means he must be skilled in some form of teaching. Why? "That he may be able by sound doctrine both to exhort and to convince the gainsayers" (Tit. 1:9).

Additionally, elders are charged with the responsibility of admonishing the church. In 1 Thessalonians 5:12 we read, "And we beseech you, brethren, to know them which labor among you, and are over you in the Lord, and admonish you." To admonish is to warn of a fault, to reprove gently but seriously, to exhort, and even to remind someone of something they may have forgotten. A faithful elder must be no respecter of persons in this duty. He is to uphold truth and right, regardless of who, when, or where; even as he knows that some will not take it very well.

Another qualification of a man who would be an elder indicates another of his duties. 1 Timothy 3:2 tells us that he must be "given to hospitality." The home of an elder should be a place of hospitality, where all are welcome. It is easy to see the wisdom of God in also requiring that an elder be "the husband of one wife." His faithful wife will have a large part to play in the hospitality of his home.

Elders are to oversee the financial matters of a congregation. This is clearly demonstrated in Acts 11:29-30, when the brethren in Antioch sent relief to the brethren in Judea who were suffering from a famine. They sent the relief into the hands of the elders.

Elders also have the responsibility to see to it that discipline of all required forms is carried out. Faithful elders, acting according to the Law of Christ, have the full authority of Christ to lead the congregation in discipline of the disorderly. They are to do so according to the pattern given by the Lord in such passages as Matthew 18:15-18, 1 Corinthians 5:4-5, 2 Thessalonians 3:6, 14-15, and Titus 3:10. It is a fearful responsibility, and it takes true courage on the part of the elders to enforce the will of God in such matters. They must keep themselves free of bias, prejudice, or personalities in problems that may arise. The Lord's will must be carried out.

January 17

Who Were These People?

In the New Testament we frequently read of two groups of people, the Pharisees and the Sadducees. Less frequently we read of another group called the Herodians. Who were these people, and what made a Pharisee a Pharisee, a Sadducee a Sadducee, and a Herodian a Herodian?

The Pharisees were the strictest sect of the Jews. In Acts 26:4-5, as Paul was presenting his defense before Agrippa, he said, "My manner of life from my youth, which was at the first among mine own nation at Jerusalem, know all the Jews; which knew me from the beginning, if they would testify, that after the most straitest sect of our religion I lived a Pharisee."

The word itself comes from the Hebrew word, *pharash*, meaning to set apart, separate. In the case of the Pharisees, that would be from anything that would hinder exact obedience to the Law of Moses.

They made their appearance in the time between the testaments, probably in the period before the Maccabean War. The Jews were beginning to adopt Hellenistic practices, showing a willingness to accept Greek customs and beliefs. The Pharisees arose as a reaction to this move away from the Law. They were first called Pharisees sometime between 135-105 B.C. At first the Pharisees were men of the strongest religious character. It could be argued that they were the best people in the Jewish nation. As the years passed, the overall quality decreased, and by the time of Jesus they were noted for their self-righteousness, hypocrisy, and their inattention to the weightier matters of the Law.

The Sadducees were comparatively few in number, but they were educated men, mostly wealthy, and of good position. They stood in opposition to the Pharisees, and while the Pharisees exercised a great deal of influence in the synagogues, the Sadducees controlled the temple.

Their name comes from Sadok (Zadok), a pupil of Antigonus Sochaeus, who was president of the Sanhedrin 260 years before Christ. Sochaeus taught that man had a duty to serve God without any hope of reward or fear of punishment. Sadok took his views even further and ended up denying the existence of heaven or hell—teaching that the soul dies with the body. The Sadducees also denied that there were angels, and interestingly, they taught that God was not concerned with man doing good or with man not doing evil. They taught that all the good man received was a result of man himself, and that all the evil man received was the result of man's own folly.

The Herodians were a Jewish party in the time of Jesus and were evidently supporters of the Herod family. It is important to remember that the Herods were not of proper Jewish descent, and they had supplanted a royal family that was not merely Jewish, but of priestly blood and rank. Additionally, the Herods took great pains to appease the Romans. The Herodians were Jews who supported this usurping family. This made them natural enemies of the Pharisees, and to a lesser extent, of the Sadducees as well.

The interesting thing is that all three of these groups, as antagonistic to each other as they were, could and did unite in their opposition to Jesus. Each in their own way perceived Jesus as a threat to their position. In Matthew 22:15-16 we read of all three groups attacking Jesus, "Then went the Pharisees, and took counsel how they might entangle Him in His talk. And they sent out unto Him their disciples with the Herodians. . . ." In verse 23 we read, "The same day came to Him the Sadducees, which say that there is no resurrection, and asked Him. . . ." In verse 34 we find, "But when the Pharisees had heard that He had put the Sadducees to silence, they were gathered together."

January 18

A Sad Thing

One Halloween I saw something that I haven't been able to get out of my mind. I guess you could say that what I saw is really "haunting" me! A group of youngsters came to our door to "trick or treat," and included in their number was a young girl who looked to be about thirteen or fourteen years of age. She was dressed up in a costume, with painted-on freckles all over her face, giggling and laughing with what appeared to be her sisters, a big bag of candy in her hand—and she was pregnant. The pregnancy was not part of her costume; it was all too tragically real.

What can you say about something like that? Young enough to be "trick or treating," old enough to be pregnant.

We all know "how" something like this happens, but what about the "why"? That little baby was the result of sin. Hebrews 13:4 clearly states, "Marriage is honourable in all, and the bed undefiled: but whoremongers and adulterers God will judge." Paul wrote in 1 Corinthians 7:2, "Nevertheless, to avoid fornication, let every man have his own wife, and let every woman have her own husband." That child on my porch was not married; that was apparent.

Who was to blame? The girl's mother was standing on the sidewalk while her children went from house to house. Does the blame reside on the parent's shoulders? Paul told us in Ephesians 6:4, "And, ye fathers, provoke not your children to wrath: but bring them up in the nurture and admonition of the Lord." Did they do their job in this case? I am not the judge, and I don't know. I must confess, I have real difficulty with that girl being out there "trick or treating" as if nothing was wrong. "Trick or treating" is something for children to engage in, and like it or not, that young girl had left her childhood behind.

Was society to blame? That young girl was bombarded continually by sexual messages. The songs to which she listened (country or rock), the television shows, movies, magazines, even commercials, all use sex to sell. It is as Paul wrote in Romans 1:32, "Who knowing the judgment of God, that they which commit such things are worthy of death, not only do the same, but have pleasure in them that do them." If she attended public school, she was being taught to be tolerant of just about every sinful, perverse lifestyle that people can dream up. So many of her peers are pregnant that high schools now offer daycare centers for the students. Pregnancy out of wedlock used to be something of which to be ashamed; now we bend over backwards to make those who put themselves in that position feel as if they have done nothing wrong. Help them, yes. But don't make them think that they haven't done anything wrong!

Was the girl to blame? Of course she was! I realize that the sex drive is a difficult thing to harness once it is allowed to get out of control, but I also realize that responsibility to control oneself resides with each of us. Ezekiel wrote, "The soul that sinneth, it shall die." She was old enough to get pregnant; she was old enough to know right from wrong.

Unless there is a general return to the standard of God's Word, a standard that used to characterize this country's morals, there will just be more pregnant "trick or treaters" in the future. Society is to blame to a certain extent. The ridiculous doctrine of humanism that now characterizes the curriculum of the schools is a classic example of "changing the glory of the incorruptible God into an image made like to corruptible man." What we are seeing now in America is the same thing Paul wrote of in Romans 1:28, "And even as they did not like to retain God in their knowledge, God gave them over to a reprobate mind, to do those things which are not convenient."

My heart went out to the girl. I looked at her and saw the young girls of our congregation. I looked at her and saw my daughter. *We have got to teach them right from wrong!* They may ultimately make the choice to commit this sin anyway, but I pray to God that they won't.

My heart went out to the baby. It's tough enough in this world, without being forced to enter it on public assistance and to face a life of poverty. In truth, it made my heart break.

Revealed by Fire

In 1 Corinthians 3:12-15 Paul wrote, "Now if any man build upon this foundation gold, silver, precious stones, wood, hay, stubble; every man's work shall be made manifest: for the day shall declare it, because it shall be *revealed by fire*; and the fire shall try every man's work of what sort it is. If any man's work abide which he hath built thereupon, he shall receive a reward. If any man's work shall be burned, he shall suffer loss; but he himself shall be saved; yet so as by fire."

I believe that the main point of this passage is evangelization, and building upon the foundation of the Lord Jesus Christ. As the gospel is presented, some will respond favorably and be true, strong Christians. Even when trials and tribulations come ("fire" so to speak), they will remain faithful, coming through those trials and tribulations even stronger than they were before. These are the "gold, silver, precious stones." They are not destroyed by "fire"; they are purified and strengthened by it.

There are others who will hear the gospel and respond favorably to it, only to fall away when difficulties arise. These are the "wood, hay, stubble." Difficulties destroy them, burn them up. Those who taught such "wood, hay, stubble" will feel loss as he sees them fall away. It is heart-rending to see someone you had a part in converting decide to abandon the Lord, but it happens. However, if the one who did the teaching remains faithful, he or she will be saved.

I think that a certain degree of "fire," of tribulation, even persecution, is good and beneficial. It has both a strengthening and a pruning effect. There are many "Christians" who are really playing at religion. They are not faithful in their attendance and cannot be counted upon to do anything other than sit in a pew one time a week for one or two hours. I am not sure what continues to motivate them for that one or two hours, but it cannot be conviction. When trials and tribulations come upon them, oftentimes they will be gone.

Every congregation can only function to its maximum capability if each member in it is doing his very best. A small congregation of faithful, dedicated members is a stronger congregation than a large one filled with lukewarm, undedicated members who lack conviction. Every member is important, and every member needs to realize that. In Ephesians 4:15-16 Paul wrote, "But speaking the truth in love, may grow up into him in all things, which is the head, even Christ: from whom the whole body fitly joined together and compacted *by that which every joint supplieth*, according to the effectual working in the measure of every part, maketh increase of the body unto the edifying of itself in love."

One very positive effect that can be derived from trials and tribulations, even outright persecution, is that they can purify and strengthen us if we let them. Nobody wants to see any Christian fall away; but at the same time, nobody wants to see a Christian "play" at religion. Oftentimes difficulties separate the wheat from the chaff.

I am reminded of the wonderful words of the Holy Spirit penned by the apostle Paul in 2 Corinthians 4:8-13. Here is what can happen to people of conviction when trials and tribulations come upon us. He wrote, "We are troubled on every side, yet not distressed; we are perplexed, but not in despair; persecuted, but not forsaken; cast down, but not destroyed; always bearing about in the body the dying of the Lord Jesus, that the life also of Jesus might be made manifest in our body. For we which live are always delivered unto death for Jesus' sake, that the life also of Jesus might be made manifest in our mortal flesh. So then death worketh in us, but life in you. We having the same spirit of faith, according as it is written, I believed, and therefore have I spoken; we also believe, and therefore speak."

Let the troubles come. We believe, therefore we speak. As Peter said before the Jewish council in Acts 4:20, "We cannot but speak the things which we have seen and heard." He made that statement after having been arrested and threatened. That's the essence of conviction.

False Teachers

There has been considerable discussion among brethren over the last several years concerning who can be rightfully labeled as a false teacher. The controversy has focused upon 2 Peter 2:1-3. That passage says, "But false prophets also arose among the people, just as there will also be *false teachers* among you, who will secretly introduce destructive heresies, even denying the Master who bought them, bringing swift destruction upon themselves. And many will follow their sensuality, and because of them the way of the truth will be maligned; and in their greed they will exploit you with false words, their judgment from long ago is not idle, and their destruction is not asleep."

There is no question that this passage has something to say about the motive behind the false teaching that a false teacher does. Looking just at verse 1 we find, "just as there will also be false teachers among you, who. . . ." The word "who" is a relative pronoun, the antecedent of which is "false teachers." It is "qualitative and intends to characterize and describe." Peter follows the word "who" by describing what these "false teachers" do and the motive behind it. Consequently, it has been argued that a brother who teachers "false doctrine" cannot be accurately described as a "false teacher" unless his motives are as wicked and insidious as those set forth in 2 Peter 2. Is that a correct idea? Does it somehow lessen the seriousness of what is occurring when a brother teaches false doctrine?

Let's notice a few things from the Scriptures. First, the opposite of false doctrine is sound doctrine—that which is true and according to the Word of God. Concerning the importance of sound doctrine, Paul wrote in 1 Timothy 4:6, "In pointing out these things to the brethren, you will be a good servant of Christ Jesus, constantly nourished on the words of the faith and of the sound doctrine which you have been following." Hence, "sound doctrine" is the very nourishment upon which a Christian feeds. In Titus 2:1 Paul exhorted Titus to "speak the things which are fitting for sound doctrine," and in verse 7 of the same chapter he urged him to "show yourself to be an example of good deeds, with purity in doctrine, dignified." In 2 Timothy 4:3-4 Paul wrote, "For the time will come when they will not endure sound doctrine; but wanting to have their ears tickled, they will accumulate for themselves teachers in accordance to their own desires; and will turn away their ears from the truth, and will turn aside to myths." This is in condemnation of those who "will not endure sound doctrine" and who "turn away their ears from the truth." The importance of "sound doctrine" of teaching and believing the truth, cannot be overemphasized.

How is false doctrine viewed in Scripture? It is condemned as being demonic. Remember John 8:44 where Jesus said, "You are of your father the devil, and you want to do the desires of your father. He was a murderer from the beginning, and does not stand in the truth, because there is no truth in him. Whenever he speaks a lie, he speaks from his own nature; for he is a liar, and the father of lies." How much more forcefully can this point be made than it is in 1 Timothy 4:1-2 where Paul wrote, "But the Spirit explicitly says that in later times some will fall away from the faith, paying attention to deceitful spirits and doctrines of demons, by means of the hypocrisy of liars seared in their own conscience as with a branding iron"?

The Bible condemns believing false doctrine. In 2 Thessalonians 2:10-12 we find, "And with all the deception of wickedness for those who perish, because they did not receive the love of the truth so as to be saved. And for this reason God will send upon them a deluding influence so that they might believe what is false, in order that they all may be judged who did not believe the truth, but took pleasure in wickedness."

The Bible also condemns teaching false doctrine, regardless of what the motive might be. In Galatians 1:6-9 we read, "I am amazed that you are so quickly deserting Him who called you by the grace of Christ, for a different gospel; which is really not another; only there are some who are disturbing you, and want to distort the gospel of Christ. But even though we, or an angel from heaven, should preach to you a gospel contrary to that which we have preached to you, let him be accursed. As we have said before, so I say again now, if any man is preaching to you a gospel contrary to that which you received, let him be accursed." 1 Timothy 6:3-5 also should be mentioned, "If anyone advocates a different doctrine, and does not agree with sound words, those of our Lord Jesus Christ, and with the doctrine conforming to godliness, he is conceited and understands nothing; but he has a morbid interest in controversial questions and disputes about words, out of which arise envy, strife, abusive language, evil suspicions, and constant friction between men of depraved mind and deprived of the truth, who suppose that godliness is a means of great gain."

The Bible even condemns supporting or encouraging those who teach false doctrine in any way whatsoever, and it doesn't do so based solely on the motive behind the false teaching. In 2 John 9-11 we are told, "Anyone who goes too far and does not abide in the teaching of Christ, does not have God; the one who abides in the teaching has both the Father and the Son. If anyone comes to you and does not bring this teaching, do not receive him into your house, and do not give him a greeting; for the one who gives him a greeting participates in his evil deeds."

If someone teaches something that is absolutely false and is not part of the "teaching of Christ," yet his motive in doing so is pure and he truly believes what he has taught—does it make it any less false or damaging? If I believe something false that was sincerely taught to me by one who was honestly mistaken, does that make it any less false? It certainly seems to me that regardless of what the motive of the teacher might be, the end result of false doctrine will be the same.

January 21

Thinking about the Family—Its Importance

What is the foundational unit of society as designed and created by God? The answer to that question is the family. In Genesis 2 we read some of the specifics of the creation account given in chapter 1. Included in Genesis 2 is the beginning of the family with Eve being created as a suitable companion for Adam, and these two being brought together and joined together by God. They were given the charge to "be fruitful and multiply, and replenish the earth" (Gen. 1:28). In this we see the formation of the basic unit of society.

It has always been true that the welfare of man on earth has risen and fallen with the recognition of the importance of that basic family unit. I say that because the emotional, physical, intellectual, and spiritual needs of every individual begin to be met in that family relationship as God designed it. It is in the home that the most important truths must be instilled. It is in the home that respect and love for God as the Creator, Sustainer, and Ruler must be formulated. It is in the home that the principles of right and wrong, respect for authority, ethical standards, and personal responsibility must be taught. This truth is found in both the Old and the New Testaments. Deuteronomy 6:6-7 tells us, "And these words, which I command thee this day, shall be in thine heart: and thou shalt teach them diligently unto thy children, and shalt talk of them when thou sittest in thine house, and when thou walkest by the way, and when thou liest down, and when thou risest up." Ephesians 6:4 puts it so simply with the words, "And ye fathers, provoke not your children to wrath: but bring them up in the nurture and admonition of the Lord."

Any time, and to the same degree, that the most important truths of life fail to be taught in the home, society as a whole will suffer. Sadly enough, many of the bad things that happen in society seem to sooner or later make their way into the church. No thinking Christian can deny that the general breakdown of the family unit in our society has begun to manifest itself more frequently within the body of Christ. We are seeing more unhappy families, more unruly children with no interest in spiritual things, more abuse of different kinds, more worldliness, more divorce. We, whose responsibility it is to shine forth as lights in the world (Matt. 5:16) are, in many instances, allowing the world to exercise the greater influence.

What can be done? There is only one answer to the problems so many of us face in our families today. We must follow the blueprint of the architect of the family, God. He designed it. He created it. If anyone would learn how to be a better husband, provider, father, and companion—let that person turn to God's Word. All of the principles and precepts needed to function in every relationship we sustain in the family are there. Is it the desire of a woman to learn to be a godly wife, a mother, and a best friend to her spouse? Then let her study God's Word and find every answer that she needs within its pages. Does a son or a daughter want to be the very best son or daughter they can be, the very best person they can be? Such will not happen by following the example of the world. It will happen by learning and clinging to God's Word. David wrote in Psalm 119:9, "Wherewithal shall a young man cleanse his way? By taking heed thereto according to thy word."

Oh, brethren, what God's word has to say about the family, and each member in it, is neither trite nor antiquated. "For the Word of God is quick, and powerful, and sharper than any two-edged sword, piercing even to the dividing asunder of soul and spirit, and of the joints and marrow, and is a discerner of the thoughts and intents of the heart" (Heb. 4:12). There is nothing like the Word of God. It is absolutely unique, and it is through its precepts that we get understanding (Ps. 119:104).

I would not dare to present myself as an expert on the family, *but God is!*

Thinking about the Family—"Submitting Yourselves One to Another in the Fear of God"

Over the years there have been many occasions when I have been asked to talk to different married couples who were experiencing problems in their marriages. On many other occasions my input was not sought or wanted, yet I could not stand on the sidelines and watch as another family disintegrated. Even those who are Christians are not immune to those kinds of problems. Very few congregations of any size that have existed for several years have escaped the heartache derived from watching a beloved married brother and sister decide to go their separate ways in violation of God's Word, or from watching a family that is loved by all degenerate into unhappiness, bitterness, and disharmony. These kinds of things take place rather frequently. Sometimes you can see it happening, other times there is no obvious indication that something is wrong until it is too late to help.

What problems seem to come up most often? I would have to agree with most experts (and I do not put myself in their company—I just have the benefit of being able to read what they say) that the number one problem in marriage is money, particularly among young people. Sometimes problems arise that have to do with the intimate side of marriage. At other times moral issues come up, when one or the other desires to engage in activities that are sinful. There are problems with the children and how they are to be raised. Sometimes couples just don't talk to each other, and when they do talk it is not about things that really matter. There are just a host of different problems that can and do come up.

It has been my experience that in each and every situation that has led to an unhappy marriage, or even to the dissolving of a family, there has been a failure to abide by Ephesians 5:21 where Paul wrote, "Submitting yourselves one to another in the fear of God."

The word translated as "submitting" (*hupotassomenoi*) has an interesting etymology. Originally it was military in meaning, describing the coming together of troops for battle under a commanding officer. Each individual soldier was to understand and stay in his proper place in the formation as instructed by his superior. Eventually it came to mean subordination in any relationship under discussion. If a person was "submitting," he was placing himself under the influence of authority—and that could be a person or position, as far as obedience was concerned. There was the subjection of one's will to that of another. This can be either voluntary or involuntary. If I were captured by an enemy and forced into a life of slavery, there would be submission, but it would not have been entered into voluntarily. But when we talk about the kind of submission required by the gospel of Christ, we are talking about submission entered into by choice. I voluntarily submit myself to Christ. I voluntarily submit myself to the oversight of the elders of the congregation of which I am a member. Indeed, I voluntarily submit myself to my brothers and sisters in Christ.

There is another aspect of *hupotassomenoi* (submitting) that needs to be considered. In some instances, and context would make this determination, it goes beyond authority and involves the "motive" behind the submitting. It involves an unselfish concern for the desires and wishes of another, even when that other person has no real authority over you. It is the antithesis of selfishness. Paul, in Ephesians 5:21, was instructing the brethren to voluntarily "submit" to one another. This means to always take the needs and feelings of the others into consideration, even more than our own. He was telling them, and us, not to be selfish, not always to demand our own will and our own way. That kind of attitude was necessary one to another in the body of Christ; can't we see how important it is in the family relationship at home?

Paul goes on to show how this works in the home in Ephesians 5:22-25, "Wives, submit yourselves unto your own husbands, as unto the Lord. For the husband is the head of the wife, even as Christ is the head of the church: and He is the savior of the body. Therefore as the church is subject unto Christ, so let the wives be to their own husbands in everything. Husbands, love your wives, even as Christ also loved the church and gave himself for it." In verse 28 we read, "So ought men to love their wives as their own bodies. He that loveth his wife loveth himself."

Whenever there is a failure to "submit" one to another in the home, problems will arise, and this lack of submission is selfishness. Yes, money often creates major problems in the marriage, but how? Several different scenarios related to this have been played out in families over the years. Sometimes there is a wife who is not satisfied with what the husband is able to provide monetarily, and she becomes bitter. Sometimes there is a husband who will not work to provide for his family. Sometimes both of them work but live way beyond their means or their needs, hence there is constant pressure to make more money. If one of them gets sick or loses their job, then they are in deep financial trouble. You don't have to look too hard to see that selfishness plays a role in each of those situations.

I have been aware of times when, through no fault of their own, families have gotten into money problems. There may have been an accident, sickness, a lay-off, or something like that. Even as the situation became very difficult, it did not create problems between the husband and wife because each one was more concerned about the feelings and the needs of the other. They were submitting to one another. So instead of fussing and fighting, they pulled together to confront their problems and work them out.

January 23

Thinking about the Family—Physical Intimacy

On occasion problems will arise in a marriage that have to do with the intimate side of the relationship. If there is no physical cause creating the difficulty, then usually it is possible to trace the disturbance back to a failure to embrace and abide by Ephesians 5:21, "Submitting yourselves one to another in the fear of God."

In 1 Corinthians 7:1-5 some very basic principles dealing with this side of marriage are set forth. Paul wrote, "Now concerning the things whereof ye wrote unto me: it is good for a man not to touch a woman. Nevertheless, to avoid fornication, let every man have his own wife, and let every woman have her own husband. Let the husband render unto the wife due benevolence: and likewise also the wife unto her husband. The wife hath not power of her own body, but the husband: and likewise the husband hath not power of his own body, but the wife. Defraud ye not one the other except it be with consent for a time, that ye may give yourselves to fasting and prayer; and come together again, that Satan tempt you not for your incontinency."

There have been instances where the intimate side of marriage has been used as a weapon. What I mean by this is that one or the other will defraud their mate, depriving them of their God-given right, until they get their own way about some matter. Surely we can all see that such behavior is as ungodly as can be and is in direct violation of the principle of Ephesians 5:21, as well as many others.

I have had people tell me over the years that they no longer find their mate physically attractive or appealing. Sometimes the mate, thinking only of him or herself, has in fact allowed their physical appearance to deteriorate, no longer even trying to make themselves attractive for their spouse. Sometimes it is just that the complainer thinks the grass is going to be greener on the other side, and they don't stop to think that maybe the stretch marks came from the bearing of children or that the little bit of a belly is just nature's way of saying you are getting older. Instead of thinking of what a joy it is to go through all of these stages of life together, they think only of the physical things that are not what true love is all about. So often this kind of complaint and problem has its birth in just plain selfishness and a failure to understand and abide by Ephesians 5:21.

How many marriages of brethren over the years have been torn asunder by adultery? More than I care to think about. When all of the rationalization has been done, and all of the excuses have been given, 99.9999% of the time it boils down to selfishness. How can there possibly be unselfish concern for the desires and wishes of the spouse, and adultery be committed? How can the one guilty of such a thing be considering the feelings and needs of his/her mate? This is all part and parcel of "submitting one to another," and the Holy Spirit through Paul used marriage to illustrate how it is supposed to work in Ephesians 5.

I have known of marriages among brethren destroyed because of moral issues. One or the other decides to engage in some activity that is contrary to God's Word. It might be drinking, gambling, pornography, or any one of a number of other things from which Christians should stay as far away as possible. When the one spouse refuses to violate God's law to placate the selfish and unholy desires of the other, trouble comes. Who causes the trouble? Is it the one who refuses to sin or the one who demands their own way, even to the extent of trying to lead their spouse into sin with them? These kinds of things are the result of a failure to apply Ephesians 5:21.

Thinking about the Family—Children

Sometimes there are problems with the discipline of the children. Why is it that some couples refuse to sit down and talk out their differences over the handling of certain parental responsibilities? Could it be that one or the other is determined it will be their way or no way? I understand that the man is the head of the family, yet at the same time I recognize that Ephesians 5:21, "submitting yourselves one to another" also applies to his relationship with his wife, and not just hers to him. The woman was created as a help "meet" for man. That means complimentary and compatible in every way. If her opinion isn't worth anything, neither is his. When there is genuine submission, real concern for the desires and the wishes of the spouse, these kinds of problems won't prove to be problems for very long.

For many of us, one of the happiest, as well as one of the most frightening, days of our lives was the day when the doctor said the test was positive and there was a baby on the way. As we looked into the eyes of our spouse and held each other close, we knew that we were embarking on a new and exciting adventure. Do you remember the feeling? Do you remember the love you felt for that person with whom you had chosen to spend your life? Do you remember the feeling of responsibility, knowing that you were going to be bringing a new life into this world? Remember the countless hours spent in discussion about how you were going to raise that child, what you would and would not do? Oh, the innocence of inexperience and youth! Remember the childbirth classes, the shopping, the showers, and all of the things that go along with the impending arrival of a new addition to a family?

What a blessing it is to be parents! The psalmist wrote in Psalm 127:3-5, "Lo, children are an heritage of the Lord: and the fruit of the womb is His reward. As arrows are in the hand of a mighty man; so are the children of youth. Happy is the man that hath his quiver full of them: they shall not be ashamed, but they shall speak with their enemies in the gate."

God's plan for the family is a wonderful thing—one man and one woman together for life, being fruitful and multiplying, bringing children into the world. Within His plan God has provided for the physical, intellectual, the emotional, and the spiritual needs of the child. To summarize how God has provided for all of these needs, we can simply say, "the parents."

The responsibility to provide for the physical needs of the child is found in such passages as 1 Timothy 5:8, "But if any provide not for his own, and especially for those of his own house, he hath denied the faith, and is worse than an infidel." When it comes to the intellectual, emotional, and spiritual needs, such passages as Deuteronomy 6:6-7 and Ephesians 6:4 show that God has placed the primary responsibility in these areas on the shoulders of the parents. When we choose to become parents, we choose to assume these responsibilities. If ever there is a situation where God would have us put the needs of others before ourselves, it is in the realm of parenting. Certainly when it comes to manifesting genuine care and concern for others, our children must be at the top of that list. Why is it that we are seeing more and more parents within the Lord's church acting like those in the world when it comes to their children and their parental responsibilities?

I truly believe with all my heart that, barring death, a child has the God-given right to grow up with both parents. Surely that truth is contained in our Lord's teaching concerning marriage in such passages as Matthew 5:32, "But I say unto you, That whosoever shall put away his wife, saving for the cause of fornication, causeth her to commit adultery: and whosoever shall marry her that is divorced committeth adultery." God's intention is that marriage be one man and one woman together for life. I truly believe that a child has the God-given right to have all of his or her needs provided through the faithful fulfillment of their responsibilities by the parents. Yet more and more we are seeing parents fail in this area and the children suffering because of it, and it is happening within the church.

January 25

Thinking about the Family— "Do Not Sin Against the Child"

There is a passage that I would like to take out of context because the wording of it fits this topic. It is found in Genesis 42:22 and is a statement Reuben made to his brothers concerning their ungodly treatment of their brother Joseph, "Spake I not unto you, saying, Do not sin against the child:

and ye would not hear? Therefore, behold also his blood is required." When marriages deteriorate into unhappiness and discontent, or when they dissolve altogether and end in divorce, the children of those marriages are being "sinned against."

A child should not be deprived of the constant presence of a mother or father. The child has the God-given right to both. A child should not have to listen to his mother or father fight. Children should never have to hear one parent try to convince them to choose over the other. A child should not have to undergo emotional problems because he or she somehow feels responsible for the ungodly behavior of his parents. A child should never have to be used as a pawn in a power struggle between two parents. I stood in a courtroom hallway and watched and listened as two "divorce" lawyers (representing two "Christians") negotiated over the children. They were actually bargaining with one another as the parents sought to *win* the battle, and the children were the bounty. A child should never have to be deprived of one set of grandparents.

There are times when a divorce is scriptural, but even then it is brought about because of sin; and it is always the children who suffer.

Even within a family that stays together there are ways that the children can be "sinned against." In our modern society, it is often the case that both the mother and the father work outside of the home. There are circumstances where this arrangement is necessary simply to provide for the necessities of life—food, clothing, shelter, etc. But there are many other situations where the primary purpose is not to provide the necessities, but to provide the luxuries. Therefore, the children often have the best toys money can buy, and all of them. They have the nicest clothes and money in their pockets, late-model cars to drive, and everything else of a material nature they desire. But they don't have their parents at home to talk to.

It certainly seems that money breeds the desire for more. Let me give you a common scenario that is often played out. There will be a married couple, both of them working and spending everything they make. Children come, but they are too far in debt to allow the mother to stop working outside of the home, so the children go into day care. Day care costs a lot of money, so every bit of extra they might have had now goes to paying for that. However, the more this couple has, the more they want. So as one credit card gets paid off, another gets filled up.

Or perhaps even more frequently, when one credit card hits its limit, another one is applied for, received, and used. Soon the old house isn't nice enough either. A new one is needed in a nicer neighborhood with a humongous monthly payment. New cars are also added to the mix, and even though they may be moving up in their companies, they are also moving deeper and deeper into debt. All overtime must be worked—although by this time many of them are now salaried, and overtime is not paid (but it is expected); both of them are constantly tired, and with that tiredness comes a certain shortness of temper. They fuss with one another; they fuss with the kids, and what the kids really wanted more than anything else was just their mom and dad.

In this common scenario, attendance at services and Bible study becomes just another demand on their limited time. Instead of being an oasis of calm and a time of spiritual refreshing, it becomes more of a chore. Before long you will hear, "I was just too tired to come," and sitting at home with their exhausted parents are the children. Their Bible study is neglected, but not their education. For as they sit at home with their parents, those children are learning. They are learning that there are other things more important than service to God. They are learning that secular work and the things it will buy are more important. They are learning that physical comfort is more important. They are learning that God fits in when it is convenient to put Him in. When this happens, the children involved are being "sinned against."

It is sad, but true, that many times couples become more spiritually minded as they get a little older and wiser. They will become more faithful in their attendance and even start to get personally involved in the work of the church. Oftentimes these same couples will suffer the terrible heartache of seeing their children leave the Lord altogether, and with tears in their eyes express a lack of understanding—"How could this have happened?" Maybe it is because, when the children were little and the foundations were being laid, the parents were more concerned about the things that matter the least. The truth of Proverbs 22:6 is seen everyday, "Train up a child in the way he should go: and when he is old, he will not depart from it."

Thinking about the Family— Teaching the Children Respect

There are few things that are as pleasant to behold as a well-behaved child who is in subjection to his or her parents. I am not talking about a perfect child, because I have never met one. I am talking about boys and girls who run and play, who have to be rebuked sometimes, who may test their parents and push the limits every now and again; these are normal kids who are just growing up. At the same time, few things are as distasteful and unpleasant to behold as a child who is in charge of his or her mom and dad—mouthy, disrespectful, disobedient, insolent, and in control. This is just another way that we can "sin against the child."

A vital parental responsibility is to teach one's child respect for authority. That begins in the home from the earliest days of the child. One of the Ten Commandments given by God through Moses to the children of Israel was, "Honor thy father and thy mother: that thy days may be long upon the land which the Lord thy God giveth thee" (Exod. 20:12). The charge to teach this command of God, as well as all of the other commands, is given to the parents (Deut. 6:6-7; Eph. 6:4). The very first authority figures that a child comes in contact with are its parents. A failure to instill a proper respect for authority on that most basic level will result in trouble with other forms of authority later on, including a respect for the authority of God.

It is not a sign of love on the part of the parents to allow their children to speak to them in a disrespectful manner. It is not a sign of love to allow the children blatantly to disobey parental commands without have to pay the consequences of such disobedience. Several passages from the book of Proverbs emphasize this fact. For instance, Proverbs 13:24, "He that spareth his rod hateth his son: but he that loveth him chasteneth him betimes." Proverbs 19:18, "Chasten thy son while there is hope, and let not thy soul spare for his crying." Proverbs 22:15, "Foolishness is bound in the heart of a child; but the rod of correction shall drive it far from him." The parents who refuse to punish a child for blatant disobedience and disrespect do their child a great injustice, and are indeed guilty of "sinning against the child."

Why are some adolescents, living in the home of their parents, allowed to decide if they will come to worship services or not? I have heard all of the supposed reasons for this, but none of them holds even a single, tiny drop of water. (a) I don't want my child to end up hating religion. (Yet, these same parents make their children go to school because they know it is best for them.) (b) My child just won't get out of bed on Sunday morning. (I always want to ask those parents, "Were you ever in the military?" They certainly have a way to get a disrespectful, lazy soldier out of bed!) (c) Why force them to go if they don't want to be there? (Because God has given the responsibility for the spiritual upbringing of the child to the parents. Who would you rather offend—God or your child? Who knows better what is good for them, God and the parents, or a teenage child?)

There must be no mistake about it. God has placed the parents in charge, not the children, and the husband is to be the head of the house! There are willful children; about that there is no doubt. But as parents we must let them know that our will is stronger. It is so distasteful to see parents manipulated by their children like puppets on a string. It is sinful to allow that to happen.

God has clearly revealed to us how He feels about indulgent parents who allow their children to run roughshod over them and neglect their responsibilities in this area. Remember Eli and his two sons, Hophni and Phinehas? 1 Samuel 3:12-14 says, "In that day I will perform against Eli all things which I have spoken concerning his house; when I begin, I will also make an end. For I have told him that I will judge his house for ever for the iniquity which he knoweth; *because his sons made themselves vile, and he restrained them not.* And therefore I have sworn unto the house of Eli, that the iniquity of Eli's house shall not be purged with sacrifice nor offering forever." Eli was punished for letting his sons misbehave and not restraining them. Let us not forget that the sons were punished as well. Hophni and Phinehas died in one day as punishment from God.

A child who grows to follow the way of righteousness generally does not happen by accident. It takes work by dedicated parents who love the Lord and love their children. Let's close this thought with the words of Solomon from Proverbs 23:15-25, "My son, if thine heart be wise, my heart shall rejoice, even mine. Yea, mine reins shall rejoice, when thy lips speak right things. Let not thine heart envy sinners: but be thou in the fear of the Lord all the day long. For surely there is an end; and thine expectation shall not be cut off. Hear thou, my son, and be wise, and guide thine heart in the way. Be not among winebibbers; among riotous eaters of flesh: for the drunkard and the glutton shall come to poverty: and drowsiness shall clothe a man with rags. Hearken unto thy father that begat thee, and despise not thy mother when she is old. Buy the truth and sell it not; also wisdom, and instruction, and understanding. *The father of the righteous shall greatly rejoice: and he that begetteth a wise child shall have joy of him. Thy father and thy mother shall be glad, and she that bare thee shall rejoice.*"

January 27

Thinking about the Family— "Honor Thy Father and Thy Mother"

In Matthew 15:1-6 we read, "Then came to Jesus scribes and Pharisees, which were of Jerusalem, saying, Why do thy disciples transgress the tradition of the elders? For they wash not their hands when they eat bread. But He answered and said unto them, Why do ye also transgress the commandment of God by your tradition? For God commanded, saying, Honor thy father and mother: and, he that curseth father or mother, let him die the death. But ye say, Whosoever shall say to his father or his mother, It is a gift, by whatsoever thou mightest be profited by me; and honor not his father or his mother, he shall be free. Thus have ye made the commandment of God of none effect by your tradition."

The main point of this passage was to show that the system of tradition, consisting of the comments of the elders upon the written Law of Moses and bound upon the people with equal force as the Law itself, was a false system. They had actually set aside the law of God in favor of their traditions in many instances, and for this Jesus strongly condemned them.

However, I want to notice the example that Jesus used to illustrate the contradiction between their "traditions" and the law of God. The law was very clear. Exodus 20:12 said to "honor thy father and mother." Exodus 21:17 said, "He that curseth his father, or his mother, shall surely be put to death." There was a great deal involved in the command to "honor thy father and mother." It included such things as assisting aged parents when they could not meet all of their needs themselves—food, clothing, shelter, and such like. Surely it also included emotional needs as well—love and comfort in the sometimes extremely trying and difficult later years.

By their traditions the scribes and Pharisees had managed to sidestep a major portion of their responsibilities. They said, "Whosoever shall say to his father or his mother, it is a gift, by whatsoever thou might be profited by me." In a parallel account, Mark 7:11 puts it this way, "But ye say, If a man shall say to his father or mother, It is Corban, that is to say, a gift by whatsoever thou mightest be profited by me; he shall be free." The idea was that by claiming that his property and goods had been solemnly set apart by a formal vow to the sacred use of the services of God, or Corban, he could not use his property in the support of his parents. He could, however, use it in support of himself. Hence, they violated God's law.

My purpose in referring to this exchange between the Lord and the scribes and Pharisees is to emphasize our responsibility to our parents as they grow older. I truly believe that God has placed the primary responsibility for aged parents upon the shoulders of their children—not the government and not the church. In 1 Timothy 5:8 we find, "But if any provide not for his own, and specially for those of his own house, he hath denied the faith, and is worse than an infidel." Who better to fulfill this responsibility than those who have been nurtured, loved, and cared for by the ones who now need help in their old age?

It is always a joy to see families present at services that consist of as many as four generations and to watch the grandchildren and great-grandchildren interact with their grandparents and great-grandparents. What a blessing it is to the children to benefit from the love and wisdom of their grandma and grandpa, or great-grandma and great-grandpa. At the same time, one needs only to look at the eyes of those older folks to see how much they benefit from the children.

No aged parent should ever want for the necessities of life when they have children who are able to supply them, and no adult should ever live in abundance while their mother and father cannot make ends meet and struggle in poverty. No aged person should ever waste away in a nursing home with no visitors while they have family alive and close by. No aged person should ever have to feel forgotten or worthless as long as his or her children or grandchildren walk this earth. That also includes those parents who no longer have any idea who their children are—even those who sit with no visible response whatsoever. They may not know who their children are, but their children know who they are.

Ephesians 5:21 tells us, "Submitting yourselves one to another in the fear of God." I truly believe that understanding this verse and applying it in our homes is a key to success. If every member of a family is always willing to take the needs and the feelings of others into consideration even above his/her own (because this is what God wants in a family), that family will be successful and happy.

January 28

I Held Your Hand

I held your hand before the preacher when we
    both said we would;
I held your hand in the delivery room when you
    said you could;
I held your hand at ball games, emergency
    rooms, and plays;
If the Lord wills, I'll hold your hand throughout
    our golden days.
When the time comes to cross over and leave this
    old land,
I pray to God we'll be together and I'll be there
    to hold your hand.

January 29

"My, How Tiresome It Is!"

The book of Malachi is a fascinating book for a number of different reasons. It is the last book of the Old Testament canon; it is the final word from God to His people before the fulfillment of that to which the entire Old Testament looked forward—the coming of the Messiah. It also depicts the spiritual condition and attitude of the people about 450 years before the coming of the Lord. It is the message of the book upon which I want to focus. There are timeless lessons contained within it. By the time of Malachi, the people had been back in Judea for over 100 years. God had brought them back just like

He said He would. The temple was rebuilt, although not to its previous glory, and the walls of the city of Jerusalem had been very recently rebuilt. They had every reason to be a worshipful, thankful people. But instead of getting better spiritually, they had gotten worse. Malachi talks about indifference on the part of God's people to the moral and ceremonial aspects of divine law. Their worship was in a state of decay. Oh, they did it, but it was not occupying the place of priority in their hearts and lives that the worship of God deserved. As a matter of fact, Malachi teaches that worship that is mere ritual is of no value at all. Worship only has value when it is the result of sincere love and adoration of God. They were giving God the leftovers, so to speak, and not the first fruits. That included the animals offered in sacrifice and the tithes that they gave. Let's look at some examples. In Malachi 1:6–8, we find:

> A son honors his father, and a servant his master. Then if I am a father, where is My honor? And if I am a master, where is My respect? Says the Lord of hosts to you, O priests who despise My name. But you say, "How have we despised Thy name? *(By the way, this is the "didactic–dialectic method"—Greg).* You are presenting defiled food upon My altar. But you say, How have we defiled Thee? In that you say, The table of the Lord is to be despised. But when you present the blind for sacrifice, is it not evil? And when you present the lame and sick, is it not evil? Why not offer it to your governor? Would he be pleased with you? Or would he receive you kindly? says the Lord of hosts."

Instead of giving God the very best, they were giving Him the worst. Why offer to God a perfectly healthy animal that would prove very profitable to themselves, when they had sick and lame animals that weren't worth nearly so much? God said that if they gave the same kind of gifts to a political ruler, it would be an insult to him and he would not accept it. How much more of an insult is it to give to God less than our best? That is the lesson. In verse 10, we read, "Oh that there were one among you who would shut the gates, that you might not uselessly kindle fire on My altar! I am not pleased with you, says the Lord of hosts, nor will I accept an offering from you." What is God saying here but that it is better to shut the gates and stay home rather than to pervert the worship by giving God less than our best?

Look at verses 13-14: "You also say, My, how tiresome it is! And you disdainfully sniff at it, says the Lord of hosts, and you bring what was taken by robbery, and what is lame or sick; so you bring the offering! Should I receive that from your hand? says the Lord. But cursed be the *swindler* who has a male in his flock, and vows it, but sacrifices a blemished animal to the Lord, for I am a great King, says the Lord of hosts, and My name is feared among the nations."

Instead of their worship being an expression of joy out of a grateful and reverent heart, they viewed worship and their part in as a burdensome chore. *Do you ever feel that way come Sunday morning, evening, or Wednesday night?* Consider 3:8, where we find, "Will a man rob God? Yet ye have robbed me. But ye say, Wherein have we robbed thee? In tithes and offerings." God is God of all, and everything is His. Yet the people were not willing to freely give their tithes and offerings as an acknowledgement of God's ownership and their stewardship.

Now we are not obligated to tithe under the New Covenant, but we are most certainly obligated to recognize God's position of ownership and ours as stewards. We are most certainly obligated to demonstrate our love and recognition in our offerings to God. In 2 Corinthians 8: 8 Paul wrote, "I speak not by commandment, but by occasion of the forwardness of others, and to prove the sincerity of your love." That statement was made in the context of a discussion of giving, and he spoke of it as proof of *"the sincerity of your love."* We are most certainly obligated to give freely and cheerfully out of a heart filled with love and gratitude. Just one chapter over, in 2 Corinthians 9:6 & 7, we find, "But this I say, He which soweth sparingly shall reap also sparingly; and he which soweth bountifully shall reap also bountifully. Every man according as he purposeth in his heart, so let him give; not grudgingly, or of necessity: for God loveth a cheerful giver."

All was not lost, however. The book closes with marvelous words of anticipation. Malachi 4:5-6 says, "Behold, I will send you Elijah the prophet before the coming of the great and dreadful day of the Lord: and he shall turn the heart of the fathers to the children, and the heart of the children to their fathers, lest I come and smite the earth with a curse." John the Baptist would come and prepare the way of the Lord.

Let's be sure that we are not guilty of apathy when it comes to our service and worship to God.

January 30

Let's Consider Together

God has gone to great lengths in His Word to assure the proper rearing of children. The first thing to be noted is that God views children as a great blessing to their parents. In Psalm 127:3-5 we read, "Lo, children are an heritage of the Lord: and the fruit of the womb is his reward. As arrows are in the hand of a mighty man; so are the children of the youth. Happy is the man that hath his quiver full of them: they shall not be ashamed, but they shall speak with the enemies in the gate."

The second thing to mention is that children are to be loved. In Paul's letter to Titus, we find that the older women were to teach the young women "to be sober, to love their husbands to *love their children*" (Tit. 2:4).

Children are to be provided for. 1 Timothy 5:8 informs us, "But if any provide not for his own, and specially for those of his own house, he hath denied the faith, and is worse than an infidel."

Children are to be corrected when necessary. Solomon wrote in Proverbs 22:15, "Foolishness is bound in the heart of a child; but the rod of correction shall drive it far from him." Proverbs 13:24 tells us, "He that spareth his rod hateth his son: but he that loveth him chasteneth him betimes."

In each step of their development, children are to be instructed in the ways of the Lord. Deuteronomy 11:18-20 says, "Therefore shall ye lay up these words in your heart and in your soul, and bind them for a sign upon your hand, that they may be as frontlets between your eyes. And teach them to your children, speaking of them when thou sittest in thine house and when thou walkest by the way, when thou liest down, and when thou risest up. And thou shalt write them upon the door posts of thine house, and upon thy gates." In the New Testament the apostle Paul made the very same point when he instructed the Ephesians, "And, ye fathers, provoke not your children to wrath; *but bring them up in the nurture and admonition of the Lord*" (Eph. 6:4).

Instructing our children in the ways of the Lord involves many things. They must be taught about God, prayerfully brought to believe in Him. They must be taught of the wonderful things of His creation and the way that he blesses us every day of our lives. Children must be taught to worship God and live the moral life that He has decreed to be right and proper. Children must be taught to be good citizens and to be in subjection to the government under which they live, and they must be taught to work.

The Passover

The Passover was the first of the three annual festivals of the Jews. It began on the evening of the fourteenth day of the month Nisan, the beginning of the fifteenth day, roughly corresponding to our Easter. Passover was followed by a seven-day festival of unleavened bread. Sometimes the name Passover was applied to all eight days. Passover commemorated the night when the Lord killed all of the firstborn of Egypt but passed over the houses of the Israelites where the blood had been sprinkled on the doorposts and the lintels.

The observance "included the following provisions: (1) the taking of a lamb, or kid without blemish, for each household on the 10th of the month; (2) the killing of the lamb on the fourteenth at even; (3) the sprinkling of the blood on doorposts and lintels of the houses in which it was to be eaten; (4) the roasting of the lamb with fire, its head and its legs and inwards—the lamb was not to be eaten raw nor sodden with water; (5) the eating of unleavened bread and bitter herbs; (6) eating in haste, with loins girded, shoes on the feet, and staff in hand; (7) the remaining in the house until the morning; (8) the burning of all that remained; the Passover could be eaten only during the night" (*The International Standard Bible Encyclopedia*, IV: 2256).

In 1 Corinthians 5:7-8 we find, "Purge out therefore the old leaven, that ye may be a new lump, as ye are unleavened. For even Christ our Passover is sacrificed for us: therefore let us keep the feast, not with old leaven, neither with the leaven of malice and wickedness; but with the unleavened bread of sincerity and truth." By its death and the sprinkling of its blood, the Passover lamb was the means of deliverance for the firstborn of the Jews on that night in Egypt so long ago.

Jesus is our Passover. The words of John the Baptist, found in John 1:29 come to mind. Seeing Jesus, he said, "Behold the Lamb of God, which taketh away the sin of the world." Like the paschal lamb, not a bone of His was broken. Like the lamb, He was without spot or blemish. Like the lamb, His blood is our means of deliverance.

It Can Be a Lonely World

In Ecclesiastes 4:8-12 we read:

There is one alone, and there is not a second; yea, he hath neither child nor brother: yet is there no end of all his labor; neither is his eye satisfied with riches; neither saith he, For whom do I labor, and bereave my soul of good? This is also vanity, yea, it is a sore travail. Two are better than one; because they have a good reward for their labor. For if they fall, the one will lift up his fellow: but woe to him that is alone when he falleth; for he hath not another to help him up. Again, if two lie together, then they have heat: but how can one be warm alone? And if one prevail against him, two shall withstand him; and a threefold cord is not quickly broken.

In writing these words, Solomon was acknowledging a need that every person has—the need for relationships. I am not talking about romantic relationships, but simply that man is a social being, and loneliness is one of the worst of human experiences.

It is sad but true that we live in a cold, lonely world. Doors must be locked to keep out those who would injure or steal. I have known some folks who were practically imprisoned by fear, afraid to go out at night because they were alone. Others have experienced deep losses such as the death of a spouse or a divorce. It can be so difficult if one feels that he is alone.

Those who seek fulfillment and contentment in material possessions are ultimately going to find themselves lonely. Our society tells us that we will feel better and happier if we have enough things. If we have the biggest house or the latest car, we will be satisfied. But I think of the Prodigal Son. He learned that someone with money and the mindset to spend it has a lot of friends more than willing to help him do it. But once the money was gone, so were the friends. How many times do we hear wealthy celebrities bemoan the fact that they can't tell if people want to be their friends because they like them, or because they like their money and prestige. It doesn't seem possible, but it is true that one can be surrounded by people and still be lonely.

When people try to fill the void in their lives with sin, they will find that that won't fill the empty spot either. When all is said and done, they are still alone. Others seek to remedy loneliness by filling all of their time with hobbies and other interests, and many of those things are good. However, the truth of the matter is that the only absolute answer to loneliness is found in serving God.

After devoting himself to a search for happiness and contentment in an attempt to find real meaning in life, Solomon's conclusion was, "Fear God, and keep his commandments: for this is the whole duty of man" (Eccl. 12:13). Only by fulfilling the very purpose for which we were created, to worship and serve God, will we find what we truly need. Even in the darkest hours as we lie awake in bed listening to the clock tick and wondering if the morning will ever come, the Christian can know that God has said, "I will never leave thee, nor forsake thee" (Heb. 13:5). As a child of God, I am never, never alone.

February 2

A Dark and Stormy Night

It was a dark and stormy night! How many times have you heard literary critics and English teachers ridicule that line as a means of introducing a story? But our focus today is upon a time that really was a dark and stormy night on the Sea of Galilee. We find the account of this dark and stormy night in Matthew 8:23-27, Luke 8:22-25, and Mark 4:35-41. It is Mark's account that we will read:

> And the same day, when the even was come, he saith unto them, Let us pass over unto the other side. And when they had sent away the multitude, they took him even as he was in the ship. And there were also with him other little ships. And there arose a great storm of wind, and the waves beat into the ship, so that it was now full. And he was in the hinder part of the ship, asleep on a pillow: and they awake him, and say unto him, Master, carest thou not that we perish? And he arose, and rebuked the wind, and said unto the sea, Peace, be still. And the wind ceased, and there was a great calm. But the men marveled, saying, What manner of man is this, that even the winds and the sea obey him?

Don't you wish you could have been there? Two different words were used by the gospel writers to describe the storm that arose. Mark and Luke use the word *lailaps*. This is defined by Thayer as "never a single gust of wind, but a storm breaking from black thunderclouds in furious gusts, with floods of rain and throwing everything topsy-turvy." Matthew used *seismos* a word that can mean an earthquake, but is also a common word for a tempest with a storm of such volume causing a shaking or commotion. Both words are meant to emphasize the severity of the storm.

The storm, which arose so quickly, raged about the small boat. The apostles of Jesus, many of them experienced fishermen, feared for their lives. Yet in the midst of such a violent storm, Jesus slept. The apostles cried out, "Master, carest thou not that we perish?" and "Lord, save us, we perish" and "Master, master, we perish." I remember reading one man describe the apostles' reaction in the following way. What good is one's faith if he loses it instead of uses it? The storm blew their faith away for a while. If we can't lay hold of our faith when we need it most, then what value is it.

Jesus arose and said, "Peace, be still," and the wind subsided and the sea became calm. The apostles said, "What manner of man is this, that even the wind and the sea obey him?" I feel very privileged to be able to answer that question so many years later. This man was Jesus, the Son of God. This was the One who said, "Let there be light" back in the days of creation, and there was light.

The sea of life that I have sailed upon has not been without storms, and if you are of any age at all, neither has yours. When the waves of despair and the winds of sorrow beat upon me at the death of my parents, the words, "Peace, be still" assumed a whole new meaning for me. I don't know what trials and difficulties you have faced and I don't know what may be causing tears to leave their traces on your cheeks, but I do know that whatever it is, as a faithful Christian the words of Jesus, "Peace, be still," can apply to whatever turmoil rages in your heart.

One last point to consider, and I don't know if I thought of this myself or heard it somewhere else—if even the wind and the sea obey him, shouldn't we?

February 3

Love, the Cross, and Giving

Love means many things to different people, but I believe that most would agree that love, by its very nature, involves giving. If I love someone, I give to that person, to the best of my ability, what that person needs the most. God is love (1 John 4:8), and therefore He gave what was most needful to the world: "For God so loved the world, that he gave his only begotten Son, that whosoever believeth in him should not perish, but have everlasting life" (John 3:16).

The love that our Lord Jesus has for mankind was also demonstrated in the most graphic and powerful way. In 2 Corinthians 8:9 we are told, "For ye know the grace of our Lord Jesus Christ, that, though he was rich, yet for your sakes he became poor, that ye through his poverty might be rich." In order to picture the incredible magnitude of the gift that Jesus gave because of his love, try to contrast what he left with what he came to and received in this world. He was rich, yet He became poor. How do we describe what Jesus had in heaven? I don't think we can, but I marvel at the significance of part of the Lord's prayer in John 17:5, "And now, O Father, glorify thou me with thine own self with the glory which I had with thee before the world was." If Jesus had left heaven and been born into the palace of Caesar and shared in the physical wealth of the whole world as emperor of Rome, He still would have been abysmally poor in contrast to what He left in heaven.

When it comes to love and giving, Jesus set the supreme example. Paul used the Lord's great gift to motivate Christians to give and to show us what giving is all about. In 2 Corinthians 8:7-9 we find:

> Therefore, as ye abound in everything, in faith, and utterance, and knowledge, and in all diligence, and in your love to us, see that ye abound in this grace also. I speak not by commandment, but by occasion of the forwardness of others, and to prove the sincerity of your love. For ye know the grace of our Lord Jesus Christ, that, though he was rich, yet for your sakes he became poor, that ye through his poverty might be rich.

Paul's continued teaching along this line led to the exhortation of 2 Corinthians 9:6-7, "But this I say, He which soweth sparingly shall reap also sparingly; and he which soweth bountifully shall reap also bountifully. Every man according as he purposeth in his heart, so let him give; not grudgingly, or of necessity: for God loveth a cheerful giver."

Jesus' gift of Himself was the ultimate expression of love. The Lord Himself said, "Greater love hath no man than this, that a man lay down his life for his friends" (John 15:13). How much greater was the Lord's gift of love when He laid down His life for those who were certainly not living as His friends? So Paul uses the Lord's gift to help us understand our giving. Once again he wrote, "I speak not by commandment, but by occasion of the forwardness of others, and to prove the sincerity of your love." Can we not see what it is that takes the sting out of giving, that makes us give sacrificially and to the best of our ability? It is love, and when we truly love, we will give appropriately. All we need to do is look to Jesus to see the clear and obvious connection between love, the cross, and giving.

February 4

Two Statements of Jesus

At the age of twelve, Jesus went to the city of Jerusalem with his parents for the feast of the Passover. When his family left the city, they thought that Jesus was with the company of those traveling together, their relatives and acquaintances. But in fact, Jesus had remained behind in Jerusalem. When they realized that he was not with them, Mary and Joseph returned to the city to look for their son. After three days they found him in the temple, sitting in the midst of the teachers. When they asked him why he had done this, Jesus answered, "How is it that ye sought me? Know ye not that I must be about my Father's business?" (Luke 2:49).

If we move ahead approximately twenty-one years to Luke 23:46, we find the second statement of Jesus that I want to consider. It is interesting that Jesus is probably not much more than a mile, if that, from where he had spoken those words in the temple so many years before, but now he is hanging on the cross. Jesus said, "Father, into thy hands I commend my spirit." The verse continues on to tell us, "and having said thus, he gave up the ghost." Think of everything that had happened between, "Know ye not that I must be about my Father's business" and "Father, into thy hands I commend my spirit." Yet, it was because of those first words and what they really meant, that Jesus could say those last. As a matter of fact, it is because of those first words that any Christian will be able to say those last words.

There is a statement that Jesus made in John 8 in the midst of a discussion that he was having with some Pharisees that I want to notice. In verse 29 Jesus said, "And he that sent me is with me: the Father hath not left me alone; for I do always those things that please him." The word "always" meant then what it means now. Have you ever thought about how often we misuse the word "always"? We might say in frustration to someone, "You always lie." From a more positive standpoint we might say, "You always have a smile on your face." But the truth is, no matter how frustrated we might be with a person, he does not, in fact, always lie. No matter how impressed we may be with someone, she does not, in fact, always have a smile on her face. The word "always" literally means "at all times." There is not a person we know who does those things that we might say they "always" do all the time—at all times without fail. Yet Jesus did, at all times without fail, do those things that were pleasing to the Father. At all times, he was "about his Father's business."

That must be our goal as well—to live our lives trying always to do the things that please the Father, always to be about our Father's business. Then the words, "Father, into thy hands I commend my spirit" take on a thrilling meaning for us. What an incredibly wonderful thing to be able to say with our last dying breath! What a tremendous peace a person must feel at that moment! That is a peace that comes from an individual taking every care, trial, and heartache and laying them at the feet of Jesus. It is a peace that comes from a person having taken every victory, success, and reason to rejoice and bowed to God in thanksgiving. It is a peace that finds God at its foundation and is sustained by unflinching and unfailing faithfulness and loyalty to him. It is a peace made possible because Jesus came here to be "about his Father's business."

February 5

What Did You Write That Day in the Sand?
By Adam Litmer

What did You write that day in the sand?
I think this thought with head in hand.
Was it something profound, or really nothing at all?
With sorrowful heart, on Thee I call.

Surrounded by people who claimed hearts that were true,
Whose actions betrayed them, as ours sometimes do;
People who knew what was right, but just didn't care,
With ungodly motives, confronted you with a dare.

What did you write, and what made you so strong?
What inner strength as You faced such a throng?
I need that strength now, as few times before.
Give ear to my plea and open the door.

It grieves my soul to see Christians rebel —
To see them so cavalier, without a thought toward hell;
Watching Christians hurt a fellow saint
Sometimes causes my heart to faint.

A fellow saint has been pained, dealt a terrible scar.
His heart is heavy and the pain has gone far.
It was a Christian who hatefully dealt him this wound,
But his faith is strong, and he still sees the boon.

But it's for me that I write these words to my Lord.
I need reassurance of Your love's impregnable cord.
When my heart is weary and this world grows dark,
There's a peace that only You can impart.

So what did You write that day in the sand?
Was it something that would strengthen and cause me to stand?
As eyes become cloudy and tears begin to fall,
With sorrowful heart, on Thee I call.

February 6

Friends

Let's briefly consider the idea of friendship today—what it means to be a friend and what it means to have a friend. I believe there to be few words in the English language that are as beautiful and as meaningful as "friend." Friends are there to share our joys and to help us with our struggles. In moments of reflection and reminiscence, we often find that they are part of our sweetest memories. In short, having friends is one of the things that makes life worthwhile.

In *Webster's New Universal Unabridged Dictionary*, there are several definitions given for the word "friend." The first two are: (1) "A person attached to another by feelings of affection, or personal regard; (2) A person who gives assistance, a patron; supporter."

When I think of such friends, I think of David and Jonathan. Understand that Jonathan was the son of King Saul, and thus the man who would have succeeded him to the throne under normal circumstances. David was the man chosen by God to take Saul's place. A person could understand if there had been an antagonistic rivalry between the two, but that was certainly not the case. In 1 Samuel 18:1 there is this beautiful expression of the friendship of these two men: "And it came to pass, when he had made an end of speaking unto Saul, that the soul of Jonathan was knit with the soul of David, and Jonathan loved him as his own soul." It is absolutely heart-wrenching to read the words of David as he lamented the death of Jonathan, his friend. In 2 Samuel 1:25-27 we find, "How are the mighty fallen in the midst of battle! O Jonathan, thou wast slain in thine high places. I am distressed for thee, my brother Jonathan: very pleasant hast thou been unto me: thy love to me was wonderful, passing the love of women. How are the mighty fallen, and the weapons of war perished." The hearts of these two men were knit together in so many ways: by courage, by love, and by covenant. What a beautiful illustration of friendship!

We must also recognize that true friends watch out for our eternal soul, and sometimes that may very well mean telling us things that are difficult to hear. Proverbs 27:6 comes to mind. It says, "Faithful are the wounds of a friend; but the kisses of an enemy are deceitful." Remember the old anti-drunk driving slogan, "Friends don't let friends drink and drive"? Well, what does a friend do, and I mean a real friend, when he sees his friend headed for spiritual trouble? He does every thing he can to stop him, within the parameters of God's word, even when it hurts his feelings to do so or brings the wrath of his friend upon him. No one likes to hear that he or she has sinned and has headed in the wrong direction. But no one is going to tell you that except a true friend. A friend's criticism may be so painful at first, hurting like an open wound, but if one can only bring himself to recognize that it is given out of love, the pain turns to gratitude.

In consideration of friends, yet another verse comes to mind—Proverbs 27:17, "Iron sharpeneth iron; so a man sharpeneth the countenance of his friend." Those whom we trust and with whom we spend the most time will have the greatest influence upon us. In this manner our friends sharpen our countenance as they provide a sounding board for our ideas. When and if those ideas are wrong or need to be redirected, true friends will tell us so. They give us encouragement and advice, which may not always be exactly what we want to hear. A friend will pick us up when we are down and try to help when we are hurting, but always based upon the principles of truth found in God's word. To have such a friend is to be blessed indeed.

February 7

Be Ye Doers and Not Hearers Only

I have a confession to make. There have been times when I have been sitting in a pew, listening to a gospel preacher deliver a sermon, and have thought, "I sure hope so and so is listening to this sermon. He or she really needs to hear this." Frankly, sometimes I wasn't even that specific in my thinking. Instead, I thought of the ubiquitous "they." "They" sure need to hear this! Have you ever done the same thing? God has warned us about the need to make application of His word to ourselves.

Do you remember the account of the prophet Nathan coming to David after his adultery with Bathsheba and the murder of her husband, Uriah? In 2 Samuel 12 Nathan told David the story of a rich man with many flocks and herds, and a poor man who had nothing save one little ewe lamb. He loved that lamb and treated it as one of the family. He held it to his bosom and it was to him as a daughter. One day a traveler came to visit the rich man and he chose not to take of his own flocks, but he took the poor man's lamb and killed it to feed his guest. Hearing that story, David was filled with righteous indignation and said in verses 5-6, "As the Lord liveth, the man that hath done this thing shall surely die: and he shall restore the lamb fourfold, because he did this thing, and because he had no pity." Nathan's response to David resonates across the ages, teaching the need to examine self first. Nathan said to David, "Thou art the man."

In the Sermon on the Mount, Jesus said in Matthew 7:3-5, "And why beholdest thou the mote that is in thy brother's eye, but considerest not the beam that is in thine own eye? Or how wilt thou say to thy brother, Let me pull out the mote out of thine eye; and, behold, a beam is in thine own eye? Thou hypocrite, first cast out the beam out of thine own eye, and then shalt thou see clearly to cast out the mote out of thy brother's eye." The lesson is clearly that the first person I need to be concerned about when it comes to applying God's word is myself. I need to make personal application of its principles before I look to anyone else.

I think of Paul's words in Romans 2:21 where he wrote, "Thou therefore which teachest another, teachest thou not thyself? Thou that preachest a man should not steal, dost thou steal?" Again we can easily see the principle. Application begins with me.

In James 1:22 we read, "But be ye doers of the word, and not hearers only, deceiving your own selves." If we look at the first phrase of this verse simply from a grammatical standpoint, it means, "keep on demonstrating yourselves to be doers of the word." The import of that statement is that it is not enough to hear the word and to receive it in that way, a person has to be obedient to it. Did you ever stop to consider that God never blessed anyone in any age or dispensation of time for simply hearing the word and simply believing it? God's blessings came when the individual's faith was exhibited in obedience and not before. It has never been enough simply to "hear" the word—or for that matter, simply to "believe" it. It must be expressed in action in life, it must be personally applied in order to bless and save. Take care to notice of whom the action is required. It is required of me. I must do what the word says personally. I must apply it to myself and so must you.

February 8

A Covenant with Our Eyes

While in my freshman year of high school, I took biology. We were assigned a special project and given some latitude in deciding what to do. I decided to go down to the butcher shop at the end of our street to see if the butcher would give me a cow's eye. I was going to dissect it and label all of its various parts. He did it for me. The butcher saved an eye from one of the cow heads that they used to have delivered and gave it to me, free of charge. I undertook the dissection, and although not germane to this short study, I will tell you that the dissection did not go well. How was I supposed to know that a cow's eye is under pressure? Once it stopped squirting liquid at me, what I already did know about the eye was reaffirmed. The physical eye is a marvelous mechanism. The relatively small human eye, not much more than an inch across, opens up a vast world for us. With it we can see distant horizons and heavenly bodies, massive mountains, rolling seas, lush rain forests, and arid deserts. With the same eye we can see minute microscopic bodies.

As one who has worn glasses since about the fourth or fifth grade, I also know that the physical eye can have serious defects. In like manner, the spiritual eye can develop some real problems if it is not properly taken care of. In Job 31:1 we find, "I made a covenant with mine eyes; why then should I think upon a maid?" To "think upon" is to look intently, the obvious implication being to look upon with lust. Job had made a pledge to himself that he would not do that. He had made a covenant with his eyes.

Think of what Jesus said in Matthew 5:27-29:

> Ye have heard that it was said by them of old time, Thou shalt not commit adultery: but I say unto you, That whosoever looketh on a woman to lust after her hath committed adultery with her already in his heart. And if thy right eye offend thee, pluck it out, and cast it from thee: for it is profitable for thee that one of thy members should perish, and not that thy whole body should be cast into hell.

If only David had made the same covenant with his eyes that Job had made, and then stuck to it, the tragic and sad story of David and Bathsheba would not have entered into the annuals of history. How many terrible situations could be avoided if we will simply make the same covenant with our eyes?

The Richest People on Earth

There is a tendency to get so involved with the affairs of this world that we can forget one of the most fundamental truths presented in the word of God. Genuine Christians are the richest people on earth. I remember a statement the Lord made to the church in Smyrna in verse 9 of Revelation 2. This was a congregation of the Lord's people who knew and experienced real, physical poverty—of the sort that most of us have never experienced. Yet Jesus said to them, "I know thy works, and tribulation, and poverty, (but thou art rich)."

True, faithful Christians are the richest people on earth, but it is not always easy to remember that, is it? If we should find ourselves in a situation where we aren't sure how we are going to pay the next month's rent, it can be hard to realize just how wealthy we really are. If a faithful child of God has to decide between the medicine he needs or a couple of meals a day, it can be pretty hard to feel rich. When our body is wracked with pain or those that we love are dealing with a terminal illness that affects our thinking seemingly every minute of the day, it can be hard to remember that no other people occupy a position as enviable on this earth as do faithful children of God.

In Ephesians 1:3 we read, "Blessed be the God and Father of our Lord Jesus Christ, who hath blessed us with all spiritual blessings in heavenly places in Christ." All spiritual blessings are found in Christ. In verses 22-23 of chapter 1 we find, "And hath put all things under his feet, and gave him to be the head over all things to the church, which is his body, the fullness of him that filleth all in all." The easiest way to understand verse 23 is to think of a tire that contains an inner tube. When the inner tube is filled with air until it is the fullness of the tire, then all of the air in the tire must be in the inner tube. In just the same way, the church is the fullness of Christ, meaning that all the glorious blessings to be found in Christ are in the church. So as members of the body of Christ, the church of Christ, faithful Christians enjoy all of the blessings that matter the most—the spiritual blessings.

Ephesians 1 gives us a partial listing of some of those blessings. In verses 3-4 we find that we have been chosen by God and predestined unto the adoption as His children. We understand that God has chosen and foreordained that those who respond in obedient faith to the gospel would be adopted as His children. In verse 11 we are told of the marvelous inheritance that awaits us. Verse 12 tells us that we have been "sealed with the Holy Spirit of promise." There are so many more blessings mentioned just in Ephesians 1, but one of them absolutely rivets my attention. In verse 7 we read, "In whom we have redemption though his blood, the forgiveness of sins, according to the riches of his grace."

How wealthy are we? We have been forgiven! Having had the price for our redemption paid by the blood of Christ, and having been washed in that blood through baptism, we are no longer separated from our Creator. If there were nothing else, that alone would make the faithful children of God the wealthiest people on earth.

To Thee I Go

There have been times in my life when I have struggled personally with prayer. But the truth is that given the nature of the world in which we live and the things that happen, there should be no more important daily part of our lives than prayer. We live in a world full of uncertainty and confusion. Today's friends may turn out to be tomorrow's enemies, and the stresses of today may very well spill over into tomorrow and mar another day with which God has blessed us.

What do we do? King David was one who had the answer. David faced critics, plots against his life, intrigues, and personal attacks from enemies that at times seemed to be all around him. He faced each day, as we all do, with uncertainty—in his case not knowing exactly who among his closest associates and friends he could ultimately and without question trust. However, David had a solution, and that solution was to pray to God.

Psalm 5 seems to be a morning prayer of David's. It begins with, "Give ear to my words, O Lord, consider my meditation. Hearken unto the voice of my cry, my King, and my God: for unto thee will I pray. My voice shalt thou hear in the morning, O Lord; in the morning I will direct my prayer unto thee, and will look up" (vv. 1-3). Friends, David was facing enemies in many different forms. He faced those who lied to him and about him. He faced those within his own house who were arrogant, filled with ungodly ambition, and even bloodthirsty. What was David's first solution? Prayer.

Prayer ought to be the first solution that comes to our minds when faced with problems. However, often our minds say differently. We think we should *do* something, fix the problem ourselves, or take on our opponents and show them a thing or two. We want to be ready to fend off their attacks on our own and perhaps, with well-chosen arguments, defeat them. All of this is based upon our taking charge and fixing the problems by ourselves. I have found myself believing that by sheer force of my will, I could fix problems or even prevent them from happening—but that is just not true.

Let's learn from David. As he faced a day of worldly challenges, he knew that the best thing to do was to lay it all in God's hands. David was a good man, a man of wisdom and strength, and as king, a man of political and military might. Yet, he turned to the Lord first. This doesn't mean that he was ignoring his own responsibilities to work on his problems and to deal with his difficulties—but it does show that David knew where real help comes from.

He concluded Psalm 5 with the words, "But let all those that put their trust in thee rejoice: let them ever shout for joy, because thou defendest them: let them also that love thy name be joyful in thee. For thou, Lord, wilt bless the righteous; with favor wilt thou compass him as with a shield" (vv. 11-12).

What Lack I Yet?

In the 19th chapter of the Gospel of Matthew, we find one of the accounts of the rich young ruler. In verses 16-20 we read:

> And, behold, one came and said unto him, Good Master, what good thing shall I do, that I may have eternal life? And he said unto him, Why callest thou me good? There is none good but one, that is, God: but if thou wilt enter into life, keep the commandments. He said unto him, Which? Jesus said, Thou shalt do no murder, Thou shalt not commit adultery, Thou shalt not steal, Thou shalt not bear false witness, honor thy father and thy mother: and, Thou shalt love thy neighbor as thyself. The young man saith unto him, all these things have I kept from my youth up: what lack I yet?

I don't know if you have ever stopped to think about it, but that is a question that most people don't like to ask or even think about. Many people, instead of being interested in knowing where improvements can be made in their lives, resent having any lack called to their attention. But it is good for all to think about this very question, "What lack I yet?" It is so important for us honestly to seek to understand where we can make improvement in our service to God and then to make it. It is so important to have the attitude that Paul demonstrated when he wrote, "Brethren, I count not myself to have apprehended: but this one thing I do, forgetting those things which are behind, and reaching forth unto those things which are before, I press toward the mark for the prize of the high calling of God in Christ Jesus" (Phil. 3:13-14). With Paul there was no room for complacency or satisfaction. There was always more that could be done and always improvement that could be made.

In 2 Peter 1:5-9 Peter wrote, "And beside this, giving all diligence, add to your faith virtue; and to virtue knowledge; and to knowledge temperance; and to temperance, patience; and to patience godliness; and to godliness brotherly kindness; and to brotherly kindness charity. For if these things be in you, and abound, they make you that ye shall neither be barren nor unfruitful in the knowledge of our Lord Jesus Christ. But he that lacketh these things is blind, and cannot see afar off, and hath forgotten that he was purged from his old sins."

What lack I yet? Well, how am I doing as far as virtue, or moral excellence is concerned? How is my knowledge? At no time in history have Christians been better educated from a secular standpoint than we are right now—yet how is the level of Bible knowledge for the average Christian today? How am I doing in the realm of self-control? If I have the knowledge of God's word, do I have the personal discipline to abide by it? How about patience? Patience is steadfastness or perseverance. Will I bravely bear up and contend against trials, temptations, and even persecution? What about godliness? Do I truly evidence reverence and respect toward God?

February 12

Work of Faith

Paul's first letter to the Thessalonians begins in verses 1-4 with the following words, "Paul, and Silvanus, and Timotheus, unto the church of the Thessalonians which is in God the Father and in the Lord Jesus Christ: Grace be unto you, and peace, from God our Father, and the Lord Jesus Christ. We give thanks to God always for you all, making mention of you in our prayers; remembering without ceasing your work of faith, and labor of love, and patience of hope in our Lord Jesus Christ, in the sight of God and our Father; knowing, brethren beloved, your election of God." For our purpose in this brief study I want to focus upon a statement found in verse three, "your work of faith."

Students of the Bible must understand that according to God the faith that saves is an obedient faith. The greatest treatise on the glorious theme of salvation by grace through faith is the book of Romans. Consider how that book begins and ends. In Romans 1:3-5 Paul wrote, "Concerning his Son Jesus

Christ our Lord, which was made of the seed of David according to the flesh; and declared to be the Son of God with power, according to the spirit of holiness, by the resurrection from the dead, by whom we have received grace and apostleship, for *obedience to the faith* among all nations, for his name." Note the phrase, "obedience to the faith." The book closes with the following words found in 16:25-27, "Now to him that is of power to stablish you according to my gospel, and the preaching of Jesus Christ, according to the revelation of the mystery, which was kept secret since the world began. But now is made manifest, and by the Scriptures of the prophets, according to the commandment of the everlasting God, made known to all nations *for the obedience of faith*: to God only wise, be glory through Jesus Christ for ever. Amen." Note again the phrase, "for the obedience of faith." In God's word, faith and obedience are inseparable if we are talking about a faith that saves.

When Paul wrote of the Thessalonians' "work of faith," the word for work denotes "a deed, an act" (*Vine's Expository Dictionary*). So Paul was writing of their deeds or acts or works. The truth is that an inactive faith will save no one. To prove a person's faith, indeed as a very part of their faith, God requires obedience. To demonstrate this truth, simply consider Hebrews 11, sometimes referred to as the Hall of Fame of Faith, and note the language used to describe saving faith. In v. 4 we find, "By faith Abel offered unto God a more excellent sacrifice than Cain." In v. 7 we read, "By faith Noah, being warned of God of things not seen as yet, moved with fear, prepared an ark to the saving of his house." In v. 8, "By faith Abraham, when he was called to go out into a place which he should after receive for an inheritance, obeyed." In v. 17, "By faith Abraham, when he was tried, offered up Isaac." In v. 29 we are told of the Israelites, that "by faith they passed through the Red Sea as by dry land." And in v. 30, "By faith the walls of Jericho fell down, after they were compassed about seven days." Surely all can see that a faith that saves is a great deal more than a simple mental assent concerning the facts of the life of Jesus.

We cannot invent good works to save ourselves. We are saved by doing God's works, not because they place God in the position of owing us our salvation, but because they are expressions of our faith. Our job is to do that which God's divine word has revealed he wants us to do. That is what the Thessalonians were doing. They were living their lives in obedience to God's revealed will. That was their "work of faith."

Is It Appropriate?

In Ephesians 4:1 Paul wrote, "I therefore, the prisoner of the Lord, beseech you that you walk worthy of the vocation wherewith ye are called." Christians are obligated to be what we profess to believe. We have been saved. We are in Christ. We are then to live as Christians are to live. We are required to move on from simply having an understanding and believing what God's purpose is for us to actually having that understanding make a difference in our lives.

Paul, in 1 Timothy 2:9-10, instructed the young evangelist to teach, "In like manner also, that women adorn themselves in modest apparel, with shame-facedness and sobriety; not with braided hair, or gold, or pearls, or costly array; but (which becometh women professing godliness) with good works." The true import of this passage is found in the word "modest." Paul referred to modest apparel. What does that mean? It means apparel that is "orderly, suitable to a character, a time, place or occasion; becoming, appropriate."

Whether we like it or not, it is true that our actions often speak much more clearly than our words when it comes to the matter of our convictions. It is easy to say something, but the question is, "Do our actions bear out what we say?" Is our walk of equal value to our claims? Are we walking worthy of the vocation wherewith we were called?

Friend, modesty has to do with more than just the way a person dresses. When we understand that the word modest refers to something that is suitable to a character, time, place and occasion, when we consider that it means appropriate, it becomes easy to see that modesty can and must be discussed in reference to all aspects of our lives. Christians are to be modest. That being the case, is the way we talk, the way we act, the way we think, the things we do for recreation—are all of these things appropriate for one who claims to be a follower of the Lord and who wears his name?

Have you ever heard what a person was wearing described as "making a fashion statement"? Have you ever heard the expression, "Clothes make the man"? There is truth to be found in those statements because what we wear says a great deal about our character and how we feel about an occasion or a function that we are attending. I believe that dressing modestly, or appropriately has become a problem for many Christians because they are using the wrong standard to determine what is modest, what is appropriate for a child of God to wear. Far too many Christians are making their fashion choices based upon what the world says is appropriate and not upon what God's word indicates is appropriate.

I realize that the Bible does not give a specific dress code, and that it is not specific about how long, short, tight, or sheer clothing should be. But I remember hearing an older preacher say something to the effect that he might not be able to clearly define pornography, but he was sure able to recognize it when he saw it. It is the same with appropriate clothing for one who wears the name of Christ. If we have truly been in the word of God and have made it so much a part of our very being that our senses have been exercised, by reason of use, to discern between good and evil—then we will be able to tell what is appropriate—modest—and what is not. The fashion designers of London, New York, and Paris do not determine what is appropriate—God does.

February 14

Valentine's Day

According to *Wikipedia*, "Valentine's Day is a holiday celebrated on February 14. In North America and Europe, it is the traditional day on which lovers express their love for each other by sending Valentine's cards, presenting flowers, or offering confectionary. The holiday is named after two among the numerous early Christian martyrs named Valentine. The day became associated with romantic love in the circle of Geoffrey Chaucer in High Middle Ages, when the tradition of courtly love flourished."

Regardless of the origin of the holiday, and some would go even further back to certain ancient fertility rites to find the seeds of its beginning, we all recognize that February 14 has become an important mid-winter day. Certainly from a financial standpoint it is a boom to greeting card manufacturers, florists, and candy makers. It is also a nice time to show your love and appreciation to your boyfriend or girlfriend, or spouse, in a special way. I say in a special way because love and appreciation should be shown every day, but a particular day set aside to focus upon something that is so important is awfully nice.

Isn't it wonderful to have a mate? Back in the account of creation found in Genesis 1 and 2, we find some interesting statements made that can help us to appreciate what we have if we have a spouse or special friend, of the opposite sex. In Genesis 1:31 we find, "And God saw everything that He had made, and, behold, it was very good. And the evening and the morning were the sixth day." However, as we move over into chapter 2 we find one thing that God saw that was not good. In verses 18-22 we are told:

> And the Lord God said, It is not good that the man should be alone; I will make him an help meet for him. And out of the ground the Lord God formed every beast of the field, and every fowl of the air; and brought them unto Adam to see what he would call them: and whatsoever Adam called every living creature, that was the name thereof. And Adam gave names to all cattle, and to the fowl of the air, and to every beast of the field; but for Adam there was not found an help meet for him. And the Lord God caused a deep sleep to fall upon Adam, and he slept: and he took one of his ribs, and closed up the flesh instead thereof; and the rib, which the Lord God had taken from man, made he a woman, and brought her unto the man.

The woman was created to be a help "meet" for man. She was created to be a companion, suitable in every way to complement man. It is obvious that man is thus compatible with the woman as they are meant to walk hand in hand together, supporting and complementing one another in this incredible journey called life. God created men and women to be monogamous; one man and one woman joined together for life. Take time on this admittedly man-made holiday to let that special person know how much you care for him or her. At the same time, make certain that you remember to thank God for his plan and for the wonderful person with whom he blessed you.

February 15

Lessons from Munoz
By Adam Litmer

The source of our time together today is an article that my son wrote about his dog, Munoz. (I am sure that football fans remember Anthony Munoz, the Hall of Fame offensive tackle for the Cincinnati Bengals.)

Who is Munoz? Munoz is my dog. Most days during the school year I take him for a walk at a nearby park in the early afternoon. No one is in the park then and I can let him run loose. From the moment he jumps out of the car to the moment he jumps back in, he seems to be running. He sniffs every fallen leaf, chases every squirrel, and makes sure every bird stays in the air where it belongs.

For the first few minutes he stays fairly close. As time goes by he moves a little further away. Eventually, he takes off. However, Munoz always likes to be where he can see me. Today, I stepped behind the wall of a shelter and peeked around at him. He was sniffing around about a hundred yards away. He glanced up and stopped dead in his tracks. He couldn't find me. I wasn't there. He turned and charged to the other end of the park. I wasn't there. I felt bad once he started letting out a few panicked barks, so I stepped from behind my hiding place. You would have thought he had not seen me in a year, as happy as he was. All he knew was that he had wandered off, following whatever had interested him, and when he paused to look up, he could no longer see his master.

There is obviously a spiritual lesson there, but I do not want to talk about the fact that Christians can wander away from their Master. I want to focus on our reaction when we glance up and realize that we cannot see him from where we stand. In John 6:16-21 we read, "And when even was now come, his disciples went down unto the sea, and entered into a ship, and went over the sea toward Capernaum. And it was now dark, and Jesus was not come to them. And the sea arose by reason of a great wind that blew. So when they had rowed about five and twenty or thirty furlongs, they saw Jesus walking on the sea, and drawing nigh unto the ship: and they were afraid. But he saith unto them, It is I; be not afraid. Then they willingly received him into the ship: and immediately the ship was at the land whither they went." Some translations say, "Then they were glad to take him into the boat."

We have got to do exactly what Munoz did. When we realize that we have wandered far enough afield that we cannot even see our Master, we've got to drop everything and sprint back the way we came until we can see him again! Indeed, it is not enough for us to go just far enough back so that we can see him, we've got to go all the way back to his side. It reminds me of Hebrews 13:12-13: "Wherefore Jesus also, that he might sanctify the people with his own blood, suffered without the gate. Let us go forth therefore unto him, without the camp, bearing his reproach."

Remember, "Let us go forth therefore unto him." Once we have found him, let us cling to his side as if our lives depended on it. In truth, they do.

Snow, *Oh No!*

Last week the possibility of snow existed. Three days before the dreaded event was supposed to take place the meteorologists at the various television stations in town started to get real excited. I recall the promo for one of the news programs where the anchor said, "SNOW is in the forecast." I am quite sure that throughout the tri-state area, people were going "Oh no, not SNOW!"

For the next three days we got to watch the impending snow event make its way across this great country. We saw computer models anticipating its inevitable arrival. Story after story appeared about the various city and county service departments gearing up to hit the roads with the salt trucks. The day before the "white death" was to come upon us, the bigger and wealthier counties were "pre-treating" the roads. I saw a local tire dealer whose sign encouraged us all not to worry about the snow, come on in and buy some new tires and that would take care of it. Without a doubt some folks made sure that they got to the supermarket to buy bread and milk. All of this for a possible snowstorm with a predicted accumulation of one, that's "1" inch. By the way, the snow did not come.

It never ceases to amaze me the amount of excitement the possibility of snow can generate. Folks spring into action getting ready for its arrival, and yet it seems that in this part of the country, it rarely turns out to be as bad as predicted. Nonetheless, the salt trucks are loaded, the snow shovels primed and in an easily accessible spot in the garage, and the refrigerators stocked with milk and bread.

There is an event that has been predicted by One whose every other prediction has turned out to be absolutely accurate and true. Jesus is coming back, and when He does it will be in judgment.

In John 5:28–29, the Lord said, "Do not marvel at this: for the hour is coming in which all who are in the graves will hear His voice and come forth—those who have done good, to the resurrection of life, and those who have done evil, to the resurrection of condemnation." So many make more preparation for the possibility of a one-inch snowfall than they do for the event that will bring this old world to an end.

Peter tells us what that day will be like, and incredibly, by their actions, most people indicate that they are more concerned about the inconvenience of slippery roads on the way to work. In 2 Peter 3:10-12 we find:

> But the day of the Lord will come as a thief in the night, in which the heavens will pass away with a great noise, and the elements will melt with fervent heat: both the earth and the works that are in it will be burned up. Therefore, since all these things will be dissolved, what manner of person ought you to be in holy conduct and godliness, looking for and hastening the coming of the day of God, because of which the heavens will be dissolved, being on fire, and the elements will melt with fervent heat.

Peter asked a marvelous question in that passage. Since all of these things are going to happen, what kind of people should we be? People of holiness and godliness, which is just another way of saying "Prepared People."

I was disappointed when I woke up on the day of the predicted snowfall. There was to be that inch on the ground when I got up, with a little more to follow during the course of the day. I sprang from my bed with the excitement of a child on Christmas day, looked out my bedroom window and all I saw was the brown, wet grass of an unusually warm and rainy winter. I was so disappointed. All preparation had been to no avail. But this I know for certain. On the great day when the Lord Himself descends from heaven with a shout, when we hear the voice of the archangel and the trumpet of God—all preparation made in anticipation of that event will have been rewarded. As Paul wrote in 1 Thessalonians 4:17-18, "Then we who are alive and remain shall be caught up together with them in the clouds to meet the Lord in the air. And thus we shall always be with the Lord. Therefore comfort one another with these words."

February 17

Turned

As the ages keep unfolding, the inexorable march of years
Pen to paper has been put, and stories did appear.
Some were false, others true, all lines meant for the reader.

But more poignant line was never penned than, "The Lord turned and
 looked upon Peter."

A man with stellar character, some flaws—oh yes, indeed—
Would curse and swear, "I know not the man" in His hour of greatest need.
The man who said, "Thou art the Christ, the Son of the Living God" could
 not stay awake.
But when Jesus turned and looked on Peter, we know his heart did break.

The crow of the cock preceded the awful look from Him
And as His eyes bore into Peter, so did Peter's sin.
Peter could have turned and run away, seeking relief with each new step,
But that's not what we are told he did; the Bible says, "He wept."

On the great and glorious morning of not four days hence
Through the mist of the early hours, four women walked
An angel they were blessed to see and listened as he talked
Go and tell His disciples, but Peter especially, That you have seen the empty
 tomb,
And they will see the Lord in Galilee

When the Lord turned and looked at Peter, I know what I'd have done.
I would have shaken my head and turned away and said he's not the one.
He said if I must die with You that will be alright with me;
But when the time did come to pass, he failed miserably.
With arrogance born of pride and lack of empathy, I probably would have said,
Peter, get away from me.

We have gone from, "The Lord turned and looked on Peter" to, "Go and
 tell him especially"
That His Lord had risen from the dead and would appear to him in Galilee.
Only the love of both Peter and of Jesus, kept Peter by His side.
With bitter tears I must admit, this same Jesus I've denied.

I have not cursed and sworn and shouted that I do not know the man
But there have been times when He needed me most I failed to say, "I can."
What of the man on the corner, did he even have a bed in which to sleep?
But I turned my head, averted my eyes, and with hand in pocket my money
 I did keep.

What about the brother who can no longer cut his grass,
Or what of the sister whose house-cleaning days are now long past?
Why can I see where Peter failed, but myself I cannot see?
"When you have done it unto one of these the least of My brethren, you
    have done it unto Me."

I want to try much harder, for His love I don't deserve;
And I know the reason I am here is to live my life to serve.
Of all the lines ever written or words spoken in the unfolding tale of history
I never want to have it written, that the Lord turned and looked at me.

February 18

"Be Ye Thankful"

When I was a youngster I attended St. John the Evangelist parochial school in Deer Park, Ohio, a suburb of Cincinnati. The first eight years of my formal education took place there. Two things in particular stand out in my memory from my first grade year. One was getting in trouble for something and having to stay inside for recess, only to be caught climbing on the old-fashioned windows and getting into even more trouble. The second was a little story that my teacher, Sister John Marie (at least it was Sister "something" Marie), told us in religion class. Please remember that this was a nun trying to teach a group of first graders a very important lesson. She did a good job, because I have never forgotten what she said. I have continually tried to put it into practice in my life since then. Here is the little story:

> One day God called two of His angels to Him and gave them an assignment. Each angel was to take a basket and go down to earth. One angel was to put every request made to God by man into his basket, while the other angel was to put every expression of thanks uttered by man into his basket. When they returned to the presence of God, the angel who had collected the requests had a full basket, even to the point of overflowing. The angel who was collecting all the gratitude had just one or two in his basket.

For some reason or other, that story has always stayed with me. It expresses in such simple terms the need to be thankful, a decidedly biblical principle. Let's read Luke 17:12-19:

> And as he entered into a certain village, there met him ten men that were lepers, which stood afar off: and they lifted up their voices, and said, Jesus, Master, have mercy on us. And when he saw them, he said unto them, Go show yourselves unto the priests. And it came to pass, that, as they went, they were cleansed. And one of them, when he saw that he was healed, turned back, and with a loud voice glorified God, and fell down on his face at his feet, giving him thanks: and he was a Samaritan. And Jesus answering said, Were there not ten cleansed? But where are the nine? There are not found that returned to give glory to God, save this stranger. And he said unto him, Arise, go thy way: thy faith hath made thee whole.

Even the Lord Jesus commented on the lack of gratitude and thankfulness displayed by nine of these ten lepers. They had been healed of a horrendous, devastating disease that caused them to be outcasts from society and that would eventually have taken their lives. As Christians, we have been "healed" of a far more terrible affliction, the affliction of sin. Its consequences are eternal. How can we not be thankful for that?

In a congregation of the Lord's people, everybody is a volunteer. The benefits we derive from being a volunteer in the Lord's army are indescribably sweet and too numerous to list, but we are all volunteers nonetheless. The people who clean the building, cut the grass, prepare the Lord's Supper table, count the money, lead the singing, serve at the Table, teach the Bible classes, and on and on—all volunteers, every one of them. We all derive benefits and blessings from each one of those actions and more. It is such a simple thing, and so encouraging for those who hear it, to remember to say, "Thank you."

> Put on therefore, as the elect of God, holy and beloved, bowels of mercies, kindness, humbleness of mind, meekness, longsuffering; forbearing one another, and forgiving one another, if any man have a quarrel against any: even as Christ forgave you, so also do ye. And above all these things put on charity, which is the bond of perfectness. And let the peace of God rule in your hearts, to the which also ye are called in one body; *and be ye thankful.*

February 19

Keep the Heart

In Matthew 12 the charge had been made against the Lord that He was casting out demons by the power of Beelzebub, the prince of the devils. It was obviously a pitiful attempt by certain of the Pharisees to deny the significance of the miracles Jesus was performing. The Lord quickly exposed their charge as utterly foolish. His comments included the statements found in Matthew 12:34-35, "O generation of vipers, how can ye, being evil, speak good things? For out of the abundance of the heart the mouth speaketh. A good man out of the good treasure of the heart bringeth forth good things: and an evil man out of the evil treasure bringeth forth evil things."

I am writing this on a computer. It is a marvelous machine, capable of doing a thousand things more than I know how to do. The computer does, however, have its limitations. It can only put out what is put into it. It needs the necessary software to be able to produce anything. For instance, I would like to be able to produce and edit digital video programs using my computer. I can do that, but not without the necessary software installed on my trusty Gateway. Yet, even with the software, what I can produce will be limited to what I put in. It reminds me of the Bible heart.

In Proverbs 4:23 Solomon wrote, "Watch over your heart with all diligence, for from it flow the springs of life," or as the King James renders it, "the issues of life." What flows from it can only be that which has been put into it. The computer that does not have the video producing software installed cannot produce videos. The heart that has been filled with only good treasure will not bring forth evil. The heart that has been filled with what is wicked will not bring forth that which is good.

So how do we "watch over the heart with all diligence"? Paul supplies us with the answer in Philippians 4:8-9, "Finally, brethren, whatever is true, whatever is honorable, whatever is right, whatever is pure, whatever is lovely, whatever is of good repute, if there is any excellence and if anything worthy of praise, let your mind dwell on these things. The things you have learned and received and heard and seen in me, practice these things; and the God of peace shall be with you."

There is the answer. Put in what is good and that is what will come out. This is not always an easy thing to do, but with care it can be accomplished. The Lord does not demand that we become hermits. He does not demand that we isolate ourselves, build walls around us and allow nothing in but the Bible. As a matter of fact, in 1 Corinthians 5:9-10 Paul wrote, "I wrote unto you in an epistle not to company with fornicators: yet not altogether with the fornicators of this world, or with the covetous or extortioners, or with idolaters: for then must ye needs go out of the world." There are good and wholesome things that this world has to offer. There is good music, good literature, good television, good movies, and other upright things in which we can freely engage. On the other hand, there is wicked music, wicked literature, wicked television, wicked movies, and a whole host of other wicked things in which we can engage if we choose.

February 20

"Remember also Thy Creator in the Days of Thy Youth"

I am sure many will recognize the title of this reading as being from Ecclesiastes 12:1. Let's examine the first seven verses of that chapter. Solomon wrote:

> Remember also your Creator in the days of your youth, before the evil days come and the years draw near when you will say, I have no delight in them; before the sun, the light, the moon, and the stars are darkened, and clouds return after the rain; in the day that the watchmen of the house tremble, and mighty men stoop, the grinding ones stand idle because they are few, and those who look through windows grow dim; and the doors on the street are shut as the sound of the grinding mill is low, and one will arise at the sound of the bird, and all the daughters of song will sing softly. Furthermore, men are afraid of a high place and of terrors on the road; the almond tree blossoms, the grasshopper drags himself along, and the caperberry is ineffective. For man goes to his eternal home while mourners go about in the street. Remember Him before the silver cord is broken and the golden bowl is crushed, the pitcher by the well is shattered and the wheel at the cistern is crushed; then the dust will return to the earth as it was, and the spirit will return to God who gave it.

"Remember" means "to mark," or "to be mindful." Quite simply, Solomon is calling for the proper respect and consideration to be given to the Creator. There is a very good reason why this should be done "in the days of your youth." The young are able to enjoy the things that this world has to offer to a greater degree, and such enjoyment should be tempered with a proper regard for the One who made it all. In youth the frailties of age have not yet come. Devotion to God in the prime of our life will serve us well when the years come and the afflictions that so often accompany age begin to beset us.

In verse 2 Solomon is comparing the light of the sun, moon, and stars to the eyes of the human body. The idea is to remember the Creator before the eyes become dim with age. Those of us who have trouble with the "fine print" can certainly appreciate Solomon's illustration. Also in verse 2, Solomon makes reference to the clouds returning after the rain. How does that fit in? Normally, after a rain the skies clear and the earth is refreshed. But sometimes it stops raining yet does not clear up. It remains cloudy and gloomy. When young, ailments may come but are generally short-lived and easily recovered from. With age comes increased ailments that do not always clear up and go away.

In verse 3, Solomon mentions frequent age-related occurrences. Hands lose their steadiness and the strong backs of mighty men begin to bend. The "grinders," or teeth, cease to work as efficiently because they become fewer in number. Once again reference is made to the fact that most of the time those who are older just don't see as well as they used to.

Verse 4 indicates what seems to be generally true—older folks just don't venture out as much any more, particularly at night. The amount of work the aged are able to do is considerably less than it used to be. With age often comes a light-sleeping pattern, which is the idea of "one will arise at the sound of the bird." The word used for "bird" in this verse indicates a small bird with a weak chirp. Hence, the smallest sound will awaken the aged. That is true even though a deterioration of hearing makes all sounds harder to hear.

Many times fear accompanies age, as Solomon points out in verse 5. The fear of high places may be from the effort required to reach them or from the lack of stability one may have once there. Also, older people are more fearful in general of what may happen to them. It is sad but true that for some criminals and thugs, older people make the most attractive targets because there is little they can do in return. The hair turns white as the blossoms of an almond tree. Oftentimes movement is difficult as the hips and legs lose their elasticity and the aged become as newly hatched grasshoppers of the spring. Without their wings they move slowly and awkwardly. The "caperberry," when it is overripe, bursts open and falls off of the plant.

In the normal process of things, death is nearer for the aged than it is for the young. The time is drawing near when they will go to their "eternal home," and be remembered by the mourners. When "the silver cord is broken and the golden bowl is crushed, the pitcher by the well is shattered and the wheel at the cistern is crushed," life on earth is over and the body decays in the grave while the soul moves on to await its final destination.

This is the normal progression of things. It is the way that God designed it. How much wiser it is to concern ourselves with spiritual things while we are most capable of serving the Lord in all ways! At the same time how important it is to remember that not all people reach "old age." Many are lost in their youth—old enough to serve the Lord but not having made that decision yet.

There is no good or reasonable explanation for a failure to put God first in all stages of life. He invites all, young and old, to come to Him and to know the peace that comes from serving the Lord.

February 21

It Made Me Tremble

I want to tell you about an event that happened several years ago, yet if I close my eyes and think about it, I can still see it as plain as day. My daughter, Rachel, was going to have a slumber party at our house in Louisville. Since the prospect of a houseful of little girls giggling till all hours of the night did not appeal to us, my son, Adam, and I made the trip to the country. "The country" for us was Rockcastle County, Kentucky, where my wife's parents lived.

No sooner had Adam and I arrived, than we were given the opportunity to participate in something that I had never done before—we were going to burn a field. Being from the city and having not one drop of country blood in me, that seemed a peculiar thing to do. But they were all excited about it, so I thought I'd go ahead and give it a try.

When we put the first torch to that field, darkness was just beginning to fall. All around the perimeter of that field, small fires were set, and with ever-increasing speed, the small fires joined with one another until there was one continuous circle of flames all racing toward the center of that field. After valiantly doing my duty of seeing to it that the fire didn't "git out" and burn up the "knob," Adam and I walked to a corner away from the fire and stood there to watch. By now darkness had completely fallen, and standing there looking in a pattern of 180 degrees, all we could see were the flames of that fire licking up against the darkened sky. It was a memorable sight and, as it turned out, both of us were thinking the same thing—this must be what hell looks like.

As I stood there watching the flames, various thoughts came to my mind. For instance, "Depart from me, ye cursed, into everlasting fire, prepared for the devil and his angels (Matt. 25:41). Also, "And if thy hand offend thee, cut it off; it is better to enter into life maimed, than having two hands to go into hell into the fire that never shall be quenched: where their worm dieth not, and the fire is not quenched. . . .And if thine eye offend thee, pluck it out: it is better for thee to enter into the kingdom of God with one eye, than having two eyes to be cast into hell fire: where their worm dieth not, and the fire is not quenched (Mark 9:44-48).

I am not sure if the fire in hell will be a literal fire, or if that is a device used by our Lord to illustrate the pain to be suffered eternally there. Personally, I lean toward a literal fire. However, whatever it will be, watching the fire that night just reminded me once again how much I don't want to go there. I am a Christian because I love the Lord and want desperately to go to heaven when I die. I am also a Christian because I don't want to go to hell.

There is one other thought going through my mind as I write these words and think back to that evening—all the while the fire was burning, I was keeping one eye on Adam. When I occasionally lost sight of him, my first thought was, "Where's Adam?" At the time, he was a young fellow, naturally curious, and he wanted to get as close to the fire as he could. It was my job, as his father, to keep him safe.

When our children are in our care, it is our job to keep them safe from hell-fire as well. Children are young, naturally curious, and as they grow there are going to be times when they are going to want to get as close "to the fire" as they can. Those of us who are parents must steer our children away from the "fire that is not quenched" even more diligently than we would steer them away from a burning field. We will do all we can to keep our children away from an earthly fire. What about the fire that no amount of water can put out?

February 22

"We Exult In Hope of the Glory of God" or "In Hope We Have Been Saved"

Perhaps you recognize the dual title of today's subject. The first is from Romans 5:1-2 where Paul wrote, "Therefore having been justified by faith, we have peace with God through our Lord Jesus Christ, through whom also we have obtained our introduction by faith into this grace in which we stand: *"and we exult in hope of the glory of God."* The second is found in Romans 8:24-25 where we find, "For *in hope we have been saved,* but hope that is seen is not hope; for why does one also hope for what he sees? But if we hope for what we do not see, with perseverance we wait eagerly for it."

We must never make the mistake of under-valuing *hope* in the life of a Christian. Hope is what enables us to rejoice; it is what makes it possible for us to exult when properly understood. In our day and time hope can be viewed as being relatively weak—more of a wish than anything. But that is not how the word is used in the Scriptures. It most certainly speaks of the desire for the thing "hoped" for; but it goes beyond that to a confident expectation. *The Dictionary of New Testament Theology* says of the noun and verb forms of "hope": "In the NT the words never indicate a vague or fearful anticipation but always the expectation of something good." *The Theological Dictionary of the New Testament* says of "hope": "Thus *elpizein* means expectation with the nuance of counting upon. . . ." Concerning the verb, Thayer writes in *Thayer's Greek-English Lexicon of the New Testament:* "In a religious sense, to wait for salvation with joy and full of confidence." Of the noun he writes, "Always in the N.T., in a good sense: expectation of good...and in the Christian sense, joyful and confident expectation of eternal salvation."

So, because of hope, we who are Christians do not fearfully await judgment for ourselves. We joyfully look forward to it, expecting salvation. One fellow wrote of it this way, "If your father was away on a long trip, you would look forward to his return. If he had written you a letter assuring you of his deep and unchanging love, you would exult in the thought of his return. If you loved him, knowing of his love for you, you'd be ecstatic about his return. You wouldn't be wringing your hands full of anxiety over his coming. You might even wring over the delay in his coming." I like that.

February 23

Matthew 5:27-37

As I begin to focus my attention upon Matthew 5:27-37, a passage of Scripture comes to mind. It is Habakkuk 2:20: "But the Lord is in His holy temple.

Let all the earth keep silent before Him." Most of the problems that have arisen concerning the verses in Matthew 5 will be avoided if individuals will simply recognize that God is God, and what He says is truth. God cannot be fooled by semantics, and His word is not to be manipulated to one's own advantage.

Jesus introduces the subject of adultery by referring to the seventh commandment, "You shall not commit adultery" (Exod. 20:14). The Law of Moses focused upon the act itself, and even called for the death penalty to be given to those involved. Jesus focused on the source of the act—the heart. He spoke of one who "looks on a woman to lust for her" as having committed adultery with her already. But where? In his heart. It is one thing to merely glance at a woman, perhaps even acknowledging that she is pretty and pleasant to see. It is another thing entirely to gaze upon her, longing for and fantasizing acts of sexual immorality with her. A classic example would the way that David looked upon Bathsheba in 2 Samuel 11:2.

There have been those who have sought to use Matthew 5:28 to divorce their spouses even when the physical act of adultery has not been committed. Such sophistry is beneath the faithful child of God. Paul Earnhart rightly described the sin of verse 28 as "the calculated cultivation of the desire to possess one to whom you have no right."

In verses 29-30 the Lord emphasizes the seriousness of avoiding any such sins of immorality in the heart. He is speaking figuratively, not literally. The point is that man would be better off spiritually to be rid of these most useful parts of the body than to have them lead him into such sins of the heart. Recognizing that Jesus is speaking metaphorically, I appreciate how Harold Fowler put it in *The Bible Study Textbook Series*, "Better maimed than damned."

As we move on to verses 31 and 32, there is no need for me to address how thoroughly studied and debated these verses have been. The Lord's statement in verse 31, "And it was said, Whoever sends his wife away, let him give her a certificate of divorce" comes from Deuteronomy 24:1. A discussion of the various views of the rabbinical schools of the time is not germane to this article. What we do need to consider is verse 32. When all of the arguments of one kind or another have been made, when all of the articles and books have been written, what our Lord's teaching boils down to is simply this, "The man who divorces his wife without cause is an accomplice to her adultery if she remarries. Fornication alone gives a person the right to divorce his spouse and remarry without sin. The one who marries a wrongly divorced person becomes an adulterer" (Kenneth L. Chumbley, *The Gospel of Matthew*, 105).

In verse 33 our Lord said, "Again, you have heard that the ancients were told, You shall not make false vows, but shall fulfill your vows to the Lord." I have not been able to find the exact wording of the traditional teaching Jesus mentions here in the Old Testament. More than likely Jesus was giving a summary of the Law's teaching concerning the making of oaths from such passages as Leviticus 19:12, a verse that gives every indication of seeking to regulate an already prevalent practice. The problem was in the application of the regulation of the Law. Apparently the scribes and Pharisees saw the teaching of the Law concerning oaths as permission not to be entirely truthful when one was not under an oath. What a shame and perversion of everything the Bible has to say about being truthful.

In verse 34 our Lord was not prohibiting the taking of oaths but lying and deception. All deceitful subtleties, lies, and ungodly semantics are shown to be exactly what they are by the observation that Jesus makes. There was not, and is not, a single thing by which a person can swear that is not ultimately tied to God and His power. Who created the heavens? Who created the earth? Who created man and by whom does Jerusalem stand? How foolish it is to think that one can play games with God or somehow manipulate Him. It is the responsibility of every child of God to be truthful, period. It does not matter if a person is under oath or not, for God is fully aware of every word he speaks, and there is no excuse for any word to be less than the truth. Yes must mean yes, and no must mean no.

February 24

"Who Would Not Fear Thee, O King of Nations?"

This title is a quotation from Jeremiah 10:7. One of the primary reasons for the destruction of the ten tribes of the Northern Kingdom of Israel was idolatry. When that kingdom was established, Jeroboam set up golden calves for the people to worship at Dan and Bethel, and proclaimed, "Behold thy gods, O Israel, which brought thee up out of the land of Egypt" (1 Kings 12:28). As Jeremiah wrote his book, the Southern Kingdom of Judah was on the brink of destruction, and idolatry was once again a primary reason. In Jeremiah 7:17-18 we find, "Seest thou not what they do in the cities of Judah and in the streets of Jerusalem? The children gather wood, and the fathers kindle the fire, and the women knead their dough, to make cakes to the queen of heaven, and to pour out drink offerings unto other gods, that they may provoke me to anger." The "queen of heaven" referred to by Jeremiah was probably Ashtoreth, the chief female deity of the Canaanites.

Time and again both the Northern and Southern kingdoms of the Jews placed something on a par with, or above, the God of heaven, Jehovah. Time and again they gave their allegiance to the gods their neighbors worshipped, and even though they were God's chosen people, they sought to be like everybody else. God viewed their consideration of anything or anybody equal to or above Him as adultery.

In Jeremiah 10:3-5 we find, "For the customs of the people are vain: for one cutteth a tree out of the forest, the work of the hands of the workman, with the axe. They deck it with silver and with gold; they fasten it with nails and with hammers, that it move not. They are upright as the palm tree, but speak not: they must needs be borne, because they cannot go. Be not afraid of them: for they cannot do evil, neither also is it in them to do good."

This reminds me so much of what had been written to this same nation by Isaiah approximately 120 years earlier in Isaiah 46:4-7, "To whom will ye liken me, and make me equal, and compare me, that we may be like? They lavish gold out of the bag, and weigh silver in the balance, and hire a goldsmith; and he maketh it a god: they fall down, yea, they worship. They bear him upon the shoulder, they carry him, and set him in his place, and he standeth; from his place shall he not remove: yea, one shall cry unto him, yet can he not answer, nor save him out of his trouble."

The point of both passages is, "Why would anyone place anything above God?" The idols that man creates are powerless. They cannot even move unless the very ones who worship them bear them about on their shoulders. They have no power to do either evil or good. It is a piece of wood with silver or gold covering it, an inanimate object with no inherent power.

February 25

Modern-Day Idols

What are some of the things that we can allow to become equal to, or above, God in importance in our lives? With what can we commit spiritual adultery, just as the children of Israel did?

How about money—or perhaps more specifically, the things that money can buy? Is there anything that money can buy that has the power to create itself? Is there anything that money can buy that possesses the ability to consistently move from one place to another without the intervention of man? Is there anything that money can buy that does not, from the moment it is created, begin to deteriorate? Isn't it foolish to allow a job, or the things that we can purchase as a result of that job, to take precedence over God? How many cars will I be able to take with me to the judgment seat of God? How much of my house, no matter how fine a house it is and no matter how beautifully decorated it might be, will enter into heaven or hell with me? I wonder if God will ask me the scores of any sporting events that I allowed to interfere with my service to Him when I face Him in judgment, or how many fish I caught on that Lord's Day morning spent on the lake?

Idolatry does not just involve images before which man falls down and worships. It includes any and all things that come between man and God; any and all things that we allow to take the Lord's rightful place of preeminence in our lives.

Jeremiah put it so well in Jeremiah 10:6-7, 10: "Forasmuch as there is none like unto thee, O Lord; thou art great, and thy name is great in might. Who would not fear thee, O King of nations? For to thee doth it appertain: forasmuch as among all the wise men of the nations, and in all their kingdoms, there is none like unto thee...But the Lord is the true God, he is the living God, and an everlasting king: at his wrath the earth shall tremble, and the nations shall not be able to abide his indignation."

We must allow nothing, absolutely nothing and no one, to come between God and ourselves. He is the true God, the living God, and there is none like unto Him.

February 26

The Mind of Christ

"Let this mind be in you, which was also in Christ Jesus: Who, being in the form of God, thought it not robbery to be equal with God: but made Himself of no reputation, and took upon Him the form of a servant, and was made in the likeness of men: and being found in fashion as a man, He humbled Himself, and became obedient unto death, even the death of the cross" (Phil. 2:5-8).

The more I study this passage, the more I marvel at our incredible Lord Jesus. Paul affirms that before He became man, Jesus was really and objectively God. Everything that was distinctly divine, Jesus possessed. John put it so simply in John 1:1 where he wrote, "In the beginning was the Word, and the Word was with God, and the Word was God." Existing "in the form of God"—possessing everything distinctly divine (the whole nature and essence of Deity)—Jesus was equal with God and was God.

Taking it one step further, Paul tells us that Jesus did not consider this equality as a robbery, or as a thing to be used to snatch or seize. You see, it was not necessary for Jesus to "snatch" or "seize" equality with God; He was already equal with God. And that being true, it was certainly not necessary for Jesus to maintain equality by force. So, being "equal with God" was not what the seizing or the snatching was about. Being "equal with God" was not the subject of the "seizing" or "snatching." The "seizing" or the "snatching" under consideration in this passage *begins* with the equality with God. It is something that would radiate from it. That is true, but what does it mean?

Jesus did not view His equality with God as a means of promoting Himself. He would not use His divinity to gain, or to profit in "an egoistic or despotic way from what and who He was." As a matter of fact, Jesus did just the opposite.

Even though man is made in the "image of God" (Gen. 1:26), how differently from Him do we act!!! We so often pursue such trivial things as position and power, and then use it to get our way and to serve ourselves, as Paul implied in Philippians 2:4, "Look not every man on his own things, but every man also on the things of others."

But Jesus is not like that, meaning that God is not like that. He didn't come demanding His rights. He didn't come seeking to assert His own position for His own benefit. He came here to give and to be spent for us. I am reminded of Paul's words in Romans 15:1-3, "We then that are strong ought to bear the infirmities of the weak, and not to please ourselves. Let every one of us please his neighbor for his good to edification. For even Christ pleased not Himself; but, as it is written, The reproaches of them that reproached thee fell on me."

Jesus, instead of acting as He could have acted (and by that, I mean using His equality with God to seize and snatch everything good on earth for His own personal benefit), acted exactly opposite of that. He made Himself of "no reputation." Some use the term "emptied" there, and that is okay as long as we understand that Jesus "emptied" *Himself*, and not that He emptied something *out* of Himself. It all relates in the context to how Jesus viewed His equality with God. He didn't lose or negate His equality with God in any way. What He *did do* was to put Himself totally and completely at the service of others, humbling Himself even to the extent of "taking on the form of a servant, and being made in the likeness of men." And continuing the thought, Jesus did that so He could die.

Paul said to let that same mind be in us. Is that difficult? Sure, it is! But it is part of what it means to be Christ-like.

February 27

A Lonely World (1)

There is one alone, and there is not a second; yea, he hath neither child nor brother; yet is there no end of all his labor; neither is his eye satisfied with riches; neither saith he, For whom do I labor, and bereave my soul of good? This is also vanity, yea, it is a sore travail. Two are better than one; because they have a good reward for their labor. For if they fall, the one will lift up his fellow: but woe to him that is alone when he falleth; for he hath not another to help him up. Again, if two lie together, then they have heat; but how can one be warm alone? And if one prevail against him, two shall withstand him: and a threefold cord is not quickly broken (Eccl. 4:8-12).

When Solomon wrote those words, he was acknowledging a need that every person has, and that is the need to be in a relationship with someone. I don't mean a romantic relationship, but just the idea that man is a social being. Solomon was rich, wise, and had taken every opportunity to experience earthly pleasure, but he knew that loneliness was among the worst of human experiences.

It is sad, but true, that in many ways we live in a cold, lonely world. Doors must be locked to keep out those who would injure and steal. A lot of people are almost imprisoned by fear—afraid to go out at night or to be alone. Others have experienced deep losses such as divorce or abandonment by a loved one. In all these situations our modern world reinforces the loneliness that all face. From death to a job loss to crime, we can find ourselves forced into ever smaller realms in which we know fewer and fewer people. In loneliness we face an empty life and uncertain future. Where does loneliness come from, and how can it be changed?

People are lonely when they place their emphasis upon material things. This society in which we live has sold people a bill of goods. It tells us that we will feel better if we have enough. If we have enough money, we will feel secure. If we have the latest car or the biggest house, we will be satisfied. With all of the advertisements pointed in that direction, the majority of Americans seem to have bought into the idea that happiness is to be gained by having enough "stuff."

Sadly, so many times people who succeed in having money and an abundance of things find themselves lonely. I think of the prodigal son from Luke 15:11-15, "A certain man had two sons: and the younger of them said to his father, Father, give me the portion of goods that falleth to me. And he divided unto them his living. And not many days after the younger son gathered all together, and took his journey into a far country, and there wasted his substance with riotous living. And when he had spent all, there arose a mighty famine in that land; and he began to be in want. And he went and joined himself to a citizen of that country; and he sent him into his fields to feed swine."

I believe the prodigal son learned that someone with money, and the willingness to spend it, will have a lot of friends more than willing to engage in the riotous living with them. But once the money is gone, so are the friends. How many times do we hear wealthy celebrities bemoaning the fact that they often can't tell if people want to be their friends because they like them, or because they like their money and prestige. A person can be surrounded by a lot of people and still be lonely. Having a lot of wealth doesn't mean we will be happy. It doesn't mean our kids will turn out well. It doesn't mean we will have a strong marriage.

February 28

A Lonely World (2)

Contentment lies in God, not in things. Paul had some things to say that need to be considered in this context. In 1 Timothy 6:6-10 he said, "But godliness with contentment is great gain. For we brought nothing into this world, and it is certain that we can carry nothing out. And having food and raiment let us be therewith content. But they that will be rich fall into temptation and a snare, and into many foolish and hurtful lusts, which drown men in destruction and perdition. For the love of money is the root of all evil: which while some coveted after, they have erred from the faith, and pierced themselves through with many sorrows."

The Holy Spirit, through Paul, was telling us the dangers of placing all of our emphasis upon money and things. Not only is a soul lost to God, but the individual experiences many sorrows. Think about it. How many fathers have pursued their careers vigorously and successfully, only to lose their families through neglect? How many mothers have worked to have more and more and to enjoy the "good life," only to lose their children? How many marriages have been destroyed because of arguments over how to spend what little was left in the checkbook, and credit cards all run up to the limit? Surely, the love of money, the pursuit of material wealth as an end in itself, isolates people and causes loneliness.

March 1

A Lonely World (3)

People who live in sin are lonely. At the root of sin, when you think about it, is selfishness. Eve was tempted by the desire to be like God in Genesis 3:6. Man is tempted when "he is drawn away of his own lust and enticed" (Jas. 1:14). Sin results in separation, isolation from God and often from our fellow man.

Nevertheless our world today continues to send the message that having fun by living in sin will make us happy. So many buy into the silly cycle of bars and clubs, drinking and dancing, and satisfying physical desire—and when all is said and done, they are still alone.

Real happiness lies in being close to God and close to others, not in pursuing selfish pleasures. I think of Moses and the statement made concerning him in Hebrews 11:24-25, "By faith Moses, when he was come to years, refused to be called the son of Pharaoh's daughter; choosing the reproach of Christ greater riches than the treasures in Egypt: for he had respect unto the recompense of the reward." Moses chose God's people over sin. He chose people, relationships that meant something, and righteousness over sin. Putting others ahead of ourselves can defeat loneliness. Selfishness brings about sin and creates loneliness and isolation even in a crowd. Selflessness creates intimacy and closeness.

March 2

A Lonely World (4)

People who have no purpose in their lives are lonely. So many folks feel so empty. They get up in the morning and go to work; they come home—day after day and year after year. They feel a sense of discomfort, wondering if that is all there is to life. They make money; they spend money. They have marriages, children, and friends. Yet they feel empty. They have no sense of a higher purpose, other than making it through another day. They feel alone.

Some folks try to fill that empty spot with social pursuits. Others get some sort of a hobby. Still others seek higher education or athletic skills; perhaps physical fitness or a thousand other pursuits aimed at hiding that feeling of aimlessness that plagues so much of mankind.

The truth is that only in God can man find a higher purpose with real quality and lasting power. Again, after devoting himself to a search for happiness and contentment, in an attempt to find real meaning in life, Solomon's conclusion was, "Let us hear the conclusion of the whole matter: Fear God, and keep his commands: for this is the whole duty of man. For God shall bring every work into judgment, with every secret thing, whether it be good or whether it be evil" (Eccl. 12:13-14).

Only by learning about God, only by submitting to God, only by following God's will for life can anyone discover real satisfaction. To pursue any other goal will ultimately end in disappointment. I believe this is part of what Jesus was saying in Matthew 16:24-25 when He said, "If any man will come after me, let him deny himself, and take up his cross, and follow me. For whosoever will save his life shall lose it: and whosoever will lose his life for my sake shall find it." When people attempt to find purpose without God they ultimately fail, no matter how noble the cause. But with God, people find both purpose and fulfillment. Any life lived without God at its center will turn out to be a lonely life.

People are lonely who do not know God. In Paul's address to the Athenians on Mars Hill in Acts 17:26-28 he said, "He made from one, every nation of mankind to live on all the face of the earth, having determined their appointed times, and the boundaries of their habitation, that they should seek God, if perhaps they might grope for Him and find Him, though He is not far from each one of us: for in Him we live and move and exist; as even some of your own poets have said, For we also are His offspring." This sums up the basic problem of loneliness. God created man to seek Him and to know Him. When man sins, he isolates himself from God. Yet, as we are created to know God and to serve Him, isolation from Him is to be without purpose, without any real satisfaction. To be isolated from God is contrary to our very reason for being. Remember Paul's words in 1 Corinthians 6:13b, "Now the body is not for fornication, but for the Lord: and the Lord for the body." Without God, we cannot fulfill our very purpose for existence, and that is the height of loneliness.

March 3

A Lonely World (5)

Man needs God. He needs His wisdom, His guidance, His power, and His mercy. When we try to exist apart from God, all of those resources are lost. We can see it in the world in which we live. Today man is trying to build a better world, leaving God out of the picture as they do so, and where has it gotten us? Without God there can be no peace, no harmony, no true happiness and contentment. The consequences of a lack of God, as seen in our world, is more selfishness, more empty pursuit of material wealth, more emotional and spiritual isolation, and more loneliness.

But all is not lost, and we are not without a solution to the devastating problem of loneliness. When man repents and turns back to God, he rediscovers his true purpose in life. Going back to Paul's address on Mars Hill, we find in Acts 17:30, "And the times of this ignorance God winked at; but now commandeth all men everywhere to repent." God wants us to acknowledge our need for Him. When we accept our need for God and to turn to Him in obedient faith, God redeems us from sin and gives our lives meaning again. That is the ultimate cure for loneliness.

In becoming a child of God through obedience to the gospel, I have found a relationship that will not fail—ever. God will sustain me, forgive me, and love me as I walk in the light of His revealed Word. As long as I remain faithful I will never lose my purpose or my direction again. I will always have a steadfast companion who will be there for me. With God I am never alone.

But there is more. When I became a Christian, I found myself part of a family that is even closer than my blood relationships. I have thousands and thousands of brothers and sisters in Christ who have also been born again. I love them, and they love me. Once added to that family, I have many relationships with many people, each one a forgiven sinner just like me. In that atmosphere, I am never alone.

Let me tell you one more practical benefit. By being a Christian—by learning to put God first, others second, and myself third—every other relationship in my life is better too.

Oh, friends, so many people are lonely and are waiting for the right person or maybe the right "cause" to come along and make them happy. They wait for the right spouse or maybe the right job—whatever. But in truth, there is nothing outside of God that can fill the hunger within the human soul permanently. No person, no cause, no amount of money or possessions can ever really cure loneliness. Only by submitting to God, only by seeking God through the Lord Jesus, only by rendering obedience to the gospel of Christ, can a person fill the void that is there.

March 4

The Lord's Supper on Sunday Evening

At the celebration of the Passover Meal before His death on the cross, our Lord Jesus instituted the Lord's Supper. In 1 Corinthians 11:23-26 Paul gives this divinely inspired account of that event: "For I received from the Lord that which I also delivered to you, that the Lord Jesus in the night in which He was betrayed took bread; and when He had given thanks, He broke it, and said, This is My body, which is for you; do this in remembrance of Me.

In the same way He took the cup also, after supper, saying, This cup is the new covenant in My blood; do this, as often as you drink it, in remembrance of Me. For as often as you eat this bread and drink this cup, you proclaim the Lord's death until He comes."

Bible students are aware of the fact that as the apostles went about teaching the church to "observe all that I commanded you" (Matt. 28:20). One of the things that they taught was that the disciples of Jesus were to partake of the Lord's Supper each first day of the week. Acts 20:7 constitutes the only example we have of *when* the early church partook of the Lord's Supper. It was upon the first day of the week. Each week has a first day; consequently, Christians are to partake of this great memorial feast every first day of the week.

In 1 Corinthians 11:18 we learn as well that this memorial is to be observed at the congregational assembly of the brethren, "For, in the first place, *when you come together as a church. . . ."* Verse 20 tells us, "Therefore when you meet together. . . ." While the congregation is assembled together on the Lord's Day, the Lord's Supper is to be partaken of. The setting is collective, but the actual partaking is individual. 1 Corinthians 11:27-29 says, "Therefore whoever eats the bread or drinks the cup of the Lord in an unworthy manner, shall be guilty of the body and the blood of the Lord. But let a man *examine himself*, and so let *him* eat of the bread and drink of the cup. For he who eats and drinks, *eats and drinks judgment to himself, if he* does not judge the body rightly." Thus, the Lord's Supper is taken when the church is gathered together—yet each member is individually responsible for partaking and for the manner in which he partakes. This is why there is no authority for taking the Lord's Supper to a sick member in a hospital or home. It is taken when the church *"comes together as a church."*

There has been considerable controversy over the years and in various locations about offering the Lord's Supper on Sunday evening for those who were not able to be with the saints at the morning service. I believe that it should be offered if there is going to be a Sunday evening service. The Bible makes it clear that it is each member's responsibility to partake of the Lord's Supper each first day of the week. If I truly cannot be at the Sunday morning service, but can gather with the saints on Sunday evening, I find nothing that would indicate that my responsibility to individually partake of the Lord's Supper has been negated. The church comes together in the evening; hence, the setting is correct. And I individually partake, and that is also correct. I would not want to appear before the Lord having denied a brother or sister the opportunity to do what God requires them to do.

What I do have trouble with is those who view Sunday evening service and the offering of the Lord's Supper as an alternative to Sunday morning. Those who think, "I can miss Sunday morning because I can always partake of the Lord's Supper on Sunday evening" clearly have a lax attitude and are abusing the opportunity. The Sunday evening offering of the Lord's Supper is not done to allow someone who was out late Saturday night to sleep in. It is not offered to make it more convenient for those who have out-of-town guests. It is not offered so vacationers can get an early start and stop somewhere in the evening to partake. It is offered for those who truly could not be there in the morning to fulfill their obligation.

March 5

How Reliable Is the Text?

Have you ever heard anybody question the reliability of the text of the Bible? By that I mean have you ever heard anyone confidently assert that we just can't be sure that we have the original words of the Scriptures, that we just can't be sure that the text is reliable? It has always amazed me that such comments are usually made by fairly well educated people who use such reasoning to defend their rejection of the authority of the Word of God. I say it amazes me because these are often the same people who have studied the works of Aristotle and Plato in philosophy classes, or labored over the works of Pliny the Younger or Caesar's Gallic War in History of Western Civilization courses.

The Bible is a work of antiquity. Even its most noted and vehement critics assign it a place of prominence among other ancient writings. It seems to me that when we are talking about something as fundamental as textual reliability, all works of antiquity must be judged by the same criteria. Let's see how the textual reliability of the Bible stacks up against other famous works of antiquity when the same standard is used.

There is a test used by scholars when dealing with ancient writings that is meant to determine the reliability and the validity of the text of such writings.

It is called the *bibliographical test*. This test is an examination of the way the text of the documents we now have has reached us. In other words, since the original documents no longer exist, or at least haven't been found, how reliable are the copies that we do have in regards to the number of manuscripts we now possess and the time between the original writing and the earliest copy in our possession?

There are over 13,000 ancient manuscripts of the New Testament. Now this is not to say that they are all complete, but at least 13,000 manuscript copies of at least portions of the New Testament do exist. There are approximately 8,000 manuscripts of the Latin Vulgate translation and close to 1,000 manuscripts for the other early version. Add to that 5,000 Greek manuscripts, and that is how we arrived at the figure of over 13,000. Besides all of these partial and full manuscripts, almost all of the New Testament can be found in quotations of early Christian writers from the second and third centuries.

Here is how the *bibliographical test* works. Let us consider the famous *Gallic War* of Caesar. It was written between 58 and 50 B.C. The earliest copy still existing was written in approximately A.D. 900, making a time span of 1,000 years from the original to our earliest copy. There are ten copies that are any good at all in existence today.

Consider Plato's famous *Tetralogies*. Plato lived from 427-347 B.C. The earliest copy we have of his work is dated from around A.D. 900, making a time span of 1,200 years from the date of writing to the earliest copy. There are seven ancient manuscripts of this work. Philosophy students have been studying Plato for years, and the professors don't seem to worry about "textual reliability."

How about Pliny the Younger's *History*? It was written between A.D. 61 and 113. The earliest known copy is from A.D. 850, making a time span of 750 years. There are seven manuscripts total.

Now, what about the New Testament? It was written between A.D. 50-95. The earliest manuscript that we have is the John Ryland MSS, dating A.D. 130. It is a portion of the Gospel of John. That is a time span of 40 to 50 years.

There is the Chester Beatty Papyri, dating A.D. 200. It contains major portions of the New Testament. Here is a time span of 110 years.

On and on we could go, from A.D. 150 to 500, including the Codex Sinaiticus of A.D. 350, containing almost all of the New Testament and over half of the Old. There is the Codex Vaticanus, dated A.D. 325 to 350. It is currently in the Vatican Library and contains nearly the entire Bible. Also existing is the Codex Alexandrinus from A.D. 400. It is in the British Museum and contains almost the whole Bible. When it is all put together, with time spans ranging from 50 years to 410 years, there are over 13,000 manuscripts of the New Testament. To deny the textual reliability of the New Testament is to reject every single work of antiquity, because there is not one that comes even close to being as well attested to as the New Testament text. Even skeptics must be honest.

March 6

Love Is. . .

John's teaching in 1 John 4:7-21 has been described as "a diamond turned round and round for different angles of light to flash on it." John writes of the source of love, its greatest manifestation, its proof in the lives of Christians, and the confidence it engenders. His teaching is so profound that I doubt anyone could ever exhaust the depth of its meaning. Each statement reflects its brilliance in so many ways that it truly is like a perfect diamond on display for all to examine and marvel at.

Paul, in 1 Corinthians 13, provides us with another view of love—a view that embraces the practical application of each of the principles that John sets forth. Paul gives us characteristics that will be manifested in the life of one who truly loves. It is one thing to say, "I have love"; it is another thing to live it.

In the midst of a discussion of miraculous spiritual gifts, Paul interjects his teaching concerning "the more excellent way," which is love. He begins with hyperbole—exaggeration for rhetorical effect, and wrote, "If I speak with the tongues of men and of angels. . . ." This simply means the highest possible degree of "tongue-speaking" ability. Yet if Paul exercised that gift without love, he was just making noise.

Paul wrote, "And if I have the gift of prophecy, and know all mysteries and all knowledge; and if I have all faith...." Once again, he exaggerates for effect.

"Mysteries" refers to those secret thoughts and plans of God hidden from human reason and that must be revealed. It reminds me of Deuteronomy 29:29, "The secret things belong to the Lord our God." No one knows all of God's thoughts, nor can we. Paul is simply making the point that all of the miraculous spiritual gifts upon which the Corinthians placed so much emphasis were nothing if they were not under girded with love. Even acts of charity and courage that appear magnificent to the eye did not benefit the one doing them at all if they were not prompted by love.

What does characterize love, and why is it so important? These are questions that Paul continued to answer, and we need to know these answers. Our eternal salvation depends upon love—God's love for us, our love for God, and our love for our fellow man. Let's see how we are doing.

"Love is patient"; other translations may have "longsuffering." It actually means to be long-tempered. We speak of a person being short-tempered. This is just the opposite. It is self-restraint that is not hasty to retaliate. It endures injuries and wrongs. What better example of this attribute of love can there be than Jesus? Peter wrote of the Lord in 1 Peter 2:23 the following, "And while being reviled, He did not revile in return; while suffering, He uttered no threats, but kept entrusting Himself to Him who judges righteously."

Do you ever feel the need to retaliate in kind to insults, slights, or injuries? I do. I am working on it, and I believe that I am getting better, but I am not there yet. How about you?

"Love is kind." The word for "kind" actually means "gentle." There is no room for harshness or roughness in love. It is not caustic or antagonistic. Do not misunderstand this point. Sometimes love demands firmness, and being kind is not the same as being wimpy. But there is never a reason to be unkind.

March 7

Love Does Not. . .

Love "is not jealous." To be jealous, as Paul uses it in 1 Corinthians 13:4, is to feel a dishonorable envy about the good in others and to have that envy manifest itself in berating and maligning the other person. Sometimes folks will be jealous, and because of that, try to belittle or tear down the one of whom they are jealous. It can be done publicly in front of a lot of people, privately with snide remarks made over the telephone, or to just one or two people. It is inexcusable.

"Love does not brag and is not arrogant." The emphasis here is on arrogance in speech. It really is boasting that is meant to do others harm. It is building myself up to tear someone else down. Love does not allow for an inflated opinion of my own importance. How can I be boastful and arrogant and try to build myself up at the expense of others, and still claim to be a follower of Jesus? Remember Paul's words in Philippians 2:3-4: "Do nothing from selfishness or empty conceit, but with humility of mind let each of you regard one another as more important than himself; do not merely look out for your own person interests, but also for the interests of others."

"Love does not act unbecomingly; does not seek its own." If I have love, I will not conduct myself in a way that is contrary to what the Lord considers decent and proper. I have a responsibility to the Lord to let my light shine in such a way that men can see my good works, and in turn glorify God. That is my responsibility. I also have a responsibility to my fellow man to give them the very best example possible. I am not going to be doing that if I am behaving in an ungodly manner. That would be the height of selfishness, of seeking my own. If I have love, I will consider the cares and needs of others and conduct myself accordingly.

"Love is not provoked; does not take into account a wrong suffered." The word "provoked" means "to be irritated or incensed." Perhaps the best way to put it is that love does not go around looking for trouble. It does not "fly off the handle" every time something does not go its way.

Additionally, love does not allow for someone to keep a running record of offenses committed against them with the idea that somewhere down the line they are going to get even. As a matter of fact, love does not allow for a person to even dwell on offenses committed against him. We cannot claim to be Christians if we hold grudges. This is another characteristic of love at which I have to work hard. It is tough to lay aside hurtful things and to truly have in my heart the desire for only the best to happen to those who hurt me. But again, I need only look to the example of my Lord to see that it can be done.

"Love does not rejoice in unrighteousness, but rejoices with the truth." The person with love finds no pleasure in sin. Such a person realizes that sin is an offense against God and is the reason Jesus died on the cross. It is no reason for joy. It should cause sorrow.

Did you ever know someone who seemed to take delight in the failures of others? Did you ever know someone who always wanted to talk about sinful things that had taken place in the life of someone else? Did you ever know anyone who seemed to find personal vindication in the sins of others? You know what I mean—one who says, "I always knew they were going to do that," or "I'm not surprised!" That is just about as unloving as you can get.

"Love bears all things, believes all things, hopes all things, endures all things." Those who have love will be able to bear whatever trials and tribulations come their way. If I have love, I am going to believe the very best about others. I will not yield to unfounded suspicions and doubts. I will also give a brother the benefit of the doubt and believe the very best about him until the evidence demands otherwise.

I am going to hope for the best in all situations, and if it doesn't always work out for the best, then I am going to be patient and steadfast in my endurance. Love demands that it be so.

March 8

"And Lot Lifted up His Eyes"

In Genesis 13 we read of Abram and Lot parting ways because the land was not sufficient to bear both of them with their families and possessions. In verse 9 Abram offered Lot the following solution to their problem, "Is not the whole land before thee? Separate thyself, I pray thee, from me: if thou wilt take the left hand, then I will go to the right; or if thou depart to the right hand, then I will go to the left."

Abram left the choice entirely up to Lot. He was free to choose where he would live, where he would raise his family. Verses 10-11 detail his choice, as well as the reasons for it. The passage says, "And Lot lifted up his eyes, and beheld all the plain of Jordan, that it was well watered everywhere, before the Lord destroyed Sodom and Gomorrah, even as the garden of the Lord, like the land of Egypt, as thou comest unto Zoar. Then Lot chose him all the plain of Jordan; and Lot journeyed east: and they separated themselves the one from the other."

There was one aspect that Lot obviously did not consider as he was making his choice. Verse 13 tells us, "But the men of Sodom were wicked and sinners before the Lord exceedingly."

So Lot lifted up his eyes and made this important life decision on the basis of what appealed to his eyes. The plain of Jordan was well watered and obviously fruitful, but we have to wonder about the cities that were located there. Later we would find that in having chosen the vicinity of these cities as the place to raise his children, Lot would actually take up residence in the city of Sodom itself. It is apparent that the moral character of these cities was well known, and yet Lot chose to live among them. Did he make his choice purely on the basis of material considerations? Did he journey east to the plain and the cities of it because he thought that that was where he would prosper the most? Whatever was the basis for Lot's decision, and we are told that he "lifted up his eyes and beheld all the plain of Jordan, that it was well watered everywhere," how it would affect his family spiritually was not his primary concern.

In our lives we are so often faced with what I would call "life decisions." They are choices that we must make that will have a profound effect upon us. Aside from the most significant choice of all—to be a Christian—consider some of these "life choices" with me. Where will I go to school, will I get married, and if so, who will I marry? Will we have children and how many? What kind of job do I want? Where do I want to live? With what congregation do I want to identify? The list goes on and on. What will be the basis upon which we make these decisions?

I think of Joseph, who, when confronted with a life decision of whether or not to commit fornication, said, "How then can I do this great wickedness, and sin against God?" (Gen. 39:9). I think of Joshua demanding a choice to be made by the Israelites and saying, "If it seem evil unto you to serve the Lord, choose you this day whom ye will serve; whether the gods which your fathers served that were on the other side of the flood, or the gods of the Amorites, in whose land ye dwell: but as for me and my house, we will serve the Lord" (Josh. 24:15). Each made his choice on the basis of what was best spiritually. So must we.

A Very Special Friend

I want to take this opportunity to tell you about a very special friend that Vicky and I have. He exhibits qualities of character that I wish I regularly displayed. He is always happy, always ready to go, and is completely loyal. When I am feeling down, he has a wonderful way of bringing a smile to my face. With the loss of Vicky's mother, he has filled a hole in her heart and has given her a wonderful companion through the days. If you haven't already guessed it, the friend that I am talking about is Othello Joseph Litmer—Ozzy the dog. When I think of unwavering loyalty, I am reminded of the wonderful woman, Ruth. After the death of her husband, Naomi, Ruth's mother-in-law, encouraged her to return to the home of her own mother. But in one of the most famous statements of the Bible, Ruth said, "Do not urge me to leave you or turn back from following you; for where you go, I will go, and where you lodge, I will lodge. Your people shall be my people, and your God, my God. Where you die, I will die, and there I will be buried" (Ruth 1:16-17a). I am amazed at the unquestioning loyalty that a dog can exhibit. He helps to remind me of attitudes and characteristics that the Bible tells me I ought to have.

When I come home from work, Ozzy will follow me around, waiting for me to say, "Hey, Oz, want to go for a walk?" He has never yet indicated the slightest hesitation. He is always ready to go even if it is 95 degrees, or if there is snow on the ground or the wind is blowing on a wintry, cold day. Sometimes when there are opportunities that arise for me to engage in some aspect of the Lord's work—to call someone, visit someone, even study with someone—I find myself hesitating. It may have been a long day, perhaps I am tired. But Ozzy is always ready to go, and all I have to do is call his name. Such readiness and willingness to go makes me think of myself and whether I would always answer, "Here am I, send me." Remember when the great Messianic prophet, Isaiah was called in Isaiah 6:8, this is what we find, "Then I heard the voice of the Lord, saying, Whom shall I send, and who will go for Us? Then I said, Here am I, send me."

He is the happiest, most loving and forgiving little fellow I have ever known. He exudes joy every day and that can make the darkest of days a little bit brighter. All he knows is that he has a warm house to live in, food every day, and people who will take him outside. I have so much more than Ozzy, but I know that I don't exude joy every day. I am certain that I don't always brighten every room I enter. But you know what? I should. It calls to mind Philippians 4:4, "Rejoice in the Lord always; again I will say, rejoice!" That little dog, he is my buddy, and he teaches me lessons every day.

March 10

Examine Ourselves

It is now well past thirty years since I graduated from high school (actually it closer to forty than thirty), but I remember those four years fondly. However, there was one aspect of those four years that I did not enjoy, and that was when the time came to face mid-term or final exams, when the time came to evaluate how much progress I had made over the preceding five months, or nine months. When I was a senior, the exams really served to determine how much progress I had made over the last four years. Intellectually, emotionally, and certainly physically, the one graduating from high school is not the same as the youngster who began that journey four years earlier. We expect that. Seniors are no longer freshmen. They have grown. They have increased in every way. They have matured, and indeed, if they had not, then we would recognize that something was wrong.

It is not so very different in the spiritual realm. All of us who are faithful children of God, no matter what age we might be, should not be the same spiritually now as we were four years ago. We all should have grown and increased in every possible measurement of spirituality and faithfulness. We should all be better Christians now than we were four years ago.

As Paul was beginning to bring the very personal letter of 2 Corinthians to a close, he wrote in 13:5, "Examine yourselves, whether ye be in the faith; prove your own selves. Know ye not your own selves, how that Jesus Christ is in you, except ye be reprobates?" Regular spiritual examinations of ourselves are important. Have we increased, have we matured, have we grown over the last four years (in keeping with the high school analogy)? I am reminded of what David wrote in Psalm 26:1-2, "Judge me, O Lord; for I have walked in mine integrity: I have trusted also in the Lord; therefore I shall not slide.

Examine me, O Lord, and prove me; try my reins and my heart." This helps us to remember that even as we conduct our own examinations to determine our spiritual growth, or lack thereof, the one who ultimately grades the test is God.

In so many places the Scriptures exhort us to love one another. One such example is our Lord's statement in John 13:34 when he said to his apostles, "A new commandment I give unto you, That ye love one another; as I have loved you, that ye also love one another." How are you doing? Have you grown in your love for your brothers and sisters in Christ over the last four years?

The Bible teaches us to be evangelistic. Jesus said, "Go ye into all the world, and preach the gospel to every creature" (Mark 16:15). How are you doing? Are you more evangelistic, more willing to tell people the Good News of Jesus Christ now than you were four years ago?

God's Word exhorts us to grow in our knowledge of His will for us. Peter wrote in 2 Peter 3:18, "But grow in grace, and in the knowledge of our Lord and Savior Jesus Christ." Do you know more of God's word now than you did four years ago? Do you have a better understanding of His will?

We can all see the point. Periodic self-examinations of our growth as Christians are both called for and helpful. They enable us to see ourselves a bit more clearly and honestly.

March 11

I Will Not Deny Thee

"I will not deny Thee"
That's what Peter said.
And the words of this great man of God
Keep ringing in my head.

Later on that selfsame night,
Peter did that very thing.
"I do not know the man!"
Through the ages those words still ring.

All was not lost for Peter
On that fateful night.
For when the Lord turned and looked at him,
Peter wept with all his might.

"I will not deny Thee."
It repeats inside my head.
For though I have not said the words,
I've done the deed instead.

Jesus left me an example,
In His steps I am to tread.
But I have not always done that,
Even in the things I've said.

"I will not deny Thee!"
Oh, no, not me.
But I have done that very thing
With what I've allowed my eyes to see.

"Love your enemies,"
Seek their greatest good.
I have not always done that,
Even when I could.

"Father, forgive them"
From the cross our Lord did say.
But what of me, I ask myself—
Have I always thought that way?

"I will not deny Thee."
To keep those words I do intend.
But there are days the cock crows for me,
And I know I've failed again.

You said to clothe the naked,
And to feed the hungry too.
At times I've turned my back on those in need,
And You said I did it unto You.

"I will not deny Thee."
Oh, Lord, help me to those words to cling!
And when I fail to do so,
Help me my contrite heart to bring.

I love You, this I know,
And in my heart I'll strive to be
One who lives, as well as says,
"I will not deny Thee."

March 12

Just Do It!

Do you remember that slogan from the Nike commercials a few years back? It was a most effective advertising campaign, because in everyday conversation folks began to urge others to "Just do it!" when there was some task that needed to be accomplished. It may not have been quite as memorable as "Where's the beef?" but it got the job done. (Quite a few of the younger people may not remember, "Where's the beef?" But believe me, it was big for a time!)

The phrase "Just do it!" seems to fit the books of 1, 2, and 3 John. In those three letters John writes a great deal about love. As a matter of fact, in 1 John 4:7-8 he wrote, "Beloved, let us love one another: for love is of God; and every one that loveth is born of God, and knoweth God. He that loveth not knoweth not God; *for God is love."*

Love is vital and foundational. To show just how important it is, let's consider the words of Paul in 1 Corinthians 13:1-3 when he was teaching the Corinthians "a more excellent way." He wrote, "Though I speak with the tongues of men and of angels, and have not love, I am become as a sounding brass, or a tinkling cymbal. And though I have the gift of prophecy, and understand all mysteries, and all knowledge; and though I have all faith, so that I could remove mountains, and have not love, I am nothing. And though I bestow all my goods to feed the poor, and though I give my body to be burned, and have not love, it profiteth me nothing."

However, a lot of Christians have an idea of love that may be consistent with the world's view, but has very little to do with the biblical view of love.

A few years back there were some little cartoons that would say, "Love is..." and follow that with something like "a soft puppy," or "a hand to hold," and other such things. They were cute and generally did give a warm feeling. But such feelings are not all that love is about, certainly not in the biblical sense. As a matter of fact, such warm and fuzzy feelings are not even necessarily considered in the biblical approach to love.

This now brings us back to 1, 2, and 3 John and the saying, "Just do it!" That expresses the idea behind biblical love a great deal more accurately than some feel-good emotion or soft pedal approach. In John's letters, love is inseparably attached to obedience—to the point that John tells us if we *say* we have love, to God or our fellow man, then "Just do it!" Let me show you what I mean. In 1 John 2:3-5 we read, "And hereby we do know that we know him, *if we keep his commandments.* He that saith, I know him, and keepeth not his commandments, is a liar, and the truth is not in him. But *whoso keepeth his word, in him verily is the love of God perfected:* hereby know we that we are in him." In other words, "Just do it!"

March 13

Just Keep on Doing It!

In 1 John 3:16-18 we find, "Hereby perceive we the love of God, because he laid down his life for us; and we ought to lay down our lives for the brethren. But whoso hath this world's goods, and seeth his brother have need, and shutteth up his bowels of compassion from him, how dwelleth the love of God in him? My little children, *let us not love in word, neither in tongue; but in deed and in truth.*" There we see it again. Folks can talk about love all they want, but it doesn't mean anything if they don't "Just do it!" By the way, what we do must be according to truth and sometimes that is really hard. Warm and fuzzy feelings are a lot easier than true biblical love.

Now we move down to 1 John 3:23-24. John wrote, "And this is his commandment, That we should believe on the name of his Son Jesus Christ, and love one another, as he gave us commandment. *And he that keepeth his commandments* dwelleth in him and he in him. And hereby we know that he abideth in us, by the Spirit which he hath given us." In other words, "Just do it!"

Let's move over to 1 John 5:2-3: "By this we know that we love the children of God, when we love God, *and keep his commandments.* For this is the love of God, *that we keep his commandments:* and his commandments are not grievous." Surely we are seeing a pattern here. If we don't do what God says, if we walk outside the realm of truth (i.e., that which is authorized), we can talk about love all we want, but we don't have it.

Look at 2 John 5-6: "And now I beseech thee, lady, not as though I wrote a new commandment unto thee, but that which we have from the beginning, that we love one another. And this is love, *that we walk after his commandments.* This is the commandment, That, as ye have heard from the beginning, ye should walk in it."

Now to show that this love must be in truth, consider 2 John 9-11: "Whosoever transgresseth, and abideth not in the doctrine of Christ, hath not God. He that abideth in the doctrine of Christ, he hath both the Father and the Son. If there come any unto you, *and bring not this doctrine,* receive him not into your house, neither bid him God speed: for he that biddeth him God speed *is a partaker of his evil deeds.*"

Finally, look at 3 John 4, a favorite passage of mine. John wrote, "I have no greater joy than to hear that my children *walk in truth.*" That is just another way of saying that they "Just do it!"

All the talk of love in the world is just that—talk—if it is not backed up with respect for, and obedience to, the truth. Otherwise, we are just kidding ourselves. It is like John wrote in 1 John 3:7, "Little children, let no man deceive you: *he that doeth righteousness is righteous,* even as he is righteous." Once again, "Just do it!"

Do I Give As Good As I Get? (1)

One of the most memorable statements that the Lord Jesus made is not found recorded in the Gospels, but rather in the book of Acts. In Acts 20:35 Paul is recorded as saying to the Ephesian elders, "I have showed you all things, how that so laboring ye ought to support the weak, and to remember the words of the Lord Jesus, how he said, It is more blessed to give than to receive." All of us receive so much; I wonder if we give as good as we get. (I know this is grammatically improper, but it makes the point efficiently.)

In the life of a congregation of the Lord's people, there will be good times and bad, especially as a congregation grows numerically. There will be times when the congregation experiences very little sickness or other trying situations, and there will be times when many of its members are sick or suffering in some other way. It is thrilling to see brethren rally to the side of those who need help, and truly demonstrate that the love we feel for one another is real, and not just spoken. I am reminded of the words from 1 John 3:17-23: "But whoso hath this world's goods, and seeth his brother have need, and shutteth up his bowels of compassion from him, how dwelleth the love of God in him? My little children, let us not love in word, neither in tongue; *but in deed and in truth*. And hereby we know that we are of the truth, and shall assure our hearts before him. For if our heart condemn us, God is greater than our heart, and knoweth all things. Beloved, if our heart condemn us not, then have we confidence toward God. And whatsoever we ask, we receive of Him, because we keep His commandments, and do those things that are pleasing in His sight. And this is His commandment, that we should believe on the name of His Son Jesus Christ, and *love one another*, as He gave us commandment."

What has John told us? He has told us that we can assure our hearts by the reality of our love one for another. If we move beyond just talking about loving one another, to manifesting that love in deed and in truth, we can still our hearts, set them at rest, knowing that we are abiding by the standard of righteousness that the Lord has left us.

March 15

Do I Give As Good As I Get? (2)

In 2 Corinthians 8 the Apostle Paul was encouraging the Corinthian brethren to be liberal in their giving to ease the burden of other brethren. In verses 13-15 he wrote, "For I mean not that other men be eased, and ye burdened: but by an equality, that now at this time your abundance may be a supply for their want, that their abundance also may be a supply for your want: that there may be equality: as it is written, He that had gathered much had nothing over; and he that had gathered little had no lack."

Paul's point in this passage was that those impoverished brethren might have their needs supplied by the brethren who were able to do so that there might be equality. Not a "ledger-like" equality—one for you and one for me; but an equality that was a relief from the burden of want. Then if a time came when the situation was reversed, those brethren who had been helped would reciprocate, relieving the burden of the Corinthians. That is the practical beauty of love among the brethren.

Who among us has not benefited from the love of the brethren? So many of us have known the joy of brethren coming to visit us in the hospital when we were sick, or having food brought to our homes at some time of crisis when we were unable to take care of that ourselves. So many of us have known the comfort of telephone calls made simply to tell us that someone was thinking about us and that we were in their prayers. So many of us have had the strong shoulders of brethren to place our weary heads upon and weep when weeping seemed to be the only thing we could do. So many of us have known the peace that comes from brothers and sisters in Christ saying, "I am here if you need me. What can I do?"

Do we give as good as we get? Remember that Jesus said, "It is more blessed to give than to receive." The person that I see in the mirror every morning has been so blessed. Do I demonstrate my love for the brethren as they have demonstrated theirs toward me? Do I go to the hospital and visit the sick, or sit with a family when surgery is going on if I can? Do I prepare food for those whose lives are just a little too hectic at the moment to be able to take care of that? Have brethren done it for me in the past? Will I pick up the phone and brighten a shut-in's day or drop them a little note of concern?

I believe that reciprocating the love of the brethren in real practical ways is like saying, "Thank you" to the Lord for all that He has done. Remember that Jesus also said, "Inasmuch as ye have done it unto one of the least of these my brethren, ye have done it unto me" (Matt. 25:40). He said as well, "Verily I say unto you, Inasmuch as ye did not to one of the least of these, ye did it not to me" (Matt. 25:46).

Baptized for the Dead

1 Corinthians 15 is one of the most encouraging and uplifting chapters found in God's Word. There were those who were denying the future resurrection of the dead. In a most powerful way, Paul presents the truth of the resurrection of the Lord Jesus and how His resurrection guaranteed the general resurrection of the dead.

Paul's progression of logic in verses 13-20 is unassailable. He argues first in verse 13 that, if there is no general resurrection of the dead, then Christ was not raised. In verse 14 he proceeds by stating an obvious truth—if Christ was not raised, then there is no point in preaching the gospel and faith in it is worthless. Indeed, verse 15 makes the point that the apostles must then be false witnesses, liars, because they were teaching that God raised up the Lord, who was not raised up if it were true that there was to be no resurrection. In verse 16, the point is again made that, if there is to be no general resurrection of the dead, then Christ was not raised. If that was the case, verse 17 drives home the point that they had believed something that was just not true. Their belief was vain and they were still dead in sins, and all of their brothers and sisters in Christ who had died in faith were, in fact, lost. If there was no resurrection, then Christians are of all people to be pitied the most. The reason is that they had put everything they were and everything they ever hoped to be on something that was just not true, and such a one deserves pity. In verse 20 Paul asserts with great boldness, "But now is Christ risen from the dead, and become the first fruits of them that slept." In other words, He is risen and all that they had believed was absolutely true. The future general resurrection that they looked forward to was assured.

In verses 29-32 Paul asked some questions that must be viewed in light of the discussion of the reality of the general resurrection of the dead. He wrote, "Else what shall they do which are baptized for the dead, if the dead rise not at all? Why are they then baptized for the dead? And why stand we in jeopardy every hour? I protest by your rejoicing which I have in Christ Jesus our Lord, I die daily. If after the manner of men I have fought with beasts at Ephesus, what advantageth it me, if the dead rise not? Let us eat and drink; for tomorrow we die."

The phrase, "baptized for the dead" in verse 29 has generated a lot of discussion and controversy. It has even given rise to the Mormon practice of baptism by proxy. In other words, people who are living can be baptized for those who have already died, thus securing, or making possible, the salvation of those who lived their lives even in opposition to Christ. I do not believe that is correct.

There are several ways of looking at this. I will give the one that is the most logical, and contextually sound, as far as I can tell. Brother Mike Willis gives the following paraphrase in his *Commentary on Paul's First Epistle to the Corinthians* (563). I believe he has expressed the meaning of the verse very well: "Otherwise what shall they do who are baptized? For the dead? (I.e., are they baptized to belong to, to be numbered among the dead, who are never to rise again?) Indeed, if the dead do not rise again at all, why are people baptized? For them? (I.e., are they baptized to be numbered among the dead who are never to rise again?)"

I believe Mike has hit the nail on the head. This expresses well the meaning in the context. It recognizes the real purpose of New Testament baptism, and it fits perfectly into Paul's argument. A person is baptized in order to be saved. That was the reason the Corinthians had been baptized, and it is the reason that all faithful Christians were baptized. If there is no resurrection from the dead, then what difference does it make whether or not a person has had his sins washed away? If there is no resurrection from the dead, why were they baptized? To simply die and perish? No! If the dead are not to be raised, then being baptized is nonsensical.

Additionally, if it were true that there was to be no general resurrection from the dead, then why did Paul and the others risk their lives every hour to spread the gospel? If there was to be no general resurrection from the dead, why was Paul willing to lay down his very life for Christ if it should prove to be necessary? Why did he go through the persecution and torment that he did if he knew that what he was preaching was not true? If there was to be no future resurrection from the dead, then there was no point in trying to live a righteous life here. What powerful reasoning! What inspiring logic!

Let's conclude with verses 51-54: "Behold, I show you a mystery; we shall not all sleep, but we shall all be changed, in a moment, in the twinkling of an eye, at the last trump: for the trumpet shall sound, and the dead shall be raised incorruptible, and we shall be changed. For this corruptible must put on incorruption, and this mortal must put on immortality. So when this corruptible shall have put on incorruption, and this mortal shall have put on immortality, then shall be brought to pass the saying that is written, Death is swallowed up in victory."

The Precious Blood of Christ

In his letter to the Ephesians, the Apostle Paul begins with a joyous presentation of some of the bountiful spiritual blessings that are enjoyed by all of those who are "in Christ." That little phrase, "in Christ," appears thirty times in the six chapters of this letter and clearly shows the importance of being in the body of Christ. Two of the blessings enjoyed by those who are "in Christ" are pointed out in Ephesians 1:7, "In whom we have redemption through his blood, the forgiveness of sins, according to the riches of his grace." Oh, the marvelous blood of the Lord Jesus Christ!

In Matthew 26, at what has come to be known as the Last Supper, Jesus instituted the great memorial of which faithful Christians partake every first day of the week, the Lord's Supper. In verses 27-28 we find, "And he took the cup, and gave thanks, and gave it to them, saying, Drink ye all of it; for this is my blood of the new testament, which is shed for many for the remission of sins." Looking forward to His death, Jesus stated that His blood would ratify the New Testament and make the forgiveness of sins possible through it.

The Hebrew writer addressed this very thing in Hebrews 9. The whole chapter deals with the superiority of the New Covenant and the superiority of the blood that sealed it. In verses 12-22 he wrote:

> Neither by the blood of goats and calves, but by his own blood he entered in once into the holy place, having obtained eternal redemption for us. For if the blood of bulls and of goats, and the ashes of an heifer sprinkling the unclean, sanctifieth to the purifying of the flesh; how much more shall the blood of Christ, who through the eternal Spirit offered himself without spot to God, purge your conscience from dead works to serve the living God? And for this cause he is the mediator of the new testament, that by means of death, for the redemption of the transgressions that were under the first testament, they which are called might receive the promise of eternal inheritance. For where a testament is, there must also of necessity be the death of the testator. For a

testament is of force after men are dead: otherwise it is of no strength at all while the testator liveth. Whereupon neither the first testament was dedicated without blood. For when Moses had spoken every precept to all the people according to the law, he took of the blood of calves and of goats, with water, and a scarlet wool, and hyssop, and sprinkled both the book, and all the people, saying, This is the blood of the testament which God hath enjoined unto you. Moreover he sprinkled with blood both the tabernacle, and all the vessels of the ministry. And almost all things are by the law purged with blood; and without shedding of blood is no remission.

With the death of Jesus, it was possible for the New Covenant to come into effect. Through His blood, the sins that were committed under the first covenant could be forgiven—all of the blood of the sacrificed animals looking forward to the time when the precious blood of Christ would be shed—and the sins committed by those living under the New Testament can be remitted.

March 18

More about the Precious Blood of Christ

The blood of the Lord was the price that was to purchase the church of Christ. In Paul's farewell address to the Ephesian elders recorded in Acts 20, he stated in verse 28, "Take heed therefore unto yourselves, and to all the flock, over the which the Holy Ghost hath made you overseers, to feed the church of God, which he hath purchased with his own blood."

Not only was the blood of the Lord said to be the purchase price of the church, but it is also represented as the price of the purchase of the kingdom. In Revelation 5:9-10 John wrote, "And they sang a new song, saying, Worthy art Thou to take the book, and to break its seals; for Thou wast slain, and didst purchase for God with Thy blood men from every tribe and tongue and people and nations. And Thou hast made them to be a kingdom and priests to our God; and they will reign upon the earth."

The church is God's kingdom on earth, and since the value of something is ultimately determined by that which someone is willing to pay for it, what is possibly worth more than the church of Christ? It is made up of those who have had their sins forgiven by being washed "with the precious blood of Christ, as of a lamb without blemish and without spot" (1 Pet. 1:19).

It was the blood of Christ that made it possible for both Jew and Gentile, all people, to be reconciled to each other and, more importantly, to be reconciled unto God in one body, which is the church of Christ. In Ephesians 2:13-16 Paul wrote, "But now in Christ Jesus ye who sometimes were far off are made nigh by the blood of Christ. For he is our peace, who hath made both one, and hath broken down the middle wall of partition between us; having abolished in his flesh the enmity, even the law of commandments contained in ordinances; for to make in himself of twain one new man, so making peace; and that he might reconcile both unto God in one body by the cross, having slain the enmity thereby."

Oh, the precious blood of the Lord Jesus Christ!

March 19

You Can't Please Everybody

Occasionally someone will ask me, "What is the hardest part of being a preacher?" There are several ways I could answer, some of which would be peculiar to one who has devoted his life to preaching the gospel, and some of which would be applicable to any child of God who does his best to try to reach others with the gospel of our Lord Jesus. However, I would have to say for me personally, the hardest part is realizing that you can't please everybody all the time, and you can't please some of the people any of the time. But knowing that intellectually and dealing with it emotionally are two different things.

Jesus made an interesting observation about the generation among whom He was living in Matthew 11:16-19, "But whereunto shall I liken this generation? It is like unto children sitting in the markets, and calling unto their fellows. And saying, We have piped unto you, and ye have not danced; we have mourned unto you, and ye have not lamented. For John came neither eating nor drinking, and they say, He hath a devil. The Son of Man came eating and drinking, and they say, Behold, a man gluttonous, and a winebibber, a friend of publicans and sinners. But wisdom is justified of her children."

The Lord's point was that the generation of people among whom He walked was never satisfied. They were like children playing in the marketplace. If they played their little pipes and sang and danced, some of the other children would complain and refuse to take part. If they changed their tactics and played at mourning, there were still those who were not happy. John came living an austere lifestyle, and there were those who did not like it, or even John himself. Jesus came and enjoyed the simple, yet completely whole-some things of life, and they didn't like that either. He went to people whom others would not, and the "holier than thou's" criticized Him for it. His point was that it was impossible to please everybody all the time, and that you couldn't please some of the people any of the time. But those who wanted nothing more than to hear the truth of God's word would hear and respond.

What a hard lesson to learn! Intellectually I know it to be true; accepting it emotionally is another story. That is one of the reasons why it is so essential that faithful brothers and sisters in Christ support one another in the work of the Lord. Over the years I have been called a cretin, Satan, the anti-Christ, stupid, and a false teacher. Just two weeks ago I was called a "Jim Jones Guy-ana freak" (whatever that is!). This particular fellow also said that I would be arrested if I ever came to his apartment again, and that if the law wouldn't take care of me, he had friends in the Mafia who would. I have been thrown out of houses, pushed and shoved, and have even been in a living room where a gun was being waved around.

I would be lying if I said that none of this stuff ever bothered me, because some of it did. Yet everything I have just mentioned came from non-Chris-tians, and I know that the truth is going to upset some of them. It is not dif-ficult to intellectually and emotionally deal with the fact that you can't please every non-Christian all the time, and that there are some non-Christians you can't please any of the time.

It is not difficult to accept intellectually that the same holds true among Christians, but this is a lot harder to accept emotionally. Among Christians there is a place for disagreements. After all, none of us is perfect. Yet among Christians there is no place for being disagreeable. Among Christians we have to make allowances for a brother or sister having a bad day and perhaps acting in an unfriendly manner. But among Christians, there is no place for general unfriendliness toward any of our number. Among Christians we have to recognize that we all have different likes and dislikes, different things that bring us satisfaction and enjoyment; and that is okay. But we must never allow personal likes and dislikes to cause animosity to exist between any of us.

Among us we are not all going to be equally pleased with every decision made by the elders, nor are we going to be equally pleased with every Bible class taught or every sermon delivered. But you know what we can always be? Loving toward one another! Encouraging toward one another! We are not going always to see eye to eye on everything, but we can all do what Paul instructed in Colossians 3:12-14: "Put on therefore, as the elect of God, holy and beloved, bowels of mercies, kindness, humbleness of mind, meekness, longsuffering; forbearing one another and forgiving one another, if any man have a quarrel against any: even as Christ forgave you, so also do ye. And above all these things put on love, which is the bond of perfectness."

March 20

Time Marches on, So Don't Waste It!

The one thing that we cannot stop is the inexorable march of time. If death does not overtake us at an early age, or the Lord does not return before that time, we will all become old with the peculiar infirmities that age brings. In striking, poetic language, Solomon describes the onset of age in Ecclesiastes 12:1-7:

Remember also your Creator in the days of your youth, before the evil days come and the years draw near when you will say, I have no delight in them; before the sun, the light, the moon, and the stars are darkened, and clouds return after the rain; in the day that the watchmen of the house tremble, and mighty men stoop, the grinding ones stand idle because they are few, and those who look through windows grow dim; and the doors on the street are shut as the sound of the grinding mill is low, and one will arise at the sound of the bird, and all the daughters of song will sing softly. Furthermore, men are afraid of a high place and of terrors on the road; the almond tree blossoms, the grasshopper drags himself along, and the caperberry is ineffective. For man goes to his eternal home while mourners go about in the street. Remember Him before the silver cord is broken and the golden bowl is crushed, the pitcher by the well is shattered and the wheel at the cistern is crushed; then the dust will return to the earth as it was, and the spirit will return to God who gave it.

Even at its very best, even if we live to a ripe old age, life is short. James wrote, "Yet you do not know what your life will be like tomorrow. You are just a vapor that appears for a little while and then vanishes away."

All of this being true, isn't it a tremendous waste of the precious time that God gives us to spend one minute of it bitter, or continually angry with someone? Isn't it a horrible waste of priceless breath to gossip, or to continue to talk about unfortunate events that have taken place within the congregation—but that have been properly and scripturally handled—refusing to move on?

We all have such a short time to teach others the gospel of Christ, to influence people for good, and to help improve each person's life with whom we come in significant contact. Isn't it terrible to allow even one minute to go by complaining about things that we could help to fix, but don't. Or to benefit so much from the labor of others and never take the time to say, "Thank you"? Now *there's* a great use of the limited number of words we will get to say in this life!

If the normal way of things continues, I will be old one day. I don't want to be ignored or unappreciated when the time comes; neither do I want to look back with a single moment of regret.

March 21

Pentecost

Pentecost was the second of the three great annual festivals of the Jews. It was celebrated on the fiftieth day after the Sabbath of the Passover week. Because the Jews were to count out those seven weeks, Pentecost was also known as the "feast of weeks." Pentecost was also referred to as the feast of harvest or the day of first fruits because it celebrated the close of the grain harvest. It was a day of joy and celebration, and even though it occurred on the first day of the week, or Sunday, it was observed as a Sabbath. All work was suspended and the people expressed their gratitude toward God on that day.

The most extraordinary Pentecost of all was the Pentecost that followed the resurrection and the ascension of our Lord Jesus. A careful reading of Acts 1:3 and Acts 2:1 indicates that there were forty days between our Lord's resurrection and His ascension into heaven, and less than ten days from the ascension to Pentecost. On that Jewish feast day, on that day of celebration, the church that Jesus had promised to build began.

Acts 2:1-4 tells us, "And when the day of Pentecost was fully come, they were all with one accord in one place. And suddenly there came a sound from heaven as of a rushing mighty wind, and it filled all the house where they were sitting. And there appeared unto them cloven tongues like as of fire, and it sat upon each of them. And they were all filled with the Holy Ghost, and began to speak with other tongues, as the Spirit gave them utterance."

The prophecies that pointed to the coming of the church, such as Joel 2:28-32, were being fulfilled. On this glorious Sunday, we find Peter exercising the "keys of the kingdom" as he effectively opened the door to the church by proclaiming Jesus to be both Lord and Christ. In response to the question, "Men and brethren, what shall we do?" Peter told those Jews assembled in Jerusalem for the celebration of the feast what to do to be saved. He said, "Repent and be baptized every one of you in the name of Jesus Christ for the remission of sins, and ye shall receive gift of the Holy Ghost" (Acts 2:38). That same day about 3,000 people were baptized for the remission of their sins and added to the church by the Lord.

The Lord's church has existed from that day forward and will continue to exist on earth as long as this old world is still here. When the Lord returns, He will deliver up the church, the kingdom, to God (1 Cor. 15:24).

March 22

Easter

I was at my local bank recently and could not help but overhear a conversation that was taking place between several of the ladies who work there (nice ladies, every one of them) and a customer. The ladies were bemoaning the fact that they were going to have to work all day on Friday and would not be able to attend Good Friday services. The customer, who seemed to be yet another very nice lady, was expressing her disappointment in not knowing where the ecumenical Good Friday service was going to take place. She just loved it when the Baptists, the Christian Church folks, the Roman Catholics, and other denominational people all got together for one big service. Altogether they were generally lamenting, "Things just aren't like they used to be."

You know, *the very fact* that there are so many different denominations claiming to worship Christ, and *the very fact* that there is such a thing as Good Friday taking place on the Friday before the Sunday that many celebrate as

Easter, all indicate that "things just aren't like they used to be." What I mean is that when Jesus established the church, there existed no such thing as different denominations. The church that Jesus established knew nothing of "Good Friday," and most certainly did not set aside one Sunday to be designated as Easter and used to commemorate and celebrate the resurrection of Jesus in a special way.

Neither Easter nor Good Friday are biblical terms. Good Friday never appears in Scripture. As far as I know, the word Easter appears in only one translation of the New Testament, and that is the King James or Authorized translation. Acts 12:1-4 says, "Now about that time Herod the king stretched forth his hands to vex certain of the church. And he killed James the brother of John with the sword. And because he saw it pleased the Jews, he proceeded further to take Peter also. (Then were the days of unleavened bread.) And when he had apprehended him, he put him in prison, and delivered him to four quaternions of soldiers to keep him; intending after *Easter* to bring him forth to the people."

The use of the word "Easter" in verse 4 is not a translation; it is a mistranslation. The word is *pascha*, which is the ordinary Greek word for "Passover." It is used twenty-nine times in the New Testament, and twenty-eight times it is translated as Passover. Only in Acts 12:4 is it translated as "Easter," and even there it is apparent to anyone even slightly familiar with Jewish feast days that the inspired writer, Luke, had the Passover in mind.

The early Christians commemorated the death and resurrection of the Lord Jesus every first day of the week by partaking of the Lord's Supper. This was done under the guidance and direction of the apostles who had been commissioned by the Lord to teach those they converted to "observe all that I commanded you." Faithful children of God continue to do the very same thing today.

March 23

More about Easter

There is absolutely no authority for one man, or a group of men, to set aside one day in the year above all others to commemorate the death and resurrection of Jesus as an official religious observance. If it is true that the Bible supplies us with "everything pertaining to life and godliness" (2 Pet. 1:3), and if it is wrong to add to or take away from the word of God (Rev. 22:18-19), and if the Bible does not mention Good Friday or Easter celebrations, what does that mean for those who engage in them?

Actually, the word "Easter" comes from the word "Eastre" or "Estera," a Teutonic goddess to whom sacrifice was offered in April. She was the goddess of spring and the dawn. Even *The International Bible Encyclopedia* (II: 889) tells us "there is no trace of Easter celebration in the New Testament." It then goes on to say, "though some would see an intimation of it in 1 Corinthians 5:7." What does that passage say? "Clean out the old leaven, that you may be a new lump, just as you are in fact unleavened. For Christ our Passover also has been sacrificed." To attempt to get Easter out of a passage that is calling for the removal of evil from among the brethren at Corinth is a classic example of going to the Scriptures to find authority for something that someone wants to do, rather than to simply find out what they say.

So here is another man-made holiday, yet all the Lord wants is for us to worship Him "in spirit and truth." There will be a lot of spirited Easter celebrations—but they are going to be real short on "truth." I am so thankful that our Lord died for us and rose from the dead. I am thankful enough to commemorate His great sacrifice as He has informed us that He wants it remembered, and not the way that I want to do it. Indeed, "The celebration of Easter was from what source, from heaven or from men?"

March 24

Conduct Matters (1)

One of my favorite books in the New Testament is the book of 1 John. In it John attacks a prevalent first-century philosophy known as Gnosticism. Without going into a great amount of detail, Gnosticism basically regarded evil as an ever-present characteristic of matter—all matter—and therefore, those who held to this view were unable to accept the doctrine of the incarnation, the assumption of flesh on the part of the Lord. Gnostics believed that it was impossible for sinless deity to occupy a material body. John addressed that false view directly in 1 John 4:2-3 when he wrote, "Hereby know ye the Spirit of God: Every spirit that confesseth that Jesus Christ is come in the flesh is of God: and every spirit that confesseth not that Jesus Christ is come in the flesh is not of God: and this is that spirit of antichrist, whereof ye have heard that it should come, and even now already is it in the world."

The majority of Gnostics embraced the following idea. Inasmuch as they regarded their bodies as evil, they concluded that their spirits were independent of them, and thus could not be defiled by anything the body did. Consequently, they could live lives of unrestrained indulgence, do whatever they desired, on the grounds that a precious jewel might be laying in a dung heap, but it was still just as precious a jewel as if it were laying in a fancy, costly box. They believed that it was inevitable that their bodies would sin and nothing they could do could change that. So, with such a clear and distinct separation between body and spirit, they were free to indulge in whatever they wanted without spiritual consequence. In the early church, some held to this view, and some today act like they do as well. The letter of 1 John repeatedly makes the point that *conduct matters*.

Let's consider 1 John 1:5-10: "This then is the message which we have heard of him, and declare unto you, that God is light, and in him is no darkness at all. If we say that we have fellowship with him, and walk in darkness, we lie, and do not the truth: but if we walk in the light, as he is in the light, we have fellowship one with another, and the blood of Jesus Christ his Son cleanseth us from all sin. If we say that we have no sin, we deceive ourselves, and the truth is not in us. If we confess our sins, he is faithful and just to forgive us our sins, and to cleanse us from all unrighteousness. If we say that we have not sinned, we make him a liar, and his word is not in us."

John's point is profoundly simple—do not claim fellowship with God and Christ, but then walk in an ungodly way. "God is light." Not "a light" or "the light," but simply "light." That is His essence; it is what He is. I don't understand all that that means, but I know that He is the "Father of light" (Jas. 1:17), He is the creator of light (Gen. 1:3), He is bathed in perpetual light (1 Tim. 6:16), and I know that it is in His marvelous light that Christians are to walk (1 Pet. 2:9). I know that "light" is used in Scripture to represent truth, purity, holiness, and goodness. I also know that "dark" is used as a figure of ignorance, superstition, and sin. And I know that, using it in that sense, there is no darkness in God—none at all; no, not even one tiny particle.

With this being true, how could anyone say that they have fellowship with God and walk in sin? It reminds me of Paul's rhetorical question in 2 Corinthians 6:14-16, "For what fellowship hath righteousness with unrighteousness? And what communion hath light with darkness? And what concord hath Christ with Belial? Or what part hath he that believeth with an infidel? And what agreement hath the temple of God with idols?" Do you not see the point? *Conduct matters!*

A man's "walk" is his continual practice, his way of life. Paul talks about "walking in newness of life" in Romans 6:4; also to "walk not after the flesh" in Romans 8:1. A person claiming fellowship with God (light), yet walking in sinful ways (darkness), has no fellowship with God. The Gnostics thought that they could do as they pleased and continue in fellowship with God. However, the truth is that to think we are not going to be held accountable for actions of the fleshly body is a spiritually fatal view, both then and now! In Christianity, doctrine and practice are inseparably connected. True, saving faith always involves belief *and obedience.*

If we keep on "walking in the light" (and that is present subjunctive, meaning that we *must* keep on walking in the light), we have fellowship with one another, and the blood of Jesus Christ cleanses us from all sin. This walk must be "as He is in the light," meaning God; and it is to walk in His righteousness, to conform to His revealed will.

Receiving the benefits of the blood of Jesus is conditional, and that is as true for the Christian as it is for the non-Christian. A Christian cannot live in sin. He or she must confess those sins and pray for forgiveness. One of the requisitions of this "walk in the light" is that a Christian will confess his sins, as he is able to comprehend and repent of them. God has always required a confession of sins by the sinner, as well as repentance, as conditions of forgiveness.

March 25

Conduct Matters (2)

John clearly shows that *conduct matters* in 1 John 2:3-6 where we find:

And hereby we do know that we know Him, if we keep His commandments. He that saith, I know Him, and keepeth not His commandments, is a liar, and the truth is not in him. But whoso keepeth His word, in him verily is the love of God perfected: hereby know we that we are in Him. He that saith he abideth in Him, ought himself also so to walk, even as He walked.

John's point is simple—those who claim to abide in Christ have the moral obligation (that is the significance of "ought" in verse 6) to conduct themselves as the Lord did to the best of their ability. "Even as He walked" means in the light, in fellowship with God, keeping His commandments. The responsibility to make our walk equal to our claim is a consistent biblical principle. Paul wrote in Ephesians 4:1, "I therefore, the prisoner of the Lord, beseech you that ye walk worthy of the vocation wherewith ye are called." *Conduct matters!*

In 1 John 2:15-16 we read, "Love not the world, neither the things that are in the world. If any man love the world, the love of the Father is not in him. For all that is in the world, the lust of the flesh, and the lust of the eyes, and the pride of life, is not of the Father, but is of the world." That to which we attach our affections dictates how we act.

John wrote of three avenues of approach that Satan uses in his efforts to seduce us to sin, to make us love the world. They are the lust of the flesh, the lust of the eyes, and the pride of life. The word "lust" denotes strong desire, and it can be either good or bad, depending upon its usage. As near as I can tell, "lust" is found thirty-eight times in the New Testament and only three times is it used in a good sense. All the other times, including here, it is used to refer to evil desires, "anxious self-seeking." It is the lowest form of worldly indulgence, referring to an animalistic desire to fulfill appetites.

The "flesh" that John was writing about is not pertaining to skin and bones, muscle and tissue. It is much deeper than that. "Flesh" in the sense of skin and bones, can be used for good or bad purposes. This is where the Gnostics got it wrong. They thought that skin and bones, muscle and tissue were inherently evil. That is just not true. When John writes about "flesh" here, he is writing about the "seat of evil desires." He is writing about uncontrolled fleshly desires and appetites. It is somewhat the idea of a man acting like an animal. Again, *conduct matters!*

The "lust of the eyes" is an inordinate and ungodly desire for something that is seen; while the "pride of life" is simply prideful boasting over possessions, achievements—the idea that I have mastery over my life. All of these things are manifested in what we do, and what we do is a very good indicator of what we are inside. *Conduct matters!*

In 1 John 3:7 John wrote, "Little children, let no man deceive you: he that doeth righteousness is righteous, even as he is righteous." I love this verse.

The plain and simple truth is that one who practices righteousness is righteous, just as the Lord claimed righteousness and lived it. It is important to understand that John is not teaching that the practice of righteousness is how one initially becomes righteous or justified. Rather, his point is that because a Christian has been begotten by God and is in the family of God, and that family practices righteousness, then the child of God is expected to practice righteousness as well. *Conduct matters!*

Further in 1 John 3:17-18 we find, "But whoso hath this world's good, and seeth his brother have need, and shutteth up his bowels of compassion from him, how dwelleth the love of God in him? My little children, let us not love in word, neither in tongue: but in deed and in truth." If we say that we are children of God, it is our responsibility to act like it. We are to manifest in our lives the love of God, and that love is manifest in what we do. Love that is in word only, and not accompanied by conduct that proves it, is useless and hypocritical. *Conduct matters!*

Have you ever heard the old expression, "Charity begins at home"? Love begins at home too—and the most important family that we have is our spiritual family. They are the people that we intend to be with eternally. Surely, all of the teaching about conduct and its importance must begin at "home," with our spiritual brothers and sisters in Christ. We are bound together by the blood of the Son of God. How we treat each other matters. How we act toward one another, how we speak to or about one another, how we pray for each other is important. It all matters.

March 26

Obscuring the View

I was once driving home from Mt. Vernon, Kentucky on I-75. There was road construction taking place just a bit north of the Mt. Vernon exit, as they worked to increase that stretch of highway from two lanes to three, as well as adding permanent barriers. As I was driving through the construction area, the rain was pouring down, and I noticed a cloud of some sort up ahead. As I got closer to the cloud, I discovered that it was where the road crew was pouring hot blacktop. As the cold rain hit that hot asphalt, it created a cloud of smoke that was incredibly thick. I thought the cloud would be the consistency of fog, until

I got into it. I could not even see the front of my truck, much less the road. It was one of the few times I was actually frightened while driving. I could not see ahead of me, and I knew no one coming up behind me would be able to see either. That smoke, so unexpected, obscured my view of where I was going.

I always want to know where I am going. I want to be able to see ahead of me. That is certainly true from a physical standpoint and, for me, it is even truer from a spiritual standpoint. I want to be able to see where I am going. It brings to mind Hebrews 12:1-2: "Wherefore seeing we also are compassed about with so great a cloud of witnesses, let us lay aside every weight, and the sin which doth so easily beset us, and let us run with patience the race that is set before us, looking unto Jesus the author and finisher of our faith; who for the joy that was set before Him endured the cross, despising the shame, and is set down at the right hand of the throne of God." I need to keep my eyes fastened firmly and resolutely upon Jesus; and if I do, I will make it to my eternal destination of choice.

There are things, however, that can come up unexpectedly and obscure the view. In the parable of the Sower, the Lord spoke of just such occurrences. In Luke 8:12-14 Jesus said, "Those by the way side are they that hear; then cometh the devil and taketh away the word out of their hearts, lest they should believe and be saved. They on the rock are they, which, when they hear, receive the word with joy; and these have no root, which for a while believe, and in time of temptation fall away. And that which fell among thorns are they, which, when they have heard, go forth, and are choked with cares and riches and pleasures of this life, and bring no fruit to perfection."

In each case the Lord is describing people whose spiritual view was obscured for one reason or another. Some very early in their spiritual progression allow Satan to cloud their view and they lose sight, even before they get started, of the only destination where eternal life is to be found. And they lose sight of the only One who can show them the way.

Others begin the walk and seem to be on fire for a time. The Lord described them as having "received the word with joy." Then temptation rears its ugly head, obscuring their view, and they don't have the fortitude to keep on going. They turn back. When I was in the midst of that cloud, I figured if I was going to get hit I was going to get hit from behind, because I was not about to turn around. It has got to be the same way spiritually. We cannot turn around, because it is certain that we will get hit head-on. If we keep on going, we may get bumped from behind, but we are still going to be ahead.

Still others embark on the journey to heaven with their eyes on the Lord, and then life hits them. It can happen unexpectedly and in so many different ways. I have known people who lost a job, falling into a terrible financial mess, and blamed it on the Lord. They lost sight of Jesus. On the other hand, I have known people who became very successful at work, focusing on the riches of this world, and losing sight of what was truly important. Things obscured their view. I have known people who have focused their eyes upon a man or woman other than their spouse, and for the fleeting pleasure that would bring, they lost sight of eternity and what was truly important.

I couldn't see anything in that cloud, and I was scared. But I'll tell you something. I had not lost sight of Jesus. So even if some eighteen-wheeler had come barreling through that cloud and run completely over my little truck, and me, it just would have meant that my journey ended sooner than I thought it would. I believe I would be in Paradise right now and wouldn't come back even if I could.

When my eyes close for the last time and I have drawn my last breath, I want to be looking at Jesus. With God's help, I will let nothing obscure the view.

March 27

The Story of the Lamb

One day a little white lamb was taking a walk with his mother, and as they walked around the farm, they came to the pigpen. A big old pig was stretched out, grunting contentedly as he wallowed in the muck and the mud of the pen. He looked absolutely happy and comfortable—so much so that the little lamb was really quite impressed. So impressed was he that he began to think he might be missing something here. So he turned to his mother, a little breathlessly because of the excitement and the wonderful idea that he had, and he asked, "Mother, may I wallow?"

Her son's question set the old mother sheep back on her heels a bit. She was both shocked and surprised to think that a son of hers would ask such a question. When she had regained her composure, she answered him very firmly, "Certainly not! Sheep don't wallow!"

Well, the little lamb wasn't convinced, and the minute his mother turned her back—zoom, there he went! He ran over to the pigpen, slipped between the rails of the fence, and felt his feet sink into the cool mud. But it was deeper than he had thought, and to tell the truth, it smelled terrible! He tried to back out, but found the mud clinging to his feet, and he could not move. He began to be frightened, and he jerked and tugged frantically, but that only got him in deeper. By now he was terrified. He wished with all of his heart that he hadn't come—that he had obeyed his mother. He thrashed and thrashed about in desperation, lost his balance, and sprawled over on his side in the evil, foul-smelling muck and mire.

The pig looked over at him and grunted in a very friendly manner, but the little lamb was frantic. He couldn't move. He could only roll his eyes, and he thought that each breath he took would be his last. Then finally, just as he had bleated weakly for the last time and given up, the farmer came along and tenderly lifted the little lamb from his death trap, cleansed him thoroughly, and restored him to his mother.

As any parent can imagine, his mother had mixed emotions. She was so thankful that he was all right, but terribly hurt that he had chosen to so blatantly disobey her. She was even more distressed to think that her own son, a beautiful white lamb, had decided to wallow.

She said to him, "I feel that you have learned your lesson. Only pigs wallow. As a sheep you are the only animal that sets the pattern of behavior above all other animals. Hogs are born to wallow, but sheep are different creatures from hogs. And *sheep don't wallow!*"

The moral of the story is obvious. As a Christian we are part of the Lord's flock. He is the Shepherd; we are the sheep. And we all need to know that *sheep don't wallow!*

This little story is pure imagination, because no sheep ever, ever wallows. Just so, the Christian will remain apart from the wickedness of the world. The wicked things of the world should hold no more appeal to the Christian than the hog wallow does for a sheep.

How many times do people who are Christians find themselves asking the "Why can't I" questions? You know what I mean. "Why can't I dance the modern dances of today?" "Why can't I drink alcoholic beverages?" "Why can't I gamble at the boats or buy a lottery ticket?" "Why can't I go mixed swimming?" "Why can't I watch any television program that I want?" "Why can't I rent or go to any movie that I would like to?" "Why can't I wear anything that I want?" "Why can't I miss services to engage in some sort of worldly activity?"

The answer is the same as the mother sheep gave to her lamb. *Sheep don't wallow!* Christians are not worldly people. We are new creatures. Paul wrote in 2 Corinthians 5:17, "Therefore if any man be in Christ, he is a new creature: old things are passed away: behold, all things are become new." A Christian has the mind of Christ, or he should have according to Philippians 2:5. Would Christ engage in modern dancing? Would Jesus drink intoxicating alcoholic beverages? Do you think Jesus would go to "the boat" or stand in line to buy a lottery ticket? Do you think that Jesus would be at the pool or the beach in a swimming suit? Do you think He would watch the same television shows that you watch? Do we really think that Jesus would miss services of His own church for anything?

The new creature in Christ has put to death the desires of the flesh. It doesn't mean he will never have those desires come into his mind again, but it does mean that he won't let them stay there when they do. Remember Paul's words of Romans 6:6-7, "Knowing this, that our old man is crucified with him, that the body of sin might be destroyed, that henceforth we should not serve sin. For he that is dead is freed from sin." Again, from the pen of Paul we find in Galatians 5:24, "And they that are Christ's have crucified the flesh with the affections and lusts." When a person becomes a Christian, truly putting to death the evil desires of the world, then the wicked things of the world will hold no more appeal to him or her than the hog wallow does to the sheep.

We are sheep in the flock of Jesus, and *sheep don't wallow!*

March 28

It Only Takes a Moment

Once I was watching a fellow clearing some land push over the trees in his way. It was pretty neat to see. He took a bulldozer, loosened the dirt around the bottom of the tree, freeing the roots, and then he just used the dozer to push them over. I don't think that even the largest of the trees took more than five minutes. As is usually the case, that got me to thinking.

I wonder how long the largest of those trees had been there. From the time the seed fell to the ground, or the sapling was planted, it had to be years and years for some of them to have grown to the size they were. Many gentle spring rains, heavy summer thunderstorms, fall frosts, and winter snows had fallen on those branches. Then, in a matter of minutes, all those years of growth ended, and what had taken so many years to build up was torn down.

That is like so many things we see in this life. How about a reputation? Good reputations take years and years to build and are so important. Solomon wrote in Proverbs 22:1, "A good name is rather to be chosen than great riches, and loving favor rather than silver and gold." He makes the same point, and elaborates upon it, in Ecclesiastes 7:1-4. Here he shows the importance of a good reputation and alludes to the time and experiences through which one builds it. He wrote, "A good name is better than precious ointment; and the day of death than the day of one's birth. It is better to go to the house of mourning, than to go to the house of feasting: for that is the end of all men; and the living will lay it to his heart. Sorrow is better than laughter: for by the sadness of the countenance the heart is made better. The heart of the wise is in the house of mourning; but the heart of fools is in the house of mirth."

How long does it take to "push over" a good reputation? Not very long at all. An ungodly act followed by a refusal to repent can greatly damage a person's reputation. Words quickly spoken with no forethought can bring the mighty oak of a reputation crashing to the ground. We all know this is true.

How about friendships? True friendships take considerable time to build. They are like the layers of growth rings we see in the trunk of a tree that has been cut down. Trust and confidence are layered into the friendship, strengthening and growing it, as the years and shared experiences go by. Proverbs 27 speaks much of the value of friendship. For instance, verse 6 says, "Faithful are the wounds of a friend; but the kisses of an enemy are deceitful." In verses 9-10 we find, "Ointment and perfume rejoice the heart; so doth the sweetness of a man's friend by hearty counsel. Thine own friend, and thy father's friend, forsake not; neither go into thy brother's house in the day of calamity: for better is a neighbor that is near than a brother far off." Verse 17 says, "Iron sharpeneth iron; so a man sharpeneth the countenance of his friend." While some may not think that verse 19 addresses the subject of friendship, I most certainly think it does. Solomon wrote, "As in water face reflects face, so the heart of man reflects man."

Does the beauty of friendship just happen? No, it takes effort and work, but it is absolutely worth it. In Proverbs 18:24 we find, "A man that hath friends must show himself to be friendly: and there is a friend that sticketh closer than a brother." Can there be a more beautiful statement of the essence of friendship than is found in Proverbs 17:17? It says, "A friend loveth at all times, and a brother is born for adversity."

How long does it take to destroy a friendship? Not very long. All it takes is for one to forget what being a friend is all about. All it takes is for one to put himself or herself before the welfare of his or her friend, to make hurtful and unkind remarks. I don't know why folks will do this, but some do. Oh my, does it hurt!

The man responsible for the removal of the trees is going to take the very best ones and sell them for lumber. A good purpose will be served. There may be a piece of furniture that results and provides comfort and beauty to a home. Some will provide warmth through being used as firewood. Still more will be ground up and used as mulch to make beautiful things grow. Several good purposes will be accomplished by the trees being torn down.

What good is accomplished when a stellar reputation is "pushed over" quickly by ungodly acts or thoughtless words? What good is accomplished when a friendship, nurtured and grown over the years, is decimated because one or the other forgot to place the welfare of his or her friend first? Through the tearing down of some things, progress is made. Through the tearing down of others, only tragedy occurs. Hold fast to that which is important and be willing to sacrifice to retain that which matters.

March 29

Hold on a Minute!

One Lord's Day evening before I got up to preach, I was sitting in the padded pew, wiping my brow with a handkerchief and thinking, "Man, it is hot in here!" I was even trying to let one of the deacons know how I was feeling by telepathy, somehow transferring my complaint across the aisle to him. He didn't get the message, so I guess I am going to have to work on that.

More to the point, after services were over I got to thinking about being a little warm and a little uncomfortable in services, and letting that bother me even for one little minute. You know what? I was ashamed. I got to thinking about our early, first-century brothers and sisters in Christ, many of whom were forced to flee their homes because of persecution—and I was worried about being a little bit warm. I got to thinking about different things that I had read in the past about the worship of the earliest Christians. For instance, in *The History of the Christian Church,* Philip Schaff wrote, "Let us glance first at the places of public worship. Until about the close of the second century the Christians held their worship mostly in private homes, or in desert places, at the graves of martyrs, and in the crypts of the catacombs. This arose from their poverty, their oppressed and outlawed condition" (II: 199).

That's not all. I got to thinking about some of the church buildings in which I have held meetings that were nowhere near as comfortable as the building I was currently in. I thought about the country buildings in which many of our older saints attended while they were growing up. There was no air conditioning, and many of them were heated by one stove that sat in the middle of the floor. I thought of the brethren in London, England, who meet in a common room in what we would call a slum. I thought of the brethren in Ireland who met in a mobile home until it was vandalized because of prejudice and persecution. I thought of the brethren in China who must meet surreptitiously because the open practice of their faith would cause them to be arrested. I thought of the brethren in India who, in some cases, meet in conditions we would consider deplorable. For that matter, I thought of brethren in the United States who meet in little rented rooms, sometimes even in a motel, just a handful of people—but they do it faithfully, carrying the bread, fruit of the vine, and song books back and forth from their homes to these rooms every week.

Yet there I was, complaining about *nothing!* We are so blessed, and I am so thankful for all of it. At the same time I realize and appreciate that there are a lot of our brethren not so blessed as far as a place to meet and the comforts thereof.

I am resolved not to utter a single complaint about being hot or cold in the church building again (except maybe to my wife). I resolve to appreciate the carpet and those padded pews, the color of the walls and the tile. I resolve to appreciate the lights, the fans, the drinking fountain, and all of the other authorized amenities that make our coming together so comfortable and easy. I know that in my prayers I need to pray for help to appreciate and not to complain.

When Bad Things Happen

Sometimes bad things happen—things that tear at our hearts and disrupt our lives. I am not saying anything that every adult does not already know. The vital issue concerning these kinds of events is not so much the event itself, but how we react to it. We can throw up our hands in despair, blame God, and quit. We can get angry and bitter, lashing out at anybody and everybody. We can wallow in self-pity and feel sorry for ourselves. Or we can trust God and His word, knowing that we can remain faithful to Him no matter what.

I think of Joseph. As a young man, the favoritism shown him by his father led to his being hated by his brothers. Genesis 37:3-4 tells us, "Now Israel loved Joseph more than all his children, because he was the son of his old age: and he made him a coat of many colors. And when his brethren saw that their father loved him more than all his brethren, they hated him, and could not speak peaceably unto him."

This hatred would lead his brothers to conspire to kill him, and only the intervention of Reuben prevented that from happening. However, they did cast him into a pit and ended up selling him to a band of Ishmaelite merchants who sold Joseph into slavery in Egypt.

Even the little children know the rest of the story. Joseph ended up in the household of Potiphar, captain of the guard in Egypt, only to be mistreated by Potiphar's wife. The statement that Joseph made in response to her unwanted advances is one of the classic statements of Scripture, and shows how a person can continue to be faithful and do what is right, even when bad things happen. In Genesis 39:7-9 we read, "And it came to pass after these things, that his master's wife cast her eyes upon Joseph; and she said, Lie with me. But he refused, and said unto his master's wife, Behold, my master knoweth not what is with me in the house, and he hath committed all that he hath to my hand; there is none greater in this house than I: neither hath he kept back any thing from me but thee, because thou art his wife; *how then can I do this great wickedness, and sin against God?*"

No matter what the circumstances are, no matter what happens, we can always do what is right. I am reminded of three other young men who certainly had bad things happen to them. We all know the story of Shadrach, Meshach, and Abednego. Taken from their homeland after Babylon had besieged Jerusalem and brought into the king's palace, they determined that they would remain faithful to the one true God. When forced with the choice to fall down and worship a golden idol that Nebuchadnezzar had set up or die, these three young men stood their ground and did what was right. Daniel 3:16-18, a passage that I have read more times than I could possibly count, still moves me to marvel at the conviction and courage of these men in the face of a very bad circumstance:

> Shadrach, Meshach, and Abednego, answered and said to the king, O Nebuchadnezzar, we are not careful to answer thee in this matter. If it be so, our God whom we serve is able to deliver us from the burning fiery furnace, and he will deliver us out of thine hand, O king. But if not, be it known unto thee, O king, *that we will not serve thy gods, nor worship the golden image which thou hast set up.*

Again, these young men show us that no matter what happens, we can be faithful. We can do what is right.

Do we have to go it alone when bad things happen? Certainly not. First of all, and most importantly, we have God by our side. He does not promise that bad things won't happen. Indeed, as we view the biblical records of various men and women of God, it appears certain that bad things will happen and that in every life there will be storms, despair, and times of anguish. What He does promise the faithful is so beautifully expressed by Paul in 2 Corinthians 12:7-9, "And lest I should be exalted above measure through the abundance of the revelations, there was given to me a thorn in the flesh, the messenger of Satan to buffet me, lest I should be exalted above measure. For this thing I besought the Lord thrice, that it might depart from me. And he said unto me, *My grace is sufficient for thee.*"

God will give us what we need to get through every problem, every single bad thing. When the Hebrew writer quoted from Joshua 1 in Hebrews 13:5, "Let your conversation (manner of life) be without covetousness; and be content with such things as ye have: for He hath said, *I will never leave thee, nor forsake thee,*" he meant it. When Paul wrote, "I can do all things through Christ which strengtheneth me" (Phil. 4:13), that wasn't just rhetoric, it was the truth. These are all statements onto which every faithful Christian can hold.

There are also truly faithful and loving brethren who will stand with their brothers or sisters in their darkest moments—on that, each of us can depend!

Paul wrote in Galatians 6:2, "Bear ye one another's burdens, and so fulfill the law of Christ." There are so many who stand ready to do just that.

So we can be faithful and we can do what is right in every situation, no matter what. Bad things do happen. When they do, trust in God, lean on Him, and let your brethren help.

March 31

"I Will Eat No Flesh While the World Standeth, Lest I Make My Brother to Offend" (1 Cor. 8:13)

This is certainly a lengthy title, but it aptly expresses the principle set forth by Paul in 1 Corinthians 8. There are several specific questions that are considered in this chapter, the details of which are not particularly germane to us. However, the underlying lesson contained therein is most assuredly applicable to you and me. The specific questions are: (a) Could a Christian attend a banquet in the temple of an idol? (b) Could a Christian eat meat sacrificed to an idol in the home of a believing or unbelieving friend? (c) Could a Christian eat meat sacrificed to an idol if he inadvertently bought it at the market?

Verse 1 sets forth a basic principle by which all questions among brethren are to be handled. It says, "Now as touching things offered unto idols, we know that we all have knowledge. Knowledge puffeth up, but charity edifieth." Any answer that they arrived at concerning these questions had to be arrived at by reasoning based upon God's word tempered by love. Isn't that how any controversy among brethren should be approached? Paul goes on and shows that in such consideration a person who thinks he has superior knowledge but does not approach the discussion with love doesn't even know the most basic thing.

Verses 4-7 emphasize that an idol is absolutely useless and meaningless. The pagan world was full of many different meaningless gods and idols, but there is only one true God. The problem was that not every Christian in Corinth had reached the same level of spiritual maturity and knowledge. Remembering that the Corinthian Christians had come out of a background of idolatry, it is easy to understand that not all of them viewed an idol as meaningless and worth nothing. Many still felt that to eat meat that had been sacrificed to an idol was to still somehow be involved in its worship. Consider verse 8: "But meat commendeth us not to God: for neither, if we eat, are we the better; neither, if we eat not, are we the worse." In other words, food didn't affect their relationship with God. The truth was that it didn't matter if they ate or not, but not all of them had that same degree of understanding and knowledge. Look at verses 9-10: "But take heed lest by any means this liberty of yours become a stumbling block to them that are weak. For if any man see thee which hast knowledge sit at meat in the idol's temple, shall not the conscience of him which is weak be emboldened to eat those things which are offered to idols?"

Again, not all Christians are at the same level of knowledge and spiritual maturity. Paul urged those who did understand the importance of idols to be mindful of their brothers and sisters in Christ who did not yet understand. They were not to let their knowledge be an occasion of stumbling to the others. Perhaps seeing their brother eat meat that had been sacrificed to an idol would prompt the less mature brother or sister to violate their own conscience and eat. Certainly the spiritually mature would not want to invite a brother or sister to their home and serve them such meat that would cause them to violate what they believed.

Verse 11 puts it so clearly. Paul wrote, "And through thy knowledge shall the weak brother perish, for whom Christ died?" That is such a powerful and logical statement. Christ died for all, including the brother or sister who had not yet achieved the same level of knowledge. That being the case, shouldn't the more knowledgeable, more mature brother be willing to forgo even something that he had the liberty to do in order to help the weaker? The obvious answer to that question is yes.

Indeed, verse 12 says, "But when ye sin so against the brethren, and wound their weak conscience, ye sin against Christ." To demand all of our rights and all of our liberties even if it creates difficulty, and by that I mean an occasion to sin, to a weaker, less knowledgeable brother, is to violate the very character of Christ and to repudiate His work.

A very simple example would be the non-religious celebration of Christmas. I believe that a Christian can engage in the secular celebration of Christmas—a tree, the giving of gifts, the gathering together with family, and so forth. I have known numerous Christians over the years who did not hold to the same view. I believe it would be sinful for me to try to force them to attend a Christmas celebration, causing them to violate their conscience.

Here is another simple example of the principle. I knew a Christian who believed it would be sinful to attend a professional baseball game because alcohol was sold there. I really believed that he was wrong, but I would not have continually invited him to a baseball game. We may have discussed it (indeed, we did), but I would not try to force him to violate his conscience. These are not the best examples, but they help to understand.

The real principle is to put the needs of others before myself. That is the real character and nature of the work of Christ. As Paul said, using Christ as the illustration, "In lowliness of mind let each esteem other better than themselves" (Phil. 2:3). To demand my own way or the exercise of all my liberties to the detriment of my brother or sister in Christ is totally un-Christlike and wrong. Thus Paul concludes 1 Corinthians 8 with the words, "Wherefore, if meat make my brother to offend, I will eat no flesh while the world standeth, lest I make my brother to offend."

April 1

I Have Prayed for Thee

When you think of the word "prayer," what comes to your mind? Is it quiet moments spent in communication with our Father in heaven? Is it a list of requests that you have made, a list of supplications and desires that you have expressed to God and are awaiting answer? Perhaps when you think of prayer the first thing to come to your mind is thanksgiving for petitions granted, for help given, and for comfort and encouragement secured.

All of these and more come to my mind when I think of prayer. I believe in the power of prayer. I know that James told us in James 5:16, "The effectual fervent prayer of a righteous man availeth much." I have found confidence in the words of 1 John 5:14-15, "And this is the confidence that we have in him, that, if we ask anything according to his will, he heareth us: and if we know that he hear us, whatsoever we ask, we know that we have the petitions that we desired of him." I know that our Father in heaven hears us, and what a blessing it is to have this avenue of communication with Him available to us and to have Him want us to use it. Paul wrote in 1 Thessalonians 5:17, "Pray without ceasing."

One of the really wonderful things about prayer is that I can pray for you and you can pray for me. Now I don't mean that I can pray "instead" of you, or that you can pray "instead" of me. I simply mean that I can offer prayer on your behalf and you can offer prayer on my behalf. We can pray for each other. Who can forget the beautiful prayer of Jesus in John 17:9, "I pray for them ('them' being the apostles, g.l.). I pray not for the world, but for them which thou hast given me; for they are thine." In verse 20 Jesus said, "Neither pray I for these alone, but for them also which shall believe on me through their word." In Luke 22:31-32 we read, "And the Lord said, Simon, Simon, behold, Satan hath desired to have you, that he may sift you as wheat: but I have prayed for thee, that thy faith fail not: and when thou art converted, strengthen thy brethren." Jesus shows us that we are to pray on behalf of others.

In Acts 12:5 we are told, "Peter therefore was kept in prison: but prayer was made without ceasing of the church unto God *for him.*" Look at what Paul wrote in Ephesians 6:18-19: "Praying always with all prayer and supplication in the Spirit, and watching thereunto with all perseverance and supplication *for all saints; and for me,* that utterance may be given unto me, that I may open my mouth boldly, to make known the mystery of the gospel." We could present a host of additional examples of brethren either praying for one another or being exhorted to do so.

Let us be certain that we follow this part of the New Testament pattern and pray for our brothers and sisters in Christ. With those who are sick, those who are bereaved, those who are shut-in, those who are weak in the faith, those who are experiencing financial difficulties, those involved in a job search, and those who can simply use a word of encouragement, there is never a lack of need for prayer. Let's remember each other several times a day as we go to our Father in prayer. It works.

April 2

Take Heed How Ye Hear

In Luke 8:18, in the context of His explanation of the parable of the Sower, Jesus said, "Take heed therefore how ye hear: for whosoever hath to him shall be given; and whosoever hath not, from him shall be taken even that which he seemeth to have." In the same account from Mark 4:24 the exhortation given is to "take heed what ye hear." By putting these two passages together we can see that the disciples were being urged to be careful about *how* they heard *what* they heard. Since both of these statements were made in the explanation of the parable of the Sower, making application is easy.

Over many years of doing daily, call-in radio programs, one of the most frustrating things was *how* so many in the listening audience heard *what* they heard. Some take such a shallow approach to God's Word that they focus on things of no real consequence and turn a deaf ear to the more sublime issues of Scripture. I could be discussing what the Bible means when it speaks of "salvation by grace through faith," only to have someone call up and ask, "Where did Cain get his wife?" I could be examining the conditional nature of salvation and the need for us to be obedient to God's commands, and someone would call wanting to know how Noah got all of the animals onto the ark.

Still others in the listening audience were so entangled with denominational error that the truth was choked out when they heard it, and they would absolutely refuse to acknowledge it as truth. I remember a classic example of this very thing. On a program one day, I was discussing a letter of disagreement that I had received from a listener. As I answered each part of the letter with the appropriate passages from the Word of God, showing that grace does not negate our need for obedience but actually instructs us to obey, callers were calling in saying, "I agree with that sister." No Scriptures were given to support their agreement. No comments were made related to the answers I had presented, just "I agree with that sister." Why did they agree? Because her letter was filled with the same old denominational errors of "salvation by faith only" and "once saved, always saved." Because that is what these people had chosen to believe, they turned a prejudiced ear to the truth when they heard it.

Did you notice that Jesus said, "For whosoever hath, to him shall be given; and whosoever hath not, from him shall be taken even that which he seemeth to have"? Everyone is responsible for *how* they hear *what* they hear.

This responsibility does not stop with those who are outside the Body of Christ. It is also the responsibility of those who are Christians. It is not uncommon at all for some brethren to be very selective about *how* they hear *what* they hear. If a lesson is presented on the need for baptism for the remission of sins, practically all the brethren will strongly agree. If a lesson is preached about the organization of the church, most again will agree. Present a lesson about the love that binds us together with the Body and the agreement is palpable.

However, present a lesson about modest apparel, and some stop listening. It is as much the Word of God as any of the other lessons, but the "cares, riches, and pleasures of this life" interfere with *how* they hear, and it affects their perception of *what* they hear. "I want to wear what I want to wear, so obviously what was preached was not the truth."

If a person preaches about social drinking, what we should or should not partake of as entertainment, what the Bible teaches about divorce and remarriage, and many other controversial subjects, hearing problems will crop up for some.

The way to deal with hearing problems, both for the Christian and for those who have been washed in the blood of the Lamb, is to be as the Bereans we read of in Acts 17:11: "These were more noble than those in Thessalonica, in that they received the word with all readiness of mind, and searched the Scriptures daily, whether those things were so."

How they heard was "with all readiness of mind." *What* they heard was "the word." After hearing "the word with all readiness of mind" they then "searched the Scriptures daily, whether those things were so." That is *how* to hear, to make sure *what* we hear is the truth. Finding it to be so, simply believe and obey it.

April 3

And the Winner Is. . .

Every year the Academy Awards presentation, the Oscars, takes place. It is estimated that the worldwide television audience is usually over one billion people. As the big night draws near, numerous articles appear in various newspapers and magazines predicting who is going to win and who is going to lose. Entire segments of television news broadcasts are devoted to what the actresses are going to wear. (I guess *somebody* cares!) I have even heard reports that as much as a week before the actual event, people begin to camp on the sidewalk outside the auditorium so they can be close enough to get a good view of the stars as they enter into the building.

When the awards are actually presented, the recipients are justifiably excited. It is a wonderful thing to be recognized as the best in your field for a particular piece of work, whether you are an actor, a director, a salesman, a doctor, a secretary, or any other profession in which you might be involved. Those statuettes are taken home, placed in a prominent location in the house, and will serve as a constant reminder that at least one time in their lives the winners were honored with the greatest and most significant award possible in their field of endeavor.

Awards are nice. Being honored for something that you have done is a wonderful feeling. Being able to look back over a body of work and say, "I have done the best I could," and then to have others say that you did well, is extremely satisfying. Imagine looking back over our work as Christians when we come to death's door and being able to say, "For I am now ready to be offered, and the time of my departure is at hand. I have fought a good fight, I have finished my course, I have kept the faith; henceforth there is laid up for me a crown of righteousness, which the Lord, the righteous judge, shall give me at that day: and not to me only, but unto all them also that love his appearing" (2 Tim. 4:6-8).

From the moment we rise from the watery grave of baptism, our new lives are to be characterized by a relentless pursuit of our goal. I do not believe it to be wrong at all to say that we labor and strive for the reward. Paul put it this way in Philippians 3:12-14, "Not as though I had already attained, either were already perfect: but I follow after, if that I may apprehend that for which also I am apprehended of Christ Jesus. Brethren, I count not myself to have apprehended: but this one thing I do, forgetting those things which are behind, and reaching forth unto those things which are before, I press toward the mark of the prize of the high calling of God in Christ Jesus."

The reward for which we strive will not be simply a constant reminder—it will be an eternal reminder—that the lives we led were pleasing to our Savior through obedience to the "gospel of the grace of God" (Acts 20:24), and in recognition of such we will share in His glory. It will not be something that we will have earned. It will be something that He gives us as a reward for having been faithful children, having fought the good fight, and having kept the faith.

When the envelope is opened by the presenter at the awards shows, everyone holds their breath in anticipation of the words, "And the winner is..." Don't you even now wait with eager anticipation to hear the words, "Come, ye blessed of my Father, inherit the kingdom prepared for you from the foundation of the world"?

Weeds

A few weeks ago I received notice that my lawn care company had been sold but that I could rest assured that I would be receiving the same great service I had always received at the same low price. Oh, boy! Anyway, that got me to thinking about weeds.

I was standing in my miniscule backyard, and it occurred to me that with this recent heat wave, the only things growing in my yard are the weeds. The grass is starting to dry up, the bare spots are not longer just dirt—they have degenerated to dust. The few flowers have withered and died, but the weeds continue to thrive. Every week I pull some out, weed-eat the ones I can't pull, and chop down the ones too big to whack with my weed-whacker. But every week they come back and seem to bring friends with them!

It reminded me of the parable of the Sower from Luke 8. Jesus said, "A sower went out to sow his seed; and as he sowed, some fell by the wayside; and it was trodden down, and the fowls of the air devoured it. And some fell upon a rock; and as soon as it was sprung up it withered away, because it lacked moisture. And some fell among thorns; and the thorns sprang up with it, and choked it. And other fell on good ground, and sprang up, and bore fruit an hundredfold."

In verse 14 Jesus gave this explanation of the thorns, "And that which fell among thorns are they which, when they have heard, go forth, and are choked with cares and riches and pleasures of this life, and bring no fruit to perfection."

For many of us the temptations that give us the most trouble are like weeds. We battle them, we fight them, we struggle with them on a daily basis, and they keep coming back. If I quit worrying about the weeds for a while and just let them go unchecked, they take over. In my yard the weeds require steady attention. Temptation is like that too. Peter wrote in 1 Peter 5:8, "Be sober, be vigilant; because your adversary the devil, as a roaring lion, walketh about, seeking whom he may devour." We simply must be vigilant, aware that Satan wants us back.

I don't know what particular temptation you might have to deal with. I don't know what it is that gives you the most trouble and causes you the most pain. I suspect that we all have something or some area in our lives that Satan attacks most frequently. But I know that none of us has to be overrun by the "weeds" of temptation. In 1 Corinthians 10:13 Paul wrote, "There hath no temptation taken you but such as is common to man: but God is faithful, who will not suffer you to be tempted above that ye are able, but will with the temptation also make a way to escape, that ye maybe able to bear it."

In my backyard I am winning the battle with the weeds. I'm not sure where they keep coming from, but they are not going to get the better of me. In my life I'm winning too. Satan is not going to get the better of me. I will not be overrun. I know where temptation comes from, and I will not let Satan win the war. We can all be like God's gardeners, rooting out the "weeds" of temptation, cultivating as perfect a life as possible, until we get to go home.

April 5

"Finally, Brethren, Farewell" (1)
2 Corinthians 13:11

2 Corinthians 13:11 is one of my favorite verses in the New Testament. As Paul was bringing this letter to a close he wrote, "Finally, brethren, farewell. Be perfect, be of good comfort, be of one mind, live in peace; and the God of love and peace shall be with you." It has become my custom to use this verse as a way of bringing gospel meetings that I hold to a close.

2 Corinthians is not an easy letter to read. It is a very emotional book filled with Paul's responses to numerous personal attacks that he had endured, as well as his response to several charges that had been leveled against him. Paul holds nothing back in this book. He meets the personal attacks head on, and answers in often stern language the charges that had been made by some against him. Yet we also note in this book some of the great, fundamental doctrines of Christianity. We see in 2 Corinthians the glory of our Lord Jesus, the majesty of His work of reconciliation, and the power of the gospel to change men. He writes of the life of service that Christianity demands and of the need to avoid sin. However, this letter is probably the least doctrinal of all Paul's letters to the churches.

Paul was a man of great passion, and that passion is never more evident than in the 2 Corinthian letter. One man wrote, "Yet it is not the events of his outward life which attract our supreme interest. It is rather the revelation, which is here made of the apostle's soul. We look into his very heart. We see his motives, his anguish, his joys, his fears, his hopes, his wounded feelings, his ardent love. Evidently the whole letter was written under the stress of strong emotion" (Charles Erdman, *The Second Epistle of Paul to the Corinthians*).

Paul was so plain in this letter, strict and to the point. When rebuke was necessary, he rebuked in language that could leave no room for misunderstanding. No one could read this letter and come away wondering what Paul believed or what he thought of any issue that he addressed within it. As a matter of fact, in 13:10 Paul wrote, "Therefore I write these things being absent lest being present I should use sharpness, according to the power which the Lord hath given me to edification, and not to destruction." The letter was meant to stimulate those guilty of making the false charges against Paul to repent, lest when he was present among them he would need to deal with those individuals severely.

Now, as forceful and as powerful as Paul was in this letter, as plain and severe as his rebukes were, did this indicate that Paul had anything but love in his heart for these brethren? No, in fact, he brings the letter to a close with a word of loving exhortation. He had had stern words for those involved in sin, and he had severely rebuked those who needed rebuking, but now he includes them all as his "brethren."

April 6

"Finally, Brethren, Farewell" (2)
2 Corinthians 13:11

"Finally, brethren, farewell." More literally that would be "Finally, brethren, rejoice." There is much in which to rejoice in being a Christian. Surely there is joy in our redemption, and we should be moved to rejoice in our union with our Lord and our Father. I am not exactly sure what Paul was saying to these brethren when he urges them to "rejoice," but perhaps he is expressing the thought, "Let my last word to you be to rejoice."

"Be perfect," or "press on to perfection." The content of the letter indicates that there was a great deal among the brethren in Corinth that needed to be fixed. Many sins had been committed and in many areas some had fallen so far short, and Paul had not hesitated to point those things out. Now he is saying, "Fix it!" Be what you ought to be; walk as the Lord would have you to walk.

"Be of good comfort." The same word can be translated as comfort or counsel. It is probable that Paul was saying they were to give heed to the things that he had written unto them. Obey his words, and know real comfort.

"Be of one mind." This takes me back to Paul's first letter to the Corinthians. In 1 Corinthians 1:10 he had written, "Now I beseech you, brethren, by the name of our Lord Jesus Christ, that ye all speak the same thing, and that there be no divisions among you; but that ye be perfectly joined together in the same mind and in the same judgment." That letter went on to address several of the issues that were causing problems and divisions among the Corinthian church. The word for "divisions" was the same word used to designate a tear in a piece of material; while the word for "perfectly joined together" came from a word meaning "to mend fishing nets." Paul was exhorting the Corinthians to fix the divisions, to mend those things that were tearing them apart. He didn't mean ignore them, or pretend that the problems didn't exist. He meant to fix them. When brethren do that, they will:

"Live in peace." Unity—how blessed it is! However, true unity is not "agree to disagree." True unity is obtained when all accept the same standard and abide therein. I am reminded of the words of Jesus in John 17:19-21, "And for their sakes I sanctify myself, that they also might be sanctified through the truth. Neither pray I for these alone, but for them also which shall believe on me through their word; that they all may be one; as thou, Father, art in me, and I in thee, that they also may be one in us: that the world may believe that thou hast sent me." An even more blessed consequence of being "of one mind" is that "the God of love and peace shall be with you."

I love 2 Corinthians 13:11. It gives me an attitude of heart to shoot for. No matter what issues must be addressed, no matter how passionate the method of addressing may be, it is always based on love.

What Do I See?

Back in the 1960s there was a musical called *"You're a Good Man, Charlie Brown."* It was a semi-hit, as I remember. It seemed to me that the person who got to play Snoopy had the best part. In the play there was a song about clouds, and the idea was "What do you see when you look at the clouds?" Poor old Charlie Brown only saw clouds, but when Linus looked at the clouds, he saw "all twelve apostles waving at me." What a great line!

Who among us hasn't, at least as children, looked up into the sky to see what we could see among the clouds? Hot summer days often remind me of times years ago spent lying on my back in the grass, looking up at the clouds as an afternoon drifted by. I never saw "all twelve apostles waving at me," but I saw dinosaurs, horses, dragons, faces, and a host of other things. I don't spend much time anymore looking at the clouds, except to see if it is going to rain. I am not altogether sure that that is such a good thing.

By this time you are probably asking yourselves, "What does all this have to do with anything?" The answer is that, while I no longer lay on my back looking at the clouds to see things, I do close my eyes from time to time, and in my mind's eye see things just as surely and as clearly as I did then.

I have spent so much time thinking about the death of Jesus, so much time studying the physiological effects of the crucifixion, so much time in the gospel accounts of the horrifying death of Jesus, and so much time in the 22nd Psalm, that when I close my eyes, I can see a crucifixion. Please don't misunderstand; I don't know what Jesus looked like. The closest that we have of a physical description of the Lord is found in Isaiah 53:2, "For he shall grow up before him as a tender plant, and as a root out of a dry ground; *he hath no form nor comeliness; and when we shall see him, there is no beauty that we should desire him."* However, I can picture—almost clearly see—the image presented in Psalm 22:13-18 where David wrote, "They gaped upon me with their mouths, as a ravening and a roaring lion. I am poured out like water, and all my bones are out of joint: my heart is like wax; it is melted in the midst of my bowels. My strength is dried up like a potsherd; and my tongue cleaveth to my jaws; and thou hast brought me into the dust of death. I may tell all my bones: they look and stare upon me. They part my garments among them, and cast lots upon my vesture." Undoubtedly the image that I see with my mind's eye has been influenced by various representations of the crucified Christ which I have seen over the years, but not any more than by the words the Holy Spirit has chosen to use to describe it. It can take my breath away! Do you find that happening to you too?

When I Close My Eyes

When I close my eyes, I can see hell, much of it coming from my study of the word "Gehenna" and the image that Jesus was using to describe such a terrible place. It was a reference to the valley of Hinnon, the garbage dump for the city of Jerusalem and a place with a terrible history. So I can picture in my mind's eye a place of "fire that never shall be quenched: where their worm dieth not, and the fire is not quenched" (Mark 9:43-48). I have seen fires burning garbage and have both seen and smelled the rotting flesh of various animals and meats that constituted part of that garbage. Just picture a city that continues to produce garbage on a daily basis. Now just picture all of that garbage burning, but each day the fire does not consume what is already there, and it just keeps getting bigger and bigger. Now just picture the fire that never goes out as being fueled by numberless souls of those who have chosen to turn their backs on Jesus. Picture the worms that feed on rotting flesh as figuratively feeding on the endless source of food the lost will be—for such will never be consumed. No Hollywood producer can present an image more frightening than the image Jesus presented with just about twenty words when translated into the English language.

When I close my eyes I can see heaven, even though I don't really have any idea of what it will look like. What I see is my perception of the vision that John saw in the book of Revelation. I can see "the holy city, the new Jerusalem" (21:2). I can picture a place of "no more death, neither sorrow, nor crying," a place where there won't be "any more pain" (21:4). I can picture streets of pure gold, and a place of continuous light. I can picture in my mind's eye a place where "there shall in no wise enter into it anything that defileth, neither whatsoever worketh abomination" (21:27). I can picture a place without sin.

I am so thankful to God that He gives us the ability to see things with our eyes closed. With that ability, it is easy to dread the very thought of going to such a place as hell. At the same time, it is easy to long to go to such a place as heaven.

I find myself being able to picture only those things that I have actually seen or read. That helps me to understand how important it is to be careful about what I read and what I allow myself to see. Sometimes when I close my eyes images appear unbidden, but they are things that I have seen before or about which I have read descriptions—like a computer, it only puts out what is put in.

April 9

It Is Notabout Me!

My continued study of the New Testament has convinced me that a vital key to my living as a faithful child of God is recognizing that I am not the most important person. It is not about me! Perhaps no passage so clearly teaches that essential truth as does Philippians 2:1-4 where Paul wrote:

> If therefore there is any encouragement in Christ, if there is any consolation of love, if there is any fellowship of the Spirit, if any affection and compassion, make my joy complete by being of the same mind, maintaining the same love, united in spirit, intent on one purpose. Do nothing from selfishness or empty conceit, but with humility of mind let each of you regard one another as more important than himself; do not merely look out for your own personal interests, but also the interests of others.

The intriguing thing that I have encountered concerning this passage is that folks will read it and come away thinking of how others are not as spiritually minded as they are, thinking, "So and so sure needs to read that and be more *like me!*" Such thinking happens to be an example of the very type of attitude Paul was seeking to eradicate from the hearts of the Philippian brethren. Actually, to summarize the passage we should realize that we need to subordinate our own interests to the interests of others. What is best for the church? What is best for my fellow Christians? Not what is best for me, or what do I personally like the best?

What better example could there possibly be of just such an attitude than the Lord Jesus? Verse 5 tells us, "Have this attitude in yourselves which was also in Christ Jesus." Jesus epitomized the attitude of selflessness, not selfishness. He was humble minded, thinking of others and not of Himself alone, or even primarily. Such an attitude was manifested in His coming to this earth and dying. Because that was true, Paul wrote in verses 12-16:

> So, then, my beloved, just as you have always obeyed, not as in my presence only, but now much more in my absence, work out your salvation with fear and trembling; for it is God who is at work in you, both to will and to work for His good pleasure. Do all things without grumbling or disputing; that you may prove yourselves to be blameless and innocent, children of God above reproach in the midst of a crooked and perverse generation, among whom you appear as lights in the world, holding fast the word of life, so that in the day of Christ I may have cause to glory because I did not run in vain nor toil in vain.

It is not my intention to offer an in-depth exegesis of this passage. Rather, I simply want to note that Paul is exhorting the Philippians to conduct themselves according to the pattern that had been set for them by Christ. Part of that humility, part of that willingness to serve others, part of that self-sacrificial attitude that should be manifested in their lives, was to "do all things without grumbling and disputing." This I do want to consider more closely.

"Grumbling" (*goggusmon*) means, "complaint, displeasure, expressed in murmurings." The word is used to describe outward wranglings of discontent. We find the same word being used in a number of different places in Scripture and looking at a few of them will help us to better understand its meaning. In John 6:41 we read, "The Jews therefore were *grumbling* about Him, because He said, 'I am the bread that came down out of heaven.'" In verse 43 we find, "Jesus answered and said to them, 'Do not *grumble* among yourselves.'" And it appears again in verse 61, "But Jesus, conscious that His disciples *grumbled* at this, said to them 'Does this cause you to stumble?'"

The second word was "disputing." There are three different views expressed concerning this word as it is used here. Some see it as meaning divided or diverse reasonings, and if silent, then equally "doubts." Others think it means divided or diverse reasonings that are expressed—a more normal idea of disputes. Still others think that it refers to inner strife of an individual's heart. I believe that the context, as well as other places in Scripture where the word is used, indicates that it has reference to open discussion—the more normal concept of disputes. One thing that we do know for certain is that in Philippians 2:14, "grumbling" and "disputing" are closely related and indicate the same basic idea of dissatisfaction and doubt.

Is it possible that any of us could be described as one who has been dissatisfied, a complainer, filled with displeasure, who has sought to push his or her own ideas and desires? The world outside is difficult enough. A congregation of the Lord's people should be an oasis where we can come and feed upon the word of the Lord, bask in the wonderful comfort of our brothers and sisters in Christ, and know that we all have the best interest of each other before self in our hearts.

Are your thoughts, your words, and your deeds truly to that end? "Have this attitude in yourselves which was also in Christ Jesus."

April 10

Think

Several years ago I had the opportunity to engage in an exchange of correspondence with a young Mormon "elder" (and I use that term most accommodatively!). The young fellow even took the Bible correspondence course offered by the congregation with which I was working at the time. Afterward he sent me a letter encouraging me to be "honest" in my investigation of the Mormon church. In reply, I sent him a number of articles I had written concerning Mormonism and Joseph Smith, its founder. I promised him that, if he could prove any statement that I had made to be incorrect, I would publicly retract it. Quite frankly, I thought that would be the end of our correspondence and did not expect a reply. However, the young man did reply, and it was the first of many such replies that I have received over the years from members of various denominations. It was, and continues to be, heartbreaking. It is not my practice to make common knowledge private correspondence, but this letter so aptly illustrates one of the major problems, not only of Mormonism, but other religious bodies as well. The letter read as follows:

Mr. Litmer,

Thanks for sending those articles, they were interesting. I'd just like to tell you that I *know* the Church of Jesus Christ of Latter Day Saints is the one true church on the earth today. And that Jesus Christ restored it through the prophet Joseph Smith. And the authority to perform the saving ordinances of the gospel was once again restored to the earth. I *know* that there is a living prophet on the earth today. His name is President Spencer W. Kimball. He has said, 'I am not the head of the church, the master Jesus Christ is the head of his church.' I *know* the Book of Mormon is the word of God. I *know* because I have read it and put to the test the promises in it. No one can say that the Book of Mormon is not true until they have read it carefully and prayed about it. Our heavenly Father is the source of all truth and if we want to know if something is true, we should go to Him and not rely on the ideas of men. I challenge you to read the book of Mormon and put the promises to the test.

I was so disappointed in this response for several reasons. First, he mentioned not one word about the documented, proven charges against Joseph Smith, Mormonism, and the book of Mormon. All that was received were the statements of "I know." How does he know? That is made clear in the letter. The Mormon church teaches its members that, if they want to know something, just ask God or the Holy Spirit, and He will tell you. This works particularly well when you want to know whether or not charges against Mormonism are true. All you have to do is just convince yourself that God told you they weren't true and all the documentation, all the evidence, and all of the cold, hard facts won't make a bit of difference. I don't mean to be harsh, but in other words, don't think for yourself, don't examine, don't investigate, just accept what your leaders tell you.

The Mormon leaders teach their people that what they say is true. And they teach their people that, if anyone disagrees with them or says they are not speaking the truth, then just ask God and God will tell you to believe your leaders and the Book of Mormon. That makes just about a perfect circle of reasoning!

This whole episode was a shame. Here was a young man entering into the prime of his life, being taught not to think for himself, not to question, not to investigate—just believe what he is told and believe it blindly. With all my heart I can honestly say that I don't want anyone to believe what I say just because I said it. I don't want anyone to believe what some "well-known" preacher might say just because he said it. I don't want anyone to believe what some elders say, just because they said it. We all have the responsibility to think and reason according to the Scriptures. If those who comprise the religious world in general would think for themselves, investigate the Scriptures themselves and not rely on others to do their thinking and reasoning for them, such sad events as these would not occur with nearly the frequency that they do.

In Acts 17:11 we read, "These were more noble than those in Thessalonica, in that they received the word with all readiness of mind and searched the Scriptures daily whether those things were so." Here were individuals who were commended for their investigation. The truth does not fear investigation—it invites it! The truth does not depend on some mystical voice whispering in your head telling you not to believe its critics. If it can't stand investigation, if it doesn't *demand* investigation, then it is not the truth. What did Jesus say? "Search the Scriptures: for in them ye think ye have eternal life: and they are they which testify of Me" (John 5:39). In 1 John 4:1 we are exhorted, "Beloved, believe not every spirit, but try the spirits whether they are of God: because many false prophets are gone out into the world."

Certainly there was never any animosity toward this young man. There was, and continues to be, real concern and sadness. How tragic not to be willing to use the reasoning powers that God gave us in the first place. "I know" is not good enough. Really, it is the old "better felt than told" philosophy. It is a "let your emotions guide you" way of thinking. That is not New Testament Christianity.

April 11

"Came the Word of God out from You?"

Bible students are aware of the fact that much of what Paul writes in 1 Corinthians deals with times when they came "together in the church," when they came "together therefore into one place" (1 Cor. 11:18, 20). We know that in chapter 11 Paul deals with whether or not a woman was required to wear a covering and with problems they were having in partaking of the Lord's Supper. In chapters 12, 13, and 14 Paul addressed the issue of miraculous spiritual gifts, what their attitude toward them should be, and what their attitude toward each other should be. In chapter 14 Paul focused on instructions that would help them to do all things "decently and in order" when "the whole church be come together into one place" (1 Cor. 14:40, 23).

Paul was primarily addressing the times when the congregation assembled for corporate worship, what they were to do, and how they were to conduct themselves at those times. Interestingly, Paul wrote concerning the Lord's Supper, prayer and singing, teaching and giving (1 Cor. 16:1-2).

In chapter 14, after writing about the orderly exercise of miraculous spiritual gifts in their assemblies, Paul wrote in verses 33-37:

> For God is not the author of confusion, but of peace, as in all churches of the saints. Let your women keep silence in the churches: for it is not permitted unto them to speak; but they are commanded to be under obedience, as also saith the law. And if they will learn anything, let them ask their husbands at home: for it is a shame for women to speak in the church. What? Came the word of God out from you? Or came it unto you only? If any man think himself to be a prophet, or spiritual, let him acknowledge that the things that I write unto you are the commandments of the Lord.

It is not my purpose to address the place of women in the worship assemblies, but rather to notice an aspect of Paul's teaching to the Corinthians that is not often talked about. The confusion and lack of order that characterized the assemblies of the Corinthians was not happening in all of the other churches. In verse 33 Paul wrote, "For God is not the author of confusion, but of peace, *as in all churches of the saints.*" That phrase brings to mind a statement that Paul made earlier in chapter 4:15-17, "For though ye have ten thousand instructors in Christ, yet have ye not many fathers: for in Christ Jesus I have begotten you through the gospel. Wherefore I beseech you, be ye followers of me. For this cause have I sent unto you Timotheus, who is my beloved son, and faithful in the Lord, who shall bring you into remembrance of my ways which be in Christ, *as I teach every where in every church.*" There was a consistency of teaching and a pattern to be followed by all of the churches wherever they were. What was happening in Corinth was different from what was taking place in all of the other churches.

In verse 36 Paul made a very interesting point. He asked the Corinthians, whose practice was different from the other churches, "What? Came the word of God out from you? Or came it unto you only?" What did he mean by that? Quite simply, if the gospel originated with the Corinthians, then the other churches were wrong, because what they were doing was different from what the Corinthians were doing. If the gospel came to the Corinthians from some other place or source, and their practice was different from all the other churches, then they were wrong. Paul went on to make the point that those who would present themselves as being particularly spiritual or who presented themselves as spokesmen of God had to acknowledge that what Paul was writing to them were, in fact, the commandments of the Lord, and not something of his own devising.

"Came the Word of God out from You?" Applied

I believe that there is a practical lesson to be learned for us today from Paul's statements found in 1 Corinthians 14:33, 36. Those who would feel free to change any aspect of the Lord's pattern for the church, whether we are talking about worship, the organization of the church, the work in which the church is authorized to engage, or the terms of admission into the body, need to answer a simple question: *Did the gospel originate with them, or did they receive it from some other source?*

The truth is that there is only one gospel of the Lord Jesus Christ. It was delivered in its entirety, with the conclusion of the book of Revelation, in the A.D. 90s. No one has the right to add to it or take away from it. No one has the right to change it in any way. If they add to it, God will "add unto him the plagues that are written in this book." If they take away from it, "God will take away his part out of the book of life, and out of the holy city, and from the things which are written in this book" (Revelation 22:18-19).

The Apostle Paul wrote in Galatians 1:6-10:

I marvel that ye are so soon removed from him that called you into the grace of Christ unto another gospel: which is not another; but there be some that trouble you, and would pervert the gospel of Christ. But though we, or an angel from heaven, preach any other gospel unto you than that which we have preached unto you, let him be accursed. As we said before, so say I now again, If any man preach any other gospel unto you than that ye have received, let him be accursed. For do I now persuade men, or God? Or do I seek to please men? For if I yet please men, I should not be the servant of Christ.

It is a serious matter to tamper with God's word in any way. If you should find yourself chafing under what you might perceive as its restrictions and limitations, or if what you desire is different from what is being done in all other faithful churches of the Lord's people, pause and ask, "Did the gospel originate with me, or did I receive it from some other source?"

A Man Born Blind (1)
John 9

In John 9 we read the account of the healing of a man who had been born blind. We do not know exactly where in the city of Jerusalem this event took place. Since we are told in verse 8 that this man "sat and begged," it is possible that it occurred near the main entrance to the temple.

As Jesus passed by, He saw this man who had been born blind. His disciples asked Him, "Rabbi, who sinned, this man or his parents, that he should be born blind?" This question gives us some insight into a commonly held belief among the Jewish people of that time. It was generally held that all suffering was retributive, the result of sin. Some have suggested that the disciples' question also indicates a possible belief in the transmigration of souls; that perhaps this man had sinned in some previous existing state. However, there is nothing to indicate that they knew this man had been blind from birth. They thought he was blind as the result of some sin in his life, or perhaps his parents had sinned before he was born and his blindness was punishment to them. (This type of thinking is also found in Luke 12:1-5.)

Jesus responded with, "It was neither that this man sinned, nor his parents; but it was in order that the works of God might be displayed in him." The Lord's answer is not to be taken to mean that the man or his parents were not sinners. It simply means that their sins were not the cause of his blindness. Rather, it was part of the providential plan of God, and through him the mighty power of God was going to be revealed. Lest any should question the "fairness" of God in this circumstance, it would be good to consider what happened with this man as pointed out in verses 35-38. The passage says, "Jesus heard that they had put him out; and finding him, He said, Do you believe in the Son of Man? He answered and said, And who is He, Lord, that I may believe in Him? Jesus said to him, You have both seen Him, and He is the one who is talking with you. And he said, Lord, I believe. And he worshipped Him."

Jesus' method of cure was somewhat unusual in this case. He spat upon the ground, made clay of the spittle, and anointed the man's eyes. Then He gave him instructions to go and wash in the pool of Siloam. Perhaps several things can be said of the Lord's approach in this case. (1) It served as an aid to the man's faith. He could feel that something was being done for him. (2) It helped to draw attention to the miracle by raising the expectation of any who saw it. (3) It also served to bring Jesus into conflict with the Sabbath traditions of the Jews, both by applying the clay and the man going to wash it off. The man obeyed the Lord, washed, and was cured.

• A word about the pool of Siloam. "Siloam (sent; specially a sending of water through an aqueduct). A pool at Jerusalem; probably identical with Shiloah, the waters of which go softly (Isaiah 8:6), and the pool of Shelah, which was by the king's garden (Nehemiah 3:15). Josephus says that it was situated at the extremity of the valley of cheesemongers, near a bend of the old wall beneath Ophlas, i.e. Ophel. The name is preserved in the Birket Silwan, which occupies the general site of the ancient pool. It is a rectangular reservoir, 58 feet long, 18 broad, and 19 deep, built of masonry, the western side of which has considerably broken down" (*Davis Dictionary of the Bible*, 763).

April 14

A Man Born Blind (2)
John 9

I would suppose that a man born blind who suddenly received his sight would have a slightly altered appearance. That, coupled with the impossibility of the cure, probably led to the confusion of his neighbors. "Is not this the one who used to sit and beg?" they asked. "This is he," some said, while others stated, "No, but he is like him." The man himself said, "I am the one." This led to the obvious question, "How then were your eyes opened?"

The man's response was direct and to the point, containing only the facts with no embellishment. "The man who is called Jesus made clay, and anointed my eyes, and said to me, Go to Siloam, and wash; so I went away and washed, and I received sight." This led his neighbors to want to see how the Pharisees would react. After all, the cure had been wrought on the Sabbath day, and Jesus had made that clay.

The Pharisees also asked the man how he had received his sight and he told them, "He applied clay to my eyes, and I washed, and I see."

The reaction demonstrates that not all of the Pharisees viewed Jesus in the same way. Some stressed the Jewish tradition in the face of the evidence and declared Jesus to be a sinner because He had done this on the Sabbath day. Others recognized the significance of the miracle and declared that a sinner could not do these things. Thus, there was division concerning Jesus even among the Pharisees.

They turned again to the man and said, "What do you say about Him, since He opened your eyes?" The healed man's response was, "He is a prophet." This was a very logical deduction and shows that the man's faith was progressing as he listened to the arguments of the Pharisees, considering carefully the ramifications of what had happened to him.

The discussion was not at all going the way the Pharisees desired it to go, so they chose to deny the cure. They denied that the man had been born blind and had miraculously received his sight. They even called for his parents and asked them, "Is this your son, who you say was born blind? Then how does he now see?"

That's a good question! The following lesson will continue this thought.

April 15

A Man Born Blind (3)
John 9

The parents answered clearly and affirmatively the first two questions. "We know that this is our son, and that he was born blind." However, they demonstrated a decided lack of courage concerning the third question. It is obvious that the Pharisees had already let it be known, however informally, that confession of Jesus would result in removal from the synagogue, the focal point of Jewish life. Fearing that, the parents said, "How he now sees, we do not know; or who opened his eyes, we do not know. Ask him; he is of age, he shall speak for himself."

Verse 24 and the statement of the Pharisees deserves special notice, "So a second time they called the man who had been blind, and said to him, Give glory to God; we know that this man is a sinner." Two different views of this statement seem possible. (1) They were very subtly urging the man to be as pious as they were. They had judged this Jesus to be a sinner and this man should go along with them. (2) They were seeking to get this man to confess that he and Jesus had concocted this story together and the whole thing was a fake. It is said that the phrase, "give glory to God," was an adjuration to a criminal to admit what he had done.

No matter how the statement of the Pharisees is understood, this healed man would have none of it. He stuck strictly to the facts he knew. He didn't know Jesus well enough to say if He was a sinner or not. But he did know that he had been blind, now he could see, and there was nothing fraudulent about it.

Seeking some way to answer the simple honesty of the healed man, the Pharisees again asked for the details of what had happened. His response is inspiring to all those who have faced skeptics. He simply asked them two questions, which laid bare their hypocrisy. First, "I told you already, and you did not listen; why do you want to hear it again?" and "You do not want to become His disciples too, do you?" This man's faith in Jesus, a man he had not known at all prior to this event, was very quickly growing under the harassing questioning of the Pharisees.

His response really upset these unbelieving Pharisees. "You are His disciple, but we are disciples of Moses. We know that God has spoken to Moses; but as for this man, we do not know where He is from." This is a powerful argument. If they could make it appear that Jesus was forsaking Moses, and that this fellow was doing the same thing by following Him, they would rightfully label him as an apostate.

April 16

A Man Born Blind (4)
John 9

What courage this formerly blind beggar demonstrated as he exposed the ungodly motives of the Pharisees! "Well, here is an amazing thing, that you do not know where He is from, and yet He opened my eyes." This remark was dripping with sarcasm. These were the Pharisees, the scholars of the law, and they couldn't draw the right conclusion from the evidence before their faces.

"We know that God does not hear sinners; but if anyone is God-fearing, and does His will, He hears him. Since the beginning of time it has never been heard that anyone opened the eyes of a person born blind. If this man were not from God, He could do nothing." There was only one conclusion that could be honestly reached. Jesus had to be from God. It is interesting that this simple man, healed by Jesus of life-long blindness, reached the same conclusion that the great Nicodemus reached in John 3:2, "Rabbi, we know that thou art a teacher come from God: for no man can do these miracles that thou doest, except God be with him."

First the Pharisees had denied that the man had been blind. Now they find themselves being outsmarted by this simple, honest man. So they attempt to use his blindness as proof of the fact that he was a sinner. As a sinner, how could he possibly teach them? With that they cast him out, meaning that he would not be welcome in the synagogue or the temple any more.

Jesus, hearing of the persecution of the man, sought him out. He had been cast out of that which pertained to Moses, but Jesus was leading him into fellowship with the Son of God. "Do you believe in the Son of Man?"

"And who is He, Lord, that I may believe in Him?" We must acknowledge that to this man the idea of knowing the Son of God, the long-awaited Messiah, was beyond his wildest dreams. But here, to an outcast from the synagogue, Jesus clearly identified Himself as "He—the Son of God." The man believed and worshipped Jesus. Since God alone deserves worship, surely this is an example of Jesus acknowledging that He was God even as He was man.

While the discussion between Jesus and the man He had healed has all the earmarks of having been private, Jesus next turned His attention to the crowds. He contrasted the physical blindness of the man who had been healed with the spiritual blindness of the Pharisees who thought they saw and understood all, but in reality refused to see. Some of the Pharisees made the application and said, "We are not blind too, are we?"

Of the Lord's reply, Augustine wrote that "If they had realized their blindness then they would have sought the Light and He would have taken away their sin, but as now they boast of their vision, their sin remained because they reject the Light."

What a wonderful chapter!

Blasphemy against the Holy Spirit (1)

In Matthew 12:31-32 we read, "Wherefore I say unto you, All manner of sin and blasphemy shall be forgiven unto men: but the blasphemy against the Holy Ghost shall not be forgiven unto men. And whosoever speaketh a word against the Son of man, it shall be forgiven him: but whosoever speaketh against the Holy Ghost, it shall not be forgiven him, neither in this world, neither in the world to come."

The parallel accounts are found in Mark 3:28-30 and Luke 12:10. Mark wrote, "Verily I say unto you, All sins shall be forgiven unto the sons of men, and blasphemies wherewith soever they shall blaspheme: but he that shall blaspheme against the Holy Ghost hath never forgiveness; but is in danger of eternal damnation: because they said, He hath an unclean spirit."

Luke wrote, "And whosoever shall speak a word against the Son of man, it shall be forgiven him: but unto him that blasphemeth against the Holy Ghost it shall not be forgiven."

The three most popular interpretations concerning the blasphemy against the Holy Spirit that are advanced are these:

1. These Pharisees committed the blasphemy against the Holy Spirit when they said that Jesus was in league with the devil and was casting out demons by the power of the devil. Those who hold this view usually maintain that it is not a sin which is committed today, but was simply this particular charge made against Jesus during His ministry.

2. It is the sin of rejecting the invitation of Jesus to become His follower. It is committed by everyone who refuses to believe and obey when they hear the gospel.

3. It is the sin of continuous malicious attacks upon Christ and the Holy Spirit. It is not a single word or insult, but a continuous assault by word or deed.

I do not accept any of these views entirely but believe a combination of the second and third views to be most correct.

In Luke 4:17-19 we find Jesus in the synagogue of the city of Nazareth. The passage says, "And there was delivered unto him the book of the prophet Isaiah. And when he had opened the book, he found the place where it was written, The Spirit of the Lord is upon me, because he hath anointed me to preach the gospel to the poor; he hath sent me to heal the broken-hearted, to preach deliverance to the captives, and recovering of sight to the blind, to set at liberty them that are bruised, to preach the acceptable year of the Lord."

This passage, as well as the statement Jesus made in Matthew 12:28, "But if I cast out demons by the Spirit of God, then the kingdom of God is come unto you," indicates to us a very important function of the Holy Spirit as far as the Lord was concerned. Jesus performed the miracles that He performed through the Holy Spirit. The gospel accounts are clear that Jesus was anointed of the Spirit and that the Spirit was a vital agent in His work. This needs to be borne in mind as we seek to understand the nature of blasphemy against the Holy Spirit from the account itself.

April 18

Blasphemy against the Holy Spirit (2)

Jesus had wrought a notable miracle in the presence of witnesses. The subject of the miracle was both blind and dumb, afflictions that were evidently brought about by the fact that he was a demoniac, possessed by a demon. But Jesus healed him, or cleansed him, "insomuch that the blind and dumb both spake and saw." The crowd of witnesses was convinced. They cried out, "Is this not the son of David?" Is not this miracle worker the Messiah? Didn't the prophecies portray Him as a worker of miracles? Who could dispute that the Spirit of God was with Jesus? Who could dispute that He was the Anointed One, the Messiah, the Christ of God?

The Pharisees did dispute it. Against the clearest of evidence, because of their pride and envy, they refused to accept what they had seen. Truly there are none so blind as those who refuse to see. To defend their opinion of the Lord and to retain some credibility in the eyes of the people, they invented the ludicrous charged that Jesus was casting out devils through the prince of the devils. Thus they blasphemously attributed the work of the Spirit of God to diabolical agency. The Holy Spirit was blasphemously identified with the very prince of demons. What had they done? They had rejected the clearest of evidence, the work of the Spirit through Jesus.

It is my conviction that the blasphemy against the Holy Spirit is the final rejection of the clearest evidence produced by the Spirit through Jesus—the miracles that He worked. Obviously such an individual will reject Jesus as well. That there is no forgiveness for such a sin, while the sinner remains involved in it, is clear. But Jesus did say, "And whosoever speaketh a word against the Son of man, it shall be forgiven him." What would that be? I believe it to be resistance to the testimony of Jesus without the demonstration of the miracles. But to speak against the Holy Spirit, to blaspheme against the Holy Spirit, is to resist that testimony when it is confirmed by the miracles.

The sin denounced as the blasphemy against the Holy Spirit is the rejection of the evidence of the Messiahship of Jesus through the work of the Holy Spirit—the miracles He performed. Can it be committed today? Yes it can, because we have the same evidence today that they had in the first century, and it is presented to us for the same reason. "And many other signs truly did Jesus in the presence of His disciples, which are not written in this book: but these are written, that ye might believe that Jesus is the Christ, the Son of God; and that believing ye might have life through His name" (John 20:30-31).

The ludicrous charge of the Pharisees had shown the condition of their hearts. A man who was truly good would not speak such wicked things. They, by their speech, had shown the abundance of their hearts, and it was wickedness. To the Pharisees, and to all, Jesus gave a warning. For every word that we speak we will be held accountable. Idle words spoken thoughtlessly, without giving true consideration to their meaning or their effect, can condemn us.

April 19

The Language of Ashdod

Nehemiah was a man who played an extremely important role in the restoration of a remnant of the children of Israel in Judea after the Babylonian Captivity. He was the cupbearer for the Persian king, Artaxerxes, a position of considerable honor and responsibility. As the cupbearer, one of Nehemiah's chief duties was to taste the wine for the king to see that it was not poisoned. He was one of the very few permitted to be in the presence of the king when the queen was also present. This position afforded Nehemiah the close intimacy with the king that enabled him to obtain the commission as governor of Judea and all the letters and edicts by which he was able to restore the walls of Jerusalem.

Zerubbabel led the first group of returnees with the intention of restoring the city and rebuilding the temple in 539 B.C. Ezra led a second group in 457 B.C. Nehemiah was the third to return, and his purpose was to build the wall of the city of Jerusalem and to accomplish certain vital reforms among the people there. He made his return in 445-444 B.C. He would serve as governor for thirteen years, returning to Artaxerxes at least once during that time. He accomplished a great deal socially, financially, politically, and especially spiritually.

Some of the accomplishments of Nehemiah included the appointment of officers for better government. He caused the people to be instructed in the Law by public readings. He celebrated the Feast of Tabernacles and observed a national fast, at which the sins of the people were confessed. The people agreed to keep the Sabbath and to contribute to the support of the Temple once again. To provide for the well being of the city of Jerusalem itself, one out of every ten of the people living outside of Jerusalem was compelled to settle within the city. The people also agreed to avoid marriages with the heathen people living in the land. It is in connection with this last circumstance to which we want to turn our attention.

In Nehemiah 13:23-27 we find:

In those days I also saw that the Jews had married women from Ashdod, Ammon, and Moab. As for their children, *half spoke in the language of Ashdod, and none of them was able to speak the language of Judah, but the language of his own people.* So I contended with them and cursed them and struck some of them and pulled out their hair, and made them swear by God, You shall not give your daughters to their sons, nor take of their daughters for your sons or for yourselves. Did not Solomon king of Israel sin regarding this things? Yet among the many nations there was no king like him, and he was loved by his God, and God made him king over all Israel; nevertheless the foreign women caused even him to sin. Do we then hear about you that you have committed all this great evil by acting unfaithfully against our God by marrying foreign women?

I find it very interesting that the children of Israel had so intermingled with those peoples living in the land that they were losing their identity. Even their own language was in danger of fading away, for the generation coming up could not speak it. What Nehemiah heard as he walked among the people was not the language of the Jews—he was hearing the language of the surrounding peoples. He was hearing "the language of Ashdod."

April 20

The Language of Ashdod—Modern Application

According to what I have read, the fastest growing segment of the publishing industry is the religious genre. Of that particular field, the fastest growing sub-category is "Christian fiction" (and I use that term very, very loosely). So-called "Christian" bookstores are springing up and doing quite well, and the major secular bookstores have increased the religious sections. It reminds me in many ways of Solomon's statement in Ecclesiastes 12:12-14 where he wrote, "But beyond this, my son, be warned: the writing of many books is endless, and excessive devotion to books is wearying to the body. The conclusion, when all has been heard, is: fear God and keep His commandments, because this applies to every person. For God will bring every act to judgment, everything which is hidden, whether it is good or evil."

Here then is the application I want to make. It is frightening to me when brethren use terms, express ideas, and promote positions that are denominational in origin and foreign to the language of the New Testament. It is frightening when we frequent "Christian" bookstores, not to purchase valid, scholarly research material (and even then we must be very careful and extremely discriminating), but to purchase the denominational pablum that lines the shelves, is designed to make everyone feel good, is filled with quaint and clever illustrations, makes us feel warm and fuzzy all over, and *is absolutely filled with error and "the language of Ashdod."* Even the so-called "Christian fiction" presents stories, told in a very convincing and exciting way, which are built around *false doctrine.*

The men whose works fill the "Christian" bestseller lists—the Colsons, Swindolls, Shullers, LaHayes—are false teachers who are doing incredible damage by leading so many people astray. I have a relative who is a devout Catholic. She asked me about Max Lucado. She told me how much she enjoys reading his books. Why? Because Max Lucado would never put anything in one of his books that would cause her to question where she is doctrinally. She can read his works, or any others found on those "Christian" bestseller lists, and come away feeling absolutely good about herself. In many cases it is not that what they have taught is false (although often it blatantly is), but what they studiously will not teach.

A steady diet of such trite, simplistic pap eventually makes its way into our language, and cute-sounding denominational catchphrases begin to take the place of simple Bible terms and truths. Instead of the "utterances of God" (1 Pet. 4:11), instead of calling Bible things by Bible names, instead of staunchly maintaining our identity as people of *the book*, we can begin to sound like everybody else. I call it "the language of Ashdod," because it has nothing to do with the language of God's people.

April 21

I Have Met Diotrephes

At first glance you may be inclined to ask yourself, "What in the world does he mean by, 'I have met Diotrephes'?" That is a good question. I use that statement in much the same way that John wrote of "the spirit of the antichrist" in 1 John 4:3. Obviously I have not met the original Diotrephes about whom John spoke in 3 John, but I have met those with his spirit or attitude.

In 3 John 9-10 we read, "I wrote something to the church; but Diotrephes, who loves to be first among them, does not accept what we say. For this reason, if I come, I will call attention to his deed which he does, unjustly accusing us with wicked words; and not satisfied with this, neither does he himself receive the brethren, and he forbids those who desire to do so, and puts them out of the church."

As one studies this short letter, it is apparent that John had previously written a letter to the church of which Gaius was a member and sent it by the hand of some brethren whom Gaius had graciously received. Diotrephes rejected both the letter and the messengers. The name of Diotrephes, while not as well known by non-Bible students as the name of Judas, has become synonymous among us for something very wicked and destructive in the church.

What did this man do? Diotrephes loved to have the preeminence. Things would go his way, or they would not go at all. You have met him too, haven't you? Maybe he is an elder, maybe a preacher, maybe a deacon or one of the other members. Truth be told, I met a Diotrephes on more than one occasion who was a woman. It is a domineering person in a local congregation who demands his or her own way, come what may.

The Diotrephes about whom John was writing had even denied the authority of an apostle as he strove to control the local church. He refused to accept what John had written in an attempt to make himself appear greater. It reminds me of a time when I preached about pride in a local congregation, only to have one such individual, feeling the sting of the Word of God, leave the auditorium, enter an adult Bible class that took place immediately afterward, and inform the class that the Bible only condemned pride of man toward God, not man toward man. Thus he rejected outright everything the Bible has to say about pride from man to man, or man over man. That is the spirit of Diotrephes!

Diotrephes sought to prejudice the minds of the faithful members of the congregation who wanted to help those sent by John, even to the extent of railroading them out of the congregation.

John wasn't afraid of Diotrephes, and faithful Christians can't be afraid of those with the spirit of Diotrephes either. Such an individual, or individuals, can only occupy positions of preeminence if other Christians let them. I am not talking about being unkind to such individuals; I am talking about being faithful to the Lord. I am talking about being concerned for their souls. Those with the spirit of Diotrephes must be stopped. God's Word is the instrument to stop them.

April 22

The Seasons of Life (1)

In Ecclesiastes 3:1-2 we find, "There is an appointed time for everything. And there is a time for every event under heaven—a time to give birth, and a time to die; a time to plant, and a time to uproot what is planted."

March is the month that ushers in spring. I love this time of year. It is the time when everything starts to come alive. The trees begin to bud and the flowers start to bloom. The air becomes filled with the sounds of all different kinds of birds and more little animals can be seen running around. It is the time of rebirth as nature shakes off the shackles of a long winter season and reasserts the beauty of life.

Have you ever noticed how the yearly cycle of life closely parallels the life of a Christian? Starting with spring and the bursting forth of life anew, it is easy to make the comparison. In John 3:3 Jesus made the following statement to Nicodemus, "Truly, truly, I say to you, unless one is born again, he cannot see the kingdom of God." When a man is born into this world he is spiritually alive, sinless, and in fellowship with the Father. However, at some point in his life he will sin; he will violate God's law. When that happens, he dies spiritually and is separated from God. Thus a new birth is required, a restoration of the fellowship with the Father that is enjoyed only by those whom He counts righteous. This "new birth" is detailed in Romans 6:3-6 where Paul wrote:

> Or do you not know that all of us who have been baptized into Christ Jesus have been baptized into His death? Therefore we have been buried with Him through baptism into death, in order that as Christ was raised from the dead through the glory of the Father, so we too might walk in newness of life. For if we have become united with Him in the likeness of His death, certainly we shall be also in the likeness of His resurrection, knowing this, that our old self was crucified with Him, that our body of sin might be done away with, that we should no longer be slaves to sin.

2 Corinthians 5:17 also needs to be noticed. Paul wrote, "Therefore if any man is in Christ, he is a new creature; the old things passed away; behold, new things have come."

Did you notice in the passage from Romans 6 the phrase, "newness of life"? Did you notice in 2 Corinthians 5:17, "a new creature" and "new things have come"? Doesn't that remind you of spring? The infant buds are bursting forth, the baby animals are coming out for their first real experience with life, and there is freshness and excitement.

Doesn't that bring to mind the new Christians, the "babes in Christ"? They are truly "born again," "all things are become new." There is a freshness and excitement to a new Christian that is something to see. Just as the trees and flowers soak up the sunshine and the rain of spring, receiving their proper nourishment to enable them to grow, so too the new Christians, "like newborn babes, long for the pure milk of the word, that by it they may grow in respect to salvation" (1 Pet. 2:2).

It is so exciting to see a new Christian. Almost in a rush, they try to fill themselves with the Word of God, as if to make up for lost time, and to reach the point of spiritual maturity where they will be equipped to handle the "meat" of the Word, and not the "milk" only. They are out in the world talking to people about their salvation, and when they are with their fellow Christians, they are asking questions, trying to grow. I enjoy spring, and I enjoy "babes in Christ."

Unfortunately, not all of the buds that come out in the spring are going to make it to maturity. Some simply won't have the root system that they need to sustain them. Others will not be able to withstand the powerful spring storms that they will have to face. Still others will have someone come along and pluck them out before they really have a chance to grow.

Unfortunately, some of the newborn "babes in Christ" are not going to make it to maturity either. I am reminded of the parable of the Sower, and specifically the Lord's explanation of it found in Luke 8:11-15:

> Now the parable is this: the seed is the word of God. And those beside the road are those who have heard; then the devil comes and takes away the word from their heart, so that they may not believe and be saved. And those on the rocky soil are those who, when they hear, receive the word with joy; and these have no firm root; they believe for a while, and in time of temptation fall away. And the seed which fell among the thorns, these are the ones who have heard, and as they go on their way they are choked with worries and riches and pleasures of this life, and bring no fruit to maturity. And the seed in the good soil, these are the ones who have heard the word in an honest and good heart, and hold it fast, and bear fruit with perseverance.

April 23

The Seasons of Life (2)

Eventually June 21 arrives, and those buds and animals that began in the spring and made it to a certain degree of maturity now enter into summer. Summer is in many ways the most difficult season of the year. I guess you could almost refer to it as the adulthood of nature. There will be periods of dryness, if not outright drought, when there will be very little rain to nourish the plants, and they will start to wilt. Some will die and not make it through;

others will be almost gone, only to revive when the rains begin again. There will be occasions of terrible storms. Sometimes those summer storms that seem to arise so quickly can be devastating in their ferocity. Whole crops can be destroyed, giant trees uprooted and torn apart, and they do not make it to fall. But I suspect that the most difficult part of summer for the plants and animals of nature is just the day-to-day process of surviving. The newness and the excitement of life wears off, and it is a matter of going day to day, sometimes in wilting heat.

But, oh, the trees that stand tall during the summer are wondrous things to behold! They provide oxygen to all of nature. They supply homes to countless animals and birds, and they supply much-needed shade to those who are weary and hot. The flowers of summer can be so beautiful that they can make us forget the heat and marvel at the wonders of God's creation.

So, too, it is in the life of a Christian. Eventually there comes a time when we are no longer "babes in Christ." There comes a time when God expects us to be functioning as adult Christians. The fervor and enthusiasm that characterized the earliest years of being a Christian are replaced by a more mature enthusiasm that is flavored by knowledge and an ever-deepening love for the Lord. I liken this to the summer in the life of a child of God. This is the day to day living of a faithful servant.

No life is completely tranquil. No life of any length is lived without experiencing pain and setbacks. There are good times and there are bad times. There are times when our faith is so strong, and there are other times when it is not quite as strong as it should, and needs, to be. There will be different "storms of life" that will confront us—being a Christian does not make us immune to having bad things happen. But even more than the wonderful peaks and the difficult valleys we will face, are the everyday struggles as we seek to serve our Lord. A mature Christian realizes that sometimes it is a matter of perseverance, a matter of just hanging in there. A mature Christian realizes that no matter how tough the walk may be, or for that matter how mundane and ordinary it may appear, he or she walks with the Lord. So day after day, week after week, month after month, and year after year the faithful Christian just keeps on going, remaining "steadfast, immovable, always abounding in the work of the Lord, knowing that your toil is not in vain in the Lord" (1 Cor. 15:58).

Consider Hebrews 12:1-13. What a wonderful lesson it teaches us concerning patience and perseverance:

Therefore, since we have so great a cloud of witnesses surrounding us, let us also lay aside every encumbrance, and the sin which so easily entangles us, and let us run with endurance the race that is set before us, fixing our eyes on Jesus, the author and perfecter of faith, who for the joy set before Him endured the cross, despising the shame, and has sat down at the right hand of the throne of God. For consider Him who has endured such hostility by sinners against Himself, so that you may not grow weary and lose heart. You have not yet resisted to the point of shedding blood in your striving against sin; and you have forgotten the exhortation which is addressed to you as sons. My son, do not regard lightly the discipline of the Lord, nor faint when you are reproved by Him; for those whom the Lord loves He disciplines, and He scourges every son whom He receives. It is for discipline that you endure; God deals with you as with sons; for what son is there whom his father does not discipline? But if you are without discipline, of which all have become partakers, then you are illegitimate children and not sons. Furthermore, we had earthly fathers to discipline us, and we respected them; shall we not much rather be subject to the Father of spirits, and live? For they disciplined us for a short time as seemed best to them, but He disciplines us for our good, that we may share His holiness. All discipline for the moment seems not to be joyful, but sorrowful; yet to those who have been trained by it, afterwards it yields the peaceful fruit of righteousness. Therefore, strengthen the hands that are weak and the knees that are feeble, and make straight paths for your feet, so that the limb which is lame may not be put out of joint, but rather be healed.

Sometimes in the summer of our lives as Christians, we just have to keep on going, regardless of what happens. In each of the letters to the seven churches in Revelation 2 and 3, Jesus ended by saying, "To him who overcomes" or "he who overcomes," and then spoke of the reward that would belong to such an individual. What Jesus was urging upon all Christians is the need to be faithful, to remain strong, to hang in there, to continue steadfast to the end.

April 24

The Seasons of Life (3)

As is the way with nature, so it is with the life of a Christian. September 23 rolls around, and fall arrives. Of all the seasons of the year, fall is my favorite. All of the leaves that have made it through the spring and the long, hot months of summer, are now winding down their lives. The closer they get to the end, the more beautiful they are. I love to walk in the woods in the fall. Truly, there is no canvas painted by man that is as beautiful as the canvas that God paints with the vibrant colors of autumn. It is as though, before they pass from this life, the leaves are determined to burst forth with one more magnificent splash of beauty to remind us of how wonderful they have been. Then they fall to the earth, and over the process of time actually make the earth more fertile so that more beautiful leaves may grow.

Faithful Christians in the autumn of their lives are the most beautiful of all. They are the ones who so long ago took root. They survived the trials and tribulations; the storms of life did not cause them to be lost, and the day-to-day grind of living faithfully did not deter them. They have now come out on the other side of the summer of their lives and are beautiful to behold. I think of the aged Apostle Paul sitting in a Roman prison. What a life he had led! He had given years of toil and service for the Lord and for his fellow man. He had taken root and hung on. He had remained steadfast and constant in his labor! Now he could say:

> For I am already being poured out as a drink offering, and the time of my departure has come. I have fought the good fight, I have finished the course, I have kept the faith; in the future there is laid up for me the crown of righteousness, which the Lord, the righteous Judge, will award to me on that day; and not only to me, but also to all who have loved His appearing (2 Tim. 4:6-8).

I love to talk with older Christians in the autumn of their lives. They are the most beautiful. We know that in just the natural way of things, their time to pass to where faith becomes sight is near—and when they do, our hearts will ache. But we will be able to grow a little bit better because they were here.

Then comes the winter, and I like to think of winter as the period of waiting for the faithful Christian who has gone on. What are they waiting for? They are waiting for Jesus to return and the beginning of a state that will never change or end. Paul put it this way in 1 Corinthians 15:50-57:

> Now I say this, brethren, that flesh and blood cannot inherit the kingdom of God; nor does the perishable inherit the imperishable. Behold, I tell you a mystery; we shall not all sleep, but we shall all be changed, in a moment, in the twinkling of an eye, at the last trumpet; for the trumpet will sound, and the dead will be raised imperishable, and we shall be changed. For this perishable must put on the imperishable, and this mortal must put on immortality. But

when this perishable will have put on the imperishable, and this mortal will have put on immortality, then will come about the saying that is written, Death is swallowed up in victory. O Death, where is your victory? O Death, where is your sting? The sting of death is sin, and the power of sin is the law; but thanks be to God, who gives us the victory through our Lord Jesus Christ.

Be a faithful Christian. It is the only life worth living, and it is the only life that promises eternal joy.

April 25

What Is Going on?

Many times I have been reminded that the Lord's church is made up of imperfect people, like me, and that we have not yet reached the goal of reflecting the character of Christ to the world. During one short period of time, I had been to four different congregations and had visitors to my home from a fifth. Let me explain what I mean from my opening statement.

In one congregation where I was asked to speak one evening, I had really looked forward to perhaps seeing one of my very best friends who preaches at another congregation in that particular city. He was not there. I found out that he wasn't there for reasons that I must say are difficult, and I am not sure how I would have handled them either. They had to do with some preachers and elders, and their actions toward each other.

I went to another congregation to preach one lesson, by request, and because of strong disagreements about a particular subject, some of the folks there would have little or nothing to do with me. And I must admit, I wasn't real tickled to be there either. It was the first time in my life as a preacher that I have been verbally heckled during the time I was being introduced. It was a different experience.

So I went to another congregation. As I walked in the door practically the first thing that was said to me by one of the preachers who was doing the speaking was that the congregation where I was about to hold a gospel meeting had cancelled a meeting that he was supposed to have there. And I was informed that they also would not announce the meeting of the congregation where I was visiting that evening.

The visitors that we had at home are dear and wonderful friends that I love with all of my heart. They are favorites of mine, if it is okay to have favorites. Solely because they care and would like to see everything taken care of as it should be, they brought up some of the darkest memories of my life that have everything to do with the ungodly way that brethren can treat each other from time to time.

So off I went to the fourth congregation, and I had a wonderful time. The attendance was very good and friends and visitors came from miles away to hear the gospel. But truth be told, certain preacher friends of mine came who would not be asked to lead in prayer at this congregation, and some of them probably wouldn't ask the preacher at this fourth congregation to lead prayer where they preach either.

What is going on?

In Galatians 5:13-15 Paul wrote, "For, brethren, ye have been called unto liberty; only use not liberty for an occasion to the flesh, but by love serve one another. For all the law is fulfilled in one word, even in this; Thou shalt love thy neighbor as thyself. But if ye bite and devour one another, take heed that ye be not consumed one of another."

When Paul begins the 15th verse with the word, "But," he is drawing a contrast between "loving thy neighbor as thyself" and "biting and devouring one another." It is a conditional sentence that assumes the "biting" and the "devouring" to be a reality, and the conclusion follows logically from that assumption. In other words, biting and devouring were already taking place among the Galatians. The Lord's church has had almost 2,000 years to stop it. How good of a job are we doing?

Brother Mike Willis gave the following explanation of verse 15 in his commentary on Galatians: "The comparison is to vicious animals biting and devouring one another until they kill each other. The word *dakno* (bite) literally means 'to bite with the teeth' and then metaphorically means to 'wound the soul, cut, lacerate, rend with reproaches.' *Katesthio* (devour) literally means 'to eat up, consume, devour, swallow.'"

How graphically the Holy Spirit describes what we can do to each other! We can pick, fuss, fight, gossip, backbite, and verbally assault until we are used up—destroyed. That can be true numerically, but more importantly, it happens spiritually. It can reach in and rip the heart out of a child of God. It can make you feel almost punch-drunk until you either withdraw into your own little protected shell, or you can find yourself doing the same kind of thing—talking about folks and being anxious to hear all the latest about everybody.

I just do not believe that this is what the Lord prayed for with the shadow of the cross looming over Him less than twenty-four hours away. Jesus prayed, "Neither pray I for these alone, but for them also which shall believe on me through their word; that they all may be one, as Thou, Father, art in Me, and I in Thee, that they also may be one in us; that the world may believe that Thou hast sent Me" (John 17:20-21).

It is so easy to get caught up in this stuff, and there have been times in my past when I have. I pray for forgiveness. Our time on earth is too short and there is too much work to do!

How Should We View the Elders?

When scripturally and completely organized, each local congregation will be overseen by a plurality of elders. The rest of the congregation is comprised of deacons and the other saints. Philippians 1:1 is the simplest statement of this organization of which I know. Paul began his letter to the church in Philippi with the words, "Paul and Timotheus, the servants of Jesus Christ, to all the saints in Christ Jesus which are at Philippi, with the bishops and deacons."

Faithful Christians recognize that between the local congregation and the Lord in heaven, there exists no other level of organization. But what are the responsibilities of the members of a local congregation toward the elders who oversee it? There are several passages that give us insight into how the Lord expects and demands that Christians treat faithful elders in the congregation of which we are members.

1 Thessalonians 5:12 says, "And we beseech you, brethren, to know them which labor among you, and are over you in the Lord, and admonish you." The idea of "knowing" the elders involves more than simply being acquainted with them. The meaning of "to know" is "to respect, highly regard, recognize and appreciate." Actually it is a sin to disrespect, dishonor, ridicule, or *destruc-*

tively criticize elders of the church. This is not to say that elders are perfect and can never be constructively criticized; but it is to say that we should help them in every way we can in their work as they "labor among us." To destructively criticize elders is to destroy their effectiveness as leaders of the Lord's people and to call into question the wisdom and authority of God's pattern.

1 Thessalonians 5:13 tells us, "And to esteem them very highly in love for their work's sake. And be at peace among yourselves." Elders who are doing the very best they can in accordance with God's word are to be loved and esteemed for their very work's sake. We should help, cooperate with, and encourage them, making their job as enjoyable as possible. The exhortation to "be at peace among yourselves" emphasizes that point. Truly, the effectiveness and the efficiency of the elders in doing their work and in causing the church to do a good work, depends upon peace and unity among the brethren. Every single member should be involved in "endeavoring to keep the unity of the spirit in the bond of peace" (Ephesians 4:3). That unity and peace cannot be attained and maintained unless *every member* is working for it. "Behold how good and how pleasant it is for brethren to dwell together in unity!" (Psalm 133:1).

April 27

Further Consideration of How We Should View the Elders

Members of a congregation have responsibilities toward the elders of that congregation. Here are a few of them.

Hebrews 13:7 commands, "Remember them which have the rule over you, who have spoken unto you the word of the God whose faith follow, considering the end of their conversation." We are to imitate, or follow, the faith of the elders. They have the responsibility to be examples to us in love, faith, liberality, attendance, study, and just in generally doing the work of the Lord. Our responsibility is to emulate them in these good things.

Hebrews 13:17 exhorts us with these words, "Obey them that have the rule over you, and submit yourselves: for they watch for your souls, as they that must give account, that they may do it with joy, and not with grief, for that is unprofitable for you." Simply put, elders are to rule in accordance with God's word, and members are to submit and obey. Their rule is not as lords over the congregation (1 Pet. 5:2-3), but as those who enforce the law of Christ.

Consider 1 Timothy 5:19. "Against an elder receive not an accusation, but before two or three witnesses." Let's face it, for some it is easy to pick at flaws and be a "mote-finder" (Matt. 7:1-5). And it is easy for some to be hypercritical of everybody but themselves, like the Pharisee in the Lord's parable of Luke 18:9-14. But members should not make, nor should we pay any attention to, idle charges against an elder. To do so is to sin. Elders are not perfect people—no one is. They can sin and even espouse error. Paul told the Ephesian elders in Acts 20:29-30, "For I know this, that after my departing shall grievous wolves enter in among you, not sparing the flock. Also of your own selves shall men arise, speaking perverse things, to draw away disciples after them." If a charge is to be brought concerning an elder, two or three witnesses must prove it. I know from experience that it is easy for shots to be taken at men in their position.

Finally, look at James 5:14, "Is any sick among you? Let him call for the elders of the church; and let them pray over him, anointing him with oil in the name of the Lord." Those who are sick are to call for the elders if they want them to come. Interestingly, this places the responsibility on the shoulders of the members. Sometimes a Christian will say, "I was sick and the elders didn't come to see me." My question has often been in response, "Did you call the elders?" When good "shepherds" learn of sick "sheep" in their fold, they will try to visit, if possible, and pray for them and see that their needs are met. However, even the best shepherds are not omniscient or omnipresent. They can't visit the sick if they don't know they are sick, nor can they be in two places at the same time.

God's pattern works, if all will abide by it. A congregation of the Lord's people should be the most peaceful, efficient body there is.

April 28

"There I Am in Their Midst" (1)

On August 17, 2001, I had the opportunity to fulfill a lifelong dream. Having been raised Roman Catholic, spent twelve years as a student in parochial schools, and toyed with the idea of a vocation as a Roman Catholic priest, I dreamed of the day when I could stand within the walls of St. Peter's Basilica in Rome. Even after learning the truth and rendering my obedience to the gospel of Christ, leaving the false religion of Catholicism behind forever, I still longed to see the center of what had been the church of my childhood. On August 17, 2001, I walked through its doors.

St. Peter's Basilica is the largest church building the world. If one did not know this upon entering into it, he would learn very quickly. On the floor of the Basilica, running down its center, the lengths of the other largest church buildings in the world are clearly marked. Thus it demonstrated for all to see that no other building can match St. Peter's in Rome.

For sheer magnitude, it is breathtaking. I cannot begin to describe the incredible artwork that adorns the building. As you enter, to the right is the beautiful marble sculpture of Michelangelo's Pieta. Seemingly without end, there is one beautiful statue after another, one beautiful painting after another, incredible woodwork, pure gold lattice and gilding, magnificent mosaics, marble figures on pillars, ceiling, and walls. There are six-foot-high letters that surround the top of the main nave, which is longer than three football fields, and this nave is enclosed by a precious bronze canopy that covers the papal altar, under which Peter is supposed to be buried. That bronze canopy is constructed from the melted statue of Colossus that once stood before the great Roman arena and from which it received its name, the Colosseum.

Near the papal altar is the statue of Peter. The feet of Peter are practically worn away from the centuries of Roman Catholic pilgrims who have filed by and run their hands across the feet of that statue, asking Peter for help and graces. Around the corner from that statue is the body of Pope John XXIII, exhumed and lying in state since his beatification, which is the first step in the process of canonization.

I could go on and on and never do this building justice in my description. Even on that Friday morning there were thousands of people there, and as I left the building, I was standing before St. Peter's Square, into which thousands upon thousands of people flock to hear the papal address. It is surrounded by columns that are topped with statues of various figures. From a physical standpoint I have never seen anything that comes even close to matching the beauty, the awesomeness, and the ornateness of the center of Roman Catholicism.

I must not fail to mention the Vatican souvenir shop, located right outside the entrance to the Square. Here a person can buy just about any kind of Roman Catholic article desired, and there is even an arrangement to have any item bought taken inside the Vatican itself, blessed, and delivered to your hotel. Statues, rosaries, books, medals, scapulars, postcards, holy cards—name it, and it is probably there.

Many, many things went through my mind as I beheld this building that at one time had meant so much to me. The emotions I felt were staggering as I beheld this monument to man-made religion. As the flashbulbs were popping, as the tour guides were speaking and pointing, as the people stood with their mouths gaping open, I thought of the Lord's statement in Matthew 8:20, "The foxes have holes, and the birds of the air have nests; but the Son of Man has nowhere to lay His head." Where did man get the idea that these visual displays mean anything at all to God? As I wandered into the souvenir shop and saw the hordes of people snatching up everything they could get their hands on, I thought of Jesus making a scourge of cords, pouring out the coins of the moneychangers, and overturning their tables while proclaiming, "Take these things away; stop making My Father's house a house of merchandise."

I saw people bowing before the crypts and the images of past popes who are entombed within the confines of St. Peter's. I thought of the ridiculous Roman Catholic distinction between the various forms of worship; cultus latriae, cultus hyperduliae, and cultus duliae. To the minds of the people bowing before those statues, there was no difference. As these people bowed before the statue of Peter and ran their hands across its feet, I knew they did not know that Peter himself had told Cornelius, "Stand up; I too am just a man!" when Cornelius had fallen at his feet in worship. They did not know it because the Roman Catholic authorities had not told them, and they were content to have it so. They did not know that Jesus had said in Matthew 23:8-12, "But do not be called Rabbi; for One is your Teacher, and you are all brothers. And do not call anyone on earth your father; for One is your Father, He who is in heaven. And do not be called leaders; for One is your Leader, that is, Christ. But the greatest among you shall be your servant. And whoever exalts himself shall be humbled; and whoever humbles himself shall be exalted."

"There I Am in Their Midst" (2)

Even though my heart aches, I am glad I went to St. Peter's Basilica in Rome. The primary reason for that gladness is something else that happened on my way there.

On August 12, I was privileged to meet with a group of brethren in London, England. I took the subway to get there, and had to walk down a street in a somewhat seedy section of town. Without a sign to announce its location or any physical beauty to attract one to it, I came to a community room in the midst of what would be called a housing project in the States. It was not well painted, nor fancy in any way. As a matter of fact it was just a room. But into this room came about forty brethren from all over London to worship. We sat on chairs that we all helped to set up. The brethren were like most brethren everywhere in that they greeted us so warmly and with such love.

Oh, we sang together, prayed together, partook of the Lord's Supper together, gave of our means together, and studied from God's Word. There was nothing there that could be called enticing or attractive from a worldly standpoint, but I know that the Lord was there. There was no other reason for anyone to be there but to worship God.

The magnificent St. Peter's Basilica in Rome is not what God is all about; but those forty or so humble brethren meeting together in a rented hall truly is. I think of us here in the United States being so often concerned about the buildings in which we meet, building more than we need, fancier than we need, to put on a good show. I am not talking about a nice and appropriate meeting place to conduct our worship to the Lord, nor am I talking about taking care of what we do have. But I am talking about really knowing what is important—and the church is not a building. It doesn't matter how big, beautiful, and ornate it may be.

St. Peter's may very well stand until the time that the Lord returns. Then that magnificent building with all of its priceless treasures will be gone. Peter told us, "But the day of the Lord will come like a thief, in which the heavens will pass away with a roar and the elements will be destroyed with intense heat, and the earth and its works will be burned up" (2 Pet. 3:10). But the true church, the church of Christ that knows nothing of magnificent buildings and priceless earthly treasures, will be delivered up to God the Father to be with the Lord forever.

April 30

Just a Normal Person

Every now and then I find myself feeling inadequate to accomplish some task for the Lord that I have the opportunity to do. Have you ever felt that way? Perhaps the chance to talk to someone at work about the Lord presented itself, and yet you just felt ill equipped to do it. Maybe you have hesitated to go door-to-door with the congregation because of the possibility of getting into a discussion with someone. Maybe somebody needed spiritually sound advice about a problem he was having, and you just didn't feel qualified to give it.

We have all felt the feeling of inadequacy at one time or another. We have all felt like we are nobody special, just a normal person working hard to get by. There are so many others better qualified, better equipped, better educated, more polished and professional who can do the work of the Lord much better than me. I would like to look at just a few normal people, "blue collar" we might call them, just working hard trying to get by, who God used in a great way.

Somewhere around 760 to 750 B.C., in the wild country west of the Dead Sea, in a wide stretch of open land known as "The Wilderness of Judea," there was a herdsman. He even referred to himself as being "among the herdsmen of Tekoa." His name was Amos. In Amos 7:14-15 he described himself in this manner, "I am not a prophet, nor am I the son of a prophet; for I am a herdsman and a grower of sycamore figs. But the Lord took me from following the flock and the Lord said to me, Go prophesy to My people Israel." Amos was just a normal person. He was not trained in any special schools for his task. When we read the book that bears his name, we just have to be impressed. Here was Amos, a native of Judea, sent to prophesy to the northern kingdom, Israel. He was certainly not fancy. His vocabulary, the figures of speech that he used, his illustrations, all spoke of the country life that he had led. He was exceedingly blunt, and it is clear that he had not learned the "fine art" of going all around a subject without ever getting right to the point. But God used him, just like He can use you and me. There is no such thing as an inadequately equipped person if that person is with the Lord, believing and obeying the truth.

Let's look at a very important list of people who we find in Matthew 10:2-4, "Now the names of the twelve apostles are these: The first, Simon, who is called Peter, and Andrew his brother; and James the son of Zebedee, and John his brother: Philip and Bartholomew, Thomas and Matthew the tax-gatherer; James the son of Alphaeus, and Thaddaeus; Simon the Zealot, and Judas Iscariot, the one who betrayed Him." To this list we should add Matthias, who was chosen to replace Judas, and Paul.

What were these men? Were they highly educated? Only Paul was what could be called a scholar. Were they wealthy? Maybe Matthew had money, having been a publican, but there is no indication that any of them were men of means. Were any of them politically influential? Simon was a zealot, a nationalist; but that background certainly does not seem conducive to being an apostle of the Lord.

So what were these men? They were normal people like you and me. They had jobs and families. They held to many of the popular misconceptions of their times. They were influenced by the society in which they lived. They made mistakes and sometimes just did not understand. At times they struggled to keep things in the proper perspective; the Lord often had to deal with their priorities. In other words, *they were normal people just like you and me.*

However, the Lord looked at the hearts of these normal people and saw anything but inadequacy. Yes, they were not the best educated, they were sometimes backward and superstitious, and often ambitious. But you know what they had? They had faith in Jesus. They believed in Him so completely, and they committed themselves to Him so totally, that they would learn any lesson and endure any hardship for Him. These "normal people" who believed in Jesus so completely were truly powerful men. They were powerful in their humble simplicity and transformed by their tenacious faith and love for the Lord.

You and I can be the same way. I'll gladly be as "normal" as the herdsman, Amos. I'll gladly be as "normal" as the fisherman, Peter, or the tax collector, Matthew. With Jesus we are all anything but "normal." "I can do all things through Him who strengthens me" (Phil. 4:13). Does that sound "normal" to you?

May 1

"Each Man Has His Own Gift from God"

In 1 Corinthians 7:1-9 the apostle Paul wrote:

Now concerning the things about which you wrote, it is good for a man not to touch a woman. But because of immoralities, let each man have his own wife, and let each woman have her own husband. Let the husband fulfill his duty to his wife, and likewise also the wife to her husband. The wife does not have authority over her own body, but the husband does; and likewise also the husband does not have authority over his own body, but the wife does. Stop depriving one another, except by agreement for a time that you may devote yourselves to prayer, and come together again lest Satan tempt you because of your lack of self-control. But this I say by way of concession, not of command. Yet I wish that all men were even as I myself am. However, each man has his own gift from God, one in this manner, and another in that. But I say to the unmarried and to widows that it is good for them if they remain even as I. But if they do not have self-control, let them marry; for it is better to marry than to burn.

We do not know all of the questions that the Corinthian brethren had written to Paul concerning marriage. However, an examination of what Paul wrote gives us a pretty good idea of at least some of what they were asking. It is apparent that the relative desirability of being married or single was involved in their questions, as well as whether or not one state or the other was required.

Paul began his answer, under the inspiration of the Holy Spirit, by showing that marriage is not a moral obligation bound upon all people. Perhaps some were saying that it was required for all to be married, or at least be in the process of looking for a mate. Paul wrote, "It is good for a man not to touch a woman." Perhaps some were teaching that celibacy was an inherently better way of life. Paul wrote, "Let each man have his own wife, and let each woman have her own husband." It is obvious from 1 Corinthians 7:1-2 that Paul is teaching that *both* states are lawful. It is no sin to marry (provided one has the right to do so), and it is no sin to remain unmarried. Some may feel that celibacy is best for them and have the gift to remain that way; let them remain single. Others, lacking that particular gift, recognize that marriage is the most desirable state for them; let them marry.

Certain things are important to remember in a discussion of this issue. First of all, the apostle Paul is not seeking to elevate celibacy above marriage. In creation God looked over what He had wrought, and said in Genesis 2:18, "It is not good for the man to be alone; I will make him a helper suitable for him." God created woman for the man and brought the two together. In Ephesians 5:22-33 the apostle Paul used the marriage relationship to illustrate the intimacy and beauty of the relationship of Christ and His church. In 1 Timothy 4:1-3 Paul said that those who "forbid marriage" were "paying attention to deceitful spirits and doctrines of demons." The Hebrew writer put it this way in Hebrews 13:4, "Let marriage be held in honor among all, and let the marriage bed be undefiled; for fornicators and adulterers God will judge."

We must also recognize that 1 Corinthians 7:26 helps us to understand the entire chapter. Paul wrote about the "present distress" that the church was undergoing and that needed to be considered when they were making a decision among these lines. But generally speaking, marriage is the way that most people should go.

May 2

Living Single

On the other hand, to remain unmarried and celibate as a choice is commended to those who have the gift of self-control. Paul is definitely looking at that ability as a gift from God, whether under "the present distress" or not. It brings to mind part of a discussion that Jesus had with some Pharisees and also with the disciples in Matthew 19. Starting in verse 9 Jesus said:

> And I say to you, whoever divorces his wife, except for immorality, and marries another woman commits adultery. The disciples said to Him, If the relationship of the man with his wife is like this, it is better not to marry. But He said to them, Not all men can accept this statement, but only those to whom it has been given. For there are eunuchs who were born that way from their mother's womb; and there are eunuchs who were made eunuchs by men; and there are also eunuchs who made themselves eunuchs for the sake of the kingdom of heaven. He who is able to accept this, let him accept it.

There are certain advantages to remaining single, provided that one has the ability to subjugate his physical desires. One who is single, quite naturally, does not have the same cares that a married individual has. Paul addressed this point in 1 Corinthians 7:32-34 when he wrote:

> But I want you to be free from concern. One who is unmarried is concerned about the things of the Lord, how he may please the Lord; but one who is married is concerned about the things of the world, how he may please his wife, and his interests are divided. And the woman who is unmarried, and the virgin, is concerned about the things of the Lord, that she may be holy both in body and spirit; but one who is married is concerned about the things of the world, how she may please her husband.

This is so whether in times of particular distress or not, but it is easy to see how in times of persecution it would be especially true.

Being single is not a state to be belittled. It can be a situation of special opportunities. Those who adopt the single state as a choice from the right motives and who possess the ability to control themselves are worthy of esteem. They can do much in the service of the Lord.

I have often found myself feeling sorry for single adults in the church. Not because they are single adults, but because of the questions they are so often asked—"So, do you have a man (or a woman) yet?" "How come you are not married?" "When are you going to get married?" And the all time insensitive statement, ranking right up there with "You have put on some weight" is "You aren't getting any younger, you know!"

Even those who by virtue of circumstances, and perhaps not by choice, find themselves compelled to live their lives as single Christians, are to be held in honor if they use it to advantage. Thankfully, we don't hear the term "old maid" much any more, but it has been my experience that some who have been called "old maids" have turned out to be the best of maids—faithful, godly women. And some men who have remained single, finding themselves unfettered by marital responsibilities, have demonstrated themselves to be patterns of excellence in the service of the Lord.

"Each man has his own gift from God!" Not everyone is the same, and aren't we thankful for that? Let each serve God according to the ability he possesses and the situation that best enables him to use it.

The Autumn Years

In my opinion, the most beautiful time of the year is autumn. What could be prettier than a tree-covered hillside bursting with color as the leaves turn? What could be more invigorating than the crispness in the air as the wind blows away the smog and haze of the dog days of summer? How interesting it is that the most majestic beauty of the leaves is not seen until the autumn, until the time when they are about to fall to the ground and be swept away. The last days of their lives are the most beautiful to behold. There is no sadness at this time because we know that the leaves will live again and the trees will once more be full.

How similar are the latter days of the faithful Christian. When the earlier days of toil and labor are but a memory, and the promised rest does not appear to be too far in the future—is there ever a time when the Christian is more beautiful than in the autumn years, especially in those days when the leaf is about to fall to the ground? What a joy to speak to a brother or sister who has just about completed the race, who has almost finished fighting the battle, and who knows that henceforth there is laid up for him or her a crown that the righteous judge will give at that day. Can anything make us feel better than the smile on the face of such a brother or sister in Christ? Can anything make us more confident of what lies beyond than the blessed assurance of one who has lived his or her life as a faithful servant of the Lord?

In 2 Corinthians 1:3-4 Paul wrote:

Blessed be the God and Father of our Lord Jesus Christ, the Father of mercies and God of all comfort; who comforts us in all our affliction so that we may be able to comfort those who are in any affliction with the comfort with which we ourselves are comforted by God.

What an incredible description of our God—"The God of all comfort; who comforts us in all our affliction. . . ."

I strongly suspect that those autumn years, and the days right before the leaf falls, is the time of life when the faithful Christian really comes to understand the meaning of "the God of all comfort." Yes, parents and friends may be long gone; spouses may have passed away as well. Maybe the body has worn out and doesn't function as it once did. Maybe the mind wanders and conversations are hard to have. But in the lucid moments, there is that comfort that comes only from a life of service to our God, "the God of all comfort." I strongly suspect that is why so many autumnal Christians have a smile on their faces.

May 4

"I Would You Were Cold or Hot!" (1)

The final of the seven letters to the churches in Revelation 2 and 3 is to the church at Laodicea. I find it to be the most disconcerting, and even frightening, of all the letters. It is found in Revelation 3:14-22, and this is how it reads:

> And to the angel of the church in Laodicea write: The Amen, the faithful and true Witness, the Beginning of the creation of God, says this: I know your deeds, that you are neither cold nor hot; I would that you were cold or hot. So because you are lukewarm, and neither hot nor cold, I will spit you out of My mouth. Because you say, I am rich, and have become wealthy, and have need of nothing, and you do not know that you are wretched and miserable and poor and blind and naked, I advise you to buy from Me gold refined by fire, that you may become rich, and white garments, that you may clothe yourself, and that the shame of your nakedness may not be revealed; and eye-salve to anoint your eyes, that you may see. Those whom I love, I reprove and discipline; be zealous therefore, and repent. Behold, I stand at the door and knock; if anyone hears My voice and opens the door, I will come in to him, and will dine with him, and he with Me. He who overcomes, I will grant to him to sit down with Me on My throne, as I also overcame and sat down with My Father on His throne. He who has an ear, let him hear what the Spirit says to the churches.

The city of Laodicea was located approximately forty-five miles southeast of the city of Philadelphia in Asia Minor, in an area famous for hot springs that emitted a lukewarm water. In the suburbs of the city there was a renowned school of medicine. It produced a very well known eye medicine called Phrygian powder. The region in which the city was found was also distinguished as the breeding ground of a special breed of sheep that produced very beautiful and glossy black wool. Most importantly, Laodicea was a center of commerce and was one of the wealthiest cities in the world. It had theaters, a magnificent stadium, fancy public baths, and a host of other leisure activities. It was a city of bankers and had a large retired community. All of these things help us to understand the condition of the church there.

As always, Jesus knew exactly what was going on in that congregation, just as He does today. This was a congregation that could not be described as "cold," meaning that they had never really experienced the power or influence of the gospel. Nor could it be said that they were "hot," meaning filled with zeal and "on fire" for the Lord. Truth be told, they were just "lukewarm," and the Lord would rather that they be cold, than to pretend to be faithful children of His. But what He truly desired was that they be hot—excited to be Christians and working hard to bring others to the Lord.

The interesting and frightening thing about this letter is that it shows just exactly how the Lord feels about a "lukewarm" attitude in a Christian. It is nauseating to Him. Did you ever notice how a cold or a hot drink may be just the thing needed to quench a thirst, but a lukewarm liquid just doesn't taste right, and can even make you gag? That is how the Lord feels toward those who are lukewarm toward him. He told the brethren in Laodicea that, if they did not repent, He would "spit you out of my mouth." Can you imagine thinking that you are a faithful Christian, but the Lord feels that way about you? That ought to be enough to make everybody sit up and do some real self-evaluation

The Lord didn't just leave it at that. He went on in verses 17-19 and told the Loadicean brethren what had brought them to this position; then he made an earnest plea for those thus afflicted to repent. Here was the problem. They figured that they were financially secure, had the things they wanted, weren't hurting for anything, and were pretty happy with themselves. This doesn't mean that the church consisted only of wealthy people, but it was a wealthy city, and the majority of the church was probably comfortably middle-class. In that socio-economic level, there is a tendency for folks to become satisfied, complacent, and rather formulaic in the way they worship God.

Personally, I believe that this happens to a large number of congregations today. Reasonably secure from a financial standpoint, and situated in a nice building in a good part of town, Christians can become pretty happy with themselves. They will have two meetings a year, one in the spring and one in the fall, with well-known gospel preachers. They support a man or two, maybe even mail out a bulletin. But individually there is very little personal evangelism taking place, and when the opportunity for evangelistic work is presented, comparatively few will show up for the work. They are actually "lukewarm" spiritually.

"I Would You Were Cold or Hot!" (2)

In Revelation 3:17, how did the Lord describe the actual spiritual condition of complacent and unmotivated Christians? He said that they didn't even know that they were *"wretched,"* which means distressed spiritually. They didn't even know that they were *"miserable,"* meaning actually to be pitied. Here they were pleased with themselves and the Lord is saying, "No, you are to be pitied, not envied." They didn't know that they were *"poor,"* spiritually speaking. From a material standpoint they were comfortable, not even realizing that the Lord was viewing them as spiritual beggars. Jesus said that they did not know they were *"blind"*—spiritually blind and unable to discern their own wretched condition. And He also called them *"naked."* They were not clothed in holiness, as they might have thought. They were standing uncovered and naked before the Lord. Wow! What a terrible picture! However, it is a picture that is repeated many times today—congregationally, and even more frequently, individually.

If I wanted to prove that I was a "lukewarm" Christian, how could I do it? Well, I could be sporadic in attendance. I could never darken the door on Sunday evenings or Wednesday nights, and I could refuse to attend Gospel Meetings or Vacation Bible School, no matter how fervently the elders pleaded for me to come. I could never read my Bible, or see to it that my children read theirs. I could neglect to sing at the one service I do attend and glance at my watch occasionally to see just how long it is taking. I could never visit the sick or write them an encouraging card. If I never talk to anybody about their salvation or invite anyone to a service or a study, that would be pretty good proof, too. I am sure you can think of many other ways that I could use to prove conclusively that I was a "lukewarm" Christian.

Here is what Jesus told the lukewarm Christians of Laodicea to do: "Buy from Me gold refined by fire, that you may become rich." The riches of the world will pass away, but faith tried by fire, tempered in the crucible of trials and tribulations through which the Lord has carried us, doesn't pass away. It is true riches.

Jesus also urged them to buy from Him "white garments, that you may clothe yourself, and that the shame of your nakedness may not be revealed." White symbolizes purity and holiness, and this reminds me of what Paul told the Philippian brethren in Philippians 4:8, "Finally brethren, whatever is true, whatever is honorable, whatever is right, whatever is pure, whatever is lovely, whatever is of good repute, if there is any excellence and if anything worthy of praise, let your mind dwell on these things."

In addition, Jesus told them to buy from Him "eye-salve to anoint your eyes, that you may see." They were blind to what they were really doing, blind to their faults and to their terrible condition. Jesus was telling them to open their eyes and see themselves as they really were, with no sugar coating. That is a tough thing to do.

I wonder how they reacted to the Lord's rebuke. Jesus made it clear in verse 19 that when He issues a rebuke and a stern chastisement, it is because of His love and concern for the individuals and should be understood as such. Even today, if all would understand the reasoning behind rebukes issued from the Word of God, there would be no getting angry, mad, or offended at sermons and lessons taken *from God's Word.* The reason for rebuke and chastisement is to turn people from sin, causing them to repent, and to be zealous (sometimes again) for the Lord.

I don't ever want the Lord to say to me, after becoming a child of His and having salvation in hand, "I know your deeds, that you are neither cold nor hot; I would that you were cold or hot. So because you are lukewarm, and neither hot or cold, I will spit you out of My mouth."

May 6

Meeting Musings

I never cease to marvel at the relationship that exists between good brethren wherever we might be. The tie that binds us together is stronger than any physical relationship could ever be. We are tied together by blood—the blood of the Lord Jesus Christ. So I sit in the homes of brethren as they share their food with me, and it is as though we have known each other for years instead of simply days. Brethren have offered me the key to their home while they were going to be away, just so I could be comfortable and have privacy. Some have shared with me burdens that they are enduring, really heavy-duty burdens and trials, and yet I looked out each night of the meeting and there they were—praising God in song and seriously listening to His word. It is a wonderful thing to be a Christian and a preacher of the gospel!

As I entered into one home during one of the gospel meetings, a little five-year-old girl went running behind a counter and hid behind her mother. When her mom asked what the problem was, she said, *"I am afraid of the preacher!"* That took me by surprise because I happen to think that I am one of the least scary people I know! However, her mom said something that got me to thinking. She said, "That's okay. A little fear is a good thing."

She was right. A little fear is a good thing. I was reminded of Hebrews 10:26-31 where we read:

> For if we go on sinning willfully after receiving the knowledge of the truth, there no longer remains a sacrifice for sins, but a certain terrifying expectation of judgment, and *the fury of a fire which will consume the adversaries.* Anyone who has set aside the Law of Moses dies without mercy on the testimony of two or three witnesses. How much severer punishment do you think he will deserve who has trampled under foot the Son of God, and has regarded as unclean the blood of the covenant by which he was sanctified, and has insulted the Spirit of grace? For we know Him who said, *Vengeance is mine, I will repay.* And again, *the Lord will judge His people. It is a terrifying thing to fall into the hands of the living God.*

God is love. 1 John 4:8 tells us that this is so. But many people choose to forget that God is also just. Romans 3:26 speaks of God as being "just and the justifier of the one who has faith in Jesus." In order for God to be "just," there must be punishment for the violation of His law, and there is. I don't want to go to hell. The very thought of it terrifies me. It should terrify everyone. There would be a whole lot fewer worldly people if they had a good and healthy dose of fear. Actually, all of those who comprise the church would be a whole lot stronger and more faithful with a bit of fear.

More Meeting Musings

At one gospel meeting, I was told of a sixteen-year-old girl who was killed in an automobile wreck. It was her friend and lab partner who told me about it. She had had her license for just a week and was driving sixty miles an hour in the rain where there was a posted thirty mile per hour speed limit. Evidently an animal of some sort ran in front of her car and she jerked the wheel. Her inexperience and lack of real preparation caused her to lose control, panic, go off the road, and end up hitting two trees. She died on the way to the hospital.

So often young people live their lives as though they are invincible. Nothing is going to happen to them, and they never consider death as something they will experience or that it could happen soon. How do we impress upon young people the urgency of obeying the Lord and living as God wants them to live? In Ephesians 6:1-3 Paul wrote, "Children, obey your parents in the Lord, for this is right. Honor your Father and Mother (which is the first command with promise), that it may be well with you, *and that you may live long on the earth.*" I know that Paul was not saying that every obedient, faithful child will live to a ripe old age, nor was he saying that every disobedient child will die in childhood. However, I do believe that he was stating a principle. The obedient child who honors his or her parents and God does not generally participate in ungodly and often dangerous activities.

How do we make young people understand that they are not invincible and that there are consequences for their actions, both good and bad? I could not help but think of Solomon's words found in Ecclesiastes 11:9-10: "Rejoice, young man, during your childhood, and let your heart be pleasant during the days of young manhood. And follow the impulses of your heart and the desires of your eyes. *Yet know that God will bring you to judgment for all these things.* So remove vexation from your heart and put away pain from your body, because childhood and the prime of life are fleeting."

Did anybody ever see an age limit on James 4:14-17? James wrote, "Yet you do not know what your life will be like tomorrow. You are just a vapor that appears for a little while and then vanishes away. Instead, you ought to say, If the Lord wills, we shall live and also do this or that. But as it is, you boast in your arrogance; all such boasting is evil. Therefore, to one who knows the right thing to do, and does not do it, to him it is sin."

The pull of the world is not lessening, it is getting stronger and stronger. At least that is the impression I get when I compare attendance at meetings now with attendance at meetings twenty years ago. People do not visit from other congregations like they used to, and it takes a more concentrated effort to get non-Christians to come. But the most distressing thing of all is that it is getting harder and harder to get the members of the congregation holding the meeting to attend faithfully. What else could be happening that is more important? Surely not television, or sports, or even school events are more important than serving the Lord and learning His word. What about the encouragement found from being with other Christians? What about being an encouragement to other Christians?

Leadership is vital to the welfare of a congregation of the Lord's people. Good, qualified, hard-working elders who lead the flock as a shepherd does his sheep can make all the difference in the world. Elders who try to drive the congregation or lord it over the flock, who make arbitrary decisions and rule with an iron fist, destroy rather than build up.

There are still churches like Sardis in the world—churches that "Have a name that you are alive, but you are dead" (Rev. 3:1).

Mom

In June my mother will have been dead for seven years. I find that hard to believe even as I write it. I miss her everyday. I am fifty-two years old and still with every event in my life—good, bad, or just different—one of the first things to go through my mind is, "I've got to call mom." I can hear her now.

"Mom, I'm going to be a grandpa. I'm not old enough to be a grandpa."

"How do you think I feel, Greg? My *baby* is going to be a grandpa!" And on and on we would go.

One of my earliest memories, and I don't even know how old I would have been at the time, occurred when I wandered down the street a little bit from our yard. I was young enough not to be allowed outside of the perimeter of our little plot of land in Deer Park, Ohio. I distinctly remember Mom grabbing me with one hand, dragging me home, all the while using the other hand to spank my bottom with a spatula, although in those days we called it a pancake turner.

I remember standing at the front door watching my brother and two sisters get on the bus for school, and then racing Mom back to her bedroom and jumping into bed. I always wanted to get her side because her pillow smelled so good. After I fell back to sleep, Mom would get up and go about her business.

All the while I was growing up, Mom was a stay-at-home mom, at least until I was in high school. She was the hardest-working woman I have ever known. In my earliest years Mom would not wear slacks. I can see her every time I read of someone in the Scriptures "girding" themselves. Mom always wore a dress of some sort, and when she was scrubbing the floors (always on her hands and knees) she would hitch that dress up in such a way to allow her to get down there and still be modest.

She collected S & H Green Stamps and also Yellow Stamps from the grocery stores, and a trip to the grocery store generally meant a piece of gum from one of the gum machines and perhaps, just perhaps, a ride on one of the bucking broncos that used to be outside almost every such store. I do believe every baseball glove I ever had as a child came from those stamps. The day I left my glove outside and it got ruined because it rained overnight resulted in a stiff lecture from both Mom and Dad. Yet somehow, with so very little money, by the time my next practice rolled around Mom had gotten me a new glove.

Even though Mom denied it up to the day she died, I remember playing in the "Turkey Bowl" football game in grade school. I was just a sixth grader playing with the seventh and eighth graders. I was playing cornerback when the opposing team ran the old Green Bay Packers sweep. That meant that everybody and their brother pulled and led that runner around end. Everyone on our team got blocked and there I was, the last bastion of hope for our team, protecting that goal line, weighing all of maybe 80 pounds. I was all set to make the tackle until a road grader hit me and down I went with a torn up knee. (Kids, get out of the way if a road grader is about to hit you.) As I lay on the field having my uniform pants cut off of me, I heard a voice. It was soft at first but gradually grew in volume. What the voice said was,

"My baby, my baby!" Lo and behold, my mom made her way onto that field. She was right with me as they loaded me into the ambulance. I acted embarrassed at the time, and continued to bug my mom about that all through her life—but I loved hearing that voice and having her hold my hand through the pain.

I also remember the times I caused my mom heartaches and the times when she would shake her head, give me a look that only she could give, or tell me that she was disappointed in me. I wish that I could take every single one of those times back and behave differently.

The high school years were tough as I rebelled and tried to assert my independence. I did a lot of things that I deeply regret, said some things to my mom that I would give almost anything never to have said, and yet as big a jerk as I was, there was Mom.

My life did not go in the direction she had anticipated. As a matter of fact, the choice I made when I was twenty-one about what I believed and what I wanted to do with my life created some disappointment and hurt feelings simply because she did not understand. However, as the years went by and we talked and studied—Mom and Dad even accompanied me to a debate I participated in at Lincoln, Nebraska with a fellow who held the same views they did—she let me know in her own special way that she was proud of me. She saw, or was aware of, most of the wonderful things that happened to me because of the choice of life that I had made. She didn't really live to see the bad.

As I write these words I miss her so much that my heart is aching and my eyes are misting over with tears. There is something very special about a mother and I am reminded of a statement that is made concerning Mary, the mother of Jesus, in Luke 2. Perhaps you remember the account of the time when Jesus was twelve years old and He accompanied His parents to Jerusalem for the feast of the Passover. When Mary and Joseph began the journey home, Jesus remained behind. They did not realize this because they thought he was with their relatives and acquaintances who were traveling with them. When they discovered that He was not there, they returned to Jerusalem and found Him three days later in the temple talking to the teachers of the Law. In verses 51-52 we find, "Then He went down with them and came to Nazareth, and was subject to them, *but His mother kept all these things in her heart.*"

Now obviously Mary remembered the miraculous circumstances of Jesus' conception and birth. She remembered the coming of the Magi and the statements of Simeon and Anna in the temple. And now she ponders and remembers this peculiar statement of Jesus and undoubtedly tries to sort out the meaning of it all in her heart.

I am not comparing myself with Jesus, but my mom kept everything I did in her heart, and I believe all good mothers do so as well. There is just something about a mom, and I believe God designed it that way. HAPPY MOTHER'S DAY!

May 9

Knocked down, but Not out

I have two windows in my office. Outside of the one that my desk faces is a little fir tree that we were required to plant as part of the landscaping. I have enjoyed watching that little tree, and it has given me the ideas to launch several other articles. A few weeks ago someone (I suspect it was kids attending a graduation party that one of our neighbors was having) decided to break off the top third of that little tree. The part that was broken off was just thrown to the ground. When I saw my little buddy so badly damaged I ran outside to check on him, only to discover that the same malicious act of vandalism had been performed on at least two other little fir trees. In each case the broken top was simply left lying on the ground.

This may sound silly to you, but I was truly saddened to see what had been done. I was looking forward to many years of watching that tree grow. I wanted to see it withstand the spring storms and the summer heat. I wanted to watch it grow large enough that snow would rest upon its branches. I found it somehow grounding and encouraging knowing that that little tree would be here long after I was gone. I thought that because it had been so damaged it would surely die, but someone who knows more about trees and shrubbery than I told me that was not necessarily so. Just because that tree was damaged doesn't mean that it cannot come all the way back.

Isn't that the way it is spiritually as well? Just because we may stumble and fall in our spiritual journey does not mean that we cannot get up and come all the way back. Just because something happens that makes us feel damaged, maybe even as though a part of us has been broken off, doesn't mean that we have to stay that way and cannot grow to our full potential. We can stumble and fall, we can sustain some significant spiritual damage and yet, depending on our attitude and willingness to repent, come all the way back and grow even beyond where we were.

Several individuals in the New Testament come to mind as examples of this very thing. I think of Peter and some of the statements he made to Jesus on the very night that our Lord was betrayed. In Matthew 26:33-35 we find, "Peter answered and said unto him, Though all men shall be offended because of thee, yet will I never be offended. Jesus said unto him, Verily I say unto thee, That this night, before the cock crow, thou shalt deny me thrice. Peter said unto him, Though I should die with thee, yet will I not deny thee. Likewise also said all the disciples."

That was quite a statement by Peter, and one in which I am certain he was absolutely confident at the time, "Though I should die with thee, yet will I not deny thee." Not too many hours later, Peter was saying concerning Jesus, "I do not know the man!" Luke 22:60-62 tells us, "And Peter said, Man, I know not what thou sayest. And immediately, while he yet spake, the cock crew. And the Lord turned, and looked upon Peter. And Peter remembered the word of the Lord, how he had said unto him, Before the cock crow, thou shalt deny me thrice. And Peter went out, and wept bitterly."

I don't know how much further a person could fall, how much more damage could be done spiritually, than to deny even a passing acquaintance with the Lord in the hour of greatest need. As Peter went out and wept bitterly, I suspect he might have felt a bit like a fir tree with the top brutally torn off. There was his arrogance and pride, lying right at his feet. But Peter came all the way back. We even find the Lord saying to him in John 21:15-17, "Feed my lambs," "Feed my sheep," and "Feed my sheep." Peter would announce the Gospel Plan of Salvation in Acts 2, and he would open the door of the kingdom to the Gentiles by doing the same thing with Cornelius and his household in Acts 10. Just because a person is down and damaged spiritually doesn't mean he or she has to stay that way.

In the Gospel of Mark we find a most interesting event in 14:51-52. This was the very same night upon which Peter denied the Lord. The location in Mark 14 was the Garden of Gethsemane and this is what we find, "And there followed him a certain young man, having a linen cloth cast about his naked body; and the young men laid hold on him: and he left the linen cloth, and fled from them naked." Most scholars believe that young man to have been none other than John Mark, the penman of the gospel.

Later, in Acts 13, we find Paul and Barnabas taking John Mark with them on their first evangelistic journey. He would depart from them before the journey was completed. The reason for his departure is not given, but Paul was certainly not pleased with it. In fact, when it became time for them to go on their second journey, Barnabas wanted Mark to go with them, but Paul refused. How much more spiritually damaged can you be than to run away from the Lord and to have the apostle Paul say, "I don't want him to go with me"? But Mark came back. First of all, he came back from having deserted the Lord to accompany Paul and Barnabas in the initial stages of that first journey. Later, he would come back from his previous failures to the point where the older Apostle Paul referred to him as a fellow worker and co-laborer in the gospel of Christ.

I hope that little broken fir tree grows strong and tall, home for the birds and a stalwart survivor of years of storms and the blistering heat of summer. Just because it is broken now doesn't mean it has to die, and just because a person may be spiritually broken doesn't mean he has to stay that way.

May 10

Every Man's Battle

In Proverbs 7:6-23, we find an account of a young man falling prey to sexual temptation. Solomon wrote:

For at the window of my house I looked out through my lattice, and I saw among the naïve, I discerned among the youths, a young man lacking sense, passing through the street near her corner; and he takes the way to her house, in the twilight, in the evening, in the middle of the night and in the darkness. And behold, a woman comes to meet him, dressed as a harlot and cunning of heart. She is boisterous and rebellious; her feet do not remain at home; she in now in the streets, now in the squares, and lurks by every corner. So she seizes him and kisses him, and with a brazen face she says to him: I was due to offer peace offerings; today I have paid my vows. Therefore I have come out to meet you, to seek your presence earnestly, and I have found you. I have spread my couch with coverings, with colored linens of Egypt. I have sprinkled my bed with myrrh, aloes and cinnamon. Come, let us drink our fill of love until morning; let us delight ourselves with caresses. For the man is not at home, he has gone on a long journey; he has taken a bag of money with him, at full moon he will come home. With her many persuasions she entices him; with her flattering lips she seduces him. Suddenly he follows her, as an ox goes to the slaughter, or as one in fetters to the discipline of a fool, until an arrow pierces through his liver; as a bird hastens to the snare, so he does not know that it will cost him his life.

This is such a sad story, but one that is played out in so many different ways in the lives of so many different men every day. Sexual temptation is every man's battle. Not all men are afflicted with sexual temptation to the same degree, and not all will succumb, but every healthy, normal male has a God-given sexual drive that he must learn to control. God's standard for sexual purity is clear and is perhaps most simply set forth in Ephesians 5:3, "But do not let *immorality or any impurity* or greed *even be named among you,* as is proper among saints."

Men receive sexual stimulation visually; we can receive gratification through our eyes. Consequently, the danger is ever present and the need for constant vigilance is paramount. The account of Proverbs 7:10 indicates that part of what enticed the young man to this woman was the way she was dressed, appealing to his eyes. It calls to mind King David and how he was aroused by gazing upon Bathsheba as she bathed in 2 Samuel 11:2. Jesus said in Matthew 5:27-28, "You have heard that it was said, You shall not commit adultery; but I say unto you, that everyone who looks on a woman to lust for her has committed adultery with her already in his heart." As men we simply must control our eyes.

If we sit down to watch television, so many of the commercials are sexually based; automobiles to snack chips are advertised by scantily clad women. This does not even take into account so many of the television shows themselves. Trips to the mall can almost require blinders. Perusal of the magazine rack during a trip to the local drugstore can be a pathway to sin. Sexual temptation seems to be everywhere, just as verse 12 of Proverbs 7 indicated, "She is now in the streets, now in the squares, and lurks by every corner." As we consider the easy availability of visual sexual gratification, perhaps the most insidious is the Internet. How many men who are Christians are struggling mightily with the temptation to click that mouse in the privacy of their home, or at the office, or in the motel when traveling for business, and pour into their hearts through the portals of their eyes every lascivious, ungodly image of women imaginable?

To many the temptation provided through their computers seems almost too much to deal with, but it is not. To sin with our eyes is a choice, and none of us has to choose to commit that sin. Job made a statement in Job 31:1 that goes directly to the issue. He wrote, "I have made a covenant with my eyes; how then could I gaze at a virgin?" Each of us can make a contract with our eyes as well, a contract that says, "I will not give in." Don't think that you cannot do it, because you can. I am not saying that it will be easy, but I am saying that one who is determined to live according to God's pattern, striving to be more like Jesus every day, can do it.

The only place where God has permitted man to fulfill his sexual desires is in marriage. Hebrews 13:4 tells us, "Let marriage be held in honor among all, and let the marriage bed be undefiled; for fornicators and adulterers God will judge." Let each man find satisfaction in the arms of his wife, for that is as God designed. Not only is he to receive sexual gratification in marriage, he is to give it as well.

Living purely in a world full of sexual stimulation is not always easy, but it can be done. We are responsible for "taking every thought captive to the obedience of Christ" (2 Cor. 10:5). I have found it helpful to drive out each thought when it first appears, refusing to let it linger, and replacing it with what is good. Paul exhorted in Philippians 4:8, "Finally, brethren, whatever is true, whatever is honorable, whatever is right, whatever is pure, whatever is lovely, whatever is of good repute, if there is any excellence and if anything worthy of praise, let your mind dwell on these things." This is wonderful advice to help every man win this battle—and we must win!

May 11

Every Woman's Battle
By Vicky Litmer

Those of us who are of a "certain age" can remember a time when some television programs were so discreet that they actually depicted married couples sleeping in separate twin beds. This certainly seems silly and comical nowadays, doesn't it? Yet look at the programming of today. There seems to be no limit at all as to what will be on television, radio, movies, or in books and magazines. How did we get from "I Love Lucy" to "Sex and the City," "Temptation Island," and other such rubbish in the course of a couple of generations? Because *people* set the standards for our entertainment, and when *people* decide on that which is reasonable and decent, it's only a matter of time until it becomes totally unreasonable and indecent.

God made men and women to be sexual beings. Since He created us with these desires, He understands them even better than we do ourselves. And He also laid down the limits by which these desires could be fulfilled. Hebrews 13:4 gives us that limit: "Let marriage be held in honor among all, and let the marriage bed be undefiled; for fornicators and adulterers God will judge." Sexual activity between marriage partners is to be the one and only recourse for sexual gratification. This is God's will.

And yet it can be so hard to obey! Men and women struggle in different ways when it comes to sexual temptation. While a man's battle begins with what he takes in through his eyes, a woman's often begins with her heart and her thoughts. And very often a woman's battle begins with a heart full of disappointment. She may be disappointed in men, circumstances, God, life, money, kids, and the future. She may turn to secret fantasies to find excitement, and the married woman may start comparing her husband with other men. Of course, when she does that her husband always comes up short. Why can't he be as witty as this one, as attentive as that one, or as romantic as someone else? Some have even gone so far as to imagine the death of their husbands, wondering about the "new, improved" husband they may someday have.

However, many women believe that just because they are not involved in a physical, sexual affair they don't have a problem with sexual immorality. But doesn't emotional and mental unfaithfulness still compromise our sexual integrity? 1 Peter 3:1-4 brings up some pertinent instructions when it comes to dealing with our hearts and minds, "In the same way, you wives, be submissive to your own husbands so that even if any of them are disobedient to the word, they may be won without a word by the behavior of their wives, as they observe your *chaste and respectful behavior.* And let not your adornment be merely external—braiding the hair, and wearing gold jewelry, or putting on dresses; but let it be the *hidden person of the heart, with the imperishable quality of a gentle and quiet spirit,* which is precious in the sight of God." God knows our very thoughts, He knows what is at our core, and we will be held accountable for that, as well as our actions.

Having "emotional affairs" is just another of Satan's methods of entangling us in sin. We may start dressing in a way of enticing men to sexual thoughts, whether we engage in any actual activity or not. Again in our entertainment, even the smartest, most accomplished, and successful women are nearly always shown in too low-cut, too tight, too short, too revealing attire—and we may find that type of "power" heady and exhilarating. And after all, a little office flirtation isn't really hurting anybody, right? The lines between what is appropriate and what is not start to blur when we allow our emotional desires and fantasies to overshadow our spirituality.

One of the biggest temptations nowadays for women who want something more stimulating in their lives can be found on the Internet. How many people have we all heard about who were led astray by someone they met online? What began as a means to find information quickly or to send notes to friends has also become one of Satan's most useful tools to lead us down the pathway of destruction. There are women who drop their kids off at school in the morning, then spend hours throughout the day "chatting" with a man they met on a web site. So often the "chats" become more personal and intimate until they are both so hooked on one another that they have to meet. This is reminiscent of the description of sin we find in James 1:13-16, "Let no one say when he is tempted, 'I am being tempted by God'; for God cannot be tempted by evil, and He Himself does not tempt anyone. But each one is tempted when he is carried away and enticed by his own lust. Then when lust has conceived, it gives birth to sin; and when sin is accomplished, it brings forth death. Do not be deceived, my beloved brethren."

As God's women, we must protect ourselves from any and every type of immorality that exists. Could you imagine the woman of Proverbs 31 allowing herself to be pulled away from her Lord by a failure to control her thoughts and emotions? All Christian women, whether married or single, have an obligation to live by God's standards, which are light years higher than man's standards. By resisting temptation when it starts, redirecting tempting thoughts, and renewing our minds we can develop an attitude such as David had when he said, "Search me, O God, and know my heart; Try me and know my anxious thoughts; And see if there be any offensive way in me, and lead me in the way everlasting" (Psa. 139:23-24).

May 12

Compromise (1)

"That which has been is that which will be, and that which has been done is that which will be done. So, there is nothing new under the sun" (Eccl. 1:9).

"Compromise" is an interesting word. Depending on the context in which it is being used, it can be a good thing or a bad thing. *Webster's New Universal Unabridged Dictionary* gives the following as one of its definitions of compromise: "A settlement of differences by mutual concessions; an agreement reached by adjustment of conflicting or opposing claims, principles, etc., by reciprocal modification of demands."

While the word itself does not appear in the Scriptures, the idea behind this definition of compromise certainly does. In the Sermon on the Mount, Jesus urged compromise under the right circumstances. In Matthew 5:25 He said, "Make friends quickly with your opponent at law while you are with him on the way, in order that your opponent may not deliver you to the judge, and the judge to the officer, and you be thrown into prison." By reaching a mutually satisfactory compromise with an opponent, or adversary, entering into the legal system could be avoided. In this sense, compromise is a good thing.

However, under certain other circumstances, compromise would not be a good thing. In fact, it can be evil. *Webster's New Universal Unabridged Dictionary* also gives these definitions and sample usages: "An endangering, esp. of reputation; exposure to danger, suspicion, etc.: a compromise of one's integrity," and, "To make a dishonorable or shameful concession: He is too honorable to compromise with his principles."

In the letters to the churches found in Revelation 2 and 3, we find that compromise in the evil sense was a problem for brethren toward the end of the first century, and it has not changed. The church at Pergamos is addressed in Revelation 2, beginning in verse 12. Jesus began the letter by affirming His intimate knowledge of their situation. He said in verse 13, "I know where you dwell, where Satan's throne is." Pergamos, having been bequeathed to the Romans in 133 B.C. by King Attalus, became the political capital of Asia and as such served as the center of Emperor worship. In this way the brethren in

Pergamos were living "where Satan's throne is." They were living in the center of Emperor worship during the reign of Domitian. Refusal to worship the Emperor meant severe persecution, even death. For the most part, the brethren there had not denied the Lord, even when death entered the church in the city via persecution.

As the letter to the church in Pergamos continues, we find the Lord's complaint in verses 14-15. He said, "But I have a few things against you, because you have there some who hold the teaching of Balaam, who kept teaching Balak to put a stumbling block before the sons of Israel, to eat things sacrificed to idols, and to commit acts of immorality. Thus you also have some who in the same way hold the teaching of the Nicolaitans."

In Numbers 22, 23, and 24, when the children of Israel came to the borders of Moab, Balak, the king of Moab, called for Balaam to come and curse the Israelites. Balaam was unable to curse the Israelites, even though he tried three times, so he counseled Balak to send forth the daughters of Moab to entice the men of Israel to join them in their idolatrous, lascivious worship. His scheme succeeded and resulted in the deaths of 24,000 Israelites.

The "teaching of Balaam" is summed up in verse 14 in three ways:

1. It taught Balak "to put a stumbling block before the sons of Israel." "Stumbling block" comes from the word *skandalon*, and it refers to the part of a trap on which the bait is placed. When it is touched, the trap springs and catches its victim. By his advice, Balaam set a trap for the children of Israel, and many got caught by it and perished. Evidently, some in Pergamos were doing things that were enticing others in the church to seek to compromise their principles and it would result in their perishing.

2. "To eat things sacrificed to idols." This was not just the eating of meats that Paul talked about in Romans 14 and 1 Corinthians 8. This was actual participation in the idolatrous feasts, compromising the truth to do so.

3. "To commit acts of immorality." Immorality was part of idolatrous worship.

There were also those in Pergamos who held to the belief of the Nicolaitans. There is little known about the Nicolaitans except that they were a sect of Gnostics who advocated participation in the idolatrous feasts and worship because they did not believe such sinful activity mattered. What it all boils down to is that there were those in the congregation at Pergamos who wanted to be Christians and yet still take part in the immoral, idolatrous practices of the day. By so doing they could avoid persecution and separation from the mainstream society of their city. It was a doctrine of compromise.

It didn't work then and it won't work now. In verse 16, Jesus told them, "Repent therefore; or else I am coming to you quickly, and I will make war against them with the sword of My mouth."

May 13

Compromise (2)

COMPROMISE! In business negotiations it can be a good thing. In the arena of government it is sometimes necessary. Even in the church brethren need to learn to be willing to make concessions with each other in matters that God has left up to our judgment to ensure peace and harmony. However, in matters of truth and in principles of right, compromise is deadly.

In Romans 12:1-2, Paul wrote, "I urge you therefore, brethren, by the mercies of God, to present your bodies a living and holy sacrifice, acceptable to God, which is your spiritual service of worship. And do not be conformed to this world, but be transformed by the renewing of your mind, that you may prove what the will of God is, that which is good and acceptable and perfect."

Literally speaking, to be "conformed to this world" is to be poured into the world's mold. Consider the second definition and sample usage of "conform" given by *Webster's New Universal Unabridged Dictionary*. It says, "To act in accord with the prevailing standards, attitudes, practices, etc., of society or a group: One has to conform in order to succeed in this company."

Did you ever have the feeling that in order to succeed in the world, be it at school or at work, or maybe just among friends and associates, you had to "conform" to the world? Did you ever feel that you had to act in accordance with prevailing standards, attitudes, and practices of society even though you knew that much of it was just not right? What happens is that we might find ourselves making shameful and dishonorable concessions and compromise our principles.

If I am going to be "poured into the mold" of anything, it must be in the mold of Christ. I need to be like Him, not the world. Every time I compromise my principles—and I have done that—I mess up that mold.

I having been serving the Lord for many years now, and I still find myself compromising with the world from time to time. The words of the Apostle Paul in 2 Corinthians 6:14-18, ring clear and true across the ages. He wrote:

> Do not be bound together with unbelievers; for what partnership have righteousness and lawlessness, or what fellowship has light with darkness? Or what harmony has Christ with Belial, or what has a believer in common with an unbeliever? Or what agreement has the temple of God with idols? For we are the temple of the living God; just as God said, I will dwell in them and walk among them; and I will be their God, and they shall be My people. Therefore, come out from their midst and be separate, says the Lord. And do not touch what is unclean; and I will welcome you. And I will be a father to you, and you shall be sons and daughters to Me, says the Lord Almighty.

May 14

This Is What God Meant!

A while back I had the opportunity to sit down and talk to an older sister in Christ who had been married for sixty-eight years. She's a quilter, and she makes some beautiful ones, but no quilt has she made as beautiful as the tapestry of the life that she and her husband have made together. Each stitch in that tapestry has been lovingly sewn. It is a picture of two godly people walking hand in hand with each other and with the Lord through the sometimes-turbulent waters of life. It is a picture complete with mountains and valleys, pleasant sun-filled meadows and dark times of sorrow. The background of this tapestry is love—love for God and love for each other.

There were just a few more stitches to be sewn and the tapestry would be completed. As we talked, it was apparent that her companion of sixty-eight years would soon be going home. It would not be the earthly home that they had shared together, but it would be to that home they had spent a lifetime preparing to enter. It would be one prepared by the Lord for those who loved Him.

Tears streamed down her face, and every one of them had a story to tell. One tear told the story of their time of courting, another of their early years as husband and wife during the days of the depression, and how their first house had been a converted chicken coop. Another told of the births of their children, while yet another told of an anxious night waiting for her beloved husband to come home from school during the great flood.

I wish you could have been there. Those tears told the story of countless biscuits baked in the wood-burning stove and of his laughter and wave as he would come home from teaching school each day. They told of the absolute trust that they had of each other. There were many trips to the barn and the chicken pens for feedings in those tears, as well as cold evenings spent around the fire quilting and studying God's Word. As I sat and talked to her, I could almost see the whole family bustling about on Sunday morning getting ready to go worship the Lord together.

There are four children, and they are all faithful members of the body of Christ. Each one of us should have had the opportunity to witness the care and help that those children gave to their mother and father in these difficult times. They have been living examples of what Paul meant when he said, "Honor your father and mother; (which is the first commandment with promise)." That kind of love and respect does not come by accident. It is a testimony to just how seriously those two beloved older Christians took the admonition to bring their children up "in the nurture and admonition of the Lord."

This dear sister and friend looked at me and said, "He's my pal." After sixty-eight years, he is still her best friend.

This particular brother and sister in Christ started life together so long ago with little more than each other and the Lord. A little over sixty-eight years later now, one has gone home to be with the Lord, and the other can't wait to join him. When she crosses over, the whole world will be poorer for it, but their legacy will live on and on.

Yes, there are problems in the world, and there are problems in the church. Yes, some brethren don't live as they should, and that is a shame. There are brothers and sisters in Christ who do not keep the vows that they made to one another and to God when they were joined in marriage. But the truth is that most brethren do. Most brethren serve the Lord together, raise their families together, and grow old together.

Sometimes the bad takes so much of our energy and attention that we can overlook and fail to appreciate the good, but the good is there.

What a Waste

Someone that I once knew died a couple of weeks ago. A homeless man was found dead behind the K-Mart in Newport, Kentucky. He had built a fire to warm himself and became so intoxicated that he fell into the fire and died. As it turned out, I knew him. He actually took over an apartment that I had had many, many years ago. We broke bread together and celebrated a few holidays together, but I had not seen or talked to him in over fifteen years. There is a natural tendency to look at his end, and the life leading up to it, and say, "What a waste!" I suppose that is true. It was a waste, but he was a very sick man, and we can at least look at what happened and know that there was a physiological reason for it. Thankfully, God is the Judge.

In the weeks that have gone by since his death, I have thought about it quite a bit. I have thought about him all alone, with nothing really but the clothes on his back, building a fire in a vacant lot behind a K-Mart to try to knock off the chill and spending what little money he had on alcohol. I have thought about all those folks who read about his death in the newspaper as they sat at the breakfast table drinking coffee and munching toast who said to themselves, "What a waste!" And I thought about Paul's words in Romans 2:21, where he wrote, "Thou therefore which teachest another, teachest thou not thyself?"

Whether a person is rich or poor, lives in a mansion or a shack, dies in a private room in a hospital receiving the best of care or behind a K-Mart all alone, if he lived his life without God by choice, his life was a waste. All the accumulated wealth of a life spent without God doesn't change that truth one little bit.

Ecclesiastes is a fascinating book that chronicles Solomon's search for meaning and fulfillment in life. He was in a position to deny himself nothing in his quest, including tremendous wealth, great learning, and physical pleasures. Consider chapter 2:1-11 where Solomon wrote:

I said in mine heart, go to now, I will prove thee with mirth, therefore enjoy pleasure: and, behold, this also is vanity. I said of laughter, It is mad: and of mirth, What doeth it? I sought in mine heart to give myself unto wine, yet acquainting mine heart with wisdom; and to lay hold on folly, till I might see what was that good for the sons of men, which they should do under the heaven all the days of their life. I made me great works; I builded me houses; I planted me vineyards: I made me gardens and orchards, and I planted trees in them of all kinds of fruits: I made me pools of water, to water therewith the wood that bringeth forth trees: I got me servants and maidens, and had servants born in my house; also I had great possessions of great and small cattle above all that were in Jerusalem before me: I gathered me also silver and gold, and the peculiar treasure of kings and of the provinces: I got me men singers and women singers, and the delights of the sons of men, as musical instruments, and that of all sorts. So I was great, and increased more than all that were before me in Jerusalem: also my wisdom remained with me. And whatsoever mine eyes desired I kept not from them, I withheld not my heart from any joy; for my heart rejoiced in all my labor: and this was my portion of all my labor. Then I looked on all the works that my hands had wrought, and on the labor that I had labored to do: and, behold, all was vanity and vexation of spirit, and there was no profit under the sun.

At first glance this almost appears to be a statement of utter despair. Solomon knew wealth like few men know it. He knew power to a degree that most men never know. He was in a position to partake of every pleasure he wanted. From a worldly standpoint, he had it all! But when it was said and done, he said it was all useless and without meaning. It was empty and vain. If Ecclesiastes had stopped there, my inclination would be to say what a depressing and discouraging book. However, Solomon didn't stop there.

What he taught us is that the life that is truly wasted and without meaning, is the life lived without obedience to God. All of the things upon which man places so much importance are vain and useless if we choose to leave God out of the picture. I think it is even worse when we deceive ourselves by giving God just a little part of our lives in order to appease our conscience and make ourselves feel good.

When it was all said and done, Solomon wrote in Ecclesiastes 12:13-14, "Let us hear the conclusion of the whole matter: Fear God, and keep his commandments: for this is the whole duty of man. For God shall bring every work into judgment, with every secret thing, whether it be good, or whether it be evil."

The life that can truly be characterized by the statement, "What a waste!" is the life lived without being a faithful Christian.

Eternal Life

Several years ago I had a discussion with an individual concerning whether or not a Christian could ever lose his or her salvation. The individual was of the firm belief that such could never happen, and the reason he presented for his conviction on the matter was rather interesting. The gentleman referred to 1 John 5:13 and clung to it tenaciously, unable or unwilling to see that it did not teach what he thought it did.

The verse says, "These things I have written to you who believe in the name of the Son of God, in order that you may know that you have eternal life." His point was that everyone who believes in the Lord Jesus Christ has eternal life—that it is a present possession of an individual, and if a person *has* eternal life, that was it. If a person has eternal life, if he or she presently possesses it, how can it ever be any different? I either have it, or I don't. That was his approach.

I tried several different ways to teach this individual that his understanding of 1 John 5:13 was not consistent with the teaching of that book itself, nor was it consistent with the teaching of the rest of Scripture. Perhaps you have encountered this argument as well. Here is what I believe the Bible to teach on the subject.

First of all, the Christian does not have eternal life as a present possession. It is a promise, as sure as it can be, but a promise nonetheless. In 1 John 2:21–25 we find:

> I have not written to you because you do not know the truth, but because you do know it, and because no lie is of the truth. Who is the liar but the one who denies that Jesus is the Christ? This is the antichrist, the one who denies the Father and the Son. Whoever denies the Son does not have the Father; the one who confesses the Son has the Father also. As for you, let that abide in you which you heard from the beginning. *If what you heard from the beginning abides in you*, you also will abide in the Son and in the Father. *And this is the promise which He Himself made to us: eternal life.*

Surely we can see that a Christian has eternal life in prospect and promise, but not in realization as of yet. We continue to have it as long as that which we have "heard from the beginning abides in" us. If we cast it off, if we reject Christ, we no longer have eternal life in prospect and promise.

I remember the gentleman reacting very negatively to this line of discussion. He said I was denying what the Holy Spirit clearly said, "that you may know that you have eternal life." So I tried to explain it in yet another way.

In Joshua 6, we find the account of the destruction of the city of Jericho by the children of Israel. In Joshua 6:2, we find these words, "And the Lord said to Joshua, See, I *have given* Jericho into your hand, with its king and the valiant warriors." The question to ask is, "Did the children of Israel have the city of Jericho when God made that statement?" No, they did not. But they had it in prospect and in promise. *If* they did what God told them to do, the city was as good as theirs. However, if they did not do what God said, even though He told Joshua, "I have given Jericho into your hand," the children of Israel would not have received it. It is exactly the same as we found in 1 John 2. If that which we have "heard from the beginning abides in" us, we will have eternal life. It is as good as ours. If it does not abide in us, we will not have eternal life.

Jesus made a statement in Mark 10:29–30 that clearly shows that eternal life does not belong to this age, but it is a possession in prospect, or promise. The passage reads, "Truly I say to you, there is no one who has left house or brothers or sisters or mother or father or children or farms, for My sake and for the gospel's sake, but that he shall receive a hundred times as much *now in the present age*, houses and brothers and sisters and mothers and children and farms, along with persecutions; *and in the age to come, eternal life.*"

Another way to consider this matter is to look at Titus 1:1–2 where Paul wrote, "Paul, a bond-servant of God, and an apostle of Jesus Christ, for the faith of those chosen of God and the knowledge of the truth which is according to godliness, *in the hope of eternal life*, which God, who cannot lie, promised long ages ago." Paul has taught that we live "in the hope of eternal life." Well, couple that with his teaching in Romans 8:24–25. In the context of a discussion of the Christian eagerly and earnestly desiring and expecting a glorious future in heaven, in other words, "eternal life," he wrote, "For in hope we have been saved, but hope that is seen is not hope; for why does one also hope for what he sees? But if we hope for what we do not see, with perseverance we wait eagerly for it."

Eternal life is coming. It is a possession of the believer now in prospect and promise. If we remain faithful to the Lord it is as good as ours; just as the city of Jericho was as good as theirs if the children of Israel did what God said. Our ultimate realization of that promise is predicated upon that which we have heard abiding in us.

Give Me My Rights!

We live in a very selfish society. It seems as though everybody is demanding "their rights," and woe be to anyone who in some way seems to infringe upon them. Folks are ready to call a lawyer and sue at the drop of a hat. It is even possible for those of us who comprise the body of Christ to fall into this "Me First" way of thinking. Paul teaches us some very valuable lessons about this way of thinking in 1 Corinthians 8, 9, and 10.

1 Corinthians 8:1-2 sets the stage for the discussion. It says, "Now concerning things sacrificed to idols, we know that we all have knowledge. Knowledge makes arrogant, but love edifies. If anyone supposes that he knows anything, he has not yet known as he ought to know."

There were some questions that evidently had been brought to Paul's attention that he was about to consider in chapter 8. Those questions revolved around the eating of meat that had been sacrificed to an idol. Remember that this was Corinth, a Gentile city filled with idolatry, and that the church there was made up of Gentiles converted from that idolatry.

The questions were: (1) Could a Christian attend a banquet in the temple of an idol? (2) Could a Christian eat meat sacrificed to an idol in the home of a believing or non-believing friend? (3) Could a Christian eat meat sacrificed to an idol if he inadvertently bought it at the market? In the very beginning Paul makes the point that any answer arrived at must be arrived at by reasoning tempered with love. Anyone strutting around thinking that he had all the answers due to his superior knowledge didn't even know the most basic thing.

In verse 4 Paul wrote, "Therefore concerning the eating of things sacrificed to idols, we know that there is no such thing as an idol in the world, and that there is no God but one." The foundational point was that idols were nothing. They were useless and meaningless. There was but one God that existed, and there was, and is, no other. However, not all of those converted Gentile Christians fully understood that yet. There were some who still viewed the eating of meat that had been part of a sacrifice to an idol as worship of that idol. They had been raised attending feasts in honor of the idols, and to suddenly change their attitude toward such was difficult. So, if they ate such meat their conscience was violated.

In verse 8 we find, "But food will not commend us to God; we are neither the worse if we do not eat, nor the better if we do eat." Paul's point was simply that food does not affect our relationship to God. What we eat doesn't make a bit of difference one way or the other. (Please understand that he is not discussing gluttony in this passage.)

Now consider verses 9-11: "But take care lest this liberty of yours somehow becomes a stumbling block to the weak. For if someone sees you, who have knowledge, dining in an idol's temple, will not his conscience, if he is weak, be strengthened to eat things sacrificed to idols? For through your knowledge he who is weak is ruined, the brother for whose sake Christ died." The brother or sister in Christ who understood that the idol was nothing and that he or she was free to eat the meat had to be very careful and considerate, lest their knowledge and understanding turned out to be an occasion of stumbling for the brother who did not understand. Perhaps he would be emboldened to do something that he believed in his heart was wrong. Christ died for the brother who had not yet arrived at that understanding. Shouldn't a brother who had such knowledge be willing to forego his liberty to eat to help the other?

Paul's conclusion to the matter is found in 8:13 and in 10:23–24 where he wrote, "Therefore, if food causes my brother to stumble, I will never eat meat again, that I might not cause my brother to stumble." Over in chapter 10, we find, "All things are lawful, but not all things are profitable. All things are lawful, but not all things edify. Let no one seek his own good, but that of his neighbor."

As a Christian, even if something is right and proper in itself when understood, if my doing it will cause another brother to stumble, then I need to let it go. I need to be willing to forego my liberty to help another. In 1 Corinthians 9 Paul demonstrated how this principle of conduct had ruled his life as an evangelist and apostle. In order to facilitate his work, he had not married, even though it was his right to do so. Being single made it much easier for Paul to move about and thus teach more the gospel of Christ. He had not required the brethren in Corinth to help in his support, even though he had the right to do so. He had foregone that right with them in order to help them. He was always willing to relinquish a personal right for the benefit of others. So should we.

"Give no offense either to Jews or Greeks or to the church of God; just as I also please all men in all things, not seeking my own profit, but the profit of the many, that they may be saved" (1 Cor. 10:32–33). Personal rights and liberties are not nearly so important as is the salvation of others. It must truly be God first, others second, and self third.

May 18

Why Lie? (1)

I have heard the statement made, "Everyone lies." I suppose that at some point in their lives, pretty much everybody has told a lie, but I deny that everybody makes a practice of it. It would be an absolute tragedy if they did. In Revelation 21:8, we are told, "But the cowardly, unbelieving, abominable, murderers, sexually immoral, sorcerers, idolaters, and *all liars* shall have their part in the lake which burns with fire and brimstone, which is the second death."

What does the word "lie" mean? It can be used as a noun and a verb. *Webster's New Universal Unabridged Dictionary* provides the following definitions that would be pertinent to this article. "1. A false statement made with deliberate intent to deceive; an intentional untruth; a falsehood; 2. something intended or serving to convey a false impression; 3. an inaccurate or false statement." As a verb, "6. to speak falsely or utter untruth knowingly, as with intent to deceive; 7. to express what is false; convey a false impression; 8. to bring about or affect by lying (often used reflexively): to lie oneself out of a difficulty; accustomed to lying his way out of difficulties." There were more definitions given but these will suffice.

I have often wondered "why" a person will lie. It seems that a reason that would encompass most of the lying that is done would be to somehow benefit the liar. Consider Ananias and Sapphira in Acts 5. These two individuals lied. As a matter of fact, Peter specifically asked Ananias in verses 3-4, "Ananias, why has Satan filled your heart to lie to the Holy Spirit and keep back part of the price of the land for yourself? While it remained, was it not your own? And after it was sold, was it not in your own control? Why have you conceived this thing in your heart? You have not lied to men but to God." Actually Ananias had lied to men, but ultimately every sin, including lying, is against God. This exchange between Peter and Ananias also helps us to understand whom the liar is acting like. It harkens back to a statement that the Lord made to certain of the Jews in John 8:44, "You are of your father the devil, and the desires of your father you want to do. He was a murderer from the beginning, and does not stand in the truth, because there is no truth in him. When he speaks a lie, he speaks from his own resources, for he is a liar and the father of it."

People will lie in a reflexive attempt to extricate themselves from trouble. Frequently, when people are confronted with a statement they made that puts them in a bad light, the reflexive lie "I didn't say that" will be uttered. It is an attempt to get out of trouble. I think of Peter and what he did as he perceived that his life was in danger if he had told the truth. Let's read Luke 22:55-60:

> Now when they had kindled a fire in the midst of the courtyard and sat down together, Peter sat among them. And a certain servant girl, seeing him as he sat by the fire, looked intently at him and said, This man was also with Him. But he denied Him, saying, Woman, I do not know Him. And after a little while another saw him and said, You also are of them. But Peter said, Man, I am not! Then after about an hour had passed, another confidently affirmed, saying, Surely this fellow also was with Him, for he is a Galilean. But Peter said, Man, I do not know what you are saying! Immediately, while he was still speaking, the rooster crowed.

Sometimes it is not so reflexive, but a well thought out, premeditated story concocted with much effort and planning. Either way, it is a sin.

Why Lie? (2)

People will lie to do harm to someone else. This still fits into the realm of lying to benefit the liar, but it is a clear sub-case. Consider what was done at the trial of Jesus in Matthew 26:59-60: "Now the chief priest, the elders, and all the council sought false testimony against Jesus to put Him to death, but found none. Even though many false witnesses came forward, they found none." This is very similar to what happened to Stephen in Acts 6:9-13:

> Then there arose some from what is called the Synagogue of the Freedmen (Cyrenians, Alexandrians, and those from Cilicia and Asia), disputing with Stephen. And they were not able to resist the wisdom and the Spirit by which he spoke. Then they secretly induced men to say, We have heard him speak blasphemous words against Moses and God. And they stirred up the people, the elders, and the scribes: and they came upon him, seized him; and brought him to the council. They also set up false witnesses who said, This man does not cease to speak blasphemous words against this holy place and the law.

I also believe that I have met people who lie because that is just what they do. They have not told the truth for so long that lying is now their normal mode of operation. With some of them, I am not even altogether sure that they realize they are lying anymore.

Every lie is a sin and an affront to God. However, lies by brethren are particularly odious. We, of all people, ought to be pure, holy, honest, and trustworthy enough to tell the truth. Paul instructs us in Ephesians 4:25, "Therefore, putting away lying, Let each one of you speak truth with his neighbor, for we are members of one another." In Colossians 3:9-10, he wrote, "Do not lie to one another, since you have put off the old man with his deeds, and have put on the new man who is renewed in knowledge according to the image of Him who created him."

May 20

But It Is the Biggest Event of the School Year!

It comes every year. You walk through the mall and see that J.C. Penney's, Sears, and Macy's have rack after rack of formals for sale, and the tuxedo rental shops are advertising special deals. Before too long a lot of young Christians across the land are going to have to answer what is, for many of them, a very difficult question: *"Should I go to the Prom?"* Please allow me to suggest a few things that might help you if you are faced with that question and that might help parents assist their teenagers in making the right decision.

First of all, a prom is a glorified dance. I know this, because I went to several of them before I learned the truth. Sure, everybody gets dressed up, trips to the beauty salon are made, flowers are given, and special pictures are taken. But before too long those expensive shoes come off the feet of the girls, and the cummerbunds will be off of the guys, along with those formal bow ties and rented coats, and it will be just like any other dance.

I hope you are not, but at this point some might be saying, "So what? What's wrong with going to a dance?" I've never seen clogging at a prom, and I don't think they square dance there, so let's admit that we are talking about modern dancing. In Galatians 5:19 Paul mentions several "works of the flesh." He wrote, "Now the works of the flesh are manifest, which are these; adultery, fornication, uncleanness, lasciviousness." There are several definitions of "lasciviousness"—lewd, wanton, unchaste bodily movements, unchaste handling. Take your pick; any one of them fits modern dancing. Indeed, any one of them may very well be the *point* of modern dancing.

Someone may be saying now, "Well, I won't dance." This little article is being written by one of the all-time non-dancers. But you know what? You will not have your eyes closed. You will be watching. Let's be honest, especially you guys. The ones you will be watching will be the best dancers, and the best dancers are generally the ones who are dancing in the most provocative way. Please, don't sin through lasciviousness or through lustful gazing. Don't put yourself in that position.

Secondly, while I haven't read about it in the newspaper or heard about it on the evening news, there must be a worldwide shortage of material. How else can we explain all the formals that do not cover the shoulder (not even with little bitty straps), or the majority of the chest, or a major portion of the thighs? If we admit that there is no shortage of material, aren't we also admitting that those formals are designed the way they are to attract attention? Maybe you wouldn't wear that kind of dress, but I guarantee you that the majority of the girls at the prom will be wearing just that kind of dress. Whatever happened to shamefacedness, or the ability to blush? Why would any young woman go out in public with half her chest, all of her shoulders, and a large portion of her thighs exposed, if not to attract attention? Now tell me, what good can possibly be said about that?

There is one more thing I want to mention. The prom had a problem attached to it that the other dances didn't seem to have to the same extent. Almost all of the guys had a Five-Step Preparatory Program that they went through for the prom. It went like this: a. Get a date; b. Rent a tux; c. Buy flowers; d. Make dinner reservations; e. Make sure you have access to something alcoholic to drink.

Now I'm sure you wouldn't do that. And hopefully your date wouldn't do that. But a whole lot of people driving to and from that prom will have done it. As I read the paper every year and read of another prom night accident, I can see that it hasn't changed one iota. It is exactly the same. What a silly waste of time, energy, and potential! Young Christians, don't take part in something that is just not good.

Paul made an interesting statement in Romans 6:21: "What fruit had ye then in those things whereof ye are now ashamed? For the end of those things is death." Maybe the Prom seems big to you now, but don't take part in something that you are just going to be ashamed of having done later on.

May 21

What Am I Supposed to Think?

On a Wednesday evening I arrive for Bible study and am standing right at the door greeting the brethren and visitors as they come in. You walk right by me, ignoring my outstretched hand and my words of greeting. What am I supposed to think?

My child comes home from Bible class and says, "Mommy, my teacher was mean to me today." What am I supposed to think? For a couple of weeks now I have been sick, and my name has been included in the announcements as being ill. I have not been able to attend the services, really haven't been able to do much of anything. Yet you have not visited me or called me or sent me a card. What am I supposed to think?

I heard in a roundabout way that you said something about me that was not very kind. What am I supposed to think?

A dear sister has been too ill to be at services for a little while now, but I see her at Wal-Mart all the time. What am I supposed to think?

I'll tell you what I am supposed to think in situations like these and any one of a hundred others that we could probably come up with. I am to think the very best of you until irrefutable evidence demonstrates otherwise. My first thought, my initial reaction, should not be negative. I should be positive about you, and you should be positive about me.

In 1 Corinthians 13 Paul was discussing the "more excellent way," the way of love. As he gave various characteristics of love, he wrote in verse 7 that love "bears all things, believes all things, hopes all things, endures all things." Two phrases in that verse are particularly applicable to this topic. The first is that love "believes all things." That is not to say that one who has love is gullible or stupid, but it is saying that when there is no absolute evidence to the contrary, love believes the best about its fellow man. If I have love, I will not give in to unfounded suspicions and doubts. I will give you the benefit of every doubt because I *want* to believe the very best about you. And if I need to know the whole story, I will come to *you* to find out.

The second phrase is that love "hopes all things." What this means is that when there is evidence of a negative nature, love goes the extra mile. It hopes for the best in its fellow man even when the evidence indicates otherwise. Putting the two of these phrases together, we can say that love, when it has no evidence, believes the best; and that love, when the evidence is adverse or negative, hopes for the best.

If you walk right by me at services without saying hello or acknowledging my presence, it could very well be that you received some bad news right before coming and your mind is a thousand miles away. You don't need a negative reaction or hurt feelings from me, you need my concern that everything is okay. If you don't call me when I am sick, maybe you just forgot—because I certainly have before! Let's always give each other the benefit of the doubt and never jump to conclusions that could be unwarranted. Love demands no less.

May 22

I Can't Believe You Said That!

As someone who has spent his entire adult life speaking for a living, I am well aware of the power of the tongue—both for good and evil. The spoken word, in the hands of a skilled craftsman, can take us to heights of ecstasy individually, and stir great multitudes of people to action. It can encourage and comfort, or bring tears of sympathy to the eyes of its hearers. It can teach and admonish in the ways of righteousness, or lead a person down the paths of iniquity. It can also wound and injure in ways equally as severe as any weapon of war ever did, and some of its wounds are more difficult to heal. The ability to communicate through the spoken word is truly one of the greatest blessings that God has given to man and it should never be used for anything but good.

In Ephesians 4:29, in the midst of Paul's discussion of certain of the attributes that are to characterize the "new self," the self "created in righteousness and holiness of the truth," he wrote, "Let no unwholesome word proceed from your mouth, but only such a word as is good for edification according to the need of the moment, that it may give grace to those who hear." In Colossians 4:6 Paul also wrote, "Let your speech always be with grace, seasoned, as it were, with salt, so that you may know how you should respond to each person." Such a magnificent blessing, given to us by God, surely requires forethought and care before we open our mouths and misuse it.

It never ceases to amaze me how thoughtlessly cruel people can be with their tongues. There was a time when I had put on quite a bit of weight. There was a reason for it that was really nobody's business, yet several people felt that it was their business to tell me that I looked fat. "Boy, you sure put on the weight, didn't you?" I guess they thought I didn't know that. But the thing is, these were statements made by brethren in a decidedly off-handed manner, and they hurt.

Since that time I have been particularly sensitive to that sort of thing and there have been so many times when I have thought, "I can't believe you said that!" I have seen young sisters reduced to tears because someone thought it was their business to comment about some weight that they had put on. I have seen young Christian mothers absolutely deflated because someone felt compelled to make a comment about their children's conduct in services—comments that were not meant to help but were just mean. I remember a time when a young sister in her mid- twenties was talking about her reasons for continuing her education. As she sat there in the midst of several secretaries, the reason she gave for going on in school was that she was much too smart to be a secretary. Well, she may have been too smart to be a secretary, but at that moment you sure couldn't have proved it by the evidence of her speech.

May 23

Memorial Day

One of the national holidays for the United States of America is known as Memorial Day. While viewed as the traditional start of the Summer Season, it is actually much more serious and significant than that. It is a day set aside to remember and commemorate those men and women who have given their lives in the military service of our country.

A memorial is simply something designed to preserve the memory of a person, event, etc. The Bible speaks of many of them. For example, in Joshua 4, after the children of Israel had crossed on dry ground through the flooded Jordan River, we find in verses 1-8:

> And it came to pass, when all the people were clean passed over Jordan, that the Lord spake unto Joshua, saying, Take you twelve men out of the people, out of every tribe a man, and command ye them, saying, Take you hence out of the midst of Jordan, out of the place where the priests' feet stood firm, twelve stones, and ye shall carry them over with you, and leave them in the lodging place, where ye shall lodge this night. Then Joshua called the twelve men, whom he had prepared of the children of Israel, out of every tribe a man: and Joshua said unto them, Pass over before the ark of the Lord your God into the midst of Jordan, and take ye up every man of you a stone upon his shoulder, according to the number of the tribes of the children of Israel: that this may be a sign among you, that when your children ask their fathers in time to come, saying, What mean ye by these stones?

Then ye shall answer them, That the waters of the Jordan were cut off before the ark of the covenant of the Lord; when it passed over Jordan, the waters of Jordan were cut off: and these stones *shall be for a memorial* unto the children of Israel for ever. And the children of Israel did so as Joshua commanded, and took up twelve stones out of the midst of Jordan, as the Lord spake unto Joshua, according to the number of the tribes of the children of Israel, and carried them over with them unto the place where they lodged, and laid them down there.

Thus the event that took place at the beginning of the Conquest of Canaan was commemorated.

Just as is the case in the United States, the Bible speaks of certain days being set apart as memorials for particular events. For instance, the Passover was established as a memorial. While we won't take the time to examine the entire passage where the institution of the Passover is explained in Exodus 12, we will notice verses 13-14:

And the blood shall be to you for a token upon the houses where ye are; and when I see the blood, I will pass over you, and the plague shall not be upon you to destroy you, when I smite the land of Egypt. And this day shall be unto you *for a memorial*; and ye shall keep it a feast to the Lord throughout your generations; ye shall keep it a feast by an ordinance forever.

The greatest memorial ever established was instituted by the Lord Jesus on the very night in which He was betrayed. At the Last Supper, with the horror of the cross literally just hours away, Jesus called upon His followers to remember the events that were about to take place. In Matthew 26:26-29 we find:

And as they were eating, Jesus took bread, and blessed it, and brake it, and gave it to the disciples, and said, Take, eat, this is my body. And he took the cup, and gave thanks, and gave it to them, saying, Drink ye all of it; for this is my blood of the new testament, which is shed for many for the remission of sins. But I say unto you, I will not drink henceforth of this fruit of the vine, unto that day when I drink it new with you in my Father's kingdom.

As Paul was describing the institution of this incredible memorial in 1 Corinthians 11, we find the additional words of Jesus, "*this do in remembrance of me,*" in verse 24; "*This cup is the new testament in my blood: this do ye, as oft as ye drink it, in remembrance of me,*" in verse 25; and "*For as often as ye eat this bread, and drink this cup, ye do show the Lord's death till He come,*" in verse 26. Faithful children of God observe this memorial every first day of the week, Sunday, just as the early church did (Acts 20:7).

Memorial Day commemorates those who fought in wars for our country and gave their lives in so doing. Jesus gave His life in battle against the most dangerous and insidious foe of all time, Satan and the evil he promotes. It was a battle that began with Adam and Eve, and from that time forth the ultimate conclusion was inevitable. In Genesis 3:14-15 we read:

> And the Lord God said unto the serpent, Because thou hast done this, thou art cursed above all cattle, and above every beast of the field; upon thy belly shalt thou go, and dust shalt thou eat all the days of thy life; and I will put enmity between thee and the woman, and between thy seed and her seed; it shall bruise thy head, and thou shalt bruise his heel.

When Jesus died on the cross, the death of this sinless, perfect man was the *bruising of his heel.* But three days later, the crushing blow to the head was delivered when Jesus rose from the dead. Because of that glorious resurrection, we will rise too. So, with humility and great gratitude, let us remember that every first day of the week is a "memorial day," as we participate in the greatest and most significant memorial known to man—the celebration of the Lord's Supper.

May 24

"Better Than Themselves"

It took me a long time to figure out what was the key to practical Christianity. By "practical Christianity," I mean living day by day in a manner that is pleasing to the Lord. The key is found in Philippians 2. The first four verses of that chapter tell us,

> If therefore there is any encouragement in Christ, if there is any consolation of love, if there is any fellowship of the Spirit, if any affection and compassion, make my joy complete by being of the same mind, maintaining the same love, united in spirit, intent on one purpose. Do nothing from selfishness or empty conceit, but with humility of mind let each of you regard one another as more important than himself; do not merely look out for your own personal interests, but also for the interests of others.

The "key" to truly living day by day as a child of God is to "regard one another as more important than self." It is to recognize that being a Christian is not about me, it is about others. It is to recognize that my conduct will result from my love for God, for the Lord, and for others.

I find it interesting that the word translated as "humility of mind" (as a noun), before Paul's time, is not found in Greek sources outside of the New Testament. When the adjective form of the word was found outside of the New Testament, it was used to describe the mentality of a slave; in other words, base, unfit and no account. The pagan Greek writers did not view humility as a virtue. But the Holy Spirit, in inspiring the New Testament writers, used the example of Jesus who was Himself, "gentle and humble in heart" (Matt. 11:29). In fact, the slave mentality was used to teach valuable and *practical* lessons about the importance of humility for the one who would be pleasing to God.

Jesus taught that true greatness in His kingdom is found in serving, not in being served. In Mark 10:42-45 we find:

> And calling them to Himself, Jesus said to them, You know that those who are recognized as rulers of the Gentiles lord it over them; and their great men exercise authority over them. But it is not so among you, but whoever wishes to become great among you shall be your servant; and whoever wishes to be first among you shall be slave of all. For even the Son of Man did not come to be served, but to serve, and to give His life a ransom for many.

Have we not all marveled as we read the account of the Son of God rising from the supper, and laying aside His garments, taking a towel and girding Himself about? "Then He poured water into the basin, and began to wash the disciples' feet, and to wipe them with the towel with which He was girded" (John 13:5). Have we understood the significance of what the Lord did that Thursday evening? With Jesus leading the way, we see that humility isn't about weakness—it is about strength.

May 25

Tragedy

A tragedy occurs at every Sunday and Wednesday evening service. Brethren who could be present are absent. Encouragement that could be received or offered is lost. Bibles that could be studied are left unopened. Songs that could be sung are neglected. All of these things are true tragedies. The worst part of all is the simple fact that it doesn't have to be. Will you meet with the brethren here every time we come together? If not, why not?

"He Takes away the First. . ."

One of the keys to understanding God's Word and interpreting it properly is to recognize the distinction between the Old and New Testaments. This goes far beyond simply knowing that one comes before the other in the Bible and that they contain different books. It involves recognizing the place of each in God's great plan and understanding what is applicable to us today in terms of authority and what is not.

One of the simplest ways to describe the difference and purpose of the two is to say that the main point of the Old Testament is that the Christ, the Messiah, was coming. The first four books of the New Testament, the Gospels, tell us that He was here. The remaining twenty-three books of the New Testament tell us that He is coming again and teach us how to live in anticipation of His arrival.

The first book of the Bible, the book of Genesis, is the book of beginnings. In it we see the beginning of the world and all things in it. We see the beginning of man and the introduction of sin into the world. We see the beginning of the Scheme of Redemption, at least as it begins to be unfolded to man with the first promise concerning it, the Protevangelium (Gen. 3:15). We also see the beginning of the Jewish nation—the nation through whom the Messiah would come.

As the Old Testament begins to focus upon the Hebrews and we move from the book of Genesis into Exodus, Leviticus, Numbers, Deuteronomy, and beyond, we find God taking steps to keep the Jewish nation racially and spiritually pure, in anticipation of the coming of the Christ. They were given a law, the Law of Moses, by which they were to be governed and a land in which to live. In the New Testament, in Galatians 3:23-24, the ultimate purpose of that Law is made clear. There Paul wrote, "But before faith came, we were kept in custody under the law, being shut up to the faith which was later to be revealed. Therefore the Law has become our tutor to lead us to Christ, that we may be justified by faith."

A great deal of the Old Testament record concerns the struggle of the nation of Israel with the Law of Moses and their failure to keep it. Time and again they would forsake the Law of God and face God's righteous wrath—God utilizing various peoples and nations to punish the Jews and turn them back to Him. Time and again we see the compassion and mercy of God as the nation would repent and God would deliver them from their oppressors. As a matter of fact, the accounts of their struggles with sin and God's dealings with them serve a tremendous purpose for us today. In 1 Corinthians 10, after writing of several of the things that the children of Israel did in the time of the Wilderness Wanderings, Paul wrote in verse 11, "Now these things happened to them as an example, and they were written for our instruction, upon whom the ends of the ages have come." In Romans 15:4 we find, "For whatever was written in earlier times was written for our instruction, that through perseverance and the encouragement of the Scriptures we might have hope."

Clearly, we can open the pages of the Old Testament, read therein, and learn tremendous lessons. Actually, we cannot fully understand the New Testament without a knowledge of what came before, what preceded it, and in a very real sense, foreshadowed it. However, when it comes to our source of authority for what we do in religion today, the Old Testament is not where we are to turn. Earlier we were in Galatians 3 and saw the ultimate purpose of the Law of Moses. If we had continued on, we would have seen the duration of the Law as well. Galatians 3:25 says, "But now that faith has come, we are no longer under a tutor." The purpose of the Old Law was fulfilled. Salvation is now available through Christ and no one is under the Law of Moses any more.

May 27

". . . To Establish the Second"

In Matthew 17, upon the Mount of Transfiguration, as Jesus appeared with Moses and Elijah in a glorified state, God stated in verse 5, "This is My beloved Son, with whom I am well-pleased, listen to Him." In Matthew 28:18 Jesus said, "All authority has been given to Me in heaven and on earth."

In the book of Hebrews, chapter 1:1-2 we find, "God, after He spoke long ago to the fathers in the prophets in many portions and in many ways, in these last days has spoken to us in His Son, whom He appointed heir of all things, through whom also He made the world."

Jesus is the source of all authority today and His authority for us is found in the New Testament, the covenant Jesus ratified with His own blood.

So much of the book of Hebrews is about the superiority of the New Testament over the Old. It is a logical presentation of many of the reasons why the Old is no longer in effect and that all who would be saved are bound to obey the New. In Hebrews 7:22 we read, "So much the more also Jesus has become the guarantee of a better covenant." In Hebrews 8:6–13 we find:

> But now He has obtained a more excellent ministry, by as much as He is also the mediator of a better covenant, which has been enacted on better promises. For if that first covenant had been faultless, there would have been no occasion sought for a second. For finding fault with them, He says, 'Behold, days are coming, says the Lord, when I will effect a new covenant with the house of Israel and with the house of Judah...and they shall not teach everyone his fellow citizen, and everyone his brother, saying, Know the Lord, for all shall know Me, from the least to the greatest of them. For I will be merciful to their iniquities, and I will remember their sins no more.' When He said, 'A new covenant', He has made the first obsolete. But whatever is becoming obsolete and growing old is ready to disappear.

We are under the New Covenant, not the Old today. To search for authority for our religious practices in the Old Testament is to fail to properly interpret God's Word.

May 28

"Cast out the Bondwoman and Her Son"

In yesterday's reading, the article dealt with the fulfillment of the Old Law and the establishment of the New. The point was made that no one is under the Old Covenant today, not the Jew and not the Gentile. All today are bound to respond in obedience to the New Covenant, the New Testament that was ratified with the blood of the Son of God.

In today's reading, I would like to look at an interesting passage in which the same point is made. I believe it illustrates how completely God's hand was in the development of His plan and that the glorious Gospel of the New Testament was always God's purpose. The passage is found in Galatians 4:21-31, and reads as follows:

> Tell me, you who want to be under law, do you not listen to the law? For it is written that Abraham had two sons, one by the bondwoman and one by the free woman. But the son by the bondwoman was born according to the flesh, and the son by the free woman through the promise. This is allegorically speaking: for these women are two covenants, one proceeding from Mount Sinai bearing children who are to be slaves; she is Hagar. Now this Hagar is Mount Sinai in Arabia, and corresponds to the present Jerusalem, for she is in slavery with her children. But the Jerusalem above is free, she is our mother. For it is written, "Rejoice, barren woman who does not bear; break forth and shout, you who are not in labor; for more are the children of the desolate than of the one who has a husband." And you brethren, like Isaac, are children of promise. But as at that time he who was born according to the flesh persecuted him who was born according to the Spirit, so it is now also. But what does the Scripture say? "Cast out the bondwoman and her son, for the son of the bondwoman shall not be an heir with the son of the free woman." So then, brethren, we are not children of a bondwoman, but of the free woman.

The book of Galatians was written to a predominately Gentile church that was being troubled by certain Jewish Christians. Those Jewish Christians were teaching a perverted gospel, bringing into it certain aspects of the Law of Moses, such as circumcision, and saying that they were necessary for salvation. The letter is a powerful denial of the validity of their teaching, as well as a forceful defense of the gospel Paul had presented to them. In chapter 4, Paul makes the point that, if those who sought to be bound by the Old Law had understood the Old Law, they would know that no one was to be under it any longer.

Paul's use of the events surrounding Abraham, Isaac and Ishmael, Sarah and Hagar, is striking. He parallels what happened with them to the difference between the Old and New Covenants to illustrate the principles involved. Consider the points of comparison. Abraham is vital in that he was the father of the Jewish race and also the man who was saved by faith and the father of the faithful. (3:6-9) The two women under consideration are Sarah—a freewoman, and Hagar—a bondwoman. The two sons were Isaac—the child of promise born to a previously barren Sarah who was past the age of childbearing, and Ishmael—born after the flesh through the natural laws of procreation by Abraham and Hagar.

The allegorical interpretation is found in what Paul, through the Holy Spirit, says the things represent. Hagar and Sarah represent the two covenants. Hagar signified the Law of Moses (the Old Covenant) that was given at Mount Sinai. The Old Law kept a man in bondage to keep that Law perfectly. In 3:23, Paul had put it this way: "We were *kept in custody* under the law." In this way, Paul could write that the Law gave birth to children destined to be slaves. The Law alone could not give spiritual freedom. Thus, those seeking salvation through perfect obedience to the Law of Moses could be referred to as "her children" in slavery with her. "Present Jerusalem" stands for earthly Jerusalem, the headquarters of Judaism.

Sarah, on the other hand, corresponds to "the Jerusalem above." Notice that this Jerusalem is free, and the children of it are free as well—free of the bondage of the Law and the guilt of sin. It is clear that this " Jerusalem above," this "heavenly Jerusalem," is the church. I know this is so from Hebrews 12:22-23 which says, "But you have come to Mount Zion and to the city of the living God, the heavenly Jerusalem, and to myriads of angels, to the general assembly and *church of the first-born* who are enrolled in heaven, and to God, the Judge of all, and to the spirits of righteous men made perfect." Those who are in the church, seeking justification through faith in Christ are "children of promise," comparing to Isaac. In the comparison, those who were seeking justification through works of the Law of Moses were slaves corresponding to Ishmael.

Paul even carries the illustration further. Just as Ishmael taunted Isaac, the Jews of the first century were persecuting the church. It is important to carry the allegory to its conclusion. Even though Abraham had been reluctant to drive Hagar and Ishmael away, God told him to do so. Paul is making the same point. Those Jewish Christians who were perverting the gospel and trying to lead the Galatians astray needed to be "cast out," clearly identified, not tolerated, withdrawn from.

What a wonderful and fascinating way to demonstrate that no one is under the Old Law today! Do you not marvel at the incredible hand of God as He brings things to fruition, as He would have them to be?

If Only . . .

I was there when it started;
I guess I just couldn't tell.
If anyone had asked me
I would have said, "They're doing well!"

When did the flame start to flicker
And the enthusiasm fade away?
I guess I just didn't see it.
I didn't know what to say.

At first it was just occasionally,
They didn't miss all the time.
A child was sick, or he had to work,
I still thought everything was fine.

After a while it got more frequent;
Their seat was empty more than not.
I should have said something then,
But that would have put me on the spot.

If only I had noticed;
If only I had tried.
I didn't do a thing to help them.
That's the truth, it cannot be denied.

Now their seat is always empty.
They have left the Lord, I don't know why.
And when I think about "If only. . . .
All I can do is cry.

"Whoever Believes in Him Will Not Be Disappointed"

In every formal, public discussion concerning the necessity of baptism for the remission of sins that I have attended, passages such as Romans 10:11 are continually brought up. The point is generally made in this way: "If baptism is necessary why does it say, 'Whoever believes in Him will not be disappointed'?"

Most often there will be an overhead projection, a beautifully made chart, listing a number of passages that mention belief and nothing else. John 3:16 is usually included: "For God so loved the world, that He gave His only begotten Son, that whoever believes in Him should not perish, but have eternal life." John 3:36 is inevitably included as well. It says, "He who believes in the Son has eternal life; but he who does not obey the Son shall not see life, but the wrath of God abides on him." John 6:40 is on all of the lists because it says, "For this is the will of My Father, that everyone who beholds the Son and believes in Him, may have eternal life; and I Myself will raise him up on the last day." Frequently the entire exchange between Jesus and Martha in John 11 is on the list as well, and we must not forget Ephesians 2:8-9, "For by grace you have been saved through faith; and that not of yourselves, it is the gift of God; not as a result of works, that no one should boast." I have even heard the argument made that a person could list four times as many passages that deal with belief than passages that deal with, or even mention, baptism. How then could baptism be essential?

In Luke 13: 3 and 5, Jesus made the exact same statement. He said, "I tell you, no, but unless you repent, you will all likewise perish." Would we be correct if we went to these verses and said that repentance is all that is necessary? The verses do not contain the word "belief," or any other form of it. We could go to Acts 17, to the midst of the Areopagus with Paul, and read his words of verses 30-31, "Therefore having overlooked the times of ignorance, God is now declaring to men that all everywhere should repent, because He has fixed a day in which He will judge the world in righteousness through a Man whom He has appointed, having furnished proof to all men by raising Him from the dead." Would we be correct if we said that

Paul only mentioned repentance in this passage, therefore repentance is all that is necessary?

For that matter, we could go to Acts 22:16 and read the words of Ananias to Saul (later to become Paul), "And now why do you delay? Arise, and be baptized, and wash away your sins, calling on His name." I don't see belief mentioned there, or repentance either. Would it be right to say that baptism to "wash away your sins" is all that is necessary? We could quote 1 Peter 3:21 which says, "And corresponding to that, baptism now saves you—not the removal of dirt from the flesh, but an appeal to God for a good conscience— through the resurrection of Jesus Christ." Would it be fair and good scholarship to say that on the basis of 1 Peter 3:21, only baptism is necessary?

The answer to every one of those questions is no. It is not right to take a verse out of the context of the entire New Testament revelation and assign to it a significance that it does not have. Yet, each one of those verses teaches the absolute truth. How can that be? The answer is simple.

John 3:16; 3:36; 6:40; and 11:25f, as well as Ephesians 2:8-9; Luke 13:3 and 5; Acts 17:30-31; 22:16, and 1 Peter 3:21, all teach the truth and do it in the following way. They are examples of synecdoche, which is a fancy name for something that we both read and use all the time. Synecdoche is a "figure of speech in which a part is used for the whole or the whole for a part, the special for the general or the general for the special, as in ten sails for ten ships or a Croesus for a rich man" (*Webster's New Universal Unabridged Dictionary*).

So, when Jesus said "that whoever believes in Him should not perish," that includes everything that is involved in belief. When the Lord said, "Unless you repent, you will all likewise perish," everything else that is involved in salvation is implied. Repent was a part being used for the whole. When Peter said, "baptism now saves you," he did not mean baptism only; everything else was implied. It was synecdoche, a part being used for the whole.

The interesting thing is that every single person I have discussed this issue with, whether in private conversation, formal discussion, public debate, or on the radio, has recognized the use of synecdoche even though they didn't know it. They have all believed that repentance was necessary. When pressed, they would all admit that confession was necessary. They simply refuse to admit, because of previously held ideas and spiritual prejudice, that the same is true of baptism.

For the faithful child of God, every single verse is his verse. Every single verse is true and teaches the truth. The faithful child of God does not have to run to a few memorized "proof-texts," because they are all our texts. That is how God intended it to be, and it is a comforting and glorious position in which to be. Every verse harmonizes perfectly with every other one. It is the marvelous presentation of truth.

"Sanctify them in the truth; Thy word is truth" (John 17:17).

"For Christ Did Not Send Me to Baptize"

Recently I attended a debate concerning the question of baptism. I believe the proposition on the evening I attended was something like "Salvation occurs before and without water baptism." A Baptist preacher was in the affirmative that night, with a young gospel preacher in the negative.

In the course of his affirmative presentation, the Baptist preacher quoted 1 Corinthians 1:17 in an attempt to prove that baptism is not necessary for salvation. The verse reads as follows, "For Christ did not send me to baptize, but to preach the gospel, not in cleverness of speech, that the cross of Christ should not be made void." Very few debates on this subject go by, at least that I am aware of, without 1 Corinthians 1:17 being brought up as a "proof-text" that demonstrates that baptism cannot be essential to salvation. After all, Paul wrote, "For Christ did not send me to baptize."

In truth, when it is kept in context, 1 Corinthians 1:17 proves the exact opposite. It is a joy to know that when you have the truth, every verse is a "proof-text" of it. For a faithful child of God, every verse is his verse. We have no particular "proof-texts," because all Scripture is the truth. As those who have only the truth to uphold and absolutely no denominational creed to defend, we don't have to back away from any verse or concede a single iota of that which is not true.

Let's look at the context of 1 Corinthians 1:17. Beginning with verse 10 we read, "Now I exhort you, brethren, by the name of our Lord Jesus Christ, that you all agree, and there be no divisions among you, but you be made complete in the same mind and in the same judgment. For I have been informed concerning you, my brethren, by Chloe's people, that there are quarrels among you. Now I mean this, that each one of you is saying, I am of Paul, and I of Apollos, and I of Cephas, and I of Christ. Has Christ been divided? Paul was not crucified for you, was he? Or were you baptized in the name of Paul? I thank God that I baptized none of you except Crispus, and Gaius, that no man should say you were baptized in my name. Now I did baptize also the household of Stephanas; beyond that, I do not know whether I baptized any other. For Christ did not send me to baptize, but to preach the gospel, not in cleverness of speech, that the cross of Christ should not be made void."

As we begin to examine the context of this passage, we note that Paul is exhorting the brethren in Corinth to unity. He exhorts that there be "no divisions" among them, "divisions" coming from the same word that is used to designate a tear in a piece of material. He exhorts them that they be "made complete," "complete" coming from a word that originally meant to mend fishing nets. So the idea was that they were not to let any tears appear in the fabric of the congregation, and where any were, they were to mend them by all being "in the same mind and in the same judgment."

Word had reached Paul that there were "quarrels" among the brethren in Corinth. Some were saying that they were "of Paul." Others were claiming to be "of Apollos," or "of Cephas," or "of Christ." So Paul simply asked them a series of rhetorical questions, the answer to each being "no." He asked, "Has Christ been divided? Paul was not crucified for you, was he? Or were you baptized in the name of Paul?" Paul was asking how they could possibly say that they were "of someone," when that person had not been crucified for them and they had not been baptized in the name of that person, or by that person's authority. What we actually are seeing are two conditions being set forth by Paul that must be met before they could truthfully say they were "of" someone: (1) that person had to be crucified for them, and (2) they had to have been baptized in the name of that person. Those two conditions were true of no one but Christ, so how could they be saying that they were "of" Apollos, or Cephas, or Paul?

As we continue on in our examination of the context of verse 17, it is quite clear and apparent to all that Paul was not making an absolute statement when he wrote, "For Christ did not send me to baptize." If he was, then he violated what he said that Christ told him. Paul said that he baptized Crispus and Gaius, and the household of Stephanas. How could he do that if, in fact, Christ did not send him to baptize?

Obviously there has to be an explanation of the first phrase of verse 17, and there is. It is a rather common grammatical device known as "elliptical construction." This is sometimes explained as a "not only, but" statement. Let me give you another biblical example of the same kind of statement. In John 12:44 we find these words, "And Jesus cried out and said, He who believes in Me does not believe in Me, but in Him who sent Me."

Now we ask, is it true that the person who believes in Jesus does not believe in God? No, that is not true. This is another example of elliptical construction. To get the true meaning, John 12:44 can be read this way, "And Jesus cried out and said, He who believes in Me, does not believe in Me only, but in Him who sent Me." We can all see that, can't we? It is a "not only, but" kind of construction. The "only" doesn't need to be supplied because it is obvious.

In exactly the same way, 1 Corinthians 1:17 is to be understood. It can be read this way, "For Christ did not send me to baptize only, but to preach the gospel, not in cleverness of speech, that the cross of Christ should not be made void." The "only" in this verse does not need to be supplied either, because it is equally obvious to all who keep it in context and who do not have a man-made doctrine to sustain.

June 1

"And Abraham Believed God. . ." (1)

Recently I heard a fellow call the gospel of John, "the gospel proclaimed," and the letter to the Romans, "the gospel explained." I thought that was an interesting way of looking at it and was prepared to hear more until I heard the fellow's approach to Romans 4—a pivotal chapter in the book. The gentleman focused on Romans 4:3, and completely missed the point. Romans 4:3 says, "For what does the Scripture say? And Abraham believed God, and it was reckoned to him as righteousness." The fellow attempted to use Abraham to prove that salvation comes at the point of belief; he even added the word "alone" in his explanation of the verse.

The quotation found in Romans 4:3 is from Genesis 15:6. It was made concerning Abram believing that God would give him an heir, a son of his old age. This statement was made even as Abram was in the land of Canaan, and that is a vital point.

As I think about the letter to the Romans, referring to it as "the gospel explained" is a pretty good way of looking at it. It is, at least in my opinion, the most profound and in-depth presentation of salvation by grace through faith in Scripture. It is also one of the most profoundly misunderstood and misused.

Romans is about faith. It is about salvation through faith. It also makes it clear that the faith that saves is not simply belief, and Abraham, the father of the faithful, is a classic example of that truth.

We are first introduced to Abraham, called Abram at the time, in Genesis 11. He was residing in Ur of the Chaldees, a city located in the lower southeastern portion of Mesopotamia on the Euphrates River. Stephen, in Acts 7:2-4, makes it clear that while he was living in Ur of the Chaldees, Abraham received his first call from God. That passage says:

> And he said, Hear me, brethren and fathers! The God of glory appeared to our father Abraham when he was in Mesopotamia, before he lived in Haran, and said to him, Depart from your country and your relatives, and come into the land that I will show you. Then he departed from the land of the Chaldeans, and settled in Haran. And from there, after his father died, God removed him into this country in which you are now living.

God called Abraham. He told him to leave the land that he knew and journey to a land that he did not know. Hebrews 11:8 tells us, "By faith Abraham, when he was called, obeyed by going out to a place which he was to receive for an inheritance; and he went out, not knowing where he was going." Abraham journeyed through Mesopotamia to Haran, a city located in the northwest portion of Mesopotamia between the Tigris and Euphrates Rivers. At the death of his father, God called him again. This is the call recorded in Genesis 12:1-3 that contains the land, nation, and seed promises. Do you know what Abraham did when he received this call? He obeyed. Genesis 12:4 tells us, "So Abram went forth as the Lord had spoken to him; and Lot went with him. Now Abram was seventy-five years old when he departed from Haran."

The pertinent question, and the key to understanding Abraham's place as the father of the faithful, is this: Would the statement found in Genesis 15:6, and quoted in Romans 4:3, ever have been made if Abraham had remained in Ur of the Chaldees? For that matter, would it have been made if Abraham had remained in Haran when the second call came? The obvious and undeniable answer to those questions is *no!* If Abraham had simply believed God alone, and had not obeyed Him, then there would have been no saving faith, only belief. Belief alone has *never* been good enough!

"And Abraham Believed God. . ." (2)

The gentleman who prompted this discussion continued in his misuse of Romans 4, by looking at verses 4-5, among others. Those verses say, "Now to the one who works, his wage is not reckoned as a favor, but as what is due. But to the one who does not work, but believes in Him who justifies the ungodly, his faith is reckoned as righteousness." His assertion was that, if Abraham had to do anything, then he wasn't justified by faith. The problem here, among many, is that he equates saving faith with belief alone, and they are not the same. Abraham was justified without the works of the Law of Moses, or the works of any man-made law, but he was most definitely justified by works. Whose works? The works that God told him to do.

In James 2, Abraham is used to demonstrate the exact opposite of what this false teacher to whom I was listening was attempting to convince people to believe. In James 2:21-24 we find, "Was not Abraham our father justified by works, when he offered up Isaac his son on the altar? You see that faith was working with his works, and as a result of the works, faith was perfected; and the Scripture was fulfilled which says, And Abraham believed God, and it was reckoned to him as righteousness, and he was called the friend of God." What kind of works was James writing about? Was he writing concerning works of the Law of Moses? No! Was he writing about works that man comes up with in an attempt to earn his salvation? No! He was writing about works of obedience to the commands of God. He was writing about doing what God says, not just believing God, but obeying Him as well.

Now let's get back to the letter to the Romans. That wonderfully profound letter practically begins and ends with a phrase that is the key to understanding the letter itself. The phrase acts as "bookends" to the wonderful library of magnificent truths taught within the pages of the letter. It is found in Romans 1:5 and in Romans 16:26. Romans 1:5 reads, "Through whom we have received grace and apostleship to bring about the *obedience of faith* among all the Gentiles, for His name's sake." Romans 16:26 says, "But now is manifested, and by the Scriptures of the prophets, according to the commandment of the eternal God, has been made known to all the nations, leading to *obedience of faith*." Without obedience, there is no saving faith!

In Romans 6:3-7, we have that wonderful teaching about baptism being a burial into the death of Christ as well as a resurrection when we come out of the water to walk in newness of life. In verses 16-18 we read:

> Do you not know that when you present yourselves to someone as slaves for obedience, you are slaves of the one whom you obey, either of sin resulting in death, or of obedience resulting in righteousness? But thanks be to God that though you were slaves of sin, you became obedient from the heart to that form of teaching to which you were committed, and having been freed from sin, you became slaves of righteousness.

When were the Romans "freed from sin"? When they "became obedient from the heart to that form of teaching."

The emphasis on obedience in Romans is all encompassing. In 2:6-8 we find, "Who will render to every man according to his deeds; to those who by perseverance in doing good seek for glory and honor and immortality, eternal life; but to those who are selfishly ambitious and do not obey the truth, but obey unrighteousness, wrath and indignation." In Romans 15:18, we read, "For I will not presume to speak of anything except what Christ has accomplished through me, resulting in the obedience of the Gentiles by word and deed."

Brethren and friends, *without obedience there is no saving faith*. Faith without obedience is simply belief, and belief alone is not good enough. "You believe that God is one. You do well; the demons also believe, and shudder" (Jas. 2:19).

June 3

Putting on a Red's Jacket

One of the listeners to a radio program I once hosted sent me a very thoughtful and kind e-mail. In it, he questioned what we have been saying that the Bible teaches concerning the necessity of baptism for salvation. One of the points that he made was, "Baptism is like wearing a Red's jacket. It shows who our loyalties are with, but it has *no* saving power. It is a human work, not an outpouring of grace." This was such a kind spirited letter from a man who is obviously deeply spiritually minded. It breaks my heart to see such a person so misled as to make a statement that is not only without scriptural support, but is absolutely contrary to what Scripture actually teaches.

In Galatians 3:26-27 Paul wrote, "For ye are all the children of God by faith in Christ Jesus. For as many of you as have been baptized into Christ have put on Christ." Elsewhere Paul taught, "For by grace are ye saved through faith: and that not of yourselves: it is the gift of God: not of works, lest any man should boast." That we are saved by grace through faith is unquestionably true. The faith that saves is faith in the Lord Jesus Christ. Those who have faith enter into a spiritual relationship with God. They are born again and become His children. This is undeniable.

Galatians 3:27 begins with the word "for," from the Greek word *gar*. That helps us to understand. Verse 27 relates to verse 26 by way of explanation. It explains how people become "children of God by faith in Christ Jesus." Everyone who has become a child of God by faith in Christ Jesus has done so through being baptized into Christ. The text says that we are "baptized into Christ."

This is the question that must be asked: "Is salvation found in Christ?" According to Ephesians 1:7, it certainly is. That verse says, "In whom (the 'whom' is Jesus, g.l.) we have redemption through his blood, the forgiveness of sins, according to the riches of his grace." If redemption, forgiveness of sins, is found "in Christ," and we are "baptized into Christ," then to argue that baptism has nothing to do with salvation is to argue that salvation is not found in Christ.

Ephesians 1:7 also tells us that our redemption is "through his blood." That begs the question, "When, or where, did Jesus shed His blood?" The answer to that is in His death on the cross of Calvary. Into what are we baptized? Romans 6:3–4 states it so plainly that a person truly needs help to misunderstand. Paul wrote, "Know ye not, that so many of us as were baptized into Jesus Christ were baptized into his death? Therefore we are buried with him by baptism into death: that like as Christ was raised up from the dead by the glory of the Father, even so we also should walk in newness of life." If baptism has nothing to do with salvation, then neither does the blood of Christ, which He shed in His death.

What about the Red's jacket? Galatians 3:27 does use a phrase associated with the idea of putting on clothing. The word "put on" means "to dress, clothe." It points to a specific event—what happened when they were baptized into Christ. In the act of baptism, they clothed themselves with Christ.

Literally, the word refers to putting on clothes; figuratively, it refers to taking on the characteristics, virtues, and intentions of Christ. What the kind writer of the e-mail has done is to focus entirely on verse 26 and the last phrase of verse 27, but dismiss the part of verse 27 that explains it all.

We often hear, as the writer included in his e-mail, that baptism is a human work. The idea behind that statement is that we are making baptism a work whereby man earns his salvation. I deny with every fiber of my being that baptism is such a work. The bold statement that baptism is a work whereby a person earns his salvation is completely contrary to what the Scriptures actually teach. Baptism is nowhere called a work, and is specifically stated not to be such a work. I get tired of people making such a bold assertion that is nowhere supported by Scripture. If something gets said often enough, people will just begin to believe it is true and repeat it like a parrot.

Consider Titus 3:4-5 where Paul wrote, "But after the kindness and love of God our Savior toward man appeared, *not by works of righteousness which we have done*, but according to his mercy he saved us, *by the washing of regeneration*, and renewing of the Holy Ghost." Baptism is not a work of man's own righteousness; it is included in God's righteousness. It is a part of God's way for making man righteous, just as much as belief is (John 6:28-29).

One might wear a Red's jacket, but that doesn't make him part of the team. I wear a Bengal's jacket, and that doesn't make me part of the team. But when I am "baptized into Christ," I become part of the team, I "put on Christ," taking on His characteristics and virtues. Being on the team and just sitting in the stands wearing a jacket are two different things.

June 4

"Not As a Result of Works, That No One Should Boast"

The title of this reading is from Ephesians 2:9. In the continuing debate with denominational preachers concerning the necessity of baptism for the remission of sins, Ephesians 2:8-9 is always brought up. One argument that is made in an attempt to deny the essential nature of baptism for salvation is to say that baptism is a human work, and salvation is not of works. In addition to

Ephesians 2:9, Romans 4:4-5 is frequently quoted. That passage says, "Now to the one who works, his wage is not reckoned as a favor, but as what is due. But to the one who does not work, but believes in Him who justifies the ungodly, his faith is reckoned as righteousness." Thus, according to the argument, since baptism is a work that humans do, it cannot be essential to salvation.

Baptism is a work, but it is not a work that man invented or came up with. In truth, baptism is no more a human work than belief. In John 6:28-29 we find the following exchange between Jesus and a multitude near the city of Capernaum: "They said therefore to Him, What shall we do, that we may work the works of God? Jesus answered and said to them, This is the work of God, that you believe in Him whom He has sent." Belief itself is called a work. Who requires it, man or God? If I believe, have I earned my salvation? Does the responsibility for my believing rest upon my shoulders or God's? If we place the responsibility upon God's shoulders, and I believe but you don't, did God fail with you? Did He arbitrarily decide that I would be a believer and you would not? Would that not make God the quintessential "respecter of persons"? The truth is that belief is a work that God has told me I must do to be saved. I am the one who must believe and when I do, I have not earned my salvation, I have simply obeyed God.

The same holds true with repentance. God requires it, He commands it. It is my responsibility to obey. In Acts 17:30 the Apostle Paul said, "Therefore having overlooked the times of ignorance, God is now declaring to men that all everywhere should repent." Who must do the repenting, God? No, I must repent. It is something that I must do! Does that then make repenting a human work, something whereby I can boast of earning my salvation? Absolutely not! It is simply doing what God said to do.

What about confession of my belief in Jesus as Lord? Does that constitute a human work whereby I merit remission of sins? In Romans 10:8-10 we read, "But what does it say? The word is near you, in your mouth and in your heart—that is, the word of faith which we are preaching, that if you confess with your mouth Jesus as Lord, and believe in your heart that God raised Him from the dead, you shall be saved; for with the heart man believes, resulting in righteousness, and with the mouth he confesses, resulting in salvation." Who must do the confessing? The answer to that question is me; I am the one who must confess. It is not something that God does for me, I must do it! Does that mean I have earned my salvation? No, I have simply done what God has commanded.

By now all who really want to see certainly can. As a matter of fact, believing, repenting and confessing are things that I must do. Baptism, on the other hand, is something that I submit to - it is the only one of these things that is done to me. But the point is, it is a work. Baptism is a work that God would have me to do to have my sins remitted. That is precisely what Peter said in Acts 2:38 in answer to the question, "Brethren, what shall we do?" Peter's answer is as true now as it was on that Jewish feast day of Pentecost that followed the ascension of our Lord into heaven. He said, "Repent, and let each of you be baptized in the name of Jesus Christ for the forgiveness of your sins; and you shall receive the gift of the Holy Spirit."

There is no legitimate reason or way to try to distinguish between belief and baptism by saying belief is a work of God and baptism is a work of man. The same can be said of those who try to make a similar distinction between repentance, confession, and baptism. All of these are required by God for salvation, originated in His mind, not man's, and are essential to salvation. To try to make such a distinction is purely arbitrary and dishonest. To say that one is an attempt to earn our salvation and the others are not is ridiculous. All of them are necessary works of obedience to God and leave no room for boasting.

As always, the Lord put it best. In Luke 17:7-10 we read:

But which of you, having a slave plowing or tending sheep, will say to him when he has come in from the field, Come immediately and sit down to eat? But will he not say to him, Prepare something for me to eat, and properly clothe yourself and serve me until I have eaten and drunk; and afterward you will eat and drink? He does not thank the slave because he did the things which were commanded, does he? So you too, when you do all things which are commanded you, say, We are unworthy slaves; we have done only that which we ought to have done.

The greatest minds of all the people who have ever lived could be combined in an attempt to devise a plan whereby we could be saved and the result would only be failure. Our salvation cannot be merited or earned. We cannot through our own works place God in our debt. When we do what He has commanded us, we have no basis for boasting. We have only done what is our duty to do.

June 5

What You Mean to Me

I wake up every morning, and the first thing I do
Is thank God for the blessing of another day with you.

We promised God so long ago that we'd walk through life as one.
So through hills and valleys we have gone,
And will forever do so until this life is done.

Through children, sickness, operations, no money,
And the loss of parents too,
There have been two that I could always count on—they are God and you.

As the years go by and we grow older, there is one thing I pray—
That you and I will go together, leave this world the same day.

With heartfelt gratitude to God on my knees I fall,
Thanking Him for all life's blessings, and you are best of all.

I promise I will nourish you and cherish you until the very end.
You are my life, you are my love, you are my best friend.

"Husbands, love your wives, just as Christ also loved the church and gave Himself up for her; that He might sanctify her, having cleansed her by the washing of water with the word, that He might present to Himself the church in all her glory, having no spot or wrinkle or any such thing, but that she should be holy and blameless. So husbands ought also to love their own wives as their own bodies. He who loves his own wife loves himself" (Eph. 5:25-28).

June 6

Do Not Let Your Anger Cause You to Sin

In Ephesians 4:26 Paul wrote, "Be ye angry, and sin not: let not the sun go down upon your wrath." There is much that we could say about this verse.

For instance, we could focus on the fact that Paul used two different terms in this verse to refer to anger. They are *orgizo*—angry, and *parorgismos*—wrath. About these words Vine wrote, "*Orgizo* from *orge* is a reasoned state of mind which is aroused or provoked to the point of being indignant or enraged by conditions impacting the individual. That arousal may or may not be sudden but it is often the result of spontaneous reaction. *Parorgismos* is a stronger form of *orge* implying a cherished anger. It is a more constant bad temper, embittered wrath, or irritated exasperation."

There are times when anger, *orge*, is justifiable, even righteous. The Bible refers to the anger of Jesus in such places as Mark 3:1-5 and John 2:13-17. Jesus was sinless, so in these cases we are seeing righteous anger. It is most certainly true that Christians should be made angry by sin, especially if we see it in ourselves. A failure to be angry with sin may be, in itself, sinful.

However, what I want to briefly focus upon is that Paul is telling us not to let anger cause us to sin. He said, "Don't let the sun go down upon your wrath." That is just another way of saying don't hang on to that anger, don't let malice and bitterness over take you. Connecting the dismissing of wrath with the setting of the sun illustrates the need to deal with that emotion quickly.

I believe that this is one of the more difficult tasks that God has enjoined upon us. As Christians, members of the body of Christ, things happen. In what is to be the closest of families, even closer than our immediate fleshly families, things can be said, actions can be taken, sin committed, and anger aroused. How we deal with that anger is equally important in God's eyes, as the sin that initially prompted it. We have a choice when anger is called for. It can be a reasoned response, controlled and free of vindictiveness or vengeance and something that we absolutely refuse to dwell upon; or it can be an emotional response that involves an almost cherished anger, something that we intend to hold on to, allowing it to build to bitterness and to destroy our inner peace and happiness.

Not only do I know what the Bible says about this kind of anger and what it can do—I personally know about this type of anger. I know that it can reach right into your heart and take away your joy. It can cause you to be blind to all the wonderful blessings we have in Christ because we can't, or won't, let the bitterness go. It can get to the point where the very thought of a particular person, or persons, can cause bad feelings to rise within us. If we have gotten to that point, we don't have to stay there. Through prayer, study, and following the Lord's pattern of conduct, we can get to the point that when the sun goes down, there will be no wrath remaining.

June 7

Just One Hour!

Jesus said through Him I'm free,
And I must say I do agree.
On Sunday morning at church I'll be,
But the rest of the week you won't see me.

Jesus understands I know what's best,
On Sunday evening I need my rest.
Wednesday night's a bad time too,
The week's half over and I've so much to do.

I sure am glad He died for me,
And from my sins He set me free.
So one hour a week I'll gladly give,
That's payment enough for the things He did.

June 8

Solomon Wasn't the Only One

Solomon wasn't the only biblical writer to teach the need to be spiritually minded while young. As a matter of fact, all of the writers who address the subject in God's Word are unanimous in teaching that the ideal time for seeking God and coming to know and obey Him is when a person is young.

In Deuteronomy 31:12-13 we find, "Gather the people together, men, and women, and children, and thy stranger that is within thy gates, that they may hear, and that they may learn, and fear the Lord your God, and observe to do all the words of this law: and that their children, which have not known anything, may hear, and learn to fear the Lord your God, as long as ye live in the land whither ye go over Jordan to possess it."

David wrote in Psalm 34:11, "Come, ye children, hearken unto me: I will teach you the fear of the Lord."

Once again, from the pen of Solomon, we find in Proverbs 4:1-4, "Hear, ye children, the instruction of a father, and attend to know understanding. For I give you good doctrine, forsake ye not my law. For I was my father's son, tender and only beloved in the sight of my mother. He taught me also, and said unto me, Let thine heart retain my words; keep my commandments, and live."

Why is it so important to love God and to obey Him while young? There are several reasons I can think of. For instance, remember Proverbs 22:6? Solomon wrote, "Train up a child in the way he should go: and when he is old, he will not depart from it." A young person is like a blank computer disk. Little by little information is put onto that disk, and it is only what goes onto that disk that can be retained. Youth appears to be the time when a person is most receptive and capable of learning. The older a person gets, the harder it becomes to learn. We've all heard the expression, "You can't teach an old dog new tricks." There is a certain degree of truth to that statement.

June 9

Help Me!

Help me to forgive
When things don't go my way.
Help me to be willing to listen,
To what others have to say.

Help me to be willing
To turn the other cheek.
Help me to be able
To recognize the weak.

Help me to be willing
To admit when I am wrong.
For such a willingness,
Is seen in those who are strong.

Help me to focus entirely on You,
When a few seemed determined,
To let me know in subtle ways,
That they don't like the sermon.

Help me to understand
That all any of us can do,
Is the very best our skills allow
As we seek to love and honor You.

Help me to recognize
A wonderful blessing that You Give,
Our brothers and sisters in Christ,
Among whom to work and live.

I don't know what tomorrow holds,
Or what the dawn may bring.
But if it be good or it be bad,
Help me lift my voice to praise and sing.

June 10

Dealing with Pride

In 1 Peter 5:5 Peter wrote, "You younger men, likewise, be subject to your elders; and all of you, clothe yourselves with humility toward one another, for God is opposed to the proud, but gives grace to the humble." Adherence to the principles set forth in this verse, and in several others that we will notice, would eliminate the overabundance of love for self—*pride*—that causes so many problems in congregations of the Lord's people.

The word for "one another" means "reciprocally, mutually." So what all Christians are to clothe themselves with is to be done reciprocally, or mutually. What we are to clothe ourselves with is "humility." It is interesting that the concept of humility, the idea of serving one another reciprocally, was unknown among the pagans of that time. Thayer writes of the expression "clothe yourselves" in this way: "to fasten or gird on one's self, the *egkomboma* was the white scarf or apron of slaves, which was fastened to the girdle of the vest *(exomis)*, and distinguished slaves from freemen; hence 1 Peter 5:5 *ten tapeinophrosunen. Egkombosasthe,* gird yourselves with humility as your servile garb *(egkomboma)* i.e., by putting on humility show your subjection to one another."

Arndt and Gingrich define "humility" as "the having of a humble opinion of one's self; a deep sense of one's (moral) littleness; modesty, humility, lowliness of mind." Putting those definitions together, one's mind is immediately drawn to Philippians 2:3-8:

> Do nothing from selfishness or empty conceit *(pride—g.l.),* but with humility of mind let each of you regard one another as more important than himself; do not merely look out for your own interests, but also for the interests of others. Have this attitude in yourselves which was also in Christ Jesus, who although He existed in the form of God, did not regard equality with God a thing to be grasped, but emptied Himself, taking the form of a bondservant, and being made in the likeness of men. And being found in appearance as a man, He humbled Himself by becoming obedient to the point of death, even death on a cross.

This is the attitude that Christians are to have one to another. It is one of mutual service. It has no room in it for arrogance, an "I am better than you" way of looking at things. It doesn't allow for a Christian to set him- or herself over and above others and expect everything to go his or her way. If I am more interested in your welfare than I am in mine, and you feel the same way about me (because in Christ it is to be mutual and reciprocal), how are there going to be problems of a non-doctrinal nature that we can't work out? The truth is, a lot of Christians just don't have that attitude.

How serious is it to fail to have and to manifest this attitude? Peter said, "For *(hoti, because)* God is opposed to the proud, but gives grace to the humble." This is all about the way we view and treat one another, and Peter says that God opposes the one who is arrogant, proud, who thinks he is better than anyone else. Thayer defines the word *huperephanos* as "especially in a bad sense, with *an overweening estimate of one's means or merits, despising others or even treating them with contempt, haughty."* On the other hand, the "humble" person is the recipient of God's favor and blessings. Brethren, *pride destroys!*

This is the way it is supposed to be, but there will continue to be strife and bitterness, biting and devouring, and congregational splits in the absence of doctrinal matters as long as some brethren look at others and see only *themselves.* Whose church is it? Does it belong to me? Does it belong to you? "Has

Christ been divided? Paul was not crucified for you, was he? Or were you baptized in the name of Paul?" (1 Cor. 1:13).

June 11

Bending the Rules

A gentleman once asked me on a radio program, "Can't you bend the rules a little bit?" My initial reaction to his question was surprise. In the context of a discussion about the need to abide within the truth of our Lord, how could someone ask if it was possible to bend the rules? But upon further reflection, it has become easy to see what would cause that man to ask such a question.

"Bending the rules" is a way of life for most people. Is it even necessary to mention how people bend the rules when it comes to obeying the laws of our land? If the speed limit is 55 on a particular road, most interpret that to mean 60. A few weeks ago I heard a highway patrolman say that the average speed on I-75 between Cincinnati and Dayton is 80 mph. Have you ever noticed how, in many instances, a yellow light no longer means slow down and prepare to stop—but rather, speed up so you can make it through the light? I have known people who prefer to be paid in cash if possible in order to avoid any record of income so that they can "bend the rules a little bit" when it comes to taxes. In sports, coaches and players regularly push the rules to the limit, even "bending them a little bit" if it means they might gain an advantage. In schools with dress codes, students make a habit of seeing just how far they can "bend the rules" and get away with it. "Bending the rules" is commonplace, and people do get away with it every single day.

But how does God feel about bending His rules? In Romans 15:4 Paul wrote, "For whatever was written in earlier times was written for our instruction, that through perseverance and the encouragement of the Scriptures we might have hope." Recognizing the value of "whatever was written in earlier times," perhaps we can find some indication of how God feels about those who "bend His rules" in the Old Testament.

Cain was evidently a "rule bender." He offered a sacrifice that was not according to God's instructions. I am sure that he felt satisfied in "bending the rules" to suit himself, but was God satisfied? Genesis 4:5-7 gives us the answer, "But for Cain and for his offering He had no regard. So Cain became very angry and his countenance fell. Then the Lord said to Cain, Why are you angry? And why has your countenance fallen? If you do well, will not your countenance be lifted up? And if you do not do well, sin is crouching at the door; and its desire is for you, but you must master it."

How about Nadab and Abihu? God told the people from where fire was to come for the burning of incense. Nadab and Abihu decided to "bend the rules a little bit," and get fire from some place other than the one God had designated. The incense was still going to burn, and it would smell the same. What was the big deal? Leviticus 10:2 tells us, "And fire came out from the presence of the Lord and consumed them, and they died before the Lord." The "big deal" was that God had given the rules and these two men "bent" them.

In the New Testament we are told not to go beyond that which is written. Paul wrote in 1 Corinthians 4:6, "Now these things, brethren, I have figuratively applied to myself and Apollos for your sakes, that in us you might learn not to exceed what is written, in order that no one of you might become arrogant in behalf of one against the other."

We are told in 2 John 9, "Anyone who goes too far and does not abide in the teaching of Christ, does not have God; the one who abides in the teaching, he has both the Father and the Son." At no time is permission ever given to "bend" the rules of God—not even just a "little bit."

A person might be a "bender of rules" all the days of his life and consistently get away with it. But when this life is over, so too is the getting away with it. We can't bend God's rules, even a little bit. "For we must all appear before the judgment seat of Christ, that each one may be recompensed for his deeds in the body, according to what he has done, whether good or bad" (2 Cor. 5:10).

June 12

Servant

"Paul, a servant of Jesus Christ..." These words appear in the first verse and letter to the Romans. Paul was writing to a church composed of people he did not know personally. He was writing to a church located in the greatest city in the world, the capital of the greatest empire in the world. Naturally, he began by presenting his credentials. One of those was that he was a servant of Jesus Christ.

The word translated "servant" is the Greek word *doulos*. It is also translated at various times as bondservant or slave. Paul thought of himself as the slave of Jesus Christ. He was a bondservant, bought with a price (1 Cor. 6:19-20), and he belonged to Jesus. No longer was he free to indulge in his own pleasures and desires. As a "slave of Jesus Christ" his duty was to do what Jesus commanded of him.

We too are "servants of Jesus Christ." We have been bought with a price and belong completely to Jesus. Our work is to do the will of the Lord and to do it without complaint. Considering what Jesus gave to purchase us to be His slaves, this is not a burden. It is a great honor.

June 13

Am I Like the Israelites?

I looked in the mirror,
And what did I see?
The Israelites in the wilderness
Looking back at me.

Why did they criticize?
Why did they complain?
Give me your attention
And I'll try to explain.

In the land of Egypt
Their lives were spared;
The rise of Joseph
Showing how God truly cared.

In prosperity and number
They grew and grew,
In the choice land of Goshen,
That God had brought them to.

At one hundred and ten
Joseph passed away,
And with a different dynasty
Came a new day.

This pharaoh knew not Joseph
And cared not what he had done.
He saw the number of Israelites
And feared that trouble had begun.

He made slaves of Joseph's people;
They labored from dawn to setting sun.
Bondage was their lot in life,
Unless something could be done.

God heard their cries of anguish,
To their pleas He turned His ears.
They would be delivered out of Egypt,
After 430 years.

Moses was their leader;
A man of God was he.
They left the land of Goshen,
Headed toward the Red Sea.

Through the mighty hand of God
The waters did divide.
On a miracle of dry ground,
They passed to the other side.

God was clearly with them.
He showed this by parting the sea.
But as they turned toward Sinai,
On each of their minds was *"ME"!*

Why did they criticize and complain,
When from bondage they had been set free?
Listen carefully,
The answer lies within the word *"ME."*

Three days into the wilderness,
Bodies of Egyptians probably still washing to the shore,

They came to a place called Marah,
And complained, "God give *ME* more!"

Water God gave to them,
But it did not stop there.
When they complained of lack of food,
He gave them bread from the air.

They complained about Moses,
Said he brought them there to die.
They each thought of no one but themselves;
They didn't even try.

We don't like his leadership,
We don't like this bread.
They didn't want to listen
To the things that God had said.

We can't take the land of Canaan;
The people are too strong.
Thus cried the Israelites in the wilderness.
They thought God had it all wrong.

Let's not be too hard on these people,
Even though they failed God's love to see,
Because each and every one of us,
Must fight that dreaded word *"ME."*

Every complaint that people offer,
All the nasty things that people say,
Almost every single one of them,
Begins the exact same way.

What about *MY* rights?
He didn't talk to *ME.*
I don't like this and *I* don't like that,
I'M number one, don't you see?

If all would simply realize
That a servant to God and others we are to be,
There would be so many less hurt feelings,
Harsh words to hear or tears to see.

So let's all try to understand,
That complaints and troubles don't need to be.
If all of us will truly believe
That the most important person is not *"ME."*

What Should I Preach?

Every once in a while someone will ask me, "How do you come up with two sermons every week?" Occasionally the question is more specific, such as, "How do you decide what to preach about?" All the preachers I know who are worth their salt give serious and prayerful thought to that matter.

There are a few basic principles that need to be considered whenever a person undertakes the task of preaching. One such principle is found in Paul's address to the Ephesian elders in Acts 20:26-27. As Paul was bidding them farewell, he made the following statement, "Therefore I testify to you this day, that I am innocent of the blood of all men. For I did not shrink from declaring to you the whole purpose of God." In order to be a faithful gospel preacher a man must be willing to preach "the whole purpose of God." By looking at the entire address of Paul at that time, it is easy to see that "the whole purpose of God," is another way of saying, "the gospel of the grace of God" (v. 24), or "preaching the kingdom" (v. 25). That responsibility includes many things. It includes preaching the facts that need to be believed (1 Cor. 15:1-8), the commands that must be obeyed (2 Thess. 1:7-8), the doctrines that must be embraced (2 Tim. 1:9-11), and the promises to be enjoyed (Acts 2:39).

Preaching "the whole purpose of God" brings other principles into play. In 2 Timothy 4:2-3, as Paul's exhorts the young evangelist, Timothy, we find:

Preach the word; be ready in season and out of season; reprove, rebuke, exhort, with great patience and instruction. For the time will come when they will not endure sound doctrine; but wanting to have their ears tickled, they will accumulate for themselves teachers in accordance to their own desires.

This simply means to preach the word when folks want to hear it, and when they don't. I have had people over the years tell me, "I don't like negative preaching." You know something; *I don't like negative preaching either!* However, if a person is going to preach "the whole purpose of God," and "be ready in season and out of season," a fair amount of that kind of preaching is going to have to be done.

With those principles in mind, the decision still has to be made as to what Sunday's sermons are going to be about. How is that decision made? In my case, several things enter into the decision. First of all, I consider what *I* need to hear. I know that I am no different from anybody else; so if I need to hear something, somebody else in attendance probably does too.

Occasionally the elders will ask me to preach on specific subjects. This usually comes about because they have seen a particular need or have perceived that it would be beneficial for the congregation to have a certain subject addressed. I have been personally blessed over the years in that I have never had a group of elders say to me, "Do not preach about. . . ." In other words, every group of elders with whom I have worked have all wanted "the whole purpose of God" to be presented, whether it was pleasant or not.

There are times when brothers and sisters in Christ have asked me to preach about a particular subject that was of special interest to them or that they thought was needed. If it is possible and appropriate for me to do so, I am always more than happy to accommodate such requests.

There are certain "seasonal sermons" that I preach as well. For instance, at some point in the early spring I will undoubtedly preach about appropriate apparel, and the reason for that ought to be easily understood. Historically, I have found myself addressing the subject of social drinking around the holiday season, due to all the parties and such to which people are invited at that time of the year.

There are times when I become aware of a problem that may exist or a situation that some may be struggling with. Experience has proven that if one person has it, others have it as well, have had it, or will struggle with it sometime in the future. The time to preach about something is when you know it needs to be heard.

Every preacher that I know of is trying to do the best job he can. I suppose that there are some who use the pulpit for personal vendettas and, quite frankly, those folks ought to just quit preaching altogether. But for the rest of us, what an awesome responsibility, whether we preach full time or occasionally. Passages such as James 3:1, "Let not many of you become teachers, my brethren, knowing that as such we shall incur a stricter judgment" must be constantly remembered and considered. Ezekiel 3:17-18 haunts me. The prophet wrote:

> Son of man, I have appointed you a watchman to the house of Israel; whenever you hear a word from My mouth, warn them from Me. When I say to the wicked, 'You shall surely die'; and you do not warn him or speak out to warn the wicked from his wicked way that he may live, that wicked man shall die in his iniquity; *but his blood I will require at your hand.*

A preacher ought to occupy the pulpit because he has something that he has just got to say, and not because he has got to say something.

June 15

Father's Day

This is the day of the year that has been set aside as a special day to focus upon fathers. When I think back upon my dad, who has been gone for many years now, I remember several characteristics more than specific events. I remember a man of responsibility, a man who got up early in the morning, day after day and year after year, to go to a job that he did not particularly like because he had a family to provide for and that was what he was supposed to do. I remember a man of integrity. If Dad said he was going to do something, he did it. I remember a man devoid of prejudice who had friends of different races and beliefs, and when I was a very young boy, that was not always as easy thing to do. I remember a man with a strong sense of what was right and what was wrong, a patriot who served his country in World War II with thirty-six straight months in the South Pacific. I don't know that he was ever more proud of me than on the day I left to serve the country in the Coast Guard. I also remember a man of gentleness, love, and kindness toward my mother. In all the years I was at home, I never saw or heard my dad treat my mother in an unkind manner. I am not sure that I ever heard my dad raise his voice to her, and he taught me never to touch a woman in anger. Dad taught me what it meant to be a man. I miss him every single day and yet I know he lives on in the things I do.

Over the years my own children have given me different things for Father's Day. One was a plaque that said, "Anyone can be a father, but it takes someone special to be a dad." Another was a little decorative pillow on which is stitched, "DAD—Strong shoulders, Saturday coach, big hugs, fixes broken toys and hearts, counselor of wisdom." I agree. Any one can be a father from a biological standpoint, as evidenced by the incredibly large number of absentee dads. We often hear of sports figures and entertainers with numerous children by numerous women. Shame on them—shame on every one of them. It doesn't make a person a man because he has fathered a child—and it certainly doesn't make him a "dad."

Next to being a Christian, I don't believe that there is a more serious responsibility given to a man in God's Word than that of being a father. A father has the responsibility to provide for the needs of his family. In 1 Timothy 5:8 Paul wrote, "But if any provide not for his own, and specially for those of his own house, he hath denied the faith, and is worse than an infidel." The word "provide" in this passage means, "to perceive before, think of beforehand, foresee, to take thought for, care for." While I believe that the primary emphasis of this verse is on material things such as food, clothing, shelter, and so on, it is a mistake to think that that is all a father is responsible for.

Far too many fathers think that their responsibility toward their children begins and ends with providing the physical needs of each child. If they go to work and bring home the paycheck, that's enough. Now, while physical things are very important, they are not the most important; at least, not as far as the child is concerned. I used to coach girls' high school basketball at a rather exclusive school. Many of those girls drove automobiles that probably cost well over half of what I made in a year. Some of them lived in houses that would have been large enough to play our games in. That is probably an exaggeration, but I think you get the point. Yet with all of their material possessions, what I found those girls to want most was their mom, and particularly their dad, to be in the stands watching them play. So many of their fathers were gone so much of the time making a living that they were forgetting to make a life.

In Ephesians 6:4 Paul wrote, "And, ye fathers, provoke not your children to wrath; but bring them up in the nurture and admonition of the Lord." Both mothers and fathers have vital roles to fulfill in the education and discipline of their children. However, fathers must not abdicate their roles as the spiritual leaders of their families. The father has the responsibility, given by God, to nurture the child. Here the primary emphasis is upon the spiritual needs of that child. How is a child going to grow to be most happy and fulfilled? By being faithful and loyal to the Lord throughout his or her life, that is how. Part of the means by which that will be accomplished is by admonition, or more literally, "putting in mind of right." As fathers, we must teach our children what is right as well as what is wrong.

Colly Caldwell, in his Commentary on Ephesians, stated it this way on page 295, "The ultimate concern of parents (fathers, g.l.) who love the Lord is the loyalty of their children to Christ. We can often force them by sheer strength or by the power of what we provide while they are very young. Will our children be good, however, when they are grown? Only by the most careful training, prayer, instruction, admonition, chastening, and loving will we do all we can to insure that (Prov. 22:6). May God bless us all, parents and children, to that end."

Many of the problems that plague our society today can be traced to far too many fathers, but nowhere near enough "dads." It is time for all men to assume their God-given responsibilities when they make the choice to father a child. For those who have, Happy Father's Day.

June 16

Prejudice (1)

My brethren, do not hold your faith in our glorious Lord Jesus Christ with an attitude of personal favoritism. For if a man comes into your assembly with a gold ring and dressed in fine clothes, and there also comes in a poor man in dirty clothes, and you pay special attention to the one who is wearing the fine clothes, and say, You sit here in a good place, and you say to the poor man, You stand over there, or sit down by my footstool, have you not made distinctions among yourselves, and become judges with evil motives? Listen, my beloved brethren: did not God choose the poor of this world to be rich in faith and heirs of the kingdom which He promised to those who love Him? But you have dishonored the poor man. Is it not the rich who oppress you and personally drag you into court? Do they not blaspheme the fair name by which you have been called? If, however, you are fulfilling the royal law, according to the Scripture, You shall love your neighbor as yourself, you are doing well. But if you show partiality, you are committing sin and are convicted by the law as transgressors (Jas. 2:1-9).

What is James addressing? The phrase, "an attitude of personal favoritism," is translated from only one word in the original language, which literally meant, "to take face." It is rendered "partiality" in verse 9. It suggests the conclusions we draw, not from the facts about a person, but from our consideration of who that person is. To illustrate this point, many times a teacher who is trying to be utterly fair and to guard against any "partiality" will block out the name of the student while grading papers. In this way he assures that what was done, and not who did it, will determine the grade given.

In 1 Timothy 5:21 we read, "I solemnly charge you in the presence of God and of Christ Jesus and of His chosen angels, to maintain these principles without bias, doing nothing in a spirit of partiality." The word, "bias," is rendered "prejudice" in the American Standard Version and that better expresses the idea in our language of today. Prejudice comes from the prefix "pre" meaning "before" and the root "judicium" meaning "judgment." *Vine's Expository Dictionary of New Testament Words* defines "prejudice" as "pre-judging, preferring one person, another being put aside, by unfavorable judgment due to partiality." Webster defines it as "an irrational attitude of hostility directed against an individual, a group, a race, or their supposed characteristics."

To put it simply, "an attitude of personal favoritism," "partiality," "bias" or "prejudice," is pre-judgment. It can manifest itself in so many ways. For instance, it can be found being based upon a person's financial status. This is the specific area about which James was writing. Is an individual poor or wealthy? It can be manifested on the basis of appearance. I am talking about someone who looks a little different, perhaps he is scarred or deformed in some way or has some unusual mannerism that sets him apart. We have all known someone who may have been a little bit different in looks or actions, and we have all heard the jokes about such a person. Folks can be awfully cruel.

Prejudice also rears its ugly head on the basis of intellect. There is a tendency to make unwarranted judgments about people if we think they are not as intelligent or as well educated as we are. It can be found on the basis of sex. There are those who think that women are inferior to men, and there are those who think that men are inferior to women. We see it based on religion as well. Some groups hate Catholics; others hate Jews. Some hate all Muslims, and on and on it goes. Now understand that we are to hate every false way, but not the people themselves. Pre-judgment because of what a person believes is wrong.

Obviously, prejudice is manifested on the basis of race as well. Racial prejudice is not something new. It has been around a very long time, and it did not begin with the white and black issue. No greater example of prejudice can be found than the prejudice that existed between the Jew and the Gentile in the time of our Lord. It had existed for some 1500 years. The Jews considered the Gentiles as base, unclean barbarians.

Peter was a man who had been born and schooled as a Jew. He also had this Jewish prejudice toward all Gentiles. In fact, it was so strong that the Holy Spirit gave Peter a direct vision, not once but three times, in order to get him to enter into the house of Cornelius, a Roman centurion of Caesarea. The conclusion was so clear and so simple: "God is not one to show partiality, but in every nation the man who fears Him and does what is right, is welcome to Him" (Acts 10:34-35). So strong was the racial prejudice of the Jews that when Peter went back to his fellow Jewish Christians they said, "You went to uncircumcised men and ate with them" (Acts 11:3). In their eyes, that was a terrible thing to do. Peter described the whole event for them, told them how he had six witnesses with him and how he had arrived at the conclusion that he did. God does not judge a man according to his race, color, or nationality, and Peter learned that we better not do it either.

In Galatians 2:11-14 we see that Peter had been eating with Gentiles. Some Jewish Christians came and Peter withdrew himself from the Gentiles, causing other Jewish Christians to do the same. The reason Peter did this was because he feared that some of the Jewish Christians would not accept his actions because of their prejudice against Gentiles. Paul stated that Peter was to be blamed, and he rebuked him. Peter had sinned. He withdrew his company because of racial prejudice, and he was wrong.

June 17

Prejudice (2)

Previously we noted that "prejudice" is defined as "pre-judging, preferring one person, another being put aside, by unfavorable judgment due to partiality" (*Vine's Expository Dictionary of New Testament Words*). Webster defined it as, "an irrational attitude of hostility directed against an individual, a group, a race, or their supposed characteristics." We considered the fact that this type of irrational pre-judging can be based upon a number of considerations, such as a person's financial status, perceived intellect, sex, religion, and race. Special attention was given to the severe racial prejudice exhibited in the days of Christ by the Jews toward the Gentiles, and we even saw Peter and Barnabas having difficulty with it.

Even today there is evidence that not all Christians have learned this lesson. Prejudice was a sin then, and it is a sin now. Today we pray for the cause of Christ, sing of the love of God, and still occasionally hear some make comments that indicate they view a particular race, or races, of people with prejudice—pre-judging them on the basis of their color.

I believe that God condemns all racial prejudice. The Lord Jesus is our example, we are to follow in His footsteps, and His great sacrifice demands that all prejudice be put aside. In 1 Timothy 2:6 we read, "Who gave himself a ransom for *all*, to be testified in due time." The benefits of His sacrifice are all-inclusive, available to anyone who will take advantage of them.

In Matthew 28:18-20 Jesus said, "All power is given unto me in heaven and in earth. Go ye therefore, and teach all nations, baptizing them in the name of the Father, and of the Son, and of the Holy Ghost; teaching them to observe all things whatsoever I have commanded you: and, Lo, I am with you always, even unto the end of the world." What does this passage teach us? It teaches that the gospel is to be taken into all the world, regardless of race, color, or nationality.

Galatians 3:26-28 expresses the truth so well. Paul wrote, "For ye are all the children of God by faith in Christ Jesus. For as many of you as have been baptized into Christ have put on Christ. There is neither Jew nor Greek, there is neither bond nor free, there is neither male nor female: for ye are all one in Christ Jesus." This is truly one of the marvelous things about Christianity. God doesn't care what color we are, what race we are, or what nationality we are, for we are all one in Christ Jesus. It is so wonderful to think that when men become reconciled to God, they are also reconciled to one another with no room for prejudices of any kind.

Prejudice (3)

If I struggle with prejudice, what can I do about it? First of all I can understand that it is a sin. Remember James 2:8-10: "If ye fulfill the royal law according to the Scripture, Thou shalt love thy neighbor as thyself, ye do well: but if ye have respect of persons, ye commit sin, and are convinced of the law as transgressors. For whosoever shall keep the whole law, and yet offend in one point, he is guilty of all."

I can determine to judge according to the facts, and not appearance. Jesus said in John 7:24, "Judge not according to the appearance, but judge righteous judgment." Respect of persons, or prejudice, is a sin that is learned. Children learn it from their parents and from other children. It is also true that judging righteous judgment must be learned as well.

I can have a proper evaluation of myself. In Romans 12:3 Paul wrote, "For I say, through the grace given unto me, to every man that is among you, not to think of himself more highly than he ought to think: but to think soberly, according as God hath dealt to every man the measure of faith." He also spoke of a mistake that people make. Folks sometimes measure themselves by themselves and compare themselves with themselves (2 Cor. 10:12). The verdict was that such people are not wise. In other words, if we can see ourselves, and others as we and they really are, then we will neither unduly adore nor maliciously defame anyone.

I can recognize the kinship of man. Since all of us are created in the image of God, and all of us have common parents in Adam and Eve, we really have no reason to look down on, or up at, anyone.

Finally, I simply need to remember and to practice what Jesus said in Matthew 7:12, "Therefore all things whatsoever ye would that men should do to you, do ye even so to them: for this is the law and the prophets." If I desire to be treated with dignity by all, regardless of my wealth or poverty, whether I am well known or unknown, whether I am a member of a majority race or a minority race (in the world the white race is in the minority), whether I am perfectly formed physically or have a defect of some kind, then I must certainly treat all others the same way.

June 19

"When Pride Cometh, Then Cometh Shame"

The title for this reading is taken from Proverbs 11:2 and asserts a basic Bible truth: When pride develops in the heart of an individual, he or she is headed for a fall. Solomon made the same point in Proverbs 16:18, "Pride goeth before destruction, and an haughty spirit before a fall." It has been my experience in life that some of the most difficult people to deal with, to teach and reach with the Word of God, are those most affected by pride.

Let's define what we are talking about. *Webster's New Universal Unabridged Dictionary* gives the following first definition of pride: "A high or inordinate opinion of one's own dignity, importance, merit, or superiority, whether as cherished in the mind or as displayed in bearing, conduct, etc." While that gives us a good idea of the attitude that I am addressing in this article, I really like what Webster's presented concerning the synonyms: "*Pride, conceit, self-esteem, egotism, vanity,* and *vainglory*" imply an unduly favorable idea of one's own appearance, advantages, achievements, etc., and often apply to offensive characteristics. 'Pride' is a lofty and often arrogant assumption of superiority in some respect: *Pride must have a fall.* 'Conceit' implies an exaggerated estimate of one's own abilities or attainments, together with pride: *blinded by conceit.* 'Self-esteem' may imply an estimate of oneself that is higher than that held by others: *a ridiculous self-esteem.* 'Egotism' implies an excessive preoccupation with oneself or with one's own concerns, usually but not always accompanied by pride or conceit: *His egotism blinded him to others' difficulties.* 'Vanity' implies self-admiration and an excessive desire to be admired by others: *His vanity was easily flattered.* 'Vainglory', somewhat literary, implies an inordinate and therefore empty or unjustified pride: *puffed up by vainglory.*"

Let's take pride and place it in the hearts of some and see what it can and will do. In Proverbs 13:10 we read, "Only by pride cometh contention: but with the well advised is wisdom." Pride generates contention in a congregation. It is a great instigator, causing those affected by it to take exception to every contradiction, every suggestion, anything that might appear to be a little different from his way of thinking.

Pride produces sinful and foolish speech. Proverbs 14:3 tells us, "In the mouth of the foolish is a rod of pride: but the lips of the wise shall preserve them." There are a couple of ways this could be looked at, both bad and harmful to the congregation where it occurs. Solomon could be saying that as a fool grows more conceited and prideful, his speech will become more insolent and unkind toward others. Or he could be saying that the man who is foolish enough to speak boastfully will feel the chastening rod of his own foolishness eventually.

Pride will also produce strife among brethren; upon that you can count. In Proverbs 28:25 we read, "He that is of a proud heart stirreth up strife: but he that putteth his trust in the Lord shall be made fat." The person filled with pride can never, or will never, say that he was wrong. Consequently, every wrong or foolish statement made requires more wrong or foolish statements to defend it. When pride will not permit a person to say that he was wrong, then he can never back up. Instead of climbing out of the hole his statements have dug, every additional statement simply makes the hole deeper.

There is an aspect of the conduct of a prideful man that is almost para-doxical in nature. One who is filled with pride is easily used. We might ask, "How can someone with a high opinion of himself be easily manipulated?" The answer is simple—appeal to that high opinion. Consider Proverbs 25:27: "It is not good to eat much honey: so for men to search their own glory is not glory." It is hard indeed for a prideful man not to pay close attention to words of praise and compliments. Praise him enough, compliment him enough, and he will be yours forever.

The kind of pride that we are writing about is a sin. Solomon wrote in Proverbs 21:4, "An high look, and a proud heart, and the plowing of the wicked, is sin." It is a dangerous, soul-condemning thing. When John was writing of the methods by which Satan tempts man to sin, he wrote in 1 John 2:15-16, "Love not the world, neither the things that are in the world. If any man love the world, the love of the Father is not in him. For all that is in the world, the lust of the flesh, and the lust of the eyes, *and the pride of life*, is not of the Father, but is of the world." This would be life's empty pride. It causes a man to cling to things that do not matter, boast of things he has not done, and to consider himself above all others.

Is there a cure for this sin of pride? Of course there is, but I do believe that this sin is particularly insidious because it is so difficult for the man filled with pride to even entertain the thought that he might need to repent. It is so difficult for the prideful man to even consider the possibility that he needs to reevaluate his position in God's creation. It is so difficult for the prideful man to finally say, "Lord, forgive me. I have been wrong."

Thoughts about the Sabbath

Conducting a religious "call-in" radio program on a daily basis is a real education. A person learns very quickly that there are certain subjects and questions that are going to come up repeatedly. One such subject is the Sabbath day.

I have heard Sunday referred to as the "Christian Sabbath." I have had Sabbatarians call in and tell me that the Roman Catholic Pope changed the Sabbath from Saturday to Sunday. Those same people have vehemently argued that God enjoined the observance of the Saturday Sabbath upon all people for all time, and that it is even today the sign of whether or not a person is a true follower of the Lord Jesus. Let's see what the Bible tells us about that day.

It is true that God rested from His work of creation on the seventh day. In Genesis 2:2-3 we read, "And on the seventh day God ended His work which He had made; and He rested on the seventh day from all His work which He had made. And God blessed the seventh day, and sanctified it: because that in it He had rested from all His work which God created and made." There is significance to this that goes well beyond the day that God rested, and we will notice that significance a little later on. What is interesting is that there is no indication whatsoever that God had made His Sabbath known to anyone prior to the giving of manna in the Wilderness of Sin as the children of Israel were journeying from Egypt to Sinai.

You might recall that the Israelites were instructed to gather the manna for five days, just enough for each day's use. On the sixth day they were to gather twice as much so that they would have sufficient food for the seventh day. In Exodus 16:23 we find, "And he said unto them, This is that which the Lord hath said, Tomorrow is the rest of the holy Sabbath unto the Lord: bake that which ye will bake today, and seethe that ye will seethe; and that which remaineth over lay up for you to be kept until the morning." In verses 29-30 we read, "See, for that the Lord hath given you the Sabbath, therefore He giveth you on the sixth day the bread of two days; abide ye every man in his place, let no man go out of his place on the seventh day. So the people rested on the seventh day."

Later, when the children of Israel arrived at Sinai and God gave them the Law, "Remember the Sabbath day, to keep it holy" was the fourth of the Ten Commandments. Consider Nehemiah 9:13-14. Nehemiah wrote, "Thou camest down also upon mount Sinai, and spakest with them from heaven, and gavest them right judgments, and true laws, good statutes and commandments: and madest known unto them Thy holy sabbath, and commandedst them precepts, statutes, and laws, by the hand of Moses Thy servant." The Sabbath was not revealed until after the children of Israel fled Egypt.

It is also extremely important to note that the Sabbath observance was enjoined upon no one but the children of Israel. It was given to them, and to them alone. In Exodus 31:12-17 we read:

> And the Lord spake unto Moses, saying, Speak thou also unto the children of Israel, saying, Verily My Sabbaths ye shall keep: for it is a sign between Me and you throughout your generations; that ye may know that I am the Lord that doth sanctify you. Ye shall keep the Sabbath therefore; for it is holy unto you: everyone that defileth it shall surely be put to death: for whosoever doeth any work therein, that soul shall be cut off from among his people. Six days may work be done; but in the seventh is the Sabbath of rest, holy to the Lord: whosoever doeth any work in the Sabbath day, he shall surely be put to death. Wherefore the children of Israel shall keep the Sabbath, to observe the Sabbath throughout their generations, for a perpetual covenant. It is a sign between Me and the children of Israel for ever; for in six days the Lord made heaven and earth, and on the seventh day He rested, and was refreshed.

Who was the Sabbath a sign between? It was a sign between God and the children of Israel—no one else. Further proof of that is found in Deuteronomy 5:15 where Moses said, "And remember that thou wast a servant in the land of Egypt, and that the Lord thy God brought thee out thence through a mighty hand and by a stretched out arm; therefore the Lord thy God commanded thee to keep the Sabbath day." Only the Israelites were required to keep the Sabbath day.

I May Be Old-Fashioned, but . . .

There has been an extremely interesting dynamic unfolding in my work as a preacher over the last several years. Many brothers and sisters in Christ, especially when I am out holding a meeting, will come to me after a sermon and say things like, "We don't hear preaching like that any more" or "That is the old-fashioned kind of preaching" or even, "We need to hear more preaching like that." On the other hand, there are several, both young and old, who don't seem to care for some of the preaching that I do.

I held a meeting recently and one of the topics I addressed was "Does It Make A Difference?" The point of the lesson was that it does make a difference what we believe, what we teach, what we practice, what church we belong to. I didn't believe it to be a particularly harsh sermon; it was just the truth and to the point. After it was over, the fellow making the final announcements did everything in his power to disarm the sermon—letting me know from the pulpit how gentle, kind, and above all non-offensive we need to be in our preaching.

Well, I may be old-fashioned, but I long for the "good old days." No, I don't want to go back to the old manual typewriters, no air conditioning, tiny little black and white televisions, and so on. But I do long for the "good old days" of morality and the "good old days" in the church. Yes, I may be old-fashioned but an awful lot of those "old things" are worth keeping, indeed must be kept, and I will go to my grave hanging on to them.

We need faith today that is based on God's word, nothing else. Paul wrote, "So then faith cometh by hearing, and hearing by the word of God" (Rom. 10:17). "I think so" doesn't mean a thing unless it is supported with contextually accurate biblical support. There is one body of things to be believed and practiced, called "one faith" (in Eph. 4:5), and there always will be only one no matter how badly some want to change it.

I may be old-fashioned, but I believe that many Christians have lost their reverence for God. In Psalm 110:9 we read, "He sent redemption unto his people: he hath commanded his covenant forever: holy and reverend is his name." I looked up the word "reverence" in *Webster's New Universal Un-*

abridged Dictionary, and the first two definitions given were "a feeling or attitude of deep respect tinged with awe; veneration" and "the outward manifestation of this feeling; to pay reverence." Just from the basis of outward manifestations alone, it is obvious that a lot of Christians have very little reverence when they come before God to worship. God is permitting us, allowing us, to come before him in organized worship after his pattern. We are not going to a ballgame, a picnic, a movie, or to the mall. We are coming before God. He deserves, and demands, our very best in every way. I may be old-fashioned, but Hebrews 12:28-29 still says, "Wherefore we receiving a kingdom which cannot be moved, let us have grace, whereby we may serve God acceptably with reverence and godly fear: for our God is a consuming fire."

June 22

Just Thinking

I guess the best way to be understanding of the shortcomings of my brethren is to look first at myself. When someone hurts my feelings, I need to ask if I have ever hurt someone's feelings. If a brother or sister fails to call me when I am sick, I need to ask if I have ever failed to call someone when he was sick. If a brother or sister in Christ lets me down, I need to ask if I have ever let someone down.

Paul put it so well when he wrote, "Thou therefore which teachest another, teachest thou not thyself?" When I do this, I just can't stay mad or upset.

June 23

Dublin

I was holding a meeting in Dublin, Ireland, several years ago. Vicky and I were staying in the home of Steve Kearney, the preacher there. His daughter, Noelle, turned seven years old the week we were there. We were staying in her room, while she slept in her mom and dad's room. Along about Wednesday,

Vicky asked Noelle how she was enjoying the meeting. She said, "I don't like the preaching part. And I don't like the question part. And I want my room back!"

Oh, well. Can't win 'em all!

June 24

Elsie Shull

Your probably didn't know her,
Her name was Elsie Shull.
And of all the sisters I have loved and lost,
I think I miss her most of all.

Elsie was in her 80's.
Her hair was white but she was ramrod straight.
"Come on, Greg, there's work to do,
Time's a-wasting and we can't be late!"

She could read me like a book,
She knew how I was feeling somehow.
With a simple word she could wipe away the tears.
Oh, Elsie, I need you now!

Maybe soon the Lord will return,
And you and I will reunite and once again embrace.
I have done all that I know to do,
And now I long to see your face.

June 25

"I Just Wasn't Thinking!"

It was late in the fourth quarter, and after an absolutely horrendous game, Brett Favre was leading the Green Bay Packers on the potential tying, or game winning, drive. The opponents were our beleaguered, bedraggled, yet oh-so-beloved, Bengals. As Favre received the snap and dropped back to pass, the official blew the play dead. Why? Because a "fan" had made it to the field and was running toward the quarterback. As Favre relaxed, the "fan" snatched the ball from his hand and took off. He was eventually tackled by security and hauled off.

Later, when his girlfriend came to pick him up from jail, it was reported that she asked him, "What were you thinking?" His response was, "I just wasn't thinking!" Allow me to say a hearty *amen* to that. However, his "lack of thinking" didn't begin when he slung his leg over the wall surrounding the field, hopped down on that cart that had been parked beneath him, and darted onto the field; his lack of thinking started way back when he decided he was going to consume alcoholic beverages.

More and more I am hearing Christians, and unfortunately many of them are young, saying that the occasional alcoholic beverage is okay. Satan must be rejoicing at the inroads he continues to make. For the one who is willing to accept what the Word of God says, 1 Peter 4:3-4 should lay the matter to rest. Peter wrote, "For the time past of our life may suffice us to have wrought the will of the Gentiles, when we walked in lasciviousness, lusts, excess of wine, revellings, banquetings, and abominable idolatries: wherein they think it strange that ye run not with them to the same excess of riot, speaking evil of you." For the one who is willing to accept it, that verse covers all levels of drinking, from the falling down drunk to the single drink in the privacy of the home. Every bit of it is just plain worldly and those who argue in support of the consumption of any amount of alcoholic beverages are "Just Not Thinking!"

June 26

Fun and Fellowship

Several years ago while driving through the south central Kentucky countryside late one Friday night, an announcement came on the radio that I had never heard before. It began with a fellow saying, "Ah, Sunday—my day of rest." He then proceeded to name all of the things that he had to do on that day. He was going to change the oil in his wife's car. He was going to cut the grass, trim the hedges, and edge the lawn. He was going to see to it that both of his cars got washed, go to the store, clean out the garage, and take his family out to dinner. In between the mention of all these chores, he kept saying, "Ah, Sunday—my day of rest."

Toward the end of the 60-second spot, another announcer came on. He said something like, "Our lives are so busy and all of us need to take a little time out for ourselves. Do you go to church on Sunday? Why not take the time for fun and fellowship? Go to church. Just a little message from your friends of the Southern Baptist Association."

Is it just me, or does this message strike you as approaching the subject of "going to church" from the wrong perspective? Throughout the entire spot, there was not one mention of God. That is not necessarily wrong. God is not mentioned in the Book of Esther either, but the whole book is about Him. Throughout the entire spot there was not one mention of worship—even though it was about "going to church." Throughout the entire spot there was no mention of the Lord Jesus. Throughout the entire spot there was not one mention of praise or thanksgiving. The complete emphasis was upon the person and "going to church" as a way to get a break from work and to have some *fun and fellowship*.

Don't get me wrong. I do have fun at services, but it is fun from the sense of enjoying worshipping my God. I enjoy studying God's Word, singing praises unto Him, partaking of the Lord's Supper, giving back a portion of that which God has blessed me, and praying. I enjoy the joint participation in worship with my fellow Christians, and I enjoy the opportunity to see and talk to everybody when the services are completed. However, what brings me here is not the idea of *fun and fellowship* (especially in the way that fellowship is being used). It is "Jesus Christ, and Him crucified" (1 Cor. 2:2). I find it incredible that the Southern Baptist Association could produce a radio spot meant to encourage people to attend "church" services and never mention the Lord. What they were using to entice people was *fun and fellowship*. I guess those folks want to improve upon what the Lord said would draw the people. He said that the drawing power was to be the cross: "And I, if I be lifted up from the earth, will draw all men unto me" (John 12:32).

I am reminded of Paul's words in Galatians 1:10. He wrote, "For do I now persuade men, or God? Or do I seek to please men? For if I yet pleased men, I should not be the servant of Christ." That radio spot was just another example of "Give the people what they want." Well, what about what God wants?

Out of the Mouths of Babes

A little four-year-old girl came in from playing outside one day and complained to her mother of a sore stomach. "That's because it's empty. It'll feel better when you have something in it," the mother soothed her.

That very afternoon the preacher stopped by the house to pick up some material that he had loaned to the mother. He complained of a severe headache. "That's because it's empty," the little girl told him. "It'll feel better when you get something in it!"

On Tuesday evening Vicky and I had the pleasure of watching Maggie and Jake for a little while. In our basement we have a little "practice putting rug," with a machine at the end that shoots the ball back to you if you put it in the hole. The kids love to play with it. After watching me putt for a little while, Maggie was able to figure out the problem even though none of the men that I have played with have been able to do so. Maggie said, "Man, you are really bad at that." Truer words have never been spoken.

Invitations

Is the practice of extending an invitation a biblical practice, or is it simply a matter of the "traditions of man"? If it is a biblical practice, is there a pattern given as to *how* it should be done, either explicitly or implicitly? If it is not a biblical practice, should we be doing it at all?

First, whenever God's Word is presented, it always carries with it an implicit call for a response, for a reaction. In John 6:45 Jesus said, "It is written in the prophets, And they shall all be taught of God. Everyone who has heard and learned from the Father, *comes to Me.*" When the Lord preached, He did so with a purpose. His preaching was designed to move people to action, to cause them to respond. In the same way, whenever we see the gospel being presented in the book of Acts, it was done to cause people to respond to it.

The preaching of the gospel was never done as entertainment or as a mere intellectual exercise. It never served a purely didactic purpose, a "for your information" reason. It always, either explicitly or implicitly, demanded a response. Consider James 1:21–25. This passage clearly shows that God wants people to react to His word:

> Therefore putting aside all filthiness and all that remains of wickedness, in humility receive the word implanted, which is able to save your souls. But prove yourselves doers of the word, and not merely hearers who delude themselves. For if anyone is a hearer of the word and not a doer, he is like a man who looks at his natural face in a mirror; for once he has looked at himself and gone away, he has immediately forgotten what kind of person he was. But one who looks intently at the perfect law, the law of liberty, and abides by it, not having become a forgetful hearer *but an effectual doer*, this man shall be blessed in what he does.

In the Old Testament, a response was called for time after time by those presenting the Word of the Lord. Think of Elijah on Mt. Carmel in 1 Kings 18:21: "How long will you hesitate between two opinions? If the Lord is God, follow Him; but if Baal, follow him." That was an invitation. It was a call to action. Just one example of Moses calling for a response is found in Exodus 32:26, where Moses stood at the gate of the camp and said, "Whoever is for the Lord, come to me!" He was calling for a response.

How about Joshua in Joshua 24:15, where he said, "And if it is disagreeable in your sight to serve the Lord, *choose for yourselves today whom you will serve*: whether the gods which your fathers served which were beyond the River, or the gods of the Amorites in whose land you are living; but as for me and my house, *we will serve the Lord.*" Think of Ezra 10:10-11, when Ezra stood before those who had returned from captivity and said, "You have been unfaithful and have married foreign wives adding to the guilt of Israel. Now, therefore, make confession to the Lord God of your fathers, and do His will; and separate yourselves from the people of the land and from the foreign wives." Again, it was a call that demanded a response. The preaching of the word of God was a call for action.

It was no different in the New Testament, where the same kind of pattern is seen. When God's word is presented, a response is called for, either explicitly or implicitly. As a matter of fact, that is why God's word is presented in the first place—to cause people to respond in obedient faith. Just think of the book of Acts, and if there is a place where the gospel was presented without a call to action, I don't know where it would be. Acts 2:38 is a classic example:

"Repent, and let each of you be baptized in the name of Jesus Christ for the forgiveness of your sins; and you shall receive the gift of the Holy Spirit." But this is just the tip of the iceberg, so to speak. Similar calls are found in chapters 3, 4, 5, 6, 7, 8, 9, 10, 11, 13, 14, 16, 17, 18, 19, 20, and so on.

Sometimes the invitations, the calls to respond, were clearly for the sake of conversion. Acts 2:38 is one case out of many. Consider Acts 18:8, where the process is clear. It says, "And Crispus, the leader of the synagogue, believed in the Lord with all his household, and many of the Corinthians when they heard were believing and being baptized." There were other times when the invitation was clearly for the purpose of restoration, and by that I mean correcting sinful behavior on the part of a Christian. Do you remember Peter's words to Simon in Acts 8:20–23? He said, "May your silver perish with you, because you thought you could obtain the gift of God with money! You have no part or portion in this matter, for your heart is not right before God. Therefore repent of this wickedness of yours, and pray the Lord that if possible, the intention of your heart may be forgiven you."

Now brethren, a call to respond, which is what an invitation is and *according to the biblical pattern*, necessarily includes a clear statement of what that response must be. It is extremely difficult for a person to respond in a biblical fashion if he does not know what that response entails. An invitation, in true biblical fashion, is not just a talk presented to fill some time or because it is traditionally done—it is a call to action. The people on Pentecost were told what they needed to do. Simon the Sorcerer was told what he needed to do. Everyone was told what he needed to do. If we are going to follow the pattern when we give an invitation, we will tell the people what to do.

June 29

Walkers

We have some new walkers at the congregation. Little folks who were crawling or taking just a few tentative steps a short time ago are now proudly marching down the aisle with great big smiles on their faces. I find it kind of funny to watch a mom or dad go chasing after a little one before services or after services—especially when that little one has just learned how to run. I confess to having urged a few on in my time.

Everybody has to go through the various stages of development. We can't expect a newborn like Samuel to be walking, or even crawling yet; but we know that in the normal course of things, he is one day going to come crawling down that aisle, and then he will be walking. And then I will be urging him to run as his mom or dad chases him.

It is the same in the spiritual realm. The Bible talks of the different stages of development. We are all familiar with 1 Peter 2:2, "As newborn babes, desire the sincere milk of the word, that ye may grow thereby." We are also well aware of the Hebrew writer's exhortation in Hebrews 5:12-14:

> For when for the time ye ought to be teachers, ye have need that one teach you again which be the first principles of the oracles of God; and are become such as have need of milk, and not of strong meat. For every one that useth milk is unskillful in the word of righteousness: for he is a babe. But strong meat belongeth to them that are of full age, even those who by reason of use have their senses exercised to discern both good and evil.

I have a niece who is almost twenty-eight years old, and she has never spoken and can barely walk. She suffers from seizures and someone must be with her at all times or she will fall. Obviously her development has not progressed as it should have in the normal course of things. It is extremely sad and a difficult task beyond my comprehension for my brother and sister-in-law. However, if I understand God's Word, Karen is as safe as she can possibly be, and her eternity is guaranteed.

I also know Christians who have not developed as they should. Some have been Christians for many, many years and are still "crawling." The sad thing about it is that it is their own choice. I dream of Karen skipping and running. Maybe she will in heaven. I also dream of those Christians who are still crawling after so many years. I dream of their seats being filled and their refusing to allow anything to interfere with their service to the Lord. I dream of them being present and accounted for at work days. I dream of them showing up at gospel meetings, both here and at other congregations. I dream of being eternally with them in heaven.

I am reminded of what Paul wrote in 1 Corinthians 9:24: "Know ye not that they which run in a race run all, but one receiveth the prize? So run, that ye may obtain." You can't run, if you are still crawling.

"The Very World of Iniquity"

Perhaps you recognize that phrase. It comes from James 3, and is part of the Bible's teaching concerning the use of the tongue. In James 1:26 we find, "If anyone thinks himself to be religious, and yet does not bridle his tongue but deceives his own heart, this man's religion is *worthless*." In James 3:5-6 we are told:

> So also the tongue is a small part of the body, and yet it boasts of great things. Behold, how great a forest is set aflame by such a small fire! And the tongue is a fire, *the very world of iniquity*; the tongue is set among our members as that which defiles the entire body, and sets on fire the course of our life, and is set on fire by hell.

Peter wrote in 1 Peter 3:10, "For let him who means to love life and see good days refrain his tongue from evil and his lips from speaking guile."

Sins of the tongue are probably the most common of all sins. The religion of people who are faithful in all other ways can be rendered useless, without worth, because of the improper use of their tongues. The tongue truly is a very small part of the body, but it can cause a great deal of trouble and result in a person being eternally lost. I am reminded of the words of Jesus found in Matthew 12:34-37:

> You brood of vipers, how can you, being evil, speak what is good? For the mouth speaks out of that which fills the heart. The good man out of his good treasure brings forth what is good; and the evil man out of his evil treasure brings forth what is evil. And I say to you, that every careless word that men speak, they shall render account for it in the day of judgment.

Surely we can all see just how important it is for us to control our tongues. We must be certain that there is not an "unwholesome word that proceeds from our mouths, but only such a word as is good for edification according to the need of the moment, that it may give grace to those who hear" (Eph. 4:29).

July 1

What about God's Name?

People are using God's name and the name of our Lord Jesus in many ways that they shouldn't. God's name is used as an expletive—a profane exclamation. It is used as a byword; in other words, when people are happy, they use God's name. When they are sad, they use God's name. If they get disappointed, out will come the name of God. Should they be surprised or suddenly excited, for some reason they use God's name. Just about anytime and for any reason, God's name is being used. Such ought not to be. No, that is not strong enough. Such is sinful!

Consider some principles set forth in God's word. In Exodus 20:7, the Third Commandment, we find, "You shall not take the name of the Lord your God in vain, for the Lord will not leave him unpunished who takes His name in vain." Specifically this refers to the taking of an oath falsely and invoking God's name as witness. However, in the greater sense, it implies a total lack of reverence for God. It is as worldly as it can be to so carelessly toss God's name around. I believe that Ecclesiastes 5:1-2 speaks to the attitude called for by the Third Commandment, as well as the entire tenor of the word of God. Solomon wrote:

> Guard your steps as you go to the house of God, and draw near to listen rather than to offer the sacrifice of fools; for they do not know they are doing evil. Do not be hasty in word or impulsive in thought to bring up a matter in the presence of God. For God is in heaven and you are on the earth; therefore let your words be few.

In Psalm 111:9 David said, "He has sent redemption to his people; He has ordained His covenant forever; holy and awesome is His name." Brethren, the only proper time to use God's name is when we are speaking to Him or about Him, and then only if it is done reverently. Using His name in any other way is sin.

We might also mention euphemisms or substitutes. Sometimes we can feel that we have accomplished the same thing by saying Gosh, or Golly, or Gee Whiz, without violating God's law. What do you think about that?

What about Lying?

Lying seems to be a convenient way to keep from getting into trouble or to make us look better than we are. A lie can so easily roll off the tongue and can even be made to appear palatable if we refer to it as a "little white lie."

Do we ever stop to think like whom we are acting when one of those "little white lies" rolls off our tongues? Jesus said in John 8:44, "You are of your father the devil, and you want to do the desires of your father. He was a murderer from the beginning, and does not stand in the truth, because there is no truth in him. Whenever he speaks a lie, he speaks from his own nature; for he is a liar, and the father of lies."

In Ephesians 4, as Paul was exhorting the Ephesian brethren, and all Christians, to "walk in a manner worthy of the calling with which you have been called," he wrote in verse 25, "Therefore, laying aside falsehood, speak truth, each one of you, with his neighbor, for we are members of one another."

It is never right to lie. Under no circumstances and regardless of the consequences, honesty is not only always right; it truly is the best policy. 2 Corinthians 8:21 tells us, "For we have regard for what is honorable, not only in the sight of the Lord, but also in the sight of men."

What about Gossip?

Have you ever been the object of gossip? I have, and I am here to tell you that it hurts. I have been in congregations where its effects were devastating. Gossip can tear down a congregation as quickly and efficiently as anything else. I have heard it said before, "Kids can be so cruel," and usually that refers to a child being picked on or having stories told about him. I think we all know that adults can be cruel too. Let's look at the wisdom of Solomon:

He who goes about as a talebearer reveals secrets, but he who is trustworthy conceals a matter (Prov. 11:13).

A perverse man spreads strife, and a slanderer separates intimate friends (Prov. 16:28).

He who goes about as a slanderer reveals secrets, therefore do not associate with a gossip (Prov. 20:19).

For lack of wood the fire goes out, and where there is no whisperer, contention quiets down (Prov. 26:20).

The prohibitions against gossip are equally clear and adamant in the New Testament. In 1 Timothy 5:9-13 the apostle Paul was writing to Timothy of certain obligations a congregation has in the realm of benevolence:

Let a widow be put on the list only if she is not less than sixty years old, having been the wife of one man, having a reputation for good works; and if she has brought up children, if she has shown hospitality to strangers, if she has washed the saints' feet, if she has assisted those in distress, and if she has devoted herself to every good work. But refuse to put younger widows on the list, for when they feel sensual desires in disregard of Christ, they want to get married, thus incurring condemnation, because they have set aside their previous pledge. And at the same time they learn to be idle, as they go around from house to house; and not merely idle, but also gossips and busybodies, talking about things not proper to mention.

We can hurt someone so badly with our tongues, and I don't know why anyone who wears the name of Christ would ever want to do it. As children of God, we are Christians all the time. Our responsibility is to strive to be what the Lord would have us to be every minute of every day. That involves controlling our tongues.

July 4

Independence Day

On July 4, 1776, the Continental Congress of the fledgling United States of America signed the Declaration of Independence. In so doing they declared the new nation's independence from the oppressive British regime, whose taxation and governmental policies had become intolerable. They did not know what road lay ahead for them, but were determined to do whatever was necessary in support of the decision they had made. The die was cast;

there could be no turning back. The path that these men had chosen would not be without cost. There would be suffering and deprivation for the general populace and there would be an enormous amount of blood shed by those men who gave their lives in battle in the pursuit of freedom. In throwing off the shackles of their former "masters," the citizens of the new United States of America were subjecting themselves to a different form of government, a new set of "masters" so to speak, chosen by the people to provide for life, liberty, and the pursuit of happiness. From these seeds shown in the beginning days would grow the mightiest nation on earth—the United States of America.

The desire of the British government to control the lives of the colonists, to derive great profit from them, and the steps they took to assure that their desires would come to pass, caused the colonies to revolt. One can see parallels between what happened then and what happens now when an individual decides to declare his or her independence and throw off the shackles of the most oppressive master of all.

Jesus referred to Satan as the "prince of this world" in three different places in the Gospel of John. In contemporary Jewish documents of the time, Satan is referred to with this descriptive phrase because he was viewed as leading the Gentile peoples—a classic example of Jewish prejudice. Daniel H. King, Sr., in his commentary on the Gospel of John (254), writes, "Here he is given the title since he is master of those who refuse to believe, in this case the Jewish political and social leadership." Make no mistake about it. When a person refuses to believe in the Lord and to obey His word, that person has subjected himself to the "prince of this world." He has made himself a subject of Satan and serves a master whose regime is so oppressive and whose ultimate reward is eternal damnation.

Consider Romans 6:15-23 where Paul wrote:

What then? Shall we sin because we are not under law but under grace? Certainly not! Do you not know that to whom you present yourselves slaves to obey, you are that one's slaves whom you obey, whether of sin leading to death, or of obedience leading to righteousness? But God be thanked that though you were slaves of sin, yet you obeyed from the heart that form of doctrine to which you were delivered. And having been set free from sin, you became slaves of righteousness. I speak in human terms because of the weakness of your flesh. For just as you presented your members as slaves of uncleanness, and of lawlessness leading to more lawlessness, so now present your members as slaves of righteousness for holiness. For when you were slaves of sin, you were free in regard to righteousness. What fruit did you have then in the things of which you are now ashamed? For the end of those things is death. But now having been set free from sin, and having become slaves of God, you have your fruit to holiness, and the end, everlasting life. For the wages of sin is death, but the gift of God is eternal life in Christ Jesus our Lord.

The time is far past for all of those who are subjects of the prince of this world, for all who are servants of Satan, to declare their independence. Such a declaration is seen and experienced as they turn in humble obedience to the Lord Jesus Christ; believing His word, repenting of their sins, confessing their faith in Jesus as the Lord, and being baptized in water for the remission of their sins. It is paradoxical that only by becoming a subject of Jesus Christ, His servant, can one truly be free.

In John 8:31-36 we read the following:

Then Jesus said to those Jews who believed in Him, If you abide in My word, you are My disciples indeed. And you shall know the truth, and the truth shall make you free. They answered Him, We are Abraham's descendants, and have never been in bondage to anyone. How can you say, You will be made free? Jesus answered them, Most assuredly, I say to you, whoever commits sin is a slave of sin. And a slave does not abide in the house forever, but a son abides forever. Therefore if the Son makes you free, you shall be free indeed.

Proclaim your independence. Become a faithful child of God, and know what true freedom in service really is. The immediate result is the best life possible on earth, and eternal salvation.

July 5

The Tongue (1)

Why should we spend any time talking about the tongue? The reason for that is simple and can be understood from noticing a few passages of Scripture. In 1 Peter 3:10 we find, "For he that will love life, and see good days, let him refrain his tongue from evil, and his lips that they speak no guile." James 1:26 says, "If any man among you seem to be religious, and bridleth not his tongue, but deceiveth his own heart, this man's religion is vain." James 3:5-6 tells us, "Even so the tongue is a little member, and boasteth great things, Behold, how great a matter a little fire kindleth! And the tongue is a fire, a world of iniquity: so is the tongue among our members, that it defileth the whole body, and setteth on fire the course of nature; and it is set on fire of hell."

When we think about it, sins of the tongue are probably the most common of all sins in all age groups. The religion of many, who are good people otherwise, is made vain or useless because of the improper use of the tongue. It truly is just a small part of the body, but it can cause a world of trouble and cause the one who fails to bridle it to be lost eternally. How serious is it? Jesus said in Matthew 12:34-37:

> O generation of vipers, how can ye, being evil, speak good things? For out of the abundance of the heart the mouth speaketh. A good man out of the good treasure of the heart bringeth forth good things: and an evil man out of the evil treasure bringeth forth evil things. But I say unto you, that every idle word that men shall speak, they shall give account thereof in the day of judgment. For by thy words thou shalt be justified, and by thy words thou shalt be condemned.

What about God's name? Folks in general have decided to use God's name and the name of the Lord Jesus in many ways in which they should not be used. God's name is used as an expletive, as a profane exclamation. It is used as a byword; in other words, when a person is happy, they use God's name. When they are sad, they use God's name. When they are angry, they use God's name. It they are disappointed, they use God's name. When surprised, people will use God's name. If they are excited, they will use God's name. Just about any time and for any reason God's name is used. It is not right.

In Exodus 20:7 we find, "Thou shalt not take the name of the Lord thy God in vain; for the Lord will not hold him guiltless that taketh his name in vain." This prohibition specifically refers to the taking of an oath falsely and invoking God's name as witness. In the greater and larger sense, it implies a lack of reverence for God. Jesus gave essentially the same prohibition in Matthew 5:33-37. I like what *The Pulpit Commentary* has to say about the Third Commandment, "Primarily, the Third Commandment forbids perjury or false swearing; secondarily, it forbids all unnecessary oaths, all needless mention of the holy name of God, and all irreverence towards anything which is God's—His name, house, day, book, laws, ministers. Whatever in any sense belongs to God is sacred, and, if it has to be mentioned, should be mentioned reverently."

The only proper time to use God's name is when we are speaking to Him or about Him, and then only if it is done reverently. To use God's name in any other way is sin. The Psalmist wrote in Psalm 111:9, "He sent redemption unto his people: he hath commanded his covenant forever: holy and reverend is his name."

I believe that Ecclesiastes 5:1-2 speaks to the attitude that is called for when using God's name: "Keep thy foot when thou goest to the house of God, and be more ready to hear, than to give the sacrifice of fools: for they consider not that they do evil. Be not rash with thy mouth, and let not thine heart be hasty to utter any thing before God: for God is in heaven, and thou upon earth: therefore let thy words be few."

What about vulgarity? If something is vulgar, it is offensive to good taste, gross or obscene. Vulgarity is an instance of coarseness of manners or language. Vulgar, vile language is found in today's magazines, novels, songs, movies, television shows, and even in some of the required reading for high school and college literature classes. Vulgarity seems to be everywhere from the factory floor to the boardrooms, from elementary school to the White House.

What does God say about it? In Ephesians 4:29 we read, "Let no corrupt communication proceed out of your mouth, but that which is good to the use of edifying, that it may minister grace unto the hearers." In Colossians 3:8 Paul wrote, "But now ye also put off all these; anger, wrath, malice, blasphemy, filthy communication out of your mouth."

How do I deal with vulgarity? How do I remove it from my life and vocabulary if I have fallen into it? When a person is vulgar, using profanity, telling dirty jokes, and generally being coarse in their speech, we have a picture of what that person is like on the inside. What we say can demonstrate what we are. Vulgarity doesn't just come out—it is the result of what is in our hearts. If our hearts are filled with filthy things, that is what is going to come out. So we must be careful about what we put into our hearts, we must be careful what we think about. That was Paul's very point in Philippians 4:8: "Finally, brethren, whatsoever things are true, whatsoever things are honest, whatsoever things are just, whatsoever things are pure, whatsoever things are lovely, whatsoever things are of good report; if there be any virtue, and if there be any praise, think on these things."

The Tongue (2)

As we continue our discussion concerning the tongue, something else to consider is *"What about lying?"* Many people have very little problem with telling a lie, particularly if it is what is called, "a little white lie." We all know what that is. That is a lie that isn't a whopper, it is just a little lie. Even the major networks will occasionally do a News Special or a segment on one of the Weekly News Magazine Programs about how pervasive lying is in our society. I was amazed several years ago when I was teaching a class of teenagers who, for the most part, had been raised attending services of the Lord's church. Almost to a person, they defended cheating in school. That is just another form of lying.

I wonder if the tendency to lie would be so strong if consideration was given to whom we are acting like when we do it. Jesus said in John 8:44, "Ye are of your father the devil, and the lusts of your father ye will do. He was a murderer from the beginning, and abode not in the truth, because there is no truth in him. When he speaketh a lie, he speaketh of his own: for he is a liar, and the father of it."

Paul wrote in Ephesians 4:25, "Wherefore putting away lying, speak every man truth with his neighbor: for we are members one of another." In Revelation 21:8, John wrote this eye-opening statement: "But the fearful, the unbelieving, and the abominable, and murderers, and whoremongers, and sorcerers, and idolaters, *and all liars*, shall have their part in the lake which burneth with fire and brimstone: which is the second death."

It is never right to lie. Under no circumstances and regardless of the consequences, honesty is always right. It truly is the best policy. It brings to mind 2 Corinthians 8:21, "Providing for honest things, not only in the sight of the Lord, but also in the sight of men."

What about gossip? I just want to present a number of passages that answer that question:

A talebearer revealeth secrets: but he that is of a faithful spirit concealeth the matter" (Prov. 11:13).

A forward man soweth strife: and a whisperer separateth chief friends (Prov. 16:28).

He that goeth about as a talebearer revealeth secrets: therefore meddle not with him that flattereth with his lips (Prov. 20:19).

Where no wood is, there the fire goeth out: so where there is no talebearer, the strife ceaseth (Prov. 26:20).

For I fear, lest, when I come, I shall not find you such as I would, and that I shall be found unto you such as ye would not: lest there be debates, envyings, wraths, strifes, backbitings, whisperings, swellings, tumults (2 Cor. 12:20).

But the younger widows refuse: for they have begun to wax wanton against Christ, they will marry; having damnation because they have cast off their first faith. And withal they learn to be idle, wandering about from house to house; and not only idle, but tattlers also and busybodies, speaking things which they ought not (1 Tim. 5:11-13).

It is so easy to hurt someone so badly with our tongues. Gossip always hurts, and to do so is to just plain sin.

If we are Christians, then we are Christians all the time and everywhere, in both what we do and what we say. "Letting our light shine" does not simply involve going around telling people what they must do to be saved. It also involves letting them see and hear how Christians live. One sure-fire way to cast reproach upon the church and ourselves is to sin with the tongue.

July 7

Sympathetic and Frustrated

At first glance, these two feelings or attitudes may appear to be at variance with one another. How can a person be both sympathetic and frustrated at the same time? The Scriptures provide us with two classic examples.

Consider the prophet, Jeremiah. Here was a man called to his prophetic work in approximately 626 B.C., twenty years before Jerusalem was partially destroyed by the Babylonians and forty years before they completed the devastation in 586 B.C. Jeremiah lived through that period of time and saw the judgment of God brought to bear upon His people of the Southern Kingdom. His task was to warn the people of the judgment to come and, as it was unfolding, explain to them why. At the same time a vital aspect of his mission was to remind them that there would be a restoration and salvation with the coming of the Christ.

Jeremiah, sometimes referred to as "the weeping prophet," was a man of deep emotion who greatly loved the people of Judah and yet felt profound frustration over their failure faithfully to serve and fear the Lord. There are times in his writings when these emotions seem to burst forth from the very depth of his being. Jeremiah 9:1-2 is one such place. There we find:

> Oh that my head were waters, and mine eyes a fountain of tears, that I might weep day and night for the slain of the daughter of my people! Oh that I had in the wilderness a lodging place of wayfaring men; that I might leave my people, and go from them! For they be all adulterers, an assembly of treacherous men.

Is not the love that Jeremiah had for his people evident? At the same time, is not his knowledge of sin and its consequences equally apparent? As John Humphries, in his *Commentary on Jeremiah* stated, "Jeremiah wishes that his head were as a lake and his eyes a flowing fountain of tears so that he could weep sufficiently for the destruction of his countrymen." Yet, immediately upon expressing that emotion, he wrote of his desire to flee from his people who continued to engage in spiritual adultery by forsaking Jehovah and going after other gods. Jeremiah would suffer tremendous abuse at the hands of the very people of God he had been sent to warn; yet he would continue to love them and weep for them.

What of Jesus? At the event that has come to be known as His Triumphant Entry into Jerusalem, the Lord also expressed the dual emotions of sympathy and frustration. As He crested the hill and began His descent of the Mt. of Olives, the city of Jerusalem lay before Him. In less than a week, He would die on a small hill outside the walls of that great city. Yet in Luke 19:42-44 we find Him saying of the population of the city:

> If thou hadst known, even thou, at least in this thy day, the things which belong unto thy peace! But now they are hid from thine eyes. For the days shall come upon thee, that thine enemies shall cast a trench about thee, and compass thee round, and keep thee in on every side. And shall lay thee even with the ground, and thy children within thee; and they shall not leave in thee one stone upon another; because thou knewest not the time of thy visitation.

What sympathy for the inevitable consequences of their sins, and what frustration over their obstinate continuance in them!

Do we not cause the Lord the same emotions that He expressed on that Sunday so very long ago? His love, compassion, and sympathy caused Him to shoulder the pain of the cross so that we could escape the inevitable consequences of our sins. Oh, how He loves us! Surely there must be the same frustration when we continue in them.

July 8

I Marvel

It is a beautiful day today, the sun is shining bright;
The vivid green of the leaf-filled trees stands out against the blue.
A cloud drifts by in wisps of white and makes me think of You.

A bird lands on my windowsill; it is a gorgeous cardinal red.
It looks inside as though it sees, then lifts its wings in flight;
I pause and smile and bow my head as I marvel at Your might.

There is a fox that lives round here—rabbits, squirrels, and a groundhog too;
So many creatures, each one unique, and adding to the glory of my view.
Why are they here? What do they do? They make me marvel as I think of You.
I'll go home later, embrace my wife, talk to my kids, and even walk my dog.
Loves fills the house where I most like to be, and I know it is Your plan.
But why do You care, and why such love? And I marvel at what You've done for man.

I frequently walk in a park that has an arboretum; I will be there today.
It is filled with sculptured trees, manicured bushes and flowers of every color and hue.
There is no way to walk the paths, smell the flowers, watch the bees, without marveling at You.

Two butterflies fly past my window as I write these lines; one white, the other of multi-shades.
You know them, don't You—the course their flights will take, the very fabric of their wings?

How can I but marvel, be filled with wonderment and be amazed, as with
praise and gratitude my heart sings?

July 9

The Continuing Cycle of Life

Recent events have caused me to think about the continuing cycle of life.
So many new little ones have been born into this world, and at the same
time, many individuals that I have known and loved for years have passed on.
With the birth this month of my new grandson, Alexander, I so badly wanted
to pick up the phone to call my mom and dad and share the joyous news
with them. However, they are not here anymore. I can just envision how my
father-in-law would have beamed with pride at the birth of the child of his
"Little King." That is what he always called my son. My in-laws are not here
anymore either, but somehow I know that they know. This is just the way life
is—some are born and some die. It is the continuing cycle of life, and it has
been so since death entered into the world.

How, then, should we view this physical cycle that we cannot change?
By embracing life and living it to its righteous fullest! I am reminded of the
gloriously simple statement found in Micah 6:8 where the prophet wrote,
"He hath showed thee, O man, what is good; and what doth the Lord require
of thee, but to do justly, and to love mercy, and to walk humbly with thy
God?"

What a wonderful event is the birth of a child! Indeed, the psalmist wrote
in Psalm 127:3-5, "Lo, children are an heritage of the Lord: and the fruit of
the womb is his reward. As arrows are in the hand of a mighty man; so are
children of the youth. Happy is the man that hath his quiver full of them: they
shall not be ashamed, but they shall speak with the enemies in the gate."

Each child is a little bundle of potential. Who knows what he or she will
turn out to be and how they will affect the world in which they live? If all
goes according to the normal order of things, they will pass through all of the
phases of life. They will come to know the joys and the sadness, the highs and
the lows of this journey, perhaps at some point even being able to rejoice in
the birth of their own child.

Inevitably, the physical journey will end. Solomon wrote in Ecclesiastes 7:1-2, "A good name is better than precious ointment; and the day of death than the day of one's birth. It is better to go to the house of mourning, than to go to the house of feasting: for that is the end of all men; and the living will lay it to his heart." In the book of Psalms, we find in Psalm 90:10, "The days of our years are threescore and ten; and if by reason of strength they be fourscore years, yet is their strength labor and sorrow; for it is soon cut off, and we fly away."

In addition to the physical death that all must face if the Lord does not return before we die, is the spiritual death. When an individual sins, he or she dies. As a matter of fact, the state in which they find themselves is referred to in Scripture as "dead in trespasses and sins" (Eph. 2:9). In this case death is really a separation—a separation between the sinner and God. Isaiah described it this way in Isaiah 59:1-2, "Behold, the Lord's hand is not shortened, that it cannot save; neither his ear heavy, that it cannot hear: but your iniquities have separated between you and your God, and your sins have hid his face from you, that he will not hear." If the situation is not changed, when physical death occurs the individual faces an eternity of torment in Hell, a place Jesus described as "where their worm dieth not, and the fire is not quenched" (Mark 9:46, 48).

That eternity of suffering can be avoided by what the Lord called being "born again" (John 3:3). One who is dead spiritually must be made alive spiritually. When a leader of the Jews by the name of Nicodemus asked Jesus "How can a man be born when he is old? Can he enter the second time into his mother's womb, and be born?" The Lord answered, "Verily, verily, I say unto thee, Except a man be born of water and of the Spirit, he cannot enter into the kingdom of God" (John 3:4-5). This process of being "born again" involves believing in Jesus (Mark 16:16), repenting of sins (Luke 13:3 & 5), confessing one's faith in Christ (Acts 8:37), and being baptized in water for the remission of one's sins (Acts 2:38). Such an individual, faithfully serving the Lord for the remainder of his or her life, will be eternally in heaven.

The physical cycle of life is unavoidable, but the only inevitable part of the spiritual cycle is that at some point we will sin. Romans 3:23 tells us, "For all have sinned, and come short of the glory of God." This does not mean that we *have to* sin, but only that we all do. Whether we are "born again" to spiritual life depends on us.

You Just Can't Make Some Folks Happy!

Both Matthew 11 and Luke 7 give us an account of a time when John the Baptist was in prison and sent two of his disciples to question Jesus. The question that John asked was, "Are You the Expected One, or shall we look for someone else?" Jesus told them to go back and report to John what they were seeing and what they were hearing. That would be ample evidence to provide the boost that John needed.

Jesus continued on and praised John and connected him to the prophecy of Malachi 4:5, which spoke of the coming again of Elijah. Then the Lord addressed the various reactions that John received and that He also was receiving, particularly among the Pharisees and the lawyers. In Matthew 11:16-19 we read:

> But to what shall I compare this generation? It is like children sitting in the market places, who call out to the other children, and say, We played the flute for you, and you did not dance; we sang a dirge, and you did not mourn. For John came neither eating nor drinking, and they say, He has a demon! The Son of Man came eating and drinking, and they say, Behold a gluttonous man and a drunkard, a friend of tax-gatherers and sinners! Yet wisdom is vindicated by her deeds.

This is quite an interesting comparison that Jesus makes. He is likening that unbelieving generation to contrary children in the marketplace who refuse to play with the other children. One groups holds up to their lips imaginary pipes as though they were playing wedding songs, but the contrary group of children refuses to play along and dance. So the first group changes and mourns and weeps and wails, playing as if at a funeral, but the contrary group won't join in that either. No matter which way they go, one group just won't accept it. It was the same with this contrary, unbelieving generation. John came neither eating nor drinking, in the solemn, austere manner of the children playing at the funeral, and the Jewish leaders would not accept it. Jesus came eating and drinking, and they wouldn't accept that either. They accused Jesus of being "a gluttonous man and a drunkard, a friend of tax-gatherers and sinners!" They couldn't be pleased—they wouldn't be pleased. However, the results of John's ministry demonstrated the wisdom of the course he had followed, and the results of Jesus' ministry were proving the wisdom of His course. But the unbelieving leaders of the Jews just wouldn't be satisfied.

I have found it to be a difficult, but important, lesson to learn. Even Jesus couldn't and didn't please everyone, and if He couldn't do it, why should we think that we could? If you are an elder of the church and don't call someone who has been missing for a while or is sick, you just don't care! If you do call, you are meddling! If a decision has to be made concerning the color of the walls of the building, or the carpet, or even the shingles on the roof, someone won't like it.

If you are an adult Bible class teacher and choose to go verse by verse, there will be some who think it should be done paragraph by paragraph, or thought by thought. If you go paragraph by paragraph or thought by thought, some will think you should go verse by verse.

If you are a preacher and try to be enthusiastic, putting all your energy into a sermon, some will say you are too loud. If you try to tone it down, some will say you are too soft. If you rebuke, you are too harsh. If you comfort and exhort, you need to be harder.

In the pew during worship there may very well be some who think you sing too loudly, or maybe off-key. If you are a parent with small children, there are inevitably going to be those who think they could do a better job than you as far as disciplining your child in services. If you try to calm a child who is acting up in the pew, some will think you should take the child out immediately. If you take the child out to administer the necessary discipline or care, then bring the child back in—and do it again if they act up again—there will be some who think you are disruptive.

On and on we could go, but I think everyone gets the idea. No matter what you do, you cannot make some folks happy. It will drive you nuts if you think you have to. I can tell you that from experience.

When you really think about it, there is only One that we must absolutely strive to please, and that is God. Paul wrote in Galatians 1:10, "For am I now seeking the favor of men, or of God? Or am I striving to please men? If I were still trying to please men, I would not be a bond-servant of Christ." The only thing we can really do is to try our very best to be pleasing to God. Be ourselves in His service and know and appreciate the fact that the God we love and serve wants us to succeed. He will not pick us apart as we sometimes tend to pick each other apart. If there is anyone who truly knows what is important and what is not—what matters and what does not—it is Him.

The Picture

I saw a picture the other day
And said, This cannot be!
What hair is left has gone to gray
That simply can't be me.

The shoulders once so firm and strong
Now seemed somehow flat
And around the waist, what was that there?
Could it have been some fat?

The eyes that once were bright and clear
Surrounded by skin so smooth
Were clouded a bit and not so bright
And the skin was filled with grooves.

The pictures digital cameras take
Can be hard to bear.
What was that growing from the ears?
Don't tell me it was hair!

How did those furrows come to be
On that forehead now so high?
I guess that really was me
And now I'll tell you why

The hair is gray and mostly gone;
That much is surely true.
But I don't care, for each hair that's gone
Means I had another day with you.

Those shoulders were a saddle
For our son and daughter too.

And even though they are not so strong
I promise they'll be there for you.

I guess that there is more of me
In places than before.
But I just think I needed it
Because I love you more and more

Yes that is hair on my ears
And on the back, that's swell.
I guess it doesn't really matter,
For now you don't see so well.

There are furrows on my forehead,
And that's okay, I guess.
For each I have earned over 31 years
Of living with the very best.

July 12

The World and Me (1)

As a Christian, what is my relationship with the world supposed to be? I am thinking of the "world" in the sense of that which is purely physical and earthly in nature, the concerns of this life as distinguished from those of the life to come. How am I supposed to feel about it?

There are several passages that help us answer this question. In John 17:14-15 Jesus prayed to His Father concerning the apostles, "I have given them thy word; and the world hath hated them, because they are not of the world, even as I am not of the world. I pray not that thou shouldest take them out of the world, but that thou shouldest keep them from the evil." In another passage, the Apostle Paul wrote, "I wrote unto you in an epistle not to company with fornicators: yet not altogether with the fornicators of this world, or with the covetous, or with extortioners, or with idolaters; for then must ye needs go out of the world" (1 Cor. 5:11).

It is a unique situation that exists between the Christian and the world. While we must be "in" the world on a daily basis simply to function in life, we must also not be "of" the world. Yet at the same time we are to function as "the salt of the earth" (Matt. 5:13). Salt acts as a preservative only of those things with which it comes in contact. Salt left in the container and kept separate from the meat will have no effect upon it.

We are the "light of the world" (Matt. 5:14). What good is light if people can't see it? A flashlight left on the store shelf never helps anyone. We have to be out "in" the world to survive and to properly function as Christians.

At the same time we must understand that because of our necessary close association with the world, there is an ever-present danger of yielding to its allurements and enticements, and that can be spiritually fatal for the Christian.

We must be the ones who wield the influence, and not the other way around. Remember the words of the Apostle Paul in 2 Corinthians 6:14-17? He wrote:

> Be ye not unequally yoked together with unbelievers: for what fellowship hath righteousness with unrighteousness? And what communion hath light with darkness? And what concord hath Christ with Belial? Or what part hath he that believeth with an infidel? And what agreement hath the temple of God with idols? For ye are the temple of the living God; as God hath said, I will dwell in them, and walk in them; and I will be their God and they shall be my people. Wherefore come out from among them, and be ye separate, saith the Lord, and touch not the unclean thing: and I will receive you.

Once again, the point is not that as Christians we cease all association with worldly people, *but that we be the ones who exert the influence for good.*

There are many approaches that can be taken when writing about the Christian's relationship to the world. From a morals standpoint, we truly must be different. We must not think, talk, or act like worldly people. The Bible indicates a profound difference that exists between those who belong to Jesus and those who do not. In Romans 8:5-9 Paul wrote:

> For they that are after the flesh do mind the things of the flesh; but they that are after the Spirit the things of the Spirit. For to be carnally minded is death; but to be spiritually minded is life and peace. Because the carnal mind is enmity against God; for it is not subject to the law of God, neither indeed can be. So then they that are in the flesh cannot please God. But ye are not in the flesh, but in the Spirit, if so be that the Spirit of God dwell in you. Now if any man have not the Spirit of Christ, he is none of his.

In 1 Corinthians 2:14 we find, "But the natural man receiveth not the things of the Spirit of God: for they are foolishness unto him: neither can he know them, because they are spiritually discerned." The practical applications of this truth, some of which we will discuss in tomorrow's reading, are enormous.

July 13

The World and Me (2)

As Christians, we are to be spiritually minded, not carnally minded. We are to mind "the things of the Spirit" and not "the things of the flesh." Obviously in order to understand this, we must understand what the word "mind" means. Some have defined it as "to be intent on." If we "mind" the things of the flesh, it means that the appetites and the desires of the flesh control our interests. The intention or the chief focus is on the satisfaction of the desires of the flesh.

Think about this for a minute. What is it that attracts our attention? What kinds of things do we find interesting? What are the types of things that we enjoy for recreation or entertainment? What kinds of things do we talk about and think about?

In Galatians 5:19-21 Paul wrote:

Now the works of the flesh are manifest, which are these; adultery, fornication, uncleanness, lasciviousness, idolatry, witchcraft, hatred, variance, emulations (or bitter resentment), wrath, strife, seditions (or divisions in the church), heresies, envyings, murders, drunkenness, revellings, and such like: of the which I tell you before, as I have also told you in time past, that they which do such things shall not inherit the kingdom of God.

A lot of the "works of the flesh" sound like an advertisement for a hit movie, a best-selling novel, or perhaps a hot prime-time drama on television. For that matter, much of it sounds like the moral conduct of many of our business leaders and national political characters. Are these the kinds of things that attract our attention, that fill our minds and our discussions?

I believe we can recognize that immoral, ungodly things happen. I believe that we can recognize that immoral and ungodly things serve as the basis for much of what is called entertainment in our world. However, being aware of it and knowing that it is out there is a lot different from taking delight in it, or making "the works of the flesh" the subject of our thoughts and intents. I don't want to know anything about the salacious details of daytime soap operas. I don't want to know about "Sex and the City," "The Sopranos," "The Shield," "NYPD Blue," or any other ungodly television programs or movies. I am well aware of the fact that many of our national leaders have demonstrated that they are immoral—even amoral. I know that, but it is not going to be fodder for conversation in my life. It is just not right for me as a follower of the Lord to focus my attention upon that kind of stuff. Our interests cannot be controlled by "things of the flesh." As Christians, we are supposed to have left those things behind, and quite frankly, the more spiritual we become, the less we will even want to think about or talk about those kinds of things.

As spiritually minded people, our interests are to be controlled by things of the Spirit, not of the world, and that takes work. It is not something that magically occurs when we rise from the waters of baptism. The old desires and passions are not just miraculously gone at that point, but we can certainly learn to "bring into captivity every thought to the obedience of Christ" (2 Cor. 10:5). How are we going to do that if we keep filling ourselves with worldly things? The answer is, we won't!

Paul told us what to think about and what to talk about in Philippians 4:8. He wrote, "Finally, brethren, whatsoever things are true, whatsoever things are honest, whatsoever things are just, whatsoever things are pure, whatsoever things are lovely, whatsoever things are of good report; if there be any virtue, and if there be any praise, think on these things."

I may not be able to keep from hearing and seeing some of these worldly things, but I don't have to invite them into my home; and I know I can keep myself from taking delight, or even interest, in them.

July 14

What's the Point of Being a Christian While Young?

As young people grow and mature, they find themselves faced with more and more decisions that they must make every day. When small children, most decisions were made for them. What they were going to wear, what they were going to eat, where they were going to go—just about everything is decided for small children by their parents. When the teenage years come, that begins to change a little bit. More and more young people are called upon to make decisions for themselves; and the further along they get in their teenage years, the more decisions they will face.

Here is where the real relevance of being a Christian for a young person comes in. In addition to the tremendous peace that comes from knowing that they are saved and will go home to heaven should the Lord return, there is real practical, everyday value in being a Christian as a teenager. It is found in helping the young person make the proper decisions in their lives—decisions that they can feel good about, decisions that will benefit them for the rest of their lives. Those who are outside of the body of Christ do not have an absolutely trustworthy standard by which to make those kinds of important decisions. If a young person makes the most important decision—to become a Christian and serve the Lord faithfully—he or she will have that guiding standard in all other questions to be faced.

The most important decision that a young person can make, that any person can make, is to be a Christian. I am not talking about being a Christian in name only. I am not talking about just getting wet in the baptistery because their friends did. I am talking about being a *real Christian*, one who steps up and assumes the responsibilities of such a life gladly. Once that decision has been truly made, then all of the other decisions of life are going to be based upon the fact that that young person is a child of God. Consider the words of David from Psalm 119:5-16:

> O that my ways were directed to keep thy statutes! Then shall I not be ashamed, when I have respect unto all thy commandments. I will praise thee with uprightness of heart, when I shall have learned thy righteous judgments. I will keep thy statutes: O forsake me not utterly. Wherewithal shall a young man cleanse his way? By taking heed thereto according to Thy word. With my whole heart have I sought Thee: O let me not wander from Thy commandments. Thy word have I hid in mine heart, that I might not sin against Thee. Blessed art Thou, O Lord: teach me Thy statutes. With my lips have I declared all the judgments of Thy mouth. I have rejoiced in the way of Thy testimonies, as much as in all riches. I will meditate in Thy precepts, and have respect unto Thy ways. I will delight myself in Thy statutes: I will not forget Thy word.

Young people have a lot of decisions to make—decisions that will profoundly affect their lives now and in the future.

They have moral decisions to make. Young people may not realize it yet, but they will learn that making a decision about whether or not to participate in certain things based upon what they know would be pleasing to God is not only right—it is eminently practical. God did not make any useless rules or regulations. He did not forbid anything because He did not want His people to have fun. Everything that God has taught is for our benefit. A young person who is a Christian will find that to be true.

There is the decision concerning college. Will I go? Where will I go? What will I study? If I choose to go away to college, is there a strong church of which I can be a part and have that ready-made network of friends with whom to associate? What am I going to study? Will my chosen course of study jeopardize my faith? There are decisions to be made related to a chosen career. What will I do? Is it upright and honest? Does it provide me with the opportunity to attend the services of the local congregation of which I am a member? Will I have to compromise my principles to be successful in this field?

Will I marry, and whom will I marry? Will he or she be a Christian? Will his or her primary concern be serving the Lord and helping me to get to heaven? Will he or she be a spiritual drag to me?

All of these are decisions that are so better made when the one making them is a Christian. It is preeminently practical and decidedly relevant to be a Christian while young.

July 15

Don't Assume the Worst

Don't assume the worst if one day I appear unkind.
It may just be that something heavy is weighing on my mind.

Don't assume the worst if to you I fail to speak.
There may be something very hard that has been going on all week.

But if to you I do these things from a heart that is hard and black—
It does you no good to worry, for God will take care of that!

Meet for the Master's Use

In 2 Timothy 2:20-21 we find, "But in a great house there are not only vessels of gold and of silver, but also of wood and of earth; but some to honor, and some to dishonor. If a man therefore purge himself from these, he shall be a vessel unto honor, sanctified, and meet for the master's use, and prepared unto every good work." The phrase, "meet for the master's use" means useful or usable for the master. "Prepared unto every good work" simply implies that one is in a state of readiness for whatever use the Lord will make of us.

We all have a duty to live so as to prepare ourselves to be fit to be used by the Lord, to live in such a way that we might be a "vessel unto honor" in the house of God. But the interesting thing is that contrary to how the world would view things, to be a "vessel unto honor" in the Lord's house does not mean that we are then to be served by others; it means to be the one who serves. The Lord made this point so clearly in Matthew 20:25-28 when he said, "Ye know that the princes of the Gentiles exercise dominion over them, and they that are great exercise authority upon them. But it shall not be so among you: but whosoever will be great among you, let him be your minister; and whosoever will be chief among you, let him be your servant: even as the Son of man came not to be ministered unto, but to minister, and to give his life a ransom for many."

Each of us, no matter where we are in our life as a Christian, needs to be about the business of preparing ourselves for the greatest amount of service we can render to the Lord. A person who is a Christian has much to do. Prepare to be the best man or woman in the sight of God that you can be. Learn to be the kind of husband or wife that the Lord would have you to be. Learn God's pattern for the family and recognize that it is one of service to one another. Learn what it is to be the kind of citizen in your communities that God wants His people to be. Being a model citizen and a contributing factor to the community in which we live is part of the work of the Lord. We are to be "subject unto the higher powers" (Rom. 13:1), and "Render therefore to all their dues: tribute to whom tribute is due; custom to whom custom; fear to whom fear; honor to whom honor" (Rom. 13:7). Christians are Christians every moment of every day. Hence, we are doing the Lord's work at home, at school, at work, and at play. The point is that all of us who are Christians, male or female, young or old, have the responsibility to live our lives in such a way as to be "meet for the Master's use, prepared unto every good work." That is the way we become "vessels unto honor" in the house of God.

July 17

"As A Jewel of Gold in a Swine's Snout"

I don't know much about farming or raising livestock of any kind, but I have on occasion seen pigs with a metal ring in their noses. Right next to a plot of land that my father-in-law used to own there lived a man who raised pigs, and I enjoyed watching them. I understand that pigs use their noses to dig or to root up things. I understand that they also find their noses to be awfully convenient when it comes to digging out a place in the muck and mire where they can wallow. But because some of them become a little too handy at rooting under a fence and getting out, sometimes the owner will "ring" them, put a metal ring in their noses to prevent them from doing that. Seeing those "ringed" pigs reminded me of a verse in Proverbs.

Let's read Proverbs 11:22: "As a jewel of gold in a swine's snout, so is a fair woman which is without discretion." Down in the country it wouldn't be all that unusual to see a ringed pig, but it would be very out of the ordinary to see a "jewel of gold" in the nose of a pig. They just do not go together, it would be incongruous, a word that fitly describes such a circumstance and is exactly the point that Solomon was making. According to *Webster's New Unabridged Dictionary*, "incongruous" means, "out of keeping or place, inappropriate; unbecoming; not harmonious in character, inconsistent." That perfectly describes a "jewel of gold in a swine's snout."

Just think of some of the things that are as inappropriate and out of place for a Christian as a gold ring in the nose of a pig. In Ephesians 4:29 Paul wrote, "Let no corrupt communication proceed out of your mouth, but that which is good to the use of edifying, that it may minister grace unto the hearers." To edify means to build up. So, simply put, anything other than that which is righteous and pure and which is meant to build up the one who hears is not harmonious in character. It is like a "jewel of gold in a swine's snout."

Consider another passage with me. In Luke 6:46 our Lord asked, "And why call ye me, Lord, Lord, and do not the things which I say?" That is a real good question. Over and over again the Bible indicates that a mark of a true and sincere follower of Jesus is obedience. One of the truly wondrous things about this is that Jesus showed us how. In Hebrews 5:8-9 we are told concerning our Lord, "Though he were a Son, yet learned he obedience by the things which he suffered; and being made perfect, he became the author of eternal salvation unto all them that obey him." So, for any person to say that he or she is a Christian and purposely to choose not to obey certain, or any, of the commands of the Lord is just as inappropriate, just as incongruous and out of character for a child of God, as is a gold ring stuck in the snout of a pig.

Surely we can all see further possible applications of this principle. I don't want any part of my life to be so out of harmony with the life the Lord expects of his people that it would resemble a "jewel of gold in a swine's snout."

July 18

Upon the First Day of the Week (1)

The inspired writer Mark gives us the following information in Mark 16:1-9:

And when the Sabbath was over, Mary Magdalene, and Mary the mother of James, and Salome, bought spices, that they might come and anoint Him. And very early on *the first day of the week*, they came to the tomb when the sun had risen. And they were saying to one another, 'Who will roll away the stone for us from the entrance of the tomb?' And looking up, they saw that the stone had been rolled away, although it was extremely large. And entering the tomb, they saw a young man sitting at the right, wearing a white robe; and they were amazed. And he said to them, "Do not be amazed; you are looking for Jesus the Nazarene, who has been crucified. He has risen; He is not here; behold, here is the place where they laid Him. But go, tell His disciples and Peter, He is going before you into Galilee; there you will see Him, just as he said to you." And they went out and fled from the tomb, for trembling and astonishment had gripped them; and they said nothing to anyone, for they were afraid. Now after He had risen early on *the first day of the week*, He first appeared to Mary Magdalene, from whom He had cast out seven demons.

On Sunday, the first day of the week, the Lord Jesus Christ rose from the dead. With this incredible display of divine power, Jesus was declared to be the Son of God (Rom. 1:4). Since then, a significance was attached to that day which has been recognized and embraced by faithful children of God to the present time and will continue to be recognized and embraced until the Lord returns. The Lord appeared to Mary Magdalene on the very day of His resurrection (John 20:11-17), and on the evening of that first day of the week, He met with His disciples, Thomas being absent (John 20:19-24). One week later, again upon *the first day of the week*, Jesus appeared in the midst of His disciples and had the following exchange with Thomas:

> "Reach here your finger, and see My hands; and reach here your hand, and put it into My side; and be not unbelieving, but believing." Thomas answered and said to Him, "My Lord and my God!" Jesus said to him, "Because you have seen Me, have you believed? Blessed are they who did not see, and yet believed" (John 20:27-29).

Fifty days after the Passover Sabbath, another *first day of the week*, the Jewish feast of Pentecost occurred. Thus the tremendous events recorded in the second chapter of the book of Acts took place upon *the first day of the week*. It was on the first day of the week that the apostles were baptized with the Holy Spirit "and began to speak with other tongues, as the Spirit was giving them utterance" (Acts 2:4). It was on that *first day of the week* that the good news of Jesus Christ as the Son of God was proclaimed, with Peter declaring, "Therefore let all the house of Israel know for certain that God has made Him both Lord and Christ—this Jesus whom you crucified" (Acts 2:36). That same day saw three thousand individuals being added to the church by the Lord as they obeyed the gospel, and it was the first time the church was spoken of as being in existence (Acts 2:41). Hence, the church was born on *the first day of the week*.

After the church began and the apostles went about fulfilling the Great Commission, making disciples and teaching them to observe all that the Lord had commanded them (Matt. 28:19-20), we find Christians coming together upon *the first day of the week* to engage in various acts of worship. Indeed, some of those acts of worship were peculiar to the *first day of the week* and were performed on no other days. On the very night in which He was betrayed, our Lord Jesus instituted the memorial feast, the Lord's Supper that would serve to commemorate His death until He returns. He used unleavened bread to represent His body, and fruit of the vine to represent His blood.

Faithful children of God do not change those elements in the observance of the Lord's Supper, but simply do as the Lord did. We look to the actions of the first century Christians under the guidance of the apostles to learn when this feast was observed.

July 19

Upon the First Day of the Week (2)

Luke, the author of the Gospel that bears his name and the book of Acts, is a recognized historian who very carefully noted the times in which the events he was recording took place. He mentions years and officials (both Jew and Gentile), helping us to understand when the biblical events took place in relation to the history of the world. He is exact and orderly in his writing, and nothing is presented without purpose. In Acts 20:6-7 we find, "And we sailed from Philippi after the days of Unleavened Bread, and came to them at Troas within five days; and there we stayed seven days. And on the *first day of the week*, when we were gathered together to break bread, Paul began talking to them, intending to depart the next day, and he prolonged his message until midnight." Johnny Stringer, in *The Truth Commentary on The Book of Acts*, makes an interesting observation about Luke's mention of *the first day of the week*:

> Luke specifies the day. As Luke describes the many events recorded in Acts, how often does he specify the day of the week on which an event occurred? How many times does he specify that a thing occurred on the second day of the week? Or the month? In view of the great importance of the first day of the week, when Luke is careful to specify that the brethren observed the Lord's Supper on that day, we must conclude that their observing it on that particular day was a matter of significance (416).

While there is little written in God's Word concerning the time and frequency of the observance of the Lord's Supper, what is written reveals a great deal. Luke makes it clear that their foremost purpose for coming together on that day was to "break bread"; it was to partake of the memorial feast. It is also at least probable that Paul tarried at Troas in order to be able to assemble with the saints there on *the first day of the week* to observe the Lord's Supper.

Another well-known reference to the *first day of the week* is found in 1 Corinthians 16:1-2, where Paul gave the following instructions to the Corinthian brethren: "Now concerning the collection for the saints, as I directed the churches of Galatia, so do you also. On the first day of the week let each of you put aside and save, as he may prosper, that no collections be made when I come."

The two passages we are considering, Acts 20:7 and 1 Corinthians 16:1-2, provide strong evidence of a regular weekly assembly of the saints that took place upon *the first day of the week*. In his *Commentary of Paul's First Epistle to the Corinthians*, Mike Willis noted:

> Hence, from the very beginning, the Lord's church has had a regular meeting on the first day of the week. That this was the church's general practice is evident from the fact that the churches of Galatia as well as the church at Corinth were commanded to prepare the collection on this day of the week.
>
> The command that the collection be taken on the first day of the week cannot be harmonized with the interpretation that this refers to every member setting aside some money at his own home. If this was to be done in the privacy of one's own home, why was a special day mentioned for doing it? The only logical reason that can be given for specifying a particular day is that this was the regular day on which the congregation assembled for worship. Hence, Paul commanded that a collection be taken at that assembly (599).

The evidence that is available to us makes it clear that the pattern established by the apostles, and followed by the church from the beginning, included a weekly assembly that took place upon *the first day of the week* for worship. Two vital parts of that time together were partaking of the Lord's Supper and the taking of a collection to finance the work of the church. Those who are determined to follow the Lord will adhere to that pattern. The relatively recent practice of substituting Saturday assemblies for gathering together on *the first day of the week* and offering the Lord's Supper as well as taking a collection at that time, are completely without scriptural authority, and are nothing more than traditions and practices created by man.

July 20

Upon the First Day of the Week (3)

The first day of the week is also referred to in Scripture as the Lord's Day. We find this in Revelation 1:10 where John wrote, "I was in the Spirit on the Lord's Day." It helps to understand John's use of this expression if we consider the only other time the Greek word for "Lord's" (*kuriakos*) appears. It is found in 1 Corinthians 11:20 which says, "Therefore when you meet together, it is not to eat the Lord's Supper." There is an obvious connection between the Lord's Supper and the Lord's Day, both of them pertaining to Christ. As we have observed, the Lord's Supper was partaken of on the *first day of the week*.

"Surely the Lord's Supper was observed on the first day of the week, and if so, it must follow that the Lord's day was the first day of the week. The Lord provided this new name for a new day on which new religious service was observed" (Homer Hailey, *Revelation*, 107).

It must be admitted that over the years various groups have denied that the early church met on the first day of the week for worship and have contended that faithful Christians have continued to meet upon the Sabbath day, the seventh day of the week. They have argued that the regular assembly on the first day of the week was, in fact, a man-made perversion of the scriptural pattern. Let's take the time to examine the primary arguments advanced by those who hold to that erroneous view, focusing upon Seventh-Day Adventism.

In my study of that false system of belief, it appears that the rejection of the regular assemblies on the first day of the week, the Lord's Day, by Christians, and the demand for the keeping of the Sabbath day by all people for all time, is based upon three basic assertions. First, that God bound Sabbath-keeping upon all men from the Garden of Eden. Second, that in the Old Testament law a distinction must be made between the Law of God and the Law of Moses, also called the eternal law and the temporary law, the moral law and the ceremonial law. Third, that the change from *Saturday* as the day of worship to *Sunday* was the result of apostasy, with the Roman Catholic Pope officially changing the day for the apostate church. Each one of these assertions rests upon the others. If even one of them proves to be false, the case for Sabbath-keeping crumbles.

Is it true that God bound Sabbath observance upon all men from the Garden of Eden? In *Who are Seventh-Day Adventists?*, the claim is made in the following way:

God established the Sabbath institution at the very beginning of man's history upon the earth when, as the climax of creation, He set the seventh day apart as a time of surcease from labor. Genesis 2:1-3. The seventh-day Sabbath was given to mankind as a memorial of the creation of the heavens and earth by the hand of God Himself. Exodus 20:11. It was also given as a sign of that personal relationship that exists between man, the creature and God, the creator. Ezekiel 20:20 (63-64).

It is true that God rested from His work of creation on the seventh day, and it is true that when God did give the Sabbath He used the same day upon which He had rested. But did He enjoin Sabbath-keeping upon all men for all time beginning in the Garden of Eden? The answer to that question is no.

Try as we might, we can find no mention of the Sabbath before Exodus 16:23. There is no indication that anyone ever kept the Sabbath before that time, or for that matter, that anyone even knew upon what day God rested before the Book of Genesis was written. We do not have to speculate about when the requirement for Sabbath-keeping was made know to man, for Nehemiah 9:13-14 tells us, "Then Thou didst come down on Mount Sinai, and didst speak with them from heaven; Thou didst give to them just ordinances and true laws, good statutes and commandments. *So Thou didst make known to them Thy holy Sabbath*, and didst lay down for them commandments, statutes, and laws, through Thy servant Moses."

July 21

Upon the First Day of the Week (4)

Since God made known the Sabbath at Sinai, it is obvious that it had not been enjoined upon anyone from the Garden of Eden. When it was finally made known at Sinai, was Sabbath-keeping bound upon all men for all time? That is the position espoused by Seventh-Day Adventism. In a pamphlet entitled *Amazing Facts That Affect You, Number 1*, the following question and answer are presented on page 6:

> *Does Sabbath-keeping affect me personally?* Answer: Yes, by all means, the Sabbath is YOUR Sabbath. God made it for YOU, and if You love Him, YOU will keep it, because it is one of His commandments. Love without commandment-keeping is no love at all (1 John 2:4). YOU must make a decision. YOU cannot escape. No one can excuse YOU. YOU yourself will answer before God on this most important matter. God asks YOU to obey NOW!

The truth is that the requirement to keep the Sabbath was bound upon no one except the Jews. We find in Exodus 31:16-17: "So the *sons of Israel* shall observe the Sabbath, to celebrate the Sabbath throughout their generations as a perpetual covenant. *It is a sign between Me and the sons of Israel forever,* for in six days the Lord made heaven and earth, but on the seventh day He ceased from labor, and was refreshed." The same point is made in Ezekiel 20:12, "And also I gave them My Sabbaths to be a *sign between Me and them,* that they might know that I am the Lord who sanctifies them." If Sabbath-keeping was truly bound upon all men of all nations for all time, how could it be a sign between God and the nation of Israel?

Does this then mean that the fact that God rested from His labor of creation on the seventh day has no significance whatsoever for the Christian today? No, for the Hebrew writer tells us in Hebrews 4:9, "There remains therefore a Sabbath rest for the people of God." In *Hebrews For Every Man,* Jay Bowman explained that Sabbath rest:

> What kind of rest is it? It is the rest God entered when He completed the creation of the universe. God has not been idle between creation and the present (John 5:17). But when He finished creating the worlds, He paused to enjoy the beauty of His creation. Man has been invited to join Him in one eternal day of reverence and wonder, a Sabbath day (Hebrews 4:9) in which all who love to worship and commune with God can enjoy the bliss and glories of their Creator. He who will have entered the ultimate rest will have taken his place with his Creator in an eternal rest. Hence, the author to his generation concludes, 'Let us therefore be diligent to enter that rest, lest anyone fall through following the same example of disobedience' (Hebrews 4:11) (91).

What of the second of the basic assertions of Seventh-Day Adventists, that there is a distinction to be made in the Old Testament Law? They assert that one must recognize a difference between the Law of God and the Law of Moses, sometimes stated as a difference between the moral law and the ceremonial law, or the eternal law and the temporary law. Passages such as Colossians 2:13-17, Ephesians 2:14-17, Galatians 3:23-25, and Galatians 4:21-31, all of which teach that the Law of Moses has been fulfilled and taken out of the way, force the sabbatarians to make this distinction in order to continue to embrace and bind Sabbath-keeping. In *Who Are Seventh-Day Adventists?,* we find this example of their teaching:

> Nor could there be a change in the Sabbath for it is an integral part of the Decalogue, the eternal and unchangeable law of God. Right in the heart of that code of morals which forbids the worship of false gods, murder, covetousness, adultery, stealing, etc., we find the command to keep the seventh day holy. Exodus 20:3-17. These commandments constitute a holy law (Romans

7:12), and they stand fast forever as the very foundation of God's government throughout the universe (Psalm 111:7, 8). The Decalogue is not confined to any age or race, but is obligatory upon all men at all times. . . .When Christ died on the cross, the laws contained in ceremonies and ordinances pertaining to the temple service and typifying the sacrifice of Christ were done away, having served their day of usefulness. They were only "shadows" of Christ, the Lamb of God (66).

We will answer the false teaching contained in that quote in tomorrow's reading.

July 22

Upon the First Day of the Week (5)

Is this distinction between the Law of God and the Law of Moses, the moral and ceremonial law, valid? Will it hold up under the microscope of Scripture? The answer is no. In Ezra 7 we find two descriptions of Ezra that bear upon this question. In verse 6 he is described as "a scribe skilled in the Law of Moses, which the Lord God of Israel had given" and in verse 12 he is described as "the scribe of the law of the God of heaven." Thus, the Lord God of Israel gave the Law of Moses, making the Law of Moses the Law of the God of heaven. In 2 Chronicles 34:14 we find that, "Hilkiah the priest found the book of the law of the Lord given by Moses." Therefore, Moses gave the Law of the Lord and the Lord God of Israel gave the Law of Moses. In the beautiful scene depicted in Nehemiah 8 when the children of Israel gathered in the square before the Water Gate to hear Ezra the scribe, we find that he read from the book of the Law of Moses (verse 1), from the book of the Law (verse 3), and from the book, from the Law of God (verse 8). There is no difference; the terms are used interchangeably.

Additional problems arise for those who make the moral and ceremonial law distinction when 2 Chronicles 31:3 is considered. It says, "He also appointed the king's portion of his goods for the burnt offerings, namely, for the morning and evening burnt offerings, and the burnt offerings for the Sabbaths and for the new moons and for the fixed festivals, as it is written *in the law of the Lord.*" Those offerings, which are most certainly ceremonial, are said to be written in the law of the Lord.

But what about the eternal and unchangeable nature of the Ten Commandments? In *Who Are Seventh-Day Adventists?*, the assertion is made that "these commandments constitute a holy law (Romans 7:12), and they stand fast forever as the very foundation of God's government throughout the universe" (66). In the booklet *Amazing Facts That Affect You, Number One*, the question is asked, "But haven't the Ten Commandments been changed?" The answer given is, "No, indeed! It is utterly impossible for any of God's laws ever to change. All ten commandments are binding today" (3). This assertion does not stand. 2 Corinthians 3:1-16 tells us:

> Are we beginning to commend ourselves again? Or do we need, as some, letters of commendation to you or from you? You are our letter, written in our hearts, known and read by all men; being manifested that you are a letter of Christ, cared for by us, written not with ink, but with the Spirit of the living God, not on tablets of stone, but on tablets of human hearts. And such confidence we have through Christ toward God. Not that we are adequate in ourselves to consider anything as coming from ourselves, but our adequacy is from God, who also made us adequate as servants of a new covenant, not of the letter, but of the Spirit; for the letter kills, but the Spirit gives life. But if the ministry of death, in letters engraved on stones, came with glory, so that the sons of Israel could not look intently at the face of Moses because of the glory of his face, fading as it was, how shall the ministry of the Spirit fail to be even more with glory? For if the ministry of condemnation has glory, much more does the ministry of righteousness abound in glory. For indeed what had glory, in this case has no glory on account of the glory that surpasses it. For if that which fades away was with glory, much more that which remains is in glory. Having therefore such a hope, we use great boldness in our speech, and are not as Moses, who used to put a veil over his face that the sons of Israel might not look intently at the end of what was fading away. But their minds were hardened; for until this very day at the reading of the old covenant the same veil remains unlifted, because it is removed in Christ. But to this day whenever Moses is read, a veil lies over their heart; but whenever a man turns to the Lord, the veil is taken away.

What was it that Paul said was fading away? What was it that he called *the ministry of condemnation*? What was it that he called the *ministry of death, in letters engraved on stones*? Was it not the Law of Moses, including the Ten Commandments, written with the finger of God (Exod. 31:18)? Did not Moses cover his face with a veil when he gave the children of Israel all the commandments that God had spoken to him on Mt. Sinai, which included the Ten Commandments (Exod. 34:33-35)? Nine of the ten commandments are to be kept today, not because they were part of the law of Moses, but because they have been incorporated, and expanded upon, in the law of Christ.

Sabbath keeping is no longer bound upon anyone, including the only people ever required to do so—the Jews.

Upon the First Day of the Week (6)

Let us consider the third major assertion made by Seventh-Day Adventism. That false system of belief teaches that the change from Saturday to Sunday as the day of worship came about as the result of apostasy, that the Roman Catholic Pope officially changed the day for the apostate church, and that those who have been faithful to the Word of God have continued to keep the Sabbath as a holy day and the day of worship. Let us notice several examples of such teaching. In "*Who are Seventh-Day Adventists?*" this view is clearly set forth in the following manner:

> In the early centuries of the Christian Church a great apostasy set in (2 Thessalonians 2:3-4), and as men and women lost their hold on the true God, the Creator of the heavens and earth, they gradually turn to a popular festival day of paganism—Sunday. The emperor Constantine, half pagan and half Christian, promulgated the first law in support of first-day observance. Later on the Roman Catholic Church placed its official stamp on Sunday as the weekly day of worship, and essayed to transfer to Sunday the sanctity heretofore attached to the Seven-day Sabbath (67-68).

In *The Gospel For Today*, Foy E. Wallace, Jr. cited *The Early Writings of Mrs. White*, page 26. She wrote, "I saw that God had not changed the Sabbath, for He never changes. But the pope had changed it from the seventh day to the first day of the week, for he was to change time and laws" (349).

In the pamphlet, *Amazing Facts That Affect You, Number One*, the following question and answer are found:

> Well, if Sunday-keeping isn't in the Bible, whose idea is it anyway? Answer: God predicted that it would happen, and it did. . . . Misguided men of long years past tampered with God's holy law and announced that God's holy day was changed from Sabbath to Sunday. This error was passed on to our unsuspecting generation as gospel fact. Sunday-keeping is a tradition of uninspired men, and breaks God's law which commands Sabbath-keeping. Only God can make a day holy. God blessed the Sabbath, and when God blesses, no man can reverse it (5).

Earlier in this presentation evidence was given from the historically reliable documents that make up the New Testament, that from the beginning the church regularly assembled upon the first day of the week for worship. In fact, two of the acts of worship were peculiar to the first day of the week, with each Christian partaking of the Lord's Supper and contributing to finance the work of the church. Thus, long before the days of Constantine, Emperor of the Western Empire from 312 to 324 and sole Emperor of the entire Roman Empire from 324 to 327, the church was meeting on the Lord's Day. Constantine had nothing whatsoever to do with choosing the day of worship for the Lord's church.

Extra-biblical sources, such as the writings of *The Anti-Nicene Fathers, Volume 1*, provide us with a wealth of additional evidence that the Lord's church met for worship upon the first day of the week, and not upon the Sabbath day. From the pen of Ignatius, in his *Epistle To the Magnesians*, written sometime between 110 to 120 A.D., we find, "If therefore, those who were brought up in the ancient order of things have come to the possession of a new hope, no longer observing the Sabbath, but living in the observance of the Lord's Day, on which also our life has sprung up again by Him and by His death" (62).

In the *Epistle of Barnabas*, thought to be from the early second century, we read, "Wherefore, also, we keep the eighth day with joyfulness, the day also on which Jesus rose again from the dead" (15).

One of the best-known examples of this evidence is found in *The First Apology of Justin*, believed to have been written in the 150's:

> And we afterwards continually remind each other of these things. And the wealthy among us help the needy; and we always keep together; and for all things wherewith we are supplied, we bless the Maker of all through His Son Jesus Christ, and through the Holy Ghost. And on the day called Sunday, all who live in cities or in the country gather together to one place, and the memoirs of the apostles or the writings of the prophets are read, as long as time permit; then, when the reader has ceased, the president verbally instructs, and exhorts to the imitation of these good things. . . . But Sunday is the day on which we all hold our common assembly, because it is the day on which God, having wrought a change in the darkness and matter, made the world; and Jesus Christ our Savior on the same day rose from the dead. For He was crucified on the day before that of Saturn (Saturday); and on the day after that of Saturn, which is the day of the Sun, having appeared to His apostles and disciples, He taught them these things, which we have submitted to you also for your consideration (67).

Upon the First Day of the Week (7)

In his *Dialogue with Trypho,* Justin makes a very interesting statement. While it does not address the regular first day of the week assembly of the saints, it does show that the early church did not require Sabbath-keeping. He wrote, "Is there any other matter, my friends, in which we are blamed, than this, that we live not after the law, and are not circumcised in the flesh as your forefathers were, and do not observe Sabbaths as you do? (10:1-3)."

A little less than two hundred years later we find Eusebius, in his *"Ecclesiastical History"* writing about the beliefs of certain heretics called Ebionites ("ebion" meaning poor in Hebrew). He wrote:

These, indeed, thought on the one hand that all the epistles of the apostles ought to be rejected, calling him an apostate from the law, but on the other, only using the gospel according to the Hebrews, they esteem the others as of but little value. They also observe the Sabbath and other disciplines of the Jews, just like them, but on the other hand, they also celebrate the Lord's day very much like us, in commemoration of his resurrection. Whence, in consequence of such a course, they have also received their epithet, the name of Ebionites, exhibiting the poverty of their intellect. For it is thus that the Hebrews call a poor man (27; 113).

It is clear that the claims of the sabbatarians for continued Sabbath-keeping are indefensible. All of the evidence indicates that those who were members of the body of Christ met regularly upon the first day of the week and not on the Sabbath day. This was the practice taught by the apostles and embraced by faithful children of God long before there was such a thing as the Roman Catholic Church. Let us all continue to embrace the first day of the week as the time for coming together in true worship.

Worship through Proclamation

When the church gathers together and the word of God is preached, is that an "act" of worship? Some would say no, that preaching is not an act of worship and that it is never presented as such in the Scriptures. I believe that the Bible teaches that the proclamation of the word of God to a gathered assembly is an act of worship and that God has viewed it as such in both the Old and New Testaments.

Beginning in 606 B.C. and concluding in 586 B.C., the Babylonians under Nebuchadnezzar carried the Southern Kingdom of Judah into captivity. Seventy years later, Darius the Mede killed the grandson of Nebuchadnezzar. Shortly thereafter, Cyrus the Persian began to allow the Jews to return to Jerusalem, just as had been prophesied. To help in this restoration of the Jews to the land, God selected four men of outstanding leadership ability. Two were prophets whose focus was primarily the rebuilding of the temple (Haggai and Zechariah). One was Nehemiah, "the governor," a social and political leader whose primary focus was the rebuilding of the walls of Jerusalem, and sort of reconstituting the people as a nation. The fourth was Ezra. He is described in Ezra 7:6 as "a scribe skilled in the law of Moses," and in Nehemiah 12:26 as "Ezra the priest and scribe."

After the reconstruction of the temple, the rebuilding of the walls, the appointment of the Levites, and the registration of the people by genealogy, the Jews gathered together in an assembly for the reading of the Book of the Law. It is one of the most famous passages from the Old Testament. Let's look at a few select verses from Nehemiah 8:

> And all the people *gathered as one man* at the square which was in front of the Water Gate, and they asked Ezra the scribe to bring the book of the law of Moses which the Lord had given to Israel. Then Ezra the priest brought the law *before the assembly of men, women, and all who could listen with understanding,* (These would have been covenant people—g.l.) on the first day of the seventh month. And he read from it before the square which was in front of the Water Gate from early morning until midday, in the presence of men and women, those who could understand; and all the people were attentive to the book of the law (vv. 1-3).

> And Ezra opened the book in the sight of all the people for he was standing above all the people; and when he opened it, all the people stood up. Then Ezra blessed the Lord the great God. And all the people answered, Amen, Amen! while lifting up their hands; then they bowed low and worshiped the Lord with their faces to the ground. Also Jeshua, Bani, Sherebiah, Jamin, Akkub, Shabbethai, Hodiah, Masseiah, Kelita, Azariah, Jozabad, Hanan, Pelaiah, and the Levites, explained the law to the people while the people remained in their place. And they read from the book of the law of God, translating (also

translatable as "explaining"—g.l.) to give the sense so that they understood the reading (vv. 5-8).

The central idea of Ezra's message is found in verse 6, "Ezra blessed the Lord, the great God. Then all the people answered, Amen, Amen! while lifting up their hands; then they bowed low and *worshiped* the Lord with their faces to the ground." The message was all about God and His word, and the people came and worshiped.

Look at the order of verse 8: (1) "They read from the book, from the law of God"; (2) "explaining to give the sense"; (3) "so that they understood the reading." That was preaching. First should come the reading of the word of God. Then comes an explanation of the sense of that reading, so that the hearers can understand. Here it was part of their worship. But that is not all. Consider Nehemiah 9:1 and 3:

> Now on the twenty-fourth day of this month the sons of Israel assembled with fasting, in sackcloth, and with dirt upon them. . . .While they stood in their place, they read from the book of the law of the Lord their God for a fourth of the day; and for another fourth they confessed and worshiped the Lord their God.

Here the very centerpiece of their worship was the reading of the book of the Law of God.

In the New Testament we find preaching associated with all the other acts of worship that brethren do together. This was so from the earliest days of the church. In Acts 2:42 we read, "And they were continually devoting themselves *to the apostles' teaching* and to fellowship, to the breaking of bread and to prayer." While I would not have said it this way, Gareth L. Reese, in his excellent book, *New Testament History, A Critical and Exegetical Commentary on the Book of Acts*, gave voice to the general consensus concerning "devoting themselves to the apostles' teaching." He wrote:

> We would say, they attended the preaching services (the times when the apostles were teaching all the doctrine of Christianity). In the Great Commission, Jesus had instructed that the converts were to be further instructed (Matthew 28:20), and this is what is being done by the apostles. The apostles, aided by the Holy Spirit, would be sharing with the new converts the wonderful truths they themselves had learned from Jesus during his earthly ministry. In due course, the apostolic teaching took written shape in the New Testament Scriptures.

Consider also Acts 20:7, "And on the first day of the week, when we were gathered together to break bread, Paul began talking to them, intending to depart the next day, and he prolonged his message until midnight." A.T. Robertson, in his critically acclaimed *Word Pictures in the New Testament*, Volume 3, said this presented a "vivid picture of Paul's long sermon which went on and on till midnight." Yes, preaching is an act of worship.

July 26

Is Prayer Worship?

Prayer offered to God in accordance with His will is one of the most common expressions of worship in the church that Jesus built. I am reminded of Acts 2:42 where we are told, "And they continued steadfastly in the apostles' doctrine and fellowship, and in breaking of bread, and in prayers." There are those who see in these words an order. The devotion of the early Christians to the teaching of the apostles is mentioned first. This, in turn, regulated their fellowship, their manner of partaking of the Lord's Supper, and their prayers.

In prayer we give voice to our reverence for God and that is in a large measure what worship is all about. By taking our petitions and thanksgiving to God we are freely admitting and acknowledging our absolute dependence upon, and trust in, Him. The early Christians were exhorted to fill their lives with prayer. Remember 1 Thessalonians 5:17, "Pray without ceasing."

In 1 Corinthians 14 we find the Apostle Paul seeking to regulate and give order to the worship assemblies of the Corinthians. The context actually begins in 1 Corinthians 11:17-18 with the words, "Now in this that I declare unto you I praise you not, that ye *come together* not for the better, but for the worse. For first of all, *when ye come together in the church*, I hear that there be divisions among you; and I partly believe it." Skipping down to verse 20 we find, "*When ye come together therefore into one place*, this is not to eat the Lord's Supper." In verse 33 we read, "Wherefore, my brethren, *when ye come together to eat*, tarry one for another."

1 Corinthians 12 and 13 deal with the matter of the exercise and duration of the miraculous spiritual gifts. Chapter 14 focuses once again on the assemblies, and how they were to conduct themselves. We see in verse 4 the phrase, "edifieth the church." In verse 5 we find, "that the church may receive edifying." Verse 12 tells us, "seek that ye may excel to the edifying of the

church." In verse 19 Paul wrote, "Yet in the church I had rather speak five words with my understanding, that by my voice I might teach others also." And as we move down to verse 23 it becomes even clearer that Paul is writing about times of assembling. It says, "If therefore *the whole church be come together into one place.*"

In his discussion of conduct and activities that are to take place in the assemblies, Paul wrote in 1 Corinthians 14:15-16, "What is it then? I will pray with the spirit, and I will pray with the understanding also: I will sing with the spirit, and I will sing with the understanding also. Else when thou shalt bless with the spirit, how shall he that occupieth the room of the unlearned say Amen at thy giving of thanks, seeing he understandeth not what thou sayest?" Prayer was a part of the worship of the first century church, and at least a portion of that was public.

Prayer was undoubtedly part of the public worship of the first century church, but we need to be very careful about it. We must not fall into the mistake of the Pharisees who tithed mint and anise and cumin, but "neglected the weightier matters of the law: justice and mercy and faith" (Matt. 23:23). As we seek to emulate the worship of the early church, and to a large measure we have succeeded in doing that, we cannot allow ourselves to be content with the mere duplication of the outward forms of prayer. Prayer must be more than just an "item" or "act" of worship that we perform in a routine kind of way.

There is so much that can be said about prayer, and the scope of this particular writing will not permit it. However, there are some things that must be said. Individually, prayer is a pretty effective measure of what we are as Christians. Prayer is commanded in many passages. Are we personally obedient to that command? Prayer is a test of our humility. A proud man may pray loudly and at great length publicly, but does he go to God on his knees, literally or figuratively, in the privacy of his own home? Prayer is a test of our faith. It evidences our trust in a personal God who really cares about each of us individually.

What about prayer congregationally? How do we compare with the early church as a church? I would like to give you a portion of a lecture given by Sewell Hall on this subject. He wrote:

> The first church was a praying church, and no doubt that had a part in its rapid growth, both in numbers and in faith. If their prayers had not been important they would not have been mentioned. . . . .I have had opportunity to observe

some growing churches that are just as strong in denouncing sin, in demanding strong preaching, and in maintaining discipline as any that are stagnant, but I have often seen in those prospering churches more emphasis on prayer. There are churches that have fairly regular prayer meetings—meetings devoted entirely to prayer: prayer for sick persons, for the lost, for God's will to be done in national emergencies, for evangelists being sent out to preach the gospel and for other special needs. In addition, they meet together in the homes of members just as the Jerusalem church met in homes for prayer (Acts 12:12). When such churches are growing, it just may be that they are growing because of their dependence on the Lord and the blessings He has promised. How does the congregation of which you are a part measure up? (*True Worship: Florida College Annual Lectures 2005, 35-36*).

Hopefully this will give us all a better understanding that prayer is in fact part of the collective worship of the church, and also of how important it truly is.

July 27

Would First Century Christians Recognize It?

It is sometimes presented as an unqualified statement of fact, "If first century Christians came into our worship assemblies today, they would not recognize it!" It is sometimes stated as a question, but when it is, it is usually rhetorical in nature; the answer is already assumed. "If first century Christians came into our worship assemblies, do you think they would recognize it?" Either way it is meant to assert that what we do today collectively in worship is not at all like what they did in the early years of the church. Never is any proof offered; the assertion is simply made. Well, saying something doesn't make it fact.

In the New Testament there is not a single passage that presents all of the elements that went into a worship assembly of the early church. However, by combining several passages that describe different elements of the worship, we can get a very good idea of what took place. Such passages as Acts 20:7, 1 Corinthians 11:17-34, 14:1-40, and 16:1-2 give us a fairly comprehensive picture of the worship of the Lord's church.

C. W. Dugmore, in his extensively documented book, *The Influence of the Synagogue Upon the Divine Office*, makes the point that the early order of

Christian worship was built up from the Jewish synagogue service with the addition of the distinctively Christian rite of the Lord's Supper. He shows that the synagogue service included Scripture readings, interspersed with Psalm chants, a sermon, prayers, and almsgiving. Dugmore then says that we find the same elements in the early accounts of Christian worship: readings, singing, preaching, praying, and giving. Add to it the distinctive practice of observing the Lord's Supper and doesn't that all sound very familiar?

The earliest account of a worship service that we have outside of the New Testament actually came from a non-Christian. It came from Pliny the Younger, who was the Roman governor of Bithynia about 112 A.D. The fullest account of a worship service that we have is from the second century, written by Justin Martyr in his wonderful *First Apology.* Justin Martyr was a Gentile by birth but born in Samaria. He lived from 114 A.D to 165 A.D. He was extremely well educated and studied in the schools of the various philosophers, eventually coming to Christianity and writing a number of works that have proven to be the most important of the second century. He was a magnificent apologist for the Christian faith. Here is what Justin Martyr wrote concerning the Lord's Day worship service of the early second century church:

> And on the day called Sunday, all who live in cities or in the country gather together to one place, and the memoirs of the apostles or the writings of the prophets are read, as long as time permits; then, when the reader has ceased, the president verbally instructs, and exhorts to the imitation of these good things. Then we all rise together and pray, and, as we before said, when our prayer is ended, bread and wine and water are brought, and the president in like manner offers prayers and thanksgivings, according to his ability, and the people assent, saying Amen; and there is a distribution to each, and a participation of that over which thanks have been given, and to those who are absent a portion is sent by the deacons. And they who are well to do, and willing, give what each thinks fit; and what is collected is deposited with the president, who succors the orphans and widows, and those who, through sickness or any other cause, are in want, and those who are in bonds, and the strangers sojourning among us, and in a word takes care of all who are in need. But Sunday is the day on which we all hold our common assembly, because it is the first day on which God, having wrought a change in the darkness and matter, made the world; and Jesus Christ our Savior on the same day rose from the dead. For He was crucified on the day before that of Saturn (Saturday); and on the day after that of Saturn, which is the day of the Sun, having appeared to His apostles and disciples, He taught them these things, which we have submitted to you also for your consideration (Apology 1, 67).

Martyr did not specifically mention singing in that passage, but he most assuredly did earlier in his Apology, 1, 13, and connected it with prayer.

Put this all together and what do we see? We see the Christians of the early second century meeting together on Sunday where they engaged in the reading of Scripture, both Old and New Testaments. The "president" (a term used simply to describe the one conducting the service) then preached, exhorting the brethren to the imitation of the good things read. Prayer was offered, to which Justin earlier in his Apology had also connected singing. The Lord's Supper was served, which is what he discussed in the two chapters preceding this passage, chapters 65 and 66. Also a contribution was made into a common treasury. So, yes, the early Christians would recognize the worship services in which we engage.

Something else that I find very interesting and important is that the extra-biblical writings of the late first century and the second century clearly indicate that the Christians did not partake of the Lord's Supper as part of a common meal. Writers such as Pliny, Justin, Clement of Alexandria, and Hippolytus make a clear distinction. They did eat common meals together, but the evidence is clear that they separated the two—even in terms of time. By the early second century the Christians were meeting early on Sunday morning for worship, including the Lord's Supper (perhaps the early gathering had to do with the persecution they were facing), and if they shared a common meal on that day, it was later on in the evening.

We can be confident that when we gather together on Sunday to worship God, we are doing what the early Christians did.

July 28

Is Singing Worship?

Bible students recognize and appreciate the fact that God has commanded His people to worship Him with music. While we are no longer under the Old Testament as a source of authority for those things we do of a religious nature, we can turn there to establish that from ancient times the people of God have praised Him with song. Consider Psalm 30:4, where David wrote, "Sing praise to the Lord, you His godly ones, and give thanks to His holy name." If we turn to 2 Chronicles 29, we find that under the Law of Moses, Jehovah, by His prophets, commanded Israel to accompany their songs with instruments of music. As they offered burnt offerings to the Lord on the altar in the temple, the assembly worshipped, the singers sang in the worship, and the trumpeters sounded. Let's read verses 25-28:

> He then stationed the Levites in the house of the Lord with cymbals, with harps, and with lyres, according to the command of David and of Gad the king's seer, and of Nathan the prophet; for the command was from the Lord through His prophets. And the Levites stood with the musical instruments of David, and the priests with the trumpets. Then Hezekiah gave the order to offer the burnt offering on the altar. When the burnt offering began, the song to the Lord also began with the trumpets, accompanied by the instruments of David, king of Israel. While the whole assembly worshiped, the singers also sang and the trumpets sounded; all this continued until the burnt offering was finished.

Perhaps the most well known passage of the Old Testament related to the worship of God with music is Psalm 150, which simply says, "Praise the Lord! Praise God in His sanctuary; praise Him in His mighty expanse. Praise Him for His mighty deeds; praise Him according to His excellent greatness. Praise Him with trumpet sound; praise Him with harp and lyre. Praise Him with timbrel and dancing; praise Him with stringed instruments and pipe. Praise Him with loud cymbals; praise Him with resounding cymbals. Let everything that has breath praise the Lord. Praise the Lord!"

When we move into the New Testament we find that God's people are still commanded to worship Him with music. However, Christians are commanded to offer God vocal music, as Ephesians 5:19 tells us, "singing and making melody with your heart to the Lord." When faithful churches of Christ worship, that is just exactly what they do—singing as authorized by God in the New Testament. According to Ephesians 5:19, the instrument for making melody to God is the heart. The heart of man involves his ability to think, reason, understand, and believe, as well as his ability to trust, hope, love, and rejoice. When we sing the praises of God and accompany that praise by the instrument ordained of God for the worship of His church, our service to Him can be acceptable. The human heart is an instrument for everyone. The Lord has provided for every child of His to make his journey to heaven by singing and striking the strings of his own heart. When a Christian does that, he has worshipped God in the way that God desires of all men, at least as far as music is concerned.

There is an aspect of our singing in worship that needs to be addressed and properly understood. When we sing it is true that we are "speaking to one another in psalms and hymns and spiritual songs" (Eph. 5:19) and that we are "teaching and admonishing one another" (Col. 3:16); but let us never forget that when we sing together in our worship of God, our singing is first unto the Lord. Colossians 3:16 concludes with "singing with thankfulness in your hearts to God" and Ephesians 5:19 concludes with "singing and making melody with your heart to the Lord." God desires us to give unto Him our full devotion and allegiance. He wants us to sing of Him and to Him. He doesn't judge the singing the same way man does. Man tends to judge it on the basis of whether it is good or bad, whether we can carry a tune or not. God judges it on the basis of whether or not it is wholehearted and offered as an act of homage and reverence to Him. Indeed, I believe that our singing in worship to God is a sacrifice to Him, the savor of which rises to the heavens. Hebrews 13:15 tells us, "Through Him then, let us continually offer up a sacrifice of praise to God, that is, the fruit of lips that give thanks to His name."

One of the basic ideas behind the word "praise" is to cause to shine. Praise means to laud, to extol, and to commend. When praises are sung, describing the glory of God, that glory will shine.

Is it possible for singing in a worship service to be done without enthusiasm? Yes, of course it is. Is it possible that some won't think of the meaning of the words but just recite them by memory? Certainly. Is it possible that some will actually be singing to impress those nearest to them with their beautiful voice? I suppose so. But when we sing with the right attitude, with God as our focus, it is a wonderful and joyously uplifting thing. And one of the really neat things about this aspect of worship as God has set it up is that even if everybody else isn't focused, I can be!

Let's bring this reading to a close with Psalm 95:1-7a:

O come, let us sing for joy to the Lord; let us shout joyfully to the rock of our salvation. Let us come before His presence with thanksgiving; let us shout joyfully to Him with psalms. For the Lord is a great God, and a great King above all gods, in whose hand are the depths of the earth; the peaks of the mountains are His also. The sea is His, for it was He who made it; and His hands formed the dry land. Come, let us worship and bow down; let us kneel before the Lord our Maker. For He is our God, and we are the people of His pasture, and the sheep of His hand.

Beautiful, isn't it?

Is Giving an Act of Worship? (1)

What is worship? Is it possible to give one all-encompassing definition in just a few short sentences? Not if you are serious about understanding what it is. We can go to *Webster's New Universal Unabridged Dictionary* and find several definitions listed there, such as, "1. Reverent honor and homage paid to God or a sacred personage, or to any object regarded as sacred; 2. formal or ceremonious rendering of such honor and homage; 3. adoring reverence or regard; . . . 6. to render religious reverence and homage to; 7. to feel an adoring reverence or regard for. . . ." This is just a sampling, there were actually ten definitions given, as well as the synonyms "honor, homage, adoration, idolatry, venerate, revere, adore, glorify, idolize, adulate."

When we turn our attention to God's word, we find that in the New Testament there are at least six different Greek words that are translated as "worship," when used as a verb. They all have different nuances in meaning. The most frequent word rendered worship is *proskuneo*, which means, "to make obeisance, do reverence to." It is used of an act of homage or reverence. The other words are *sebomai*, meaning to revere; *sebazomai* meaning to honor religiously; *latreuo* meaning to serve, to render religious service or homage; *eusebeo* meaning to act piously towards; and *therapeuo* meaning to serve, do service to.

In the Old Testament the principle word for worship is *shahah*, appearing at least 95 times. It contains both the ideas of the physical acts of worship as well as the volitional and emotional idea as well. The context determines more or less clearly which idea is intended.

Examination of the Old Testament concept of worship shows that it is the "reverential attitude of mind or body or both, combined with the more generic notions of religious adoration, obedience, service." Examination of the New Testament idea of worship shows that it is "a combination of the reverential attitude of mind and body, the general ceremonial and religious service of God, the feeling of awe, veneration, adoration." It is a massive subject, the study of which had better not be taken lightly.

The worship of God is enjoined upon all men. The book of Psalms is filled with general calls to worship. Jesus, in John 4:23-24, said,

But the hour cometh, and now is, when the true worshippers shall worship the Father in spirit and in truth: for the Father seeketh such to worship him. God is a Spirit: and they that worship him must worship him in spirit and in truth." In Revelation 19:10, we read, "And I fell at his feet to worship him. And he said unto me, See thou do it not: I am thy fellow servant, and of they brethren that have the testimony of Jesus: worship God: for the testimony of Jesus is the spirit of prophecy.

There is a question that has been bandied about recently concerning the giving of our means upon the first day of the week, about the contribution. It has been questioned whether or not this is an act of worship. Is it an act of reverence or homage? Is it an act of service, an act of piety? All of this must be taken into consideration as one seeks to answer that question, for all of it is involved in both the New and Old Testament teaching concerning worship.

July 30

Is Giving an Act of Worship? (2): The Old Testament

Romans 15:4 tells us, "For whatsoever things were written aforetime were written for our learning, that we through patience and comfort of the Scriptures might have hope." We can, and must, learn a great deal from the Old Testament, including some wonderful principles about worship. Surely what happened with Cain in Genesis 4 and with Nadab and Abihu in Leviticus 10 teach us the seriousness of worshipping God in the way that He has set forth. These passages, as well as others, show us that when God gives a pattern for worship, it behooves man to abide by it.

Let's consider Deuteronomy 12. In this chapter worship laws were set forth as Moses restated that which God had given to him. The chapter starts in verses 1-4 by stating that when they entered the land of Canaan, all pagan sanctuaries and other paraphernalia were to be destroyed. Next come verses 5-14, which state:

But unto the place which the Lord your God shall choose out of all your tribes to put his name there, even unto his habitation shall ye seek, and thither thou shalt come: and thither ye shall bring your burnt offerings, and your sacrifices, and your tithes, and heave offerings of your hand, and your vows, and your free will offerings, and the firstlings of your herds and of your flocks: and there ye shall eat before the Lord your God, and ye shall rejoice in all that ye put your hand unto, ye and your households, wherein the Lord thy God hath blessed thee. Ye shall not do after all the things that we do here this day, every man whatsoever is right in his own eyes. For ye are not as yet come to the rest and to the inheritance, which the Lord your God giveth you. But when ye go over Jordan, and dwell in the land which the Lord your God giveth you to inherit, and when he giveth you rest from all your enemies round about, so that ye dwell in safety; then there shall be a place which the Lord your God shall choose to cause his name to dwell there: thither shall ye bring all that I command you: your burnt offerings, and your sacrifices, your tithes, and the heave offering of your hand, and all your choice vows which ye vow unto the Lord. And ye shall rejoice before the Lord your God, ye, and your sons, and your daughters, and your menservants, and your maidservants, and the Levite that is within your gates; forasmuch as he hath no part nor inheritance with you. Take heed to thyself that thou offer not thy burnt offering in every place that thou seest: but in the place which the Lord shall choose in one of thy tribes, there thou shalt offer thy burnt offerings, and there thou shalt do all that I command thee.

Thus, legitimate *worship* could only take place at that spot that the Lord would designate. The phrase "the place which the Lord shall choose" appears six times in Deuteronomy 12, not to mention eleven other times in the book. At that place, at that sanctuary (if I may use that term), all tithes, gifts, and sacrifices were to be presented in worship.

Verses 15-28 make the point that slaughtering and the eating of meat for ordinary meals could take place anywhere. However, religious meals were restricted to that central place which the Lord would choose.

Verses 29-32 warn the Israelites that they must not emulate the detestable idolatrous worship practices of the Canaanite. From this passage there can be no argument that the giving of money, as well as other goods, was viewed by God, indeed commanded by God, as worship.

Let's not stop here, though. Let's go to Numbers 18 and consider verses 24-29. The passage says:

But the tithes of the children of Israel, which they offer *as an heave offering* unto the Lord, I have given to the Levites to inherit: therefore I have said unto them, Among the children of Israel they shall have no inheritance. And the Lord spake unto Moses, saying, Thus speak unto the Levites, and say unto them, When ye take of the children of Israel the tithes which I have given you from them for your inheritance, then ye shall offer up an heave offering of it for the Lord, even a tenth part of the tithe. And this your heave offering shall be reckoned unto you, as though it were the corn of the threshing floor, and as the fullness of the winepress. Thus ye also shall offer an heave offering unto the Lord of all your tithes, which ye receive of the children of Israel; and ye shall give thereof the Lord's heave offering to Aaron the priest. Out of all your gifts ye shall offer every heave offering of the Lord, of all the best thereof, even the hallowed part thereof out of it.

Thus the tithes of the Israelites were referred to as a "heave offering" and the tenth of the tithes that the Levites had received they also had to offer to God as a "heave offering." Friends, the "heave offerings" were part of the peace offerings, offered in worship to God. The peace offerings indicated right relations with God, and expressed fellowship with Him, gratitude and a sense of obligation. The heave offerings were that which was lifted up, dedicated in service to Jehovah, consecrated to Him. Once again, without possible argument, the giving of the tithes, including money as well as other things, was considered an offering, a sacrifice to God. It was an act of worship, which was to be done in the legitimate place for worship.

July 31

Is Giving an Act of Worship? (3): The New Testament

This principle of giving as an act of worship (and yes, there are acts of worship—indeed, worship can be partially defined as an act of reverence or homage) is also found in the New Testament and reemphasized as such.

Most Bible students are familiar with 1 Corinthians 16:1-2. However, I am afraid that many have not gone deeply enough in their study of this passage to understand or know all of its ramifications. The passage says, "Now concerning the collection for the saints, as I have given order to the churches of Galatia, even so do ye. Upon the first day of the week let every one of you lay by him in store, as God hath prospered him, that there be no gatherings when I come."

We first consider the word "collection." That word is *logeia* and was thought to have been derived from *lego* and to be a word distinctive to the New Testament. This is a point made in *Thayer's Greek English Lexicon*. However, additional work by archaeologists, particularly Adolf Deissmann, has produced papyri that tell a different story. We now know that the word *logeia* was derived from the word *logeuo* (I collect) and was commonly used in Paul's day. Deissmann wrote, "We find it used chiefly of religious collections for a god, a temple, etc., just as St. Paul uses it of his collection of money for the 'saints' at Jerusalem" (Adolf Deissmann, *Light From the Ancient East*).

What is the big deal? The importance of this discovery is to prove that Paul used the word just as his contemporaries used it. The normal usage of the word was that of a collection in the "formal" sense. He wasn't telling the Corinthians to put a little money away every week in a jar at home. Rather, just as faithful Christian scholars had asserted all along, he was instructing them to take a formal collection on the first day of every week.

Some have argued that this passage only authorizes taking a collection to relieve the needs of the poor saints among the brethren and not for general purposes. "This passage was never used to show *all* of the scriptural usages of the first-day-of-the-week collection. Instead, it has been used, and properly so, as the only passage in the Bible to tell how churches raised their funds in the New Testament. Other passages imply a common treasury (2 Cor. 11:8; Phil. 4:14-16; 1 Tim. 5:9; etc.). We can know how the money in those treasuries was raised only from this passage. We must consult other New Testament passages to understand all of the things for which the collection can be scripturally spent" (Mike Willis, *First Corinthians*, 597).

One would wonder why giving as worship, so clearly set forth in the Old Testament (and we will see it set forth equally clearly in the New), is now being questioned. Where in the New Testament is singing designated as worship? Where is partaking of the Lord's Supper said to be worship? We all recognize and understand that these things are indeed acts of worship, and we understand and recognize that from passages such as 1 Corinthians 11, 12, 13, 14 that these things are done when the whole church comes together into one place, or in the assembly. We also recognize that the only authorized time to partake of the Lord's Supper and to take that formal collection (remember now, a formal collection has been proven to be the way the word was used in Paul's time) is on the first day of the week. Men may do those two things on other days, but not by faith. Faith comes by hearing and hearing by the Word of God (Rom. 10:17).

Brother Robert Turner, in his wonderful little magazine, *Plain Talk*, answered a question about giving and the collection that is pertinent to this article. It appeared in the February 1967 edition of his paper. I know that Brother Turner hit the nail right on the head. Here are the questions and his answers:

Brother Turner: Years ago I heard of a brother who said collection should be taken only for some specific purpose. Recently I have heard this repeated, and the whole idea of church treasury questioned. Please comment on this.

Reply:

This is an age-old hobby-horse, repeatedly raised. Lipscomb had to deal with it in his day....

It is true that we give for specific purposes—i.e., the *treasury* is not the *end* or *purpose* for giving. As saints of God, we have obligations to meet, work to do. Some of this work is done distributively, as individuals (Galatians 6:6) and some is done collectively (Philippians 4:15). To act collectively there must be a pooling of our means and/or abilities; and money is the medium of exchange by which this is usually done. . . . The treasury (pooled fund) is just a means to the end we may act collectively in whatever work is proposed. . . .

If I didn't believe God had a full time work which He wants His saints to do collectively, I certainly would not consider a continuous 'collection' or treasury necessary. 1 Corinthians 16:1-2 stipulates <u>purpose</u> for the 'laying by' on the first day of every week. They had a treasury to help the needy saints. The 'collection' of vs. 1, and the 'gathering' (KJ) of vs. 2, are from "logeuo" and refer to a 'religious collection' as for a god or temple. This *was* what some today sneeringly refer to as a 'church' collection; but it had a specific purpose as we have seen. Philippians 4:15 and other passages show there were *other purposes* for the pooling of funds, such as supporting preachers.

Saints who work and worship together scripturally have divine purposes, either specifically or generically, for all they do. It is to the end that these divine purposes may be carried out—collectively—that the treasury exists, is used, and must be replenished. . . .

To question the whole idea of a 'church treasury' is to question the God-given privilege and obligation of saints to function collectively. It is a shameful end to which some of my brethren have come. Fighting abuses of the 'church treasury'—and there are such—they are casting God's plan aside. Echo, THEY SHALL NOT PASS!"

I can but add a hearty and heartfelt *amen!*

We have seen Philippians 4:15 mentioned repeatedly in this discussion. Let's read it through verse 18:

Now ye Philippians know also, that in the beginning of the gospel, when I departed from Macedonia, no church communicated with me as concerning giving and receiving, but ye only. For even in Thessalonica ye sent once and again unto my necessity. Not because I desire a gift: but I desire fruit that may abound to your account. But I have all, and abound: I am full, having received of Epaphroditus the things which were sent from you, an odor of a sweet smell, a sacrifice acceptable, well pleasing to God.

This was an act of giving done collectively by the brethren in Philippi, made possible through the continuous collection (consider 2 Cor. 11:8-9). Their contribution was considered by the Holy Spirit to be a sacrificial offering to God, a sacrifice acceptable to God. This is language borrowed from the Old Testament, such as Noah offering burnt offerings upon the altar and "the Lord smelled a sweet savour" (Gen. 8:20-21). This was worship.

Make no mistake. An in-depth study of the matter demonstrates that God views giving of our means as worship! He always has, He always will.

August 1

Leading Like Paul

The greatest qualities of leadership manifest themselves in the crucible of conflict and controversy. The Thessalonians were given the opportunity to witness and benefit from the leadership of Paul in difficult circumstances. Acts 17:1-9 details Paul's work in the city of Thessalonica and tells of certain unbelieving Jews, moved by jealousy, instigating an uprising. They made the following charge against Paul and his traveling companions in verse 8, "These who have turned the world upside down have come here too." In 1 Thessalonians 2, Paul reminded the brethren of his conduct when he had been among them. Verses 1-12 contain valuable lessons for us all.

For you yourselves know, brethren, that our coming to you was not in vain. But even after we had suffered before and were spitefully treated at Philippi, as you know, we were bold in our God to speak to you the gospel of God in much conflict. For our exhortation did not come from error or uncleanness, nor was it in deceit (vv. 1-3).

A true leader does not operate in secret, and the result of his efforts is apparent. In spite of a life of service that involved tremendous physical suffering and danger, Paul had continued to wield the only weapon he used in "turning the world upside down"—the gospel of the Lord Jesus Christ. Just as he had done everywhere the opportunity presented itself, Paul preached the gospel in Thessalonica with boldness born out of his trust in God. He would not allow opposition to silence him for he was presenting the simple, powerful truths of the gospel. A true leader in the service of God does not engage in verbal gymnastics and tricks of semantics. He presents the truth in as clear a manner as possible. I do not believe that those who heard Paul came away failing to understand where he stood on any gospel related issue.

> But as we have been approved by God to be entrusted with the gospel, even so we speak, not as pleasing men, but God who tests our hearts. For neither at any time did we use flattering words, as you know, nor a cloak for covetousness—God is witness. Nor did we seek glory from men, either from you or from others, when we might have made demands as apostles of Christ (vv. 4-6).

What motivates a leader in the cause of Christ? What motivated Paul? He had been "approved by God to be entrusted with the gospel." Albert Barnes, in *Barnes Notes On The New Testament*, represented the point Paul was making in the first clause of verse 4 in this way, "Since there had been committed to us an office so high and holy, and so much demanding sincerity, fidelity, and honesty, we endeavored to act in all respects in conformity to the trust reposed in us." Oh, that we all would realize this! Being a leader for Christ is about service, and as far as being pleasing is concerned, the One we must strive to please is God. The man who seeks the praise of men is not mature enough to be a leader. The Bible speaks of those who would tickle the ears of their hearers, but such serve Satan and not the ones to whom they speak, and certainly not God.

> But we were gentle among you, just as a nursing mother cherishes her own children. So, affectionately longing for you, we were well pleased to impart to you not only the gospel of God, but also our own lives, because you had become dear to us. For you remember, brethren, our labor and toil; for laboring night and day, that we might not be a burden to any of you, we preached to you the gospel of God (vv. 7-9).

Having mentioned methods that he did not use among them, Paul now talks about the approach that he used. He was "gentle." Please do not mistake that for timidity. Gentleness is a "fruit of the Spirit" (Gal. 5:23), and Paul's use of the word here reminds me of his statement to Timothy in 2 Timothy 2:24, "And a servant of the Lord must not quarrel but be gentle to all, able to teach, patient." A leader in the cause of Christ must have genuine affection for those he leads. So strong was Paul's affection for these people that he was willing to impart to them the gospel (which is in itself strong proof of love), but he was willing to do it even when it meant danger to himself. A true leader will do what is best and most needful in a particular situation.

As Paul concluded his comments related to his conduct in verses 10-12, what he said must be embraced by leaders in the church today. Our conduct must be holy, just, and blameless. How can we lead if our conduct brings discredit or dishonor to the cause of Christ? The answer is, "We can't," any more than a father can lead his children if his conduct does not match what he says.

August 2

"Are We There Yet?"

Is there any parent among us who has not heard these words? My father's customary answer to that question was, "With every turn of the wheel, we're a turn of the wheel closer." As I recall, even as a six- or seven-year-old, I understood that my dad was telling me to just sit back and be patient for another ten or fifteen minutes. Then it was time to ask once more, "Are we there yet?" only to hear the response, "With every turn of the wheel, we're a turn of the wheel closer."

That is the way it is in our journey to heaven. Sometimes I feel like the trip there is never going to end, and with eager anticipation I find myself praying, "Even so, come Lord Jesus." But, "With every turn of the wheel, we are a turn of the wheel closer." Whatever the day brings, we are getting closer to our destination. Every turn of the wheel brings us closer to the time when "The Lord Himself will descend from heaven with a shout, with the voice of the archangel, and with the trumpet of God: and the dead in Christ shall rise first. Then we who are alive and remain shall be caught up together with them in the clouds to meet the Lord in the air, and thus we shall always be with the Lord" (1 Thess. 4:16-17).

I long for the day when faith becomes sight, but I am not there yet. I am reminded of Paul's statement in Philippians 3:12-14: "Not that I have already obtained it, or have already become perfect, but I press on in order that I may lay hold of that for which also I was laid hold of by Christ Jesus. Brethren, I do not regard myself as having laid hold of it yet; but one thing I do: forgetting what lies behind and reaching forward to what lies ahead, I press on toward the goal for the prize of the upward call of God in Christ Jesus." The eager anticipation in Paul's words is apparent. However, those same words indicate that Paul knew that if he ever stopped in his journey, if his "wheels quit turning," he wasn't going to get there.

It is imperative that we all keep in mind the truth that we have not yet taken hold of our ultimate ambition. Heaven is out there prepared for us, but like a runner who expends every ounce of energy pushing and straining for the finish line, we have got to keep on working.

Let's all examine ourselves and make sure that we are still on course. Let's make sure that the "wheels are still turning." Is the person we see in the mirror someone who is honestly "reaching forward to what lies ahead"? Is that person who is looking back at us someone who is really "pressing on toward the goal for the prize of the upward call of God in Christ Jesus"? Is our reflection in the mirror the reflection of someone who truly loves the brethren? Is it someone who visits the sick, makes calls of encouragement, refuses to gossip, and always gives the benefit of the doubt? That person looking back at us—is it someone who never misses a service that he or she is physically able to attend, who participates in all the works of the church that he or she can, and who looks for things to do in God's service?

At the time of the Lord's ascension into heaven, the Bible tells us that "two men in white clothing" stood beside the apostles. I believe it is obvious that these were angels. But more important than who they were is what they said, "Men of Galilee, why do you stand looking into the sky? This Jesus, who has been taken up from you into heaven, will come in just the same way as you have watched Him go into heaven" (Acts 1:11). Does that thrill your heart? "Come, Lord Jesus!"

August 3

Sometimes Good People Have Bad Days

One of my favorite passages of Scripture is found in Jeremiah 20:7-9. By the time this statement is made, it is probable that Jeremiah had been preaching his message of doom for the southern kingdom for over twenty years, and what he had said had not yet come to pass. His was a most unpopular message that caused him to suffer much mistreatment at the hands of the people. He was a man feeling intense emotional conflict. His love for God compelled him to preach the truth as God gave it to him; his love for the people caused him great anguish of heart as he thought about "the terror on every side" that God assured him was coming. At the same time, he was feeling very alone in his labors. In Jeremiah 15:17-18 he wrote, "I sat not in the assembly of the mockers, nor rejoiced; I sat alone because of thy hand: for thou hast filled me with indignation. Why is my pain perpetual, and my wound incurable, which refuseth to be healed? Wilt thou be altogether unto me as a liar, and as waters that fail?" So here is what Jeremiah wrote in 20:7-9:

O Lord, thou hast deceived me, and I was deceived: thou art stronger than I, and hast prevailed; I am in derision daily, every one mocketh me. For since I spake, I cried out, I cried violence and spoil; because the word of the Lord was made a reproach unto me, and a derision, daily. Then I said, I will not make mention of him, nor speak any more in his name. But his word was in mine heart as a burning fire shut up in my bones, and I was weary with forbearing, and I could not stay.

Here is an example of a very good man having a very bad day. But he was not the first, nor would he be the last. Elijah was a great man of God, a bold proclaimer of truth, who sometimes had serious problems maintaining his confidence in his ability to do what God was telling him to do and in the success of his efforts. Remember him under the juniper tree after Queen Jezebel threatened his life? I Kings 19:4 tells us, "But he himself went a day's journey into the wilderness, and came and sat down under a juniper tree: and he requested for himself that he might die; and said, It is enough; now, O Lord, take away my life; for I am not better than my fathers." This was a very good man having a very bad day.

How about John the Baptist? Here was a man of extraordinary character, "filled with the Holy Ghost" (Luke 1:15). Here was a man who had told Herod the king that it was not lawful for him to have his brother Philip's wife. Here was a man who said of Jesus, "Behold the Lamb of God, which taketh away the sin of the world" (John 1:29). He also said, "I saw the Spirit descending from heaven like a dove, and it abode upon him. And I knew Him not: but he that sent me to baptize with water, the same said unto me, Upon whom thou shalt see the Spirit descending, and remaining on him, the same is he which baptizeth with the Holy Ghost. And I say, and bare record that this is the Son of God" (John 1:32-34).

There came a time when John was unjustly arrested and cast into prison by Herod. His time in prison evidently caused him frustration and impatience to the extent that he sent two of his disciples to Jesus to question Him as to whether He truly was the One or should they look for someone else. Luke 7:19-20 tells us, "And John calling unto him two of his disciples sent them to Jesus, saying, Art thou he that should come, or look we for another? When the men were come unto him, they said, John the Baptist hath sent us unto thee, saying, Art thou he that should come, or look we for another?" The Lord's response was, "Blessed is he, whosoever shall not be offended in me" (Luke 7:23). He was encouraging John not to stumble over this issue. The

Lord would take care of things in His own way and according to His own timetable. John was a great man who had a bad day.

Turning our attention once again to Jeremiah 20, we recognize the sense of frustration and impatience. Jeremiah had preached long and hard and had seen very few visible results. He was ready to quit. It reminds me of Moses' reaction when the people complained about the manna in Numbers 11. His frustration and impatience were summarized in verse 15 when he said to God, "And if thou deal thus with me, kill me, I pray thee, out of hand, if I have found favor in thy sight; and let me not see my wretchedness." Those who are truly concerned about the work of the Lord, whether they are preachers, elders, deacons, or members, will feel this frustration from time to time. However, it doesn't mean that a good man has become a bad man. It simply means that a good man might be having a bad day.

Jeremiah couldn't quit, and neither can we. His love and devotion to God and His word meant that it was like a fire in his bones, and it proved to be harder not to speak than to speak. Jeremiah was a man who had something to say and he had to say it. There was a truth that Jeremiah knew and he expressed it in 20:11 where he wrote, "But the Lord is with me as a mighty terrible One: therefore my persecutors shall stumble, and they shall not prevail: they shall be greatly ashamed; for they shall not prosper: their everlasting confusion shall never be forgotten." Jeremiah knew that to be true, but it wasn't always at the forefront of his mind. Sometimes good people have bad days.

August 4

"Elijah Is Come Already"

For a brief but thrilling time in the early part of the first century A.D., the wilderness of Judea resonated with the preaching of John the Baptist: "The voice of him that crieth in the wilderness" (Isa. 40:3). John came as the messenger of the Lord to prepare the way before Him (Mal. 3:1) and "to make straight in the desert a highway for our God" (Isa. 40:3).

Malachi had written, "Behold, I am going to send you Elijah the prophet before the coming of the great and terrible day of the Lord. And he will restore the hearts of the fathers to their children, and the hearts of the children to their fathers, lest I come and smite the land with a curse" (Mal. 4:4-6). John was the fulfillment of that prophecy.

As these prophecies related to John and the coming of the Messiah began to be fulfilled, an angel of the Lord appeared to a certain priest named Zacharias, the husband of Elizabeth, as he was performing his priestly service before God. The angel told Zacharias that his prayers had been heard and that he and Elizabeth would be blessed with a son. In addition, the angel said, "And it is he who will go as a forerunner before Him in the spirit and power of Elijah, to turn the hearts of the fathers back to the children, and the disobedient to the attitude of the righteous; so as to make ready a people prepared for the Lord" (Luke 1:17).

"The spirit and the power of Elijah." When we consider Elijah, prophet to Israel in the days of Ahab, we see a man of fervent zeal with the courage to speak out against the false religions that were turning the people away from Jehovah. He was a man of boldness who would say what needed to be said without regard for the consequences to himself. His mission was to restore the affections of his people to their God and to reestablish respect for His law. Elijah's job was to create once again a right relationship between parents and children and to turn them to the true religion of their ancestors. By so doing, they would be ready to receive the Messiah, because when He came they would be able to see that He was the fulfillment of God's promises and the realization of the hope of their fathers. He came preaching repentance and the fruits thereof, manifested in a complete return to Jehovah. That is what John did as well. He came preaching repentance and demanded fruits thereof. He called for a return to God's way and warned of destruction to come should the people refuse. He prepared the way for the coming of the Lord.

I want to take special note of the preaching of John the Baptist. He was a man with something to say, a message that desperately needed to be delivered, and he had the courage to say it. What really required courage on the part of John, and it is the same thing that truly requires courage on the part of every faithful gospel preacher today, was the willingness to *make it practical and to make the necessary application.*

When John was confronted with the religious leaders of his day, men responsible for the perversion of God's law who were creating a religious atmosphere prophetically referred to as "a dry ground" by Isaiah, he did not couch his message in language so generic that no one could understand or be offended. "O generation of vipers, who hath warned you to flee from the wrath to come? Bring forth fruits worthy of repentance" (Luke 3:7-8).

When John was asked what he meant, or what the people should do, he gave practical answers that were applicable to their lives. He did not fill his response with the smooth sounding religious slogans and catchphrases of his day. John said that if they had two coats and another had none, share with him. If they had food and someone was hungry, give him some. To the tax collectors, John said to just do their jobs and stop the dishonest conduct. To soldiers, his response was essentially the same. When it was a matter of God's law concerning marriage, John did not speak in such a way that everybody could go away feeling good about whatever condition they were in, nor did they have to go away wondering what the truth was. John stood before Herod and said, "It is not lawful for you to have your brother's wife" (Mark 6:18).

Preaching and teaching must be practical. It must be of such a nature that the listeners can make application to their lives, or it is of little to no value. The gospel is eminently practical, and it is meant to be life changing, but not if we water it down for fear of upsetting or offending someone. What I *need* to know is what God wants me to do. I *need* to know if I am wrong. I *need* to know if I am sinning, if I am practicing something that God has not authorized, or if I am believing a false doctrine. I *don't need* someone to tickle my ears by telling me just what I want to hear. I *don't need* someone who will make me feel comfortable in sin. I *don't need* to hear a sermon and come away wondering what in the world that guy was talking about. I *don't need* cute and catchy religious slogans. *I need good sound gospel preaching that will lift my spirit, fill my soul, and help to make me a better Christian! I need God's Word, and I need to know how it applies to me!*

August 5

The Machine

I told my son,
It's a machine, don't worry, it won't hit you,
Stand in there like a man.

The machine wound up and threw the ball,
It hit him in the hand.

The first of many times I've had to say, "I'm sorry."

Winning the Battle, but Losing the War

Did you ever meet someone who just loved to be involved in discussions and debates, the hotter the better? It can be about any subject because the thrill is in the exchange itself—to counter arguments, to anticipate your opponent's line of reasoning, to have all your faculties focused and working in harmony to win that discussion. As an old high school debater and an arguer from way back, I can say that that is fun. But when it comes to discussing the Scriptures and trying to lead someone to Christ, we can win the battle but lose the war.

When we talk to someone about religion, what is to be our objective? Is our objective to show how much we know about the Bible? Is it to show the person just how "ridiculous" his beliefs are? Is it to "eat them alive" and have them reduced to silence in the face of our verbal assault with *the truth*? Is it to win the argument at all cost no matter how loud I might have to get? We all realize that the answer to each one of those questions is *"No!"* When we talk to others about religion, it must be out of love for their soul and with the earnest desire that they might faithfully serve the Lord all the remaining days of their lives and go to heaven when they die. As I look back on my years as a Christian and a preacher, and there are only nine months' difference in the two, I don't ever remember being defeated in an argument, especially in the early years. I would just keep going until I wore the other guy out. I won all the battles, but because of my approach, I have lost a lot of wars. Everybody has to answer for what they do, but how many people did I turn away from the Lord by "winning the argument"?

In Proverbs 15:1, Solomon wrote, "A soft answer turns away wrath, but a harsh word stirs up anger." In Proverbs 25:15 we find, "By long forbearance a ruler is persuaded, and a gentle tongue breaks a bone." I have a responsibility as a Christian to control my temper and my voice when discussing God's word with anyone. Such a discussion, when truly understood, is never about me. It is always about the one I am trying to teach. If I am trying to win the argument, or if I let such a discussion degenerate into an argument, then it is about me, and that is just about as selfish as I can get.

I am reminded of Paul's exhortation found in Colossians 4:6 where he wrote, "Let your speech always be with grace, seasoned with salt, that you may know how you ought to answer each one." Our job is to reflect the will of God in our speech. We must say those things that will provide spiritual and moral benefit to those who are listening to us. Never is that more important than when we are trying to teach someone the gospel. What I say may be the truth. It may very well be just the right answer. But, brethren, the way I say it can make all the difference in the world.

In Proverbs 15:23 we find, "A man has joy by the answer of his mouth, and a word spoken in due season, how good it is!" And again, from chapter 25:11, we read, "A word fitly spoken is like apples of gold in settings of silver."

If we just think of the tremendous patience Jesus showed in His discussions with people, even those who were sent specifically to ensnare Him in His words, there really is no excuse for losing our tempers or trying to win the argument when discussing salvation with anyone.

August 7

I Saw You
(Written on the Occasion of our Anniversary)

I saw you for the first time
On that special day—
All in white and on your father's arm,
And that image has never faded away.

I held your hand in the delivery room,
I wanted to share your pain.
When it was all over you smiled at me,
And said you'd gladly do it all again.

We often moved from place to place,
And sometimes you didn't want to go.
But you went with me out of love,
And I want you to know, I know.

The kids are all grown now,
We have done the best we could.

All the mistakes have been made together,
Just like we promised God we would.

I can't get by on looks anymore,
Now it has to be wit and charm.
But I want you to know you are as beautiful
As the day I saw you on your father's arm.

August 8

A Centurion Appeals for Help

In Matthew 8:5-13 and Luke 7:1-10 we find the remarkable account of a Roman centurion appealing to Jesus for help because of his sick servant who was nearing death. A centurion was a Roman officer with command over a "century," 100 men more or less. This centurion was recognized by the Jews of Capernaum as a good man. Their assessment of him is found in Luke 7:4-5, "That he was worthy for whom he should do this: for he loveth our nation, and he hath built us a synagogue."

By combining the two accounts we can see that the centurion first sent the elders of the Jews to Jesus with his request. Next he sent some of his friends. Out of respect for Jesus he had his friends ask the Lord to heal his servant from a distance, merely speak the word and his servant would be healed. In this way Jesus would not even have to come into his home. Finally, the centurion went to Jesus personally.

What he said is such a marvelous example of faith. When Jesus heard it, He said, "I have not found so great faith, no, not in Israel." The centurion first declared his own unworthiness to even come to Jesus, much less to have Jesus actually come and enter into his home. He also recognized that such a thing was totally unnecessary, for Jesus had only to say the word and his servant would be healed. Notice that the centurion understood the whole thing to be a matter of authority, and authority was a field in which he had some experience. He said, "For I also am a man set under authority, having under me soldiers, and I say unto one, Go, and he goeth; and to another, Come, and he cometh; and to my servant, Do this, and he doeth it."

This man's statement is truly amazing. To paraphrase his words, he was saying, "I understand that this whole matter is one of authority. I know about authority in my own life. I have a certain degree of authority and people under my authority respond to it. But you have authority over all things. You can do whatever you think is right and proper. You don't even have to come to my home. All that is necessary is for you to speak the word and it will be done." Even Jesus marveled at this man's faith and understanding. What an example of faith! What a depth of understanding!

I thrill to Jesus' final words of love, compassion, and kindness to this centurion, "Go thy way; and as thou has believed, so be it done unto thee." That very hour the centurion's dear servant was healed.

August 9

Love Demonstrated

God's entire plan for man is built upon love. John 3:16 tells us, "For God so loved the world, that He gave His only begotten Son, that whosoever believeth in Him should not perish, but have everlasting life." God didn't just say that He loved man—He demonstrated it with the greatest manifestation of love that the world will ever know. Consider 1 John 4:7-12: "Beloved, let us love one another: for love is of God; and every one that loveth is born of God, and knoweth God. He that loveth not knoweth not God; for God is love. In this was manifested the love of God toward us, because that God sent His only begotten Son into the world, that we might live through Him. Herein is love, not that we loved God, but that He loved us, and sent His Son to be the propitiation for our sins. Beloved, if God so loved us, we ought also to love one another. No man hath seen God at any time. If we love one another, God dwelleth in us, and His love is perfected in us." Once again John made the point that God demonstrated His love by what He did. He sent His Son to die for us.

It is an easy thing to say, "I love God." It is something else altogether to prove it. In 1 John 5:2-3 we find, "By this we know that we love the children of God, when we love God, and keep His commandments. For this is the love of God, that we keep His commandments: and His commandments are not grievous." Does my conduct demonstrate my love for God? Do I do even the simplest things that He has asked me to do? Do I study His Word regularly? Do I faithfully attend all of the services of the congregation that I am physically able to attend, considering my brethren "to provoke unto love and good works"? It is so easy to say, "I love God," but does the evidence of my conduct back that up? Jesus said in John 14:15, "If you love Me, keep My commandments." Verse 21 says, "He that hath My commandments, and keepeth them, he it is that loveth Me: and he that loveth Me shall be loved of My Father, and I will love him, and will manifest Myself to him." And in verse 24 the Lord said, "He that loveth Me not keepeth not my sayings." When it comes to God, is my love real or is it in word but not in deed?

Think of this as it relates to our fellow man. Once again from the passage in 1 John 3, we all know and understand that if I am standing next to someone who is starving to death, and I have the capability of giving him something to eat, but don't—I can say that I love him all I want, but it is just not true! James wrote in James 2:14-17, "What doth it profit, my brethren, though a man say he hath faith, and hath not works? Can faith save him? If a brother or sister be naked, and destitute of daily food, and one of you say unto them, Depart in peace, be ye warmed and filled; notwithstanding ye give them not those things which are needful to the body; what doth it profit? Even so faith, if it hath not works, is dead, being alone." It all fits in together. How can I say I love my fellow man if my conduct doesn't prove it? The answer is simple—I can't!

We have something that man needs more than food, clothing, or shelter. We have the truth. We have the gospel of the Lord Jesus Christ. That gospel is all about love—demonstrated love on the part of God. The question is, are we going to demonstrate our love by telling people about it? Are we going to love "in deed and in truth"?

If I understand the Scriptures correctly, I believe that God is telling us to put our money where our mouth is, so to speak. One of the most scathing rebukes ever issued by the Lord dealt with the hypocrisy of the Pharisees and is found in Matthew 23:2-4: "The scribes and the Pharisees sit in Moses' seat: all therefore whatsoever they bid you observe, that observe and do; but do not ye after their works: *for they say, and do not.* For they bind heavy burdens and grievous to be borne, and lay them on men's shoulders; *but they themselves will not move them with one of their fingers.*"

"For they say, and do not"! Seven times in the remaining verses of that chapter Jesus would say, "Woe unto you, scribes and Pharisees, hypocrites!"

To say something like "I love you" or "I love God" or "I love my fellow man" is easy. God wants it to be real, proven and demonstrated by our conduct.'

August 10

Shake off the Dust

There is an expression used from time to time in the New Testament, and each time it is used it carries essentially the same meaning. The expression to which I am referring is, "shake off the dust of your feet." As near as I can tell, we find it first in Matthew 10. In this passage the Lord is sending His apostles out among the Jews. He told them, "And as ye go, preach, saying, The kingdom of heaven is at hand."

He gave them other instructions as well, part of which are found in verses 11-15. Look at what Jesus said:

> And into whatsoever city or town ye shall enter, inquire who in it is worthy; and there abide till ye go thence. And when ye come into an house, salute it. And if the house be worthy, let your peace come upon it: but if it be not worthy, let your peace return to you. And whosoever shall not receive you, nor hear your words, when ye depart out of that house or city, *shake off the dust of your feet*. Verily I say unto you, It shall be more tolerable for the land of Sodom and Gomorrah in the day of judgment, than for that city.

What an interesting expression, "Shake off the dust of your feet." It makes us wonder where it came from and what it meant to the apostles. The expression came from an action that was often taken by pious Jews of the time when they were returning from Gentile, pagan territory. They would not even want the dust of such territory clinging to their sandals. They wanted to make it clear that they had removed completely the unclean elements from their person. Consequently, when individuals and towns to whom the apostles journeyed refused to accept the truth, the apostles were to move on. With the shaking of the dust off of their feet they were essentially declaring the unresponsive individuals and towns as unholy and pagan.

The Apostle Paul practiced the same symbolic action when leaving regions and people who rejected the truth of the gospel. In Acts 13, Paul and Barnabas were preaching in Antioch of Pisidia. Many of the Gentiles believed, but certain of the Jews created a problem. In verses 50-51 we find, "But the

Jews stirred up the devout and honorable women, and the chief men of the city, and raised persecution against Paul and Barnabas, and expelled them out of their coasts. But they shook off the dust of their feet against them, and came unto Iconium." Later, in Acts 18, Paul was in the city of Corinth and preaching in the synagogue of the Jews. As Paul pressed more strongly the truth that Jesus was the Christ, we find this happening in verse 6, "And when they opposed themselves, and blasphemed, he shook his raiment, and said unto them, Your blood be upon your own heads; I am clean: from henceforth I will go unto the Gentiles." This was an act that those Jews would long remember. They knew what the shaking off of the dust meant, and in case they didn't get it, Paul made it clear: "Your blood be upon your own heads: I am clean."

I believe that there are some things we can learn from the expression, "Shake off the dust of your feet." Number one relates to the responsibility we have to take the gospel to all whom we can. All we can do is to take it to them; whether or not they respond favorably is up to them. Secondly, we are going to have to make a judgment call. When the gospel is rejected, should others suffer because we fail to move on? When the truth has been presented and questions asked and answered, if the response is negative, then there are others who need to hear. Move on.

I believe that this can happen within the Lord's church as well. Occasionally people will leave the truth of God's word. They need to be taught as the process of their leaving is beginning to take place. They need to be taught and encouraged right up to the time that they leave. Even after they have left and the called-for disciplinary action has been taken, as long as they will truly study with an eye toward learning the truth and embracing it once again, they need to be taught. But a point of diminishing returns can be reached where it now becomes a mockery and manipulative. When such occurs, it is time to move on. Others who have never heard the gospel may not get the chance because so much time, energy, and effort is put forth with those who knew the truth and forsook it. There comes a time to shake off the dust of your feet and move on. There are so many people who need to hear the truth and so little time to get the job done.

"Watch Ye, Stand Fast in the Faith, Quit You Like Men, Be Strong" (1 Cor. 16:13)

There are times when I get weary,
Oh, yes, I surely do.
Sometimes the end I cannot see.
But then I hear You say, "Watch Ye."

The sword has gotten heavy
And with tear-stained eyes I fear I will not last,
But I will pick it up and hoist it high,
For I hear You say, "Stand fast."

When Satan's darts are falling
And beneath their weight I start to bend;
I can not, will not, let him win,
For I hear You say, "Quit you like men."

I marvel sometimes at things that are said,
Things that are just so cruel and wrong.
I want to say, Enough, no more.
But I hear You say, "Be strong."

Snapshots of Jesus (1)

There is no question that the New Testament teaches that Jesus was God in the flesh. In 1 Timothy 3:16 Paul wrote, "And without controversy great is the mystery of godliness: *God was manifest in the flesh*, justified in the Spirit, seen of angels, preached unto the Gentiles, believed on in the world, received up into glory." When Jesus walked through the valley of the River Jordan, climbed the foothills and mountains of Judea, or traversed the Plain of Esdraelon, He was treading upon that which He had Himself created. This truth could not be more clearly stated than it is in Colossians 1:15-17. Concerning Jesus, Paul wrote:

> Who is the image of the invisible God, the firstborn of every creature: for by him were all things created, that are in heaven, and that are in earth, visible and invisible, whether they be thrones, or dominions, or principalities, or powers: all things were created by him, and for him: and he is before all things, and by him all things consist.

I marvel at the very idea of the divine Jesus. The words of John 1:14 thrill and astound me: "And the Word was made flesh, and dwelt among us, (and we beheld his glory, the glory as of the only begotten of the Father,) full of grace and truth." What Jesus revealed to us about the nature and character of God while here in the flesh is far beyond the scope of this article. Indeed, reams could be written about what was meant in the exchange between Philip and Jesus in John 14:8-9, "Philip saith unto him, Lord, show us the Father, and it sufficeth us. Jesus saith unto him, Have I been so long time with you, and yet hast thou not known me, Philip? *He that hath seen me hath seen the Father:* and how sayest thou then, Show us the Father?"

Yet contained within the pages of the gospels are simple statements that can almost be overlooked. I like to think of these as snapshots of Jesus. They give us brief but wonderful glimpses into His humanity. Not only does the Bible teach us that Jesus was fully God on earth, it also teaches us that He was fully man. I do not understand all that is involved in such an incredible idea; I simply know that it is true. A few statements from the letter to the Hebrews emphasize this point. In Hebrews 2:16-18 we find:

> For verily He took not on Him the nature of angels; but He took on Him the seed of Abraham. Wherefore in all things it behooved Him to be made like unto His brethren, that He might be a merciful and faithful high priest in these pertaining to God, to make reconciliation for the sins of the people. For in that He Himself hath suffered being tempted, he is able to succour them that are tempted.

From Hebrews 4:15 we read, "For we have not an high priest which cannot be touched with the feeling of our infirmities; but was in all points tempted like as we are, yet without sin."

One such snapshot of Jesus is found in Luke's account of His birth. In Luke 2:7 we read, "And she brought forth her firstborn son, and wrapped him in swaddling clothes, and laid him in a manger; because there was no room for them in the inn." It came to pass in the days surrounding the birth of Jesus that a decree had come forth from the emperor of Rome, Octavian, Caesar Augustus, that a census should be taken of all of the world under Roman rule. The purpose of this enrollment was to assist in the work of taxation and also to determine how many were subject to military service. Octavian ruled in Rome from 31 B.C. to A.D. 15.

Joseph and Mary, both of the lineage of David, and Mary about to be delivered of a child, made their way to Bethlehem, the city of David, to be enrolled. As I envision this scene of the humble carpenter and his very pregnant wife making the arduous eighty mile journey from Nazareth to Bethlehem for enrollment in the city of their great ancestor, I am reminded of Isaiah 11:1. There we find, "And there shall come forth a rod out of the stem of Jesse, and a Branch shall grow out of his roots." The world did not know that the house of David, referred to as the "stump" or "stem of Jesse," cut down and brought low as evidenced by the poverty and obscurity of Joseph and Mary, was about to have the Branch spring forth of it and be raised to greater heights than it had ever known during the time of David.

While in the city of Bethlehem, Jesus was born. It was not in a palace of royalty, surrounded by the best physicians and midwives of the day and eagerly anticipated by the subjects of the king. Jesus was born in a stable because the enrollment had brought such a large number of people to Bethlehem and there was no room for Mary and Joseph in the inn. The first bed for the King of kings was a feeding trough for animals. Were there sheep, donkeys, and cows witnessing His entrance into the world? I don't really know, but could there possibly have been a clearer expression of His humanity than the humble circumstances of His birth? What a snapshot of Jesus—a tiny infant, wrapped in narrow strips of cloth (swaddling clothes), lying in a manger.

August 13

Snapshots of Jesus (2)

The wonder I feel at the humanity of Jesus has not diminished over time; in fact, it has only grown more profound. How could God in the flesh, the glorious and only begotten Son of God, feel the same physical sensations that I feel? How could He have been thirsty, hungry, or tired? How could He be touched with human sadness, sorrow, and even fear? Well, the Bible tells us that "in all things it behooved Him to be made like unto His brethren…" (Heb. 2:17). Let's continue to notice snapshots of Jesus, short statements made concerning Him in the Scriptures that speak volumes about His humanity.

Matthew 28:23-27, Mark 4:35-41, and Luke 8:22-25 all give us the account of Jesus calming the Sea of Galilee when a great and violent storm had arisen, threatening the lives of the apostles as they sailed on its waters. For our purpose, we will look at four verses from Mark's account; verses 35-38:

And the same day, when the even was come, He saith unto them, Let us pass over unto the other side. And when they had sent away the multitude, they took Him even as He was in the ship. And there were also with Him other little ships. And there arose a great storm of wind, and the waves beat into the ship, so that it was now full. And He was in the hinder part of the ship, asleep on a pillow: and they awake Him, and say unto Him, Master, carest thou not that we perish?

It had been a busy day in the life of the Lord. As "even" descended upon Him, Jesus and His disciples entered into a boat and began to make their way across the Sea of Galilee, traveling from the northwest corner to a point about midway on the eastern side. We know this because of where the boat landed, the country of the Gadarenes. Under normal conditions this would have been a journey of about two hours with a favorable light wind helping the boat along.

There is a statement made by Mark that is often overlooked in discussions of this event, yet I find it to be one of those snapshots of Jesus. It gives us insight into His humanity and into the nature of His ministry. In describing their departure, Mark wrote, "And they took Him even as He was in the ship." What do you suppose was meant by "even as He was"? Could that not mean without food or time to procure food? Isn't it probable that it means without rest and exhausted from the day's labor? It indicates the humanity of Jesus and calls to mind another such reminder that He felt as we feel and experienced the same physical sensations. In John 4 we find the account of Jesus and the Samaritan woman—an event that took place at Jacob's well. In verse 6 we read, "Now Jacob's well was there. Jesus therefore, being wearied with his journey, sat thus on the well: and it was about the sixth hour." Notice the expression that Jesus "sat thus on the well." The "thus" of John 4:6 is very much like the "even as He was" of Mark 4:36; exhausted, worn out by the tremendous strain and effort of His ministry. I often ask myself, "How could that be?" But then I know that He felt those things for me. He felt those things in order that He might be the perfect high priest.

The small flotilla set off. Mark informs us "there were also with Him other little ships." Since we do not read of these other ships reaching the country of the Gadarenes with Jesus, the indication is that they were soon scattered and left or were perhaps frightened by the signs of the gathering storm and turned back. As the journey proceeded, there is another snapshot: "And He was in the hinder part of the ship, asleep on a pillow." Our Lord, the Son of God, retired to the stern of the boat, laid His head upon a pillow, and slept, even as the storm began to rage around them. Remember that several of the apostles were experienced fishermen who undoubtedly had experienced storms for which the Sea of Galilee was well known. Yet even these men were fearful for their lives with this storm. Still, Jesus slept. How tired He must have been! How exhausting were His labors! How humbling it is for me to view such evidence of His humanity.

Later, less than twenty-four hours from His death, Jesus cried out in the Garden of Gethsemane, "O my Father, if it be possible, let his cup pass from Me" (Matt. 26:39). The horrible pain of the scourging, the unspeakable agony of the cross, were all within hours for the Lord now. Here is a snapshot of Jesus that is heart-wrenching to see. Hebrews 5:7 lends depth and color to the snapshot. It says, "Who in the days of His flesh, when He had offered up prayers and supplications with strong crying and tears unto Him that was able to save Him from death, and was heard in that He feared." There was crying, there were tears, and there was fear. It wasn't fear of the unknown as some have suggested. Jesus knew exactly what was going to happen and what the result would be. But He feared the pain, He feared the agony just as you and I would. Yet our Lord concluded His statement back in Matthew 26:39 by saying, "Nevertheless not as I will, but as thou wilt."

Snapshots of Jesus—short statements that speak volumes about His humanity. They should cause our hearts to swell with gratitude and our souls to sing His praise.

August 14

Why Shepherds?

In Luke 2 we find the account of the birth of our Lord and Savior, Jesus. In the hill country pastures around the city of Bethlehem, shepherds were watching over their sheep by night. As they watched, suddenly an angel of the Lord came upon them and there was a great brightness as the glory of the Lord shone around them, and they were very afraid.

I have asked myself from time to time, why appear to shepherds? I do believe that there is significance to this. First, they were Jews; but why not appear to the scholars in Jerusalem, or the elders of the people? Why not announce the birth to the influential Jewish leaders, perhaps at the meeting of the Sanhedrin? Interestingly, at this time shepherds were held in low esteem by the people. According to the Talmud (in the treatise "The Sanhedrin"), shepherds were not even allowed to be used in courts as witnesses. Why appear to men of such low estate?

I believe that it serves to demonstrate something about the very nature of Christianity. It is for all men, from the least to the greatest. It recognizes no class distinction in terms of the love of God and the availability of salvation.

On that day, in the city of David, a Savior was born. He was Christ—the Anointed One. The shepherds were given a sign to confirm their faith and to assist them in identifying the child. They would find Him lying in a manger, a feeding trough for animals, wrapped in swaddling clothes.

Suddenly there was a multitude of heavenly beings praising God with the words, "Glory to God in the highest, and on earth, peace, good will toward men." Can there be any question of the appropriateness of this praise? God had brought His Son into the world for man's salvation. All that He had promised He was bringing to fulfillment.

With haste the shepherds made their way to Bethlehem to see the thing that the angels had made known to them. They found Mary and Joseph, and the child Jesus lying in a manger just as they had been told. With that these men, on one of the lowest rungs of the social scale, became the first preachers of Jesus. They told abroad what had been told to them and those who heard it wondered at what they had been told.

How thankful we should be that God does not abide by the barriers, walls and prejudices that we erect between each other!

August 15

Why Do We Say What We Say?

This is a subject about which I have thought quite a bit over the years, and last week something came up that made me decide to write about it. I received a call from someone close to me and he told me that someone had told him why a particular preacher had been asked to leave a congregation where he was working. As you can imagine, the reason given was such to stimulate all kinds of conjecture and suspicion.

The first thought that went through my mind was, "Why is this stuff being talked about?" It was none of my business, none of the caller's business, and certainly none of the business of the one who was spreading the word, whether it was true or not. I wondered why it was said, what was the purpose? It certainly wasn't love or honest concern for the brother involved, so why was it ever said?

I wonder that about a lot of things that are said. Why do we say what we say? In Ephesians 4:29 we find, "Let no corrupt communication proceed out of your mouth, but that which is good to the use of edifying, that it may minister grace unto the hearers." Corrupt communication can be defined in many ways. It can and does include bad language, low or worthless comments, rotten statements, and foul speech. It is the kind of language that tears down rather than builds up and accomplishes nothing but to bring the ungodly thoughts that are in the mind of the speaker to the mind of the hearer.

Let us suppose that I know something that is not particularly good about someone. If I get on the phone and tell someone else what I know, and the person I tell is not that individual, then why in the world did I say it? I have racked my brain, but I cannot come up with one single good reason for doing that, and certainly not one reason with which God would be pleased.

The Bible is replete with warnings about the danger of allowing destructive speech and less than edifying language to make its way into our lives. Jesus said in Matthew 12:36, "But I say unto you, that every idle word that men shall speak, they shall give account thereof in the day of judgment." Solomon said, "Be not rash with thy mouth, and let not thine heart be hasty to utter any thing before God: for God is in heaven, and thou upon earth: therefore let thy words be few."

Even if something is true, we must ask ourselves why we say it. Our purpose is to reflect the will of God in our speech. We are charged with the responsibility to say those things that will provide spiritual and moral benefit to those who hear; in other words, to give grace to the hearers. In Proverbs 25:20 Solomon wrote, "He who sings songs to a heavy heart is like one who takes off a garment on a cold day, and like vinegar on a wound." Thus, Solomon shows that the wise and proper use of the gift of speech even includes knowing when to speak and when to keep quiet. Sometimes I believe that folks get to thinking that truth is truth no matter when it is spoken, and in a certain sense, that is true. However, just because something happens to be true doesn't mean that saying it is always fitting or needed, and it certainly doesn't mean that saying it is always to edification.

Why do we say what we say? Is it ever right to gossip, to engage in idle talk about the personal affairs of others? *No!* Is it ever right to bring something to someone's attention if my true motive for saying it is to cause someone pain? *No, it is not!* Is it ever right to bring the shortcomings of an individual to someone else's attention to build myself up or to make them think less of the individual? *No, it is not!* Is it ever right to use the God-given blessing of speech in an effort to hurt someone? *No, it is not!*

Staying in Proverbs 25, let's read verses 9-12:

> Debate thy cause with thy neighbor *himself*, and discover not a secret to another: lest he that hear it put thee to shame, and thine infamy turn not away. A word fitly spoken is like apples of gold in pictures of silver. As an earring of gold, and an ornament of fine gold, so is a wise reprover upon an obedient ear.

Sometimes it is necessary to give *constructive* criticism to an individual, but even then we had better be certain in our hearts that it is truly meant by us to be constructive and not destructive. I might tell someone something that he needs to know, and it might even prove to be constructive criticism, but if I do it to tear him down or to hurt him, I have sinned just as surely because my motive was wrong.

August 16

Teaching Our Children to Work

Parents have the responsibility given to them by God, and they owe it to their children, to teach them to work. Young people need to be taught that work is not a punishment, but that man was created to work. Indeed, work is essential to the happiness of man; it is part of the way that God created us. In Genesis 2:15, before any sin had been committed, we find, "The Lord God took the man, and put him into the Garden of Eden to dress it and to keep it." In a wonderful and perfect state, God gave man work to do.

The great man of wisdom, Solomon, had a lot to say about work and the vital place it plays in the happiness and fulfillment of man. In Proverbs 10:4-5 we find, "He becometh poor that dealeth with a slack hand: but the hand of the diligent maketh rich. He that gathereth in the summer is a wise son."

Proverbs 13:4 says, "The soul of the sluggard desireth, and hath nothing: but the soul of the diligent shall be made fat." Proverbs 13:11 says, "He that tilleth his land shall be satisfied with bread." Solomon wrote in Ecclesiastes 9:10, "Whatsoever thy hand findeth to do, do it with thy might; for there is no work, nor device, nor knowledge, nor wisdom, in the grave, whither thou goest." And in Ecclesiastes 11:6 we are told, "In the morning sow thy seed, and in the evening withhold not thine hand: for thou knowest not whether shall prosper, either this or that, or whether they both shall be alike good."

In the New Testament the principle remains the same. Paul instructs us in Ephesians 4:28, "Let him that stole steal no more: but rather let him labor, working with his hands the thing which is good, that he may have to give to him that needeth." 1 Thessalonians 4:11-12 makes the point so clearly in this way, "Study to be quiet, and to do your own business, and to work with your own hands, as we commanded you; that ye may walk honestly toward them that are without, and that ye may have lack of nothing." 2 Thessalonians 3:10-12 says, "For even when we were with you, this we commanded you, that if any would not work, neither should he eat. For we hear that there are some which walk among you disorderly, working not at all, but are busybodies. Now them that are such we command and exhort by our Lord Jesus Christ, that with quietness they work, and eat their own bread."

The point is well taken. Part of teaching our children the way of the Lord is to teach them the need to work. It is a good thing for young people to be given tasks to perform in the home while they are little. In this way the foundation is laid. A parent who never requires any work of his children while they are growing up in the home has not done those children any favors. In fact, they may have taken a step in raising a lazy child who will grow to be a lazy adult.

As a child grows and reaches the age when he can legally obtain a job, it is a good thing for him to do. He learns responsibility, the value of a dollar, and the pride of doing a job well. It certainly makes you proud as a parent to see your child go out and get his first job. Haven't we all smiled when we had to explain to our child who FICA is and why they took all of that money?

However, brethren, in all of this there is something to which we need to give careful consideration. The most important lesson that we are to teach our children is that God comes first—not school, not sports, not recreation, and not a job. It has been my observation that when children are allowed to take a job that causes them to miss services on a regular basis, nothing good ever comes of it. The teenage years are often the time when children are struggling with some major issues, and where God fits into their lives is one of them. I truly believe, parents, that we need to help them understand that of all there is in this world to enjoy and appreciate, God is the only One who gives it all meaning. What good are the things money can buy without God? What good is the satisfaction that comes from doing a job if that job has required God to take a back seat? Being at services, being with Christians, studying God's Word, and just being in the godly environment is more important than any secular job.

I know from experience that a child can find a job that does not require him or her to miss services. I know as well that many employers are actually happy to give a young person the time off on Wednesday evenings and Sundays to attend services. Many of them are happy to have young people who attend worship services working for them, because those kinds of kids usually have a certain moral standard by which they live. I also know from experience that an employer who will not do that with a young person is not worth working for in the first place.

It is tough to make the right decisions as we raise these precious gifts from God. But there is one thing that is absolutely certain—if we teach our children that God comes first above all else, and that nothing can take His place, it will all turn out okay.

August 17

Wondrous Journey
By Adam Litmer

Not a care as sin consumed me,
Not a care as I stood bound.
Wretched, lost, condemned, and guilty,
When through grace by Christ was found.
Then His light pierced through the darkness,
From sin's chains I'm finally free!
Blest, forgiven, marching upward,
Wondrous grace has rescued me.

Praying daily, faith grows stronger,
With His Word I cannot fall.

Time grows short; Oh, how much longer,
Till we hear archangel's call?
Will you be among that number
Who will meet Him in the air?
Blessed thought when comes life's troubles:
Where He is I'll soon be there.

If the sun should cease its shining,
If the stars fall from the sky,
If the oceans dry to nothing,
If the winds should fail and die;
Still my faith will never waver,
And my love will not grow cold!
How can I turn from my Savior,
Who has promised streets of gold?

As the years keep multiplying,
As smooth flesh begins to line,
As old mem'ries fade in darkness,
Head on pillow one last time.
Still my thoughts will soar to heaven!
Wondrous treasure for me stored!
As the angels come to greet me,
Final thought: "O, thank you, Lord."

August 18

The Feast of Tabernacles

The Feast of Tabernacles was the last of the three great annual Jewish festivals. It was kept for seven days in the Jewish month Tishri, corresponding to September/October of our calendar. During the festival the children of Israel were to dwell in booths, or tabernacles, made of boughs of trees and branches of palm trees. This really served a twofold purpose. The festival came at the close of the harvest season when all of the produce of the fields, vineyards, and olive groves would have been harvested, so it was a celebration and reminder of the agricultural life. However, it also served as a reminder of the

Exodus from Egypt and the wandering of the Jews in the wilderness, a time of dwelling in tents.

It is interesting that most of the neighboring pagan nations also had festivals and celebrations at the time of harvest—many of them containing the most unholy fertility rites and similar activities. But the Feast of Tabernacles had the idea of deliverance and so in its very purpose had little resemblance to the debauchery of the pagan festivals.

The Jewish festivals focused the mind of the people upon God and upon His continual care for them and their dependence upon Him. They were to be celebrations of joy and thanksgiving.

Every day in the life of a Christian is a day of joy and thanksgiving. Does that mean that no day will be filled with pain and sorrow brought about by the trials and difficulties of this world? No, but it does mean that, as a Christian, I know that "every good gift and every perfect gift is from above, and cometh down from the Father of lights, with whom is no variableness, neither shadow of turning" (Jas. 1:17). I also know that, as a Christian, I have been delivered from the power of darkness and translated into the kingdom of God's dear Son (Col. 1:13). I also know that I am simply a pilgrim passing through and that this world is not my home. In a very real sense the home I live in now is simply a "tabernacle," a temporary dwelling. Jesus has gone to prepare my permanent dwelling place.

"Let not your heart be troubled: ye believe in God, believe also in me. In my Father's house are many mansions: if it were not so, I would have told you. I go to prepare a place for you. And if I go and prepare a place for you, I will come again, and receive you unto myself; that where I am, there ye may be also" (John 14:1-3).

August 19

Criticize

A tale of pain and sorrow will in these words be outpoured.
And even though I hesitate to hurt or wound a heart,
But truth be told what will unfold is no more than most endure.

A task is given, a work is undertaken, and to its completion you put your hand.
Countless hours are expended; diligent concentration is the rule,
For you there is no other way; you always do the best you can.

No one knows the care you used as you labored at your task.
You put your heart, your soul, your mind and spirit into what you did,
With sweat and maybe tears, and certainly with prayer, you finished it at last.

I guess they do not see the pain, the hurt or anguish in your eyes.
They don't know how empty you feel, or how the proverbial wind was taken
    from your sails,
When those who did not do the work sit back and criticize.

Constructive words do have their place when ability and spirits they are
    meant to rise.
No one is perfect, that's for sure, and maybe I could do better,
But I do not understand the mind of one who looks to criticize.
When you sit and debate, talk and pray, and seek the counsel of the wise,
Spending innumerable hours making sure the decisions are best for all,
It breaks your heart and robs your sleep when they sit back and criticize.

There's no telling the good will a hearty "thank you" or "good job" buys;
The smiles, the joy, the determination to jump right in again.
But I don't think that's what they are looking for, those who sit back and criticize.

I guess the goal of these sad souls is to show us who is wise.
To help, encourage, to uplift is not the point—
No, there is no good that is meant or comes from those who sit back and criticize.

August 20

Is the Ending of the Life of an Unborn Baby Ever Justified?

At first glance, the answer to the question contained in this title might appear obvious and easy. I would imagine that most would say, "No," and do so rather quickly. Most of the Christians that I know would say that they oppose abortion and believe it to be murder. So do I. However, I have been disturbed by what I perceive as a steadily changing attitude among some who wear the name of Christ. More and more frequently I am hearing evidence of the influence of the world in the thinking of brothers and sisters concerning this subject. Is the ending of the life of an unborn baby *ever* justified?

First of all, there are a few points that need to be established. In Genesis 1:27 we find, "And God created man in His own image, in the image of God He created him, male and female He created them." All human beings are created "in the image of God." Indeed, that is what makes man absolutely unique in the creation of God. No other part of God's creation possesses such worth and value simply by virtue of being. At what point in the developing process does the child become "in the image of God"? Is it at conception? Is it sometime during the gestation period? Is it when the child is born, or perhaps at its first birthday? Being made "in the image of God" is what makes a human being human. Thus, the importance of the question we are considering. When does a developing child become human? I believe that the Bible gives us the answer.

In Jeremiah 1:4-5 we read, "Now the word of the Lord came to me saying, 'Before I formed you in the womb I knew you, and before you were born I consecrated you; I have appointed you a prophet to the nations.'" This passage declares that God "knew" Jeremiah and consecrated him before he was born. That is hardly indicative of an inhuman mass of tissue that at some point would become human. Much to the contrary, it indicates that God viewed Jeremiah as a distinct person, a human being, while in his mother's womb.

In Psalm 139:13-16 we find:

For thou didst form my inward parts; Thou didst weave me in my mother's womb. I will give thanks to Thee, for I am fearfully and wonderfully made; wonderful are Thy works, and my soul knows it very well. My frame was not hidden from Thee, when I was made in secret, and skillfully wrought in the depths of the earth. Thine eyes have seen my unformed substance; and in Thy book they were all written, the days that were ordained for me, when as yet there was not one of them.

This whole psalm has as its theme the inescapable presence of God. It shows that, no matter where we go, we cannot flee from God. He knows and is aware, and this knowledge and awareness extends even into the womb. It is a knowledge best described as personal. We can note that David used the first person pronouns in the psalm, "I," "me," and "my." As he penned this psalm under the inspiration of the Holy Spirit, it is apparent that David regarded God to have been at work with him personally, as a distinct human being developing within his mother's womb. He was not viewed as an inhuman mass of tissue that at some later point would become human.

There are many other passages to which we could turn that would make the same point. We could examine Job 10:9-12 and the fascinating meeting of two unborn children when the pregnant Mary brought the child Jesus into the home of her pregnant cousin, Elizabeth. We could write of the very human emotion displayed by the unborn John within his mother's womb. All of this is found in Luke 1:39-45. But let us consider this question. From the moment of conception to the time of birth, what has been added to that child that was not there in the beginning? From the moment of conception, all that the child needs is proper nourishment and a safe environment in which to grow. At conception, the genetic code is present and God is aware. This is another human being, made in His image.

Strange sounds are being heard among brethren indicating that life in the "give me my rights" generation and the incessant clamoring of the pro-abortion forces are having an effect. From the mouths of a small, but growing, number of brethren comes the distressing idea that they are personally opposed to abortion but would never deny anyone else the right to make that choice. I believe that such a statement is the statement of a coward, afraid or ashamed to take a stand. Solomon wrote in Proverbs 24:10-12:

> If you are slack in the day of distress, your strength is limited. Deliver those who are being taken away to death, and those who are staggering to slaughter, O hold them back. If you say, "See, we did not know this," does He not consider it who weighs the hearts? And does He not know it who keeps your soul? And will he not render to man according to his work?

When brethren make that kind of statement the world is winning, and they will have to answer for such an attitude.

Occasionally I hear a brother or sister argue that, while they are opposed to abortion, it is a different matter altogether when the pregnancy is the result of rape. I have always found it interesting that our society has generally determined that a guilty rapist is not subject to the death penalty for his crime, yet allows the innocent child that is conceived as a result of that rape to be executed. The only one whose "rights" are not considered in such circumstances is the unborn child's. The Bible clearly shows that God considers the developing child to be a person, a human being. What possible justification can there be for dealing with one crime by committing another? Terminating the life of that child would be murder. Jesus told us in Matthew 5:21-22:

> You have heard that the ancients were told, "You shall not commit murder" and "Whoever commits murder shall be liable to the court." But I say to you that everyone who is angry with his brother shall be guilty before the court; and whoever shall say to his brother, Raca, shall be guilty before the supreme court; and whoever shall say, "You fool," shall be guilty enough to go into the fiery hell.

Jesus not only condemned murder, He condemned the very heart that would permit it!

There is another position that some brethren have started taking lately. They say that if the mother's life is in danger should the pregnancy continue, and the baby is going to die anyhow, then a "medical procedure" would be in order to end the life of the baby and yet permit the mother to live. Others simply say that if the life of the mother is in danger if she continues to carry the baby, then ending the life of that unborn child is justified. I do not believe either of these situations justifies the killing of the baby.

One would wonder, "How is the life of the baby going to be ended?" Will it be by suction or by D&C? In each method the baby is going to be cut to pieces inside the mother and either suctioned out or removed piece by piece. Will it be by poisoning? Will a large needle filled with a concentrated salt solution be inserted into the baby's amniotic sac and released? The poisoned baby will die a horrible death and the next day be delivered by the mother. It might even be called a "candy apple baby" because that salt solution will have burned away the baby's outer layer of skin and the dead baby will be bright red. Perhaps it will be by Caesarian section. If that is the case, the baby will simply be removed through the abdominal wall and discarded, along with the placenta.

"But what if the baby is going to die anyhow?" comes the argument. "Shouldn't you save the mother?" Allow me to present the following scenario. Suppose we have a terminally ill person who is "going to die anyhow" and has done nothing wrong except get sick. We also have an individual who has a failing heart and will die if he doesn't receive a transplant. Is anyone justified in killing the terminally ill person who is "going to die anyhow" in order to use the heart to save another? If someone says, "That is different," the only difference is location and age. The baby is in the womb while the other is out.

Is the person outside of the womb more of a person, or more human, than the baby in the womb? If you justify the ending of that child's life to "save the mother," you are saying that one is worth more than the other, or that one is more "human" than the other. Any action taken that would purposely end the life of that child before his or her death comes naturally would be murder. If I were a pro-abortionist, I would love to have a Christian make such an argument in a debate. The debate would be mine!

Who has the right to place relative value on life? Who has the right to say that the mother's life is worth more than the baby's? There are things that are more important than life, my friends. It is *never* justified to end the life of an unborn baby!

August 21

What is the Difference between Submitting and Agreeing?

In *Webster's New Twentieth Century Diction of the English Language*, the first definition of the word "agree" is "to be of one mind; to harmonize in opinion; as, all parties agree in the decision." One of the definitions of the word "submit" as found in the same dictionary is "to be submissive, obedient, humble, etc.; to acquiesce in the authority of another."

These two definitions best fit the context of this question. When the Bible speaks of "submitting," as in Ephesians 5:21, 22, and 24, it involves the turning over of the will to another. The word itself was originally a military word that referred to the lining up of soldiers for battle under a commanding officer. The submission required by the gospel is because of a conscious choice made to enter into a relationship with another, knowing that the other person has the right to make binding decisions within that relationship. To truly "submit," I will acquiesce to those decisions, whether I agree with them or not.

However, the submission of Ephesians 5 goes beyond simple acquiescence and includes motive. The submission occurs out of a willing, unselfish consideration of the desires and wishes of another. It involves putting someone else before myself. We can easily see how that is not the same as agreeing. I may submit in something that I agree with completely, and that is easy. Submitting when I do not agree is another story, and in doing so I truly turn my will over to another.

Forgetting What Lies behind

In Philippians 3:13-14 Paul wrote, "Brethren I do not regard myself as having laid hold of it yet; but one thing I do: forgetting what lies behind and reaching forward to what lies ahead, I press on toward the goal for the prize of the upward call of God in Christ Jesus."

What did Paul mean by "forgetting what lies behind"? Did he mean that he literally forgot all that had gone before in his life, both good and bad? Absolutely not. Paul remembered the bad things in his life. He referred to himself in 1 Timothy 1:13 as "formerly a blasphemer and a persecutor and a violent aggressor." He said to King Agrippa in Acts 26:9, "So then, I thought to myself that I had to do many things hostile to the name of Jesus of Nazareth." He also remembered the good things he had accomplished and the work in the Lord he had done. In 2 Corinthians 3:2 Paul wrote to the Corinthians, "You are our letter, written in our hearts, known and read by all men." His point was that the Corinthian church itself authenticated Paul's work and fidelity to the Lord.

So what did Paul mean? Simply that he would not allow the things of the past, both good and bad, to interfere with his present work. Paul would not allow his past accomplishments to obscure his view of the present. He would not use what he had done in the past to vindicate what he was presently doing. Paul would not boast of previous successes because he still had work to do. May God help us all to have that same attitude. If I live in the past, I will miss the goal.

Atonement

Beginning at 6:00 on Friday evening, September 21, and ending Saturday, September 22 at 6:00 pm, was the Jewish high holy day of Yom Kippur—the Day of Atonement. While the date changes year to year, Yom Kippur is the most solemn day of the Jewish year and the only fast that was actually required under the Law of Moses. We read about the establishment of this day in Leviticus 16.

On this day the sins of the priests and the sins of the people were called to mind and atonement made for them. Atonement essentially has two meanings. One is that of reconciliation between people or beings that are at variance with one another; and second, it is used with reference to that which produces the reconciliation—generally a sacrifice designed for that purpose. On the Day of Atonement the High Priest made atonement for "all the iniquities of the children of Israel, and all their transgressions in all their sins" (Lev. 16:21). First, atonement would be made for the priests who served as mediators between God and the people, and the sanctuary itself was also cleansed because it had been ceremonially defiled by the fact that sinful men worked within it.

The New Bible Dictionary (Wm. B. Eerdmans Publishing) gives the following account of the events of the day:

> To prepare for the sacrifices of the day, the high priest put aside his official robes and dressed in a simple white garment. He then offered a bullock as a sin offering for himself and the priesthood. After filling his censer with live coals from the altar, the high priest entered the Holy of Holies, where he placed incense on the coals. The incense sent forth a cloud of smoke over the mercy seat, which served as a covering for the ark of the covenant. The high priest took some of the blood of the bullock and sprinkled it on the mercy seat and on the ground in front of the ark. In this way atonement was made for the priesthood.
>
> The high priest next sacrificed a he-goat as a sin offering for the people. Some of the blood was taken into the Holy of Holies, and it was sprinkled there in the manner in which the sin offering for the priests had been sprinkled (Lev. 16:11-15).
>
> After purifying the Holy Place and the altar of burnt offering with the mingled blood of the bullock and the goat (Lev. 16:18-19) the high priest took a second goat, laid his hands upon its head, and confessed over it the sins of Israel. This goat, commonly called the scape goat, was then driven into the desert, where it symbolically carried away the sins of the people.
>
> The carcasses of the two burnt offerings, the bullock and the he-goat, were taken outside the city and burned. The day was concluded with additional sacrifices.

The Day of Atonement occurred each year with the high priest making those offerings for his own sins and the sins of all the people. This served to demonstrate the fact that the actual blood that would provide for the perfect atonement had not yet been shed. That perfect atonement would be provided through the sacrifice of the Lord, Jesus Christ. The Book of Hebrews, in chapters 9 and 10, shows us the true significance of the Day of Atonement as it looked forward to the coming of Christ.

In Hebrews 9:7-12 we find:

> But into the second went the high priest alone once every year, not without blood, which he offered for himself, and for the errors of the people: the Holy Ghost this signifying, that the way into the holiest of all was not yet made manifest, while as the first tabernacle was yet standing: which was a figure for the time then present, in which were offered both gifts and sacrifices, that could not make him that did the service perfect, as pertaining to the conscience; which stood only in meats and drinks, and divers washings, and carnal ordinances, imposed on them until the time of reformation. But Christ being come an high priest of good things to come, by a greater and more perfect tabernacle, not made with hands, that is to say, not of this building; neither by the blood of goats and calves, but by his own blood he entered in once into the holy place, having obtained eternal redemption for us.

Verses 24-28 complete the idea:

> For Christ is not entered into the holy places made with hands, which are the figures of the true; but into heaven itself, now to appear in the presence of God for us: nor yet that he should offer himself often, as the high priest entereth into the holy place every year with blood of others; for then must he often have suffered since the foundation of the world: but now once in the end of the world hath he appeared to put away sin by the sacrifice of himself. And as it is appointed unto men once to die, but after this the judgment; so Christ was once offered to bear the sins of many; and unto them that look for him shall he appear the second time without sin unto salvation.

Today when a penitent believer is immersed in water for the forgiveness of his or her sins, he or she contacts the sacrificial blood of the Lord Jesus Christ. In so doing, reconciliation between the sinner and God takes place, made possible through the atoning sacrifice of Jesus the Christ. Praise be to God!

August 24

Is It Ever Really "Just Right"?

I am sitting in my office looking out the window and seeing something that we have not seen around this area for a very long time—RAIN. I am 53 years old and can remember a few droughts over the years, but nothing that compares to the severe lack of rain we have experienced this summer. Exacerbating the situation has been the intense heat. This has been the hottest summer in recorded history in our area, and oh, have I complained!

Yes sir, I admit it. I have been miserably hot this summer. I have bemoaned the loss of my lawn (because I refuse to spend the money to water it). I have gotten sick on a golf course because I did not drink enough water on a day that was pushing 100 degrees—who plays golf when it is that hot anyway? I have repeatedly said, "I can't wait for winter and snow."

How about you? Have you found yourself complaining about the weather this summer? Have you found yourself actually anxious for winter to get here, and are you even looking forward to snow? I believe that probably most of us have had something or other to say about the weather.

The funny thing is that along about the middle of February, especially if it has been a particularly cold and snowy winter, many of us will be saying, "I can't wait for spring. I am so tired of all of this snow and having to put on a heavy coat every time I go out. It makes it hard to get in and out of the car."

If next spring is particularly rainy, along about the middle of May many of us will be saying, "When is it going to stop raining? My grass is growing so quickly I can't keep up with it. It is just too wet to mow. I can't wait for summer and some dry weather." I freely admit that my voice will probably join in the chorus.

I wonder why that is? Why is it that so many of us always seem to want things to be just a little bit different? Frankly, I suspect that some of us are just prone to complaining. It really doesn't matter what the weather is or how things are going at work, at home, or at our local congregation, some of us are just prone to complaining. That is unfortunate, for the Bible teaches us that we must learn to be content—not complacent, but content. In Philippians 4:11-13 Paul wrote, "Not that I speak in respect of want; for I have learned, in whatsoever state I am, therewith to be content. I know both how to be abased, and I know how to abound: every where and in all things I am instructed both to be full and to be hungry, both to abound and to suffer need. I can do all things through Christ which strengtheneth me." What a blessing it is if we can learn to be thankful, happy and content with whatever the day might bring. After all, it is another day that we have been granted.

However, I believe that there may also be another reason why things don't ever seem to be "just right." God has given us a wonderful world in which to live. Yes, there is suffering, pain, and ugliness to contend with. Yes, we wonder sometimes at the brutality and wickedness of some. But there is also so much that is good, beautiful, and even awe-inspiring in this world that God has created. Yet, deep inside of us all, there is an innate desire for something even greater. I believe it is an inborn desire to be with our Father in heaven, a yearning to go home to that glorious place that the Lord has prepared for us. I believe it is part of our nature as those who have been created in the image of God.

So there is never really going to be complete satisfaction with this world in which we live, because this world is not really our home and our lives here are not really what we are all about. We are just passing through on a journey to a glorious, magnificent, and marvelous place. I am reminded of the passage found in Hebrews 11:13-16:

> These all died in faith, not having received the promises, but having seen them afar off, and were persuaded of them, and embraced them, and confessed that they were strangers and pilgrims on the earth. For they that say such things declare plainly that they seek a country. And truly, if they had been mindful of that country from whence they came out, they might have had opportunity to have returned. But now they desire a better country, that is, an heavenly: wherefore God is not ashamed to be called their God: for He hath prepared for them a city.

August 25

Sitting in the Pew
By Jeff Graves

I know how you feel, sitting in your pew.
I know what you're thinking because I was just like you.

What will I have to give up to be again born?
Is it not better to have the rose rather than the thorn?
It would be embarrassing to admit my faults and start anew.
I know how you feel; I was just like you.

Satan tried to convince me that what I was doing was good;
I was saying a prayer each night, just as I should.
I had an empty feeling as if something special was lost.
And Satan's message was… giving up the world isn't worth the cost.

I thought about Jesus and what He went through,
Dying for all, even for those with doubts sitting in the pew.
Imagine a Father who loved you so He gave up His Son.
Jesus died for all, not just for one.
As I thought about what it meant to confess and be baptized
I thought of morning, how from dark the sun would rise.
How no matter if it were raining or the clouds above were gray,
There was always light on the horizon to signify the day.

I made a choice that forever changed my life—
I chose Jesus and turned away from Satan's strife.
You see Jesus loved me before I knew Him.
In His eyes my light shined, and was never made dim.

What a wonderful gift to be loved that much,
To know all in my life has been blessed by God's touch.
You see, I was there wondering and wavering, sitting in the pew.
Yes, I gave reasons and excuses, just like you.

Now in hard times when I ask God to give me strength and lead the way,
Through my faith I know he heard what I had to say.
What a feeling to have guidance from above!
What a blessed feeling to know that kind of love!

So as you waver and wonder what to do,
Remember that Satan is holding you in that pew.
I tell this story, not to tell you what to do—
I tell this story because I was once just like you.

August 26

The Benefit of the Doubt

Have you ever met someone who always places the worst possible interpretation upon every word said and every action taken by his or her brethren? Statements can be twisted to mean something they didn't really mean, and motives for harmless actions will be called into question. If there is a good way to look at something and a bad way to look at something, some folks are just always going to choose the bad.

Paul sets forth characteristics of love in 1 Corinthians 13:4-7: "Love is patient, love is kind, and is not jealous; loves does not brag and is not arrogant, does not act unbecomingly; it does not seek its own, is not provoked, does not take into account a wrong suffered, does not rejoice in unrighteousness, but rejoices with the truth; bears all things, believes all things, hopes all things, endures all things." While every one of these attributes is applicable to the main point of this article, two of them particularly stand out. They are, "does not take into account a wrong suffered" and "believes all things."

When Paul writes, "Does not take into account a wrong suffered," or as the King James Version renders it, "Thinketh no evil," he is introducing a characteristic of love that is vital for brethren to properly deal with one another. Since the Lord's church is made up of imperfect people, there will be times when someone will get their feelings hurt, when something stupid will be said, when someone will do something wrong. Someone with love does not dwell upon those kinds of things. The idea behind "thinketh" or "take into account" is "to ponder; let one's mind dwell on." The word has a technical and an ordinary meaning. It was used in the technical sense in business dealings and referred to entering a debt on a ledger. If Paul had the technical meaning in mind, he was saying that someone with love does not keep a running record of offenses against themselves with a view toward payment. If the ordinary meaning is what Paul had in mind, then the idea is that the one who loves does not allow his or her mind to dwell on offenses. To do that allows bitterness and resentment to build.

Paul's statement in 1 Corinthians 13:7 where love "believes all things," directly addresses the point we are discussing. He is not saying that the person with love is easily deceived. In his commentary on 1 Corinthians, John Calvin commented on this by saying that the Christian is not to be so stupid as to cast aside wisdom and discernment so as to let people find it easy to cheat him; he does not forget how to distinguish white from black (*The First Epistle of Paul the Apostle to the Corinthians*).

However, the real point is that when there is no conclusive evidence to the contrary, the one with love always believes the very best about his brethren. Unfounded suspicions and doubts do not cloud such a person's judgment. He or she is always ready and willing to give their brethren the benefit of the doubt and believe the very best about them. When all of us refuse "to take into account a wrong suffered," and when all of us "believe all things," life is so much more enjoyable. And that is just how God designed it to be.

August 27

Trapped, But Not Bound

Several years ago I had the wonderful opportunity to go to a nursing home every Saturday morning with a group of fellow Christians and sing, pray, and study God's Word together with a number of the people who lived there. One Saturday we were studying in the 16th chapter of the book of Acts. Our particular focus was upon Paul and Silas being imprisoned in the city of Philippi. Verses 22-25 tell us:

> And the multitude rose up together against them: and the magistrates rent off their clothes, and commanded to beat them. And when they had laid many stripes upon them, they cast them into prison, charging the jailor to keep them safely: who, having received such a charge, thrust them into the inner prison, and made their feet fast in the stocks. And at midnight Paul and Silas prayed, and sang praises unto God: and the prisoners heard them.

As we examined that passage and the situation in which Paul and Silas found themselves, I simply made the point that their actions served to illustrate the fact that as children of God we can have joy no matter what our circumstances might be. Looking at the crowd of residents who had gathered together that morning to study with us, I noticed one older woman. She was bent over, obviously unable to straighten her body, and tied into a wheelchair. She could barely lift her head. Yet when I mentioned that circumstances do not control the true joy of a Christian, she smiled and nodded her head as best as she could.

As I looked at that woman, I could not help but to compare her with Paul and Silas. Those two great men of God had their feet made fast in the stocks; they were trapped as men in the inner prison, but their souls and spirits were not and could not be bound. Here was this older woman, trapped in a wheelchair by a body that would no longer function as it used to. I thought of her childhood, and the way I imagined that she used to run and play with the wind blowing through her hair. I thought of her as a young woman, beautiful to look at and so full of promise. Perhaps she had married and raised children; I really did not know. But now her time was drawing near and all of those physical things that she used to do, her body would not permit her to engage in anymore. She was trapped, but not bound.

Nursing homes are paradoxical to me. I have spent so much time in them over the years and have witnessed some of the saddest scenes I could ever imagine. At the same time, I have learned such wonderful lessons about what it means to have our citizenship in heaven and our souls anchored there. So many older brothers and sisters in Christ, trapped in bodies that just would not function properly, have held my hand, smiled, and helped me to understand just exactly what Paul meant when he wrote, "For I reckon that the sufferings of this present time are not worthy to be compared with the glory which shall be revealed in us" (Rom. 8:18). Though whatever happens to our bodies, whether it be accident, sickness, or just the accumulative effects of age may trap us physically, the spirits of faithful Christians cannot be bound.

August 28

Choices and Decisions

Choices and decisions—we all face them and make them every day. Some are of little importance, and whatever we decide is of no real consequence. For instance, what am I going to have for breakfast or lunch, what clothes should I wear today (as long as they are appropriate for one seeking to serve God), and so on, are all choices and decisions that we must make. However, what we choose concerning such matters makes very little difference. They are not decisions concerning right or wrong; they are choices concerning preferences.

There are times in our lives when we are called upon to make choices that have eternal consequences, when we are called upon to decide between what is right and what is wrong. I am reminded of the choice that Joshua called upon the children of Israel to make after the conquest of the land of Canaan had been completed. In Joshua 24:14-15 we find Joshua saying:

> Now therefore fear the Lord, and serve Him in sincerity and in truth: and put away the gods which your fathers served on the other side of the flood, and in Egypt; and serve ye the Lord. And if it seem evil unto you to serve the Lord, choose you this day whom ye will serve; whether the gods which your fathers served that were on the other side of the flood, or the gods of the Amorites in whose land ye dwell: but as for me and my house, we will serve the Lord.

Who can forget the stirring words of Elijah and the decision that he called for as he stood on Mt. Carmel and asked the children of Israel, "How long halt ye between two opinions? If the Lord be God, follow Him: but if Baal, then follow him?" (1 Kings 18:21).

Doesn't it seem that we usually think of the "big" things, the "big" decisions if we think of choices in the terms of eternity at all? Will I be a Christian? Now that's a big one. Whom will I marry? That's a big one in terms of eternity, for our spouse has a tremendous influence on our life. But what about the seemingly "little" things? What movie am I going to watch? It may seem so small, but it can be a choice between right and wrong. Would God be pleased with my sitting there looking at and listening to what I have decided to make my entertainment choice? There's a magazine I would like to buy, but does it promote worldliness and ungodly people? That is a question between right and wrong, and that makes it a question of eternal consequences.

Perhaps it would be good for us to be much more careful in the choices and decisions that we make. It may very well be that decisions we make in a rather off-handed manner can be of greater consequence that we thought. It is possible that some choices that we give very little thought to can, upon closer analysis, prove to be a choice between what is right and what is wrong.

August 29

Sometimes Silence Is Golden

Solomon gave tremendous words to live by in Ecclesiastes 5:2. He wrote, "Do not be hasty in word or impulsive in thought to bring up a matter in the presence of God. For God is in heaven and you are on the earth; therefore let your words be few." I believe that Solomon was telling us to think before we speak. Why am I about to say what I am about to say? It doesn't mean that everything we say has to be profound and of great significance. It doesn't mean that there can be no general conversation. But it does mean that I need to think before I speak. It does mean that every word that comes out of my mouth needs to be a good word, a word that is wholesome in content and design. It does mean, "That every idle word that men shall speak, they shall give account thereof in the day of judgment" (Matt. 12:36).

It has taken me a long time to learn (and I am still learning it) that sometimes the best thing I can do is to keep my mouth shut. That is hard for me to do because if I didn't like talking, I wouldn't be a preacher. But I can think of a lot of times when I just need to be quiet. For instance, if I am going to talk without thought just to hear the sound of my voice, I need to keep quiet. If I am about to say something mean, then I need to keep quiet. If I am about to answer a Bible question when I really don't know the answer, I need to be quiet. If I am about to take a shot at someone by my words, I need to just be quiet. If I am about to engage in spreading something that I know about someone else, it is time to keep my mouth shut. If I am about to say something that is not true, I need to keep my mouth shut. If I am losing my temper, I need to be quiet. We could probably all go on and on listing times when we know the right thing to do is to be quiet.

Let's conclude with the powerful teaching of James 3:2-12:

For we all stumble in many ways. If anyone does not stumble in what he says, he is a perfect man, able to bridle the whole body as well. Now if we put the bits into the horses' mouths so that they may obey us, we direct their entire body as well. Behold, the ships also, though they are so great and are driven by strong winds, are still directed by a very small rudder, wherever the inclination of the pilot desires. So also the tongue is a small part of the body, and yet it boasts of great things. Behold, how great a forest is set aflame by such a small fire! And the tongue is a fire, the very world of iniquity; the tongue is set among our members as that which defiles the entire body, and sets on fire the course of our life, and is set on fire by hell. For every species of beasts and birds, or reptiles and creatures of the sea, is tamed, and has been tamed by the human race. But no one can tame the tongue; it is a restless evil and full of deadly poison. With it we bless our Lord and Father; and with it we curse men, who have been made in the likeness of God; from the same mouth come both blessing and cursing. My brethren, these things ought not to be this way. Does a fountain send out from the same opening both fresh and bitter water? Can a fig tree, my brethren, produce olives, or a vine produce figs? Neither can salt water produce fresh.

August 30

The Invitation

How many invitations will we receive
Throughout our threescore and ten?

Certainly more than we can count
Or ever hope to attend.

As children there are birthday parties
Celebrations galore.
As adults there are business meetings,
Conferences and more.

We get invited to Grand Openings,
Not to mention Close Out Sales.
Even at the doctor's
We are invited to the "scales."

Most don't really matter
In the grand scheme of things;
But there is one invitation
That through the ages rings.

"Come unto Me"
Is how it began,
This invitation of
Nail-scarred hands.

"All ye that labor"
Know life at its best.
Lay the heavy burdens down
For He will give us rest.

"Take My yoke upon you"—
This is only right
For He certainly lifted us
On that dark and terrible night.

"And learn of Me"
Help me to learn,
Help me to see
Your anguish on the bitter tree.

"My yoke is easy"—
This is so true
But only through the love
Displayed by You.

"My burden is light"
On our dark and sin-filled night
You reached down and lifted us
And filled the world with light.

August 31

"He Is Not Here"—Hope

In Luke 1:1-6a, we read, "Now upon the first day of the week, very early in the morning, they came unto the sepulcher, bringing the spices which they had prepared, and certain others with them. And they found the stone rolled away from the sepulcher. And they entered in, and found not the body of the Lord Jesus. And it came to pass, as they were much perplexed thereabout, behold, two men stood by them in shining garments: and as they were afraid, and bowed down their faces to the earth, they said unto them, Why seek ye the living among the dead? He is not here, but is risen."

"He is not here, but is risen!" Have more significant or thrilling words ever been uttered? I don't think so. The very word "gospel" means "good news"—but have you ever stopped to consider that what makes it good news is the resurrection? Without the resurrection the story ends in terrible tragedy. However, because of the resurrection, it ends in unparalleled triumph and joy. The resurrection was not some kind of abstract thing that the early Christians believed; it was not just some philosophical or theological concept that the apostles preached. It was an undeniable truth with incredibly far-reaching consequences. The empty tomb existed. The risen Lord was seen by a multitude of people. The apostles boldly said, "We have seen him," and they were willing to die in support of that truth.

There came a time when some in the church at Corinth were saying that there would be no resurrection from the dead. In no uncertain terms Paul attacked that blasphemous teaching in 1 Corinthians 15. For the sake of space, let us read only verses 12-19:

Now if Christ be preached that he rose from the dead, how say some among you that there is no resurrection of the dead? But if there be no resurrection of the dead, then is Christ not risen: and if Christ be not risen, then is our preaching vain, and your faith is also vain. Yea, and we are found false witnesses of God; because we have testified of God that he raised up Christ: whom he raised not up, if so be that the dead rise not. For if the dead rise not, then is not Christ raised: and if Christ be not raised, your faith is vain; ye are yet in your sins. Then they also which are fallen asleep in Christ are perished. If in this life only we have hope in Christ, we are of all men most miserable.

Paul's point is so simple. If there is some valid reason to believe that Christians will not be raised, then Jesus was not raised. If that is the case, then all of the faithful preaching that had been done, as well as the faith it produced, was worthless. All were still in their sins, anyone who had died as a Christian had died hopelessly deluded, and anyone foolish enough to continue in such a belief was of all men most miserable. But there was no good reason to deny such a well-attested-to fact as the resurrection of Jesus, and there was no good reason to deny the indescribable power of God.

Now, in 1 Peter 1:3-4 we find, "Blessed be the God and Father of our Lord Jesus Christ, which according to his abundant mercy hath begotten us again unto a lively hope by the resurrection of Jesus Christ from the dead, to an inheritance incorruptible, and undefiled, and that fadeth not away, reserved in heaven for you." It is because of the resurrection of Christ that we have hope—a living, lively hope. It isn't based upon a lie. It is the truth, and it absolutely changes the life of a Christian. If Jesus had simply died and remained in the grave, what would be the point? But because our Lord rose from the dead, we have the "hope of eternal life" in Titus 1:2 and 3:7. We have the hope of going home to the incorruptible, undefiled inheritance that awaits the faithful children of God.

September 1

Do You Ever Stop Being a Parent?

One of the great stories of the Bible is the story of Joseph, the favorite son of Jacob. His brothers did horrible things, selling Joseph into slavery and deceiving his father into believing that he was dead. Yet Joseph would rise to second in all of Egypt and to a position in which he actually saved his family from perishing in time of great famine. In Genesis 50:19-20 we find Joseph telling his brothers, "Fear not: for am I in the place of God? But as for you, ye thought evil against me; but God meant it unto good, to bring to pass, as it is this day, to save much people alive."

Joseph in Egypt is a wonderful account of the magnificent providence of God. However, I want us to notice his father and ask ourselves, "Do you ever stop being a parent?" When Joseph's brothers brought his coat of many colors to Jacob, having dipped it in the blood of a goat, they convinced their father that he was dead. In Genesis 37:33-35 we see Jacob's reaction, "Joseph is without doubt rent in pieces. And Jacob rent his clothes, and put sackcloth upon his loins, and mourned for his son many days. And all his sons and all his daughters rose up to comfort him; but he refused to be comforted; and he said, For I will go down into the grave unto my son mourning. Thus his father wept for him." Many years later, when Jacob was reunited with Joseph in Egypt, we are told that he said to his son, "Now let me die, since I have seen thy face, because thou art yet alive" (Gen. 46:30). Do we ever stop being a parent?

I think of David, the second king of God's united people, and what happened with one of his sons. David had a son named Absalom. He is described in 2 Samuel 14:25 in the following way: "But in all Israel there was none to be so much praised as Absalom for his beauty: from the sole of his foot even to the crown of his head there was no blemish in him." This incredibly gifted and blessed young man would betray his father, David, and seek to usurp his position as king. As events unfolded, Absalom would meet his death hanging by his hair from a great oak tree. When informed of the death of his rebellious, ungrateful and ungodly son, David "went up to the chamber over the gate, and wept: and as he went, thus he said, O my son Absalom, my son, my son Absalom! Would God I had died for thee, O Absalom, my son, my son!" (2 Samuel 18:33). Do we ever stop being a parent?

Consider the parable of the Prodigal Son in Luke 15. This young man demanded his inheritance, took what he was given, and wasted it all in ungodly living in a far country. He lived a life that was completely opposed to what his father had taught him. When he hit rock bottom and thought to return to his father's house as no more than a servant, did he encounter a cold heart and a closed door? No. As a matter of fact, Luke 15:20 tells us, "And he arose, and came to his father. But when he was yet a great way off, his father saw him, and had compassion, and ran, and fell on his neck, and kissed him." In verse 24 we find, "For this my son was dead, and is alive again: he was lost and is found. And they began to be merry."

The answer to the question, "Do we ever stop being a parent?" is no. Even if our children go astray and we can no longer support them or their lifestyle, we are still their parents, praying and hoping for their return. If they remain faithful and serve the Lord, even when they are no longer under our roof or care, we can join with John in saying, "I have no greater joy than to hear that my children walk in truth" (3 John 4).

September 2

The Vase

On the shelf it sits as it has for years,
The vase given us by friends.
It doesn't hold flower or decorative arrangements;
It holds memories.

Why is it that a beautiful thing
By virtue of the years gone by
Begins to lose its magnetism—
It no longer draws the eye?

When it began I just can't say,
What day, what hour, what minute.
Maybe someone hit the shelf, maybe too many memories,
But at some time that beautiful vase developed a crack in it.

I just didn't notice, none of us did,
I guess 'cause it was always there.
But that crack that had its foundation marred
Began its strength to tear.

It's funny how a thing of beauty
Upon which your eyes did often rest,
Can begin to lose its strength and you not see,
Can begin to fail each test.

I guess it could hold no more memories,
Its strength just was no longer there,

As the crack began to widen
And with other cracks to share.

One day I happened to glance in the direction of the shelf,
Intending the vase to see.
But it was gone; it was not there
And in its place were pieces.

I cried the day the vase shattered
And broken fragments of memories seemed scattered with the
    pieces.
Its just a vase, rarely noticed, we'll get a new one, you'll see.
They missed the point because I know—that broken vase is me.

September 3

What Is Most Important?

In the western world, success is generally measured in terms of accomplishments. It doesn't always have to be financial success that draws the praise and honor of our fellow man. Men of great intellect such as Albert Einstein, Jonas Salk, and others have gained fame and admiration through the results of their study and research. Men of great military power are looked to for security and confidence. Entire nations often praise as heroes their military leaders. Elite athletes, men and women who can run, jump, throw, catch, and generally display physical prowess at the highest levels, are held up as role models. Children and adults wear replicas of their jerseys, or shoes that bear their names, and declare that they want to be like them. Those of great wealth, especially those who started with little and through hard work and determination built their fortunes, are often the subjects of books and articles extolling their great achievements. This is all good and it all has its place—but none of these things is what is truly the most important.

At a very dark time in the history of the children of Israel, God, through the prophet Jeremiah, stated in such a clear fashion what is really important. Before too long the capital city of Jerusalem would be destroyed, with the temple of Jehovah essentially leveled by the mighty Babylonian army. Large numbers of the citizens of Judah would be carried into Captivity. If ever there was a time when the people needed to understand the difference between what was significant and what was most significant, what was important and what was most important, now was the time. This is what God told them:

> Thus saith the Lord, Let not the wise man glory in his wisdom, neither let the mighty man glory in his might, let not the rich man glory in his riches: but let him that glorieth glory in this, that he understandeth and knoweth Me, that I am the Lord which exercise lovingkindness, judgment, and righteousness, in the earth: for in these things I delight, saith the Lord (Jer. 9:23-24).

Truth be told, the man who walks with God is the man who understands what is most important. He may never have great wisdom from the worldly standpoint, never lead armies or win awards for his athletic abilities. This person may never enjoy a great amount of wealth and relatively few people may know his name. But I submit to you that God knows such a person, and that the world is a better place because of the life of every person who knew what was most important. Such a person has done something great.

September 4

Why?

There is a question that is addressed in the Old Testament many times and in different ways. The question is, "Why do the wicked prosper?" In Job 21:7-15 this ancient man of God asked:

> Wherefore do the wicked live, become old, yea, are mighty in power? Their seed is established in their sight with them, and their offspring before their eyes. Their houses are safe from fear, neither is the rod of God upon them. Their bull gendereth, and faileth not; their cow calveth, and casteth not her calf. They send forth their little ones like a flock, and their children dance. They take the timbrel and harp, and rejoice at the sound of the organ. They spend their days in wealth, and in a moment, go down to the grave. Therefore they say unto God, Depart from us; for we desire not the knowledge of thy ways. What is the Almighty, that we should serve Him? And what profit should we have, if we pray unto him?

Job's friends had come to him in his suffering and afflictions and spoke of the difficulties of the wicked. Eliphaz, Zophar, and Bildad all spoke to Job of the hardship and early demise of the wicked and of the security and prosperity of the righteous. Their obvious implication was, if Job would simply come clean with whatever wickedness was in his life that had caused all of his problems, everything would be just fine. However, Job responded by showing that the same blessings of a material nature come upon the upright and the wicked. Frankly, he wanted to know why.

The 12th chapter of Jeremiah begins with the words, "Righteous art thou, O Lord, when I plead with thee: yet let me talk with thee of thy judgments: Wherefore doth the way of the wicked prosper? Wherefore are all they happy that deal very treacherously? Thou hast planted them, yea, they have taken root: they grow, yea, they bring forth fruit: thou art near in their mouth, and far from their reins." It is essentially the same question, "Why do the wicked seem to prosper?"

In a little different approach, the prophet Habakkuk just could not understand why God delayed His judgment against the wicked. Consider Habakkuk 1:2-4:

O Lord, how long shall I cry, and thou wilt not hear! Even cry out unto thee of violence, and thou wilt not save! Why dost thou show me iniquity, and cause me to behold grievance? For spoiling and violence are before me: and there are that raise up strife and contention. Therefore the law is slacked, and judgment doth never go forth: for the wicked doth compass about the righteous; therefore wrong judgment proceedeth.

Truthfully, I have wondered the same thing myself. Why is it that some of the most ungodly people appear to be so prosperous from a material standpoint? Why does God permit them to carry on, for they bring nothing of truly lasting value to the world and oftentimes cause great harm? It is hard sometimes not to ask those questions. I think of the Lord's statement in Matthew 5:45, "That ye may be the children of your Father which is in heaven: *for He maketh his sun to rise on the evil and on the good, and sendeth rain on the just and the unjust.*" I want to know "Why?" Why do the wicked get the same material blessings as those who are trying their best to serve God?

The answer is found in God's word. If we had continued on in Jeremiah 12, we would have found God informing His great prophet that he was guilty of failing to see the end. God would take care of it in His own time. Jeremiah 12 ends with the statement, "But if they will not obey, I will utterly pluck up and destroy that nation, saith the Lord." God told the prophet Habakkuk to hang on; He would take care of it in His own time and in His own way. Habakkuk 2:2-3 shows us this, "And the Lord answered me, and said, Write the vision, and make it plain upon tables, that he may run that readeth it. For the vision is yet for an appointed time, but at the end it shall speak, and not lie: though it tarry, wait for it; because it will surely come, it will not tarry."

So what do we do? Live by faith and let God handle it; that is what we do. If we move just one verse forward in Habakkuk 2 we find, "Behold, his soul which is lifted up is not upright in him: but the just shall live by his faith." It calls to mind Micah 6:8: "He hath showed thee, O man, what is good: and what doth the Lord require of thee, but to do justly, and to love mercy, and to walk humbly with thy God?" That is the answer. Humbly walk in obedience to God and completely trust Him. He is in control, and He is infinitely just and righteous.

September 5

Frustrated?

Have you ever had one of those days? You know what I mean, the kind of day where nothing seems to be working the way you intended it to. This day was just such a day. I had a wonderful idea of what to put in a certain space in the bulletin. I worked and messed with the computer, but it would not let me put what I wanted to put right there. That computer was behaving like a recalcitrant child, and even though I am sure there was something I could have done to fix the problem, I did not know what it was.

Here I was, being frustrated by a machine! That computer cannot get up and walk out of my office (although I have thought of giving it assistance in a rapid departure out of the window from time to time). I am sure that my little Gateway laptop does not possess artificial intelligence, so it can't think for itself. All it can do is what I tell it to do, and if it doesn't do it, it means that I am not telling it correctly.

I wonder *how frustrated God gets* when we don't do what He tells us to do. We *do* possess intelligence. We *can* understand what God says, and we *can* do it. We are not machines. If we don't follow God's commands, it is because we don't want to.

September 6

The Desk

I recently purchased a new desk for my home office. I was in the market for a good desk, a "piece of furniture" kind of desk that would be the last desk I would ever buy. I was stunned at the prices traditional furniture stores were asking for their desks, so I went to a rather large manufacturer of sturdy furniture at a reasonable price. The only catch is that you must assemble the furniture yourself or pay a large assembly fee. The salesman assured me that it would take about three or four hours to put it together.

After approximately ten hours of labor on that incredibly heavy desk, I was at the point where it could now be turned right side up and the drawers put into place. It took both my son and me to lift that desk and to turn it right side up. As we turned it, the top of that desk that I had spent a considerable amount of money for and had expended 10 hours of my life assembling, came off. Yes, that is right. It came right off, ripping the connectors out of the wood.

After maneuvering the bottom part of the desk into place, we put the top back on it as best as we could. Then we began to insert the drawers. Since the runners for the drawers were numbered in the directions but not in actuality, it turned out that we had to remove some and change them around in order to get the drawers to function properly. Upon closer examination, it turned out that the desktop was warped, thereby putting constant pressure on the connectors, and that is why it came off. My wife, bless her heart, said, "It is still a beautiful piece of furniture and no one will ever know"; and she is right. It is a beautiful piece of furniture and if we ever have to move it, at least I'll know that the top comes off.

In many ways my experience with the desk is a lot like life in general. It rarely goes as smoothly as we would like and sometimes it even seems like the top comes off! Little adjustments have to be made along the way, and sometimes we have to redo something in order to get it right. As we move along with a smile upon our face, most will never know the ups and downs, the struggles and difficulties, that have gone together to make us what we are. That desk is not perfect, and neither am I.

If we are faithful children of God that doesn't mean that we are perfect. None of us is. But as His children, the time will come when we will be perfect. John tells us in 1 John 3:1-2:

> Behold, what manner of love the Father hath bestowed upon us, that we should be called the sons of God: therefore the world knoweth us not, because it knew Him not. Beloved, now are we the sons of God, and it doth not yet appear what we shall be: but we know that, when He shall appear, we shall be like Him; for we shall see Him as He is.

We shall be like Him, in a resurrected body, fit to live eternally with the Lord in heaven. That is perfection.

Give Me Your Heart

God has always demanded that if we are going to give Him anything, what He wants is our very best. Insincere worship and service is an abomination to Him, and the Bible teaches that we can engage in "religious" things and still have God reject them.

In the days of the prophet Joel, God called upon the Israelites to forsake their ungodly practices and turn back to Him in repentance. The book itself speaks of a horrific locust plague that came upon the land, which the prophet used to warn of even greater punishment that would come at the hands of invading armies if the people did not repent. In Joel 2:12-13 we find these words: "Therefore also now, saith the Lord, turn ye even to me with all your heart, and with fasting, and with weeping, and with mourning. *And rend your heart, and not your garments*, and turn unto me the Lord your God: for he is gracious and merciful, slow to anger, and of great kindness, and repenteth him of evil."

The prophet Amos, prophesying to the northern kingdom of Israel not so long before they would be destroyed for their idolatry, wrote about their insincere worship and how God felt about it. Jehovah severely rebukes the people of Israel through the prophet in Amos 5:21-26:

> I hate, I despise your feast days, and I will not smell in your solemn assemblies. Though ye offer Me burnt offerings and your meat offerings, I will not accept them: neither will I regard the peace offerings of your fat beasts. Take thou away from me the noise of thy songs; for I will not hear the melody of thy viols. But let judgment run down as waters, and righteousness as a mighty stream. Have ye offered unto Me sacrifices and offerings in the wilderness forty years, O house of Israel? But ye have borne the tabernacle of your Moloch and Chiun your images, the star of your god, which ye made to yourselves.

They had continued in the outward signs of their religion. They continued with the sacrifices and other rituals. However, the other things that they did, such as worshipping false gods, indicated that their hearts were not right before God.

In the Sermon on the Mount, Jesus spoke of those who performed what would appear to be good, holy, and righteous acts, but did these things from a heart that was not right. In Matthew 6:1-4 Jesus spoke to those who did acts of charity, but not because it was the right thing to do or out of a pure motive. He said that they did what they did, "that they may have glory of men." In Matthew 6:5-13, Jesus spoke about prayer, and those who actually did it so "that they may be seen of men."

Giving God lip service and engaging in token acts of religiosity may convince our fellow man that we are spiritually minded individuals, but God knows the truth.

September 8

Responsibility

We live in a day and a time when no one seems to want to take responsibility for their own actions and very few want to hold individuals accountable for what they have done. If a person commits a crime, it is society's fault. If a person engages in behavior that is detrimental to their health such as drinking, smoking, overeating, or taking illicit drugs—it is not because they are doing something wrong. It is because they are sick, suffering from a disease of some sort. No one wants to take responsibility. The rallying cry of the day seems to be, "Don't blame me!"

This isn't a new phenomenon. It has been occurring since man first appeared on the earth. When God confronted Adam for eating the forbidden fruit, his response was, "The woman whom thou gavest to be with me, she gave of the tree and I did eat." So Adam blamed Eve, and even God Himself. When Eve was questioned she responded with, "The serpent beguiled me, and I did eat." It wasn't her fault; it was the serpent's fault.

God told the people of Judah that they could blame no one else for their defeat and captivity at the hands of the Babylonians. In Jeremiah 31:29-30 we find, "In those days they shall say no more, The fathers have eaten a sour grape, and the children's teeth shall be set on edge. But every one shall die for his own iniquity: every man that eateth the sour grape, his teeth shall be set on edge." Later, while actually in the Babylonian Captivity, God told His people through the prophet Ezekiel, "What mean ye, that ye use this proverb concerning the land of Israel, saying, The fathers have eaten sour grapes, and the children's teeth are set on edge? As I live, saith the Lord God, ye shall not have occasion any more to use this proverb" (Ezek. 18:2-3).

I suppose that there is some comfort to be found in not accepting responsibility for our own actions, particularly if there will be negative consequences for doing so. It is understandable when a small child is caught in the midst of some transgression and responds by saying, "I didn't do it," or perhaps, "It is not my fault." After all, a small child is in the process of learning to accept responsibility. It is a sad thing indeed when an adult seeks to shift the blame.

There is a basic and consistent principle taught throughout God's word. It is clearly stated in Galatians 6:7-8. Paul wrote, "Be not deceived; God is not mocked: for whatsoever a man soweth, that shall he also reap. For he that soweth to his flesh shall of the flesh reap corruption; but he that soweth to the Spirit shall of the Spirit reap life everlasting." We are personally responsible for the things we do or don't do.

Ultimately, it will not matter if we have convinced others and ourselves that the sinful things we have done are just not our fault. Paul wrote in 2 Corinthians 5:10, "For we must all appear before the judgment seat of Christ: that every one may receive the things done in his body, according to that he hath done, whether it be good or bad." It is so much better, as well as being pleasing to God, to simply accept responsibility for our actions. Repent when repentance is called for; make the necessary corrections. In God's sight we are responsible for what we do.

September 9

The Temptation in the Wilderness

The well-known account of the Lord's temptation in the wilderness is found in Matthew 4:1-11, Mark 1:12-13, and Luke 4:1-13. We must understand the reality of what Jesus went through. The temptations were real. Having taken upon Himself humanity, the reality of the temptations and the possibility of failure were things that Jesus had to face. Hebrews 4:15 tells us, "For we have not an high priest which cannot be touched with the feeling of our infirmities; but was in all points tempted like as we are, yet without sin." Hebrews 2:17-18 says, "Wherefore in all things it behooved Him to be made like unto His brethren, that He might be a merciful and faithful high priest in things pertaining to God, to make reconciliation for the sins of the people. For in that He Himself hath suffered being tempted, He is able to succour them that are tempted."

There are those who would say that since Jesus was God on earth, He did not feel temptation the way that we do. I believe that misses the point entirely. No one knows temptation to the extent that Jesus did. At some point all of us have given in and succumbed to temptation. Jesus reached that point and went beyond, never failing. Do we want to know how to endure temptation? Look to the One who experienced it at its zenith and never gave in.

By combining Matthew and Luke's accounts, we know that immediately following His baptism, Jesus, full of the Holy Spirit, was led by the Spirit into the wilderness to be tempted by the devil. There He fasted for forty days and forty nights. After that time of isolation and deprivation, Jesus was hungry. Thus the stage was set for the first recorded temptation.

"If thou art the Son of God, command that these stones become bread." This brings to mind the "lust of the flesh" that John speaks of in 1 John 2:16. Jesus was hungry. Would He use His miraculous powers in a selfish way? He certainly could have turned the stones into bread, but He did not.

The Lord's response is a lesson for all people for all time. He quoted Deuteronomy 8:3. He said, "Man shall not live by bread alone, but by every word that proceedeth out of the mouth of God." In His answer Jesus showed that that which is most important is not physical in nature, but spiritual. He who lives by bread only does not truly live, but he who places God's Word before his physical needs has attained spiritual maturity.

The second temptation according to Matthew (Luke places it third) was for Jesus to be placed on a high pinnacle of the temple. There the devil said, "If thou art the Son of God, cast thyself down: for it is written, he shall give His angels charge concerning thee: and, On their hands they shall bear thee up, lest haply thou dash thy foot against a stone." This calls to mind John's words, "the pride of life" in 1 John 2:16. What was the temptation? Satan, by misusing Scripture (Ps. 91:11-12), was tempting Jesus to endanger His life for no other purpose than to prove the protection of and close communion with His Father. Again, our Lord responded with Scripture. He quoted Deuteronomy 6:16. Who is man to tempt God? What He says He will do! That is enough!

The third temptation (second in Luke) has the devil taking Jesus to an exceedingly high mountain and showing Him all the kingdoms of the world and the their glory. Luke tells us that was done in a "moment of time," illustrating the supernatural aspect of what was happening. To Jesus Satan said, "To thee will I give all this authority, and the glory of them: for it hath been delivered unto me; and to whomsoever I will I give it. If thou therefore wilt worship before me, it shall all be thine." This brings to mind John's words of 1 John 2:16, "the lust of the eyes." "From the standpoint of Christ's humanity, how overwhelming the temptation! It was the world's honors to one who had for thirty years led the life of a village carpenter: it was the world's riches to him who had not where to lay his head" (*The Fourfold Gospel*, 97).

In answer Jesus again quoted Scripture, this time Deuteronomy 6:13, "Thou shalt worship the Lord thy God, and Him only shalt thou serve." He demanded that Satan depart, which he did, and the angels came and ministered to the Lord.

Contained within the pages of God's Word is everything we need to endure temptation. Let's fill ourselves with that Word. It will sustain us and help us in the hour of trial and temptation.

September 10

Psalm 119 (1): Blessed

We are going to spend the next twenty-two days learning many of the glorious and uplifting lessons to be found in the 119th Psalm. Let's note the peculiar organization of the psalm. The psalm contains twenty-two stanzas that correspond to the twenty-two letters of the Hebrew alphabet. Each one of the stanzas is comprised of eight verses, and each one of the verses begins with the same Hebrew letter. While we do not see it in English, it is a most powerful form of presentation in Hebrew.

The overall theme of this beautiful Psalm is the Law of God, and stanza by stanza various qualities and attributes of God's revealed message are discussed and illumined.

Aleph

Blessed are the undefiled in the way, who walk in the law of the Lord. Blessed are they that keep His testimonies, and that seek Him with the whole heart. They also do no iniquity; they walk in His ways. Thou hast commanded us to keep thy precepts diligently. O that my ways were directed to keep thy statutes! Then shall I not be ashamed, when I have respect unto all thy commandments. I will praise thee with uprightness of heart, when I shall have learned thy righteous judgments. I will keep thy statutes: O forsake me not utterly.

There is one way for a man to be truly blessed or happy. That is to have every step of the way guided by the testimonies, precepts, statutes, commandments, and righteous judgments of God. There is but one way to accomplish that, and that is to seek the Lord with our whole heart. Mere lip-service or a token acknowledgment of the requirements of God's word is not sufficient to procure all that God has prepared for His people. While the blessings to be found in following God's ways should be motivation enough for us to immerse ourselves in them, doing so is commanded by God.

An important point to note is the call to have respect unto "all" of God's commandments. It is not for us to pick and choose only those things that we might like, but to recognize that all of it is from God and for our benefit. The more we learn of God's Word and the more we come to know of its nature and life-changing influence, the more we are moved to praise Him. I believe that an "upright heart"—one that is molded and formed by the Word of God like a vessel is molded by the potter—not only is constant in its praise of God but also is itself a thing of praise. Just to behold someone who has allowed himself to develop the "upright heart" is to behold someone whose very life serves to praise God. As the prayers of the saints are compared to the smoke of incense rising up before God (Rev. 8:3-4), so too the very life of one with an "upright heart" rises up as praise to Him.

Oh, my friend, the one who determines to live his life walking in the path of God's Word will never have occasion to be ashamed. He or she will not find disappointment in their hopes; they will be realized. For the one who walks in the "law of the Lord" will not be left alone—God will be with us.

Psalm 119 (2): What Shall a Young Man Do?

Beth

Wherewithal shall a young man cleanse his way? By taking heed thereto according to Thy word. With my whole heart have I sought Thee: O let me not wander from Thy commandments. Thy word have I hid in mine heart, that I might not sin against Thee. Blessed art Thou, O Lord: teach me Thy statutes. With my lips have I declared all the judgments of Thy mouth. I have rejoiced in the way of Thy testimonies, as much as in all riches. I will meditate in Thy precepts, and have respect unto Thy ways. I will delight myself in Thy statutes: I will not forget Thy word.

There are many temptations and trials that seem to be more pronounced among the young. Their knowledge is small, but their passions often run deep. They may have the very best of intentions but lack the wisdom and strength to sustain them in times of temptations. I would not want to be a young man again, even if I could turn back the hands of time.

Young people today are faced with temptations that are not necessarily different, but perhaps more accessible. Television shows that are geared toward young people, much of the music that is being produced with them in mind, video games, movies and advertisement, are filled with sex and violence. Respect for God is often mocked, and the Internet, with sites such as MySpace, gives them an outlet to engage in the kind of behavior that so many influences have taught them is the thing to do. So young women post pictures of themselves with clothing and make-up meant to make them appear sexy. Young men present themselves in as worldly a manner as possible because the world has led them to believe that that sort of thing makes them attractive and appealing.

The passions of young people have always been strong, but hormones do not excuse ungodly behavior, even though practically everything they see, hear, and read about in media that is especially directed at them promotes ungodliness and sin. Solomon wrote in Ecclesiastes 11:9, "Rejoice, O young man, in thy youth; and let thy heart cheer thee in the days of thy youth, and walk in the ways of thine heart, and in the sight of thine eyes: but know thou, that for all these things God will bring thee into judgment." Solomon wasn't encouraging ungodliness. He was encouraging the young to understand that they are responsible for their actions and that they will reap what they sow.

So what is a young person to do? Turn to God and His Word. I know that is not always easy. I know that there are so many influences trying to pull the young away from God. The only possible hope a young person has to truly be happy is through God's way. It is sad that it often takes bad experiences and even tragic circumstances to occur before a young person learns that what this world has to offer will not ultimately satisfy and can be here one day, and gone the next.

Parents, grandparents, guardians, and all who love them, help the young to seek the Lord with their whole heart and give it permanent residence there. Encourage them to come to understand that no one can take away what God's Word will give them and how fickle the riches of this world truly are. Help them to find the true delight to be found in walking in God's way.

September 12

Psalm 119 (3): Remove from Me Reproach and Contempt

Gimel

Deal bountifully with thy servant, that I may live, and keep thy word. Open Thou mine eyes, that I may behold wondrous things out of Thy law. I am a stranger in the earth: hide not Thy commandments from me. My soul breaketh for the longing that it hath unto Thy judgments at all times. Thou hast rebuked the proud that are cursed, which do err from Thy commandments. Remove from me reproach and contempt; for I have kept Thy testimonies. Princes also did sit and speak against me: but Thy servant did meditate in Thy statutes. Thy testimonies also are my delight and counselors.

The psalmist prays for long life that he might spend it keeping God's Word. He prays that, in that long life, his eyes of understanding would be continually opened that he might come to know the wondrous truths revealed therein. Even though the psalmist says, "Deal bountifully with Thy servant, that *I* may live," it is obvious that the points of his pleadings can apply to all of God's servants.

The true servant of God is a "stranger" or "sojourner" on this earth. Our citizenship is in heaven, and we are just passing through. In the great chapter of faith, Hebrews 11, we find in verses 12-16:

> These all died in faith, not having received the promises, but having seen them afar off, and were persuaded of them, and embraced them, and confessed that they were strangers and pilgrims on the earth. For they that say such things declare plainly that they seek a country. And truly, if they had been mindful of that country from whence they came out, they might have had opportunity to have returned. But now they desire a better country, that is, an heavenly: wherefore God is not ashamed to be called their God: for He hath prepared for them a city.

As is so often the case, those who are strangers or foreigners in a particular country are viewed with suspicion and even outright hostility. If this happens simply because a person is from a different place or looks and speaks differently, how much more profound will it be when a person's very essence is different. That is the way it is for a child of God. A child of God no longer thinks like the world, talks like the world, dresses like the world, or acts like the world. Consequently, he will feel the reproach and contempt of those in the world. Even those in positions of authority will speak with derision of Christians whose conduct condemns their own. Jesus Himself was "despised and rejected of men" (Isa. 53:3), and the Apostle Paul wrote, "Yea, and all that will live godly in Christ Jesus shall suffer persecution" (2 Tim. 3:12).

So, faithful servants of the Lord, take heart. We walk a path that others have walked before us. It is a blessed path that we trod. At the same time, it is surely a cursed thing to refuse to walk in God's commandments. Don't fall for the teaching of the worldly. Don't go to the ungodly for advice and direction. "God's word is His witness or testimony to grand and important truths which concern Himself and our relation to Him: this we should desire to know; knowing it, we should believe it; believing it we should love it; and loving it, we should hold it fast against all comers" (Spurgeon, *The Treasury of David*, VI: 14). There will we find true counsel.

Psalm 119 (4): Elevate My Life, Make Me Strong

Daleth

My soul cleaveth unto the dust; quicken thou me according to Thy word. I have declared my ways, and Thou heardest me; teach me Thy statutes. Make me to understand the way of Thy precepts: so shall I talk of Thy wondrous works. My soul melteth for heaviness: strengthen Thou me according unto Thy word. Remove from me the way of lying: and grant me Thy law graciously. I have chosen the way of truth: Thy judgments have I laid before me. I have stuck unto Thy testimonies: O Lord, put me not to shame. I will run the way of Thy commandments, when Thou shalt enlarge my heart.

The psalmist recognizes his own imperfections and his own struggles. He struggled with things of the flesh; he struggled with the temptations of that which was earthly, carnal. His request was that the Lord would revive him, or help him to live a life according to His Word. He was willing to confess all of his faults, all of his failures, all of his foibles—knowing that God would hear him.

However, the psalmist was not perfect, and even after laying his heart before the Lord, he would still fall short. Hence, he wrote, "My soul melteth for heaviness." The word "melteth" can be translated as "weeps." Tears would flow from his eyes from the burden he bore as a result of his failures. One can almost hear the psalmist beseech the Lord to "take my shortcomings away, help me to follow the path that I have chosen, which is Your Word."

Have you ever felt the conflict, the frustration, of determining that you would live according to God's precepts and His commandments, only to come up short because of the pull of the world? There is not a perfect Christian. We are simply forgiven people who still fail from time to time. Oh, the call of the carnal is so strong!

Have you ever felt the tracks of tears upon your cheeks as the grief of failing to walk as you promised God touches your heart? Take courage, God will help. All we can do is to strengthen our resolve to choose the truth of God as the guiding principle of our lives. In so doing, determine with even greater fervency to stick to that which God has testified to being right and proper.

Be like the psalmist. "Run the way of His commandments." Make up for any lost time spent in serving the flesh.

Psalm 119 (5): Help Me to Learn

He

Teach me, O Lord, the way of Thy statutes; and I shall keep it unto the end. Give me understanding, and I shall keep Thy law; yea, I shall observe it with my whole heart. Make me to go in the path of Thy commandments; for therein do I delight. Incline my heart unto Thy testimonies, and not to covetousness. Turn away mine eyes from beholding vanity; and quicken Thou me in Thy way. Stablish Thy word unto Thy servant, who is devoted to Thy fear. Turn away my reproach which I fear: for Thy judgments are good. Behold, I have longed after Thy precepts: quicken me in Thy righteousness.

Jeremiah wrote in Jeremiah 10:23, "O Lord, I know that the way of man is not in himself: it is not in man that walketh to direct his steps." It is obvious that the psalmist recognizes and deeply appreciates that very truth. Hence we see this wonderful prayer and plea.

It has been said that the psalmist knew two things—"First, that there was something he must and would learn, for all his well-being depended upon it; and this something was the Word of God, which he calls now by one name and now by another. But he knew a second thing, and that was—he could never teach himself; God must teach him" (*The Pulpit Commentary*, VIII: 130).

Think about the pursuit of the knowledge of God's Word. How many begin to study the Scriptures, perhaps even establishing a daily Bible reading and time to meditate upon the meaning of what has been read, only to fail to continue in their resolution? I have done that, and I believe the psalmist had probably done it too. Therefore he wrote, "…and I shall keep it unto the end."

So many will read God's Word, study its meaning, and then proceed to pick and choose those parts that they want to keep. The psalmist promised that he would keep the law of God with his "whole heart." There can be no holding back. With God and His Word, it is all or nothing.

Isn't it possible for us to know what God would have us to do, but fail to do it from time to time? Is it not possible that by coveting things of the world we will be turned from our devotion to God and His ways? Certainly it is, and that is why the psalmist prayed to God for help to go in His paths and for assistance in keeping his heart focused.

There is so much in the world that is just not true. There is so much that is worthless and that has no lasting or redeeming value. Frankly, it is easy to become caught up in those kinds of things, and when we do, our feet wander from the path of right. Have you not felt as the psalmist did? Haven't you asked the Lord for help in keeping the worthless things of the world from taking over your life? Pause for a moment and ask the Lord to help you find and cling to the life and vitality that is found only in walking in the righteousness of God's precepts.

September 15

Psalm 119 (6): Help Me to Teach

Vau

Let thy mercies come also unto me, O Lord, even thy salvation, according to thy word. So shall I have wherewith to answer him that reproacheth me: for I trust in thy word. And take not the word of truth utterly out of my mouth; for I have hoped in thy judgments. So shall I keep thy law continually for ever and ever. And I will walk at liberty: for I seek thy precepts. I will speak of thy testimonies also before kings, and will not be ashamed. And I will delight myself in thy commandments, which I have loved. My hands also will I lift up unto thy commandments, which I have loved: and I will meditate in thy statutes.

I do not know to what situation the psalmist may be specifically referring, but he is asking God to manifest His lovingkindness to him in his deliverance. With God's mercy being so clearly demonstrated in his life, he would have a ready and easy answer to give to any who would rebuke him for trusting in God and in His Word. With "the word of truth" on his lips, he will go forth knowing the true freedom that is only experienced by those who voluntarily seek, not by constraint or compulsion, to obey God's precepts. As opportunities present themselves, he would speak of God's Word from the least to the greatest, even before kings. By the lifting up of his hands, he shows the commandments of God absolute reverence and respect.

The words of the psalmist reflect the attitude that is to be displayed by a child of God. We have been abundantly blessed with all spiritual blessings through the marvelous grace of God. "If a man knows that God's salvation has come to him, he has that in his conscious possession which will make him despise, as mere idle tales, all and every reproach of the scoffer and unbeliever. They may as well deny or decry the light of the sun as to do the like for that salvation in which the soul rejoices" (*The Pulpit Commentary*, VIII: 130). A child of God must never be ashamed of the "good news" of Jesus Christ, for it is "the power of God unto salvation to everyone who believeth" (Rom. 1:16). At any and all times, we must look for the opportunities to tell others of the glorious truths found in God's Word. As Peter wrote in 1 Peter 3:15, "But sanctify the Lord God in your hearts: and be ready always to give an answer to every man that asketh you a reason of the hope that is in you with meekness and fear."

September 16

Psalm 119 (7): Comfort Me

Zayin

Remember the word unto thy servant, upon which thou hast caused me to hope. This is my comfort in my affliction: for thy word hath quickened me. The proud have had me greatly in derision: yet have I not declined from thy law. I remembered thy judgments of old, O Lord; and have comforted myself. Horror hath taken hold upon me because of the wicked that forsake thy law. Thy statutes have been my songs in the house of my pilgrimage. I have remembered thy name, O Lord, in the night, and have kept thy law. This I had, because I kept thy precepts.

Where does the psalmist look for comfort? He looks to God's Word and the promises that are found therein, and to their gracious fulfillment. The knowledge of His word and the security of those promises, enabled the psalmist to endure any afflictions that came upon him, including ridicule and mockery from those too proud to submit themselves to God's laws. He had filled his heart with examples of how God had dealt with people from of old, and he knows that God's judgments have always been righteous. Indeed, hot indignation fills him as he thinks of those who turn their backs upon God's law, because of both the affront to God and the punishment that awaits them. Perhaps his feelings are similar to those expressed by Ezra in his prayer to God as he confessed the sins of the children of Israel in Ezra 9:6, "O my God, I am ashamed and blush to lift up my face to thee, my God: for our iniquities are increased over our head, and our trespass is grown up unto the heavens." In the difficult journey of life, God's precepts have been songs to lift his soul and to ease the fears of night.

The life of a faithful child of God is a journey, a pilgrimage that is filled with many peaks and valleys. God does not promise that all difficulties will be removed from our paths. He does promise, however, that in the most difficult of times, comfort can be found in the truths His Word contains. When others are making fun of us for trying to live a righteous life, we can take comfort from the fact that Jesus was mocked as well. Remember that the Lord said, "The disciple is not above his master, nor the servant above his lord. It is enough for the disciple that he be as his master, and the servant as his lord" (Matt. 10:24-25). When we are filled with consternation over the sinful lives of others and the horrible fate that awaits them, we can be comforted by the fact that even Jesus "committed himself to him that judgeth righteously" (1 Pet. 2:23). When we find ourselves confronted by sickness, pain, or surpassing sorrow, we can take comfort from knowing that God's grace is sufficient to get us through (2 Cor. 12:9). So, sing the song of God's great Word upon the mountaintops and in the valleys. It will get us through.

September 17

Psalm 119 (8): A Companion of the Faithful

Heth

Thou art my portion, O Lord: I have said that I would keep thy words. I intreated thy favor with my whole heart: be merciful unto me according to thy word. I thought on my ways, and turned my feet unto thy testimonies. I made haste, and delayed not to keep thy commandments. The bands of the wicked have robbed me: but I have not forgotten thy law. At midnight I will rise to give thanks unto thee because of thy righteous judgments. I am a companion of all them that fear thee, and of them that keep thy precepts. The earth, O Lord, is full of thy mercy: teach me thy statutes."

A recurring emphasis of Psalm 119 is the closeness of God and His Word. Indeed, some would even say that God cannot be separated from His Word. If considered from that standpoint, then when the psalmist says that God is his portion, the proof that he offers is that he keeps His Word. It is a personal type of thing. The psalmist writes that God is "his portion," that he had said that "he" would keep His words. God's favor was something that the psalmist would personally seek, and that means there would be times of introspection when he would need to adjust his conduct that his feet might walk in God's appointed paths. Even times of trials and persecutions would not cause him to forget who he was and Whom he followed. At all times, even in the night seasons, he would be thankful unto God. All who reverence God keep His precepts and are all companions one of another.

It has been said that Martin Luther encouraged all Christians to respond to temptation by saying, "I am a Christian." Can we not also answer every temptation with the words and determination of "Thou art my portion, O Lord: I have said that I would keep thy words?" In this firm resolve a faithful Christian is never alone. We have countless brothers and sisters in Christ who are our companions in the faith. It calls to mind an event that took place in the life of Jesus when He was twelve years old. With a large company of people, the Lord and His family went to the city of Jerusalem for the feast of the Passover. Those going to the same place traveled together, undoubtedly enjoying the company and encouragement of each other. All faithful Christians are traveling together, companions in reverence for God and obedience to His Word. Where are we going? We are going to heaven, a prepared place for saved people. We are going home.

September 18

Psalm 119 (9): It Is Good That I Have Been Afflicted

Teth

Thou hast dealt well with thy servant, O Lord, according unto thy word. Teach me good judgment and knowledge: for I have believed thy commandments. Before I was afflicted I went astray: but now have I kept thy word. Thou art good, and doest good; teach me thy statutes. The proud have forged a lie against me: but I will keep thy precept with my whole heart. Their heart is as fat as grease; but I delight in thy law. It is good for me that I have been afflicted; that I might learn thy statutes. The law of thy mouth is better unto me than thousands of gold and silver.

It seems as though the psalmist is summarizing his life up to this point by acknowledging that God had dealt well with him. Even the difficult times of his life, the times of affliction, served to his good. There are excellent uses that can be made of adversities, and the psalmist speaks to this. By difficulties he was made stronger. Often when life is going along very well, with few obstacles in our path and prosperity is ours, it is easy to drift in small increments away from God. Adversity helps us to remember just how badly we need the Lord. Let the wicked attack. Adversity had made him strong and had taught the psalmist that no precious thing this world has to offer can compare with the value of the law of God.

What use will we make of afflictions and adversity? Will we use them as stairs that take us higher and closer to God, or will we allow them to serve as a staircase upon which we stumble? The Hebrew writer tells us in Hebrews 12:6, "For whom the Lord loveth he chasteneth, and scourgeth every son whom he receiveth." In verse 11 he wrote, "Now no chastening for the present seemeth to be joyous, but grievous: nevertheless afterward it yieldeth the peaceable fruit of righteousness unto them which are exercised thereby."

Thomas Washbourne, 1606-1687, wrote the following poem that is quoted by C.H. Spurgeon in *The Treasury of David*, VI: 172:

Affliction Brings Man Home

Man like a silly sheep doth often stray,
Not knowing of his way,
Blind deserts and the wilderness of sin
He daily travels in;
There's nothing will reduce him sooner than
Afflictions to his pen.
He wanders in the sunshine, but in rain
And stormy weather hastens home again.

Thou, the great Shepherd of my soul, O keep
Me, my unworthy sheep
From gadding: or if fair means will not do it,
Let foul, then, bring me to it.

Rather then I should perish in my error,
Lord bring me back with terror;
Better I be chastised with thy rod
And Shepherd's staff, than stray from thee, my God.

Though for the present stripes do grieve me sore,
At last they profit more,
And make me to observe thy word, which I
Neglected formerly;
Let me come home rather by weeping cross
Than still be at a loss.
For health I'd rather take a bitter pill,
Than eating sweet-meats to be always ill.

September 19

Psalm 119 (10): Being an Example

Yod

Thy hands have made me and fashioned me: give me understanding, that I may learn thy commandments. They that fear thee will be glad when they see me; because I have hoped in thy word. I know, O Lord, that thy judgments are right, and that thou in faithfulness hast afflicted me. Let, I pray thee, thy merciful kindness be for my comfort, according to thy word unto thy servant. Let thy tender mercies come unto me, that I may live: for thy law is my delight. Let the proud be ashamed; for they dealt perversely with me without a cause: but I will meditate in thy precepts. Let those that fear thee turn unto me, and those that have known thy testimonies. Let my heart be sound in thy statutes; that I be not ashamed.

What a beautiful stanza this is! As God's creation, the psalmist prays that God would give him understanding that he might know completely his ways, and in living in them, be an example to all the believers. He knows that every judgment of God is according to His righteousness and that even in times of affliction, he has come to know and appreciate the sustaining power of God's Word. Nevertheless, he prays for God's continued mercy and kindness that he might maintain the exemplary life of one who walks in God's way. Let his God-fearing life be a source of confusion and turmoil for those who speak evil of him falsely, but at the same time, let it draw all others of like-minded faith to him.

The Christian is called upon to lead a life of example, one that will cause others to want to live the same type of life and to enjoy the same wonderful blessings. In the Sermon on the Mount, Jesus said, "Let your light so shine before men, that they may see your good works, and glorify your Father which is in heaven" (Matt. 5:16). Timothy was exhorted to be an example to all the believers in word, in his manner of life, in love, spirit, faith, and purity (1 Tim. 4:12). Believers strengthen each other by the lives that they live, but we can also attract others by our example. Peter wrote about husbands who, refusing to be moved by the Word, can be won by the example of their wives. In 1 Peter 3:1-2 we find, "In the same way, you wives, be submissive to your own husbands so that even if any of them are disobedient to the word, they may be won without a word by the behavior of their wives, as they observe your chaste and respectful behavior." There is the incredible power of the example that is given by those who walk in the light of God's Word.

September 20

Psalm 119 (11): In the Depths

Kaph

My soul fainteth for thy salvation: but I hope in thy word. Mine eyes fail for thy word, saying, When wilt thou comfort me? For I am become like a bottle in the smoke; yet do I not forget thy statutes. How many are the days of thy servant? When wilt thou execute judgment on them that persecute me? The proud have digged pits for me, which are not after thy law. All thy commandments are faithful: they persecute me wrongfully; help thou me. They had almost consumed me upon earth; but I forsook not thy precepts. Quicken me after thy loving kindness; so shall I keep the testimony of thy mouth.

C.H. Spurgeon called this part of Psalm 119, "...the midnight of the psalm, and very dark and black it is." But he also went on to say, "Stars, however, shine out, and the last verse gives promise of the dawn." The psalmist is writing out of the depths. It is apparent that his enemies have persecuted him and attacked him wrongfully, doing so because of his determination to walk according to God's way. Even though he has remained firm in his resolve, his enemies have succeeded in dragging his spirits down. He describes himself as being like "a bottle in the smoke." The idea is that of a wineskin hanging over a fireplace that becomes shriveled and discolored by the heat and the smoke. That is quite a graphic illustration. Yet he did not give up. Even in his difficulties and even in the depths of despair, he remained faithful to God's testimonies. He knew that in continuing to glorify God by his obedience, God would preserve his life and keep him in His care.

Have you ever been "down in the depths"? Have you ever spent a number of sleepless nights, perhaps even what could be called "the midnight of your life," tossing and turning because of the way others have treated you? And why have they treated you so wrongfully? Because you were determined to be obedient to God. We can take solace from the fact that there have been many great men of God who have found themselves "in the depths" because of the way they were treated by the ungodly. In each case they were mistreated because of their faithfulness to God. Consider Elijah, who after his great stand for God on Mount Carmel, had his life threatened by Jezebel. In 1 Kings 19:10 we find him in a cave, having fled for his life. God asked him, "What doest thou here, Elijah?" His answer was, "I have been very jealous for the Lord God of hosts: for the children of Israel have forsaken thy covenant, thrown down thine altars, and slain thy prophets with the sword; and I, even I only, am left; and they seek my life, to take it away." He wasn't the only one left, and neither are we. Later, Elijah was taken up by a whirlwind into heaven. I believe that an occasional trip to the depths can make us appreciate the lifting power of God's Word even more. The time will come when the faithful servants of God will also go to heaven. "For the Lord himself shall descend from heaven with a shout, with the voice of the archangel, and with the trump of God: and the dead in Christ shall rise first: then we which are alive and remain shall be caught up together with them in the clouds, to meet the Lord in the air: and so shall we ever be with the Lord" (1 Thess. 4:16-17).

Psalm 119 (12): Unchangeable and Constant

Lamed

Forever, O Lord, thy word is settled in heaven. Thy faithfulness is unto all generations: thou hast established the earth, and it abideth. They continue this day according to thine ordinances: for all are thy servants. Unless thy law had been my delight, I should then have perished in mine affliction. I will never forget thy precepts: for with them thou hast quickened me. I am thine, save me; for I have sought thy precepts. The wicked have waited for me to destroy me; but I will consider thy testimonies. I have seen an end of all perfection: but thy commandment is exceeding broad.

The Word of God is unchangeable and unaffected by the continued passage of time. The psalmist views the permanence of the world that God created and perceives it as an indication of the permanent faithfulness of God's precepts. It is man's responsibility to continue faithfully in obedience to God's ordinances, for all have been created to be His servants. Having something as unchangeable and constant as the Word of God enabled the psalmist to remain constant himself in the ups and downs of life. He knows from his experience of life that all earthly "perfection" has an end; it will reach its limits and regress. However, there are no limits to God's Word. It will endure forever and be forever true.

Man's knowledge is constantly changing. The textbooks that were used in science classes when I was in school are no longer being used. Knowledge has increased and previously held "scientific facts" or "theories" have been proven to be wrong. I remember the days of black and white television with no remote controls. It seems that everything changes. What was true yesterday in the world may not be true tomorrow. Look at a map or globe from thirty years ago. There are so many different countries, boundaries have changed, and governments have both risen and fallen. What can we hold on to? The answer is simple—the immutable Word of God. Jesus said in Matthew 24:35, "Heaven and earth shall pass away, but my words shall not pass away." The religions of man seem to be in a constant state of flux, with new doctrines and ideas being set forth all the time. God's Word says the same thing now as it did when it was first revealed. Man's beliefs have changed, man's dogmas have changed, and man has sought to make religion in his own image. God's Word has not and will not change. What else do you know that is like that?

Psalm 119 (13): "O How I Love Thy Law"

Mem

O how love I thy law! It is my meditation all the day. Thou through thy commandments hast made me wiser than mine enemies: for they are ever with me. I have more understanding than all my teachers: for thy testimonies are my meditation. I understand more than the ancients, because I keep thy precepts. I have refrained my feet from every evil way, that I might keep thy word. I have not departed from thy judgments: for thou hast taught me. How sweet are thy words unto my taste! Yea, sweeter than honey to my mouth! Through thy precepts I get understanding: therefore I hate every false way.

The affection and the enthusiasm that the psalmist had for the Word of God and what it has and can continue to do for him is made abundantly clear in this stanza of the psalm. He occupies himself with the study of that Word. In so doing, he has been made wiser than his enemies, superior in understanding to His teachers, and deeper in intelligence than the elders of the people. The fact that he lives his life refraining from evil and ungodliness springs from his abiding desire to follow and obey God's judgments. It is the Word of God that has taught him everything that he needs to walk faithfully. As James E. Smith said, "The Lord himself was his teacher, not men. The psalmist loved each one of God's words, individually and together. They were like the sweetest substance available as he fed on them day by day. His complete absorption of the precepts of God gave him the ability to discern between good and evil, right and wrong, and therefore he came to love all that was good and to hate every false way.

When Jesus was being tempted in the wilderness in Matthew 4, Satan said to Him in verse 3, "If thou be the Son of God, command that theses stones be made bread." The answer that Jesus gave in verse 4 coincides so beautiful with the entire sentiment of Psalm 119:97-104. Jesus said, "Man shall not live by bread alone, but by every word that proceedeth out of the mouth of God." Without the Word of God, life is empty and has no real meaning. In our topsy-turvy world, many do not have an appreciation for what the Word of God is, or what it can do. All the secular education in the world may make a man more intelligent and give him great knowledge of things of relative importance—but it will never make him wise. God's Word is where true wisdom is to be found. It will teach us not only what is right and what is wrong and give us the ability to recognize the difference—it will give us the wisdom to live according to that discernment. "All things that pertain to life and godliness" are found within its pages and it "thoroughly furnishes unto all good works" (2 Pet. 1:3, 2 Tim. 3:17).

September 23

Psalm 119 (14): Determination

Nun

Thy word is a lamp unto me feet, and a light unto my path. I have sworn, and I will perform it, that I will keep thy righteous judgments. I am afflicted very much, quicken me, O Lord, according unto thy word. Accept, I beseech thee, the freewill offerings of my mouth, O Lord, and teach me thy judgments. My soul is continually in my hand: yet do I not forget thy law. The wicked have laid a snare for me: yet I erred not from thy precepts. Thy testimonies have I taken as an heritage forever: for they are the rejoicing of my heart. I have inclined mine heart to perform thy statutes always, even unto the end.

The psalmist compares God's Word to a light by which he guides his life and he has sworn with an oath his determination to follow it. In afflictions, he is determined to continue according to the Word of the Lord. Even in times when the psalmist felt that his very life was in danger, as expressed by "my soul is continually in my hand" or "my life is continually in my hand" he would not allow himself to act in a manner contrary to what he knew God's law to be. No, the psalmist had chosen the testimonies of God as his heritage, his portion, his estate, and he would cling to them no matter what. As a man rejoices in the possession of his earthly, physical inheritance, the psalmist found the Word of the Lord to be the real cause for rejoicing. He was determined to perform the statutes of God always—"even unto the end."

What about us? How do we view the Word of the Lord? The psalmist described it as "a lamp unto my feet, and a light unto my path." In the time of the writing of the psalm, and still today in parts of the world, the roads were poorly lighted (if at all) and rough and uneven. Consequently there was the danger of falling, twisting an ankle, or hurting one's self in some other way. Lamps were used to enable the traveler to see clearly. They were actually held down by the feet, close to the ground, giving light so that each step could be carefully placed. That is what the light of the Word of God does for us. If we will allow it to do so, it will illuminate every step in our pilgrimage on earth. Every false way will have the light of truth cast upon it and none will be able to hide. It is our responsibility to determine that we will follow it, that we will perform it, that we will keep it and not forget its precepts. It is our portion, our heritage, and in it we can rejoice. This is something to which all faithful children of God must set our hearts. We must be determined that we will live by God's statutes all the days of our lives—even unto the end.

September 24

Psalm 119 (15): Hating the Evil Way

Samech

I hate vain thoughts: but thy law do I love. Thou art my hiding place and my shield: I hope in thy word. Depart from me, ye evildoers: for I will keep the commandments of my God. Uphold me according unto thy word, that I may live: and let me not be ashamed of my hope. Hold thou me up, and I shall be safe: and I will have respect unto thy statutes continually. Thou hast trodden down all them that err from thy statutes: for their deceit is falsehood. Thou puttest away all the wicked of the earth like dross: my flesh trembleth for fear of thee: and I am afraid of thy judgments.

Others frequently translate "vain thoughts" as "double-minded" and that sheds light on the meaning of the first verse of this stanza. One cannot be a follower of God and a follower of Satan. Perhaps the psalmist has in mind those who practiced a form of worship according to the Law but also gave themselves over to a practice of certain aspects of heathenism and idolatry. Such must not be tolerated and certainly not joined with in their ungodliness. The psalmist recognizes his need of God and His strength to enable him to resist the false ways of the ungodly, and he prays that he would not be put to shame by the failure of the hope to which he clings. "The acts of judgment against the wicked and the laws in accordance with which they are punished cause the psalmist to tremble with fear" (James C. Smith, *The Wisdom Literature & Psalms*, 415).

An awful lot of people who call themselves Christians want to live their lives with one foot in the church and one foot in the world. It cannot be done. It is as the Lord said in Matthew 6:24, "No man can serve two masters: for either he will hate the one, and love the other; or else he will hold to the one, and despise the other. Ye cannot serve God and mammon." Just as was the case with the psalmist, that which will enable us truly and fully to serve the Master is our study of, use of, and practice of the Word of God. How do we come to know what is right and what is wrong? How do we learn truly to tell the difference and to have the courage to act on that knowledge? The answer is through the Word of God. I am reminded of what the Hebrew writer wrote in Hebrews 5:12-14, "For when for the time ye ought to be teachers, ye have need that one teach you again which be the first principles of the oracles of God: and are become such as have need of milk, and not of strong meat. For everyone that useth milk is unskillful in the word of righteousness: for he is a babe. But strong meat belongeth to them that are of full age, even those who by reason of use have their senses exercised to discern both good and evil." Surely as our knowledge increases, so too does our understanding of the reward that awaits the faithful child of God, as well as our understanding of the judgments of God that await the ungodly. That knowledge can also, and should, act as further motivation to faithfulness.

September 25

Psalm 119 (16): Deliver Me

Ayin

I have done judgment and justice: leave me not to mine oppressors. Be surety for thy servant for good: let not the proud oppress me. Mine eyes fail for thy salvation, and for the word of thy righteousness. Deal with thy servants according unto thy mercy, and teach me thy statutes. I am thy servant; give me understanding, that I may know thy testimonies. It is time for thee, Lord, to work: for they have made void thy law. Therefore I love thy commandments above gold; yea, above fine gold. Therefore I esteem all thy precepts concerning all things to be right; and I hate every false way.

The psalmist knew that he was trying to the best of his ability to walk according to God's statutes and precepts. Therefore, he pleads with God to "be surety," to be his Defender, to be his Champion and to represent him before his enemies. The expression "mine eyes fail for thy salvation," indicate how eagerly and longingly the psalmist watched and waited for the deliverance that God had promised. Once again, that longing brings him back to the most basic request, "teach me thy statutes." It is apparent that the vast multitude pay little attention to God's testimonies and walk according to their own desires. The ungodliness of the masses causes him to urge God to act, obviously implying some act of righteous judgment against those who view as nothing the law of God. But the interesting thing is, the less regard men have for God's commandments, the more value the psalmist places upon it. There is nothing of an earthly nature that he holds above the Word of God, and that makes him turn his face from every false way.

There are times in the lives of all faithful children of God, perhaps in those quiet moments spent alone with God in prayer, when we feel compelled to say, "Lord, I am doing the best I can. I need You to stand between me and those who make fun, who persecute and belittle. Lord, why don't You just come back and reward those who have followed and loved You, and punish those who have not?" We can rest assured that the Lord will return according to God's timetable, but He has given us His word to deliver us even now. There is no circumstance, no situation of any nature that can arise, from which we cannot find deliverance in God's Word. Oh, the circumstance may not change, but through the Word we can find the strength to rise above it. By way of example, when Paul and Silas were in the Philippian prison, with their feet made fast in the stocks, they were singing praises to God at midnight. They were severely oppressed, but they were delivered long before the earthquake struck and broke their bonds. Since the Word contains "all things that pertain to life and godliness" (2 Pet. 1:3), there is nothing to which it cannot supply the answer and from which it cannot deliver. Take heart!

Psalm 119 (17): God's Word Is Food and Light to the Faithful

Pe

Thy testimonies are wonderful: therefore doth my soul keep them. The entrance of thy words giveth light; it giveth understanding unto the simple. I opened my mouth, and panted: for I longed for thy commandments. Look thou upon me, and be merciful unto me, as thou usest to do unto those that love thy name. Order my steps in thy word: and let not any iniquity have dominion over me. Deliver me from the oppression of man: so will I keep thy precepts. Make thy face to shine upon thy servant; and teach me thy statutes. Rivers of waters run down mine eyes, because they keep not thy law.

The "testimonies of God" are those things to which God gives testimony that they are good and righteous, including all of His commands, precepts, statutes and such like contained within His Word. As soon as man allows them to enter into his soul, they immediately illuminate his way, just as a light held down at the level of one's feet. The more the psalmist came to know of God's commandments, the more he wanted them. The statutes of God became his sustenance; they became his food for the spirit. He calls upon God's mercy and speaks of his response to it: ordering his steps according to God's Word, keeping His precepts. The more he feeds upon God's Word and feels the light of God's presence through it, the more sorrow the psalmist feels for those who do not know the benefit of the food and light provided by God's Word. His sentiment is not one of self-righteous superiority, but that of Jeremiah who felt sorrow because of the ultimate end of those who do not keep God's law.

As I consider this stanza of the beautiful 119th Psalm, I am reminded of a wonderful prophecy concerning Jesus found in Isaiah 9:6. The passage says, "For unto us a child is born, unto us a son is given: and the government shall be upon his shoulder: and his name shall be called Wonderful, Counselor, The mighty God, The everlasting Father, the Prince of Peace." In the beginning of John's gospel, the "Wonderful" Jesus is called "The Word," the *Logos*, the personal manifestation of God on earth. Everything about Him is wonderful. He is our spiritual food. In John 6:35 Jesus said, "I am the bread of life: he that cometh to me shall never hunger: and he that believeth on me shall never thirst." In verse 51 the Lord stated, "I am the living bread which came down from heaven: if any man eat of this bread, he shall live for ever: and the bread that I will give is my flesh, which I will give for the life of the world." Jesus was calling upon all to avail themselves of this spiritual food. He was calling upon all to accept, assimilate, yes, even devour Jesus and all He represents and teaches; for He is the very source of spiritual life. In John 9:5 Jesus said, "As long as I am in the world, I am the light of the world." It is so simple. If we do not wish to walk in darkness, if we desire to be able to see clearly the way of righteousness that leads to heaven, follow Jesus.

September 27

Psalm 119 (18): Help Me to Know Purity

Tsadhe

Righteous art thou, O Lord, and upright are thy judgments. Thy testimonies that thou hast commanded are righteous and very faithful. My zeal hath consumed me, because mine enemies have forgotten thy words. Thy word is very pure: therefore thy servant loveth it. I am small and despised: yet do not I forget thy precepts. Thy righteousness is an everlasting righteousness, and thy law is the truth. Trouble and anguish have taken hold on me: yet thy commandments are my delights. The righteousness of thy testimonies is everlasting: give me understanding, and I shall live.

God is fundamentally righteous, and that righteousness is manifested in His word. Every precept, every statute, every commandment of God "proceeds from a disposition towards and a mode of dealing with men which is strictly determined by His holiness, and beyond measure faithfully and honestly designs the well-being of man" (Keil and Delitzsch, *Commentaries on the Old Testament, Psalms*, III: 260). The psalmist is so filled with love for God's Word that when he sees others rejecting it he is filled with emotion. *What else is as pure as God's Word?* No matter what happens, God's Word stands undefiled and solid, like metal purified in a crucible. Come difficulties and trouble into his life, the psalmist (small and insignificant as he is) will delight in the Word and live in that understanding.

In John 2:14-17 we find an account of Jesus cleansing the temple at Jerusalem very early in His public ministry. Filled with righteous indignation at the abuse of His Father's house, Jesus fashioned a whip out of several small cords and unleashed His divine wrath upon those who prostituted God's house. He drove out the sheep and the oxen and those who tended them. He turned over the tables of the moneychangers, spilling their coins onto the floor of the Court of the Gentiles. He told those who sold doves to remove them from the temple and with divine authority and justification he said, "Make not my Father's house a house of merchandise." At that time, His disciples remembered a very similar statement to the one we saw in Psalm 119:139, "For the zeal of thine house hath eaten me up; and the reproaches of them that reproached thee are fallen upon me" (Ps. 69:9). How can we not be moved when we see the purity of God's Word and the religion set forth therein sullied and corrupted by man? No one has the right to pick and choose those parts of God's revealed Word that they will obey and cast aside those that they will not. No one has the right to change even one word of God's will and ruin its purity. Let us have the courage to stand like Jesus when we see that which is good and pure and holy defiled by those who feign righteousness but will not submit themselves to the righteousness of God.

September 28

Psalm 119 (19): To Thee I Cry

Qoph

I cried with my whole heart; hear me, O Lord: I will keep thy statutes. I cried unto thee; save me, and I shall keep thy testimonies. I prevented the dawning of the morning, and cried: I hoped in thy word. Mine eyes prevent the night watches, that I might meditate in thy word. Hear my voice according unto thy lovingkindness: O Lord, quicken me according to thy judgment. They draw nigh that follow after mischief: they are far from thy law. Thou art near, O Lord; and all thy commandments are truth. Concerning thy testimonies, I have known of old that thou hast found them for ever.

I find this to be the stanza of prayer. Note "how" the psalmist prayed. He "cried with his whole heart." There is in the word "cried" the sense of sincerity or earnestness, there is a certain plaintive quality to it, an utter giving of one's self in petition to God. He meets the morning with prayer and even through the night watches, his mind and heart are upon God. He pleads for God to hear him in his supplications according to His lovingkindness and the principles set forth in His word. He prays for help when those who do not love God's way, but rather love ungodliness, draw near; and he is confident of God's answer. He will be there. The psalmist knows that he could have this confidence because God's testimonies were of old and established forever.

Oh, that we all could have the attitude of constant prayer as was manifested by the psalmist. Not only that, but the same confidence that God will hear. Paul wrote to the Thessalonians in 1 Thessalonians 5:17, exhorting them to "pray without ceasing." Faithful children of God are urged to have the same prayerful attitude as the psalmist. We have a direct line to God, and we know that He hears our prayers. There is no static on the line and there will be no "dropped calls" as we seek to serve Him faithfully. Jesus spoke to the earnestness, the sincerity, and the confidence that should characterize our prayers in Mark 11:24-25 when He said, "Therefore I say unto you, what things soever ye desire, when ye pray, believe that ye receive them, and ye shall have them. And when ye stand praying, forgive, if ye have ought against any: that your Father also which is in heaven may forgive you your trespasses." Child of God, remember that the "effectual fervent prayer of a righteous man availeth much" (Jas. 5:16). Call to Him at any time. He will hear.

September 29

Psalm 119 (20): Consider Thou Me

Resh

Consider mine affliction, and deliver me: for I do not forget thy law. Plead my cause, and deliver me: quicken me according to thy word. Salvation is far from the wicked: for they seek not thy statutes. Great are thy tender mercies, O Lord: quicken me according to thy judgments. Many are my persecutors and mine enemies; yet do I not decline from thy testimonies. I beheld the transgressors, and was grieved; because they kept not thy word. Consider how I love thy precepts: quicken me, O Lord, according to thy lovingkindness. Thy word is true from the beginning: and every one of thy righteous judgments endureth for ever.

There is at the beginning of this stanza an appeal very similar to the presentation of a legal case. The request is that God consider his affliction, much as God had considered the affliction of His children in Egypt so many years before. There was much to be said on the side of the psalmist, for he asks God in His consideration to remember how he had lived. He had not forgotten the law of God. He had not declined from the testimonies of the Lord and he had lived by His precepts. On the other hand, he found himself oppressed by the wicked, by those who did not keep, or even seek, God's statutes. He asked God to "consider the evidence" and in His lovingkindness and mercy recognize and reward him for the love he had for the divine precepts and his continued determination to walk in them. If he were to add up all of God's precepts, statutes, commandments, laws, and testimonies, the combined total and common denominator of them all would be truth.

The time will come when we will all stand before the Great Judge and there will be a final "consideration" of us all. Paul wrote of this time in 2 Corinthians 5:10, "For we must all appear before the judgment seat of Christ: that every one may receive the things done in his body, according to that he hath done, whether it be good or bad." Every single one of us would be lost if it were not for the lovingkindness and tender mercies of God. In this life it is our responsibility to live in obedience to the commands of God. The Hebrew writer tells us in Hebrews 5:8-9, "Though he were a Son, yet learned he obedience by the things which he suffered; and being made perfect, he became the author of eternal salvation unto all them that obey him." No true believer of God's Word can minimize the importance of obedience. Without it we are lost. But does this mean that at the judgment seat of Christ we should proudly stand and ask Him to consider how very good we have been and to give us our just reward since we have earned our salvation? No, beloved, no! Instead, remember the words of Jesus in Luke 17:7-10 and embrace and live by the attitude there called for:

> But which of you, having a servant plowing or feeding cattle, will say unto him by and by, when he is come from the field, Go and sit down to meat? And will not rather say unto him, Make ready wherewith I may sup, and gird thyself, and serve me, till I have eaten and drunken; and afterward thou shalt eat and drink? Doth he thank that servant because he did the things that were commanded of him? I trow not. So likewise ye, when ye shall have done all those things which are commanded you, say, we are unprofitable servants: we have done that which was our duty to do.

Psalm 119 (21): Seven Times a Day Do I Praise Thee

Shin

Princes have persecuted me without a cause: but my heart standeth in awe of thy word. I rejoice at thy word, as one that findeth great spoil. I hate and abhor lying: but thy law do I love. Seven times a day do I praise thee because of thy righteous judgments. Great peace have they which love thy law: and nothing shall offend them. Lord, I have hoped for thy salvation, and done thy commandments. My soul hath kept thy testimonies: and I love them exceedingly. I have kept thy precepts and thy testimonies: for all my ways are before thee.

The psalmist devotes this stanza to praising God and extolling the incredible virtues of His matchless Word. There appears in this stanza no requests or petitions. Even in the midst of persecution by those of influence and position, God's Word was still that which filled his heart, gave him joy like someone who has found great treasure, and was the basis of his confidence and hope. "Seven times a day do I praise thee." He does not praise God in the morning and evening alone. In fact, he does not praise God even three times a day. No, his praise goes up to God seven times a day. The significance of that statement is that he repeatedly, ever and consistently, offers praise to God. In other places seven is viewed as the complete number—perhaps that is how it is to be viewed here. His complete life was devoted to the praise of God. The psalmist speaks of what comes from immersing oneself in the Word of God, great peace and the protection from stumbling. What an interesting way to end this stanza. The psalmist had endeavored to live his life according to God's precepts and testimonies, and he appeals to God as the omniscient and omnipresent One who knew each of his steps.

When a child of God gives himself wholeheartedly to a study of God's Word, there will be times when his spirit will be filled with so much wonder and joy that he cannot help but burst forth in praise to God. The statement made in Acts 2:46-47 so aptly describes what can, and should, be the daily attitude of the faithful: "And they, continuing daily with one accord in the temple, and breaking bread from house to house, did eat their meat with gladness and singleness of heart, praising God, and having favor with all the people." Praising God—that is what the life of a Christian is. It is a life spent in obedience to His Word, a life devoted to His service and to His glory and praise, not ours. I am reminded of the words of the twenty-four elders seen in John's vision around the throne of God in Revelation 4:11. Let the faithful join voices with them in saying, "Thou art worthy, O Lord, to receive glory and honor and power: for thou hast created all things, and for thy pleasure they are and were created."

October 1

Psalm 119 (22): The Lost Sheep and the Shepherd

Taw

Let my cry come near before thee, O Lord: give me understanding according to thy word. Let my supplication come before thee: deliver me according to thy word. My lips shall utter praise, when thou hast taught me thy statutes. My tongue shall speak of thy word: for all thy commandments are righteousness. Let thine hand help me; for I have chosen thy precepts. I have longed for thy salvation, O Lord; and thy law is my delight. Let my soul live, and it shall praise thee; and let thy judgments help me. I have gone astray like a lost sheep; seek thy servant; for I do not forget thy commandments.

The glorious 119th psalm comes to a close with petitions of great fervor and urgency. The psalmist prays for greater understanding and the deliverance from the oppression and persecution that he has so frequently mentioned in this psalm. He writes of using his tongue to praise God and to teach others of His Word, because every word of God is righteous. One cannot help but be moved by the last four verses of the psalm. Help me, the psalmist writes, for I have made the choice to accept thy precepts. Deliver me, he cries, from the evil of the world in which he lived. If ever I should go astray like a lost sheep, seek me as the Great Shepherd.

The study of the 119th psalm serves to reinforce and strengthen our understanding of just how much we need God and the support He provides us in His Word. It causes us to join our voices with that of the psalmist as we offer petition after petition to our heavenly Father, for He alone is able to help us in every circumstance of life. We cannot make it successfully through this world without Him and the guidance He has given us through His revelation. We are told in 2 Timothy 3:16-17, "All Scripture is given by inspiration of God, and is profitable for doctrine, for reproof, for correction, for instruction in righteousness: that the man of God may be perfect, thoroughly furnished unto all good works." We need His helping hand. We need His deliverance from the evil of the world in which we live. I am reminded of the words of Jesus in His beautifully moving prayer found in John 17:15-16 where He prayed, "I pray not that thou shouldest take them out of the world, but that thou shouldest keep them from the evil. They are not of the world, even as I am not of the world." And finally, should we ever go astray, O that He, as the Great Shepherd, will bring us back. Jesus said, "I am the good shepherd: the good shepherd gives his life for the sheep" (John 10:11). Praise God!

October 2

The Rich Fool

And one of the company said unto him, Master, speak to my brother, that he divide the inheritance with me. And he said unto him, Man, who made me a judge or a divider over you? And he said unto them, Take heed, and beware of covetousness: for a man's life consisteth not in the abundance of the things which he possesseth. And he spake a parable unto them, saying, The ground of a certain rich man brought forth plentifully: and he thought within himself, saying, What shall I do, because I have no room where to bestow my fruits? And he said, This will I do: I will pull down my barns, and build greater; and there will I bestow all my fruits and my goods. And I will say to my soul, Soul, thou hast much goods laid up for many years; take thine ease, eat, drink, and be merry. But God said unto him, Thou fool, this night thy soul shall be required of thee: then whose shall those things be, which thou hast provided? So is he that layeth up treasure for himself, and is not rich toward God (Luke 12:13-21).

In this account, an individual asked the Lord Jesus to arbitrate a dispute he was apparently having with his brother. Under the Law of Moses, when an estate with two sons was being divided, the elder brother received two-thirds, while the younger brother received one-third (Deut. 21:17). We don't know if this was a younger brother complaining or an elder brother who had not received the two-thirds portion that was to be his according to the law. But which it was does not really matter because the Lord's response concerning covetousness shows that no matter who it was, covetousness was the root of the problem.

The request made of Jesus is indicative of an erroneous view concerning His mission and purpose. The people generally saw it as earthly—related to material things. In actuality, Jesus was seeking to turn people away from the earthly and physical and the lust for those things, to the spiritual and heavenly. He was not here to act as an arbiter or judge in secular matters.

Covetousness was what made one of those brothers say, "Divide" and it was covetousness that made the other say, "No." Covetousness is an unlawful desire for the property of another, a greedy and unlawful desire for anything. It is expressly called idolatry in Colossians 3:5. How silly it is to be so desirous of material goods when all the goods in the world cannot lengthen a man's life or preserve it in any way.

The parable itself shows that all the earthly possessions the man had did not save him. In fact, his earthly possessions led to his condemnation because of his attitude toward them. He wasn't dishonest. His wealth was apparently gained honestly from the fruitfulness of his lands. His abundance was so great that he did not have sufficient room to store his goods. So he tore down his old barns and built bigger ones and decided to take things easy, "Thou hast much goods laid up for many years; take thine ease, eat, drink, and be merry." The man was demonstrating selfishness and a perverted sense of what was important. Six times the man used the pronoun "I," and said nothing about what he could do with his goods to benefit anybody else. His love of his possessions is shown by the use of the personal pronoun "my" five times.

God called this man a fool. He was a fool because (a) he devoted all of his attention to gaining earthly goods, (b) he hoarded instead of giving and sharing, (c) he obviously did not think of his duty to God or his fellow man, (d) he thought he could feed his spirit with earthly things, (e) he evidently forgot, or never considered, that death ends earthly pleasures (no matter how abundant they might have been) and brings judgment.

What would happen to all of those goods that he had placed so much emphasis upon while on earth? They would just be left behind for other people to argue about. Perhaps even to have someone say, "Master, speak to my brother, that he divide the inheritance with me." Oh, that all could come to understand and to appreciate the transient nature of material wealth. As Paul wrote in 1 Timothy 6:7, "For we brought nothing into this world, and it is certain that we can carry nothing out."

October 3

Psalm 139: "Lord, I Believe"

Moments of quiet meditation can serve to give us greater understanding and insight into the awesome character of Jehovah. The meditations of a mature spiritual mind delve even more deeply, basking in the revealed truths and realizing that, "Such knowledge is too wonderful for me; it is too high, I cannot attain to it" (verse 6). Psalm 139 appears to contain the ruminations of a deeply reflective mind, and if I were to seek to describe the results of his contemplations in one word, it would be "comfort."

The Psalm begins with both a realization and a celebration of the glorious omniscience of God. What a comforting thought to this mature man of God to appreciate the fact that he is surrounded by God in every way and every day. Only Jehovah knows every act of our lives and every thought of our hearts, whether those thoughts find expression in our words or not. Even as thoughts and ideas begin to formulate in our minds, even before they have found full expression, they are known to God. The psalmist calls to mind, in his meditation, the action of winnowing of wheat and he sees in it God's scrutiny of his ways. Every life has good and bad in it; every life has wheat and chaff, and God knows it all. He is surrounded by God, both to help and restrain, and yet he has freedom to act as he desires with the knowledge that God knows. His omniscience is beyond his ability to grasp and leads the psalmist to consider the omnipresence of God.

"Where can I go from Thy Spirit? Or where can I flee from Thy presence?" (v. 7). I do not believe that the Psalmist is asking these questions out of a desire to flee and escape the presence of God. He is stating the natural flow of his meditations—as God knows all things, He is necessarily everywhere. What a comforting thought to the mature child of God! He is never alone. Who among us has not felt alone or spent a seemingly endless night in turmoil over some event in our lives waiting for the relief that the first ray of sunlight seems to offer? It is certain that David felt that way at several points in his life, perhaps the most memorable being referred to in the first verse of the 22nd Psalm, "My God, my God, why hast Thou forsaken me? Far from my deliverance are the words of my groaning." These words would be uttered by the Lord from the cross as they found their ultimate fulfillment. For David, the meditation of quieter, calmer moments helped him to understand that he was never alone. God is everywhere. He fills the heavens above and the realms below. Escape from His presence is not possible. Perhaps for the enemy of God such a thought is dreadful and terrible, but that is not the case for the child of God. He can know that wherever he might be, God's guiding hand is there to direct his steps and the right hand of His power to uphold him.

Even before the psalmist knew anything of this world, or anything of God, God knew him. As he developed within the womb of his mother, God was there. The words the psalmist uses to describe God's involvement with him in his earliest stages help us to understand how he could but burst forth with the words, "I will give thanks to Thee, for I am fearfully and wonderfully made; wonderful are Thy works, and my soul knows it very well" (v. 14). Consider the word "weave" in verse 13. Properly, it means to knit together and in a wonderful sense describes the weaving together of the bones, sinews, and all such things that make up a human being. In verse 16, one word is translated as "my unformed substance." It means that which is rolled or wrapped together, and what an intriguing way to describe an embryo! Everything is folded up, so to speak, and as the child develops within its mother, God oversees the unfolding of all of its parts. Indeed, God knows the beginning, the development, and the ending of all things. Does this preclude free will, or remove all matter of choice? No, it simply emphasizes once again the magnitude of the omniscience and omnipotence of God.

At what point could the psalmist exhaust the thoughts of God and thereby have no more reason to meditate upon them? They are inexhaustible and as numberless as the sand of the sea. As he closes his eyes at night his final thoughts are of God's ways. When he awakens in the morning he recognizes that he is in the presence of God and occupies himself with meditation of Him.

As the psalmist considers yet again the omniscience and omnipresence of God, it is apparent that the idea of the wicked comes to his mind. Surely as

God knows all things and is everywhere, His eye is upon the wicked as well. God knows their evil words and ungodly acts. He knows of their rebellion. In his contemplation of the wonders of God, the actions of the wicked are repulsive to the psalmist. He knows that judgment will come upon the wicked. In other psalms David had often expressed his need for God to sustain him in the face of persecution and abuse at the hands of those who did not love God. What a comfort to be assured in the quiet moments of meditation that both the godly and the ungodly will be properly rewarded.

And so, as this great psalm comes to a close, the psalmist does not seek to hide from the presence of God; he embraces it, calling upon God to search him and try him. He wants any wavering way pointed out to him, any course that might lead him away from God corrected. I believe it to be probable that he understands that living his life according to God's statutes now is to live in the everlasting way—the way to eternal life. His prayer is that God would lead him in that path.

"Blessed Are the Poor in Spirit"

The first of the Beatitudes that we find in the great Sermon on the Mount is, "Blessed are the poor in spirit: for theirs is the kingdom of heaven" (Matt. 5:3). When Jesus spoke of the poor, He was not speaking of what a person had or didn't have; He was describing what a person is, and there is an important difference.

In the New Testament, two words are used to express degrees of poverty. One word (*ptochos*) means total destitution, absolute poverty. The other word (*penichros*) means having only the bare necessities of life. We could perhaps describe this person as needy. The word our Lord used was the first. Jesus was saying, "Blessed are the spiritually destitute, those who are utterly helpless, for they are the ones who will gain access into the kingdom of heaven.

The point that Jesus was making is this: we must feel our total dependence upon God rather than upon ourselves. We must come to the place where we recognize our absolute spiritual helplessness apart from God. We must reach the point where we are willing to say, as Jeremiah did in Jeremiah 10:23, "O Lord, I know that the way of man is not in himself; it is not in man that walketh to direct his own steps." Those who are not willing to bow in humble submission to the will of God will never enjoy the blessings of citizenship in the kingdom of heaven. Entrance is gained by an attitude of humility and recognition of our own insufficiency. Such an attitude leads us to ask, "Lord, what would You have me to do?" and then being prepared and anxious to do it.

There is a beautiful old song entitled "Be With Me Lord," the first verse of which so aptly expresses the mindset of one who truly is "poor in spirit." It says, "Be with me, Lord, I cannot live without Thee. I dare not try to take one step alone. I cannot bear the loads of life unaided. I need Thy strength to lean myself upon."

October 5

"Blessed Are They That Mourn"

The second of the Beatitudes that Jesus presented in the Sermon on the Mount was "Blessed are they that mourn: for they shall be comforted." This is not a verse of consolation for those who have lost loved ones. Nor is it a proof-text for the "mourner's bench" idea of praying through for one's salvation. It is a reference to those who mourn because of sin. It is a reference to those who are mourning over the lost condition of their souls. This describes an individual with a broken heart, broken because of the realization of his sin. To such a one, comfort is promised. It is important to understand that comfort is promised because one who is truly mourning over sin will be moved to do whatever it takes to be freed from that condition.

All must come to realize and appreciate how awful, how truly horrendous, sin is and the terrible state of the person who is lost in it. When the great prophet, Isaiah, was called to his prophetic office, his first response was, "Woe is me! For I am undone; because I am a man of unclean lips, and I dwell in the midst of a people of unclean lips: for mine eyes have seen the King, the Lord of hosts." This did not mean that Isaiah had been particularly vulgar or blasphemous in speech. It meant that his conscience was keen and sensitive.

In Luke 5 we find the account of the Lord telling Peter to let down his net once more into the sea even though Peter had toiled all night and caught nothing. When he obeyed there was such a great number of fish that the net was breaking and not only Peter's boat but the boat of his partners as well were so completely filled with fish that they began to sink. Peter's response was to fall down at the Lord's knees and say, "Depart from me; for I am a sinful man, O Lord" (Luke 5:8). Even though Peter said, "Depart from me," separation from Jesus was the furthest thing from his mind. It is the extreme expression of humility as he declared himself utterly unworthy of remaining even another minute in the presence of the Lord. Peter's statement actually contained a fervent appeal that in spite of his human frailty and sinfulness, Jesus would permit him to remain in His presence.

That brings us back to the Beatitude. It calls to mind Isaiah's prophecy found in Isaiah 61:1-3. It says, "The Spirit of the Lord God is upon me; because the Lord hath anointed me to preach good tidings unto the meek; he hath sent me to bind up the broken hearted, to proclaim liberty to the captives, and the opening of the prison to them that are bound: to proclaim the acceptable year of the Lord, and the day of vengeance of our God; to comfort all that mourn; to appoint unto them that mourn in Zion, to give unto them beauty for ashes, the oil of joy for mourning, the garment of praise for the spirit of heaviness; that they might be called trees of righteousness, the planting of the Lord, that he might be glorified." Jesus fulfilled that prophecy by making salvation available through His death and resurrection. The second Beatitude is an announcement of that coming fulfillment.

In contrast to those who mourn over their soul's condition is the statement of Luke 6:2, "Woe unto you that are full! For ye shall hunger. Woe unto you that laugh now! For ye shall mourn and weep." These are the ones with no feeling of godly sorrow brought about by their sins. They may be delighting in the things of the world now, oblivious to their true spiritual condition, but eventually they will mourn and weep. For them there will be no comfort.

"Blessed Are the Meek"

The third of the Beatitudes that Jesus presented in the Sermon on the Mount was, "Blessed are the meek: for they shall inherit the earth." Meekness is so frequently misunderstood. The Greek word translated as "meek" (*praus*), describes a condition of the mind and heart. Vine writes, in his *Expository Dictionary of New Testament Words* (5), "In its use in Scripture, in which it has a fuller, deeper significance than in non-scriptural Greek writings, it consists not in a person's outward behavior only; nor yet in his relations to his fellow-men; as little in his mere natural disposition. Rather it is an inwrought grace of the soul; and the exercises of it are first and chiefly towards God. It is that temper of spirit in which we accept His dealings with us as good, and therefore without disputing or resisting."

Vine also writes of this quality of character being displayed in the face of men, even evil men, out of a sense that these, with the insults and injuries they may inflict, are used by God for chastening and purifying His elect.

I cannot think of an example of the attribute of meekness being exemplified in a person more completely than it was by Jesus. Remember that the Lord Himself said, "I am meek and lowly in heart" (Matt. 11:29), and then demonstrated it in the most difficult moments of His life. In the Garden of Gethsemane, with the cross less than a day away, Jesus prayed, "O my Father, if it be possible, let this cup pass from me: nevertheless not as I will, but as thou wilt" (Matt. 26:39). On the cross itself, Jesus cried out, "Father, forgive them; for they know not what they do" (Luke 23:34).

Look to Jesus to see meekness and to learn that it is not synonymous with weakness. Those who possess it do not show resentment or threaten when they are wronged. It is an evenness of spirit, level temperament. It is in many ways the opposite of bitterness and violence. Jesus said that those who had such a disposition would "inherit the earth."

Here again, many have misunderstood what Jesus meant. The "inheritance of the earth" is a proverbial expression used to suggest great and bountiful blessings. The Jews used the expression to denote any great blessing. Originally it meant the Land of Canaan, but soon came to refer to the totality of

God's blessings. It has absolutely nothing to do with the future inheritance of this old physical earth. This old earth will ultimately be destroyed. Peter tells us in 2 Peter 3:10, "But the day of the Lord will come as a thief in the night; in the which the heavens shall pass away with a great noise, and the elements shall melt with fervent heat, the earth also and the works that are therein shall be burned up."

When Jesus said, "Blessed are the meek, for they shall inherit the earth" He was saying that those who possessed the character attribute of meekness would be in His kingdom and would receive God's blessings here and now, as well as in the future heavenly land of promise. This would be true, for meekness would move the ones who truly possess it to gladly accept and obey the Lord's teachings without disputing or resisting.

"Blessed Are They Which Do Hunger and Thirst after Righteousness"

The fourth of the Beatitudes our Lord delivered in the Sermon on the Mount was, "Blessed are they which do hunger and thirst after righteousness: for they shall be filled" (Matt. 5:6). Perhaps one of the easiest ways to understand what Jesus was saying is to paraphrase His words, "Blessed are those who vehemently desire to be right before God, for they will obtain it."

Whenever I read this particular verse, my mind is drawn back to the time when our children were infants. I well remember the urgency with which they informed my wife and me that it was time to eat, and it did not matter when it was or where we were. I believe Peter used just such an occurrence to describe the type of desire that must characterize the approach of a Christian to the Word of God. In 1 Peter 2:2 he wrote, "As newborn babes, desire the sincere milk of the word, that ye may grow thereby."

What does it mean to "hunger and thirst after righteousness"? Let us first notice righteousness, a word that is used a couple of different ways in the New Testament. In Romans 1:16-17 we find, "For I am not ashamed of the gospel of Christ: for it is the power of God unto salvation to every one that believeth; to the Jew first, and also to the Greek. For therein is the righteousness of God revealed from faith to faith: as it is written, The just shall live by faith." Here we see it used to describe what can be called God's saving righteousness. The righteousness of God by faith is revealed in the gospel in order to produce saving faith in those who hear it.

Righteousness is also used to refer to personal righteousness. Matthew 5:20 is one such place. Jesus said, "For I say unto you, That except your righteousness shall exceed the righteousness of the scribes and Pharisees, ye shall in no case enter into the kingdom of heaven."

Hungering and thirsting indicates the degree of desire. My infant children, and now my little grandson, wanted nothing so badly as to eat when they were hungry. It was their most vehement desire. When the source of food was made available to them, they would latch on to it and not let go. Hungering and thirsting after righteousness shows that a person must want to come, he must desire it and need it as strongly as he does nourishment for the body. When that kind of attitude is manifested, the Lord promises that it will be filled.

Let's not make the mistake of thinking that this attitude is only meant to characterize the new Christian, or even perhaps the person who is sincerely searching for the truth. It must characterize a Christian from the moment he is born again until he goes home to be with the Lord. Without the proper nourishment, my children would not have grown to adulthood, and my son would not have been able to present me with my grandson. My grandson needs the proper nourishment in order to make me a great-grandpa some day. The one who quits hungering and thirsting for physical nourishment dies. It is no different in the spiritual realm.

October 8

"Blessed Are the Merciful"

The fifth Beatitude given in the Sermon on the Mount is, "Blessed are the merciful, for they shall obtain mercy." Jesus attached a great, and often overlooked, significance to mercy. So frequently the Lord would quote Hosea 6:6, "For I desire mercy, and not sacrifice; and the knowledge of God more than burnt offerings."

Many of the Jewish religious leaders in the time of the Lord were, for all intents and purposes, men without mercy. In His stirring rebuke of the scribes and Pharisees recorded in Matthew 23, in verse 23 we find Jesus saying, "Woe unto you, scribes and Pharisees, hypocrites! For ye pay tithe of mint and anise and cumin, and have omitted the weightier matters of the law, judgment, mercy, and faith: these ought ye to have done, and not to leave the other undone."

The Roman world in which Jesus lived was extremely unmerciful, particularly to slaves and children. Slaves were treated as no better than property and could be put to death at the whim of their owner. Unwanted children were simply discarded in the streets of the larger cities. Against this backdrop, Jesus taught the importance and transcendent value of mercy. One of the best explanations that I have found of this mercy that Jesus calls for in a citizen of His kingdom is, "To be merciful is to have the same attitude to men as God has, to think of men as God thinks of men, to feel for men as God feels for men, to act towards men as God acts toward them." (I do not remember the author of that statement. I truly wish that I did for it is wonderfully practical. g.l.) It is the opposite of self-centeredness and selfishness.

Jesus said that the merciful would obtain mercy. This is a basic principle. If we want God to be merciful to us, we must be merciful to others. James put it so simply in James 2:13, "For he shall have judgment without mercy, that hath showed no mercy; and mercy rejoiceth against judgment." Perhaps the next time we are tempted to look with disdain upon someone who's conduct has gotten him into trouble, we will remember that our conduct got us into trouble too. All of us have sinned, and were it not for the grace and mercy of God, we would have no hope.

October 9

"Blessed Are the Pure in Heart"

The sixth of the glorious Beatitudes from the Sermon on the Mount is, "Blessed are the pure in heart: for they shall see God." To be "pure in heart" is to have a singleness of mind, an honesty that has no hidden motives, no selfish interests. It is to be true and open in all things. The "heart" means "the inner man, the faculty and seat of intelligence." Consequently, Jesus was saying, "Blessed are those whose understanding is clear, whose spiritual vision is singular, and whose motive is honest; for they shall see God."

When I think of one who manifested this kind of purity of heart, I think of the good king, Josiah. In 2 Kings 22:1-2 this description is given of him, "Josiah was eight years old when he began to reign, and he reigned thirty and one years in Jerusalem. And his mother's name was Jedidah, the daughter of Adaiah of Boscath. And he did that which was right in the sight of the Lord, and walked in all the way of David his father, and *turned not aside to the right hand or to the left.*"

Consider also Jesus. What singleness of mind He had—an honesty that had no hidden motives and absolutely no selfish interests. Paul exhorts us in Philippians 2:5-8 to have the same singleness of mind and purpose. He wrote, "Let this mind be in you, which was also in Christ Jesus: who, being in the form of God, thought it not robbery to be equal with God: but made himself of no reputation, and took upon him the form of a servant, and was made in the likeness of men: and being found in fashion as a man, he humbled himself, and became obedient unto death, even the death of the cross." He had come to do His Father's will, and that is exactly what He did. In the carrying out of His mission, it was said of Jesus that no "guile was found in His mouth" (1 Pet. 2:22).

All that we know of God's will for us and all that we know of the Lord Jesus, we know through the revealed Word. Those who know and love the truth, who follow it with a singleness of mind and with no ulterior motive but a love for God and a desire to be eternally with Him—these are the pure in heart. They will "see God." Simply, they will have a relationship with God, both here on earth and ultimately in heaven.

October 10

"Blessed Are the Peacemakers"

The seventh of the Beatitudes that Jesus presented in the magnificent Sermon on the Mount is, "Blessed are the peacemakers: for they shall be called the children of God." I recall sitting at the feet of a Gospel preacher listening to him present a sermon about the Beatitudes. When he began to explain this particular one, he told of an event that took place when he was a child in grade school. In his Bible class they had been talking about the Beatitudes and the idea of a peacemaker just intrigued him. During recess one day at school, he saw two boys fighting on the playground. Thinking that this was his opportunity to be a "peacemaker," he stepped between the boys in an effort to stop their fighting. He said that both of the boys then turned their attention to him instead and gave him a good whipping. At that point he began to realize that perhaps he did not understand what Jesus meant.

Jesus was not talking about a diplomat who negotiates agreements between countries. He was not talking about a judge or arbiter who settles disputes and disagreements among men. He was talking about peacemakers who preach the gospel of peace and show the world the way back to God.

When a man sins he separates himself from God. In Isaiah 59:1-2 we read, "Behold, the Lord's hand is not shortened, that it cannot save; neither his ear heavy that it cannot hear: but your iniquities have separated between you and your God, and your sins have hid his face from you, that he will not hear." There is a need for a restoration to take place. That is the function of the peacemaker. He preaches and teaches the gospel of peace and thereby helps to reconcile the sinner to God. Paul wrote, "And that he might reconcile both unto God in one body by the cross, having slain the enmity thereby. And came and preached peace to you which were afar off, and to them that were nigh" (Eph. 2:16-17). Those who spread the good news of the peace that Jesus made available through His death are peacemakers—makers of peace between God and man.

Romans 10:14-1 states, "How then shall they call on him in whom they have not believed? And how shall they believe in him of whom they have not heard? And how shall they hear without a preacher? And how shall they preach, except they be sent? As it is written, How beautiful are the feet of them that preach the gospel of peace, and bring glad tidings of good things!" All who proclaim the gospel of peace, all who make known to others the possibility of reconciliation to God and the restoration of peace, are the peacemakers. This includes everyone who teaches someone the gospel of Christ. These shall be called "the children of God." Are you a peacemaker?

"Blessed Are They Which Are Persecuted for Righteousness' Sake"

The eighth and final Beatitude of the Sermon on the Mount given by the Lord is, "Blessed are they which are persecuted for righteousness' sake: for theirs is the kingdom of heaven" (Matt. 5:11). It is a foolish thing to believe that being a faithful child of God is always going to be an easy thing. In fact, the Bible assures us that that will not be the case. In 2 Timothy 3:12 Paul stated this truth so simply. He wrote, "Yea, and all that will live godly in Christ Jesus shall suffer persecution." All who commit to standing firmly upon the word of God and the spiritual and moral truths it contains will find themselves subject to abuse.

As we move on in Matthew 5 and look at verse 11, we find that the persecution will take many different forms. It will not always be some sort of corporal abuse. It can, and often does, take the form of verbal abuse. The verse says, "Blessed are ye, when men shall revile you, and persecute you, and shall say all manner of evil against you falsely, for my sake." Why should we expect it to be any different, when we consider the treatment our Lord received even as He hung on the cross? Having already endured the incredible physical abuse of the scourging and in the midst of the horrendous pain of the crucifixion itself, we find in Matthew 27:39-44:

> And they that passed by reviled Him, wagging their heads, and saying, Thou that destroyest the temple, and buildest it in three days, save thyself. If thou be the Son of God, come down from the cross. Likewise also the chief priests mocking him, with the scribes and elders, said, He saved others; himself he cannot save. If he be the King of Israel, let him now come down from the cross, and we will believe him. He trusted in God; let him deliver him now, if he will have him: for he said, I am the Son of God. The thieves also, which were crucified with him, cast the same in his teeth.

As we look at verse 12 of Matthew 5 we find, "Rejoice, and be exceeding glad: for great is your reward in heaven: for so persecuted they the prophets which were before you." Satan has always done his best to intimidate and silence the voice of those who proclaim the word of God. I am reminded of Jesus looking over the city of Jerusalem and saying, "O Jerusalem, Jerusalem, which killest the prophets, and stonest them that are sent unto thee; how often would I have gathered thy children together, as a hen doth gather her brood under her wings, and ye would not!"

So be brave when persecution of any form comes upon you due to your being a faithful child of God. Know that you are not alone and that many men and women of God who have gone before have suffered greatly for their faith. Indeed, rejoice and be glad; not because being persecuted is enjoyable or feels good, but because it is frequently a step in the path that leads to heaven. Surely, no matter what, heaven will be worth it all.

October 12

Fill the Waterpots

In a village called Cana
In the land of Galilee
An event took place so long ago
That calls out to you and me.
A day of joy and happiness;
A wedding was taking place.
And in the crowd of celebrants
Was Jesus with the rest.

A day of smiles and congratulations,
Of that there is no doubt.
But a problem was beginning—
The wine was running out.

Mary told Jesus,
Even though it was not yet His time,
That their host was facing embarrassment
Because they had no wine.

What would Jesus do?
I don't believe Mary really knew.
But to the servants Mary said,
Whatever He says, Do.

At the words of this man
Just who He was they did not know
The servants filled the waterpots
Until they began to overflow.

Most probably know the story
Of what took place that day
The water was changed into wine
That was better in every way.

It isn't upon the miracle that I want us to focus
(Although it was glorious, that is true);
It is upon what Mary said,
Whatever He says, Do

If you had been a servant on that day
And Mary said, Whatever He says, Do
Would you have been so quick to act
And filled the waterpots too?
There is a tremendous lesson to be learned
From those nameless men that day
For they did as Jesus told them to do
And they did it right away.

These men did not know who Jesus really was
Or why He'd come, that's true.
But you and I can't say that
Because we really do.

As we learn more and more
Of what Jesus said and what is true
Do we hear the voice of Mary
Whatever He says, Do?

This life is all we have;
It is the chance we've got.
Let's make sure we use the time
To fill the waterpot.

Hebrews: "Let Us . . ." (1)

The book of Hebrews is a wonderful book having a theme that can be summed up in one word—better. The Hebrew writer was exhorting a group of Jewish Christians not to go back into the practice and trappings of Judaism. However, the message is applicable to anyone who would consider leaving the truth of Christianity and going back into whatever they had come out of. Why would anyone want to turn back? In the Hebrew letter we are shown the superiority of Christ to the Old Testament prophets, to angels, to Moses, to Joshua, to Abraham, to Levi and Aaron, and to all of the priests who served under the Law of Moses. The letter is a call to those Jewish Christians, and to all Christians of all time, to hold onto their faith, to not turn back, for anything and everything is inferior to serving the Lord as a faithful Christian.

In the letter there is a phrase that appears at least twelve times. The phrase is, "Let us." Over the next several days I would like to look at the passages where this phrase is used. What we will see when we examine these passages is the Hebrew writer making his primary point and following it with a warning and an exhortation. An exhortation is simply a statement or address of urgent advice or recommendation. So that is what we will be seeing, pieces of urgent advice or recommendations for conduct.

One of the minor themes of Hebrews is rest, and chapter three introduces that subject. The Promised Land of Canaan is presented as a figure of the rest that God will ultimately provide for His faithful followers. The idea is that the Israelites would be entering into a "rest" when they entered into the Promised Land. However, Hebrews 3 ends with the words, "For some, when they had heard, did provoke: howbeit not all that came out of Egypt by Moses. But with whom was he grieved forty years? Was it not with them that had sinned, whose carcasses fell in the wilderness? And to whom sware he that they should not enter into his rest, but to them that believed not? So we see that they could not enter in because of unbelief."

We know what happened. Because of their unbelief none of the adults who came out of the Egyptian bondage, passing through the Red Sea (except for

Joshua and Caleb), made it into the Promised Land. All of the rest perished in the wilderness. That brings us to Hebrews 4:1, "Let us therefore fear, lest, a promise being left us of entering into his rest, any of you should seem to come short of it."

October 14

Hebrews: "Let Us. . . " (2)

Let us therefore fear, lest, a promise being left us of entering into his rest, any of you should seem to come short of it (Heb. 4:1).

"Let us fear." Why should Christians fear, and in what sense is the Hebrew writer using the word? Simply because the great and glorious rewards that are laid up for us in heaven—the ultimate rest that God has prepared for His faithful followers—can be forfeited as long as we live in this flesh. We have a powerful and aggressive enemy in Satan who will do all he can within the realm of his influence to keep us from entering into eternal rest. Just consider what awaits us: a glorious rest that the seventh day, the Promised Land, and even the church merely prefigured. The exhortation is to greater diligence in life because eternal rest awaits us.

The urgency of this advice cannot be overemphasized. The most important thing of all is going to heaven, and we are not there yet. Faithful Christians are on the way, but we are not there yet. The Apostle Paul wrote in Philippians 3:13-14, "Brethren, I count not myself to have apprehended; but this one thing I do, forgetting those things which are behind, and reaching forth unto those things which are before, I press toward the mark for the prize of the high calling of God in Christ Jesus."

Again, we are not there yet. And the possibility of falling off of the path should cause us to fear, because quite frankly nothing is more frightening, but in a good way, in the sense of causing us to strive with all that is in us to be pleasing to God. That takes us to the next "let us" of Hebrews.

Let us labor therefore to enter into that rest, lest any man fall after the same example of unbelief (Heb. 4:11).

The word "labor" can also be translated as "strive." It is a word describing intense concentration of the energy necessary to reach a desired goal. It demands everything we have, but always with the recognition and appreciation of the fact that we can't do it alone and that we are not earning our salvation. We could never enter into that rest without the marvelous grace of God having made it available, and the greatest manifestation of that grace was the death of the Son of God. If we go to heaven, it will be because of the blood of Christ. However, it is not going to happen automatically simply because we call ourselves Christians, no more than those who were Hebrews automatically entered into the Promised Land. No! We must want to go to heaven so intensely that we are willing to "strive" for it, willing to do all that God tells us is necessary to reach that desired goal.

That takes us to the next "let us" of the book of Hebrews. Hebrews 4:14 tells us, "Seeing then that we have a great high priest, that is passed into the heavens, Jesus the Son of God, let us hold fast our profession."

October 15

Hebrews: "Let Us . . ." (3)

Seeing then that we have a great high priest, that is passed into the heavens, Jesus the Son of God, let us hold fast our profession (Heb. 4:14).

The point the Hebrew writer was making is that being a Christian is no place for a coward. The "profession" or "confession" of the faith we possess is a treasure beyond price.

In Matthew 13:44-46 Jesus said, "Again, the kingdom of heaven is like unto treasure hid in a field; the which when a man hath found, he hideth, and for joy thereof goeth and selleth all that he hath, and buyeth that field. Again, the kingdom of heaven is like unto a merchant man, seeking goodly pearls: who, when he had found one pearl of great price, went and sold all that he had, and bought it." The faith that we embrace cannot be taken lightly, easily dismissed, or abandoned. It cannot be compromised or changed. The Hebrew brethren, and we right along with them, are being urged to "hold fast" to the faith. Grab on to the truth and hang on. Don't let anybody or anything pull you away. Don't let anyone disrupt or corrupt your walk with false teaching—not family, not friends, not anyone. Throughout this book the weight of responsibility for faithfulness sits right upon the shoulders of the believer. We are constantly and repeatedly exhorted and admonished to hold it fast, to glory in it, and to exhort others to do the same. Don't let anything or anybody rob us of our faith; as a matter of fact, advertise it. Hold it fast and hold it forth.

Now we move to Hebrews 4:16, for the next "Let us." The verse says:

Let us therefore come boldly unto the throne of grace, that we may obtain mercy, and find grace to help in time of need.

In order to really get the point of this exhortation, it is important to remember to whom this letter was originally written. It was written to Hebrew Christians. Verses 14-15 help us to understand, "Seeing then that we have a great high priest, that is passed into the heavens, Jesus the Son of God, let us hold fast our profession. For we have not a high priest which cannot be touched with the feeling of our infirmities; but was in all points tempted like we are, yet without sin."

What a glorious thought! "Boldly come unto the throne of grace." That is God's throne where Jesus is seated. It is the throne of grace, the source of mercy and love for us. Now, considering that it was written to people whose minds were full of the imagery of the Levitical system, and the idea of the high priest on the Day of Atonement, the only one permitted to enter into the Most Holy Place; well, this exhortation suggests the grandeur of the position occupied by a Christian. It is a position that no one *but* a Christian occupies. No practitioner of Judaism holds the same position.

"Let us therefore" (Christians, that is), trusting in the divine power and the human sympathy of our Lord Jesus, "draw near" as priests ourselves in fellowship with our High Priest—not having to remain standing afar off as the Jews did. "Let us draw near to the throne of grace," no symbolic mercy seat this, no, but the very center of divine sovereignty and love.

Thanks be to God!

Hebrews: "Let Us . . ." (4)

Therefore leaving the principles of the doctrine of Christ, let us go on unto perfection; not laying again the foundation of repentance from dead works, and
of faith toward God, of the doctrine of baptisms, and of laying on of hands,
and of resurrection of the dead, and of eternal judgment. And this we will do,
if God permit (Heb. 6:1-3).

In verse 1 we find another "let us"—an exhortation, which is a statement
or address of urgent advice or recommendation. The New American Standard
Version says, "Therefore leaving the elementary teaching about the Christ, let
us press on to maturity. . . ." while the American Standard Version renders it,
"Wherefore leaving the doctrine of the first principles of Christ, let us press
on unto perfection." Here is a challenge, a word of exhortation, for these
Christians to leave, or go beyond, the elementary teachings of the gospel.
This is not because they are unimportant, but because they are like the ABC's
that a student leaves as he goes on and progresses in his education. Now understand that unless the student fully understands those ABC's, his education
cannot go on. But "leaving the doctrine of the first principles," they were
to "press on unto perfection." In other words, they were to move on to full
growth and spiritual maturity.

Why is it so important to grow? Why is it so necessary to progress beyond
the first principles, never forgetting them because they are so well known
and ingrained in us that they are a part of us? Why is it essential to grow to
spiritual maturity? Because the possibility of apostasy is real and threatening;
even to believers "who were once enlightened, and have tasted of the heavenly
gift, and were made partakers of the Holy Ghost, and have tasted the good
word of God, and the powers of the world to come, if they shall fall away, to
renew them again unto repentance; seeing they crucify to themselves the Son
of God afresh, and put him to an open shame" (Heb. 6:4-6). That is why it is
so important to go on to perfection—to spiritual maturity.

The consequences of leaving the truth are terrible and horrendous. This is
graphically illustrated by what is done to land that is productive versus what
is done to land that is unproductive. Hebrews 6:7-8 tells us, "For the earth
which drinketh in the rain that cometh oft upon it, and bringeth forth herbs

meet for them by whom it is dressed, receiveth blessing from God: but that which beareth thorns and briers is rejected, and is nigh unto cursing; whose end is to be burned."

My friends, Christians are encouraged to "go on unto perfection." That is continuous action, a striving toward a goal, and that goal is perfection. That is not sinless perfection, but rather it is to move from adolescence into full, mature spiritual adulthood. This is an appeal, an urgent piece of advice, a recommendation for them, and all Christians, to become better at recognizing true teaching from false, to be better able to distinguish the lie from the truth, and to stand on the truth. Grow, my friends, grow!

October 17

Hebrews: "Let Us. . ." (5)

Having therefore, brethren, boldness to enter into the holiest by the blood of Jesus, by a new and living way, which he hath consecrated for us, through the veil, that is to say, his flesh; and having an high priest over the house of God; let us draw near with a true heart in full assurance of faith, having our hearts sprinkled from an evil conscience, and our bodies washed with pure water (Heb. 10:19-22).

One man called this exhortation "an invitation to intimacy." I like that very much. Notice the basic elements of the relationship sustained by Christians in this exhortation. First, there is confident faith. The Jewish Christians are reminded that in their original acceptance of Jesus as Lord they had done so with confident faith. Again, verses 19-20 say, "Having therefore, brethren, boldness to enter into the holiest by the blood of Jesus, by a new and living way, which he hath consecrated for us, through the veil, that is to say, his flesh." The idea is that of the temple or tabernacle and the priestly functions performed there. Unlike the priests under the Law of Moses, who with great alarm and fear passed through the veil into the holy of holies, they as Christians had confidently entered into an intimate relationship with God through the death of his Son—through the blood of Jesus. Why would they ever want to go back?

In verse 20 we see the words "a new and living way." The word "new" used in that verse means "freshly killed" or "newly slain." This sacrifice of Jesus was not just warmed-over Judaism or patched-up Judaism, no sir! The fact that it is "living" indicates that it is neither temporary nor provisional, as Judaism was. No, its end is life—complete absolution for the guilt of sin.

Another element of the relationship of a Christian is that in the process of becoming priests, with access to the holy of holies and the presence of God, they had had their "bodies washed with pure water," a reference to New Testament baptism. Priests under the Law of Moses were consecrated to the priesthood by, among other things, a complete washing of their bodies before putting on their priestly attire. Believing, penitent people are inducted into Christ, thus becoming priests, by baptism.

Also, their hearts had been "sprinkled from an evil conscience." Under the Law of Moses, Aaron and his sons were consecrated to the priesthood by the blood of sacrificial animals at the same time their bodies were washed and they put on their priestly attire. Christians are actually cleansed by the blood of Jesus Christ.

Finally, for our consideration today, as Christians they have "an high priest over the house of God." That high priest is Jesus. Consecrated as priests by the blood of our great High Priest, Christians have access to the presence of the Father who dwells in heaven. Why would anyone ever want to turn back or abandon these glorious truths in any way?

October 18

Hebrews: "Let Us . . ." (6)

Let us draw near with a true heart in full assurance of faith, having our hearts sprinkled from an evil conscience, and our bodies washed with pure water (Heb. 10:22).

As Christians we have this glorious unrestricted access to God through our High Priest, Jesus Christ. This privilege also involves a duty—to maintain this personal and close relationship with our Father. To Christians, God cannot be some abstract, purely intellectual concept. He has to be so much more than that. He is a living, all-wise, all-powerful, ever-present Father. We are priests, consecrated to Him, and God has to be as real to us as the air we breathe and the next beat of our hearts. This is true in all aspects of our lives, but the context of the passage we are considering emphasizes the times when faithful Christians assemble together to worship God.

This takes us to the next "Let us" found in Hebrews 10:23: "Let us hold fast the profession of our faith without wavering; for he is faithful that promised."

The New American Standard Version makes the meaning of this statement much easier to understand. In that translation, it is rendered, "Let us hold fast the confession of our hope without wavering, for He who promised is faithful."

The exhortation is to hold fast to the confession of our hope as unbending and unwavering. When this letter was written, there were some Jewish Christians who were "forsaking Christ" and returning to Moses and the Law. Today, Christians commit sin of the same nature when they turn from New Testament truth that they had understood and embraced with "confident faith" to fallacious, man-made doctrines and practices.

In Hebrews 10:24-25 we find the next "Let us":

And let us consider one another to provoke unto love and to good works: not forsaking the assembling of ourselves together, as the manner of some is; but exhorting one another: and so much the more, as ye see the day approaching.

As Christians, we are to "consider" one another. The word means "diligently inspect." It emphasizes the fact that we are indeed "our brother's keeper." We are fellow citizens in the kingdom of God.

We are to diligently inspect one another in order to "provoke," which means to "incite, excite, or stimulate." As Christians we are to seek to stimulate our brothers and sisters to a state of excitement about their relationship and service to God. We are to excite and stimulate each other to "love and good works." The word for "love" used there is *agape*. It is a love that always seeks the highest good of its object. Those "good works" are simply good and noble works, as determined by God, by which a Christian demonstrates that love. A very important way that we "hold fast the confession of our hope" and "consider one another to provoke unto love and to good works" is by assembling with faithful brothers and sisters in Christ to worship God together.

October 19

Hebrews: "Let Us . . ." (7)

Wherefore seeing we also are compassed about with so great a cloud of witnesses, let us lay aside every weight, and the sin which doth so easily beset us, and let us run with patience the race that is set before us, looking unto Jesus the author and finisher of our faith; who for the joy that was set before him endured the cross, despising the shame, and is set down at the right hand of the throne of God (Heb. 12:1).

What magnificent imagery—the life of a Christian presented as a race that is run in an arena filled with cheering spectators who have run the race of a life of service to God and have won! We are in a race. We entered it when we obeyed the gospel; believing, repenting, confessing, and being baptized for the remission of our sins. It is a race that we must win. We can't quit, and we can't leave the designated course.

With those who have gone before us figuratively cheering us on and saying, "You can do it, you can make it," "let us lay aside every weight." The word translated as "weight" is found only here in the New Testament. Its usual meaning is that of a weight, or a burden. To understand the imagery, think of the Olympics. The runners in the races carry nothing and wear nothing that would hinder them in the race. Even their clothes are made so as not to impede their running. They seek to remove anything that could be a hindrance. For the Christian it means to lay aside everything and anything that gets in the way, or impedes our progress toward the finish line.

Not only are we to "lay aside every weight," we are also to do away with "the sin that doth so easily beset us." This is another instance where we find a word that appears only here in the New Testament. It is the word translated as "easily besets" or "easily entangles." It means "standing well around." Think about that. It is the sin that is near, that is, at hand. It is the sin to which we are most exposed. It is going to be different for each of us. There is always a weak point at which we are particularly vulnerable. There is where we need to be especially guarded, aware of the danger.

Having laid aside the weights and the sin that does so easily beset us, "Let us run with patience the race that is set before us." The race we run is not a sprint; it is a long distance race. The word for "race" is *agona* the word from which we get the word "agony." The race of life is often an agonizing, grueling course and it requires each of us to "hang in there" if we are going to win. The "patience" with which we are to run means getting in there and doing it—persevering and enduring.

Beyond this cloud of spectators, waiting at the finish line, is Jesus. He sees, He knows, He understands, and He intercedes on behalf of His people that we might win the prize. "Looking unto Jesus" means focusing all of our spiritual vision upon the Lord. Peter walked on water until he took his eyes off of Jesus. We can win if we keep Him firmly in our sights.

October 20

Hebrews: "Let Us . . ." (8)

For the bodies of those beasts, whose blood is brought into the sanctuary by the high priest for sin, are burned without the camp. Wherefore Jesus also, that he might sanctify the people with his own blood, suffered without the gate. Let us go forth therefore unto him without the camp, bearing his reproach (Heb. 13:11-13).

Over the last several days we have focused our attention upon the phrase, "Let us" that preceded urgent words of advice and teaching in the letter to the Hebrews. Try to place yourself in the position of a Jewish Christian in the first century. Suppose that you are feeling pressure to return to the practice of Judaism, the religion in which you were raised. You have read this letter up to this point and have undoubtedly felt the force of its arguments. There is no refuting the logic of this letter, but perhaps you hesitate to make up your mind and finally and forever lay aside the practice of Judaism. Your family, friends, and most of your former associates remain practicing Jews. Relatively speaking, there are very few Christians, especially in your day-to-day life. You are dealing with non-Christians, and predominately Jews, for your livelihood. Being a Christian brings slander, slurs, and other forms of persecution—sometimes physical abuse. In short, there is a stigma attached to being a Christian, a reproach. You could lay it all aside and even be welcomed back into full fellowship with your fellow Jews as one who saw the error of his way. Just turn your back on Jesus and things can be as they were. To combat this, the Hebrew writer made one final exhortation.

The word "camp" found in verses 11 and 13 would bring to the mind of a Hebrew Christian the camp of the Israelites as they wandered in the wilderness. To go outside the camp was to go outside the perimeter of their encampment. Later, the city of Jerusalem would become, for all intents and purposes, that camp. In a lesser sense, any congregation or assembly of Jews could be considered that "camp." The words, "Let us go forth therefore unto him without the camp" or "outside the camp" implied a couple of things: (1) It was to turn their back on any relationship or fellowship that stood in the way of doing God's will (in this particular case that would have been the "camp" of Judaism); (2) To accept whatever reproach, whatever consequence that might come for doing so.

My friends, the words, "Let us go forth therefore unto Him without the camp" or "Let us go outside the camp" require courage, conviction, faith, and the willingness to suffer and accept ridicule and reproach. There can even be the possibility of death. But the Christ that is to be followed "outside the camp" is constant and unchanging. Hebrews 13:8 tells us, "Jesus Christ, the same yesterday, and today, and forever." Faithful Christians have an altar (Heb. 13:10) referring to the blood of Christ, where true and effective atonement can and does take away the guilt of sin. Faithful servants of the Lord can simply follow Him. He led the way outside of the camp when He was offered outside of the city of Jerusalem for our sins. Finally, the faithful Christian has a continuing city (Heb. 13:14), one that will never be destroyed, awaiting us in heaven. Why would anyone, anytime, or anywhere, ever want to turn his back on Jesus?

October 21

Telephone, Telegraph, *Tell Me?*

When I was younger, we used to joke about people who simply could not keep any information that they had to themselves. We used to say that the quickest ways to get news around were the telephone, telegraph, and tell "so and so." I guess to be more accurate today we would have to say telephone, cellular phone, e-mail, and tell so and so. Even though we used to joke about it, the truth is that it really is not funny. One thing the Bible clearly teaches us is the need to control our tongues and not to feel compelled to tell everything we know.

Good news travels fast. Bad news travels faster, and gossip travels the fastest of all. I wonder why that is, especially in light of all that the Word of God has to say about it. Let's take a short trip through the book of Proverbs and see what God has to say about this matter.

First of all, there are wonderful uses for the tongue. Consider Proverbs 8:6-10 where Solomon wrote:

> Listen, for I shall speak noble things; and the opening of my lips will produce right things. For my mouth will utter truth; and wickedness is an abomination to my lips. All the utterances of my mouth are in righteousness; there is nothing crooked or perverted in them. They are all straightforward to him who understands, and right to those who find knowledge. Take my instruction, and not silver, and knowledge rather than choicest gold.

God has given us the ability to communicate with speech, and that serves as a glorious medium of instruction. We know that "faith comes by hearing, and hearing by the Word of God" (Rom. 10:17). From our tongues can come forth words of righteousness, meant to uplift, build, and encourage others. Indeed, our tongues can be used as the medium through which the Gospel of the Lord Jesus is spread and the availability of salvation made known to all. Proverbs 11:30 tells us, "The fruit of the righteous is a tree of life, and he who is wise wins souls."

Look at a few statements found in Proverbs 10. Verses 11-14 tell us, "The mouth of the righteous is a fountain of life, but the mouth of the wicked conceals violence. Hatred stirs up strife, but love covers all transgressions. On the lips of the discerning, wisdom is found, but a rod is for the back of him who lacks understanding. Wise men store up knowledge, but with the mouth of the foolish, ruin is at hand."

Why is it that some folks just feel that they have to tell everything they know—and in many cases, not even being sure if it is true or not? I am exaggerating for effect here, but in years gone by there have been times when I have preached on a particular subject, addressed some specific controversy or some unusually hot topic, and, before the final Amen was said, what I had said had been broadcast (and never accurately) several states away.

"A Small Inflamed Swelling of the Skin"

When I was a young person between the ages of 13 and 19 inclusive, oftentimes the most traumatic experience of the day was looking into the mirror in the morning. This was occasionally difficult because from time to time, no matter how many precautions I had taken, as I looked in the mirror I would be greeted by a "small inflamed swelling on the skin"—a pimple.

(I would have entitled this article, "A Pimple," but I didn't think anybody would read something with that title!)

After the initial wave of disgust, frustration, and depression passed by, I would set out to take care of that imperfection on my complexion as quickly and efficiently as possible. Out would come the washcloth and the soap, both of which would be applied in rigorous fashion to the afflicted area. Out would come the alcohol and any other medicines designed to eradicate the offending blemish. I did not want that blemish, it did not belong on my face, and it detracted from the natural beauty that was mine. Well—it sure didn't help!

The point I am trying to make is this: Whenever we look in the mirror and see an imperfection or a blemish, whether it be dirt or a pimple or any such thing, and it is possible for us to do something about it, we do something! We don't get mad at the mirror for showing us the blemish; neither do we just quit looking in mirrors because we don't want to see. Every one of us does what we can to remove the imperfections.

Doesn't it just make sense for us to feel the same way about spiritual blemishes and imperfections and about the mirror that points them out to us? In James 1:22-25, we find:

> But prove yourselves doers of the word, and not merely hearers who delude themselves. For if anyone is a hearer of the word and not a doer, he is like a man who looks at his natural face in a mirror; for once he has looked at himself and gone away, he has immediately forgotten what kind of person he was. But one who looks intently at the perfect law, the law of liberty, and abides by it, not having become a forgetful hearer but an effectual doer, this man shall be blessed in what he does.

There is no better mirror than God's Word. Nothing can be hidden from it, and the reflection it gives is sharp and three-dimensional. God's Word goes far deeper than the outside, physical appearance; it cuts to the core of the matter and shows what causes the imperfections. The Hebrew writer stated it this way in Hebrews 4:12-13, "For the word of God is living and active and sharper than any two-edged sword, and piercing as far as the division of soul and spirit, of both joints and marrow, and able to judge the thoughts and intentions of the heart. And there is no creature hidden from His sight, but all things are open and laid bare to the eyes of Him with whom we have to do."

When I look in that mirror, either through personal study and reading or through preaching, and see a spiritual blemish in my life, I need to do something about it right away. It is foolish and useless to get mad at the mirror, the Word of God, or to try to convince myself that it does not say what it says. We do not try to rationalize away a pimple; why do some try to rationalize away a spiritual blemish pointed out by God's Word? It doesn't do any good to get mad at the one holding the mirror either, any more than it does to get mad at the bathroom wall on which the mirror hangs at home. That is not going to take care of the spiritual blemish or the pimple. It also doesn't do any good to say, "Well, I am just not going to look into God's Word anymore," as some will do. A failure to look into the mirror of God's Word is just going to make that spiritual blemish get worse.

No, the only reasonable thing to do is to use God's Word as the mirror it is intended to be. Let it show us what we really are, and then make any necessary corrections to remove all blemishes.

One other point that needs to be made is this: When I look in the mirror at home, it is my face that I need to see. Sometimes if my wife is looking in the same mirror at the same time, I will ask her to move over a little bit. Why? Because it is my face that I need to see. It is the same way with God's Word. When I am listening to it or studying privately from it, mine is the face that I need to see. I don't need to see your face, or Vicky's face, or anyone else's. I need to see what I am, and make any necessary adjustments before I am in a position to point out any spiritual blemishes you may have. Remember the statement of the Lord in Matthew 7:5? Jesus said, "You hypocrite, first take the log out of your own eye, and then you will see clearly to take the speck out of your brother's eye."

Surely our spiritual complexions are of much greater importance than our physical. Everything we need to have the "smoothest" of spiritual complexions is to be found in the "mirror" of God's Word.

Why Did Jesus Have to Die?

Over the years I have often been asked, "Why did Jesus have to die?" The question is usually followed by some comment about God being able to choose any way for man to be saved, so why choose the way that He did. I believe that to be a great question, and one that needs to be answered.

In Hebrews 2:9 we find, "But we see Jesus, who was made a little lower than the angels for the suffering of death, crowned with glory and honor; that He by the grace of God should taste death for every man." Moving down to verses 14-18 we read:

> Forasmuch then as the children are partakers of flesh and blood, he also himself likewise took part of the same; that through death he might destroy him that had the power of death, that is, the devil; and deliver them who through fear of death were all their lifetime subject to bondage. For verily he took not on him the nature of angels; but he took on him the seed of Abraham. Wherefore in all things it behooved him to be made like unto his brethren, that he might be a merciful and faithful high priest in things pertaining to God, to make reconciliation for the sins of the people. For in that he himself hath suffered being tempted, he is able to succour them that are tempted.

It was necessary for Jesus to become man, to become flesh, to take "on him the seed of Abraham" in order that He might "make reconciliation for the sins of the people." Again, the question might be asked, "Why?"

When a person is born into this world, that person is pure, pristine spiritually, absolutely undefiled, and in fellowship with God. At some point in that person's life, if he continues to grow and develop mentally, he will sin. When he sins, he has taken that which was pure and holy, in fellowship with God, and has defiled it. In a sense, by sin, a person separates himself from God. The only thing that could redeem what was taken from God was a person who was pure and holy, absolutely undefiled. That person was Jesus. In Hebrews 4:1 we are told, "For we have not an high priest which cannot be touched with the feeling of our infirmities; but was in all points tempted like as we are, yet without sin."

The simplest explanation that I have heard is this. In the area of the country where I live, there is an exclusive men's clothing store called Joseph A. Banks. They sell very expensive clothing. Suppose that I go into that store and steal one of their $100.00 dress shirts. I wear that shirt the following day and my pen leaks in the pocket, staining it with ink. At lunch I spill some of the chili I am eating, and consequently there is a large brown spot just above where the shirt is generally tucked into the pants. On the way home from work, I get a flat tire and as I am changing it, grease gets on both of the sleeves.

The next day my conscience begins to bother me, so I decide to take that shirt, in its current condition, back to the store. As I walk in and hand that shirt back to the sales person, explaining that I had stolen it and now wanted to give it back, I believe that we all can recognize that I am not giving back that which I had taken. What I took was pure, pristine and undefiled; what I was attempting to give back was soiled, marked, and defiled. The only thing that could truly restore to the Joseph A. Banks store what was taken was a pure, pristine shirt of the exact same kind that had not been soiled in any way. Perhaps in such a simple way, this can help us to understand the necessity of the death of Jesus.

October 24

A Grandson's Tribute
By Adam Litmer

The news came Sunday night, Grandpa had died.
I stood there speechless, my mouth open wide.
In that moment my world went black;
But memories poured in and, as usual, you brought the light back.

These few lines cannot be sufficient to tell you what you mean to me.
But I'll give it a shot, because I want the world to see.
And I take comfort knowing where you are now.
But even so, here's one last message from "your buddy and your pal."

A man like you can't be found every day.
I smile through my tears remembering the things you used to say.

I'll never forget your charm or your wit,
Like when I'd hurt myself and you'd ask, "When'd you first notice it?"

My sorrow now is almost too much to bear,
But paradise is a wonderful thought, and I know that you are there.
I'm walking around your farm as I write, wondering what to do.
And I'd give anything if, for just one last time, I could walk this field with
  you.

A relationship like ours is so very rare,
I wish everyone could have what we share.
I wanted to be like you so much, and you tried to show me how,
Taking a line from one of your favorite commercials—"Grandpa, can you
  hear me now?"

Your journey on earth is now complete,
And in paradise you have taken your seat.
So from your grandson and your best friend I write this with a sigh—
Until we meet in heaven, Grandpa, goodbye.

I love you, Grandpa.

October 25

Help Me to Love As Jesus Loved

No one who has ever walked this earth has loved more fully, completely, and deeply as Jesus did. In Galatians 2:20 Paul wrote, "I am crucified with Christ; nevertheless I live; yet not I, but Christ liveth in me: and the life which I now live in the flesh I live by the faith of the Son of God, who loved me, and gave himself for me." Jesus loved mankind enough to die for us. In fact, He loved us to the greatest possible degree because self-sacrifice is the highest expression of love. The Lord Himself said, "Greater love hath no man than this, that a man lay down his life for his friends" (John 15:13). One day later, Jesus gave His life even for those who hated Him.

In 1 John 3:16 we find, "Hereby perceive we the love of God, because he laid down his life for us." Pay close attention to the reason given for Jesus laying down his life. It was "for us." That word "for" comes from the Greek word *huper* which means "on behalf of." I apologize for not remembering the individual's name who provided this graphic illustration of the meaning of that word in the following way: "The picture in the preposition is of one who sees, for example, another who has fallen, wounded, in grave danger, and about to perish, and who rushes to him, stands over him, fights in his behalf, and enters the fray in his stead. This, and more, Jesus did for us in his death on the cross."

If we are going to walk in the footsteps of Jesus, if we are going to be of the same mindset as He was; we are going to have to love as He loved. Most Bible students are familiar with the Lord's statement found in John 13:34, "A new commandment I give unto you, That ye love one another, as I have loved you, that ye also love one another." Jesus' love involved incredible sacrifice, and our love, if we are to love as Jesus, must be sacrificial as well.

Just imagine a situation in which all practiced sacrificial love toward one another. I am not even thinking about such taking place in the world. Just think of what would happen if this actually took place in the church. Just think of what it would be like if we all would actually prefer each other instead of self, if we would all esteem each other better than self. What a wonderful thing it would be if all of us who are faithful children of God would seek each other's welfare and profit, indeed, if we would all be willing to lay down our lives for each other. Does this describe an unattainable utopia on earth? Perhaps, but it is undoubtedly a goal toward which every Christian should strive.

October 26

Honor Thy Father and Thy Mother

It has always been God's desire that we honor and respect our parents. Back at the giving of the Ten Commandments, God decreed in Exodus 20:12, "Honor thy father and thy mother: that thy days may be long upon the land which the Lord thy God giveth thee." In Ephesians 6:1-3 Paul wrote, "Children, obey your parents in the Lord, for this is right. Honor thy father and mother; (which is the first commandment with promise;) that it may be well with thee, and thou mayest live long on the earth."

We owe our existence to our parents. They sacrificed for us, trained and loved us. They loved us even when we were not particularly loveable. They took care of us when we were not particularly deserving. They disciplined, encouraged, and loved us when we were rebellious and unkind. When the going got rough, as it inevitably does, they did not shirk their responsibilities. When we failed, they were constant; when we acted without the proper concern and respect, they loved us still. How can we ever forget that? There came a time in my father's life when he no longer recognized me and he had lost control over his bodily functions—but he was still my dad, he will always live in me, and I owe him so much.

Some in New Testament times were guilty of the same disregard for parents that characterize so many in our society today. In Mark 7:9-13 we find Jesus saying to a certain group of Pharisees, "Full well ye reject the commandment of God, that ye may keep your own tradition. For Moses said, Honor thy father and thy mother; and, Whoso curseth father or mother, let him die the death: but ye say, If a man shall say to his father or mother, It is Corban, that is to say, a gift, by whatsoever thou mightest be profited by me; he shall be free. And ye suffer him no more to do ought for his father or his mother; making the word of God of none effect through your tradition, which ye have delivered: and many such like things ye do."

The Law of Moses clearly demanded respect and support for one's parents. But by their tradition the Pharisees had circumvented this law. According to their tradition, an individual could declare a possession "corban" or "given to God." Thus a Jew could declare part of his estate, by which his parents could be profited, or cared for, as a gift to God and thereby be freed from his obligation to his parents. What of parents who are abandoned today by ungrateful children, or placed in homes and never visited, or whose deaths are eagerly awaited so that the inheritance can be gotten? The Scriptures teach that parents deserve respect and honor and should be treated as special. This is to be always so, but especially as they age and are no longer able to care for themselves. I was so blessed to have the parents that I did, and I miss them terribly. There is truly not a day that goes by that they are not in my thoughts.

Putting On Your Game Face

I truly enjoy many sports. When I was younger I participated in a number of them. I still enjoy playing, but the games I play now are a bit more sedate. In the field of sports, we often hear of individuals "putting on their game face." What that means is that a person becomes mentally prepared to play. It is focusing your attention, concentrating on the task at hand so that you can go out and perform at your highest level. Other thoughts and concerns are set aside; everything centers on the game. I have found an interesting parallel to that in the life of a Christian. I believe the faithful child of God has to put on his or her game face as well in order to successfully run the race of life.

The first four verses of Colossians 3 indicate the need for a Christian to have a goal and a point upon which to focus. The passage says, "If ye then be risen with Christ, seek those things which are above, where Christ sitteth on the right hand of God. Set your affection on things above, not on things on the earth. For ye are dead, and your life is hid with Christ in God. When Christ, who is our life, shall appear with him in glory." Since we die with Christ when we are baptized into his death and become dead to sin, we also rise with him to walk in newness of life—a spiritual life. That being true, then our affections and our desires are to be set upon those things which are above, upon heavenly, spiritual matters. That is, we should so live our lives as to seek those things. We should so run as to obtain those things. We should so strive as to secure them.

Consider the next five verses of Colossians 3. Beginning with verse 5 we read, "Mortify therefore your members which are upon the earth; fornication, uncleanness, inordinate affection, evil concupiscence, and covetousness, which is idolatry: for which things sake the wrath of God cometh on the children of disobedience: in the which ye also walked some time, when ye lived in them. But now ye also put off all these; anger, wrath, malice, blasphemy, filthy communication out of your mouth. Lie not one to another, seeing that ye have put off the old man with his deeds."

In order for Christians truly to seek those things which are above, truly to set our affections on things above and not on things on the earth, we are going to have to set aside those things which before occupied our minds and were the objects of our desires and affections. All of those sinful activities, attitudes and thoughts that characterize the non-Christian must be set aside; they must be put off in order that we might focus upon the task at hand. I guess we could say that laying such things aside enables us to "put on our game face." When a Christian puts on his or her game face it means that he or she has become serious and focused about the task at hand.

If you have obeyed the gospel of Christ, you have "made the team" so to speak. Now it is time to get serious and win. Paul wrote, "I press toward the mark for the prize of the high calling of God in Christ Jesus" (Philippians 3:14). That beautifully describes the idea behind "putting on your game face."

October 28

The Gospel Is for Everyone

I want to tell you of a young man many years ago who was a theater arts major in college. Religiously he was nothing—totally carnal. He drank with the worst of them, smoked with the worst of them, cussed with the worst of them, and ran around with the worst of them. But he met a young woman that he thought was kind of special, began to attend services of the Lord's church with her, and a wondrous thing happened. The gospel of the Lord touched his heart and moved him to obedience.

In Matthew 9:9-13 we read the following account:

And as Jesus passed forth from thence, he saw a man, named Matthew, sitting at the receipt of custom: and he saith unto him, Follow me. And he arose, and followed him. And it came to pass, as Jesus sat at meat in the house, behold, many publicans and sinners came and sat down with him and his disciples. And when the Pharisees saw it, they said unto his disciples, Why eateth your Master with publicans and sinners? But when Jesus heard that, he said unto them, They that be whole need not a physician, but they that are sick. But go ye and learn what that meaneth, I will have mercy, and not sacrifice: for I am not come to call the righteous, but sinners to repentance.

As one studies the gospel records, we find publicans and sinners linked together frequently and for good reasons. Publicans (professional tax collectors) were often moral reprobates. When Jesus went to Matthew's home to eat, a number of publicans and sinners joined in the meal. This prompted the scorn of the Pharisees, "Why eateth your Master with publicans and sinners?"

Jesus went right to the heart of the matter. "They that be whole need not a physician, but they that are sick. But go ye and learn what that meaneth, I will have mercy, and not sacrifice: for I am not come to call the righteous, but sinners to repentance." There is a lot to be found in that statement. Obviously Jesus was the physician, contextually the publicans where the ones who were sick; and the scribes and Pharisees the ones who were "whole." But the "whole" and the "righteous," as applied to the Pharisees and the scribes, was their own estimation of themselves. They were certain that they were healthy spiritually, but they were desperately sick and did not even know it. The parable the Lord told in Luke 18 graphically depicted the sinful, self-righteous view that so many of the Pharisees had of themselves. In verses 10-11 we find, "Two men went up into the temple to pray; the one a Pharisee, and the other a publican. The Pharisee stood and prayed thus with himself, God, I thank thee that I am not as other men are, extortioners, unjust, adulterers, or even as this publican." So many believed that they were spiritually healthy, and were so smug about it—as though God's word was theirs and theirs alone. But Jesus came to help everyone, and the Good News about Him is for everyone today. The charge that He associated with "publicans and sinners" was to His glory, not to His shame. He went to them because they needed Him. Out of this association came Matthew, faithful apostle and writer of the first gospel.

I thank God that many Christians understand who the gospel is for—everybody. I write that because I was that young man described in the beginning of today's article.

October 29

Both Lion and Lamb

In the Scriptures Jesus is referred to as the Lamb of God and as the Lion of the tribe of Judah. Both designations are accurate. When personally attacked, Jesus was as a lamb. I am reminded of the statement found in Isaiah 53:7, "He was oppressed, and he was afflicted, yet he opened not his mouth: he is brought as a lamb to the slaughter, and as a sheep before her shearers is dumb, so he openeth not his mouth." However, when the truth of God was being attacked, He was "the lion of the tribe of Judah."

It seems that a lot of people think it is kind of sissy to be a Christian. In so many families you will find that the wife is a child of God, but not the hus-band. Somehow worshipping and serving the Lord is not considered manly. Nothing could be further from the truth. It takes a courageous person to truly be a faithful child of God. It takes a courageous person to walk as Jesus walked. The Lord's presentations in the defense of the truth were unassailable and unwavering. He did not back down from controversy, and when it was time to begin the final push toward the cross, we are told that Jesus "stead-fastly set His face for Jerusalem."

Jude tells us that we must be of the mindset that we will "earnestly contend for the faith which was once delivered unto the saints" (Jude 3). That means that sometimes you just have to stand up and be counted. The word of God is referred to as "the sword of the Spirit" in Ephesians 6:17. What is a sword used for? It is used for battle. Following in the footsteps of Jesus, having the mind of Christ and walking as he walked, we must expect a certain amount of controversy and conflict.

Alexander Campbell was a great religious reformer. He pointed people back to the Bible as their sole source of authority. He often found himself embroiled in religious controversy. Concerning that, he wrote something that I believe is important for all faithful Christians to understand. Here are Campbell's words:

> If there was no error in principle or practice, then controversy, which is only another name for opposition to error, real or supposed, would be unnecessary. If it were lawful, or if it were benevolent, to make a truce with error, then op-position to it would be both unjust and unkind. If error were innocent and harmless, then we might permit it to find its own quietus, or to immortalize itself. But so long as it is confessed that error is more or less injurious to the welfare of society, individually and collectively considered, then no man can be considered benevolent who does not set his face against it. In proportion as a person is intelligent and benevolent, he will be controversial, if error exists around him. Hence the Prince of Peace never sheathed the sword of the Spirit while He lived. He drew it on the banks of the Jordan and threw the scabbard away.

To walk as Jesus walked, we must be ready to stand and to "keep that which is committed to our trust" (1 Tim. 6:20).

"In Deed and in Truth"

You may not recognize this short statement. It is but a portion of a verse found in 1 John 3:18, and is part of a passage that teaches the importance of action as it relates to love. John teaches us that conduct matters, and that love which is not demonstrated by actions is not really love at all. John wrote, "Hereby perceive we the love of God, because He laid down His life for us; and we ought to lay down our lives for the brethren. But whoso hath this world's goods, and seeth his brother have need, and shutteth up his bowels of compassion from him, how dwelleth the love of God in him? My little children, let us not love in word, neither in tongue; but in deed and in truth" (1 John 3:16-18).

I suspect that one of the easiest things in the world to do is to say, "I love you." For such a statement to be true, however, is another story altogether.

I recently spoke at a funeral. It seems I have been doing quite a bit of that lately, as dear friends, brothers, and sisters in Christ have passed from this life. But such events also give me the opportunity to learn. I have seen incredible acts of love as some were drawing near to death. I have seen sons and daughters care for their dying parent in the face of great personal hardships. I have seen spouses literally "give themselves," "spend and be spent," in the service of their dying mate. I have seen brethren, with no blood relationship to the dying person (except through the "blood of the Lamb"), change the clothing of a dying saint who has lost all control of his or her bodily functions. I have seen folks travel a great distance to be at a funeral, just to let the surviving family members know how much they care. I have seen so many people say, "I love you," and demonstrate it so clearly.

At the same time, I have seen things that cause me to shake my head and thank God that I am not the judge. I have seen children of the deceased just weep and wail and put on quite a show, crying out how much they loved their mom or dad—but their actions while Mom or Dad were still alive declare this to be a lie. They were rebellious, selfish, and ungodly; and from the time they were old enough to do so, they brought their parents nothing but heartache. I had such children come up to me after the funeral service, tears streaming down their cheeks, and say, "That was beautiful! That was just what Mom (or Dad) would have wanted you to say." What I had said was a call for them to come back to the Lord, to be faithful, or at least to honor the memory of their departed parent by godly living. Yet almost before the last bit of dirt hit the top of the vault, they were right back to the lifestyle they had chosen. Does this sound as though I am angry? I guess I am. I hate the hypocrisy of it all.

October 31

Costumes and Masks

Today is Halloween. Over the past month I suppose I have been in the Halloween store practically every time my wife and I have gone to the mall. I just like looking at the costumes and the masks. Some of the costumes are quite elaborate, with people going to great lengths to conceal their identity, and that is part of the fun. I remember a party I attended several years ago where we never did guess who two individuals were until the very end when they removed their masks. Tonight our house will be visited by everybody from Harry Potter to Spiderman. It is all part of the fun.

In real life, however, concealing one's true identity is not funny. In the spiritual realm such efforts are called hypocrisy. Our Lord warned His disciples to be careful and watchful for those who were not what they appeared to be. In Matthew 7:15 Jesus said, "Beware of false prophets, which come to you in sheep's clothing, but inwardly they are ravening wolves." Paul warned the Galatians of "false brethren unawares brought in" (Gal. 2:4). These were people who were hiding their true identities; they were not what they appeared to be. Peter wrote of "false prophets" and "false teachers" who would speak with "feigned words" in 2 Peter 2:1 and 3. John urged us to "believe not every spirit, but try the spirits whether they are of God; because many false prophets are gone out into the world" (1 John 4:1).

Since we are followers of the Lord Jesus Christ, we are to be what we appear to be. There can be no pretense; there can be no hypocrisy. With us, what you see must be what you get. As a Christian, what comes out of my mouth is to be something on which the listener can absolutely count. In Matthew 5:33–37 Jesus said:

Again, ye have heard that it hath been said by them of old time, Thou shalt not forswear thyself, but shalt perform unto the Lord thine oaths: but I say unto you, Swear not at all; neither by heaven; for it is God's throne: nor by the earth; for it is his footstool: neither by Jerusalem; for it is the city of the great King. Neither shalt thou swear by thy head, because thou canst not make one hair white or black. But let your communication be, Yea, yea; Nay, nay: for whatsoever is more than these cometh of evil.

As a Christian, if I say "No," I must mean "No." If I say, "Yes," I must mean, "Yes."

Every minute of every day, of every week, of every year, I am a Christian. Christianity is not confined to the four hours a week I spend at services. It is at home and it is at work; it is at school and at play. I am a Christian when I go to the grocery store and when I fill my gas tank at the gas station. It is not a mask that I put on as I pull into the parking lot at the church building, and then take off as soon as I get out onto the highway. I cannot claim to be a Christian on Sunday and Wednesday night, and keep company with the devil the rest of the week. The idea of "putting on Christ" in baptism that Paul spoke of in Galatians 3:27, is not the same as "putting on a costume" once or twice a year. It is to be a permanent adornment.

I like the way that Paul put it in Ephesians 4:1 where he wrote, "I therefore, the prisoner of the Lord, beseech you that ye walk worthy of the vocation wherewith ye are called." In other words, if we are going to call ourselves Christians, then we need to live like Christians. In Colossians 1:10, he wrote, "That ye might walk worthy of the Lord unto all pleasing, being fruitful in every good work, and increasing in the knowledge of God." It is just the idea of actually being what we appear, or claim, to be. No masks and no costumes; just the real me.

November 1

The Apostles

I find that a study of the twelve men chosen by the Lord to be His apostles, along with Matthias and Paul, always serves to lift my heart and encourage my spirit. In Luke 6:12-16 we find, "And it came to pass in those days, that he went out into a mountain to pray, and continued all night in prayer to God. And when it was day, he called unto him his disciples: and of them he chose twelve, whom also he named apostles; Simon, (whom he also named Peter), and Andrew his brother, James and John, Philip and Bartholomew, Matthew and Thomas, James the son of Alphaeus, and Simon called Zelotes, and Judas the brother of James, and Judas Iscariot, which also was the traitor."

After spending the night in prayer, Jesus made the choice of these twelve men to serve as His especially chosen messengers. As the gospel accounts unfold, we find that, generally speaking, these were men who had not enjoyed the benefits of higher education. We find them manifesting many of the popular Jewish prejudices and superstitions of the time. There were times when they displayed a carnal ambition, a desire to hold positions of preeminence and prestige. In Mark 9:33-35 we find one such instance. We are told, "And he came to Capernaum: and being in the house he asked them, What was it that ye disputed among yourselves by the way? But they held their peace: for by the way they had disputed among themselves, who should be the greatest. And he sat down, and called the twelve, and saith unto them, If any man desire to be first, the same shall be last of all, and the servant of all." This would continue to be a problem, for less than twenty-four hours before Jesus died on the cross, these men who had walked with Him for three years, argued among themselves who would be the greatest (Luke 22:24).

They were often slow to understand things that Jesus repeatedly taught them. One that would have been most frustrating to me was their continued failure to grasp what the Lord meant when He told them what was going to happen to Him. At various times Jesus told the twelve that He would be betrayed into the hands of the chief priests and the scribes and be condemned to death. He told them that he would be delivered into the hands of the Gentiles who would mock Him, scourge Him, and finally crucify Him. He told them that after three days He would rise again. Yet, Luke 18:34 tells us, "And they understood none of these things: and this saying was hid from them, neither knew they the things which were spoken."

There have been times when I have wondered why Jesus put up with these men and their obvious failings. Why didn't He replace them with men of greater education and sophistication who would seemingly be able to more immediately grasp the nuances of His teaching? But then I remember 1 Samuel 16:7 where a basic difference between God and us is pointed out, "But the Lord said unto Samuel, Look not on his countenance, or on the height of his stature; because I have refused him: for the Lord seeth not as man seeth; for man looketh on the outward appearance, but the Lord looketh on the heart." Jesus knew these men. He knew their hearts. They would come to the point where they believed so completely in Jesus and committed themselves to Him so entirely, that they would learn any lesson, endure any hardship, and even die for Him if necessary.

These men give me hope because they weren't perfect either. However, because of their association with Jesus and His effect upon them, they would grow to be men whose work has changed the world. The work that I can do for the Lord may not be of the magnitude of these men, but I can help to change my little corner.

November 2

The Apostle Andrew

Andrew was a man whose life before meeting Jesus can best be described as simple. By combining Mark 1:29-30 with John 1:44, we learn that Andrew was the brother of Simon Peter and that he lived in a house in the city of Capernaum with Peter, Peter's wife, and mother-in-law. Capernaum was a city located on the northwestern shore of the Sea of Galilee and that body of water played a major role in Andrew's life. Andrew was a fisherman along with his brother, Peter, and in partnership with James, John, and their father, Zebedee. To put it simply, he was a working man just like most of us. It encourages me to see God use that normal man to perform some very extraordinary things. No one is insignificant in the sight of God.

John 1:35-42 gives us some valuable insight into the character and priorities of Andrew. The passage tells us,

Again the next day after John stood, and two of his disciples; and looking upon Jesus as he walked, he saith, Behold the Lamb of God! And the two disciples heard him speak, and they followed Jesus. Then Jesus turned, and saw them following, and saith unto them, What seek ye? They said unto him, Rabbi, (which is to say, being interpreted, Master,) where dwellest thou? He said unto them, Come and see. They came and saw where he dwelt, and abode with him that day: for it was about the tenth hour. One of the two which heard John speak, and followed him, was Andrew, Simon Peter's brother. He first findeth his own brother Simon, and saith unto him, We have found the Messiah, which is, being interpreted, the Christ. And he brought him to Jesus.

We can easily see Andrew's concern about spiritual things. He appears to have been a man with balance in his life. He did not neglect his responsibility to work for a living, but at the same time he did not neglect the most important aspect of any life—the spiritual. He was a disciple of John, one who took the time to learn and to follow the teachings of that great man. This demonstrates his commitment. When he heard John identify Jesus as "the Lamb of God," and then spent the day with the Lord, Andrew was willing to commit to Jesus, being convinced that He was the Messiah. Do not mistake this seemingly rapid change as an indication that Andrew lacked depth or was wishy-washy. What this shows is a depth of perception on his part. This normal working man grasped in a very short time what many "brilliant" scholars over the years have failed to understand or believe.

It is important to note as well that Andrew was a seeker of truth. He had previously been in the wilderness with John, seeking God's word from that great prophet. Andrew actively sought the companionship and teaching of the Lord when John pointed him in that direction. As far as I can tell, Andrew gives us the first example of the fervent evangelistic zeal that overwhelms the heart of one when he or she finds Jesus. "He first findeth his own brother Simon, and saith unto him, We have found the Messiah, which is, being interpreted, the Christ."

There is a tradition that Andrew died as a martyr in the town of Patra, crucified on an X-shaped cross. No one knows for certain. What is important is what we learn of this apostle of the Lord, this fisherman who became a fisher of men.

November 3

The Apostle Philip

What do we know about Philip, the apostle? There are four passages in the Gospel of John that give us some insight into the man. The first is found in John 1:43-51. While this passage would seem to deal primarily with Nathanael and the Lord, there are a few statements found within its verses that tell us much about Philip. For instance, in verse 45 notice the first three words, "Philip findeth Nathanael." Having "found him, of whom Moses in the law, and the prophets, did write, Jesus of Nazareth, the son of Joseph," Philip could not wait to tell another. Even the skeptical response by Nathanael, "Can there any good thing come out of Nazareth?" did not discourage him. Philip answered, "Come and see."

What a lesson that is for us today. "Come and see." Let us take people to the source of truth, let them see Jesus for themselves. In other words, let the glorious light of the gospel do the talking, let the unassailable evidence of the gospels convince the unbeliever. What better lesson can we learn from Philip than to search out unbelievers, tell them of Jesus, and invite them to "come and see?"

In John 6:1-13 we find the feeding of the 5,000 (and that numbered only the men). In verses 5-7 we find, "When Jesus then lifted up his eyes, and saw a great company come unto him, he saith unto Philip, Whence shall we buy bread, that these may eat? And this he said to prove him: for he himself knew what he would do. Philip answered him, Two hundred pennyworth of bread is not sufficient for them, that every one of them may take a little." In his dealings with Nathanael, Philip had distinguished himself with his evangelistic fervor and his confessed faith in the Lord, but as with all of us, he still had room for growth and understanding. In the feeding of the 5,000, Philip was learning to trust implicitly in the Lord even when there didn't seem to be any answer to the problem.

In John 12:20-22 we are told, "And there were certain Greeks among them that came up to worship at the feast: the same came therefore to Philip, which was of Bethsaida of Galilee, and desired him, saying, Sir, we would see Jesus. Philip cometh and telleth Andrew: and again Andrew and Philip tell Jesus." Perhaps these Greeks approached Philip because he had a Greek name. I find it interesting that these men approached Philip, a member of the closest associates of Jesus, with their request. Does this not indicate a certain degree of approachability, a quality of character that did not discourage people from coming to him? I have known Christians with such a "separatist" attitude that people were hesitant to come to them. What a shame it would be to have people put off by such an attitude when what they wanted to do was to "see Jesus."

Finally, in John 14:6-8 we read, "Jesus saith unto him, I am the way, the truth, and the life: no man cometh unto the Father, but by me. If ye had known me, ye should have known my Father also: and from henceforth ye know him, and have seen him. Philip saith unto him, Lord, show us the Father, and it sufficeth us." Note Philip's eagerness and willingness to believe, along with his confidence that Jesus could fulfill such a request.

Philip is seen to be a sincere, zealous, easily approached man with a simple, "come and see" attitude. Did he have weaknesses? Yes, but our Lord would use him.

The Apostle Thomas

One of the most frequently mentioned apostles, but usually in a negative way, was Thomas. While we are not told a great deal about the man himself, we find a few events recorded in the Gospel of John that give us some insight into the character of this often criticized man.

In John 11:7-16 we find the Lord determined to go to Bethany in the region of Judea because of the death of His friend, Lazarus. The journey He desired to make could have proven to be extremely dangerous because of the antagonism felt toward Jesus by many of the prominent Jews in the region. Of all of the apostles, it was Thomas who said at that time, "Let us also go, that we may die with him" (v. 16). Here he demonstrated courage, and not simply courage, but loyalty as well. Thomas said, "Let us also go, that we may die with *him*." Thomas was willing to die with Jesus. I pray that I would be of the same mind and show the same degree of such fine attributes.

John 14:1-5 is another passage that grants us some insight into the heart of this man. In this famous passage, Jesus spoke of going to prepare a place for His disciples and promised that He would return. The gospels indicate to us that at the time of this statement, the apostles were confused and even disturbed by the way events had been going and by some of the teaching that Jesus had done. They did not know where Jesus was going, they did not understand what was meant by His promise to return, and they certainly did not know how they were going to get to where He was going. But it was Thomas who said, "Lord, we know not whither thou goest; and how can we know the way?" He wanted to know the answer. He was too honest and too earnest to simply sit there as though he understood when he did not. So he expressed his lack of understanding and his question prompted one of the most memorable of the Lord's statements in verse 6, "I am the way, the truth, and the life; no man cometh unto the Father, but by me."

In John 20:19-27 we find the famous passage in which Thomas said, "Except I shall see in his hands the print of the nails, and put my finger into the print of the nails, and thrust my hand into his side, I will not believe" (v. 25). Because of this statement, Thomas has been branded a doubter. Indeed, his name has become associated with someone who simply will not believe—a "Doubting Thomas." I am not so certain that that reputation is warranted. No one wanted to believe any more than Thomas, yet his reaction was that of a careful man, one who demanded proof. Notice that Thomas prefaced his statement of unbelief with the word "except." His unbelief was conditional. If he saw the same evidence that had convinced the other apostles, he would believe.

Eight days later Jesus appeared again to the disciples and this time Thomas was present. He saw the print of the nails, beheld the wound in the side of the Lord, and said, "My Lord and my God" (John 20:28). Thomas made this Great Confession. There was no doubt now. This was Jesus, His Lord and his God. The resurrection convicted Thomas that Jesus was God in the flesh.

Thomas is also called Didymus which means "twin." I know nothing of his physical twin, but we can all be his "spiritual" twin by being courageous and loyal to Jesus, by seeking for greater understanding of the Lord's words, and by being convicted by the evidence that Jesus is our Lord and our God.

November 5

The Apostle Bartholomew

Bartholomew's name appears only four times in the New Testament and each time it is in one of the lists of the apostles. This would seem to indicate that we know very little about this man, but that is not necessarily true. By investigating a little further into the matter, we can learn much. In the lists of the apostles found in Matthew and in Mark, Bartholomew is paired with Philip. In the gospel according to John, nothing is said of the apostle Bartholomew.

However, we do find John mentioning someone in connection with Philip, and that person's name is Nathanael. Let's look a bit more closely.

In John 21:1-2 we find, "After these things Jesus showed himself again to the disciples at the sea of Tiberias; and on this wise showed he himself. There were together Simon Peter, and Thomas called Didymus, and Nathanael of Cana in Galilee, and the sons of Zebedee, and two other of his disciples." First we see from this passage that like all of the apostles, except Judas Iscariot, Nathanael was a Galilean. Second, we find that he, like the other apostles, was a witness of the resurrected Christ. A third interesting fact has to do with the name Bartholomew. It is not what we would call a "first name"; it is a last name. Bartholomew means "son of Tolmai." These considerations have led many scholars to identify Bartholomew with Nathanael—making his name Nathanael Bartholomew—or Nathanael, son of Tolmai. About Nathanael we can ascertain much from the Scriptures.

In John 1:44-51 we read:

Philip findeth Nathanael, and saith unto him, We have found him, of whom Moses in the law, and the prophets, did write, Jesus of Nazareth, the son of Joseph. And Nathanael said unto him, Can there any good thing come out of Nazareth? Philip saith unto him, Come and see. Jesus saw Nathanael coming to him, and saith of him, Behold, an Israelite indeed, in whom is no guile. Nathanael saith unto him, Whence knowest thou me? Jesus answered and said unto him, Before that Philip called thee, when thou wast under the fig tree, I saw thee. Nathanael answered and saith unto him, Rabbi, thou art the Son of God; thou art the King of Israel. Jesus answered and said unto him, Because I said unto thee, I saw thee under the fig tree, believest thou? Thou shalt see greater things than these. And he saith unto him, Verily, verily, I say unto you, hereafter ye shall see heaven open, and the angels of God ascending and descending upon the Son of man.

Let's notice a few things. Nathanael was brought to the Lord by someone else, a follower of Jesus. That can be said of all who are Christians. Someone cared enough and was faithful enough to tell us about the Lord. This emphasizes our need to do the same, care enough and be faithful enough to tell someone about Jesus. We might also note that Nathanael's belief and commitment were not based merely on Philip's opinion. Remember that he said, "Can there any good thing come out of Nazareth?" Perhaps that appears to be an unreasonable bias, but what sets Nathanael apart is that when Philip said, "Come and see," Nathanael went and saw. A lot of people allow their bias and previously held notions to keep them from investigating the truth.

Not Nathanael. Jesus even said, "Behold, an Israelite indeed, in whom is no guile." When Nathanael recognized that Jesus possessed supernatural knowledge, his conclusion was, "Rabbi, thou art the Son of God; thou art the King of Israel."

Jesus told him that he would see greater things than these. If my understanding that Bartholomew and Nathanael are one and the same person, then Nathanael walked with Jesus through his earthly ministry. He saw Jesus heal the sick, cast out demons, calm the sea, and raise the dead. He had his confession of faith so profoundly confirmed by the Lord's resurrection.

So the picture is that of a simple man, possessed with a deep honesty and integrity, willing to investigate for himself and make an honest evaluation. Once having made that evaluation, he was willing to commit to it and live by it. I don't know that a person could do much better than that.

November 6

The Apostle James, the Son of Zebedee

James, along with his brother John and his father, Zebedee, were fishermen by trade who were in partnership with Simon Peter. In Luke 5:1-11 we read of a most interesting event. These men had been fishing on the Sea of Galilee throughout the night and had caught nothing. As they were on shore mending their nets, the Lord, being pressed by the multitude of people, entered into Simon's boat and asked him to push out a little from the land; thus from Simon's boat the Lord taught the multitude on the shore. At the conclusion of his teaching, Jesus instructed Simon to launch out into the deep and let down his nets. While hesitant to do so, Simon followed the words of the Lord and was rewarded with a tremendous catch of fish, so large that his nets were not able to contain it. Simon summoned his partners, including James, to assist him. They were astonished by the catch and Simon, James, and John left all and followed Jesus. Matthew 4:18-22 gives us additional information about James, including that marvelous statement of the Lord, "Follow me, and I will make you fishers of men."

These two passages give us some insight into James. He had witnessed, indeed participated in, a wonderful miracle. When the call to follow Jesus came, Matthew tells us that he and his brother, John, "immediately left the ship and their father, and followed him." When the evidence demanded it and the call was made, James responded. James was gainfully employed in an honest profession, and that was good. However, when the best came, he recognized it and responded. It is not always a question of choosing between good and bad, sometimes it is a question of choosing between what is good and what is best and being wise enough to make the right choice. Together with his brother John and with Simon Peter, James would be part of the "inner circle" of the apostles.

In Mark 3:17 James and John were called by Jesus, "The Sons of Thunder." An event that took place in the ninth chapter of Luke helps us to understand this a little better. As Jesus was journeying to Jerusalem, he sent messengers before him into a Samaritan village to make ready for him. The villagers would not receive him. In verses 54-56 we find, "And when his disciples James and John saw this, they said, Lord, wilt thou that we command fire to come down from heaven, and consume them, even as Elijah did? But he turned, and rebuked them, and said, Ye know not what manner of spirit ye are of. For the Son of man is not come to destroy men's lives, but to save them. And they went to another village.

We see a man who was still learning. The nature of the work that Jesus had come to do, as well as the nature of the work that James had been called to perform, was not yet clear to him. Perhaps for him, temper was a problem; but he was growing.

In Mark 10:37 we find James and John making the following request of Jesus, "Grant unto us that we may sit, one on thy right hand, and the other on thy left hand, in thy glory." Thus pride and ambition show themselves in the life of James. This does not mean that James was a bad man—much to the contrary. He simply did not yet understand. He was seeking a place of prominence, because he did not yet realize that true greatness in the Lord's kingdom is determined by service.

If we look at James closely, we see a man who was by no means perfect, but who continued to learn and to grow. He came to understand who Jesus truly was, and he was willing to give up all and follow him wherever. There were moments of weakness and error, as we all have. Yet after the resurrection of Jesus, no one stood more firmly than this man. In Acts 12:1-2, we see what became of James. "Now about that time Herod the king stretched forth his hands to vex certain of the church. And he killed James the brother of John with the sword." James was the first apostle to die for Jesus. What an example for us to emulate! Be willing to learn and to grow, make corrections in our lives as needed, and be convicted—even if it means that we must die.

November 7

The Apostles—Thaddeus and James, the Son of Alphaeus

Let's consider two men found in the list of the apostles given in Luke 6:12-16. There we find,

And it came to pass in those days, that he went out into a mountain to pray, and continued all night in prayer to God. And when it was day, he called unto him his disciples: and of them he chose twelve, whom also he named apostles; Simon, (whom he also named Peter,) and Andrew his brother, James and John, Philip and Bartholomew, Matthew and Thomas, James the son of Alphaeus, and Simon called Zelotes, and Judas the brother of James, and Judas Iscariot, which also was the traitor.

Consider Thaddaeus. Perhaps you might be thinking, "I didn't see the name Thaddaeus in that list." In the passage with which we began, this man is identified as Judas, the brother of James. It is interesting that some writers have referred to Thaddaeus as "Trinomious" or the "man with three names." He is called Thaddaeus, Judas the brother of James, and Lebbaeus. While we know very little about this man, the one time he is singled out in the gospels gives us a slight glimpse into his thinking. In John 14:21-22 we read, "He that hath my commandments, and keepeth them, he it is that loveth me: and he that loveth me shall be loved of my Father, and I will love him, and will manifest myself to him. Judas saith unto him, not Iscariot, Lord, how is it that thou wilt manifest thyself unto us, and not unto the world?"

There is little doubt that, based upon his question, Thaddaeus still held a decidedly earthly view of Jesus. His desire was that Jesus manifest himself to the world, not as a suffering Savior, but as a ruling king. That was the generally held concept of the Messiah by the Jews at that time, and the apostles had a very difficult time divorcing themselves from those previously held views.

Here was a man, ordinary to all appearances, who did not grasp everything immediately or completely, but the Lord chose him as an apostle. There is a tradition (how reliable it is I do not know) that says Thaddaeus preached the gospel in Edessa near the Euphrates River and was very successful. He preached the gospel in other areas as well, only to die a martyr's death at Ararat by being shot through with arrows.

Even less is known about James, the son of Alphaeus. Some believe he may have been the brother of Matthew, or Levi, who is also called the son of Alphaeus in Mark 2:14. Still others identify him with James the Less of Mark 15:40, but none of these can be absolutely proven.

There are traditions about this James that are interesting, but they are only traditions. It is said that this James preached in Palestine and in Egypt. According to one tradition, James was crucified in Egypt. Yet another says that he died a most unusual death—having his body sawn into pieces. Again, no one knows for certain.

Neither James the son of Alphaeus nor Thaddaeus would have been considered great men from a purely worldly perspective. They were not rich or powerful, at least as far as we know. I find this fascinating. Jesus could have used the chief rulers of his people, but John 12:42 tells us that many of them were afraid to confess him for fear that the Pharisees would expel them from the synagogue. He could have used the wise of the world, but Matthew 11:25 indicates that perhaps their much learning got in the way of their believing the simple truth. He could have used the rich, but if the rich young ruler in Matthew 19 is any indication, placing Jesus ahead of their wealth was difficult. So he used ordinary people, people like me and perhaps you. When one is willing to give himself over to the Lord like clay in the potter's hands, there is no limit to what the Lord can accomplish.

November 8

The Apostles—Matthew and Simon the Zealot

In Luke 5:27-31 we are introduced to another individual selected by Jesus to be one of His apostles. This man was named Levi, but he is much better known as Matthew. The passage says:

And after these things he went forth, and saw a publican, named Levi, sitting at the receipt of custom: and he said unto him, Follow me. And he left all, rose up, and followed him. And Levi made him a great feast in his own house: and there was a great company of publicans and of others that sat down with them. But their scribes and Pharisees murmured against his disciples, saying, Why do ye eat and drink with publicans and sinners.

What was a publican? They were employees of a group of men, or an individual man, who was a member of the *publicani*. These were wealthy men of Rome who took care of the taxes and saw to it that they were collected in the provinces. This was a source of profit for them. Publicans were men hired by the *publicani* to do the actual collecting of the taxes. Tax collectors were generally looked down upon as their occupation lent itself to greed, extortion, and fraud. For a nationalistic people like the Jews, these men were collecting taxes for an occupying foreign government—Rome. Matthew was a member of this group of people, yet Jesus chose him to be one of the twelve.

In Luke 6:12-16 we find a listing of the original twelve apostles. The last one named in verse 15 was Simon called Zelotes. We know very little about this man except that he was a zealot. What was a zealot? The Zealots were fanatical Jewish Nationalists who rigorously clung to the Mosaic Law. Initially they were brave men who disregarded the suffering involved in their struggle to preserve what they saw as the purity of their religion and to preserve what they understood to be their God-given right to possess the land of Palestine.

This is the type of background from which Simon came. He was a nationalist, a man devoted to the Mosaic Law, with a hatred for all things Roman. Considering his selection as one of the twelve, doesn't it make the selection of Matthew even more unusual? Or considering the selection of Matthew, doesn't that make the selection of Simon seem peculiar?

In both cases I think the lesson to be learned is not so much from the men themselves, but from the fact that Jesus chose them. It took the Lord to see the potential in both, a potential that perhaps others might not have seen. Matthew would hardly have appeared to be the type of individual who would have been willing to follow Jesus. He was a publican by choice, and his lifestyle would have given no indication of the possibility of a deep religious conviction. On the other hand, Simon was a man whose background nurtured hatred for his enemies, not love. For a zealot, violence would not have been out of the question as the means to the desired end.

Perhaps the next time we hesitate to approach a particular individual, or a group of people, having convinced ourselves that they are not the types of people to whom the gospel would appeal, we would do well to give them a chance. Remember Matthew and Simon. God does not look upon people as we do. We are so often swayed by appearances, but the Lord looks on the heart.

November 9

The Apostle John

John, along with his brother James and his father Zebedee, was a fisherman by trade. They were in partnership with Peter and Andrew. Very early in the Lord's public ministry, John was called to be a "fisher of men," and he immediately forsook all and followed Jesus. In addition to being one of the original twelve apostles, John, with James and Peter, was privileged to be part of what I choose to call "the inner circle." As such, he was present at times when the other nine apostles were not. John was privileged to see some things they did not see, to hear some things they did not hear.

What can we learn of the character of this man? There are a number of passages that help us to understand the personality of John. One such passage is Mark 3:17, where John and his brother James were referred to by Jesus as "the Sons of Thunder." Other passages indicate that this was probably a phrase the Lord used to describe his temperament. For instance, in Luke 9:49-50 we read, "And John answered and said, Master, we saw one casting our devils in thy name; and we forbade him, because he followeth not with us. And Jesus said unto him, Forbid him not: for he that is not against us is for us." In verses 51-56 we find John, along with his brother James, asking the Lord if they should call down fire from heaven to consume a village of Samaritans who would not receive Jesus. In Mark 10:35-37 we find evidence of earthly ambition in John as he and his brother requested that they might be given the seats on the right and left hand of the Lord in glory.

After the death, resurrection, and ascension of Jesus, John is often found in the company of Peter. These two men healed the lame man before the temple gate that was called Beautiful in Acts 3. In Acts 4 they stood boldly before the Jewish council, the Sanhedrin, and said, "Whether it be right in the sight of God to hearken unto you more than unto God, judge ye. For we cannot but speak the things which we have seen and heard." Acts 8 reveals that it was Peter and John who traveled to Samaria to impart the miraculous gifts of the Holy Spirit unto those who had received the word of the Lord by the preaching of the evangelist, Philip. We know from Galatians 2:9 that John was viewed as being a "pillar" of the church in Jerusalem. When all of this is considered together, we see a working man with a certain fiery disposition and a degree of earthly ambition. He was also a man of deep religious conviction, and in that his personality served him well. He felt deeply, and he believed deeply. When the call came he responded immediately. He was privileged to be part of that inner circle. When courage was called for, he was there and he showed the ability to lead.

There is another aspect to the character of John that needs to be considered. I believe that in John 13:23 he is referred to as the disciple "whom Jesus loved." I believe that it was John who stood near the cross of Jesus and to whom the Lord entrusted the care of his mother. In John 19:26-27 we find, "When Jesus therefore saw his mother, and the disciple standing by, whom he loved, he saith unto his mother, Woman, behold thy son! Then saith he to the disciple, Behold thy mother! And from that hour the disciple took her unto his own home."

It was John who ran with Peter to investigate the story of the empty tomb. It was also John who first recognized the Lord when he appeared to the apostles along the seashore as they were fishing. What we read of John seems to indicate that perhaps he was the closest of all of the Lord's associates on earth. Of no other are such terms of endearment used. He was not a perfect man, yet he is described as "the disciple whom Jesus loved."

Our certain knowledge of John ends on the Isle of Patmos where we leave him, a brother and companion in the tribulation and the kingdom. Near the conclusion of the book of Revelation John wrote, "And I John saw these things, and heard them." In Acts 4:13 the statement was made concerning Peter and John, "and they took knowledge of them, that they had been with Jesus." By emulating the best of the qualities of John, people will be able to look at us and know that we too walk with Jesus.

The Apostle Matthias

After the ascension of our Lord into heaven, Peter stood up in the midst of the disciples, about 120 in number, and spoke of the suicide of Judas and the need to fill his place among the apostles. Acts 1:16-26 tells us:

> Men and brethren, this Scripture must needs have been fulfilled, which the Holy Ghost by the mouth of David spake before concerning Judas, which was guide to them that took Jesus. For he was numbered with us, and had obtained part of this ministry. Now this man purchased a field with the reward of iniquity; and falling headlong, he burst asunder in the midst, and all his bowels gushed out. And it was known unto all the dwellers at Jerusalem; insomuch as that field is called in their proper tongue, Aceldama, that is to say, The field of blood. For it is written in the book of Psalms, Let his habitation be desolate, and let no man dwell therein: and his bishoprick let another take. Wherefore of these men which have companied with us all the time that the Lord Jesus went in and out among us, beginning from the baptism of John, unto that same day that he was taken up from us, must one be ordained to be a witness with us of his resurrection. And they appointed two, Joseph called Barsabbas, who was surnamed Justus, and Matthias. And they prayed, and said, Thou, Lord, which knowest the hearts of all men, show whether of these two thou hast chosen, that he may take part of this ministry and apostleship, from which Judas by transgression fell, that he might go to his own place. And they gave forth their lots; and the lot fell upon Matthias; and he was numbered with the eleven.

I do not believe that I have ever seen an article written about Matthias, and the reason why is that there is very little information known about him. The passage we have looked at from Acts 1 is all that there is. However, there is a quality of character that this man obviously possessed that is indicated by his time spent as a disciple of the Lord. In order to be considered as a replacement for Judas, the individual had to "have companied with us all the time that the Lord Jesus went in and out among us, beginning from the baptism of John, unto that same day that he was taken up from us, must one be ordained to be a witness with us of his resurrection."

Matthias had been a disciple of Jesus for approximately three years. During that time he was not part of the specially chosen twelve, the men that Jesus called apostles. The fact that he was not one so chosen by the Lord did not prevent him from following and serving the Master. Many have great difficulty being in what may be considered a position of secondary importance, at least as man may view it. For some, only a position of prominence will satisfy. Not so with Matthias.

I look at Matthias and I see the vast number of people who make up the army of the Lord. Not everyone occupies a position of perceived prominence. Not all are deacons, elders, or preachers, but each individual member is equally important. The men and women who make up the majority of the Lord's church live their lives serving the Lord to the best of their ability whether or not it is recognized by any one on this earth. There would be no church without men like Matthias.

November 11

The Apostle Judas Isacariot

In Zechariah 11:12-13, a portion of a beautiful Messianic prophecy, we read, "And I said unto them, If ye think good, give me my price; and if not, forbear. So they weighed for my price thirty pieces of silver. And the Lord said unto me, Cast it unto the potter: and a goodly price that I was prised at of them. And I took the thirty pieces of silver, and cast them to the potter in the house of the Lord." The betrayal of our Lord Jesus for the price of a servant who had been gored by an ox (according to Exod. 21:32) was prophesied. Someone would betray the Savior. That brings us to the apostle whose name has become synonymous with traitor—Judas.

What type of person would become the central figure in the betrayal of our Lord? The Scriptures give us some insight into his character. In John 12:3-6 we find, "Then took Mary a pound of ointment of spikenard, very costly, and anointed the feet of Jesus, and wiped his feet with her hair: and the house was filled with the odor of the ointment. Then saith one of his disciples, Judas Iscariot, Simon's son, which should betray him, Why was not this ointment sold for three hundred pence, and given to the poor? This he said, not that he cared for the poor; but because he was a thief, and had the bag, and bare what was put therein." While indicating a concern for the poor and less fortunate, Judas was, in fact, a thief.

We see this love of money manifested in a most horrific way. In Matthew 26:14-16 we read, "Then one of the twelve, called Judas Iscariot, went unto the chief priests, and said unto them, What will ye give me, and I will deliver him unto you? And they covenanted with him for thirty pieces of silver. And from that time he sought opportunity to betray him." So with malice afore-thought, Judas waited for the right time to present itself to betray his Lord and Master.

At the Last Supper, as Jesus and his apostles were gathered in the upper room, Jesus announced to them, "Verily I say unto you, that one of you shall betray me" (Matt. 26:21). What type of man would join his voice with the other apostles and say, "Master, is it I?" as Judas did in verse 25, having already made the agreement to do just that with the chief priests? Only one of a devious and sinister nature could do so. Later, that same night, as the act of betrayal was being carried out, Judas identified the Lord in the Garden of Gethsemane by saying, "Master, master" and kissing him. My heart aches to think of Jesus saying to this man, "Judas, betrayest thou the Son of man with a kiss?" (Luke 22:48).

In Matthew 17:1-5 we are told, "When the morning was come, all the chief priests and elders of the people took counsel against Jesus to put him to death: and when they had bound him, they led him away, and delivered him to Pontius Pilate the governor. Then Judas, which had betrayed him, when he saw that he was condemned, repented himself, and brought again the thirty pieces of silver to the chief priests and elders, saying, I have sinned in that I have betrayed innocent blood. And they said, What is that to us? See thou to that. And he cast down the pieces of silver in the temple, departed, and went and hanged himself."

Was Judas forced to do what he did? No, he had the disposition to do it but also the freedom of choice. It was not God choosing and manipulating this man to betray his Son. Luke 22:3 and John 13:2, 27 all indicate that Satan took advantage of this man's lack of character and influenced him to perform his heinous act. Yet, even having done this infamous deed, Judas still could have been forgiven and been a stalwart follower of Jesus. Peter denied the Lord, but when confronted with the reality of his sin, he went out and wept bitterly. His life from that point on was a life of service. Judas had the same opportunity, but he went out and hanged himself. Recent efforts have been made to portray Judas as a sympathetic character. He was not; he did what he did by choice.

The Apostle Peter

The best known of the original twelve apostles was Peter. Peter was a working man, a fisherman by trade. Along with his brother Andrew, he was in partnership with Zebedee and his sons, John and James. There was in Peter's personality a certain degree of impulsiveness. He occasionally spoke and acted without thoroughly thinking something through. We see this in Luke 22:33 where Peter told Jesus, "Lord, I am ready to go with thee, both into prison, and to death." John 18:10 informs us that as Jesus was being taken in the Garden of Gethsemane, Peter drew his sword and cut off the right ear of the High Priest's servant, Malchus.

With Peter we also see a certain depth of perception and the courage to act upon his convictions. It was Peter who answered the question of Jesus in John 6, "Will ye also go away?" with the marvelous statement recorded in verses 68-69, "Lord, to whom shall we go? Thou hast the words of eternal life. And we believe and are sure that thou art that Christ, the Son of the living God." It was Peter who answered the Lord's question, "But whom say ye that I am?" in Matthew 16:15, with the words, "Thou art the Christ, the Son of the living God" (v. 16).

It is important that we address Peter's denial. In Mark 14:26-28 Jesus told his disciples that they would all be offended because of him and would scatter into the night. In v. 29 Peter said, "Although all shall be offended, yet will not I." Perhaps we could say that in the downward move to denial, the first step was overconfidence. Moving further on in Mark 14 we find in verses 30-31, "And Jesus saith unto him, Verily I say unto thee, that this day, even in this night, before the cock crow twice, thou shalt deny me thrice. But he spake the more vehemently, If I should die with thee, I will not deny thee in any wise. Likewise also said they all." It certainly indicates that Peter was the first to say, "I will die before I deny thee." Thus we note how Peter spoke rashly, without considering the cost of his words before he spoke them. Impulsiveness and overconfidence won out over clear thought and sound judgment. Step two had been taken.

Mark 14:37 shows us step three: "And he cometh, and findeth them sleeping, and saith unto Peter, Simon, Sleepest thou? Couldest not thou watch one hour?" When Peter awoke to find himself confronted by men carrying swords and staves, and also being confronted by his own failure to stay awake with his Lord, Peter reacted violently. Many Christians react very strongly when confronted with their own failures.

Step number four is found in Luke 22:54, "Then took they him, and led him, and brought him into the high priest's house. And Peter followed afar off." A person cannot follow "afar off," for he tends to lose sight of the one he is following. In verses 55-61 of Luke 22, just as the Lord had said, Peter denied him three times. Verses 60-61 give us the heart-rending details of that final denial, "And Peter said, Man, I know not what thou sayest. And immediately, while he yet speak, the cock crew. And the Lord turned, and looked upon Peter. And Peter remembered the word of the Lord, how he had said unto him, Before the cock crow, thou shalt deny me thrice."

However, Luke 22:62 tells us, "And Peter went out, and wept bitterly." I can sympathize with the tremendous guilt and overwhelming sorrow that Peter must have felt when Jesus turned and looked at him, and all that Jesus had said came flooding back into his mind. The simple look of the Son of God cut Peter to the heart. Instead of wallowing in self-pity or throwing his hands up in despair, this man acknowledged his sin and rose from it to become the Peter whose very name speaks of strength and conviction. He rose to a place of faithfulness in the eyes of God, to a place of stalwart service in the work of the Lord. Peter would later write words that illustrate a profound change in the attitude of this man. In 1 Peter 5:6 he wrote, "Humble yourselves therefore under the mighty hand of God, that he may exalt you in due time."

November 13

The Apostle Paul

Paul was born in the city of Tarsus of Cilicia sometime close to the beginning of the first century. As was customary for Jewish boys, he learned a trade, that of a tent-maker. Paul wrote in Acts 22:3, "I am verily a man which am a Jew, born in Tarsus, a city in Cilicia, yet brought up in this city at the feet of Gamaliel, and taught according to the perfect manner of the law of the fathers, and was zealous toward God, as ye all are this day." Paul described himself in Philippians 3:5 as "circumcised the eighth day, of the stock of

Israel, of the tribe of Benjamin, an Hebrew of the Hebrews; as touching the law, a Pharisee."

The first we read of Saul (later called Paul) is in Acts 7 in connection with the stoning of Stephen. We are told that the clothes of those involved in the stoning were laid at the feet of a young man whose name was Saul. Acts 8:1 informs us, "And Saul was consenting unto his death." His initial reaction toward his fellow Jews who became Christians was decidedly hostile. Many years later as Paul stood before King Agrippa, he candidly admitted as much in Acts 26:9-11: "I verily thought with myself, that I ought to do many things contrary to the name of Jesus of Nazareth. Which thing I also did in Jerusalem: and many of the saints did I shut up in prison, having received authority from the chief priests; and when they were put to death, I gave my voice against them. And I punished them oft in every synagogue, and compelled them to blaspheme; and being exceedingly mad against them, I persecuted them even unto strange cities." Yet, by the time of his death, Paul had preached the gospel to countless Jews and Gentiles and had written, by inspiration, at least thirteen books of the New Testament. What happened to this man? What had brought about such a profound change?

On his way from Jerusalem to the city of Damascus for the purpose of arresting those he found to be Christians, Paul miraculously met the Lord on the road. After identifying Himself, the Lord told Paul to go into the city of Damascus where he would be told what to do. After three days he was visited by a disciple named Ananias, who told him what to do, culminating with that marvelous exhortation, "And now why tarriest thou? Arise, and be baptized, and wash away thy sins, calling on the name of the Lord." (Acts 22:16).

Paul was a specially chosen messenger to the Gentiles. Even though he had not accompanied the other apostles with the Lord while Jesus was here on earth, Paul had been a witness of the resurrected Christ and an apostle chosen by Jesus "as one born out of time." That which he taught came from the Lord, and not from men. In Galatians 1:11-12 Paul wrote, "But I certify you, brethren, that the gospel which was preached of me is not after man. For I neither received it of man, neither was I taught it, but by the revelation of Jesus Christ."

What can one write about Paul in the confines of an article such as this? My mind is drawn to 2 Corinthians 11:23-28. There we read,

Are they ministers of Christ? (I speak as a fool) I am more; in labours more abundant, in stripes above measure, in prisons more frequent, in deaths oft. Of the Jews five times received I forty stripes save one. Thrice was I beaten with rods, once was I stoned, a night and a day I have been in the deep; in journeyings often, in perils of waters, in perils of robbers, in perils by mine own countrymen, in perils by the heathen, in perils in the city, in perils in the wilderness, in perils in the sea, in perils among false brethren; in weariness and painfulness, in watchings often, in hunger and thirst, in fastings often, in cold and nakedness. Beside those things that are without, that which cometh upon me daily, the care of all the churches.

At times it appears that Paul's life was filled with tension, pain and suffering, yet the message he brought was one of peace, harmony, joy, and happiness. There was a contentment and purpose that Paul felt that nothing else could match. He wrote in Philippians 4, a letter he wrote from a Roman prison, "Not that I speak in respect of want: for I have learned, in whatsoever state I am, therewith to be content. I know both how to be abased, and I know how to abound: everywhere and in all things I am instructed both to be full and to be hungry, both to abound and to suffer need. I can do all things through Christ which strengtheneth me."

By applying those same principles in our lives, we will be able to meet the challenges that Paul presented to us in that same chapter of Philippians. In verse 9 he wrote, "Those things, which ye have both learned, and received, and heard, and seen in me, do: and the God of peace shall be with you."

November 14

"You Are the Lord, You Alone"
(Nehemiah 9:6)

By Adam Litmer

"You are the Lord, You alone."
You with the power to change heart of stone.
You who set sun and moon with tremendous might.
You who shatter darkness with piercing light.

"You have set your glory" above the earth.
You have shown mercy through a Savior's birth.
I consider "the moon and stars, which you have set in place,"
As I gaze in wide wonder up into space.

"What is man that You are mindful of him?"
With his passions and lusts, spurred by whim.
But you know the value of my poor soul's worth,
So I shout, "How majestic is your name in all the earth!"

"I will give thanks to the Lord with my whole heart."
And I will ask for strength to do my part.
I will give ear to your words and every behest,
For "the Lord is a stronghold for the oppressed."

The righteous need not fear what they will do,
For "those who know your name put their trust in you."
But I fear for those who spurn and mock my Lord.
He has said, "If a man will not repent, God will whet His sword."

"For the Lord is righteous; he loves righteous deeds."
So give me courage to take Your word abroad, planting the seeds.
Refreshed and strong, each morning I awaken,
"Because He is at my right hand, I shall not be shaken."

November 15

Loving God While Young

It is important to love and obey God while young, for it is a time when God can be most easily remembered. A young person has not had the time or opportunity to be hardened or disillusioned by a lifetime of viewing things from the wrong perspective. A young person has not yet been burdened with the worries of "making a living." Most young people have not yet been burdened with illnesses and disease that so often accompany advancing years.

It is important to love and obey God while young because He deserves it. He is the Creator and Provider of all things that we need and enjoy. Colossians 1:16-17 tells us, "For by Him were all things created, that are in heaven, and that are in earth, visible and invisible, whether they be thrones, or dominions, or principalities, or powers: all things were created by Him, and for Him: and He is before all things, and by Him all things consist."

Unfortunately, many teenagers just don't see how being a Christian can be useful to them—they just don't see how it is relevant in their lives. They see it as just "going to church" and interfering with a lot of other things they would rather be doing. (Did you ever notice how many school activities seem to take place on Wednesday night?) They see spiritual activities like worship and Bible study as something that Mom and Dad "make" them do. But I'll tell you something—Christianity as a way of life (and that is what it is) just makes sense.

Just think of some of the young people who played very important parts in Bible history and who are presented as outstanding examples, not just to young people, but also to all people. Think of Shadrach, Meshach, and Abednego of Daniel 3. Consider seventeen-year-old Joseph in Genesis 37, and then not much older in Genesis 39. How about Jesus at the age of twelve in the temple (Luke 2:41-52)? There is also the young evangelist Timothy to whom Paul wrote two letters. These are all examples of people who greatly affected the lives of others while they were young. All young people can be that way as well. They can greatly affect not only their own lives, but also the lives of their family, acquaintances, and friends.

November 16

"Neither Could They Blush"

In Jeremiah 6 there is a picture painted of a powerful enemy force invading the land of Judah from the north. The "evil that appeareth out of the north" (v.1) was Babylon. The chapter speaks of preparation for their coming that Judah would make, but it would all be to no avail. The nation of Judah would be conquered. The time of retribution was coming. Jeremiah told the people why this was going to happen and appealed to them to return to the ways of the Lord, but they continued to refuse and their wickedness remained.

The chapter ends with Jeremiah comparing the attempts to bring Judah to repentance to the refining of metals. All attempts to "refine" them had failed. Therefore they were going to face the Lord's wrath as "rejected" or "reprobate" silver.

In verses 10-15 of Jeremiah 6, the prophet goes into some detail concerning why this was going to happen to the southern kingdom of Judah. In verse 15 there is a statement found that I want to notice in particular. The verse says, "Were they ashamed when they had committed abomination? Nay, they were not at all ashamed, neither could they blush: therefore they shall fall among them that fall: at the time that I visit them they shall be cast down, saith the Lord." Did you notice the phrase "neither could they blush"?

According to *Webster's New Universal Unabridged Dictionary*, the first two definitions of blush are "to redden, as from embarrassment or shame" and "to feel shame or embarrassment." Christians must not make the same mistake that the citizens of the nation of Judah did, and lose our ability to "feel shame or embarrassment."

Let me give you a few things to consider. Does the widespread acceptance of homosexuality still cause you to blush, or do you now find yourself watching television shows or going to movies where the main sympathetic character or characters are practicing homosexuals, and where much of the humor comes at the expense of those who would oppose it?

Have you maintained your ability to be embarrassed, the ability to blush, over how you may appear it public? Is your sense of style and fashion determined by God and His standards, or is it determined by modern entertainers who appear in public (obviously as part of their appeal) dressed as what God called Judah from a spiritual standpoint, harlots?

Is it possible that the lyrics of modern music—including almost an entire genre of music—can cause you to be embarrassed, to blush to think that people would even sing of such things, or will you go on listening because it "doesn't bother you"? If that is the case, you have lost your ability to blush.

On and on we could go with question after question, but certainly most can see that a great deal of what just twenty years ago was considered cause for blushing, cause for shame and embarrassment, no longer causes folks to even bat an eye. The "things written aforetime were written for our learning" (Rom. 15:4). We must learn from the people of the nation of Judah and never lose our ability to feel shame, to be embarrassed, to blush.

Sabbath Keeping No Longer Required

With the death of the Lord Jesus, the Law of Moses was fulfilled, and no one is under it any longer. Paul wrote in Galatians 3:23-25 the following, "But before faith came, we were kept under the law, shut up unto the faith which should afterwards be revealed. Wherefore the law was our schoolmaster to bring us unto Christ, that we might be justified by faith. But after that faith is come, we are no longer under a schoolmaster." In Colossians 2:14-17 Paul wrote:

> Blotting out the handwriting of ordinances that was against us, which was contrary to us, and took it out of the way, nailing it to His cross; and having spoiled principalities and powers, He made a show of them openly, triumphing over them in it. Let no man therefore judge you in meat, or in drink, or in respect of an holy day, or of the new moon, or of the Sabbath days; which are a shadow of things to come; but the body is of Christ.

The truth of the matter is that no one, including the Jews, is bound to keep the Sabbath any longer.

What we have looked at thus far is sufficient to answer the false assertion that the Roman Catholic Pope changed the Sabbath day from Saturday to Sunday. In the first place, the Sabbath day has not been changed. It is still the seventh day, or Saturday, but no one is required to keep it. Biblically, there is no such thing as the "Christian Sabbath." The first century church came together on the first day of the week, or Sunday, to perform various acts of worship that were peculiar to that day. Acts 20:7 shows us that they partook of the Lord's Supper on the first day of the week, and 1 Corinthians 16:1-2 show us that they "gave of their means," or contributed financially, on the first day of the week. The Lord Jesus rose on the first day of the week, and since Pentecost was the fiftieth day after the Sabbath of the Passover week, the church was begun on the first day of the week (Acts 2).

What about the significance of the seventh day, the day that God rested? Is there significance to it beyond the Sabbath day enjoined upon the Jews? I believe the answer to that question is yes.

In Hebrews 4:1-10 the Hebrew writer writes of several things that fore-shadowed heaven:

> Let us therefore fear, lest, a promise being left us of entering into His rest, any of you should seem to come short of it. For unto us was the gospel preached, as well as unto them: but the word preached did not profit them, not being mixed with faith in them that heard it. For we which have believed do enter into rest, as He said, As I have sworn in my wrath, if they shall enter into My rest: although the works were finished from the foundation of the world. For He spake in a certain place of the seventh day on this wise, And God did rest the seventh day from all His works. And in this place again, if they shall enter into My rest. Seeing therefore it remaineth that some must enter therein, and they to whom it was first preached entered not in because of unbelief: again, He limiteth a certain day, saying in David, Today, after so long a time; as it is said, Today if ye will hear His voice, harden not your hearts. For if Joshua had given them rest, then would He not afterward have spoken of another day. There remaineth therefore a rest to the people of God. For he that is entered into his rest, he also hath ceased from his own works, as God did from His.

In this lengthy passage, the benefits and joys of being in the church are spoken of as foreshadowing heaven. The rest of the seventh day of creation is spoken of as foreshadowing heaven. The Promised Land is spoken of as having foreshadowed heaven, and so is the Sabbath day. The point is, however, that all of these things, including the church, look forward to that "Sabbath rest" that awaits all faithful children of God in heaven.

So, can we learn anything from God's use of the Sabbath day? Absolutely! Is any one bound to keep it today? No!

November 18

Justifying Self

In Luke 10:25-29 we find, "And, behold, a certain lawyer stood up, and tempted him, saying, Master, what shall I do to inherit eternal life? He said unto him, What is written in the law? How readest thou? And he answering said, Thou shalt love the Lord thy God with all thy heart, and with all thy soul, and with all thy strength, and with all thy mind; and thy neighbor as thyself. And he said unto him, Thou hast answered right: this do, and thou shalt live. But he, willing to justify himself, said unto Jesus, And who is my neighbor?"

Luke's account sets the stage for what came after. We have a "certain lawyer." Lawyers were a very learned group of scholars, usually Pharisees, who specialized in the exposition of the Law. We are told that this particular individual asked his question to test, tempt, or make trial of Jesus. It was a good question, "What shall I do to inherit eternal life?"

Jesus' response placed the burden upon the man himself. He was a lawyer, a student of the Law. What did the Law say? His answer was from Deuteronomy 6:5 and Leviticus 19:18. Jesus commended the lawyer's answer, but also made a fine distinction. The answer was correct, but the man had to do more than just say it. He had to do it, he had to live it. But then we find that "willing to justify himself," the lawyer said to Jesus, "Who is my neighbor?"

Why did this lawyer feel the need to justify himself? Was it because Jesus had answered his question so skillfully that he now felt foolish for having asked it? Perhaps. However, and much more probable it seems to me, was because what he knew to be the truth and the way he was actually living did not match up. This exchange prompted the beautiful and famous parable of the Good Samaritan in Luke 10:30-37.

There are occasions when justifying ourselves is acceptable and even called for (for example, if we are falsely accused of some sin). Even the apostle Paul justified himself on several occasions. In fact, it could be said that a major portion of the highly personal 2 Corinthian letter shows Paul doing just that. But it seems to me in a lot of instances, we seek to justify ourselves when we are wrong and don't want to admit it; when we don't want to make the necessary changes, apologies, or whatever else we should do. Instead, there is a tendency to make excuses, to blame others, even to attack others, and to ask questions meant to divert attention from our failings. This isn't unusual; it happens all the time. Why is it that we are often this way, seeking to justify ourselves? Could it be pride, arrogance, and stubbornness—an unholy trinity if ever there was one?

The truth is this desire to seek to justify ourselves is one that we should have begun to confront, remove, and overcome when we became Christians by obeying the gospel. Note what Jesus said in Luke 9:23-24: "If any man will come after me, let him deny himself, and take up his cross daily, and follow me. For whosoever will save his life shall lose it: but whosoever will lose his life for my sake, the same shall save it." Do you see any self-justification there? Actually, Jesus calls for the exact opposite.

"They Had Been with Jesus"

In Acts 3 we read of an event that took place not very long after the church had been established. As Peter and John entered in the temple, they encountered a forty-year-old man who had been lame from birth, and he requested charity from them. Verses 6-8 tell us what happened: "Then Peter said, Silver and gold have I none; but such as I have give I thee: in the name of Jesus Christ of Nazareth rise up and walk. And he took him by the right hand, and lifted him up: and immediately his feet and ankle bones received strength. And he leaping up stood, and walked, and entered with them into the temple, walking, and leaping, and praising God."

Going into the temple, Peter and John boldly proclaimed the gospel of Jesus, attributing the miracle to Him, convicting the people of His murder, and declaring that God had raised Him from the dead. They asserted that all of this had been foretold by the prophets. Their words did not fall on deaf ears, and not everyone who heard them that day received the word gladly. Certain leaders of the Jews had them arrested and placed in hold until the next day when they were brought before the Sanhedrin.

Before the most powerful men in the Jewish nation, Peter proclaimed that the miracle had been performed by the authority of the Lord Jesus Christ, whom, even though they were guilty of crucifying Him, God had raised from the dead. Notice the reaction of the Sanhedrin. Acts 4:13 says, "Now when they saw the boldness of Peter and John, and perceived that they were unlearned and ignorant men, they marveled; and they took knowledge of them, that they had been with Jesus."

There was something about Peter and John that was different, something about them that puzzled the Sanhedrin, something more than they were able to discern. We are even told that they marveled at the boldness of Peter and John, whom they perceived to be ignorant and unlearned men. They certainly had not studied in any of the great rabbinical schools. But the verb that is translated "took knowledge" is an imperfect tense verb, which probably doesn't mean much to you except in this way—it means that one by one the rulers began to realize the reason for their boldness; they had been with Jesus. What a wonderful thing to have said about them! They have been with Jesus!

Christians ought always to remember that we are being watched. The world does "take knowledge" of what we say and what we do. The question is—when they do, what do they see? Do they see men and women of great moral courage who will stick to the truth with an unwavering steadfastness of principle, as the Lord did? To be a Christian takes courage and it always has. In our society it takes courage to stand for the Lord's standard of right—to stand opposed to gambling, drinking of alcoholic beverages, mixed swimming, abortion, and on and on we could go. It takes courage to stand up and speak for the Lord no matter how offensive what the Lord had to say might be to those listening. When these kinds of subjects come up at work, school, the grocery store, or wherever, will those around us be able to tell that "we have been with Jesus"?

November 20

It Is Not Too Late

In Titus 2 there is a passage found that was a favorite of someone who was so dear to my heart. In verses 3-5 we find, "The aged women likewise, that they be in behavior as becometh holiness, not false accusers, not given to much wine, teachers of good things; that they may teach the young women to be sober, to love their husbands, to love their children, to be discreet, chaste, keepers at home, good, obedient to their own husbands, that the word of God be not blasphemed." I cannot think of a time in my life when the exhortation of this passage was more desperately needed.

Things have changed related to how our society views the role of women; some of it has been good and some of it has been bad. There is no question that women need to be, and deserve to be, treated as equals with men because they are equal to men. Paul wrote in Galatians 3:28, "There is neither Jew nor Greek, there is neither bond nor free, there is neither male nor female: for ye are all one in Christ Jesus." God views men and women as equals; Jesus died for both. God has given men and women different roles to perform, but he has not decreed one sex superior to the other. The woman was created to be a help "meet" for man—meaning compatible in every way—mentally, emotionally, spiritually, and physically.

What is so disturbing is that all of the sinful and ungodly things that used to be primarily associated with men, women are now doing. Today, some women make it a point to curse like any man. Thirty years ago, especially within the Lord's family, it was rare indeed to hear of a woman leaving her children and her husband for another man. Now it happens frequently. Do you remember when only men got tattoos? With equality has come a loss of femininity. So many women no longer want to look, act, talk, walk, or dress like a woman. So many now take offense at such passages as 1 Peter 3:7, "Likewise, ye husbands, dwell with them according to knowledge, giving honor unto the wife, as unto the weaker vessel, and as being heirs together of the grace of life; that your prayers be not hindered."

From an academic standpoint, most of the younger women of today are better educated than those who are older, but that does not mean they are wiser. You won't find a college class that teaches the young women to be sensible in the godly sense, or that encourages them to love their children and their husbands. Where is the college class that teaches a young woman to remain sexually pure because it is the right thing to do, or that being a homemaker is an honorable and dignified work in the sight of God? Show me the college catalogue that has a class listed in which women are taught to recognize their husbands as the head of the house.

The older, faithful sisters in Christ have been given a vitally important task. Older sisters, you must not fail, because if you don't fulfill this responsibility that God has given you, no one else will.

November 21

The Night of Preparation

On the very night in which he was betrayed, Jesus did a number of things that were not understood by his apostles until later, but they were all vital to their understanding the very nature and order of the church that Jesus was about to begin. This Thursday night was a night of preparation.

In John 13:4-5 we read of an incredible act: "He riseth from supper, and laid aside his garments; and took a towel, and girded himself. After that he poured water into a basin, and began to wash the disciples' feet, and to wipe them with the towel wherewith he was girded." As this evening progressed, Jesus took a towel, wrapped it around himself, bent down, and began to wash the feet of his apostles. The Jewish tradition was that a person would wash himself before a feast so that only his feet would need to be washed at his arrival. The Lord, no doubt in response to the tradition, took upon himself the function of the lowest household slave who was usually assigned this task. It can be said that he wrapped himself in the garment of a slave.

Incredible but true—the Creator washes the feet of his creation. In John 1:3 we are told, "All things were made by him, and without him was not anything made that was made." What an incredible contrast! Jesus was God and yet he lowered himself to wash the dust of the road from the feet of his apostles. I believe that not only was this kind of submission to be the motive for Jesus coming to the cross—it is the message of the kingdom. Jesus said, "If any man will come after me, let him deny himself." In Matthew 20:27-28 the Lord said, "And whosoever will be chief among you, let him be your servant: even as the Son of man came not to be ministered unto, but to minister, and to give his life a ransom for many."

Friends, this is what it is all about. This is the essence of what it means to be a Christian. I am reminded of Philippians 2:3-8: "Let nothing be done through strife or vainglory: but in lowliness of mind let each esteem other better than themselves. Look not every man on his own things, but every man also on the things of others. Let this mind be in you, which was also in Christ Jesus: who, being in the form of God, thought it not robbery to be equal with God: but made himself of no reputation, and took upon him the form of a servant, and was made in the likeness of men: and being found in fashion as a man, he humbled himself, and became obedient unto death, even the death of the cross."

On that great night of preparation, Jesus continued on and said to his apostles, "Ye should do as I have done to you" (v. 15). He said, "I have given you an example" (v. 15). And the Lord also said, "If ye know these things, happy are ye if ye do them." He was preparing his apostles for the life of service as His followers demanded of them. Has His action prepared us as well?

Thank You

Think of the power of gratitude. Think of the power of thankfulness. It is a subject about which the Bible has a lot to say. Over and over we are exhorted to display thankfulness to God. In Psalm 50:14 we read, "Offer unto God thanksgiving; and pay thy vows unto the most High." Psalm 69:30-31 indicates God's desire for thankfulness from man, "I will praise the name of God with a song, and will magnify him with thanksgiving. This also shall please the Lord better than an ox or bullock that hath horns and hoofs."

The New Testament is filled with calls for us to remember to be thankful. Consider Ephesians 5:18-20, "And be not drunk with wine, wherein is excess; but be filled with the Spirit; speaking to yourselves in psalms and hymns and spiritual songs, singing and making melody in your heart to the Lord; giving thanks always for all things unto God and the Father in the name of the Lord Jesus Christ."

Colossians is filled with exhortations to gratitude. Let's look at Colossians 2:6-7, "As ye have therefore received Christ Jesus the Lord, so walk ye in him: rooted and built up in him, and established in the faith, as ye have been taught, abounding therein with thanksgiving." In chapter 3:15-17 we find, "And called in one body; and be ye thankful. Let the word of Christ dwell in your richly in all wisdom; teaching and admonishing one another in psalms and hymns and spiritual songs, singing with grace in your hearts to the Lord. And whatsoever ye do in word or deed, do all in the name of the Lord Jesus, giving thanks to God and the Father by him." And chapter 4:2 tells us, "Continue in prayer, and watch in the same with thanksgiving."

Everything we have, everything we are, and everything we can be, is because of the wondrous gifts of God. James 1:17 says, "Every good gift and every perfect gift is from above, and cometh down from the Father of lights, with whom is no variableness, neither shadow of turning." I remember when I was a young child, maybe in the first grade, the nun who was my teacher told a little story. While the details of the story were simply made up, the moral of it has stuck with me to this day. She told of two angels being sent out by God. One was given a basket in which to collect all the requests that man had made that day. The other was given a basket to collect all of the expressions of thanks from man. The one with the requests had an overflowing basket. The one with the expressions of thanks had but one. I never forgot that lesson.

Thanksgiving and gratitude are not to be confined simply from man to God. There are so many examples of gratitude from man to man. I think of what Paul wrote in Romans 16:1-4, "I commend unto you Phoebe our sister, which is a servant of the church which is at Cenchrea: that ye receive her in the Lord, as becometh saints, and that ye assist her in whatsoever business she hath need of you: for she hath been a succourer of many, and of myself also. Greet Priscilla and Aquila my helpers in Christ Jesus: who have for my life laid down their own necks: unto whom not only I give thanks, but also all the churches of the Gentiles."

I never cease to be amazed at the power of a "thank you." I have been in stores where the clerk waiting on me seemed to be in the worst possible mood and on the brink of biting someone's head off. But when I thanked them for their help, a smile lit up their face. A simple "thank you" to brethren for work done, for effort put forth, means so very much, and it doesn't cost me a thing. As a matter of fact, I get something back from it. I get the satisfaction of seeing a smile on the face of someone who might have thought that nobody noticed.

November 23

Words of Exhortation from 1 Thessalonians 5:14-22—"Warn Them That Are Unruly"

Now we exhort you, brethren, warn them that are unruly, comfort the feeble-minded, support the weak, be patient toward all men. See that none render evil for evil unto any man; but ever follow that which is good, both among yourselves, and to all men. Rejoice evermore. Pray without ceasing. In everything give thanks: for this is the will of God in Christ Jesus concerning you. Quench not the Spirit. Despise not prophesyings. Prove all things; hold fast that which is good. Abstain from all appearances of evil.

As Paul begins to bring his first letter to the brethren in Thessalonica to a close, he presents a list of exhortations to the church there. His words of advice and recommendation echo across the ages as being vitally important for those who would walk in the pathway of Jesus. Because they are so important and practical, the next several daily devotions will be used to examine these words from the pen of Paul, beginning with "warn them that are unruly."

The word unruly (*ataktos*) has been translated in various ways, such as idle, lazy, and disorderly. The idea behind the word is that of not keeping order. W.E. Vine says that "it was especially a military term, denoting 'not keeping rank, insubordinate.'" William Barclay wrote that the word "originally described a soldier who had left the ranks." These definitions help us to understand the type of person that is being described by Paul. He is referring to a Christian who chooses to no longer walk according to the standard of behavior that the Lord has set forth. It is a person who is walking out of step with the promises that he made to the Lord when he became a Christian. When a person renders his obedience to the gospel of our Lord Jesus Christ and is washed by His blood, cleansed of his sins, he is making a commitment to live faithfully according to God's revealed will. Unfortunately, many times those promises are not kept.

What is the immediate responsibility of a brother or sister in Christ toward the one who is no longer walking in step, who has broken ranks, and is living in sin? As difficult as it may seem, given the fact that most people do not like confrontation of any kind, the responsibility of the faithful Christian is to warn such a one of the danger of the course he is choosing. I am reminded of Paul's words in Galatians 6:1, "Brethren, if a man be overtaken in a fault, ye which are spiritual, restore such an one in the spirit of meekness; considering thyself, lest thou also be tempted." You might note that the attitude displayed in approaching the sinning brother or sister is so important. It is not to be an accusatory, holier-than-thou verbal assault, but rather one that evidences a sincere concern for his soul.

It is sad, but true, that many will talk about that person and the sinful things he or she is doing, but they won't talk to that person. Paul's exhortation was not to tell everybody else, or anybody else, about the brother or sister walking disorderly, but to warn that individual. Our concern is to be for the soul of the unruly brother or sister, not to make him or her a topic of discussion. So, if you know someone who fits Paul's description, don't talk *about* him—talk *to* him.

November 24

Words of Exhortation from 1 Thessalonians 5:14-22—"Comfort the Feebleminded"

"Comfort the feebleminded" or the "fainthearted." What an interesting and important exhortation that Paul gives to Christians. You know someone who is fainthearted, a word that literally means "small-souled." The literal meaning does not indicate that such a person has less capacity for spiritual thought and growth, but rather that the person is despondent, disheartened, discouraged.

Life as a Christian is not always easy, and the Lord did not promise that it would be. It is not a life that will be free of all difficulties. As a matter of fact, some trials and difficulties will arise because of being a Christian. Paul wrote to Timothy in 2 Timothy 3:12, "Yea, and all that will live godly in Christ Jesus shall suffer persecution." Even great men of God suffered moments of discouragement and despondency. I think of Elijah, after his great victory for God against the prophets of Baal on Mt. Carmel in 1 Kings 18, sitting under a juniper tree after his life was threatened by Jezebel and saying, "It is enough; now, O Lord, take away my life; for I am not better than my fathers" (1 Kings 19:4). He cried out, "I have been very jealous for the Lord God of hosts: for the children of Israel have forsaken thy covenant, thrown down thine altars, and slain thy prophets with the sword; and I, even I only, am left; and they seek my life to take it away" (1 Kings 19:10). But Elijah was not alone and was soon to be accompanied by Elisha.

It is so very probable that you know a brother or sister in Christ who is hurting, who is disheartened. Perhaps it is a struggle with temptation that seems to be getting the best of him. It may very well be some difficulty in his family. He may be the brunt of jokes and unkind remarks at work or school because he stands for what is right and good. There are things that happen that hurt and discourage. No Christian walks through this life without receiving wounds. Some are easily shaken off; some are not. How important it is for them to know that someone else has walked the same path, someone else has felt the same sting, someone else has wept. It is not that they are tempted to leave the Lord, but it may be that they are just getting tired.

Do you know what a hand on the shoulder or an encouraging word can do for such a person? Of course you do, if you have been a Christian for any length of time. I love what Albert Barnes wrote in *Barnes' Notes of the New Testament*. Concerning "comfort the feebleminded" he wrote, "There is no one who would not reach out his hand to save a child borne down a rapid stream; yet how often do experienced and strong men in the Christian faith pass by those who are struggling in the 'deep waters,' where the proud waves have come over their souls!"

My friend, be the hand that the disheartened can grasp that will help to pull them out of the depths of discouragement or despondency. You have been there, and a brother or sister has helped you.

November 25

Words of Exhortation from 1 Thessalonians 5:14-22—"Support the Weak"

"Support the weak." Such a simple exhortation, but one that is vital to the spiritual health of the individual Christian and to that of a faithful local congregation. Not all Christians have attained to the same level of spiritual maturity. A classic case that was widespread in the first century had to do with whether or not Christians could eat meat that had been sacrificed to idols. In 1 Corinthians 8:4-9 we find:

> As concerning therefore the eating of those things that are offered in sacrifice unto idols, we know that an idol is nothing in the world, and that there is none other God but one. For though there be that are called gods, whether in heaven or in earth, (as there be gods many, and lords many,) But to us there is but one God, the Father, of whom are all things, and we in him; and one Lord Jesus Christ, by whom are all things, and we by him. Howbeit there is not in every man that knowledge: for some with conscience of the idol unto this hour eat it as a thing offered unto an idol; and their conscience being weak is defiled. But meat commendeth us not to God: for neither, if we eat, are we the better; neither, if we eat not, are we the worse. But take heed lest by any means this liberty of yours become a stumblingblock to them that are weak.

The problem that the brethren who were described as weak were experiencing was not with their belief in Jesus as the Savior or in their belief that there was only one God. The problem was that they had not yet grown to the level of spiritual maturity that enabled them to understand the consequences of their newfound beliefs. So the stronger Christians, the more spiritually mature Christians, were not to reject such a brother or sister, but provide them with the support they needed to grow in the faith. The idea of "support" can be described as the stronger brother picking up one end of the burden as the weaker brother picks us the other. Together, they bear that burden.

Every congregation, no matter how large or small, has people who are at different levels of spiritual growth. Not everybody is going to be at the same point in knowledge, strength in the face of temptation, or courage when confronted with persecution. Those who are stronger have the responsibility to hold to, cleave to, stick to such a person as he grows in the grace and knowledge of the Lord Jesus Christ.

Doesn't this present a beautiful picture? As Paul wrote in Romans 15:1, "We then that are strong ought to bear the infirmities of the weak, and not to please ourselves," we can envision a congregation of the Lord's people. In that congregation are people at all points along the path to spiritual maturity, and yet those who are stronger do not look down upon those who have not attained the same level, and those who are weaker do not despair. Together they are all striving for the same goal, and if one brother can help another get there by supporting and encouraging him in his growth, then that is what he will do.

So remember, support the weak; help them as they grow in knowledge, strength, courage, and spiritual maturity. Not one of us began this journey to heaven as a mature Christian.

November 26

Words of Exhortation from 1 Thessalonians 5:14-22—"Be Patient Toward All Men"

"Be patient toward all men." I am not sure about you, but I want to be patient, and I want to be patient *now*. We have all heard something similar to that and have chuckled, but I suspect that patience is a virtue with which many struggle. It is so important for a Christian to be patient in our dealings with others, both within and without the body of Christ.

The explanation of patient that appears in *Thayer's Greek English Lexicon of the New Testament* is to "persevere patiently and bravely in enduring misfortunes and troubles; to be patient in bearing offences and injuries of others; to be mild and slow in avenging." Thus, it is at the opposite end of the spectrum from becoming easily exasperated or being short-tempered. In 1 Corinthians 13:4 we find that patience, or longsuffering, is one of the attributes of true love and emphasizes the trait of self-restraint, the ability to control one's self even when wronged or injured by another.

When I think of patience, quite frankly I think of God and the very fact that mankind still exists as being evidence of just how patient He is. Peter tells us in 2 Peter 3:9, "The Lord is not slack concerning his promise, as some men count slackness; but is longsuffering to usward, not willing that any should perish, but that all should come to repentance." With all of the terrible and horrendous things that man does, and yet God continues to give opportunity for repentance, what possible cause could I have to fail to be patient?

What better example of being patient could we have than our Lord Jesus? In 1 Peter 2:21-23 we read, "For even hereunto were ye called: because Christ also suffered for us, leaving us an example, that ye should follow his steps: who did no sin, neither was guile found in his mouth: who, when he was reviled, reviled not again: when he suffered, he threatened not; but committed himself to him that judgeth righteously: who his own self bare our sins in his own body on the tree, that we, being dead to sins, should live unto righteousness: by whose stripes ye were healed."

How many local churches have been torn apart because of a lack of patience by some within its number? How many potential converts to Christ have been driven away because the one attempting to teach them grew impatient with their questions and apparent lack of progress? How many Christians have flown off the handle, so to speak, and reacted harshly and rashly to a perceived injustice or slight at work, only to have a fellow employee think, "If that is the way Christians act, I want no part of it!"

I like the way that Matthew Henry expanded upon this particular exhortation in his commentary on 1 Thessalonians. He wrote, "We must bear and forbear. And this duty must be exercised towards all men, good and bad, high and low. We must endeavor to make the best we can of everything, and think the best we can of everybody."

Words of Exhortation from 1 Thessalonians 5:14-22—"See That None Render Evil for Evil"

"See that none render evil for evil unto any man; but ever follow that which is good, both among yourselves, and to all men." One of the amazing things about the word of God is that the standard of righteousness it sets forth is so different from that which most of the world has adopted. In our "me first" society, the practice is not only to return evil for evil, but many live by the motto of "do unto others before they can do unto you." Nothing could be more different from the example the Lord set for us and from the pattern of life that He demands of His disciples.

In Matthew 5:38-45 we read:

Ye have heard that it hath been said, An eye for an eye, and a tooth for a tooth: but I say unto you, That ye resist not evil: but whosoever shall smite thee on thy right cheek, turn to him the other also. And if any man will sue thee at the law, and take away thy coat, let him have thy cloak also, and whosoever shall compel thee to go a mile, go with him twain. Give to him that asketh thee, and from him that would borrow of thee turn not thou away. Ye have heard that it hath been said, Thou shalt love thy neighbor, and hate thy enemy. But I say unto you, Love your enemies, bless them that curse you, do good to them that hate you, and pray for them which despitefully use you, and persecute you; that ye may be the children of your Father which is in heaven: for he maketh his sun to rise on the evil and on the good, and sendeth rain on the just and on the unjust.

Surely what is prohibited is the taking of vengeance. We have the God-given right to defend ourselves, protect our families, even seek the assistance of the government under which we live, for government has been ordained by God as "a revenger to execute wrath upon him that doeth evil" (Rom. 13:4). However, if even such is done out of an evil desire for revenge, we are no longer abiding within God's standard. God did not promise that all aspects of His standard of righteousness were going to be easy, but He did provide us with the greatest example of just this kind of attitude. In 1 Peter 2:21-23 we find, "For even hereunto were ye called: because Christ also suffered for us, leaving us an example, that ye should follow his steps: who did no sin, neither was guile found in his mouth: who, when he was reviled, reviled not again; when he suffered, he threatened not; but committed himself to him that judgeth righteously."

One of the challenges of being a Christian is learning to live by this rule. Not only are we to resist the temptation to retaliate in kind when evil has been done to us, we are actually to return good instead. The good referred to in 1 Thessalonians 5:15 is that which is beneficial, so it is teaching us not only to refuse to seek vengeance, but to actually seek to do that which would benefit the evildoer. That is not always a simple thing to do, nor is it limited only to those who are members of the body of Christ. If we would be faithful and Christ-like followers of our Lord, we must manifest this attitude toward all men. Paul stated it so well in Romans 12:17-19: "Recompense to no man evil for evil. Provide things honest in the sight of all men. If it be possible, as much as lieth in you, live peaceably with all men. Dearly beloved, avenge not yourselves, but rather give place unto wrath: for it is written, Vengeance is mine; I will repay, saith the Lord."

November 28

Words of Exhortation from 1 Thessalonians 5:14-22—"Rejoice Evermore"

"Rejoice evermore." The idea that Christians, of all people, should rejoice always fills Paul's writings. In the Philippians letter Paul wrote, "Rejoice in the Lord alway: and again I say, Rejoice" (Phil. 4:2). Paul even found cause for rejoicing in his sufferings. Consider Colossians 1:23-24, "If ye continue in the faith grounded and settled, and be not moved away from the hope of the gospel, which ye have heard, and which was preached to every creature which is under heaven; whereof I Paul am made a minister; who now rejoice in my sufferings for you, and fill up that which is behind of the afflictions of Christ in my flesh for his body's sake, which is the church."

The exhortation does not mean that a Christian is to always be giddy, filled with mirth, and laughing all the time. However, it does call for recognition of the fact that we serve the Lord Jesus, that we are saved, and that this world is not our final destination. Just a quick glance at the first chapter of Paul's letter to the Ephesians gives us so many reasons why we should always have joy within our hearts. As Christians, God "hath blessed us with all spiritual blessings in heavenly places in Christ" (v. 3). We "have redemption through his blood, the forgiveness of sins, according to the riches of his grace" (v. 7). Through Christ Jesus "we have obtained an inheritance" and "were sealed with the Holy Spirit of promise" (vv. 11, 13). There is so much more for us to enjoy as we go through life with our eyes firmly upon the Lord Jesus Christ and our eternal home with him that is our ultimate destination.

With all this being true, how is it possible for Christians to live their lives with a dour disposition, walking about with downcast eyes and looking as though the weight of the whole world is resting upon their shoulders? While we live in the world, and the events of the world do affect us, we are not of the world. Consequently, even when bad things happen, Christians recognize "that the sufferings of this present time are not worthy to be compared with the glory which shall be revealed in us" (Rom. 8:18).

November 29

Words of Exhortation from 1 Thessalonians 5:14-22—"Pray Without Ceasing"

"Pray without ceasing." To understand what Paul meant by the exhortation to "pray without ceasing," we need only to examine Paul's personal use of prayer in this letter to the Thessalonians and the second letter to the Thessalonians. The idea is to always be of a prayerful attitude, to have the kind of disposition that would cause us to go to our Father in prayer at every opportune time and not to grow weary in this, but to remain consistent and persistent.

In 1 Thessalonians 3:11-13 we find Paul praying in written form, "Now God himself and our Father, and our Lord Jesus Christ, direct our way unto you. And the Lord make you to increase and abound in love one toward another, and toward all men, even as we do toward you: to the end he may stablish your hearts unblameable in holiness before God, even our Father, at the coming of our Lord Jesus Christ with all his saints." What a beautiful prayer that seems to be almost spontaneous on Paul's part as he told the Thessalonians of his deep concern for them and how thankful he was when he received word of them from Timothy. In chapter 5, as Paul was bringing to a close his first letter to the Thessalonians, he wrote in verse 23, "And the very God of peace sanctify you wholly; and I pray God your whole spirit and soul and body be preserved blameless unto the coming of our Lord Jesus Christ." In the 2 Thessalonian letter, we find brief prayers in 1:11; 2:16; 3:5 and 16. All of this goes to show us how deeply ingrained prayer was in the very character of Paul. He was constantly aware of God's presence and of his own need for communication with him.

Consider some of the different ways that our Lord taught the need for persistence in prayer. I thrill to his words in Luke 11:9-13:

> And I say unto you, Ask, and it shall be given you; seek, and ye shall find, knock, and it shall be opened unto you. For every one that asketh receiveth; and he that seeketh findeth; and to him that knocketh it shall be opened. If a son shall ask bread of any of you that is a father, will he give him a stone? Or if he ask a fish, will he for a fish give him a serpent? Or if he shall ask an egg, will he offer him a scorpion? If ye then, being evil, know how to give good gifts unto your children: how much more shall your heavenly Father give the Holy Spirit to them that ask him?"

In his commentary on Philippians and Colossians from the *Truth Commentary Series*, Walton Weaver made a comment concerning Paul's exhortation in Colossians 4:2, yet another example of the importance Paul placed upon prayer in the life of a Christian. Paul wrote, "Continue in prayer, and watch in the same with thanksgiving." About this Weaver wrote, "Perseverance in prayer is needed as long as God's people are in need and the God who promises is still in heaven." I believe that summarizes the tenor of the New Testament teaching on prayer very well.

November 30

Words of Exhortation from 1 Thessalonians 5:14-22—"In Everything Give Thanks"

"In everything give thanks: for this is the will of God in Christ Jesus concerning you." I remember very few things from my first grade year of parochial education at Saint John's the Evangelist in Cincinnati, Ohio, but one thing has stuck with me over these many years. My teacher told us all a story about

God summoning two angels into his presence and giving them each a job to do. One was to take a basket and go to earth, bringing back all of the requests that people made of God. The other was to take a basket and bring back all of the "thank you's" that people made to God for blessings received and prayers answered. As the story went, the angel collecting requests brought back a basket that was overflowing; while the angel collecting thank you's had but a few at the bottom of his basket. It was a silly, simple story told to a group of first graders, but I have never forgotten it.

As the years went by, how surprised I was to learn that the Lord had taught the very same lesson at the conclusion of an event that took place in his life, recorded for us in Luke 17:11-17. There we find

> And it came to pass, as he went to Jerusalem, that he passed through the midst of Samaria and Galilee. And as he entered into a certain village, there met him ten men that were lepers, which stood afar off: and they lifted up their voices, and said, Jesus, Master, have mercy on us. And when he saw them, he said unto them, Go show yourselves unto the priests. And it came to pass, that, as they went, they were cleansed. And one of them, when he saw that he was healed, turned back, and with a loud voice glorified God, and fell down on his face at his feet, giving him thanks: and he was a Samaritan. And Jesus answering said, Were there not ten cleansed? But where are the nine?

Let us not forget that God desires our thanks, He wants us to be appreciative and to express that appreciation. I am reminded of Hebrews 13:15 where we are told, "By him therefore let us offer the sacrifice of praise to God continually, that is, the fruit of our lips giving thanks to his name."

Wilbur Fields, in his book, *Thinking Through Thessalonians*, wrote, "It has been well observed that it is backwards to have only one day a year for Thanksgiving, and three hundred sixty-four for grumbling. We ought to have one day a year for expressing our grumbles, groans, grunts, and grouching, and three hundred sixty-four days a year for blessing the Lord who satisfies our mouth with good things" (149).

It is my prayer that I never forget to say "thank you" to God. The image from the story that I was told so long ago of the angel with the almost empty basket has never left my mind and I hope that it will never leave yours.

Words of Exhortation from 1 Thessalonians 5:14-22—"Quench Not the Spirit. Despise Not Prophesyings"

"Quench not the Spirit. Despise not prophesyings." On the Jewish feast day of Pentecost, the very day upon which the church began and about which we can read in Acts 2, the apostles were baptized with the Holy Spirit. We are told in verses 3-4, "And there appeared unto them cloven tongues like as of fire, and it sat upon each of them. And they were all filled with the Holy Ghost, and began to speak with other tongues, as the Spirit gave them utterance." As the apostles received the revelation of the word of God, they were able to confirm that word "with signs and wonders, and with divers miracles, and gifts of the Holy Ghost" (Heb. 2:4). We learn as well that the apostles were able to pass on the miraculous gifts of the Holy Spirit through the laying on of their hands (Acts 8:18).

The miraculous gifts of the Holy Spirit are named in 1 Corinthians 12:8-10, and were in operation and very important in the early days of the church. It is apparent that there were those in the church in Thessalonica who possessed miraculous gifts of the Holy Spirit, including the ability to prophesy. As the complete word of God had not yet been revealed, it was the work of a prophet to act as a spokesman for God. What the prophet had to say was extremely important, for he was revealing the will of God. Paul was exhorting the Thessalonians to utilize the miraculous gifts that they had been given and not to suppress or extinguish them. However, the fact that they could "quench the Spirit" indicates that those brethren who possessed miraculous spiritual gifts in the first century were able to control them, just as Paul taught in 1 Corinthians 14:32, "And the spirits of the prophets are subject to the prophets." Also the fact that they could "despise the prophesyings" indicates that even though these were revelations of the will of God, the people could still choose to reject them or to treat them with contempt.

Since 1 Corinthians 13:8-13 teaches that the miraculous spiritual gifts would cease when the revelation of God's word was complete, and since the gifts were passed on by the laying on of the apostles' hands, we should not look for miraculous spiritual gifts to be in operation today. However, we can still "quench the Spirit." The Holy Spirit was the agent of revelation. Paul tells us in 1 Corinthians 2:12-13, "Now we have received, not the spirit of the world, but the spirit which is of God; that we might know the things that are freely given to us of God. Which things also we speak, not in the words which man's wisdom teacheth, but which the Holy Ghost teacheth; comparing spiritual things with spiritual." It was through the work of the Spirit that we can now pick up a Bible and come to know what it is that God would have us to do to be pleasing to Him.

Will a person do what God's word says to do? That is the question. To know what God would have me to do through the Spirit-revealed word, and to refuse to do it, is to effectively quench the Spirit's message to me and to despise that revealed word. Christians quench the Spirit if we refuse to obey the word of God and choose to live earthly, carnal lives.

The Bible also warns us to "grieve not the holy Spirit of God" (Eph. 4:30), which is done in much the same way. As Colly Caldwell pointed out in his commentary on Ephesians from the *Truth Commentary Series* (222), "Any time we disobey God, violate the commandments delivered by the Spirit, show ingratitude or a rebellious attitude, or neglect to do our duty before God, we grieve the Spirit."

December 2

Words of Exhortation from 1 Thessalonians 5:14-22—"Prove All Things; Hold Fast That Which Is Good"

"Prove all things; hold fast that which is good." To "prove all things" is to test all things, and it is an exhortation that is repeatedly found in the New Testament. In 1 John 4:1 we find, "Beloved, believe not every spirit, but try the spirits whether they are of God: because many false prophets are gone out into the world." Paul wrote in Philippians 1:9-10, "And this I pray, that your love may abound yet more and more in knowledge and in all judgment; that ye may approve things that are excellent; that ye may be sincere and without offence till the day of Christ." Just as a metallurgist subjects metal to various tests to determine its value and true nature, so too must the follower of Christ examine everything that is presented as truth or something to be practiced in the name of religion in the light of God's word.

How many people are what they are religiously because it is what their mothers and fathers always believed, or it has been the religion of their families for generations? The fact that the family has "always believed" something, or a well-known preacher has declared something to be true, does not make it true. There are many people in the world who teach things in the name of religion that are just not according to God's word, and while they will have to answer for the false teaching they have done, the Bible places the responsibility on all individuals to determine if what they hear is true or not.

In the first century there were a number of Jewish Christians who taught the false doctrine that Gentiles (non-Jews) had to obey certain aspects of the Law of Moses in order to be saved, including being circumcised. What they were teaching was wrong. God required no such thing. The church in Galatia was troubled by such teaching, and in Galatians 1:8-9 Paul wrote, "But though we, or an angel from heaven, preach any other gospel unto you than that which we have preached unto you, let him be accursed. As we said before, so say I now again, If any man preach any other gospel unto you than that he have received, let him be accursed." The false teacher would be held accountable for the error that he taught, but those who believed it would also be held accountable. In verse 6 of Galatians 1, Paul wrote, "I marvel that ye are so soon removed from him that called you into the grace of Christ unto another gospel." In Galatians 5:4 we find, "Christ is become of no effect unto you, whosoever of you are justified by the law; ye are fallen from grace."

It is our God-given responsibility to place everything under the microscope of God's word. Albert Barnes in *Barnes' Notes On the New Testament*, made the following comments about "prove all things." He wrote, "They were carefully to examine everything proposed for their belief. They were not to receive it on trust; to take it on assertion; to believe it because it was urged with vehemence, zeal, or plausibility. In the various opinions and doctrines which were submitted to them for adoption, they were to apply the appropriate tests from reason and from the word of God; and what they found to be true they were to embrace; what was false they were to reject."

It does very little good to determine what is true and good, what is according to God's standard, if one does not then believe it and practice it. The exhortation is as much to you and me as it was to the brethren in Thessalonica so many years ago. "Prove all things; hold fast that which is good."

December 3

Words of Exhortation from 1 Thessalonians 5:14-22—"Abstain From All Appearances of Evil"

"Abstain from all appearances of evil." For those who lived in a pagan society given over to idolatry, the command to "hold off" (Gr., *apecho*) from all appearances of evil would have been very difficult. These were people who had come out of idolatry, and they were not to give the impression that they still held to any aspect of those false religious practices and beliefs. They could do this with the Lord's help. In 1 Thessalonians 3:3 Paul wrote, "But the Lord is faithful, who shall stablish you, and keep you from evil."

While most of us do not live in a pagan society today, we do live in an idolatrous society in the sense that many people let wealth, possessions, even sports and entertainment, take the place of God in their lives and that, my friends, is idolatry. As Christians we are commanded to, "Let your light so shine before men, that they may see your good works, and glorify your Father which is in heaven" (Matt. 5:16). Consequently, we must avoid every appearance of evil. There are places a Christian should not go, activities in which a Christian should not engage, even for legitimate reasons, if such could be misconstrued as participation in evil.

I find it interesting that the New Testament refers to Christians as "saints" (Rom. 2:7; 1 Cor. 1:2). Saints are people who have been sanctified, set apart, separated from sin and consecrated to God. In the Old Testament, certain items that were used in the temple worship of God were "set apart," sanctified, consecrated to God. To use any of those items in a profane manner, or in any way that was not according to the purpose for which they were created, was to defile the item itself and to have committed sin. In a very special way, Christians correspond to that today.

In Romans 6:13 Paul wrote, "Neither yield ye your members as instruments of unrighteousness unto sin: but yield yourselves unto God, as those that are alive from the dead, and your members as instruments of righteousness unto God." In verse 19 of the same chapter we find, "I speak after the manner of men because of the infirmity of your flesh: for as ye have yielded your members as servants to uncleanness and to iniquity unto iniquity; even so now yield your members servants to righteousness unto holiness." It is not right to take that which is sanctified, separated to God and holy, and use it in a way that would corrupt and defile it. As Christians we are to be instruments of righteousness unto God, and it is our responsibility to avoid all sin, and even to conduct ourselves in such a way as to avoid even the very appearance of it. There is that overused cliché, "What would Jesus do?" that is rather flippantly tossed about today. However, when it comes to something questionable that has the potential to give the appearance of evil, it is a good idea to ask ourselves if the Lord would do it? If the honest answer is no, then neither should we.

December 4

The Marriage Relationship (1)

In Genesis 1:31 we read the glorious account of creation, "And God saw all that He had made, and behold, it was very good. And there was evening and there was morning, the sixth day." The one situation that was not "good," God had taken care of. In Genesis 2:18-25 we find,

Then the Lord God said, It is not good for the man to be alone; I will make him a helper suitable for him. And out of the ground the Lord God formed every best of the field and every bird of the sky, and brought them to the man to see what he would call them; and whatever the man called a living creature, that was its name. And the man gave names to all the cattle, and to the birds of the sky, and to every beast of the field, but for Adam there was not found a helper suitable for him. So the Lord God caused a deep sleep to fall upon the man, and he slept; then He took one of his ribs, and closed up the flesh at that place. And the Lord God fashioned into a woman the rib which He had taken from the man, and brought her to the man. And the man said, This is now bone of my bones, and flesh of my flesh; she shall be called woman, because she was taken out of man. For this cause a man shall leave his father and his mother, and shall cleave to his wife; and they shall become one flesh. And the man and his wife were both naked and were not ashamed.

Thus God instituted marriage with the first man and woman, Adam and Eve. We can immediately see that celibacy, and by that I mean not only abstaining from sexual activity but also remaining unmarried, while acceptable for some (Matt. 19:11-12), is not an inherently better state. God ordained marriage and saw that it "was very good." The Hebrew writer tells us, "Let marriage be held in honor among all, and let the marriage bed be undefiled."

December 5

The Marriage Relationship (2)

The Bible indicates that there are certain things necessary to constitute a marriage. First of all, there must be the intention to live together as husband and wife. We can see that with a man leaving his father and mother and cleaving to his wife. The woman must leave her father and mother as well and cleave unto her husband. This obviously indicates an intention to be married, an agreement between them to be husband and wife.

A second point that seems clear to me is simply this—since God's Word tells us that we are to be subject to the law of the land under which we live (Rom. 13-6), whatever that law would require for marriage God would also require, provided God's law is not violated. When we think about the divorce that Moses permitted because of the hardness of the hearts of the Israelites, we can see that a writing of divorcement for the protection of the woman was required to end a marriage. The wedding feast in John 2 and the parable of the ten virgins in Matthew 25 indicate that there was a certain point at which people were recognized as being married.

While on the subject of what constitutes a marriage, I have, after considerable study, changed my views. I used to believe that three things were necessary to constitute a marriage—the intention, the legal aspect, and the cohabitation or sexual intercourse. I no longer believe that the sexual intercourse is necessary to "constitute a marriage." I do believe it to be a duty of, and a blessing for, those who are already married. When in a wedding ceremony the person officiating pronounces them husband and wife, they really are husband and wife at that point, and I would pray that that would have been before cohabitation in the sexual sense. Matthew 1:24-25 says, "And Joseph arose from his sleep, and did as the angel of the Lord commanded him, and took her as his wife, and kept her a virgin until she gave birth to a Son; and called His name Jesus." They were married, husband and wife, a good while before the sexual act took place.

It is important to understand that when the requirements are met, that man and woman are married. It may be a marriage God approves of, in which case both individuals involved had a right to be married to each other; or it may be a marriage that God does not approve of, but it is still a marriage. Romans 7:3 speaks of a woman being "joined to another man." It is "to become another man's" and can properly be translated as "married to another man" while her husband lives. She is really married, even though God obviously would not approve. God did not approve of Herod's marriage to his brother Philip's wife, yet in Mark 6:17 the Holy Spirit saw fit to have Mark use the word "married" to describe the relationship between Herod and Herodias.

December 6

The Marriage Relationship (3)

What would constitute a marriage of which God would approve? It seems sad to have to say this, but in order to be approved by God a marriage has to be between a man and a woman. The current practice of two men or two women "marrying" one another is just another example of what happens when people lose all respect for God. Having lost respect for God, they lose respect for their fellow man. Having lost respect for their fellow man, individuals lose respect for themselves. Romans 1:19-32 details the kind of thinking that has resulted in these modern "perversions" of God's plan.

A man or woman who has never been married would have a right to be married. A man or woman who has lost a spouse through death would have the right to marry. A man or woman who has put away a spouse for fornication, being innocent, would have a right to marry. I believe that a man and woman who were in a marriage God approved of, but divorced each other and are now reconciling, would have a right to marry each other. When both parties in the marriage fit into one of these categories, when they have the intention to live together as husband and wife, and when they meet the legal requirements of the government under which they live, they are in a marriage of which God approves.

If one or both of the parties in a marriage do not fit into one of the categories mentioned above, but they have the intention to live together as husband and wife and meet the legal requirements of the government under which they live, they are married—but it is a marriage of which God disapproves.

In order to understand a vitally important point in this discussion, we need to look at Romans 7:2-3. Teaching about marriage is not Paul's primary point in this passage, but what he says will help us to make an essential distinction. The passage reads as follows, "For the married woman is bound by law to her husband while he is living; but if her husband dies, she is released from the law concerning the husband. So then if, while her husband is living, she is joined to another man, she shall be called an adulteress; but if her husband dies, she is free from the law, so that she is not an adulteress, though she is joined to another man."

Notice, the woman is "bound" by the law to her husband as long as he lives. That is the "bond." Jesus spoke of it as "God has joined together." When a couple that has a right to marry meets all of the requirements, God is the third party to that marriage. He "binds" them together. The bond is the covenant with God that joins the man and the woman.

Now in Romans 7:3 the woman in the illustration "marries" another man, or "is joined to" another man while her original husband is still alive. The word translated as "marries" in the King James and "is joined to" in the New American Standard is *ginomai*. It means "to become" and it is to become another man's. This shows that there is a biblical distinction between the "bond" and the "marriage." Marriage is the intention to live together as husband and wife, coupled with meeting the legal requirements. God doesn't have to "approve" of it in order for it to be a marriage. It is still spoken of in the Scriptures as a "marriage," whether God approves or not.

Hopefully you can see how important it is to understand the distinction between the "bond" and the "marriage." There are marriages that God approves (some brethren call them "scriptural marriages") and marriages that God disapproves ("unscriptural marriages"). In either case, God recognizes (is aware of) that the parties have entered a marriage. An unapproved marriage must end. A marriage that God does not approve is sinful and cannot be minimized by someone saying, "It isn't really a marriage in God's sight."

December 7

The Marriage Relationship (4)

Regardless of what some may say today, God has decreed that the man is to function as the head of the house. This is not to say that the man is inherently better than the woman. It is not to say that God loves men more than women, nor is it to say that the woman is to be the slave of the man. It is simply to say that God has given the man a different function within His ordained marriage, and that function is to be the head of the wife and the family. This position of headship is not a pedestal from which the man is to issue orders; rather, it is a position of tremendous responsibility.

In Ephesians 5:23-25 Paul wrote, "For the husband is the head of the wife, even as Christ is the head of the church: and he is the savior of the body. Therefore as the church is subject unto Christ, so let the wives be to their own husbands in everything. Husbands, love your wives, even as Christ also loved the church, and gave himself for it." There is a great deal involved in "husbands, love your wives, even as Christ also loved the church, and gave himself for it."

The man is to give honor to his wife as the weaker vessel, and he must recognize that he is to be her protector. He must also realize that she is an heir of the promise with him, provided they are both Christians. They are equal in God's sight. In Galatians 3:28-29 we find, "There is neither Jew nor Greek, there is neither bond nor free, there is neither male nor female: for ye are all one in Christ Jesus. And if ye be Christ's, then are ye Abraham's seed, and heirs according to the promise."

The husband is required to treat his wife with the proper care and respect, or his prayers will not be heard. A simple reading of 1 Peter 3:7 shows this to be true, "Likewise, ye husbands, dwell with them according to knowledge, giving honor unto the wife, as unto the weaker vessel, and as being heirs together of the grace of life: that your prayers be not hindered." Make no mistake about it, the husband owes his wife love, honor, care, and respect just as certainly as he owes her the physical necessities of life. Love, honor, care, respect, and such like, are things that no amount of money can buy or that no amount of material things can replace.

December 8

The Marriage Relationship (5)

In the God-ordained family, the man has the primary responsibility, given to him by God, to provide for the physical needs of his family. 1 Timothy 5:8 tells us, "But if any provide not for his own, and specially for those of his own house, he hath denied the faith, and is worse than an infidel." Consider also 1 Thessalonians 4:9-12 where Paul wrote, "But as touching brotherly love ye need not that I write unto you: for ye yourselves are taught of God to love one another. And indeed ye do it toward all the brethren which are in all Macedonia: but we beseech you, brethren, that ye increase more and more; and that ye study to be quiet and to do your own business, and to work with your own hands, as we command you; that ye may walk honestly toward them that are without, and that ye may have lack of nothing."

I believe it is clear that the man of the house is to work so that he and his family may have lack of none of the things they need and that he may be able to pay his honest debts. He is to "study to be quiet," perhaps meaning that he is not to go about fulfilling this obligation with whining and complaining, but that he is to get out and get busy. However, in fulfilling this responsibility to provide for the physical needs of the family, no husband should ever forget that the physical needs are only a part of what God expects him to provide. Do not forget love, honor, respect, and care.

Let's look now at 1 Corinthians 7:1-4, "Now concerning the things whereof ye wrote unto me: It is good for a man not to touch a woman. Nevertheless, to avoid fornication, let every man have his own wife, and let every woman have her own husband. Let the husband render unto the wife due benevolence: and likewise also the wife unto the husband. The wife hath not power of her own body, but the husband: and likewise also the husband hath not power of his own body, but the wife." Having a loving wife, one with whom the man can share the intimacies of marriage, is the greatest protection we can have against the sin of fornication, and what a wonderful blessing it is! But the man must realize that he is to render due benevolence to his wife, just as she is to render it to him. He is also to realize that she has power over his body, just as he has power over hers. This side of marriage is not designed to be a "one-sided" thing, and the man must realize this.

The woman was created for man. She was created as a suitable companion for him, to fill his most vital needs. She is a part of the very nature of man and must be treated as God intended for her to be treated. As Paul wrote in Ephesians 5:28, "So ought men to love their wives as their own bodies. He that loveth his wife loveth himself."

December 9

The Marriage Relationship (6)

God views the addition of children to a family as a great gift. In Psalm 127:3-5 the psalmist wrote, "Lo, children are an heritage of the Lord: and the fruit of the womb is his reward. As arrows are in the hand of a mighty man; so are the children of the youth. Happy is the man that hath his quiver full of them: they shall not be ashamed, but they shall speak with the enemies in the gates." When the God-ordained marriage is blessed with children, there are added responsibilities that fall upon the shoulders of the father. These added responsibilities are not a burden; they are simply part of God's plan.

When a man becomes a father, he now must provide not only for his wife, but for his children as well. In 1 Timothy 5:8 Paul wrote, "But if any provide not for his own, and specially for those of his own house, he hath denied the faith, and is worse than an infidel." He must provide them with food, clothing, shelter, and all of the other physical things necessary to their well-being.

However, a father owes his children much more than the physical necessities; he owes them things that money just cannot buy. A father owes his children leadership, guidance, and a good example. His children must be able to look to him for advice and counsel. Remember that in Ephesians 6:4 the Bible says, "And, ye fathers, provoke not your children to wrath: but bring them up in the nurture and admonition of the Lord." Much is involved in this statement. Many men feel that since they go out and earn the living, the rest of the responsibility as far as the children are concerned rests with the mother. That is not the case in the God-ordained home. While she shares the responsibility of teaching the children, God puts the first duty on the father as the head of the household to bring his children up in the "nurture and admonition of the Lord."

To be an example, to be the guiding influence that a father is to be, there must be time spent with the children. So many fathers, either because of work or social activities (clubs and associations), spend very little time with their children. We certainly would not be pleased with a schoolteacher who didn't spend the necessary time with our children. We would feel that that individual was not doing the job. Well, God places the primary responsibility for the children's "education" upon the father. As one who has spent many years coaching children of all ages, I can tell you that the happiest, most well-adjusted kids were those whose parents spent time with them. The father who always has something else to do instead of spending time with his children is just too busy. All the money in the world cannot do for the children what a father's presence and interest in their lives can do.

In addition, there is the matter of discipline. So often when discipline is mentioned, the immediate thought is punishment of some form or another. That is just a part of discipline, not all of it. Solomon wrote in Proverbs 22:6, "Train up a child in the way he should go: and when he is old, he will not depart from it." Discipline, when used as a noun, means "training which corrects, molds, strengthens, or perfects." When used as a verb, it means "to develop by instruction and exercise, to train in self-control and obedience." It can also mean "to punish, to chastise." A father's responsibility is to set certain guidelines for his children to follow, and then discipline them to follow those guidelines. In this way children learn self-control, restraint, and respect for authority. Occasionally, corporal punishment will be necessary. In Proverbs 13:24 the Bible says, "He that spareth his rod hateth his son; but he that loveth him chasteneth him betimes." This is a responsibility that is assumed when a man becomes a father.

Fathers, our children need us much more than they need things, and God expects us to supply that need.

The Marriage Relationship (7)

As we turn our attention to the woman in the marriage relationship, we do so recognizing that what God actually has to say about her position and function within the family has been under tremendous attack. My heart goes out to the godly woman in the marriage relationship—a woman whose price is "far above rubies" (Prov. 31:10). Her invaluable contributions to society are not recognized and appreciated by those in the world and are becoming less and less appreciated by those in the church. She is, however, a woman whom God calls "blessed" and worthy of praise.

1 Peter 3:1-6 tells us,

Likewise ye wives, be in subjection to your own husbands; that, if any obey not the word, they also may without the word be won by the conversation *(manner of life, g.l.)* of the wives; while they behold your chaste conversation coupled with fear. Whose adorning let it not be that outward adorning of plaiting of hair, and of wearing of gold, or of putting on of apparel; but let it be the hidden man of the heart, in that which is not corruptible, even the ornament of a meek and quiet spirit, which is in the sight of God of great price. For after this manner in the old time the holy women also, who trusted in God, adorned themselves, being in subjection unto their own husbands: even as Sarah obeyed Abraham, calling him lord: whose daughters ye are, as long as ye do well, and are not afraid with any amazement.

The woman's place in the marriage and in the home can be summarized by the word, "subjection." It is, first and foremost, subjection to the will of God and His will is that she be in subjection to her husband. The husband also must be in subjection to the will of God, and it is His will that the man be the head of the family. In Ephesians 5:22-24 Paul wrote, "Wives, submit yourselves unto your own husbands, as unto the Lord. For the husband is the head of the wife, even as Christ is the head of the church: and he is the savior of the body. Therefore as the church is subject unto Christ, so let the wives be to their own husbands in everything." In the marriage relationship, the man cannot abdicate his position of headship; nor can the woman usurp that position and still be in subjection to the will of God.

This position of subjection does not mean that the woman in the marriage

relationship is secondary to the man. It does not mean that she is less important than the man, less skilled than the man, less intelligent than the man. It
does not mean that she is "less" anything in God's eyes, with the exception of
being physically weaker. Peter wrote in 1 Peter 3:7, "Likewise, ye husbands,
dwell with them according to knowledge, giving honor unto the wife, as unto
the weaker vessel, and as being heirs together of the grace of life; that your
prayers be not hindered." Being physically weaker, it is God's will that the
husband treat her with honor, or great care. Shame on any man who would
ever raise his hand in anger against his wife and strike her with it.

The position of subjection is one of function. The man and the woman are
equal in God's eyes. Speaking of salvation, of being "in Christ" Paul wrote,
"There is neither Jew nor Greek, there is neither bond nor free, there is neither male nor female; for ye are all one in Christ Jesus" (Gal. 3:28). However,
each has a different role to perform.

December 11

The Marriage Relationship (8)

The true beauty of a woman in the marriage relationship is not seen merely
by looking at her physical appearance, although she does take care of herself;
it is seen by who and what she is. She adorns herself with that which is truly
beautiful, a meek and quiet spirit. Manifesting that meek and quiet spirit, she
exerts a tremendous influence for good upon her husband. *Oh, that women of
today could understand that!* Being the godly wife that God desires is not being
a mousy nobody who exists for no other purpose than to fulfill every whim
of her husband. She is to be a "help meet" for him. She was created from him
and for him, and they perfectly complement each other. Peter even made the
point that if she should be married to one who is not a Christian, one who
has not yet been touched to the point of obedience by the Word of God, he
may very well be won for the Lord by the wonderful influence of the good
and godly life he sees his wife lead.

As was the case with the husband, so it is with the wife. It is within the
marriage relationship that God has placed the blessing of physical intimacy.
In 1 Corinthians 7:1-5 the mutual nature of this aspect of the relationship is
clearly taught. The woman has the responsibility to "render due benevolence"

to the husband, and the husband must "render due benevolence" to the wife. This aspect of the marriage relationship must never be used as a weapon by either party.

December 12

The Marriage Relationship (9)

One aspect of the marriage relationship with which God's Word deals extensively, yet is receiving less and less attention today, is the primary function of the woman in the marriage. While I do not believe the Bible prohibits a wife from working outside of the home, unless by doing so she neglects her primary responsibilities, it is vital to understand, believe, and appreciate that her primary area of God-given responsibility in the marriage is in the home.

In Titus 2:4-5 Paul wrote, "That they may teach the young women to be sober, to love their husbands, to love their children, to be discreet, chaste, keepers at home, good, obedient to their own husbands, that the word of God be not blasphemed." Again, from 1 Timothy 5:14 we find, "I will therefore that the younger women marry, bear children, guide the house, give none occasion to the adversary to speak reproachfully." Notice the phrases "keepers at home" and "guide the house." God places the primary responsibility for earning the income the family needs upon the shoulders of the man, and He places the primary responsibility for the care of the home upon the shoulders of the woman. They have different functions, but each is vitally important.

There are so many today who believe that God's way does not allow a woman to utilize all of the abilities He has given her. Many argue that this makes a woman little more than a domestic servant and does not permit her to have meaning and purpose in her life. Many speak of wanting to "have a career," not realizing that the role God has given to the woman in marriage is the most noble of "careers."

Let us take the time to look at Proverbs 31:10-31, the epitome of the woman who is a keeper of the home and one who guides the house. Has any CEO ever been praised in such a way by God?

Who can find a virtuous woman? For her price is far above rubies. The heart of her husband doth safely trust in her, so that he shall have no need of spoil.

She will do him good and not evil all the days of her life. She seeketh wool, and flax, and worketh willingly with her hands. She is like the merchants' ships; she bringeth her food from afar. She riseth also while it is yet night and giveth meat to her household, and a portion to her maidens. She considereth a field, and buyeth it: with the fruit of her hands she planteth a vineyard. She girdeth her loins with strength, and strengheneth her arms. She perceiveth that her merchandise is good: her candle goeth not out by night. She layeth her hands to the spindle, and her hands hold the distaff. She stretcheth out her hand to the poor; yea, she reacheth forth her hands to the needy. She is not afraid of the snow for her household: for all her household are clothed with scarlet. She maketh herself coverings of tapestry; her clothing is silk and purple. Her husband is known in the gates, when he sitteth among the elders of the land. She maketh fine linen, and selleth it; and delivereth girdles unto the merchant. Strength and honor are her clothing; and she shall rejoice in time to come. She openeth her mouth with wisdom; and in her tongue is the law of kindness. She looketh well to the ways of her household, and eateth not the bread of idleness. Her children arise up, and call her blessed; her husband also, and he praiseth her. Many daughters have done virtuously, but thou excellest them all. Favor is deceitful, and beauty is vain: but a woman that feareth the Lord, she shall be praised. Give her of the fruit of her hands; and let her own works praise her in the gates.

There is not much I can add to this great tribute. The godly woman in the marriage relationship gives herself wholeheartedly to the task of caring for her home. It has been said that the man has the responsibility to provide for the things of the home, and the woman has the responsibility to make a home out of whatever he is able to provide. She is not ashamed of the work that she does, for it is the work that God would have her to do—a work of the utmost importance. She is industrious and makes her home a welcome place for her husband, a place to which he wants to come home. She looks well to her household, and she does not have the time to partake of idleness.

December 13

The Marriage Relationship (10)

Is there anyone or anything more highly praised in God's Word than the godly woman of the house? 1 Timothy 2:5 tells us, "Notwithstanding she shall be saved in childbearing, if they continue in faith and charity and holiness and sobriety." Oh, how the role of the woman expands when the children begin to arrive. In 1 Timothy 5:14 we find, "I will therefore that the younger women marry, bear children, guide the house, give none occasion to the adversary to speak reproachfully." It has been said that the hand that rocks the cradle rules the world. While that is not exactly true, who can overestimate the importance of the position of the mother?

Speaking purely from a physical standpoint alone, I used to make my living loading and unloading cartons of paper from trucks. These cartons ranged in weight from approximately thirty-five pounds to over fifty pounds. I can say without hesitation that I would rather do that for ten hours a day than try to keep up with a little baby all by myself for one whole day. What a job! A child needs personal attention and care just for their physical needs throughout the day, and as the "keeper of the home," this falls primarily upon the woman.

But even beyond the physical necessities to which a mother must attend for her children is the emotional and spiritual training she must give them. In terms of time, she is with them much more than the father, and the influence she can have on her children is tremendous. Consider 2 Timothy 1:5, "When I call to remembrance the unfeigned faith that is in thee, which dwelt first in thy grandmother Lois, and thy mother Eunice, and I am persuaded that is in thee also." Two godly women in the life of Timothy had a great influence on his spirituality, his grandmother and his mother. In the long hours that a mother and her children spend together, there are so many opportunities to talk about Jesus and all the other people in the Bible. There are so many opportunities to teach the difference between right and wrong. What a great lesson we can learn from Deuteronomy 6:4-7, "Hear, O Israel: The Lord our God is one Lord: and thou shalt love the Lord thy God with all thine heart and with all thy soul, and with all thy might. And these words, which I command thee this day, shall be in thine heart: and thou shalt teach them diligently unto thy children, and shalt talk to them when thou sittest in thine house, and when thou walkest by the way, and when thou liest down, and when thou risest up." Who better to do the teaching during those early years than the mother?

I am afraid that with today's society and economy, many children are growing up without mothers in the real sense of the word—or in the sense that God intended. So many mothers go back to work immediately after the baby is born, so right from the beginning the child misses the influence of a loving mother. Even when they return home from work in the evening, oftentimes they are too tired to give the children the individual, undivided attention that they need and deserve. Too many children are being raised by babysitters, not their mothers, and a mother will never get the opportunity to have such a profound effect upon her children again. Young mothers need to be taught that if there is any way possible, the most important thing that they can do, and the duty that God has given them, is to stay at home and raise the children. If work outside the home is absolutely necessary for the family to have the basics of life, so be it. However, the most important job for the woman in the God-ordained family relationship is in the home.

So the woman in the God-fearing home is to be honored by the faithful fulfillment of her responsibilities. Hers is not a second-class position, and those who say it is are just ignorant of God's Word. What the world needs are more women who will fill their divinely appointed position, which is uniquely theirs.

December 14

The Marriage Relationship (11)

It is inevitable when two people live together in the most intimate relationship known to man—marriage—disagreements between them are going to arise. This is nothing new, and it is not a sign that the marriage is "on the rocks." It may even be possible to classify some of these disagreements as arguments, and that is not necessarily a bad thing either. Paul wrote in Ephesians 4:26, "Be ye angry, and sin not: let not the sun go down upon your wrath." Paul is instructing us never to let our anger cause us to sin. When there is a disagreement, it is best to talk about it and to work it out verbally. It is sinful and counterproductive to let it fester inside of us until it affects our attitudes and disposition toward our spouse.

But what happens when those disagreements become sharp and contentious? What happens when the home has become a battleground of sorts, and that perfect, harmonious love-nest that was envisioned when the vows were taken degenerates into a situation filled with wrath and bitterness, heartache and pain?

When and if such happens, remember that it did not get that way overnight, and it probably will not be fixed overnight. In order for a marriage of Christians to reach that point, one or both of them has to have left God outside the door. It wouldn't get to such a state if God's will had been followed by both of them, and in order to fix it, God is going to have to be re-enthroned in that marriage.

Brethren, I am not an expert on this subject, but there are certain principles taught in God's Word, and *He is the expert.* He shows us that there are certain things that should be done and certain things that should not be done to fix a marriage in which there is a lot of fighting and unhappiness. Let's consider a few things that *should not* be done.

Reading from the New King James Version, the canon of the Old Testament practically comes to a close with these words from Malachi 2:16, "For the Lord God of Israel says that He hates divorce. . . ." Jesus, in Matthew 19:6 said, "What therefore God hath joined together, let not man put asunder."

One of the most clearly taught truths in the Word of God is that divorce is unacceptable behavior as far as God is concerned. There is only one reason for a divorce and remarriage that God would approve, and that is adultery—fornication on the part of one partner in the marriage.

All of this being true, when fighting erupts in the marriage of two Christians, there is no excuse for bringing up divorce. I have been amazed at the loose use of the "threat" of divorce that has been made over the years by those who are members of the body of Christ. The world may throw the threat of divorce around quite easily. They may try to use it as a club to beat a partner over the head with, figuratively speaking, but a Christian must *never, never* do that! To do so is sinful, reprehensible, and cruel.

December 15

The Marriage Relationship (12)

If fighting does begin to take place in a marriage of Christians, or a Christian to a non-Christian, it must *never, never* become physical. I am reminded of Paul's words in Ephesians 5:28-29, "So ought men to love their wives as their own bodies. He that loveth his wife loveth himself. For no man ever yet hated his own flesh; but nourisheth and cherisheth it, even as the Lord the church." I don't know of anyone in his right mind who purposely beats or hurts his own body in anger. God tells men to love their wives as their own bodies, and in Ephesians 5:25 Paul wrote, "Husbands, love your wives, even as Christ also loved the church, and gave himself for it." I just cannot see hitting in anger someone for whom you would die. There is simply no way to justify hitting a spouse, whether male or female.

Often when trouble arises within a marriage of Christians, one or both of the parties involved will begin to talk to others about the situation. It is good to seek the advice of those older and wiser (we will discuss going to the elders when we discuss things that should be done), but it is not good to go from person to person telling everyone what is going on. I am personally convinced that some go from person to person, giving their own version of problems in their marriage, until they find someone who will tell them what they want to hear. Solomon wrote in Ecclesiastes 5:3, "For a dream cometh through a multitude of business; and a fool's voice is known by a multitude of words."

Whenever fighting and unhappiness plague a marriage, the whole point is to make it right—not to win the fights. The focus must be getting the marriage to fit the pattern that God, the Creator of the marriage relationship, designed. Don't look for people who will make you feel good in your particular side of the fight; look for those who understand that the most important thing is to make the marriage the way it ought to be.

December 16

The Marriage Relationship (13)

In continuation of our discussion on what to do when fighting and serious contention breaks out in a marriage, let's look at some of the things that *should* be done.

When you are fighting with your spouse and the family life is disrupted, when home is not exactly the place you want to be, it may seem that God doesn't really care. *He does!* Pray! God will help. John wrote in 1 John 5:14-15, "This is the confidence that we have in him, that, if we ask anything according to his will, he heareth us; and if we know that he hear us, whatsoever we ask, we know that we have the petitions that we desired of him." In James 4:10 we find, "Humble yourselves in the sight of the Lord, and he shall lift you up."

Understand that God answers prayers in the way He sees fit. He also answers in His own timeframe. Do not despair if it does not immediately get better or suddenly work out. But know this, God will give you the strength to do what is right and bear up under the strain until it does work out. Remember Paul's statement in 2 Corinthians 12:8-9, writing of his "thorn in the flesh"? He said, "For this thing I besought the Lord thrice, that it might depart from me. And he said unto me, My grace is sufficient for thee: for my strength is made perfect in weakness. Most gladly therefore will I rather glory in my infirmities, that the power of Christ may rest upon me."

It *never* becomes necessary to do something that is wrong in God's sight to deal with a bad marriage situation. God promises sufficient strength to endure and to do what is right.

If things go wrong in the construction of a building, the builders go back to the blueprints and make sure that each step has been properly followed. If things are going wrong in a marriage, go to God's Word. Each partner in the marriage must be honest enough to look at God's Word, examine himself or herself in the light of it, and see where they, personally, need to make changes. See James 1:23-25.

Seek help and advice from the proper people. Who in the church is responsible for the spiritual well being of every one of the members? According to Hebrews 13:17, it is the elders. They are elders by virtue of meeting the qualifications set forth in 1 Timothy 3 and Titus 1. Those qualifications demand a certain degree of wisdom and experience. They are husbands and fathers. They have done, and are doing, a good job in their homes. That doesn't mean that they have been, or always are, perfect—but it does mean that they have done a good job in order to be qualified. Go to them for help. They care and are the best equipped to be of assistance.

I believe another source of assistance of which the Bible speaks, especially for the younger women, is the older women. In Titus 2:4 one of the things the older women are to do is to teach the young women "to love their husbands." There is a lot involved in that. An older, faithful sister who has successfully navigated the sometimes-turbulent waters of marriage can be an invaluable source of help. Notice I said invaluable, not infallible; and make sure they are *faithful* older sisters.

Make the Number One priority God. Next in line should be your spouse and in making the marriage work as God designed it. When #1 is right and #2 is right, then priority #3 (myself) will be just fine too.

The Marriage Relationship (14)

Whenever a marriage has reached the point of polarization, where it is no longer the husband and wife working together but two locked in combat, what is to be done? The man and woman are so very unhappy, the children are suffering tremendous emotional stress, and it usually also means that the family, or part of it, has become sporadic in attendance at services. When a civil word barely passes between the man and the woman, it is pretty safe to say that not a lot of Bible study is going on there either. When it has reached that point, you can also count on the fact that very little prayer is being offered by the husband for the wife, or the wife for the husband, because if it were, the anger and hatred would subside. You cannot remain bitter toward one for whom you are praying. So what is to be done?

Over the years I have been amazed at the advice brethren have given one another to deal with these marriages that have been allowed to go to seed. The most incredible one of all is, "Go ahead and get a divorce. It just means you can't get married again." Worse advice has never been given. Whenever a marriage is broken by divorce someone is always guilty of sin. One does not have the biblical right to walk out of his marriage in search of an illusive happiness. The sins of a mate may leave an innocent Christian very few options. However, both the innocent and the guilty should remember: There is only one reason given in God's word for divorce and remarriage. It is found in Matthew 5:32 and Matthew 19:9. That one reason is fornication. Divorcing and remarrying for any other reason is sinful. If an individual marries after they have divorced for a reason other than fornication, they have committed sin; adultery is what the Bible calls it. But we must understand that a divorce and remarriage for any reason other than fornication is a sin!

Some have advised a brother or sister to go ahead and get a divorce for a reason other than fornication (there is sin #1, both in the doing and in the advising), and then in the future, if their former spouse marries someone else, they would be free to marry. That is absolutely not true! If we look at Matthew 19:9, without the exception clause, the meaning is clear. If a person has been divorced for a reason other than fornication, they cannot remarry without sin. The passage says, "Whosoever shall put away his wife and shall marry another, committeth adultery: and whoso marrieth her which is put away doth commit adultery."

Divorce and remarriage is not an option where no fornication has been committed.

I have actually known of some who thought they could manipulate their way around God's law of marriage and divorce by denying their spouse his or her God-given conjugal rights until that person became so frustrated he or she went out and committed adultery. It is incredible that such conduct would need to be discussed in a series of articles dealing with brethren, but such has been done and that advice has been given. 1 Corinthians 7:1-4 clearly shows that the denying of those rights to one's marriage partner is sin! We cannot commit a sin in order to cause another to commit a sin, whereby we might benefit! How do members of the Lord's church even think of such things?

Others have advised, "Well, don't get a divorce, but just separate and live apart." I have even heard some call it a "legal separation." I suppose you can get such a thing via the laws of the land, but not in God's law. Again, 1 Corinthians 7:1-4 would clearly show that such conduct is wrong, sinful, and ungodly.

It is possible for a couple to separate for a period of time, but not indefinitely. But this separation must be by *mutual* consent, for the purpose of giving themselves to *prayer and fasting,* and they *must* come together again to avoid the temptation to commit adultery that Satan would place before them. Look at 1 Corinthians 7:5 where Paul wrote, "Defraud ye not one the other, except it be with consent for a time, that ye may give yourselves to fasting and prayer, and come together again, that Satan tempt you not for your incontinency."

Others have advised couples to remain in the same house (for the sake of the children and recognizing that they have no right to divorce) to live essentially in a platonic relationship. That is not God's design for marriage. That is in violation of 1 Corinthians 7:1-4. That is putting a band-aid on a gaping wound. It is not fixing the problem; it is compounding it. When a marriage of a brother and sister is falling apart, the goal is to fix it, not to destroy it. The marriage would not be in that state if they had walked consistently with God in the marriage in the first place. The marriage will never be fixed by leaving God out of the solution.

The Marriage Relationship (15)

In every marriage that I have attended or conducted, somewhere in the ceremony the phrase, "till death do you part" was mentioned. In each of those weddings both the bride and groom said, "I do," or "I will" or "Yes"; some affirmation of their vow to stay together until "death" caused them to part.

In practically every wedding that I have attended, and certainly in every one that I have conducted, Matthew 19:4-9 has been read,

> And he answered and said unto them, Have ye not read, that he which made them at the beginning made them male and female, and said, For this cause shall a man leave father and mother, and shall cleave to his wife: and they twain shall be one flesh? Wherefore they are no more twain, but one flesh. What therefore God hath joined together, let not man put asunder. They say unto him, Why did Moses then command to give a writing of divorcement, and to put her away? He saith unto them, Moses because of the hardness of your hearts suffered you to put away your wives: but from the beginning it was not so. And I say unto you, Whosoever shall put away his wife, except it be for fornication, and shall marry another, committeth adultery: and whoso marrieth her which is put away doth commit adultery.

Therefore, in each wedding there has been the recognition that God does not approve of divorce, that it can be rightfully entered into for only one reason, and to do otherwise is to sin before God. In each wedding both the bride and the groom have recognized that only death can end a marriage without sin having been committed, and in each wedding both the bride and the groom have vowed before man and God that they would stay together in the marriage relationship until one of them died.

All of that being true, does it make the slightest bit of sense to be mean or unkind to each other? Having vowed to live together until one dies, what can there possibly be that is worth arguing about to the point of nastiness? Having worked hard to fall in love when no promise before God had been made, doesn't it just make sense to keep working hard to stay in love once we have vowed before God that we were going to love, honor, and cherish that person?

Nearly every wedding I have attended or conducted has involved a younger couple. In practically all of those weddings a prayer has been offered in which thanks were expressed, on behalf of the couple, for one another. As you see them gaze into one another's eyes, as you see the smiles, the tender touches, and expressions of affection, you just know that they are as thankful to God at that moment as they can possibly be. I wonder at what point so many stop being thankful.

It is such a simple thing, but I guarantee that if you start the day by thanking God in your morning prayers for your husband or wife, and if you close the day doing the same thing, it is going to be a whole lot easier to keep that feeling alive. Why is so much emphasis placed upon what we don't have? If I am truly thankful for someone, I am not going to mistreat him or her. On the contrary, I will protect and cherish that person. You may not be blessed with the wealthiest husband or the most beautiful wife. He may not be a CEO, and she may not be the world's best cook. He might have a pot belly and be losing his hair, and her beautiful brunette hair might be getting gray; but the husband and wife belong to each other. God joined them together. Oh, brethren, let us always be thankful for what we do have and not worry about what they are not.

December 19

And
By Adam Litmer

And to love your God
And to stoke the flame
And to sleep at night, dreaming of a new name.

And to walk by faith
And to despise your sight
And to spend a life trying to do what's right.

And to sink to knees
And to bow to pray
And to pour your heart into every word you say
And to rise back up
And to stand refreshed
And to smile, knowing He watches every breath.

And to face the world
And to feel no fear
And to wake each day with conscience that is clear.

And to shout for joy
And to sing in praise
And to know He's pleased with every note you raise.

And to read His Word
And to imbibe His light
And to know you've been armed for every fight.

And to breathe your last
And to face the end
And to know through His grace you'll stand again.

And to be with God
And to pass gates of pearl
And to be with Him Who has overcome the world.

December 20

Better Off

There is an expression that I have used more times than I could count when comparing those who were wealthy with those who were not. I have often referred to the wealthy as being "better off" than those who were not so wealthy. I recently saw that expression in a magazine, and seeing it in writing made me pause and really think about it. Describing those who are wealthy as being "better off" than those who are not really hits at the essential, fundamental evil and error that is behind covetousness—that the quality of life is comprised of and based upon the amount of things that we possess. That being the case, the more we have, the better off we are. Isn't that the very fallacy that Jesus addressed in the Sermon on the Mount when he said, "Is not the life more than meat, and the body than raiment?" (Matt. 6:25). The answer to that question is yes, life is more than meat and the body is more than raiment or clothing.

The value of our lives, what we are worth, is not measured by what we own. If that were not true, if what we owned really did determine if we were "better off" than those with less possessions, then think of what the answer would have to be to the question that Jesus asked in Mark 8:36. Jesus asked, "For what shall it profit a man, if he shall gain the whole world, and lose his own soul?" If being "better off" is determined by the amount of our possessions, then the answer to the Lord's question would have to be "everything." But that is not the answer. A man who loses his own soul may be the wealthiest man on earth, but he is not "better off" than the beggar who is saved. No one thing, or combination of things, is worth even one soul. Someone once said that it is not what we own that matters; it is what owns us.

I am reminded of Luke 12:13-21, which perfectly sets forth the point of our devotion today. There we find:

> And one of the company said unto him, Master, speak to my brother, that he divide the inheritance with me. And he said unto him, Man, who made me a judge or a divider over you? And he said unto them, Take heed, and beware of covetousness: for a man's life consisteth not in the abundance of the things which he possesseth. And he spake a parable unto them, saying, The ground of a certain rich man brought forth plentifully: and he thought within himself, saying, What shall I do, because I have no room where to bestow my fruits? And he said, This will I do: I will pull down my barns, and build greater; and there will I bestow all my fruits and my goods. And I will say to my soul, Soul, thou hast much goods laid up for many years; take thine ease, eat, drink, and be merry. But God said unto him, Thou fool, this night thy soul shall be required of thee: then whose shall those things be, which thou hast provided? So is he that layeth up treasure for himself, and is not rich toward God.

The poorest Christian in this world's goods is wealthy beyond measure in that which truly matters.

True Glory—Or What Is Most Important

I'd like to begin our thought for today by turning to the book of Philippians 3:1-8. In this passage Paul shows us where the true trust, true boasting, true glorying of the faithful child of God takes place. Paul shows us what is truly important—what is most important. The passage says:

> Finally, my brethren, rejoice in the Lord. To write the same things to you, to me indeed is not grievous, but for you it is safe. Beware of dogs, beware of evil workers, beware of the concision. For we are the circumcision, which worship God in the spirit, and rejoice in Christ Jesus, and have no confidence in the flesh. Though I might also have confidence in the flesh. If any other man thinketh that he hath whereof he might trust in the flesh, I more: circumcised the eighth day, of the stock of Israel, of the tribe of Benjamin, an Hebrew of the Hebrews; as touching the law, a Pharisee: concerning zeal, persecuting the church; touching the righteousness which is in the law, blameless. But what things were gain to me, those I counted loss for Christ. Yea doubtless, and I count all things but loss for the excellency of the knowledge of Christ Jesus my Lord: for whom I have suffered the loss of all things, and do count them but dung, that I may win Christ.

Consider what Paul has done. He has listed those things that to the Jew of that time were of utmost importance. He was writing of things that in their eyes made them so much better than those who were outside of the covenant, those who had not been circumcised. He wrote of his heritage and the fact that if confidence and boasting could be derived from things of the flesh, he had more to have confidence and to boast about than just about anybody else. He was a Hebrew, pure and simple. Concerning the Law of Moses, he was a Pharisee. Remember, Paul had studied at the feet of Gamaliel, and "was taught according to the perfect manner of the law of the fathers" (Acts 22:3). He had been so zealous for the law that he had persecuted the church. Yet, when he came to a knowledge of the Lord, Paul saw all of those things in a completely different light. What he had counted as gain, what he had gloried in and trusted in, he now counted as loss. Weighing the one against the other, he had been able to determine the true value.

In verse 8 Paul had written, "I count all things but loss for the excellency of the knowledge of Christ Jesus my Lord." That would include any and everything of a worldly nature upon which he might have placed his confidence—his power, worldly possessions, position among his peers; anything when compared to the surpassing value of the knowledge of Christ Jesus his Lord.

What is this "knowledge of Christ Jesus" that Paul said was of surpassing value? To have the "knowledge of Christ" means a great deal more than just knowing something about Jesus. Paul had come to know Christ by trusting Him, by loving Him, and by being loved by Him. He had come to know Christ by obeying Him, by relying upon Him, and by serving Him. That is the "knowledge of Christ Jesus" that Paul was talking about. It reminds me of something that Jeremiah wrote so many years earlier in Jeremiah 9:24, "But let him that glorieth glory in this, that he understandeth and knoweth me, that I am the Lord which exercise lovingkindess, judgment, and righteousness, in the earth: for in these things I delight." Nothing is of greater value

That is why Paul gave up what he had so much confidence in before and counted it but rubbish. He went on in Philippians 3 and explained why: in verse 8, that he "might win Christ"; in verse 9, that he might be "found in him"; in verse 10, that he might "know him"; in verse 11, that he "might attain unto the resurrection of the dead"; and in verse 14, that he might have the "prize of the high calling of God in Christ Jesus."

In closing, if everything of a worldly nature upon which we place so much importance was to be taken away, so what? If we lose our health, we still have Jesus. If we lose our ability to make a living, we still have Jesus. If we lose our material possessions, we still have Jesus. If we lose our jobs, we still have Jesus. If we have family problems, we still have Jesus. If we lose those close to us by death, we still have Jesus. There is nothing else like it.

December 22

"He That Winneth Souls Is Wise"

"The fruit of the righteous is a tree of life; and he that winneth souls is wise" (Prov. 11:30). The book of Proverbs begins by extolling the importance of wisdom. Indeed, Proverbs 1:1-4 tells us, "The proverbs of Solomon, the son of David, king of Israel; to know wisdom and instruction; to perceive the words of understanding; to receive the instruction of wisdom, justice, and judgment, and equity; to give subtilty to the simple, to the young man knowledge and discretion." All of this leads us to the basic question, "Why is one who wins souls described as wise?"

There are so many different approaches that could to taken to answer that question, but the clearest answer given in the Scriptures is that the one who works to save souls recognizes just how valuable a single soul is. In Mark 8:36-37 Jesus said, "For what shall it profit a man, if he shall gain the whole world, and lose his own soul? Or what shall a man give in exchange or his soul?" Just by looking at what the Lord had to say, it is easy to see that if it were possible to take everything that this world has to offer, and I mean *everything*, and place it on one side of a balance, while placing on the other side one single soul—your soul, my soul, or anybody's soul—it is the soul that would tip the balance. It is the soul that would far outweigh the things of the world.

I have often heard it said that the value of anything is determined by what someone is willing to pay for it. I remember when my son was about ten years old. We lived down the street from a sports card/comic bookstore. My son would take all of his money and run to that store and buy baseball cards. He would come home and tell me that the proprietor of the shop had told him that the card he had just purchased for $1.00 was worth $50.00 on the market. I could not get my son to understand that if it was truly worth $50.00, the shop owner would not have sold it to him for $1.00. The value of a thing is determined by what someone is willing to pay for it.

What is the value of a soul? That is clearly pointed out in Philippians 2:5-8, "Let this mind be in you, which was also in Christ Jesus; who, being in the form of God, thought it not robbery to be equal with God: but made himself of no reputation, and took upon him the form of a servant, and was made in the likeness of men: and being found in fashion as a man, he humbled himself, and became obedient unto death, even the death of the cross." What is the value that Jesus places upon a soul? He was willing to give his own life to redeem it. In 2 Corinthians 5:21 we are told, "For he hath made him to be sin for us, who knew no sin; that we might be made the righteousness of God in him."

Surely with statements such as these no one can question the value of a soul, a value determined by God in the giving of his Son. This is what makes a soul winner wise. He or she is seeking to win that which is of the greatest value and the most importance.

"I Spake unto You in Your Prosperity"

In Jeremiah 22:21, we find one of the many reasons for the downfall of the southern kingdom of Judah. God said to the people of that kingdom, and to the capital city of Jerusalem, "I spake unto thee in thy prosperity; but thou saidst, I will not hear. This hath been thy manner from thy youth, that thou obeyedst not my voice." In this verse we see a problem that has been characteristic of mankind from the beginning, not just the citizens of the southern kingdom of Judah. So very often in periods of great material prosperity, people lose their willingness to listen to God. They lose their concern, if they ever had it, about God and spiritual matters. When financial problems are few, the economy is humming along, cars, vacations, and large houses are plentiful, and people have the financial wherewithal to do pretty much whatever they want, why think about God?

The letter to the Romans tells us that the things "written aforetime were written for our learning, that we through patience and comfort of the Scriptures might have hope" (Rom. 15:4). This generation in which we live needs to look long and hard at what happened to the children of Israel, remembering that "all these things happened unto them for ensamples: and they are written for our admonition, upon whom the ends of the world are come" (1 Cor. 10:11). Technology may change but people don't, and great prosperity provides the same danger today that it did in the days preceding the destruction of Jerusalem and the carrying away into Babylonian captivity of the southern kingdom of Judah.

In Deuteronomy 8:11-14a we find, "Beware that thou forget not the Lord thy God, in not keeping his commandments, and his judgments, and his statutes, which I command thee this day: lest when thou hast eaten and art full, and hast built goodly houses, and dwelt therein; and when thy herds and thy flocks multiply, and thy silver and thy gold is multiplied, and all that thou hast is multiplied; then thine heart is lifted up, and thou forget the Lord thy God. . . ."

What a warning! Yet, in a little over 700 years later, the northern kingdom of Israel would be destroyed, partially because they had done the very things

Moses had warned about. For all intents and purposes, they "forgot the Lord their God." We began by talking about Judah, and one of the reasons for their downfall some 860 years after the warning of Moses was, "I spoke to you in your prosperity, and you said, I will not hear."

Things haven't changed much. The tendency to turn to God only in time of need is still so strong. The warnings of Scripture exhort us to utilize times of wealth and prosperity to bring us closer to God in thanksgiving for all of his blessings, rather than to forget that all that we have ultimately comes from him.

December 24

There's No Place Like Home

There is an old saying that is heard quite frequently, "There is no place like home." I may be showing my age, but I can still close my eyes and see Dorothy clicking together the heels of those ruby slippers and saying over and over, "There's no place like home." We were all born somewhere—we all grew up somewhere.

When my mother and my father died, I felt funny, different. It was as though I had been cut adrift and no longer had a place to call home. Home had always been where Mom and Dad were. Home was where I grew up, but now they were gone and somebody else was living in our house. But as time went by and the more fervently I prayed about it, I came to realize that everything was going to be okay. The reason I say that is because from the moment I rose from the waters of baptism some thirty-two years ago, this old earth was no longer my home.

I suppose that for my children, both of whom are grown and out on their own, where my wife and I live is home. However, they are both faithful Christians, and like all Christians they long to go home; but it is not to Kentucky, Tennessee, Florida, Michigan, Missouri, New Mexico, or any other place on this earth. We should all be yearning to go home—to our real home—and not just for a time or a visit, but for eternity.

In Hebrews 11, a chapter sometimes referred to as the Hall of Fame of Faith, we find in verses 13-16:

These all died in faith, not having received the promises, but having seen them afar off, and were persuaded of them, and embraced them, and confessed that they were strangers and pilgrims on the earth. For they that say such things declare plainly that they seek a country. And truly, if they had been mindful of that country from whence they came out, they might have had opportunity to have returned. But now they desire a better country, that is, an heavenly: wherefore God is not ashamed to be called their God: for he hath prepared for them a city.

I am a faithful Christian, a child of God, and my citizenship is in heaven. While I live on earth and enjoy life, I must never forget that I am just passing through, and that there is a true, prepared home that awaits me in eternity. I often find myself turning to the words of the Lord as he spoke to his apostles on the very night in which he was betrayed that we find in John 14:1-3: "Let not your heart be troubled: ye believe in God, believe also in me. In my Father's house are many mansions: if it were not so, I would have told you. I go to prepare a place for you. And if I go and prepare a place for you, I will come again, and receive you unto myself; that where I am, there ye may be also."

There is a prepared home, awaiting us in heaven, that Peter described as "an inheritance incorruptible, and undefiled, and that fadeth not away, reserved in heaven for you" (1 Pet. 1:4). What more could a child of God ask for?

December 25

Christmas

This is the time of the year when most people who believe that Jesus was the Son of God celebrate His birth. While I must say I am thankful every day for His coming into this world, all must admit that no one knows what day Jesus was born. In fact, all of the evidence given in the Gospel records related to His birth makes it fairly certain that it was not on December 25. Additionally, we can search the New Testament from the day the church began in Acts 2 all the way through the remainder of the Bible, and we will find no indication whatsoever that the early church, under the direction and guidance of the inspired apostles, ever celebrated the Lord's birth as a special religious "holy day," or in any way at all.

One thing that simply amazes me concerning the birth of the Lord Jesus Christ in that stable in Bethlehem is the fact that it took place at all. Just to think that "the Word was made flesh, and dwelt among us, (and we beheld his glory, the glory as of the only begotten of the Father, full of grace and truth" (John 1:14) is beyond my finite mind to fully comprehend.

In Colossians 1:15-17 we find concerning Jesus, "Who is the image of the invisible God, the firstborn of every creature: for by him were all things created, that are in heaven, and that are in earth, visible and invisible, whether they be thrones, or dominions, or principalities, or powers: all things were created by him, and for him: and he is before all things, and by him all things consist." When we think about it, the very One who at the beginning said, "Let there be light: and there was light" (Gen. 1:3) came to this earth and was born as a baby in the humblest of settings. How is this possible? How can I grasp this great truth?

Consider 1 Timothy 3:16 where Paul wrote, "And without controversy great is the mystery of godliness: For God was manifest in the flesh, justified in the Spirit, seen of angels, preached unto the Gentiles, believed on in the world, received up into glory." For our purpose today, I am focusing upon "God was manifest in the flesh." The love that Jesus had that would cause him to leave the glory that he had with the Father before the world was and come to this earth as a human being (yet still God) boggles my mind. By the way, a large part of the religious world refers to Mary as the mother of God. Mary had nothing to do with the divinity of Jesus. He was both God and man, and it was solely the fleshly part that involved Mary; that which was "conceived in her is of the Holy Spirit" (Matt. 1:20).

I am thankful that Jesus was born into this world, indeed I am. I am thankful enough to do just what the church He founded did in the first century. I celebrate his death every first day of the week as I partake of the Lord's Supper in commemoration of his great sacrifice. That is what we are called upon to commemorate, celebrate, and remember.

Insight
By Vicky Litmer

In Mark 6 we read the account of Jesus feeding the 5,000 with five loaves and two fish. His disciples who were with Him during this amazing miracle were eyewitnesses to the gathering up of twelve baskets of leftovers. How it must have inspired their faith to see such a thing!

Immediately after this event, the disciples got into a boat to go to the other side of the Sea of Galilee to Bethsaida while Jesus went to a mountain to pray. During the early morning hours the wind gathered so much strength that the disciples had to strain at the oars. Jesus walked toward them on the sea, and believing they were seeing a ghost, the disciples became very frightened. When Jesus identified Himself and got into the boat with them, the wind immediately stopped and the disciples were greatly astonished. The reason for this astonishment is given in verse 52, "For they had not gained any insight from the incident of the loaves, but their heart was hardened."

How many times over the years could I have applied this verse to my own circumstances? How many times has God seen me through trials, difficulties, temptations, and sorrows? And yet there are still so many times when I allow doubt and anxiety to overwhelm me. When I can't imagine how a certain situation is going to turn out well, it means that I have not gained any insight from the care and comfort that God has shown me in the past. When I pray with doubting in my heart, it means I have gained no insight from the compassion and mercy that God has always extended to me. My heart becomes hardened to the magnitude of God's love for me, and I lose the peace and joy that should always characterize me as God's child. Does this also happen to you? How I pray that this insight should fill my heart, in times both good and bad.

"Cease striving and know that I am God" (Ps. 46:10). Oh, blessed Lord, forgive me my unbelief! Increase my faith!

Why Do I Do What I Do?

Of all of the public discourses of the Lord recorded for us in the gospels, the Sermon on the Mount is my personal favorite. The entire sermon is about God, about how people who place God first and foremost and above everything and everybody, will act. It addresses the attitudes that spring forth from that kind of perspective. It deals not only with what Christians are to do and not do, but it delves into the reason why—why we are what we are, and why we do what we do. It is a wonderful sermon that calls upon us to put aside all the fluff and all of the frills and all of the pretenses, and see ourselves as God sees us.

In Matthew 6:1 Jesus said, "Take heed that ye do not your alms before men, to be seen of them: otherwise ye have no reward of your Father which is in heaven." The Lord then continued on and illustrated His warning by addressing three areas that, at first glance, would appear to be evidence of great religious piety and zeal: charity, prayer, and fasting.

Looking at this, one has to wonder what attraction charity, prayer, and fasting would hold for someone who is acting because of the wrong motive. But the Lord shows that people can and do perform acts that may appear to be admirable and even deeply spiritual, but in reality are just self-serving wickedness. For example, what do you suppose was the difference between the following two individuals that our Lord spoke of in Luke 18:9-12 and Luke 21:1-4?

In Luke 18:9-12 we read, "And he spake this parable unto certain which trusted in themselves that they were righteous, and despised others: two men went up into the temple to pray; the one a Pharisee, and the other a publican. The Pharisee stood and prayed thus with himself, God, I thank thee, that I am not as other men are, extortioners, unjust, adulterers, or even as this publican. I fast twice in the week, I give tithes of all that I possess."

In Luke 21:1-4 we find, "And he looked up, and saw the rich men casting their gifts into the treasury. And he saw also a certain poor widow casting in thither two mites. And he said, Of a truth I say unto you, that this poor widow hath cast in more than they all: for all these have of their abundance cast in unto the offerings of God: but she of her penury hath cast in all the living that she had."

The difference was *motive*. Why did they do what they did? Jesus shows that it is possible to do the most noble-appearing thing and do it for a corrupt reason. Just worshipping and being generous do not provide a man a ticket to heaven. As a matter of fact, Satan will follow a person right into the place of prayer and turn his very worship into sin. A man must keep his heart pure and his love true. Ultimately, God must be behind it all.

December 28

"If Any Man Aspires to the Office of Overseer"

Bible students will immediately recognize this statement from 1 Timothy 3:1. Paul is about to set forth the qualifications for a man who could be appointed to the work of elder, or overseer, in a congregation of the Lord's church. Obviously, one of the qualifications is the aspiration to, or the desire for, the work.

To be an elder in the Lord's church is the most important function to which a man can aspire in this world. It is to be uniquely responsible for the spiritual welfare of the people who make up the congregation. The Hebrew writer wrote in Hebrews 13:17, "Obey your leaders, and submit to them; for they keep watch over your souls, as those who will give an account. Let them do this with joy and not with grief, for this would be unprofitable for you." It is to uniquely follow in the footsteps of the Good Shepherd, for elders are called upon to "shepherd" the flock. 1 Peter 5:1-4 tells us, "Therefore, I exhort the elders among you, as your fellow elder and witness of the sufferings of Christ, and a partaker also of the glory that is to be revealed, shepherd the flock of God among you, exercising the oversight not under compulsion, but voluntarily, according to the will of God; and not for sordid gain, but with eagerness; nor yet as lording it over those allotted to your charge, but proving to be examples to the flock. And when the Chief Shepherd appears, you will receive the unfading crown of glory."

So when a man "aspires to the office of an elder," or as the King James states it, "desires the office of a bishop," what is it that he desires or aspires to?

He aspires to an incredible commitment of time, energy, and devotion. If that is not truly his aspiration, then whatever he is aspiring to is not the scriptural office of an elder.

A man who would be an elder aspires to constant self-examination. He aspires to a position in which he will have to evaluate honestly and repeatedly this work in the office in the light of God's word. In Titus 1:9, included in the set of qualifications put forth there, we read, "holding fast the faithful word which is in accordance with the teaching, that he may be able both to exhort in sound doctrine and to refute those who contradict." The man who desires the office of a bishop needs to know that he is going to continually have to ask himself, "Am I performing my God-given duties as an elder in a manner with which God would be pleased?" He is going to have to constantly "look intently at the perfect law, the law of liberty" and honestly determine if what he sees is actually the kind of elder God would have him to be.

The man who aspires to be an elder is aspiring to a position where he will not only be continually looked at and examined by others, he actually has to invite that examination. We have already looked at 1 Peter 5:1-4, but again we notice verse 3 specifically, "nor yet as lording it over those allotted to your charge, but proving to be examples to the flock." The one who aspires to the office of an elder needs to know that he is desiring a position in which God expects him to say to those given to his charge, "Follow me, as I follow Christ."

This so closely relates to the elder as a shepherd. Remember Jesus' words in John 10:4, "When he puts forth all his own, he goes before them, and the sheep follow him because they know his voice." That is the idea of being an example.

A man who aspires to be an elder in the Lord's church must know that he aspires to a position that is without power and glory—at least, as the world views power and glory. He aspires to a position in which he must truly place all others ahead of and before himself. Can you picture a greater responsibility on earth than being in a position to stand before God and give an account for each individual member of the congregation? The man who would be an elder must realize that it will be the most important thing that he does.

Is this meant to scare off young men who are moving so surely toward qualifying themselves? No, absolutely not. But know that it is not a game, and for the ones who perform faithfully, great will be their reward in heaven.

What Goes in Will Come out

Our Lord made a profound statement in a discussion with certain Pharisees in Matthew 15. The Pharisees were concerned that on a particular occasion the Lord's disciples did not engage in the traditional ceremonial cleansing before eating. It was a man-made tradition, not a commandment of God. After dealing with the Pharisees, Jesus explained to His apostles what He meant in His reply in verses 17-20, "Do not ye yet understand, that whatsoever entereth in at the mouth goeth into the belly, and is cast out into the draught? But those things that proceed out of the mouth come forth from the heart, and they defile the man. For out of the heart proceed evil thoughts, murders, adulteries, fornications, thefts, false witness, blasphemies: these are the things which defile a man: but to eat with unwashen hands defileth not a man."

What comes out from the heart is only that which has been put in.

Generally we think of this in terms of the "big" stuff (I am using that expression only for emphasis): fornication, adultery, murder, lies, and so forth. But what about thinking the worst of a brother or sister in Christ, or failing to give him the benefit of the doubt? How about gossiping or talking behind the back of a brother or sister? What about harboring a grudge or refusing to talk to a fellow Christian? Where does that sort of ungodliness come from? It comes from the heart, and the only thing that comes out of the heart is what has been put into it.

There is just no way around it. Sooner or later what we think about, what we dwell upon, what we put into our hearts, is going to express itself. Solomon wrote in Proverbs 23:7, "For as he thinketh in his heart, so is he." Is there any real difference, ultimately, between actual murder and killing the reputation of a brother or sister through gossip? Not if I understand God's Word, there isn't. Both will condemn the doer to hell, and both are evidence that the heart is not right in the sight of God.

There are some things we can hide in this life from each other and some things we can't. It just seems that sooner or later an ungodly heart, made that way through what has been put into it, is going to express itself. We close with Solomon's words from Proverbs 27:19, "As in water face reflects face, so the heart of man reflects man."

Hope

The hope that we enjoy as Christians is made possible through the grace of God. In 2 Thessalonians 2:16-17 we read, "Now may our Lord Jesus Christ Himself and God our Father, who has loved us and given us eternal comfort and *good hope by grace*, comfort and strengthen your hearts in every good work and word." It is a living hope that will not die away because it is based upon the risen Christ, who lives forever and ever. Remember Peter's words of 1 Peter 1:3? He wrote, "Blessed be the God and Father of our Lord Jesus Christ, who according to His great mercy has caused us to be born again to a *living hope* through the resurrection of Jesus Christ from the dead."

This isn't a fairy tale, nor is it whistling in the dark. It isn't a dream or a vain delusion. It is the truth. Because Jesus rose from the dead, the Christian knows that he will rise too. "If we have hope in Christ in this life only, we are of all men most to be pitied. But now Christ has been raised from the dead, the first fruits of those who are asleep. For since by a man came death, by a man also came the resurrection of the dead. For as in Adam all die, so in Christ shall all be made alive. But each in his own order: Christ the first fruits, after that those who are Christ's at His coming, then comes the end, when He delivers up the kingdom to the God and Father, when He has abolished all rule and all authority and power" (1 Cor. 15:19-24).

In what sense can it be said "in hope we have been saved"? Hope is what causes us to endure. Because of the earnest expectation of the glorious future in heaven and full release from the bondage of corruption, we are patient and endure. Without this hope, I don't believe we would or could endure.

In Hebrews 6:17-20 we read, "In the same way God desiring even more to show to the heirs of the promise the unchangeableness of His purpose, interposed with an oath, in order that by two unchangeable things, in which it is impossible for God to lie, we may have strong encouragement, we who have fled for refuge in laying hold of the hope set before us. This hope we have as an anchor of the soul, a hope both sure and steadfast and one which enters within the veil, where Jesus has entered as a forerunner for us, having become a high priest forever according to the order of Melchizedek."

Hope anchors our souls in eternity. It keeps us from focusing all of our attention upon the here and now. It serves to remind us that we are but "strangers and exiles" on this earth; looking for that "better country, that is a heavenly one" (Heb. 11:13, 16).

December 31

Does It Really Matter?

Many years ago my wife and I had the opportunity to go to Ireland. I had been invited there to present a series of lectures on the subject of Roman Catholicism. It was a wonderful trip from the standpoint of getting to see places and things that we had never seen before, and from getting to speak on that particular subject in a country that has been described as the "heart" of Catholicism.

After each presentation, a time was set aside for any questions from the audience. Toward the end of the week's lectures, the Catholic wife of one of the members raised her hand and asked, "Why do you all take it so seriously?" With that short question, that woman stated what appears to be the most common of all attitudes about religion that we encounter today. Why take it so seriously?

We had all better take it seriously because it matters what we believe. John wrote in 1 John 4:1, "Beloved, believe not every spirit, but try the spirits whether they are of God: because many false prophets are gone out into the world."

We had all better take it seriously because it matters what we teach. Peter made that clear in 1 Peter 4:11, with the words, "If any man speak, let his speak as the oracles of God. . . ."

We had all better take it seriously because it matters how we worship. Jesus limited the scope of acceptable worship in John 4:24 when he said, "God is a Spirit: and they that worship him must worship him in spirit and in truth."

We had all better take it seriously because it matters what church we are part of. Jesus promised in Matthew 16:18, "I will build my church," and He did. In 1 Corinthians 1:10 Paul wrote, "Now I beseech you, brethren, by the name of our Lord Jesus Christ, that ye all speak the same thing, and that there be no divisions among you; but that ye be perfectly joined together in the same mind and in the same judgment." In verse 13, he wrote, "Is Christ divided? Was Paul crucified for you? Or were ye baptized in the name of Paul?" He isn't saying anything different to us today.

As a matter of fact, my friends, I wrote every article and every poem in this book because we had all better take it seriously. Salvation is at stake, and this life is the only chance we get.

CPSIA information can be obtained
at www.ICGtesting.com
Printed in the USA
FSHW020649271120
76189FS